Glencoe Accounting

ADVANCED COURSE
THIRD EDITION
TEACHER'S EDITION

CONCEPTS/PROCEDURES/APPLICATIONS

Donald J. Guerrieri
Norwin Senior High School
North Huntingdon, Pennsylvania

F. Barry Haber
Fayetteville State University
Fayetteville, North Carolina

William B. Hoyt
Wilton High School
Wilton, Connecticut

Robert E. Turner
McNeese State University
Lake Charles, Louisiana

GLENCOE
Macmillan/McGraw-Hill

New York, New York Columbus, Ohio Mission Hills, California Peoria, Illinois

To the Teacher

The purpose of this Teacher's Edition is to help you use *Glencoe Accounting: Concepts/Procedures/Applications, Advanced Course, Third Edition* to the best advantage in planning for and teaching the advanced accounting course. The *Teacher's Edition* consists of two parts: (1) an opening section of background information and teaching suggestions and (2) the complete student textbook with teacher annotations printed in blue in the left margin.

Send all inquiries to:

Glencoe Division, Macmillan/McGraw-Hill
936 Eastwind Drive
Westerville, OH 43081

Teacher Edition ISBN: 0-02-803643-3

Printed in the United States of America.

1 2 3 4 5 6 7 8 9 10 RRD-W 01 00 99 98 97 96 95 94

Contents

Teacher's Edition

PART 1 THE GLENCOE ADVANCED ACCOUNTING PROGRAM

Glencoe Accounting: Concepts/Procedures/ Applications, Advanced Course, Third Edition is a program that addresses the needs of students who want a strong foundation in basic accounting theory and procedures, but also want to know about computerized accounting systems. The *Glencoe Accounting* program incorporates the traditional methodology of teaching accounting with current applications of computer technology. This combination ensures that students will achieve mastery of basic accounting concepts and procedures while they gain computer literacy and a general understanding of how to use the computer to perform various accounting activities.

Objectives

Glencoe Accounting is a comprehensive program designed to help students meet two broad objectives: (1) preparation for occupational life and (2) preparation for life in general. Falling within these broadly stated goals are a number of more specific objectives:

1. To help students understand the basic accounting principles and procedures that are applied to accounting records kept for businesses that operate in the private enterprise economy of the United States.
2. To help students explain and appreciate the importance of profit in helping to ensure continued business operations.
3. To provide an understanding of the three major types of business organization in a private enterprise economy and how accounting procedures differ for the three forms.
4. To provide students with an understanding of the procedures used in the accounting systems of departmentalized, branch, and manufacturing businesses and not-for-profit organizations.
5. To provide students with means to analyze and interpret financial statements.
6. To provide students with an awareness of the role the computer can play in maintaining accounting records.
7. To help students understand the types of on-the-job activities that are required of entry-level accounting workers.

Components of the Glencoe Accounting Program

Glencoe Accounting is a two-year program that includes student textbooks, workbooks, and extensive supplemental materials for both manual and computerized activities.

First-Year Course

The first-year course materials include the following components:

1. Student textbooks (complete 28-chapter textbook, and abridged 20-chapter textbook)
2. Teacher's Wraparound Edition of the 28-chapter textbook
3. Chapter Reviews and Working Papers
4. Teacher's Edition of the Chapter Reviews and Working Papers
5. Source Documents for textbook mini practice sets
6. Teaching Transparencies
7. Solution Transparencies
8. Printed Chapter Tests
9. Printed Unit Tests
10. Test Bank with test bank software
11. Tech Prep Strategies in Accounting
12. Strategies for Teaching Global and Multicultural Perspectives in Accounting
13. Strategies for Teaching Ethics in Accounting
14. Skills Improvement Activities
15. Blackline Masters
16. Demonstration Problems
17. Math Review for Accounting
18. Student Study Plans
19. Lesson Plans
20. Posters
21. Southwest Airlines Case Studies
22. Business Simulations
23. Spanish Resource Materials
24. Accounting Dictionary
25. Accounting Contest Review
26. Microcomputer Software
27. Multimedia

A more extensive discussion of these materials is found in the *Teacher's Wraparound Edition* of the first-year course.

Advanced Course

Glencoe Accounting, Advanced Course, Third Edition is intended for use in the second-year accounting course. The advanced course materials include:

1. 25-chapter student textbook
2. Teacher's Edition of student textbook
3. Chapter Reviews and Working Papers
4. Teacher's Edition of the Chapter Reviews and Working Papers
5. Source Documents for textbook mini practice sets
6. Teacher's Resource Manual
7. Student Study Plans
8. Printed chapter tests
9. Printed unit tests
10. Test Bank with test bank software
11. Blackline Masters
12. Demonstration Problems
13. Skills Improvement Activities
14. Business Simulation
15. Microcomputer Software

In addition, some items, such as the video, Tech Prep Strategies in Accounting, Math Review for Accounting, Strategies for Teaching Global and Multicultural Perspectives in Accounting, Strategies for Teaching Ethics in Accounting, and the dictionary, may be used with either the first-year or the advanced course.

A complete listing of the components of the two-year program is included in a current Glencoe catalogue.

Glencoe Accounting, Advanced Course

A brief description of some of the components of the advanced course follows. A more complete description is included in the *Teacher's Resource Manual.*

Student Textbook

Glencoe Accounting, Advanced Course, Third Edition is a textbook on financial accounting—the procedures and systems used to record transactions and to prepare reports such as the balance sheet and the income statement. The textbook is organized with learning in mind, allowing students to review the accounting cycle before moving on to more advanced procedures and applications.

The student textbook is organized into 6 units with 25 chapters.

Unit 1—The Accounting Cycle

The first unit of the textbook reviews the basic principles and procedures that students learned in their first-year study of accounting. In Chapter 1, students begin by reviewing the basic accounting equation, the rules of debit and credit for the various types of accounts, and the steps in the accounting cycle. Then students review the first five steps in the accounting cycle as they analyze, journalize, and post various business transactions for a closely held merchandising corporation. In Chapter 2, students review the final five steps in the accounting cycle. Students complete a ten-column work sheet with adjustments, prepare financial statements, journalize and post adjusting and closing entries, and prepare a post-closing trial balance.

Unit 2—Accounting for Assets, Liabilities, and Equity

The chapters in Unit 2 elaborate on many of the transactions and procedures first introduced in Units 5 and 6 of the first-year textbook. The content of the chapters in the unit is organized to follow the order accounts are presented on the balance sheet.

Chapter 3 covers cash, marketable securities, and uncollectible accounts receivable. Students briefly look at internal controls businesses use to protect their cash and two cash funds commonly used in the business: the change fund and the petty cash fund. They next study the recording of transactions for marketable securities such as U.S. Treasury bills. The major portion of the chapter discusses uncollectible accounts receivable. The direct write-off method is presented first, followed by the allowance method.

In Chapter 4, students learn about notes receivable. They determine the maturity date and maturity value of notes, as well as learn how to record notes receivable in a business's accounting system. Both interest-bearing and non-interest-bearing notes are discussed in the chapter. Students also learn how to handle dishonored notes receivable and discounted notes receivable. Finally, students learn how to account for accrued interest income.

Chapter 5 begins with a brief review of the Merchandise Inventory account, the importance of proper inventory management, and the periodic and perpetual inventory systems. Students next learn how to determine the cost of the ending inventory by four different methods: specific identification, fifo, lifo, and weighted average cost. Students also learn how to estimate the value of the inventory using the gross profit and retail methods. A brief discussion of investments is included at the end of the chapter.

Chapter 6 introduces students to accounting for long-term assets. In this chapter, students learn how to record the initial costs of such long-term assets as equipment, buildings, and land. Then they learn how to calculate the annual depreciation on plant assets by four depreciation methods: straight-line, units-of-production, double-declining-balance, and sum-of-the-year's-digits. They also learn how to account for the disposal of plant assets and how to report depreciation on the financial statements and plant asset records. At the end of the chapter, there is a brief discussion of such intangible assets as organization costs, goodwill, copyrights, and trademarks.

Chapter 7 discusses current liabilities. Students first look at the net amount method of recording invoices. Next, students learn to account for interest-bearing and non-interest-bearing notes payable. In this section, students also learn how to handle the renewal of a note payable and how to account for accrued and prepaid interest expense. Other current liabilities are also examined in this chapter. These include payroll liabilities, salaries payable, and unearned revenue.

Chapter 8 looks at long-term liabilities, specifically mortgage notes and bonds. Students learn how to record transactions involving mortgage notes payable. They also learn how to account for the issuance of bonds at face value, at a premium, and at a discount and how to account for bond interest payments. The various transactions involving a bond sinking fund are then discussed and illustrated.

Chapters 9 and 10 look at the stockholders' equity of a publicly held corporation. Chapter 9 discusses the characteristics, advantages, and disadvantages of the corporate form of business organization. Students then learn how corporations raise capital by issuing stock and how to record various stock transactions in the accounting records.

In Chapter 10, students learn the procedures required for the declaration and payment of dividends, both cash and stock. They also learn how to account for stock splits and treasury stock. Finally, students learn how to record the entries for the appropriation of retained earnings.

Chapter 11 covers the end-of-period activities for a publicly held corporation. The adjustments discussed in the unit are reviewed; then students go on to complete an eight-column work sheet. The corporation's financial statements are prepared, including the statement of stockholders' equity (which replaces the statement of retained earnings).

Unit 3—Understanding Business Information

In Chapter 12, students learn how to use three different techniques to analyze the information contained on financial statements. These techniques include horizontal analysis, vertical analysis, and ratio analysis. Chapter 13 discusses the preparation of the fourth major financial statement prepared by businesses today: the statement of cash flows. This statement provides information not readily found elsewhere: the effect on cash of the operating, investing, and financing activities of a company. This statement replaces the statement of changes in financial position that was previously required by the FASB.

Unit 4—Accounting for Other Forms of Organization

This unit discusses two other forms of organization: the partnership and the not-for-profit organization. In Chapter 14, students are introduced to the partnership form of business organization and to the transactions required to form, dissolve, and liquidate a partnership. In Chapter 15, students learn several methods that can be used to allocate the partnership's net income or loss among the partners.

Chapters 16 and 17 focus on the accounting system used by organizations that are not set up to earn profits for their owners or organizers. The major emphasis of the two chapters is on the budgeting process and the financial statements that are prepared by not-for-profit organizations.

Unit 5—Special Accounting Systems

The chapters in Unit 5 cover specialized accounting procedures. These specialized systems include procedures used by businesses to report departmental and branch operations, to control purchases and cash payments, and to record and report on manufacturing operations.

The procedures and financial statements of a departmentalized business are discussed in

Chapter 18. Students learn how accounting records are kept by department and how to prepare departmental income statements.

In Chapter 19, students learn about one centralized accounting system used by businesses with more than one branch. Students learn how to record transactions within that system, including transactions that occur between branches. Then they learn how to prepare separate branch financial statements and combined financial statements.

In Chapter 20, students learn about an accounting system some businesses use to control their purchases and cash payments. They are introduced to the various components of the voucher system and learn how to record business transactions within that system.

The final two chapters in the unit focus on the special accounting procedures followed by manufacturing businesses. In Chapter 21, students are introduced to the differences in accounting for merchandising and manufacturing businesses. The financial statements prepared by a manufacturing business are introduced here so that students can better understand how costs flow through the accounting system.

In Chapter 22, students learn about two major cost accounting systems: job order and process. Students compare and contrast the two systems as they learn how to record transactions within both.

Unit 6—Accounting for Business Decisions

Unit 6 covers managerial and cost accounting. In Chapter 23, students learn how costs behave in relation to business activities. Variable, fixed, and mixed costs are introduced, and students see how those costs change as production is increased or decreased. Graphs are used throughout the chapter.

Understanding the relationships among costs, volume, and profit is the topic of Chapter 24. Students learn how to perform cost-volume-profit (C-V-P) analysis. Owners and managers use this analysis for planning and to help them make decisions about what to sell, what to produce, and what production facilities to use.

How owners and managers go about setting selling prices for products or services is the subject of Chapter 25. Students learn about the factors that influence pricing decisions and how to use common cost-plus pricing and labor and materials pricing methods.

Additional supplemental problems are located after Chaper 25. These problems can be used for remedial purposes or for extra credit.

Teacher's Edition of the Student Textbook

This *Teacher's Edition* of the student textbook contains all the pages from the student book plus an additional section in the front of the book. This additional section includes:

1. A description of the components of the Glencoe advanced accounting program.
2. A section describing the features of the *Glencoe Accounting* program and suggestions on how to use those features to their best advantage.
3. Chapter-by-chapter teaching suggestions and answers to the end-of-chapter vocabulary, review questions, and skills-improving activities.

The *Teacher's Edition* of *Glencoe Accounting, Advanced Course* is a unique teaching aid. It offers you the complete student textbook plus already recorded teaching annotations and answers to chapter activities—all in one handy volume. The *Teacher's Edition* contains a wealth of teaching suggestions, both in the front section of the book and on the textbook pages. Teacher annotations are printed in blue in the left margin of the student textbook pages. Perhaps its greatest advantage to you, though, is its inclusion of key answers to end-of-chapter activities. Answers to the vocabulary, review questions, and skills-improving activities are included in the front section of the *Teacher's Edition*. Teacher annotations of key dollar amounts (balance amounts, column totals, and so on) are printed in the margin alongside the exercises and problems.

Teacher's Resource Manual

The *Teacher's Resource Manual* contains useful background information and supplemental material that you can use as you plan and teach your advanced accounting course. The *Manual* contains a more complete description of the two-year accounting program; guidelines on organizing your accounting course and the amount of time required for application activities, simulations, and microcomputer activities; a sample course outline; detailed curriculum objectives for a competency-based program; and information on integrating microcomputer activities in the advanced accounting program. The *Teacher's Resource Manual* includes information on careers in accounting, more detailed accounting procedures and theories that you can use as enrichment material, and additional "Improving Your Skills" activities.

The *Teacher's Resource Manual* also contains a wealth of blackline masters you can use to enrich or individualize your classroom. Chapter study guides provide a detailed list of the activities you wish students to complete for each chapter. Three or more demonstration problems are included for each chapter. You may wish to make a transparency of a demonstration problem to use as you present a new procedure to the class. You can also use these problems as short quizzes, as make-up work, as extra practice, or as a review of chapter material. Objective tests and problem tests for each unit in the textbook and audit tests for each of the five application activities are also included in blackline-master form. Answers to these tests, as well as the separately printed chapter tests, are also included here. The *Teacher's Resource Manual* also contains blackline masters of all of the accounting forms used in the textbook. Finally, a basic math review is included for students whose business mathematics skills need more attention.

Chapter Reviews and Working Papers

The *Chapter Reviews and Working Papers* allows students to use realistic accounting stationery to complete the end-of-chapter applications. Accounting stationery, forms, or space are provided for the completion of all exercises and problems. Extra forms are included as space allowed.

Also included is a two-page chapter review that consists primarily of objective questions about the content of a chapter.

Answers to all chapter review pages and end-of-chapter problems are contained in the *Teacher's Edition* of the *Chapter Reviews and Working Papers*.

Business Simulation

One business simulation accompanies the second edition of *Glencoe Accounting, Advanced Course*. The most appropriate place for the use of this simulation, titled *Heritage Home Center, Inc.,* is following Chapter 11. A short, one-page description of the simulation appears at that point in the student textbook.

Chapter Tests

A separate test booklet contains a test for each of the 25 chapters in the student textbook. Each test is a combination of objective questions and application problems. Answers to these chapter tests are contained in the *Teacher's Manual.*

Microcomputer Software

A fully integrated accounting software program is available for use in completing the microcomputer-designated textbook problems and application activities and the business simulation. The software is similar to commercially available accounting software and includes fully integrated general ledger, accounts receivable, accounts payable, payroll depreciation, and cost of inventory. The integrated program will complete financial statement analysis and includes a pop-up calculator for computation. Problems from this textbook for which beginning template data has been prepared are identified in the textbook by an icon.

Template disks are also available for completing designated problems on commercially available spreadsheet software. The designated textbook problems are also identified in the textbook by an icon.

Finally, a computerized tutorial program helps students study textbook and study guide material chapter by chapter. For each chapter of the textbook, students reinforce their knowledge of the material just studied with objective questions, exercises, problems, and a chapter summary. Exercises and problems in the student textbook serve as models for those in the tutorial program. The models are identified in the student textbook.

PART 2 TEACHING THE ADVANCED ACCOUNTING COURSE

The accounting teacher plays an essential role in motivating students and helping them succeed in their study of accounting. Recognizing this important role, we have developed the student and teacher materials for *Glencoe Accounting* to give you maximum flexibility in accommodating the needs of your students within the constraints of the time allotted for your course.

Accounting students benefit from a variety of teacher input: introduction of new accounting concepts and procedures through oral explanation, demonstration of new procedures and applications, and encouragement and immediate feedback on performance. Accounting can best be taught in a step-by-step, systematic way. New learning is based on old, and each day builds on the previous one. Students need to know where they have been, where they are going, and how the system fits together.

The teacher's approach to instruction should, in general, follow a three-step pattern.

1. Always review old learning to be sure students are ready to move on to a new topic.
2. Demonstrate new concepts/procedures. Students learn much of their accounting by following teacher demonstrations and solving relevant assignment materials.
3. Interpret all procedures as an integral part of the overall accounting cycle. Frequent reference to the accounting equation is important, for the accounting equation is a model around which all accounting procedures are built. Too often students learn the effects of transactions on the accounting equation early in their study, only to have the teacher fail to relate new and advanced learning to the soon forgotten fundamental equation. Remind students often that every transaction can be analyzed in terms of the accounting equation and that every transaction is related to the balance sheet or the income statement.

Individualizing Instruction

Teachers in all disciplines must accommodate their instruction to students who work and learn at different rates. The *Glencoe Accounting* program has been developed to minimize this common but plaguing problem. Of greatest benefit to you and your students is the organization of the textbook. It uses the traditional accounting cycle approach to introduce students to new concepts and procedures. This step-by-step approach gives students the necessary guidance they need to look for the continuity and interrelationships of the accounting process.

End-of-chapter materials are designed to allow you to make assignments that are geared to individual students. There are numerous exercises and problems for students to complete. The problems are graded in difficulty, with the last problem in each chapter classified as a "challenge" problem. In-text application activities integrate procedures learned over several chapters. An appendix includes reinforcement problems for use by students needing additional work.

In addition to in-book materials, there are several optional activities that may be completed by students at their own pace. One simulation accompanies the advanced accounting program, intended for use after students have completed Chapter 11. There are also numerous microcomputer activities including a tutorial program, an integrated accounting software program for completing textbook activities and simulations, and template diskettes that can be used with spreadsheet software. (A more complete discussion of the microcomputer software is included in the *Teacher's Resource Manual.*)

Using The Glencoe Advanced Accounting Program

The student materials and teaching aids in the *Glencoe Accounting, Advanced Course* program were designed to be both comprehensive and convenient to use. The following paragraphs describe the primary features of the student textbook.

The student textbook lends itself to student comprehension and independent learning. As you look through the textbook, you will notice that information is presented in an easy-to-follow, well-organized matter. Explanations are written in simple, direct style and are frequently accompanied by illustrations and examples that visually reinforce new concepts. The readable typesize and variety of examples and illustrations, as well as the effective use of full-color printing invite student reading.

Glencoe Accounting, Advanced Course is composed of 6 units with 25 chapters. A solid review of the rules of debit and credit and a six-step method for analyzing transactions are presented in the first chapter of the textbook. This emphasis on transaction analysis—which continues throughout the textbook—helps students understand *why* a particular transaction has certain effects on a business's accounts. Such a solid foundation leads to an easier understanding of how a transaction is recorded properly.

The first unit reviews and reinforces those concepts learned in the first-year course. Each subsequent chapter presents new information for students that builds upon prior learning. For example, the discussion of uncollectible accounts included in Chapter 3 builds and expands upon material introduced in Chapter 23 of the first-year textbook. The order of the topics in Unit 2 follows the order of presentation of accounts on a familiar financial statement, the balance sheet.

In addition to the organization of the textbook, a number of other features that have been found to be helpful to accounting students have been built into the program. These features are described below.

Chapter Objectives

To help students read with a goal in mind, the learning objectives for each chapter are listed on the first page of the chapter. These objectives are clearly stated in language the students can understand. Urge students to use the objectives to help them set a purpose to their own reading and study.

Vocabulary Development

Vocabulary development is essential to the learning process. Words whose meanings are unknown or vaguely known to students defeat understanding. Like most disciplines, accounting has its own special language. The extent to which students master this new language determines their success in the accounting course.

The student textbook tackles the problem of vocabulary development in a variety of ways. As a preview for teachers and students, the new terms in each chapter are listed on the first page of the chapter (see, for example, page 3). These terms are defined where introduced within the chapter. When a term is first used, it is printed in bold type and highlighted in yellow. This calls students' attention to the definition. You may find it helpful to students to list the terms on the chalkboard before you begin each new chapter and to explain the meaning of each term. Many studies in reading comprehension have shown that the ability to retain what is read is enhanced if one is familiar with the terminology used. A vocabulary exercise is included as part of the end-of-chapter activities.

Aids to Reading Comprehension

Reading comprehension is the ability to grasp the meaning intended in written material. Reading comprehension requires a variety of skills—extruding essential facts, grasping concepts, comparing facts and concepts from one passage to another, making inferences, applying information to different situations. The student textbook includes several features to enhance students' reading comprehension.

An especially important aid to student learning is immediate feedback. A means of gaining that feedback independently is provided in the student textbook through the inclusion in each chapter of two or more "Check Your Learning" activities. These activities follow major sections of a chapter and include questions or problems that require students to apply what they have just learned. (See page 6 for an example of a "Check Your Learning" activity.) To provide immediate feedback, answers to the "Check Your Learning" activities are included in the back of the student textbook. Students are encouraged to compare their answers with those in the textbook and then to find out why they may have answered a question incorrectly by re-reading the appropriate section of the text narrative.

Frequent examples and illustrations are also used to reinforce comprehension of accounting concepts and procedures. When a new accounting concept is introduced, students are shown how it is applied to the keeping of accounting records in an illustration that shows each step in the new procedure (for example, see page 7). Where appropriate, the text narrative integrates the new procedure with concepts or procedures learned earlier.

Another feature of the student textbook that enhances comprehension is the use of "Remember" notes within the text narrative (see page 4 for an example). Some students find it difficult to summarize the major concept of a section of text narrative and to integrate that concept with prior learning. The "Remember" notes provide a concise summary (usually one or two sentences) of an important concept or procedure to help students identify material that is especially important for them to know.

Other means of aiding reading comprehension are the use of analogies and examples (see page 7). In addition, new accounting procedures are explained in a clear, step-by-step fashion (see page 7).

"Accounting Tips" appear throughout the textbook and provide students with practical advice on such things as writing neatly when preparing accounting records or remembering to clear a calculator before adding a column of figures. "Accounting Notes" provide interesting facts on business or the practice of accounting. At the end of each chapter is an enumerated summary of the major concepts presented in the chapter.

End-of-Chapter Activities

After studying a chapter, students are given a variety of end-of-chapter activities to test their comprehension and mastery of the chapter material. The first end-of-chapter activity is a vocabulary review. Students are asked to write sentences (to reinforce writing skills) defining each new term in a chapter.

The next end-of-chapter activity is a section of review questions. These questions may be answered directly from the text narrative, again serving to point out and reinforce key accounting concepts. The questions are generally arranged in the order in which their answers are discussed in the chapter.

The review questions are followed by a short activity that encourages students to improve their skills in critical areas such as decision-making, analysis, math, communications, human relations, and problem solving.

Following the skills-improving activity are exercises and problems that require students to apply the accounting procedures they have learned. There are two to four short, single-focus exercises and five or more problems for each chapter. The problems are arranged in an ascending order of difficulty or complexity, allowing you to select problems to meet your students' needs. Each subsequent problem requires students to apply additional procedures. In appropriate chapters, one or more problems have been set up to allow solution on a microcomputer. The final problem(s) in each chapter challenges students' understanding of accounting concepts and procedures. These challenge problems are designated by a "maze" icon.

An important point to make here about the end-of-chapter problems is that, with few exceptions, the problems do not "piggyback" on one another; that is, the solution to one problem is rarely needed to complete another problem, especially from one chapter to another. This feature allows you to assign problems as needed without worrying about whether preceding problems have been completed or whether students have retained their solutions. The exception to this falls in those chapters dealing with end-of-fiscal-period activities. In those chapters, students may need a work sheet or a financial statement in order to complete the next step in the cycle. Obviously, this procedure is more meaningful when students can see the relationship of the end-of-fiscal-period activities.

Reinforcement Activities

There are five in-book activities that allow students to apply the accounting procedures that they have learned. These "Mini Practice Sets" are provided at appropriate intervals in the textbook to give students the opportunity to integrate their knowledge of accounting concepts and procedures studied in two or more chapters. One of the mini practice sets (Application Activity 1) provides an opportunity for students to work through an entire accounting cycle.

Other Features

Also included in the student textbook is a glossary of the terms defined in the textbook. A comprehensive index is helpful to students as they study new accounting concepts and need to refer to earlier, related material.

UNIT 1

THE ACCOUNTING CYCLE

Chapter 1 Reviewing the First Five Steps of the Accounting Cycle

Teaching Suggestions

This chapter reviews the first five steps of the accounting cycle: collecting and verifying data on source documents, analyzing business transactions, journalizing business transactions, posting each entry to the general and subsidiary ledger accounts, and preparing a trial balance. Essentially, this chapter reviews Chapters 11 through 15 of *Glencoe Accounting, First Year Course, Second Edition.*

The Basic Accounting Equation

This section reviews some important accounting terms and the basic accounting equation. Remind students that total assets must equal total equities. Stress the fact that the basic accounting equation forms the foundation for all accounting concepts, procedures, and applications.

Double-Entry Accounting

Review the concept of double-entry accounting. Mention the fact that compound entries often occur. Recite in class the rules of debit and credit for asset, liability, and owner's equity accounts found on page 4.

When reviewing the revenue, cost of merchandise, and expense accounts, discuss with students the concept that these are all temporary capital accounts. Recite in class the rules of debit and credit for the temporary accounts as presented on page 5.

The Steps in the Accounting Cycle

This section lists the ten steps in the accounting cycle. Go through each step and briefly discuss the procedures to be followed in each.

Review with students the chart of accounts for Campers Unlimited on page 2. Point out the six classifications of accounts, and review selected account titles in each classification. A good review of the account titles in the Stockholders' Equity section would also be helpful.

Collecting and Verifying Source Documents

Point out the importance of source documents and the fact that the accountant must have proof that a transaction took place. Ask students to define and explain such source documents as invoices, receipts, and memorandums. If possible, have samples of these documents to show students.

Analyzing Business Transactions

Remind students that the left side of a T account is always the debit side and the right side is always the credit side regardless of the account classification. Encourage students to follow the six-question approach for analyzing transactions. Remember that this approach is designed to take students through the cognitive process needed to analyze transactions. Tell students that they should continue to analyze each transaction rather than memorizing the accounts that are debited and credited.

Journalizing Business Transactions

Recording transactions in a journal provides a chronological record of all transactions. This part of the review deals with a business that uses special journals. Review with students the four special journals and discuss the types of transactions entered in each. Also, discuss the general journal and have students name the types of transactions that are usually entered in that journal. Point out in each case why a transaction is not appropriate for the special journals.

It also may be helpful to students to briefly discuss why a business would use the special journals and why using them saves time in the posting process. As each special journal is presented, point out the special amount columns and discuss why those accounts were selected as special amount column headings.

In the presentation of cash payments, mention the following procedures for the internal control of cash: (1) All cash payments must be authorized and supported by a source document; (2) all checks should be prenumbered and should be signed only after the amounts and the payee have been entered on the check; and (3) all voided checks must be accounted for.

When presenting the employer's payroll taxes, it is best to review the payroll procedure and to explain the difference between Salaries Expense and Payroll Tax Expense. Also, point out that only the employer pays state and federal unemployment taxes in most states.

Posting

Point out that the ledger accounts are used to organize information and to summarize changes caused by business transactions. Remind students that the posted date should always be the same as the date recorded in the journal. Also remind students that the procedure for posting is to enter the data in the ledger account, moving from left to right.

Discuss with students why the amounts entered in the General Debit and General Credit columns of the cash receipts, purchases, and cash payments journals must be posted to the general ledger separately.

Remind students that totaling, proving, and ruling a special journal take place before the column totals are posted. The total in a special amount column is posted to the account named in the column heading.

Explain to students why the amounts must be posted to the controlling accounts (Accounts Receivable and Accounts Payable) in the general ledger as well as to the individual accounts in the subsidiary ledgers.

Proving the Accuracy of the Subsidiary Ledgers

Be sure students understand that the total of the balances of the subsidiary ledger accounts must agree with the balance of the controlling account in the general ledger. On a schedule of accounts receivable or accounts payable, all accounts are listed, even those with zero balances.

Preparing the Trial Balance

Emphasize that the purpose of a trial balance is to prove the equality of the debits and credits in the general ledger. Refer back to the concept of double-entry accounting. Point out that if the trial balance does not prove equal, errors have been made. An outline of typical errors is presented in Chapter 2.

Answers to Chapter Activities

Building Your Accounting Vocabulary

account An account is a record that shows the increases and decreases in, and the balance for, a specific asset, liability, or owner's equity item.

accounting cycle The accounting cycle consists of the activities a business completes within a fiscal period to keep its accounting records in order.

assets Assets are items of value owned or controlled by a business.

basic accounting equation The basic accounting equation is: Assets = Liabilities + Stockholders' Equity.

cash payments journal The cash payments journal is a special journal used to record all transactions in which cash is paid out.

cash receipts journal The cash receipts journal is a special journal used to record all transactions in which cash is received.

contra account A contra account is an account whose balance decreases another account's balance.

controlling account A controlling account is a general ledger account whose balance must equal the total of all of the account balances in a subsidiary ledger.

correcting entry A correcting entry must be made when an error in an entry has been posted to the general ledger.

cost of merchandise Cost of merchandise includes the accounts that are used to record the actual cost to the business of the merchandise that will be resold to customers.

credit A credit is an amount entered on the right side of an account.

debit A debit is an amount entered on the left side of an account.

double-entry accounting Double-entry accounting is a financial recordkeeping system in which every business transaction affects the balance in at least two accounts. For every debit, there must be an equal credit.

expenses Expenses are the amounts paid for goods and services that are used to operate a business.

fiscal period A fiscal period is the time covered by an accounting report.

general journal A general journal is a two-column journal in which all types of transactions can be recorded.

journal A journal is a chronological record of a business's transactions.

liabilities Liabilities are the creditors' claims to the assets of a business.

posting Posting is the process of transferring amounts from a journal to ledger accounts.

purchases journal The purchases journal is a special journal that is used to record all transactions in which items are bought on account.

revenue Revenue is the income earned from the sale of goods and services.

sales journal The sales journal is a special journal used to record only the sale of merchandise on account.

source document A source document is a paper prepared as evidence that a transaction took place.

stockholders' equity Stockholders' equity is the owners' claims to assets held in a corporation.

subsidiary ledger A subsidiary ledger is a ledger that is summarized in a controlling account in the general ledger.

trial balance A trial balance is a proof of the equality of debits and credits in the general ledger.

Reviewing Your Accounting Knowledge

1. Business transactions are important because each transaction changes the financial position of the business.
2. Permanent account balances are carried from one accounting period to the next. Temporary accounts are used for only one fiscal period. Examples of permanent accounts are asset, liability, and stockholders' equity accounts such as Cash in Bank, Office Equipment, and Accounts Payable. Examples of temporary accounts are revenue, cost of merchandise, and expense accounts such as Sales, Rent Expense, and Purchases.
3. The six classifications of accounts found in a chart of accounts are **(a)** Assets, **(b)** Liabilities, **(c)** Stockholders' Equity, **(d)** Revenue, **(e)** Cost of Merchandise, and **(f)** Expenses.
4. The first five steps in the accounting cycle are:
   a. Collect source documents and verify the data on them.
   b. Analyze business transactions.
   c. Journalize business transactions.
   d. Post each entry to the ledger accounts.
   e. Prepare a trial balance.
5. The six questions that can be used to analyze business transactions are:
   a. Which accounts are affected?
   b. What is the classification of each account?
   c. Is each account increased or decreased?
   d. Which account is debited, and for what amount?
   e. Which account is credited, and for what amount?
   f. What is the complete entry?
6. The descriptions of the four special journals follow.
   a. A sales journal is used to record only the sale of merchandise on account.
   b. A cash receipts journal is used to record all transactions in which cash is received.
   c. A purchases journal is used to record all transactions in which items are bought on account.
   d. A cash payments journal is used to record all transactions in which cash is paid out.
7. A general journal is used to record transactions that cannot be recorded in special journals.
8. A cash discount is calculated by taking the percent of the total merchandise sold, not including sales tax.
9. The two controlling accounts in the general ledger are Accounts Receivable and Accounts Payable.
10. A schedule of accounts receivable is prepared to prove the accuracy of the subsidiary ledger.
11. The steps to prove cash are:
    a. Record the beginning balance in the Cash in Bank account.
    b. Add the total cash received during the month.
    c. From the subtotal, subtract the cash payments for the month.
    d. Compare this figure against the balance of the last check stub in the checkbook.
12. The accounts are listed in the trial balance in the order in which they appear in the chart of accounts.

Improving Your Decision-Making Skills

Suggested answers follow; students' answers will vary.

1. Need to get a job to earn a living.
2. Find out what jobs are available.
3. Find out what jobs are available by looking at the classified section of the local newspaper or by contacting an employment agency.
4. From the list of jobs available, determine the ones for which I am qualified and in which I am interested.
5. Selected three positions for which I am qualified.
6. Contact the companies to set up a job interview.

Chapter 2 Reviewing the Final Five Steps of the Accounting Cycle

Teaching Suggestions

This chapter reviews the final five steps of the accounting cycle: completing the work sheet, preparing the financial statements, journalizing and posting the adjusting entries, journalizing and posting the closing entries, and preparing a post-closing trial balance. This chapter will give students a good review of the end-of-period activities for a merchandising business.

End-of-Fiscal-Period Work

Discuss with students the purpose of the end-of-period reports: to provide information on the financial position of the business. Mention that sound business decisions cannot be made without accurate financial information.

Preparing a Ten-Column Work Sheet

Stress the purpose of preparing a trial balance before any other work can be completed. Point out that the work sheet is the beginning of the end-of-period work and will be used to prepare the financial statements.

When discussing the common errors that may occur, it is good to review each type of error and to make sure that students know what they are looking for. A review of Chapter 6, pages 107–121, of *Glencoe Accounting, First Year Course, Second Edition* may be helpful.

This chapter reviews the adjustments that must be made for a merchandising business. Discuss with students the fact that consumed assets are an expense of doing business.

As each adjustment is reviewed, emphasize why the adjustment is being entered on the work sheet. Remind students that they must identify the accounts that need adjustment and should enter the adjustments from the top of the work sheet down. Point out that the work sheet is a working document and that all adjustments will later be journalized and posted to the general ledger.

This chapter reviews only the adjustments for merchandise inventory, supplies, prepaid insurance, and federal income tax. The adjustments for depreciation and uncollectible accounts will be presented in later chapters.

Discuss how the amounts in the Adjusted Trial Balance section are extended and why. Emphasize that first all permanent accounts are extended to the Balance Sheet section and then all temporary capital accounts are extended to the Income Statement section.

Stress the importance of proper totaling and ruling. Discuss why the net income is entered in the Debit column of the Income Statement section and in the Credit column of the Balance Sheet section. Also, review a net loss and discuss why the amounts are entered in the opposite columns.

Preparing the Financial Statements

Remind students that it is important for a business to be consistent in the method it uses to prepare its financial statements so that proper analysis can be done. Review the work sheet as the source of information for preparing these statements. Remind students to take information from the proper sections of the work sheet in preparing financial statements. Adjustments will affect account balances entered in the Trial Balance section of the work sheet.

The Income Statement

Discuss the purpose of preparing this statement. Review the five sections of the income statement and the amounts included in each section. Use demonstration problem 2-2 to walk students through the Cost of Merchandise Sold section of the income statement. Try to stress the logical sequence of entries rather than memorizing the sequence of account titles. Be sure students understand the differences among *cost of merchandise available for sale, cost of delivered merchandise, cost of merchandise sold,* and *gross profit on sales.* Point out that amounts are calculated from left to right and entered on the income statement.

The Statement of Retained Earnings

Remind students that this statement is prepared for a business organized as a corporation. Emphasize that the purpose of this statement is to report the changes that have taken place in the Retained Earning account during the fiscal period.

The Balance Sheet

Point out that this is a report of the balances of the permanent accounts as of a specific date. Remind students that the information for preparing the balance sheet is taken from the Balance Sheet section of the work sheet and from the statement of retained earnings. Use the work sheet to point out the up-to-date balances that are reported for all the accounts that were adjusted. Discuss why the balance of the retained earnings account must be taken from the statement of retained earnings rather than the work sheet.

Review with students the order of preparing the financial statements. Use a chart such as the one that follows.

First Statement
Income Statement
↓
Amount of Net Income or Loss → **Second Statement**
Statement of Retained Earnings
↓
Balance of Retained Earnings → **Third Statement**
Balance Sheet

Updating the General Ledger Accounts

Review the need to journalize and post the adjusting entries. Point out that the adjustments on the work sheet appear only on that working document. They have not yet been recorded in any of the general ledger accounts. Be sure students remember to journalize the adjusting entries by matching the amounts indicated by the small letters in parentheses.

Closing Entries

Stress that the temporary accounts start the fiscal period with zero balances. Emphasize that all revenue, cost of merchandise, and expense accounts must have zero balances to start a new fiscal period. Also point out that the Retained Earnings account in the general ledger must be brought up to date.

Answers to Chapter Activites

Building Your Accounting Vocabulary

adjusting entries Adjusting entries are the journal entries made to update the balances in all general ledger accounts affected by adjustments.

adjustment An adjustment is an amount that is added to or subtracted from an account balance to bring that balance up to date.

balance sheet A balance sheet reports the final updated balances of all asset, liability, and stockholders' equity accounts as of a specific date.

beginning inventory The beginning inventory is the merchandise on hand at the beginning of the fiscal period.

closing entries Closing entries transfer the balances of the temporary accounts to a permanent general ledger account.

cost of merchandise sold The cost of merchandise sold is the actual cost to the business of the merchandise sold to customers during the period.

ending inventory The ending inventory is the merchandise on hand at the end of the fiscal period.

gross profit on sales The gross profit on sales is the amount of profit made during the fiscal period before expenses are deducted.

income statement An income statement is a report of the net income or net loss earned by the business during the fiscal period.

net income Net income is the amount left after expenses for the period are subtracted from revenue.

net loss A net loss occurs when the expenses are greater than the gross profit on sales for the period.

net purchases Net purchases is the amount of all costs related to the merchandise purchased during the fiscal period.

net sales Net sales is the amount of sales for the period less any sales discounts and sales returns and allowances.

operating expenses Operating expenses are the costs that expire or the costs that are incurred to earn revenue for the business.

operating income Operating income is the taxable income of a corporation, or the amount of income before federal income taxes.

post-closing trial balance A post-closing trial balance is prepared to prove the equality of the debits and credits in the general ledger after the adjusting and closing entries have been posted.

statement of retained earnings The statement of retained earnings reports the changes that occurred in the Retained Earnings account during the fiscal period.

work sheet A work sheet is a working paper used to collect information from the general ledger for use in preparing the financial statements for the period.

Reviewing Your Accounting Knowledge

1. A work sheet is prepared first because the work sheet collects information from the general ledger that is needed to prepare the financial statements.
2. At the end of the fiscal period, certain account balances are not up to date. These account balances must be brought up to date before the financial statements are prepared.
3. The Merchandise Inventory account must be adjusted to bring the account up to date so that the balance is the cost of the ending inventory.
4. The purpose of the financial statements is to summarize the changes that have taken place during the period and report the financial condition of the business at the end of the period.
5. The three financial statements prepared by a merchandising business organized as a corporation are the income statement, the statement of retained earnings, and the balance sheet.
6. The cost of merchandise sold is determined by subtracting the amount of the ending inventory from the cost of merchandise available for sale.
7. The income statement is prepared first because the amount of net income or loss reported on the income statement must be included on the statement of retained earnings.
8. The two stockholders' equity accounts of a corporation are Capital Stock and Retained Earnings. The Capital Stock account represents the total amount of investment in the corporation by its stockholders. The Retained Earnings account represents the increase in stockholders' equity from net income held by the corporation.
9. The closing entries must be journalized and posted to transfer the balance of the temporary accounts to a permanent general ledger account, leaving the temporary accounts with zero balances.
10. The temporary general ledger accounts are closed into the Income Summary account.
11. There are ten steps in the accounting cycle.

Improving Your Analysis Skills

If no adjustment is made for Supplies to record the supplies used up during the fiscal period, the Supplies Expense account balance and the total operating expenses on the income statement will be understated. Therefore, the amount of Net Income will be overstated. On the balance sheet the balance of the asset Supplies will not equal the inventory of supplies on hand at the end of the fiscal period.

Mini Practice Set: Application Activity 1 A Complete Accounting Cycle for a Merchandising Business

Application Activity 1 is a comprehensive activity that requires students to complete an accounting cycle for a merchandising business that is organized as a corporation. In this activity, students are required to analyze and record the business transactions for Aqualand, Inc., a store that sells tropical fish and related equipment and supplies. Students must decide which journal to use to record each of the business transactions, including payroll. They must also post to the general ledger and the accounts receivable and accounts payable subsidiary ledgers. They then proceed through the remaining steps of the accounting cycle.

The accounting stationery needed to complete this activity is included in the student book of working papers. Most students should be able to complete the activity manually in three to five class periods.

UNIT 2

ACCOUNTING FOR ASSETS, LIABILITIES, AND EQUITY

Chapter 3 Cash, Marketable Securities, and Accounts Receivable

Teaching Suggestions

This chapter covers the assets that are most closely associated with a business's liquidity. These assets include cash, short-term investments, and accounts receivable. Students will learn about internal control procedures to safeguard cash, two cash funds (the change fund and the petty cash fund), accounting for short-term investments, and two methods of accounting for uncollectible accounts receivable.

Accounting for Publicly Held Corporations

Bring in several pages from the financial section of a daily newspaper or *The Wall Street Journal*. As students look at the stock reports, tell them that all companies listed there are publicly held corporations. You may also bring to class several annual reports of publicly held corporations.

Accounting for Cash

When explaining the internal controls of cash, refer to the list of examples and have students point out how each example helps to protect cash. Mention that when the records of a business are being audited, internal controls of cash and other assets are reviewed in detail.

The Change Fund

When introducing the change fund, point out that any business using a cash register, such as a supermarket or other retail store, needs to keep a small amount of money in the cash register for making change. The change fund consists of varying denominations of bills and coins. Ask students whether any of them use a change fund in their after-school jobs.

The size of a change fund depends on the size of the business. The change fund for a supermarket or department store may be as much as $2,000, while the change fund for a small sporting goods store may be as little as $50.

Draw T accounts on the chalkboard for Change Fund and Cash in Bank. Use the T accounts to analyze and illustrate the entry to establish a change fund. Be sure to emphasize that a new asset account, Change Fund, is created and that it is debited only once: when the business first establishes the fund.

Explain to students that occasionally errors are made in making change to customers. The amount of cash in the cash register will not agree with the amount recorded on the register tape. There may be too little or too much cash in the register. The difference is recorded in an expense account called Cash Short and Over. Draw a T account on the chalkboard for Cash Short and Over. Emphasize that this account has no normal balance. Cash shortages are considered to be expenses of the business; therefore, they are recorded as debits to Cash Short and Over. Cash overages are considered to be revenue for the business; therefore, they are recorded as credits to the accounts.

The Petty Cash Fund

Students have learned that one way to protect cash is to deposit all cash receipts and to pay all bills by check. However, it is impractical to write checks for small amounts, such as payments for postage stamps or small purchases of office supplies. Instead, businesses use a petty cash fund for making cash payments for small, incidental purchases and payments. Some working students may have some experience with a petty cash fund. If so, ask them what they can tell the class about it.

When explaining how to establish and replenish the petty cash fund, to make the experience as realistic as possible, bring to class a petty cash box, play money, and petty cash vouchers.

As with the change fund, the size of the petty cash fund depends on the size of the business and on past experiences. Therefore, a petty cash fund may be as small as $25 or as large as several hundred dollars.

Emphasize that the petty cashier is the only person who should have access to the petty cash fund and the authority to disburse cash from the fund.

After establishing the petty cash fund, guide students through the reconciliation of the petty cash fund and the journal entry that is made to replenish the fund.

Marketable Securities

Bring to class several pages from the financial section of a daily newspaper or *The Wall Street Journal*. Have students look at the New York Stock Exchange and U.S. Government Securities sections of the financial section. Point out that marketable securities consist primarily of U.S. government securities such as Treasury bills and the securities of large corporations. Mention that investments in marketable securities earn a return, interest income.

Accounting for Accounts Receivable

Point out several advantages of selling to customers on credit (increase sales, keep up with competition, earn income from interest on charge accounts). Also mention that there is one major disadvantage (not all money owed by customers will be collected). The remainder of this chapter deals with two methods of providing for uncollectible accounts.

The Direct Write-Off Method

Point out to students that a considerable amount of time often elapses (usually one year or more) during which a business attempts to collect an overdue account. At some point, management must decide to consider the account "uncollectible."

Use T accounts to analyze the direct write-off entry. Mention that, under this procedure, the Bad Debts Expense account is debited at the time the account receivable is determined to be uncollectible. The entry (1) removes the uncollectible account receivable from the accounting records and (2) charges the amount to an expense account of the business.

Point out that a person whose account was written off may later pay the amount owed. Discuss with students the fact that this account is no longer an expense of the business and must be reinstated as an account receivable. This may be the first time some students have experienced a credit entry in an expense account. It may be helpful to explain that this will reduce the balance in the expense account.

Matching Bad Debts Losses with Sales

Review the matching principle with students. Discuss the fact that if a bad debt is written off over a year after the original sale occurred, the revenue for the period is not being matched with the expenses to produce that revenue. The sale is recorded in one period and the expense in a later period. Point out the need for alternative methods.

The Allowance Method

Discuss why it is necessary to estimate bad debts expense when the allowance method is used. Analyze the procedure using T accounts. Stress why Allowance for Uncollectible Accounts rather than Accounts Receivable must be credited. Point out that the balance of Allowance for Uncollectible Accounts represents bad debts that are yet to be determined.

Point out that with the allowance method the revenue for the period is being matched with the potential bad debts expenses incurred in the same period. Although the uncollectible amount is only an estimate, the matching principle is being used.

Estimating Bad Debts Expense

Emphasize that under the allowance method, the amount of bad debts is merely an estimate. Have students name additional factors that could cause any estimate to be off. You might also have students brainstorm various methods a business could use to estimate its uncollectible accounts.

The Percentage of Net Sales Method

When discussing this section, point out that the business must have statistics from prior years to determine the percentage to be used. Be sure students understand why the percentage is calculated on net sales and not on total recorded sales for the period.

Ask students to explain why the percentage used to calculate bad debts expense is higher when only the charge sales are considered. After the section has been discussed, have students estimate some bad debts expenses based on both net sales and net charge sales.

Ask students if they feel one method is more accurate than the other.

The Aging of Accounts Receivable Method

When discussing Figure 3-12, be sure students understand that, as the time periods of the age groups increase, the amount still to be collected decreases. However, the percentage of uncollectible accounts within the age groups increases. The preparation of an aging schedule could be extremely time consuming if there were a large number of accounts receivable and if the schedule had to be prepared manually. Today, however, computers enable even larger businesses to age their accounts in a relatively short period of time.

Installment Accounts Receivable

Point out that sometimes the finance charges (interest earned) on installment sales exceed the profit made on the sale. Introduce the revenue accounts Installment Sales and Finance Charges and the asset account Installment Accounts Receivable. Discuss the differences between these accounts and Sales, Interest Income, and Accounts Receivable. Discuss the term *down payment* and how it relates to installment sales; also discuss why businesses require a down payment.

Answers to Chapter Activites

Building Your Accounting Vocabulary

aging of accounts receivable method The aging of accounts receivable method for estimating the total uncollectible accounts examines and classifies each customer's account according to its due date.

allowance method The allowance method of accounting for uncollectible accounts matches potential bad debts expenses with sales made during the same fiscal period.

book value of accounts receivable The book value of accounts receivable (Accounts Receivable minus Allowance for Uncollectible Accounts) is the amount the business can reasonably expect to receive from its charge customers.

change fund A change fund is an amount of money, consisting of varying denominations of bills and coins, that is used to make change in cash transactions.

direct write-off method The direct write-off method removes an uncollectible amount from the accounts receivable subsidiary ledger and from the controlling account when the business decides that the account is not going to be paid.

installment sales When a business sells goods or services and allows the customer to pay for their purchases over a period of time, the sale is referred to as an installment sale.

marketable securities Cash that is not needed for immediate operations is often invested in a short-term investment called marketable securities.

matching principle The matching principle states that revenue for a fiscal period must be matched against the expenses incurred in earning that revenue during the same fiscal period.

other revenue Other revenue is nonoperating revenue—revenue that a business receives or earns from activities outside its normal operations.

percentage of net sales method The percentage of net sales method for estimating uncollectible accounts assumes that a certain percentage of the current period's net sales will be uncollectible.

petty cash fund Cash a business keeps on hand with which to make small cash payments is called a petty cash fund.

publicly held corporation A publicly held corporation is one whose stock is widely held, has a large market, and is usually traded on a stock exchange such as the New York Stock Exchange.

uncollectible account An uncollectible account is an account receivable that cannot be collected and becomes an expense of the business.

Reviewing Your Accounting Knowledge

1. Internal controls are procedures a business sets up to protect its cash and other assets. Because cash is so liquid, it is important to protect it from loss, waste, theft, forgery, and embezzlement.
2. When a check is written to establish a change fund, the asset account Change Fund is debited and the Cash in Bank account is credited.
3. The Cash Short and Over account is classified as an expense account. Cash shortages result in losses or expenses to the business and are recorded as debits to Cash Short and Over. Cash overages rep-

resent gains or revenue and are recorded as credits.

4. The Petty Cash account is usually debited only once—at the time when the fund is first established.
5. A company would invest in marketable securities when it finds it has more cash on hand than it needs to pay current bills.
6. Bad debts are considered to be an expense for a business because they decrease ownership equity by decreasing the revenue earned.
7. The two methods that can be used to account for uncollectible accounts are the direct write-off method and the allowance method.
8. The allowance method is considered to be more effective than the direct write-off method because the allowance method enables the firm to follow the matching principle by matching the potential bad debts expense with sales made during the same period.
9. Since a business doesn't know for sure which accounts won't be collected, Accounts Receivable can't be credited directly for the estimated uncollectible amount.
10. Allowance for Uncollectible Accounts is classified as a contra asset account.
11. When an account is written off under the allowance method, the book value does not decrease because both Accounts Receivable and Allowance for Uncollectible Accounts are decreased by the amount of the write-off.
12. Two methods of estimating that can be used to estimate the uncollectible amounts are (a) the percentage of net sales method and (b) the aging of accounts receivable method.

Improving Your Human Relations Skills

If I were Rick Jaworski, I would first talk with Cynthia about the importance of being at work on time every day. During the conversation, I would be positive and emphasize the value of developing good work habits. Rick should also explain why company policy allows him to come to work at a different time. However, it would be best for Rick to be at work at the same time as Cynthia during the early part of her training time. With Rick reporting a little late each day, Cynthia may think that it is permissible for her to be a little late. After Cynthia feels comfortable performing her responsibilities, then Rick can return to his flex-time schedule.

Chapter 4 Notes Receivable

Teaching Suggestions

This chapter covers the use of notes receivable by businesses. Students will learn how notes are received, how to determine the maturity date, how to calculate interest, how notes are discounted at the bank, and how dishonored notes are handled.

Promissory Notes

Emphasize the reasons businesses will accept promissory notes from customers. Discuss with students the wide use of notes and how common they are in everyday business. This might be a good time to have a local banker or business person come in and explain how promissory notes are handled. Use Figure 4-1 to discuss each part of a note.

Calculating Interest on a Note

Review with students the arithmetic skills needed to calculate interest. Write on the chalkboard the formula for computing interest ($I = P \times R \times T$), and discuss each part of the formula. Be sure to point out that the time of a note is expressed as a fractional part of a year either in months (12) or days (365). Furthermore, you may want to tell students that interest rates are always stated on an annual basis for consistency and to allow for comparison between one financial institution and another.

Some students may find it easier to calculate the interest if the time fractions are converted to decimals. If so, demonstrate how to convert a fraction, such as 60/365, into a decimal. When converting to decimals, carry the calculation only to three decimal places. Point out that if the time period is less than a year, the decimal will be less than 1.00.

Notes Receivable

Explain to students some of the reasons why businesses often accept notes receivable from customers. Analyze the transaction for recording the receipt of a note receivable using T accounts and then illustrate the entry using the general journal.

Review the calculation of interest before analyzing the receipt of cash in payment of the note receivable. Analyze the transaction using T accounts.

Dishonored Notes Receivable

Explain to students that dishonoring a note does not relieve the maker of the obligation to pay and every legal means should be taken to collect the note. Discuss with students why a separate account is set up rather than just keeping the note in the Notes Receivable account. While returning the note (plus interest) to the customer's Accounts Receivable account would provide a record of the customer's payment record, the note still represents a *legal, written* promise to pay a certain amount of money and should be recognized in the accounting records as such.

Students may have difficulty understanding why the interest earned on the note is included in the amount debited to Notes Receivable Past Due and credited to Interest Income. Remind students that the interest was actually earned yet never received. Income should be recorded at the time it is earned (revenue principle).

Discounting Notes Receivable

Be sure students understand the meaning of discounting a note receivable and why a business would do this. Point out that the business endorses the note and turns it over to the bank for cash. You may want to discuss the phrase *to the order of* with students.

After completing the computational work on the chalkboard in arriving at the proceeds of a note, analyze the journalization of a discounted note receivable first in T account form. Be sure to explain carefully to students the amount recorded as interest income is the net amount or the difference between interest income and the bank discount.

The entry for dishonoring a discounted note receivable is often confusing for students. Take each part of the transaction and examine and discuss it using T accounts. Point out that the principal plus the amount of interest earned is debited to the Notes Receivable Past Due account. The protest fee is an expense of the business and is not included in this amount.

Answers to Chapter Activites

Building Your Accounting Vocabulary

accrual basis of accounting The accrual basis of accounting recognizes revenue when earned and expenses when incurred.

accrued revenue Accrued revenue is revenue that has been earned but not yet received and recorded.

bank discount The bank discount is the interest charge the bank deducts in advance at the time the note is issued. The remaining amount is given to the borrower.

conservatism Conservatism is a fundamental guideline of accounting. Conservatism is applied when amounts that are least likely to overstate income or assets are used to report the financial position of a business.

contingent liability A contingent liability exists when the endorser of a discounted note, by virtue of the endorsement, agrees to pay the note at maturity if it is not paid by the maker. The liability of the endorser is contingent, or depends upon, the possible dishonoring of the note by the maker.

discount period The discount period is the period of time between the discount date and the maturity date of the note.

discounting notes receivable Discounting notes receivable takes place when a business sells its notes receivable to a bank for cash rather than holding the notes until maturity.

dishonored note A note is dishonored when the maker of the note fails to pay or renew the note at the maturity date.

draft A draft is an order by one party (the drawer) to another party (the drawee) to pay a certain sum of money to a third party (the payee).

face value Face value is the amount written on the "face" of a promissory note.

interest Interest is a fee charged for the use of money.

interest rate The interest rate is the amount of interest expressed as a percentage of the principal.

interest-bearing note A note that requires the principal plus interest to be repaid at maturity is called an interest-bearing note.

issue date The issue date is the date on which the note is written.

maker The maker of the note is the person or business promising to repay the principal and interest.

maturity date The maturity date is the due date of the note; that is, the day on which the note must be paid.

maturity value The maturity value is the principal plus the interest that must be paid on the maturity date.

notes receivable A note receivable is a promissory note accepted by a person or a business.

payee The payee is the person or business to whom a note is payable.

principal The principal is the amount being borrowed.

proceeds The proceeds is the amount the borrower actually receives. It is the maturity value minus the bank discount.

promissory note A promissory note is a written promise to pay a certain sum of money on demand or on a specific date.

protest fee A protest fee is the bank charge to the endorser for a discounted note that is dishonored. It must be paid along with the maturity value.

term The term of a note is the length of time between the issue date and the maturity date, or the length of time the borrower has to repay the note.

trade acceptance When one party orders another party to pay a certain sum of money at some later date and the second party agrees to do so in writing on the face of the instrument, the document is known as a trade acceptance.

Reviewing Your Accounting Knowledge

1. A promissory note is a formal legal document that serves as proof of a debt.
2. The equation for calculating interest is: Interest = Principal × Interest Rate × Time, or I = PRT.
3. A business usually accepts a note receivable when the credit sale is 30 days or more.
4. Notes Receivable Past Due is a current asset account. The amount entered in this account is the maturity value of the past due note, which includes the principal plus interest.
5. The amount of interest the bank charges (called the *bank discount*) for discounting the note is subtracted from the maturity value of the note in order to determine the proceeds.
6. Notes Receivable Discounted is classified as a contra asset account. On the balance sheet, it is reported as a deduction from Notes Receivable to show the book value of notes receivable.
7. If the proceeds of a note are greater than the face value, the difference is interest income and is recorded in the Interest Income account.
8. The liability of the endorser is contingent upon (depends upon) the possible dishonoring of the note by the maker.
9. When a discounted note receivable is dishonored, the maturity value of the note is debited to the Notes Receivable Past Due account.
10. An adjusting entry is required for accrued interest income because revenue should be reported in the fiscal period in which it is earned.

Improving Your Communications Skills

Suggested answers follow; students' answers will vary considerably.

1. by 4 P.M. on July 28
2. a secretarial desk and swivel chair
3. 9:00 A.M. on August 9
4. our branch office in the upper level of the Greengate Mall
5. Brenda Starr, our new employee
6. at extension 601
7. four colors: gray, yellow, red, and white
8. please notify me no later than Monday
9. business has increased by 17%
10. has been in business for seven years

Chapter 5 Inventories and Investments

Teaching Suggestions

This chapter covers the periodic and perpetual inventory systems. It also covers four different methods that can be used to assign costs to the ending inventory. Two methods for estimating the value of the ending inventory are also presented.

Merchandise Inventory

This section discusses the importance of having an accurate inventory valuation system. Inaccurate inventory data will cause inaccurate reporting on financial statements. Neither the income statement nor the balance sheet will present an accurate financial picture of a business.

Managing the Inventory

The importance of having the proper quantity of merchandise on hand for customers should be stressed. Ask students what they or their parents do when the merchandise they want is not available in stores. Have students name some other problems they may think of that occur when the inventory is too high or too low.

Determining the Quantity of Inventories

The periodic inventory system is most familiar to students. Ask students if they have ever taken an inventory themselves or have ever seen one being taken. A discussion as to the amount of time needed to complete a physical inventory will help students understand why most businesses cannot perform this activity very often. Discuss the need to perform a physical count of all merchandise at least once a year.

Discuss with students several advantages of having a perpetual inventory system. Stress the advantage a business has over its competition if it has access to inventory data on an up-to-date basis. Mention that even larger stores can now set up perpetual inventory systems using computers and electronic cash registers.

Assigning Costs to the Ending Inventory

Point out that very few firms can assign the exact cost to all items in their inventories. As a result, estimated costing methods are usually used.

When presenting the specific identification costing method, point out that it is the most accurate because the exact cost of each item is known and assigned. Point out the time-consuming aspects of this type of system unless the business is one that deals in unique items or relatively high-priced, low-volume items.

This may be the first time students have had the opportunity to calculate an inventory using the first in, first out costing method. Be sure to put many examples on the board and have students calculate several inventory amounts.

To present the last in, first out costing method, have students calculate inventory amounts using the same examples they used for the fifo method. This will be a beginning for comparison.

Review the mathematical procedures to follow when making the calculations for the weighted average cost method. Offer several examples. Discuss with students why this is a "weighted" method. This concept is often difficult for students.

Comparing Inventory Methods

Point out to students that there is no "right" or "wrong" inventory costing method; rather, a business chooses a particular method to best meet its needs under certain economic conditions. A discussion on long-term and short-term economic projections and price trends may be helpful.

Spend time discussing the effects of the different methods on the cost of merchandise sold. From this point, discuss the differences in gross profit. This section may prove difficult for students, so some time should be taken for discussion and examples.

Reporting Inventory Using the Lower-of-Cost-or-Market Rule

Students may understand how to determine which ending inventory value is lower, but they often do not see the advantage for the business of using the lower amount.

You might also tell students that the lower-of-cost-or-market rule might not be used when the inventory cost is calculated by the fifo method. That ending inventory value already approximates market cost.

Estimating the Value of Inventories

Point out that the two methods of estimating inventory values are not meant to replace the periodic inventory; rather, they are a means of preparing interim financial reports when a physical count of merchandise is not possible.

Take students through the mathematics involved in the retail method of estimating inventories. Be sure to emphasize the purpose of doing this procedure. Take students through the steps on page 129. Stress the sequence and have students think each step through.

Mention that the gross profit method is an alternative procedure to the retail method. Remind students that the purpose of both methods is to estimate the value of the ending inventory. To use the retail method, the retail price of the beginning inventory and the retail price of net purchases must be determined. In the gross profit method, amounts on past financial statements must be examined to determine the gross profit percentage. This procedure may be easier for businesses that have been established for a few years.

Inventory Valuation and the Financial Statements

This is a good time to reinforce the importance of accurate inventory amounts and the need to perform a physical inventory at least once a year. Take students through the error on the income statement and discuss the problem. Point out that just because they offset each other at the end of the second year, this is no justification for such an error.

Ask students to name other amounts on the financial statements that also will be incorrect due to this error. They should name the capital balance on the statement of changes in owner's equity (or the balance of Retained Earnings for a corporation) and the value of the ending inventory as reported in the Assets section of the balance sheet. Note that if the ending inventory is understated, the value of total assets for the business will also be understated.

Answers to Chapter Activites

Building Your Accounting Vocabulary

first in, first out method (fifo) The first in, first out inventory costing method assumes that the first items purchased were the first items sold.

gross profit method The gross profit method of estimating the value of inventory uses the percentage of gross profit the company has made over a given period of time.

investments Investments are long-term assets that are not intended to be converted to cash or to be used in the normal business operations within the next accounting period.

last in, first out method (lifo) The last in, first out inventory costing method assumes that the most recently purchased articles are sold first.

market value Market value is the current price that is being charged for similar items in the marketplace.

markup The markup is the dollar amount a retailer adds to the cost of merchandise to arrive at the selling price.

periodic inventory system A periodic inventory system is one in which the amount of goods on hand is determined by counting them.

perpetual inventory system A perpetual inventory system is one in which the business keeps a constant, up-to-date record of the amount of merchandise on hand.

retail method The retail method of estimating the value of inventory is used by retail businesses and is based upon the ratio of cost to retail. The beginning inventory and net purchases are recorded at both cost and retail value.

specific identification method The specific identification method of inventory costing determines and assigns the actual cost of each item in the inventory.

weighted average cost method The weighted average cost method determines the cost of inventory by assigning an average unit cost to all like items in the ending inventory.

Reviewing Your Accounting Knowledge

1. The cost value of Merchandise Inventory must be determined to prepare accurate and realistic financial statements.
2. A business benefits by having effective inventory management procedures because it should be able to determine which items need to be reordered and also to schedule purchases to take advantage of discounts and sales.
3. With a periodic inventory system, a business makes a physical count of all items in stock periodically during the year. In a perpetual inventory system, a record of the number of items on hand is constantly being kept.
4. A periodic inventory must be taken to verify the balances shown on the inventory records. This will determine losses due to theft or breakage.
5. The specific identification method is the most realistic method because it determines and assigns the actual cost to each item in the inventory.
6. The term *weighted* means that the greater the number of units bought at a specific price, the greater the influence that purchase has on the average cost.
7. An advantage of using the lifo method is that it will yield the smallest taxable

income in a period of rising prices. A disadvantage of the lifo method is that taxes would be higher if prices fall.

8. The lower-of-cost-or-market rule is used if the replacement cost of the inventory is lower than the cost calculated by using an inventory costing method.
9. A firm might estimate the value of its inventory if taking a physical inventory is too time consuming and expensive or if the actual inventory has been destroyed.
10. The gross profit method is used if the retail prices of the beginning inventory and net purchases are not readily available.
11. If the beginning inventory is understated, the net income will be overstated.
12. Short-term investments are invested for a few weeks or months. In long-term investments, it is assumed that the cash will not be needed in the near future.

Improving Your Problem-Solving Skills

I would explain to Lisa that all salary information is confidential and that as the payroll clerk I cannot tell her how much her supervisor makes. I would also explain that I could lose my job if I were to divulge such information about any employee. I would suggest that Lisa talk with someone in personnel who might be able to provide a job description and possibly the salary range for a supervisory position.

Some other types of information that should remain confidential about an employee are benefits selected, beneficiaries named, withholding allowances claimed, age, medical history, and performance evaluations. These items are personal and should be known only by people such as payroll clerk, human resources employees, and supervisors who need the information to perform their jobs.

Chapter 6 Property, Plant, and Equipment Assets and Intangible Assets

Teaching Suggestions

In this chapter, students will acquire an understanding of the accounting procedures required for plant assets. They will learn how to calculate depreciation using four depreciation methods. They will also learn how to record adjusting entries for depreciation and the entries needed when plant assets are disposed of.

Property, Plant, and Equipment Assets

When introducing this section, emphasize the difference between current assets and property, plant, and equipment assets. Ask students to identify the property, plant, and equipment assets in the classroom. Then ask them to offer examples of plant assets used in business.

Determining the Cost of Property, Plant, and Equipment

Explain to students that the original cost of a piece of equipment often includes more than its invoice price. The original cost could include such things as sales taxes, freight charges, insurance costs while the equipment is in transit, and installation costs.

Point out to students that land is classified as a property, plant, and equipment asset when it is used in the normal operations of the business. Make sure students understand that land—unlike other property, plant, and equipment assets—has an unlimited useful life and does not wear out.

Discuss with students why a separate account is set up for buildings. Point out that any costs expended to make a building usable would also be debited to the building account.

Students may be confused by the concept of "land improvements." Point out that land improvements are expenditures that improve the value and usefulness of the land. While land improvements will be used over several accounting periods, they do have a limited life (unlike land) and will eventually be replaced.

Allocating the Cost of Plant Assets

Point out that it is impossible at the time of purchase to know (1) how long a plant asset will last (useful life) and (2) the value of the asset when it is discarded or replaced (its disposal, or salvage, value).

Also make sure that students understand that depreciation does not represent the physical deterioration of a plant asset or the decrease in the market value of the asset over time. It is simply a means of allocating the *cost* of the asset over the years in which it is used.

Discuss with students some factors that might affect a plant asset's useful life. Point out that an asset's estimated useful life may (and often does) differ from its potential life. For example, a typewriter may have a potential life of ten or more years. However, one company may find that it is wise to trade in its old typewriters on new ones every four years. For this company, the typewriter's useful life is four years.

Methods of Calculating Depreciation

As you introduce each method, write each formula on the board. Then work through the calculations with students to be sure they understand the mathematics involved.

The Straight-Line Method

Point out that the straight-line method is appropriate when the plant assets are used in about the same amount in each accounting period. An equal share of a plant asset's depreciable cost is then allocated to each period in which the asset is used.

It may be easier for some students to calculate the depreciation by using the straight-line rate. Walk students through the calculations as follows. First, determine the straight-line depreciation rate by dividing 1 by the number of years in the asset's useful life. Then multiply the depreciable cost by the depreciation rate to determine the annual depreciation.

The Units-of-Production Method

Make sure students understand that the units-of-production method is based on how much the asset is used. Ask students to name other ways of expressing a plant asset's useful life; for example, miles driven or units produced. Use demonstration problem 6-2, then have students calculate the depreciation expense for several years using the same per-unit rate.

The Double-Declining-Balance Method

Point out that the double-declining-balance method is an *accelerated* depreciation method in which the depreciation expense is computed at twice (double) the straight-line rate. Also point out that the calculations are based on the plant asset's book value. The business disregards disposal value when calculating the annual depreciation. When this method is used, the book value of the plant asset never reaches zero. The asset is not depreciated beyond its disposal value.

Sum-of-the Years'-Digits Method

The sum-of-the-years'-digits method is also an accelerated depreciation method. A higher amount of depreciation is taken on the plant asset in its early years.

The textbook presents one method of determining the denominator of the fraction used in the calculations. The denominator can also be found by using the following formula:

$$S = \frac{N(N + 1)}{2}$$

In the formula, *S* stands for the sum of the digits (the denominator of the fraction) and *N* stands for the number of years in the asset's useful life.

Use the table on page 151 as the basis for a comparison of the four depreciation methods. You may wish to prepare a graph on which all four methods are plotted.

Calculating Depreciation for Less Than One Year

You might point out to students that since time is not a factor in calculating depreciation with the units-of-production method, it is not included in the table on page 152. Also, be sure that students understand that the annual depreciation must be calculated first. The partial-year depreciation is then calculated on the full-year amount.

Recording Depreciation Expense

Emphasize that the adjusting entry for depreciation affects two accounts: Depreciation Expense and Accumulated Depreciation. Students should understand that each plant asset account (such as Delivery Equipment or Office Furniture) has (1) a depreciation expense account and (2) an accumulated depreciation account.

Plant Asset Records

Using Figure 6-3, point out to students (1) how the annual depreciation was determined, (2) how the accumulated depreciation was determined, and (3) how the book value was determined.

Disposing of Plant Assets

Throughout this section, make sure students understand why depreciation must be recorded before the plant asset is disposed of.

Discarding Plant Assets

Remind students that a fully depreciated plant asset is retained in the accounting records until it is discarded or otherwise disposed of. It is not removed from the accounting records when its book value reaches zero.

Even though a plant asset has a book value, it may be inadequate for business use. If the business discards that plant asset, it incurs a loss since it is giving up something of value. Make sure students understand why the amount of the loss is debited to an expense account.

Selling Plant Assets

Analyze the loss transaction with students using T accounts on the board. Make sure students understand that it is the difference between the cash received and the book value of the asset that determines whether there is a loss or gain on the transaction.

Analyze the gain transaction using T accounts. Make sure students understand why Gain on Disposal of Plant Assets is a revenue account. To check understanding, give students several examples, and have them determine whether the business has incurred a loss or a gain on each transaction.

Exchanging Plant Assets

According to Accounting Principles Board (APB) Opinion No. 29, losses on the exchange of plant assets should be recognized in the accounting records but gains should not. Income tax laws and accounting principles differ on this procedure. According to the Internal Revenue Code, when an old asset is traded in on a similar asset, the gain or loss on the exchange must be absorbed into the cost of the new asset. The gain on an exchange would be deducted from the cost of the new asset; a loss on an exchange would be added to the cost of the new asset. This textbook presents the exchange of plant assets according to APB Opinion No. 29.

This may be a good time to discuss the accounting guideline of *conservatism*. According to this guideline, accountants should always take the "safer route" or the alternative that is least likely to overstate income. It is for this reason that losses on the exchange of plant assets are recognized in the accounting records. Analyze the loss transaction with students using T accounts on the board. Work through the mathematics carefully so students understand why the business has a loss. Then give students other examples and have them calculate the amount of the loss.

Since gains should not be recognized, stress that the recorded value of the new asset is equal to the book value of the old asset plus any cash paid out. Analyze both transactions on the board using T accounts. Make sure students understand that even though the business is paying out cash, it has a gain on the second transaction.

Answers to Chapter Activities

Building Your Accounting Vocabulary

accumulated depreciation Accumulated depreciation is the total amount of depreciation that has been recorded up to a specific point in time.

appraisal value Appraisal value is the estimated worth of an asset such as property.

book value The book value of an asset is its original cost minus the accumulated depreciation. It is the value according to the records of the business.

current assets Current assets are the assets that are either used up or converted to cash during the normal operating cycle of the business.

depreciable cost The depreciable cost of an asset is the estimated amount to be depreciated: the original cost less any disposal value.

depreciation Depreciation is a systematic procedure for allocating the cost of plant assets to the accounting periods in which the business receives service from those assets.

double-declining-balance method The double-declining-balance method is an accelerated method of deprecation that allows larger amounts of depreciation to be taken during the early years of an asset's useful life.

intangible assets Intangible assets are long-lived assets having no physical substance.

property, plant, and equipment Property, plant, and equipment are long-lived assets that are used in the production or sale of other assets or services and benefit the business for several accounting periods.

salvage value The salvage value is the estimated value of a plant asset at the time of its disposal.

straight-line method The straight-line method of depreciation assumes that depreciation depends only on the passage of time. An equal amount of depreciation is charged off during each year of a plant asset's useful life.

sum-of-the-years'-digits method The sum-of-the-years'-digits method is an accelerated method of depreciation that uses fractions based on the number of years in the plant asset's estimated useful life.

units-of-production method The units-of-production method of depreciation is based on the idea that depreciation is a result of use, not time.

Reviewing Your Accounting Knowledge

1. Current assets are either used up or converted to cash during one accounting period. Property, plant, and equipment assets are long-lived and are used in the production or sale of other assets over several accounting periods.
2. The initial cost of a property, plant, and equipment asset includes all normal costs necessary to acquire and install it: for example, sales tax, freight charges, insurance costs in transportation, unpacking and assembling costs, legal fees, real estate agent fees, and demolition costs.
3. Land is treated differently from other plant assets because it is considered to have an unlimited life. It does not wear out and therefore is not depreciable.
4. Land improvements are depreciable and therefore must be separated from Land. These improvements include the cost of driveways, parking lots, trees, fences, and outdoor lighting.
5. Depreciation is an estimate because the useful life of a plant asset cannot be accurately determined.
6. The three factors that must be known before a plant asset's depreciation expense can be calculated are (1) the depreciable cost, (2) the estimated useful life of the asset, and (3) the method of depreciation used.
7. An accelerated depreciation method allows larger amounts of depreciation to be taken during the early years of an asset's useful life. The double-declining-balance method and the sum-of-the-years'-digits method are both accelerated depreciation methods.
8. The two accounts involved in recording the adjusting entry for depreciation are Depreciation Expense and Accumulated Depreciation.
9. Companies use different methods of depreciation because one method may result in higher earnings being reported on financial statements. For tax returns, another method results in a lower net income and lower taxes.
10. Plant assets are divided according to type. A plant asset record card is prepared for each plant asset; a group of similar plant assets become a plant asset ledger. Some items listed on a plant asset record include purchase date, original cost, estimated useful life, depreciation method, general ledger account, disposal value, annual depreciation, and accumulated depreciation.
11. Gains and losses on the sale of plant assets are not listed in the Revenue or Operating Expenses sections; they are not a result of normal business operations.
12. When similar plant assets are exchanged, losses on the exchange are recorded but gains are not recognized.

Improving Your Math Skills

1. 0.5000	**6.** 0.6250
2. 0.8750	**7.** 0.4167
3. 0.5556	**8.** 0.0800
4. 0.2500	**9.** 0.1500
5. 0.2727	**10.** 0.8571

Mini Practice Set: Application Activity 2 Accounting for Current and Long-Term Assets

Application Activity 2 is a comprehensive activity involving Chapters 3 through 6. Students will calculate the amounts for end-of-period adjustments and complete a work sheet and balance sheet for Fast Gifts, a retail merchandising business organized as a closely held corporation. This is a good review of the activities involving uncollectible accounts, notes receivable, merchandise inventory, and depreciation of plant assets.

The accounting stationery needed to complete this activity is included in the student book of working papers. Most students should be able to complete this activity manually in four to five class periods.

Chapter 7 Accounts Payable, Notes Payable, and Other Current Liabilities

Teaching Suggestions

This chapter shows how accounts payable and notes payable are used by many businesses today. Students will learn how interest-bearing notes payable are issued to gain more time on accounts payable; to purchase merchandise or other assets; and to borrow money. They will also learn how non-interest-bearing notes payable are discounted at the bank and then paid at maturity.

Notes Payable

Present an example of a business going to a bank to borrow $6,000. Discuss the transaction and use T accounts to analyze the entry. Review with students the terms *maker* and *payee* in the discussion.

Interest-Bearing Notes Payable

Point out that the purpose of reclassifying the amount owed from Accounts Payable to Notes Payable is to establish written evidence of the amount owed and the amount of interest that will be charged. Emphasize that the only time the Notes Payable account is increased is when a promissory note is issued. Also mention that businesses normally do not keep a subsidiary ledger for notes payable as they do for accounts payable.

Using T accounts, analyze the payment of an interest-bearing note payable. When completed, review the entry recorded in the cash payments journal.

Non-Interest-Bearing Notes Payable

Point out that a non-interest-bearing note payable actually carries an interest charge. The interest is paid in advance—at the time the note is issued.

Discuss why banks deduct the interest in advance. Be sure students understand that this process is called *discounting a note*. After teaching students how to compute a non-interest-bearing note problem, a good question to ask them is this one. If they had to borrow money from the bank, would *they* prefer an interest-bearing note or a non-interest-bearing note?

While discussing the issuance of a note, you may want to test students' knowledge of how to determine the amount of interest. Have students calculate the interest and the proceeds for several non-interest-bearing notes.

The Discount on Notes Payable account may be confusing for students. Explain to them that (1) it is a contra liability account and it reduces the balance of the Notes Payable account; (2) it has a normal debit balance and is increased on the debit side and decreased on the credit side; and (3) its balance shows the amount of future interest expense. Point out that although the interest is deducted in advance, the Interest Expense account is not debited until the note payable is paid.

Use T accounts when analyzing the cash payment of a non-interest-bearing note payable transaction. Students will have difficulty understanding why the amount of the check to be written must be for the maturity value or face value of the note and not for the amount of the proceeds. Students seem to think the check should be written for the amount of the proceeds. They think that if they were to write the check for the amount of the maturity value, they would be paying the interest twice. To help them overcome this difficulty, you may want to use the following illustration. Ask students what total amount of money the bank would receive from us for (1) an interest-bearing note and (2) a non-interest-bearing note.

	Interest-Bearing Note	Non-Interest-Bearing Note
Principal	$2,000	
+ Interest	+ 50	
Maturity Value	$2,050	$2,000
– Bank Discount		– 50
Proceeds		$1,950

With an interest-bearing note, the total amount of money to be paid back is $2,050. With a non-interest-bearing note, the total amount is $2,050 (maturity value + amount of bank discount initially withheld).

Renewal of an Interest-Bearing Note Payable at Maturity

Sometimes the maker of a note payable is unable to pay the note at maturity. When this occurs, the note is often renewed for a designated number of days, but at a higher rate of interest. The interest rate is higher because the second note is more of a risk to the payee.

Answers to Chapter Activities

Building Your Accounting Vocabulary

accrued expense An accrued expense is an expense incurred in one fiscal period but not paid until a later fiscal period.

current liabilities Current liabilities are debts or obligations that a business expects to pay off in one year or within the business's normal operating cycle, whichever is longer.

discounting a note payable A note payable is discounted when the bank requires the borrower to pay the interest at the time the note is issued. The bank deducts the interest (bank discount) from the face value of the note and gives the difference (proceeds) to the borrower.

long-term liabilities Long-term liabilities are liabilities that are not due during the next fiscal period or operating cycle.

net amount method The net amount method of recording invoices assumes that the business always takes advantage of cash discounts; therefore, invoices are recorded at their net amount (total invoice amount less the cash discount).

non-interest-bearing note payable A non-interest-bearing note payable is a note from which the interest is deducted in advance.

note payable A note payable is a promissory note issued by a person or a business.

prepaid expense An expense paid in advance is called a prepaid expense.

unearned revenue Revenue received in advance but not yet earned is called unearned revenue.

Reviewing Your Accounting Knowledge

1. The accounts are classified as follows: Accounts Payable is a current liability; Bonds Payable is a long-term liability; Dividends Payable is a current liability; Notes Payable usually is a current liability; Salaries Payable, is a current liability; Unearned Rent is a current liability
2. A business may prefer to record invoices at their net amount to help management determine when discounts are not taken.
3. On the maturity date, the maker of an interest-bearing note must pay the maturity value (principal + interest). For a non-interest-bearing note, the maker must pay the maturity value or face value of the note.
4. The proceeds for a non-interest-bearing note are calculated by deducting the bank discount from the face value of the note.
5. The book value of notes payable is the difference between the two accounts Notes Payable and Discount on Notes Payable.
6. An adjusting entry must be made to record the amount of accrued interest expense chargeable to the current fiscal period.
7. An accrued expense is an expense incurred in one fiscal period but not paid until a later fiscal period. A prepaid expense is an expense paid in advance.
8. The accounts are classified as follows: Discounts Lost is an expense account; Interest Expense is an expense account; Discount on Notes Payable is a contra liability account; Salaries Payable is a current liability; Rental Income is a revenue account.
9. To record an adjusting entry for accrued salaries, debit Salaries Expense and credit Salaries Payable.
10. Unearned revenues are reported on the balance sheet as a current liability.

Improving Your Decision-Making Skills

Don't be a follower; be a leader! Take pride in yourself and at the same time please management by wearing appropriate business clothes. Set an example for your co-workers to follow.

Chapter 8 Long-Term Liabilities

Teaching Suggestions

In this chapter, students will learn about another method of acquiring funds available to a corporation: bonds and mortgage notes. Students will learn how to journalize transactions involving bonds payable and mortgage notes payable and how to report these liabilities on the corporate financial statements. Students will also learn how the corporation uses a sinking fund to pay off the bonds when they come due.

Mortgage Notes

Explain to students that a business may go to a bank and issue a mortgage note just as their parents may have done when they purchased their home. Write the following terms on the board and define them for students: mortgage, mortgagor, mortgagee, and mortgage contract.

Explain the textbook illustration of Meadow Link Golf Club needing additional cash to expand the golf course from 9 to 18 holes. Use T accounts on the chalkboard to illustrate the transactions to issue a mortgage note and to make a mortgage payment.

Borrowing Money by Issuing Bonds

First, point out why corporations issue bonds by giving students some concrete examples with which they can identify. You might explain how, as a company grows, its demand for more funds grows. Have students list as many methods of financing growth and expansion as they can. When borrowing is mentioned, discuss the problems a large corporation might face if it wished to borrow $25 million, for example. Bonds enable the corporation to divide the total loan among many lenders. Point out that these lenders could be individuals as well as institutions (such as banks).

You may want to give students a brief overview on how bonds are issued. You may want to use your school district as an example. Your school district wants to construct a new high school. Since it cannot raise the millions of dollars through taxation to finance the project, it issues bonds. However, instead of selling the bonds itself, it will hire an investment firm (an underwriter) to sell the bonds.

Types of Bonds

Bring an example of a bond contract to class. Have students read the section of the contract that identifies the type of bonds issued. Use this contract as a means of pointing out the differences among (1) term and serial bonds, (2) registered and coupon bonds, and (3) secured and unsecured bonds.

You might have students list several reasons why corporations prefer to issue registered bonds. Mention how interest is paid when the bond is a registered bond and when it is a coupon bond. Registered bondholders receive a check in the mail from the corporation; coupon bondholders must submit the coupon attached to the bond to a commercial bank to receive the interest due. A corporation usually pays the total interest due on coupon bonds to an agent, such as a bank. The agent, in turn, pays the interest to bondholders for coupons that are presented.

Accounting for Bonds Payable

Discuss with students how the market interest rate changes. You might have several students research the Treasury bill rates for the past three months. They can use *The Wall Street Journal* or some other financial publication to obtain the information they need. Have students prepare a weekly listing of the interest rates. Then direct students to examine these problems:

1. How do corporations establish a rate of interest for a bond issue?
2. Once a corporation establishes a rate of interest, will it agree with the market rate at the time the bonds are to be issued? Why or why not?
3. If a corporation selected a 9% interest rate, suppose that, on the day the bonds are to be issued the current market rate is 8%. What might an investor be willing to do to get the higher interest rate offered by the corporation if all other factors to be considered are equal?

Discuss with students why investors are willing to pay a premium for a bond. Refer them to their research on the interest rates.

Discuss why it is sometimes necessary to issue bonds at a discount. Make sure students understand how the discount is amortized at the end of the fiscal period.

Accrued Bond Interest

Point out that bonds are not always issued with interest payment dates that coincide with the end of a corporation's fiscal year. Compare this to issuing a note payable that matures during the next fiscal period. The bond interest that has accrued as of the end of the fiscal period must be recorded (matching principle).

Use T accounts to illustrate the journal entries needed for the first full year of the bond issue: the first interest payment on September 30, the adjusting entry on December 31, and the second interest payment on March 31. Point out that the September 30 and March 31 entries will not change during the life of the bond issue. The adjusting entry for the accrued interest payable will also be the same every fiscal year.

Bond Sinking Fund

Discuss and illustrate the following transactions that affect the bond sinking fund:

1. Annual deposit to the sinking fund. Point out that Mayfaire will actually deposit a total of $150,000 over the ten years of the bond issue. The company expects to earn the additional monies (approximately $50,000) by investing that cash in income-producing securities. Ask students what types of securities the company could invest in.
2. Investing the sinking fund cash. Point out to students that Mayfaire invested $9,900 of the $15,000 it had deposited in the fund in December.
3. Recording earnings from sinking fund investments. Point out that Mayfaire will be receiving earnings on its investments at various times during the year. Depending on the type of investment, Mayfaire may receive cash monthly, quarterly, semiannually, or annually.
4. The sale of a sinking fund investment for more that the purchase price. Mayfaire can also earn a profit on its investments if it sells them for more that their purchase price. Of course, the company could also lose by selling its investments for less than their purchase price. In that case, the difference between the cash received and the purchase price would be debited to an account titled Loss on Sale of Sinking Fund Investments.
5. Issuing a check from the sinking fund to retire a bond issue. Point out that, at the end of the ten years, there should be enough cash in the sinking fund to retire the entire bond issue. If there is not, the company may have to make an additional deposit to bring the balance up to $200,000.

Answers to Chapter Activities

Building Your Accounting Vocabulary

amortize Amortize means to write off the bond premium or bond discount to the Bond Interest Expense account.

bond A bond is a promise to repay a certain amount (the principal) at a specified date and to pay interest at set times.

bond certificate A bond certificate is evidence of the corporation's debt issued to the bondholder.

bond indenture A bond indenture is a binding agreement (contract) between the corporation and the bondholders that defines the rights, privileges, and limitations of bondholders.

bond issue A bond issue is the total amount of bonds issued at the same time.

call price The call price is the amount the corporation agrees to pay for the bonds that are redeemed.

callable bonds Callable bonds are bonds that a corporation has the option of redeeming.

carrying value The carrying value is the amount at which the corporation is "carrying" the bond issue on the corporate records. It is the present value of the bond issue.

contract rate The rate of interest stated in the bond indenture is called the contract rate.

coupon bond A coupon bond has an interest coupon attached to the bond certificate. A coupon bond is sometimes called a *bearer bond* because the interest coupon is payable to the bearer or holder of the coupon.

discount If the issue price is less than the face value, the bonds are issued at discount.

face value When the contract rate and the market rate are the same, bonds are issued at face value.

leverage When the bond-issuing corporation is able to earn a greater return on the money it raises than it has to pay out in interest, it is known as leverage.

market interest rate The market interest rate is the rate a borrower (the corporation) is willing to pay and lenders (investors) are willing to accept for the use of money.

mortgage A mortgage is a formal, legal agreement in which the borrower agrees to repay the amount owed plus interest over a 5-to-30-year period.

premium If the issue price of the bonds is more than the face value, the bonds are issued at premium.

registered bond When the name of the owner of a bond is recorded in the issuing corporation's records, the bond is called a registered bond.

secured bond A bond that is covered or backed up by corporate assets, such as buildings or equipment, is called a secured bond.

serial bond A bond within a bond issue that has a series of maturity dates is called a serial bond.

sinking fund A sinking fund is a special fund used to pay off the bond issue when it comes due.

term bond A term bond is a bond that becomes due at the same time as all bonds within a bond issue.

underwriter An underwriter is an investment firm that buys the bond issue from the corporation and, in turn, sells the bonds to the general public.

unsecured bond An unsecured bond or debenture is a bond that is issued on the corporation's credit standing. It is not backed up by the assets of the corporation.

Reviewing Your Accounting Knowledge

1. A business will usually issue a mortgage note when it needs a large sum of money to purchase land, buildings, or equipment.
2. No, a bondholder is not an owner of a corporation but a creditor. A corporation borrows money from a bondholder when a bond is sold and promises to repay the principal at a specified date and to pay interest at set times.
3. The underwriter is an investment firm that purchases the entire bond issue from the corporation and, in turn, sells the bonds to the general public. The trustee makes certain that the corporation fulfills all of its responsibilities to the bondholders.
4. The bond indenture defines the rights, privileges, and limitations of bondholders. The document describes such things as the bond interest rate, maturity date of the bonds, interest payment dates, and characteristics of the bonds.
5. Two advantages of bonds are that (a) interest payments to bondholders are tax-deductible expenses and (b) bondholders are creditors of the corporation and have no say over the corporation's operations. Two disadvantages of bonds are that (a) bond interest payments are fixed expenses that must be paid to bondholders and (b) the corporation must eventually repay the principal of the bonds it issues.
6. Coupon bonds are called *bearer bonds* because the interest coupons are payable to the bearer or holder of the coupon.
7. The market interest rate on bond interest changes from day to day. Therefore, if the interest rate is favorable, investors may be willing to purchase bonds at either face value or at a premium. If rates are not favorable, the bonds will not be popular and investors may be able to purchase the bonds for less than face value or at a discount.
8. Bonds selling at 103 are being sold at a premium that is good for the corporation, because it means that investors are willing to pay an amount equal to 103% of the face value.
9. The carrying value of bonds is the face value plus any premium or less any discount. It represents the amount at which the corporation is "carrying" the bond issue on the corporate records.
10. Amortization of a bond discount *increases* the total interest expense because the interest incurred over the life of the bond issue will be greater than the contract rate. On the other hand, amortization of a bond premium *decreases* the total interest expense because the interest incurred over the life of the bond issue will be less than the contract rate.
11. When corporations issue bonds with interest payment dates that do not coincide with the end of the corporation's fiscal year, an adjusting entry must be made at the end of the fiscal period to record the accrued interest expense.
12. A corporation may want to redeem or call back a bond issue with a high contract interest rate and replace it with a bond issue with a lower contract issue rate.

Improving Your Analysis Skills

1. Expenses such as rent, advertising, utilities, and employee salaries increased more than sales.
2. The purchase price of merchandise increased but the selling price remained the same or was not increased enough.
3. The cost of ending merchandise inventory was understated the second year, causing the net income to be understated.

Mini Practice Set: Application Activity 3 Accounting for Liabilities

Application Activity 3 requires students to record and post transactions affecting current and long-term liabilities such as notes payable, bonds, and sinking fund for Metro Sports World, Inc., a publicly held corporation. Metro Sports World is a retail merchandising business that sells sporting goods and athletic equipment.

A partial general ledger has been opened in the student working papers. The account titles and account numbers have also been entered on the work sheet. At the end of the fiscal period, after all transactions have been recorded and posted, students will prepare a trial balance on the work sheet, and then enter the adjustments affecting selected current and long-term liabilities.

The accounting stationery needed to complete this activity is included in the student working papers. Most students should complete the activity manually in three to four class periods.

Chapter 9 Stockholders' Equity: Contributed Capital

Teaching Suggestions

In this chapter, students will learn about the characteristics, advantages, and disadvantages of corporations. They will learn how corporations raise capital and how to journalize transactions for the issuance of stock.

Point out to students that each of them will, at some time in his or her life, work for, own an interest in, or transact business with a corporation. For this reason, they should appreciate the economic impact that corporations have on their lives.

The Nature of a Corporation

Discuss Chief Justice Marshall's definition of a corporation with the class. Point out that, by law, a corporation is a separate legal being or entity, with all the rights, duties, and responsibilities of a person (except voting and marrying). Because of this status, a corporation may buy, sell, or inherit property. A corporation may be held responsible for its actions, to the point of being sued or punished for crimes.

Remind students that although most major businesses in the United States are organized as corporations, size is not a requirement. Many small businesses are also organized as corporations.

Forming a Corporation

One significant difference between corporations and sole proprietorships and partnerships is in their formation. It is relatively easy to form a sole proprietorship or partnership because there are few, if any, legal constraints. Before an organization can legally function as a corporation, it must file an application with the state in which it plans to do most of its business. Only after the application is approved by the state may the organization begin its business operations.

Most corporations are either privately held or publicly held corporations. Emphasize the difference between the two. Bring or have students bring to class the financial section of the newspaper. Point out that all of the companies listed on the various stock exchanges are publicly held corporations. You may want to take a few minutes to explain the data reported for a listed stock.

Organization costs can be carried on the corporate books for as long as forty years. However, the IRS permits corporations to amortize their organization costs as tax-deductible expenses over a period of not less than five years. For this reason, most corporations have adopted the five-year amortization period.

Present the management of a corporation by going over the organization chart in Figure 9-2 with students. Discuss with them how the board of directors and officers gain their positions. As an analogy, you may want to compare your school district with a corporation. For example, the voters in a community elect school board members, who oversee the educational process and establish school policies. The school board members hire administrators such as the superintendent, business manager, principals, and so on, who manage the school district and carry out school board policies. Be sure students understand the stockholders' rights listed in Figure 9-2. Dividends will be discussed in greater detail in Chapter 10. Mention that stockholders who do not attend the corporation's annual meeting may assign their voting rights to another individual via a proxy.

Capital Stock

A corporation usually is authorized to issue more stock than it plans to sell at the time of its organization. This enables the corporation to issue additional stock in the future without having to apply to the state for permission to do so.

Many investors prefer to buy common stock because of the voting privileges, growth possibilities, and options of buying additional shares of newly issued stock (pre-emptive right). Be sure students understand the difference between par-value stock and no-par stock. One disadvantage of par-value stock is that the investor may believe the par value represents the worth of the stock. In reality, stock is usually issued and sold for amounts higher than its par value.

As its name implies, preferred stock is granted some type of preference over common stock. This preference is usually in the form of payment of dividends. Be sure to explain that this preference does not guarantee a dividend; it guarantees only that preferred stockholders will receive a dividend first if a dividend is declared.

Issuing Stock

Remind students about the difference between par-value and no-par stock.

No-Par Stock

One of the main reasons for the development of no-par stock was to avoid the abuses that occurred when par-value stock was issued. Many people were confused about the meaning of par value, thinking that it represented the actual worth of the stock rather than simply the value that was assigned to it by the corporation's charter. Investors are less likely to be confused about the value of the property and the stock if there is no par value printed on the stock certificates.

The concept of legal capital may be difficult for students to understand. Remind them that stockholders of a corporation have limited liability. They are liable for the debts of the corporation only up to the amount of their investment. Creditors cannot look to the assets of the individual stockholders to satisfy their claims. Creditors' rights, however, must be protected. Legal capital represents the investment in assets that are available to meet creditors' claims.

Stock Subscriptions

If students have difficulty understanding stock subscriptions, you might compare it to buying something on layaway. In that instance, you choose an item, which the store sets aside for you. You then make regular periodic payments towards the total purchase price. Only when you have completely paid for the item will the store turn it over to you.

Since the stock will not be issued until it is completely paid for, the capital stock account cannot be credited. Instead, the total amount of the stock subscription is credited to the Common (or Preferred) Stock Subscribed account. Bring in notices from the financial section of the newspaper that advertise stock subscriptions, if these are available.

Answers to Chapter Activities

Building Your Accounting Vocabulary

articles of incorporation The application submitted by a person or persons to incorporate in a particular state is called the articles of incorporation.

authorized capital stock Authorized capital stock is the maximum number of shares that a corporation may issue according to its charter.

board of directors The board of directors of a corporation govern and are responsible for the affairs of the corporation.

charter The corporate charter is the articles of incorporation that have been approved by the state. It is, in essence, a legal contract between the state and the corporation, defining how the business may operate.

common stock When a corporation issues only one type of stock, it is called common stock.

corporation A corporation is an artificial legal being that may own property, enter into contracts, sue and be sued, and so on. It is a separate legal entity that has a continuous existence separate from that of its owners, the stockholders.

double taxation Double taxation refers to the fact that corporations must pay income taxes on their earnings and stockholders must pay personal income taxes on dividends that are distributed to them from those earnings.

issued shares Issued shares are those shares that have been sold to stockholders.

legal capital Legal capital represents the minimum amount of the capital contributed by the stockholders that must be kept in the business in order to give some protection to creditors.

no-par stock No-par stock is stock that does not have a dollar value printed on the stock certificates.

outstanding stock Outstanding stock is stock that is actually in the hands of stockholders.

par-value stock Par-value stock is stock that

has a specific value that is printed on the stock certificates.

pre-emptive right Pre-emptive right is the right of existing stockholders to subscribe to, or purchase, additional shares, when they are issued, in proportion to their present holdings.

preferred stock Preferred stock is a type of capital stock that has certain preferences over common stock. Preferred stockholders are paid dividends, at a set rate, before common stockholders. Preferred stockholders also receive their share of the corporations assets before common stockholders if a corporation goes out of business. Preferred stockholders, however, usually do not have voting rights.

stated value The stated value is the value assigned to a share of no-par stock by the corporation's board of directors.

stock Stock represents the shares of ownership in a corporation.

stock certificate A stock certificate is a document that shows how many shares of corporation stock are owned by a particular stockholder.

stockholders Stockholders are the owners of a corporation.

stockholders' ledger The stockholders' ledger is a subsidiary ledger showing the name and address of each stockholder and the number of shares owned.

stock subscription A stock subscription is a stockholder's contract to buy a certain number of shares of stock on an installment basis for an agreed upon price.

Reviewing Your Accounting Knowledge

1. A corporation is a separate legal entity in every respect, having a continuous existence separate from its owners. It may own property, enter into contracts, and sue or be sued in the courts.
2. Advantages of the corporate form of business organization include (a) limited liability of stockholders, (b) ease of raising capital, (c) ease of transferring ownership, (d) continuous existence, and (e) professional management. Disadvantages include (a) additional taxes and (b) additional governmental regulation.

   The greatest advantage is the limited liability of its owners—the stockholders. The greatest disadvantage is the double taxation on earnings.
3. Examples of organization costs include (a) fees paid to the state, (b) attorneys' fees, (c) promotional costs, (d) travel expenses, and (e) charges for printing stock certificates. Organization Costs is an intangible asset. Organization costs are written off as an expense over a period of years.
4. Capital stock represents the total amount invested in the corporation by its stockholders. Retained earnings represents the earnings held by the corporation and not distributed to stockholders as dividends.
5. Common stockholders have a right to vote on issues at the corporation's annual meetings. They also elect the board of directors, receive dividends, and share in the distribution of assets if the corporation is liquidated.
6. Preferred stockholders have the following advantages over common stockholders: (a) They receive their dividends before common stockholders; (b) they are assured of a stated, uniform rate of dividends; and (c) If the corporation goes out of business, preferred stockholders receive their share of the corporation's assets before common stockholders.

   Preferred stockholders incur the following disadvantages: (a) They usually cannot vote at the corporation's annual meetings, and (b) their dividends are limited to the regular rate unless the preferred stock is participating preferred stock.
7. The balance in the Capital Stock account represents the par value of all stock issued to stockholders.
8. If a corporation sells its stock at a price above par, the amount of the excess represents a part of the stockholders' investment. It does *not* represent a profit to the corporation.
9. The par value is a value that is actually printed on the stock certificate. The stated value is the value that has been assigned to no-par stock by the corporation's board of directors.
10. A corporation may issue stock on a subscription basis to accommodate investors who wish to purchase stock without paying for it right away. This may allow more shares to be sold.
11. Common Stock Subscribed is a temporary stockholders' equity account. It is used to record the par or stated value of the stock subscribed to but not yet issued. When the subscribers have completely paid for all their shares, the firm records the issuance of the stock by debiting the Com-

mon Stock Subscribed account and crediting the capital stock account.

Improving Your Human Relations Skills

Talk with Gail and Jeff, and explain how their negativism is starting to bother you. Point out that a negative attitude is harmful to them, their co-workers, and to the company. Suggest that rather than just complaining about what they don't like, they should look for ways to improve the workplace. They should (1) identify some problem situations, (2) come up with ideas for alleviating the problems, and (3) present their ideas to their supervisor.

Chapter 10 Stockholders' Equity: Earnings and Distributions

Teaching Suggestions

This chapter continues the accounting concepts, procedures, and applications for publicly held corporations. The chapter's main focus is on stockholders' equity: earnings and distribution. In this chapter, students will learn how corporations distribute their earnings to stockholders and, also, how a corporation reacquires and reissues shares of its own stock. Students will also learn how corporations can appropriate retained earnings for specific purposes.

Dividends

Remind students that stockholders are the owners of a corporation and are entitled to share in the profits of the business. Stress that dividends are not guaranteed. Mention that some corporations pay dividends regularly while others do not. Emphasize that the size and frequency of dividends depend upon the corporation's earnings, the amount of cash it has available, and the plans and policies of the corporation's board of directors.

Only the board of directors can determine whether to pay a dividend to stockholders. The board of directors is under no obligation to distribute the total amount of its earnings to stockholders. In fact, it would be foolish to do so. The corporation must retain some of its assets for emergencies, for future distributions to stockholders as dividends in those years when earnings are not sufficient to pay normal dividends, and—most important—for use in expanding operations.

Cash Dividends

Emphasize that both the balance in the Retained Earnings account and the balance in the Cash in Bank account must be sufficient to cover the amount of the proposed dividend. Often the corporation will have a large balance in the Retained Earnings account but not in the Cash in Bank account. Remind students that a cash dividend decreases the balance in both of these accounts.

Stress that preferred stock dividends have first claim to any dividend declared by the board of directors. Therefore, the total amount available for a common stock dividend may depend upon the amount paid to preferred stockholders.

Today most corporations prefer to debit a separate dividend account for each class of stock rather than debiting the Retained Earnings account directly. Dividends—Preferred and Dividends—Common are the two accounts used in this chapter. Stress that these two dividend accounts will be closed to the Retained Earnings account at the end of the fiscal period.

Stock Dividends

When presenting this section, discuss the advantages to a corporation of issuing stock dividends rather than cash dividends. Make sure students understand that when a stock dividend is declared, the percentage refers to the number of outstanding shares, not to the stock's market value.

Point out that the Retained Earnings account is debited directly for a stock dividend. The Dividends accounts are *not* used for stock dividends.

Point out that Common Stock Dividends Distributable is a stockholders' equity account rather than a liability account. A stock dividend declaration transaction is simply a rearrangement of the amounts in the stockholders' equity accounts. It will not decrease the total assets and therefore is not a liability that must be paid.

Explain why the Paid-in Capital in Excess of Par account is used when a stock dividend is declared. Remind students that the common stock account is used to record par value of the stock. The amount of the stock dividend is calculated on the market value of the stock, not on its par (or stated) value. Any excess over par must be credited to the paid-in capital account.

Stock Split

Point out to students that corporations split stock to lower its market value. As the market price of stock increases, some investors become increasingly less willing (or able) to buy the stock. By increasing the number of outstanding shares and lowering the market price, the corporation is making its stock more attractive—and more affordable—for investors.

Treasury Stock

The procedures involved with treasury stock are often confusing for students. Because a corporation cannot own part of itself, the balance in the Treasury Stock account cannot be considered an asset of the corporation. As a contra stockholders' equity account, it reduces the corporation's total paid-in capital and retained earnings.

When a corporation resells its treasury stock, it may be sold at cost, above cost, or below cost. The Paid-in Capital from the Sale of Treasury Stock account is debited if the treasury stock is sold below cost and credited if sold above cost. The Treasury Stock account is credited when the stock is sold.

Appropriating Retained Earnings

Point out to students that the board of directors of a corporation sometimes wishes to restrict a certain amount of retained earnings for a specific purpose. Give students several examples, and explain each one.

Introduce the new account Retained Earnings Appropriated for *(purpose)*. Point out that the balance in the Retained Earnings account represents unappropriated retained earnings and can be used for a cash or stock dividend. Mention that although retained earnings is appropriated, it does *not* represent a separate cash fund.

Point out that when the objective of the appropriated retained earnings has been accomplished, the retained earnings no longer need to be restricted. An entry is made that reverses the appropriation and returns the amount to the Retained Earnings account.

Answers to Chapter Activities

Building Your Accounting Vocabulary

appropriated retained earnings Appropriated retained earnings are retained earnings that the board of directors has restricted for a specific purpose.

cash dividend A cash dividend is a distribution in the form of cash paid by a corporation to stockholders as a reward for their investment.

dividend A dividend is a distribution of earnings—either in the form of cash or shares of stock—that a corporation makes to its stockholders.

stock dividend A stock dividend is a distribution of shares of its own stock that a corporation makes to its stockholders.

stock split A stock split is a deliberate split in the par or stated value of a corporation's stock and the issuance of a proportionate number of additional shares.

treasury stock Treasury stock is stock that has been issued by the corporation and then reacquired and held.

Reviewing Your Accounting Knowledge

1. The *date of declaration* is the date on which the board of directors votes to declare a dividend. The *date of record* is the date as of which the ownership of shares is determined. The *date of payment* is the date on which the dividend is actually paid.
2. Journal entries for dividends must be made on the date of declaration and the date of payment.
3. The minute book is a written narrative record of all actions taken at a corporation's official meetings. The minute book is important because it usually contains all details relating to the purchase of plant and equipment, bank loans, officer's salaries, etc.
4. Following are the three requirements that must be met before a corporation can pay a cash dividend: (a) There must be a sufficient balance in the Retained Earnings account against which cash dividends are charged; (b) there must be an adequate balance in the Cash in Bank account to cover the cash dividend; and (c) there

must be a formal declaration by the board of directors.

5. Dividends is a temporary contra stockholders' equity account. It is used to summarize the dividends declared by the corporation during the fiscal period. At the end of the fiscal period, the balance of the Dividend account is closed to the Retained Earnings account. In this way, it is very similar to a sole proprietor's or partner's withdrawals account.
6. A cash dividend is the distribution of cash to stockholders. A stock dividend is a distribution of shares of a company's own stock to its stockholders.
7. Cash dividends decrease both an asset account Cash in Bank and a stockholder's equity account Retained Earnings. A stock dividend merely transfers a dollar amount from Retained Earnings to the paid-in capital accounts. Therefore, the total stockholders' equity is unchanged.
8. A corporation may choose to make a stock dividend because it may wish to give its stockholders some return on their investments but does not wish to distribute cash or other assets that are needed to finance future expansion.
9. A stock dividend is a distribution by a corporation of its own stock to its stockholders. A stock split is a deliberate split in the par or stated value of a corporation's own stock and the issuance of a proportionate number of additional shares.
10. A corporation may buy back its own stock to (a) have stock available to reissue to employees under a bonus or stock-purchase plan; (b) support the market value of the stock if it is unusually low; or (c) have shares available for exchanges of stock if the corporation acquires other companies.
11. The accounts are classified as follows: Dividends Payable is a current liability account; Common Stock Dividend Distributable is a temporary stockholders' equity account; Treasury Stock is a contra stockholders' equity account; Paid-in Capital from Sale of Treasury Stock is a stockholders' equity account; Bonus to Employees is an other expense account.
12. When the board of directors of a corporation wishes to earmark (appropriate) part of retained earnings for some specific purpose, the board passes a resolution (which is recorded in the minute book) restricting a certain amount of retained earnings for a specific purpose.

Improving Your Communications Skills

1. John completed the task by the end of the day.
2. Everything we did that day was a waste of time.
3. The attorney accepted the case.
4. The store offered a discount.
5. The technician serviced the computer.
6. The sales manager dictated and signed the letter.
7. The applicant canceled the interview.
8. The copy center repaired the copier.
9. About a dozen people reviewed the draft of the report.
10. Helen threw the stack of papers into the wastebasket.

Chapter 11 Work Sheet and Financial Statements

Teaching Suggestions

The purpose of Chapter 11 is to pull together the topics presented in Unit 2. The chapter discusses the adjustments required and the preparation of the work sheet and financial statements for a publicly held merchandising corporation.

The Eight-Column Work Sheet

Students should understand that the account balances in the general ledger have no significance for managers, stockholders, and creditors as they are listed. The accountant therefore must organize the data in the general ledger to determine how well a business has done. The purpose of the work sheet is to assemble all the financial data needed to prepare the end-of-period financial statements and the adjusting and closing entries.

Remind students that all general ledger accounts are listed on the work sheet, whether or not those accounts have balances at the end of the period. Also remind students that many of the accounts with zero balances in the Trial Balance section will be used during the adjustment process.

The trial balance is a check on the equality of debits and credits in the general ledger. If the trial balance totals are not equal, errors have occurred that must be corrected before the end-of-period work can be continued.

Remind students that adjustments are planned and entered on the work sheet. The work sheet adjustments, however, do not update the accounts. The accounts can be updated only by the journalizing and posting of the adjusting entries.

Remind students to label the debit and credit parts of each adjustment with small letters in parentheses. This is done to more easily match up the debit and credit parts of the adjusting entries.

Again, remind students that the totals of the Debit and Credit columns in the Adjustments section must be equal. If they are not, the errors must be found before the work sheet can be continued.

Completing the Work Sheet

Up until this point, students have been using a ten-column work sheet that included an Adjusted Trial Balance section. However, this section will now be deleted to save time in completing the work sheet. Therefore, it is imperative that students extend the proper amounts to the last four columns of the work sheet. Remind students to begin with line 1 and extend all amounts to either the Balance Sheet section or the Income Statement section. Guide students through this new learning experience carefully.

Remind students that the difference between the Income Statement Debit and Credit columns and between the Balance Sheet Debit and Credit columns must be the same amount. If it is not, an error has been made that must be found and corrected.

Preparing End-of-Period Financial Statements

Now is the time to reinforce the idea of why the work sheet is called a tool of the accountant. The work sheet provides the data needed to prepare the three major financial statements: the income statement, the statement of stockholders' equity, and the balance sheet.

The Income Statement

Ask students to explain why the income statement is the first financial statement prepared at the end of the period. Students should realize that the data presented on the income statement are needed to complete other financial statements.

Point out the Other Revenue and Other Expenses sections of the income statement in Figure 11-2. Income and expenses that occur from transactions outside the normal operations of a merchandising business are reported in these two sections. Also point out that, on the income statement of a corporation, income taxes are reported separately. In this way, readers of the statement can more easily see the corporation's taxable income.

The Statement of Stockholders' Equity

Up to this point, students have prepared a statement of retained earnings for closely held corporations. Explain to students that today, instead of the statement of retained earnings, many corporations prepare a statement of stockholders' equity. The statement of stockholders' equity reports changes that have taken place in all of the stockholders' equity accounts during the period. Point out the specific columns for the preferred stock, common stock, treasury stock, retained earnings, and paid-in capital on the statement of stockholders' equity in Figure 11-3.

The Balance Sheet

Since the balance of the Retained Earnings account must be taken from the statement of stockholders' equity, students should understand why that statement is prepared *before* the balance sheet. Also, remind students that the balance sheet is prepared *as of a specific date* (unlike the income statement and statement of stockholders' equity) and reports the final balances of all permanent accounts. Take some time to discuss the location of the various new accounts introduced in this unit.

Notes to Financial Statements

Take a few minutes to review Figure 11-5 with students. Explain to them that it is customary for businesses to provide additional financial information that is used to support the financial statements. You may wish to have several annual reports of companies available for students to examine.

Completing the Accounting Cycle

Remind students that the purpose of the post-closing trial balance is to prove the equality of debits and credits in the general ledger *after* the adjusting and closing entries have been journalized and posted. Briefly review the post-closing trial balance in Figure 11-7 with students.

Answers to Chapter Activities

Building Your Accounting Vocabulary

accrual An accrual is the recognition of revenue or expenses that have gradually increased over time but have not yet been recorded.

deferral A deferral is a delay in recognizing revenue for cash already received or an expense for a bill already paid.

notes to financial statements The notes to financial statements contain additional information that explains significant matters not disclosed in the financial statements and the accounting policies followed by the organization.

statement of stockholders' equity The statement of stockholders' equity reports the changes that have taken place in all of the stockholders' equity accounts during the period.

Reviewing Your Accounting Knowledge

1. Adjustments must be made at the end of the accounting period to bring certain accounts up to date.
2. An accrual is the recognition of revenue or expenses that have gradually increased over time but that have not yet been recorded. Examples of accruals include the interest on a note receivable that matures during the next fiscal period and the salary expense incurred during the current fiscal period but not paid until the next period. A deferral is the delay in recognizing revenue for cash already received or an expense for a bill already paid. Examples of deferrals include prepaid expenses such as insurance and unearned revenue such as rent received in advance.
3. Some adjustments normally made at the end of the accounting period are: accrued interest income, estimated bad debt losses, depreciation, prepaid interest expense, accrued interest expense, accrued salaries, unearned rental income, federal income taxes, merchandise inventory, supplies.
4. Interest Receivable is debited and Interest Income is credited to record the adjustment for accrued interest income.
5. Bad Debts Expense is debited and Allowance for Uncollectible Accounts is credited for the adjustment for the estimated uncollectible amount using the allowance method.
6. Accumulated Depreciation is credited for the annual depreciation on a plant asset.
7. The balance in Discount on Notes Payable is the prepaid interest expense chargeable to the next fiscal period.
8. Unearned Rent is classified as a liability.
9. A corporation's taxable income may differ from the net income on its income statement for the following reasons:
   (a) A corporation may use one depreciation method for financial accounting purposes and another depreciation method for income tax purposes.
   (b) A company may include certain types of revenue on its income statement but not on its tax return.
   (c) A corporation may record certain types of expenditures as assets and therefore not include them on the income statement but list them on a tax return as expenses.
10. The three financial statements prepared by a merchandising corporation are the income statement, the statement of stockholders' equity, and the balance sheet.
11. The statement of stockholders' equity reports the changes that have taken place in all of the stockholders' equity accounts during the period.
12. The balance of the Dividends account is closed into Retained Earnings at the end of the period.
13. Notes to financial statements are prepared to provide additional information that explains significant matters not disclosed in the financial statements and the accounting policies followed by a corporation.

Improving Your Problem-Solving Skills

What the co-worker is doing is not dishonest. However, she should not borrow cash from the fund because it was established for making small business cash disbursements only. Furthermore, what she is doing might lead to dishonesty. If the supervisor found the fund short, she might blame your friend for the shortage and fire her.

Mini Practice Set: Application Activity 4 Accounting for a Publicly Held Corporation

Application Activity 4 requires students to complete the end-of-fiscal period work sheet and financial statements for Jet Star Products, Inc., a publicly held merchandising corporation.

A trial balance has been completed on the work sheet in the student working papers. Students will enter the required adjustments and complete the eight-column work sheet. They will use the data on the work sheet to prepare an income statement, statement of stockholders'equity, and a classified balance sheet. They will then complete the accounting cycle by recording and posting the adjusting and closing entries. In the new fiscal period, students will record and post various transactions relating to corporate income tax, stocks, and dividends.

The accounting stationery needed to complete this activity is included in the student working papers. Most students should be able to complete the activity manually in four to five class periods.

UNIT 3 UNDERSTANDING BUSINESS INFORMATION

Chapter 12 Analyzing and Interpreting Financial Statements

Teaching Suggestions

The annual financial reports published by many corporations are often difficult to understand. They require a thorough analysis to dig out the data needed to answer specific questions and to find meaningful relationships within each report or from one report to another. To enable students to see the real world of analyzing and interpreting financial statements, obtain samples of annual and interim financial statements and the analysis of each statement by a corporate accountant.

Interpreting Financial Data

Financial statements that are classified are easier to analyze than those that are not separated into related categories or classifications. You may want to bring into class examples of several annual reports to show students how published financial statements are classified.

Horizontal Analysis

Explain horizontal analysis to students. To help build confidence, remind them that calculating the percentages is simply an arithmetic function. You may want to review for students the calculations of a few percentages using the comparative income statement in Figure 12-1.

Working Capital

Discuss how working capital is an important measure of a company's liquidity. Illustrate how lack of working capital can lead to the failure of a business.

Ratio Analysis

Accountants rely on analysis and use of ratios to find out more about a company than would be possible simply by reading the financial data as presented. The process of comparing a set of figures and establishing their relationship enables one to gain a better understanding of a going concern. Ratios highlight unusual, unexpected, or otherwise unexplained, changes in a business's performance.

Published comparative ratio information may be acquired from two basic groups or agencies. One group, which includes Dun & Bradstreet and Robert Morris Associates, compiles financial data for a number of individual industries. The other group, generally trade associations, compiles information for a particular industry or group of industries.

Dun & Bradstreet, Inc., has been publishing "Key Business Ratios" annually since 1932 in *Dun's Review and Modern Industry*, a monthly magazine. Robert Morris Associates, founded in 1914, has developed ratio studies for over 225 lines of business. The most important specialized industry sources for ratio data are national trade associations. These associations publish ratio statistics covering a wide range of industries.

Financial ratios allow interested parties to make relative evaluations. Ratios, however, are only guidelines and can serve as warning signs. Students should be given some cautions. First, a simple ratio does not provide enough information to judge a firm; rather, a group of ratios is required. Second, ratios must be applied consistently over time to make meaningful comparisons.

The ratios in this chapter are but a few of the ratios that can be calculated in analyzing financial data. The primary aim of this chapter is not to turn students into analysts but to show them what happens to the financial data they have learned to record and report. Reinforce the concept that the financial data reported by a company presents a picture of that company's financial results. For public corporations, the picture is there for anyone who wants to see or who knows how to analyze the parts of the picture.

Ratios can be divided into three general groups: (1) liquidity ratios, (2) profitability ratios, and (3) financial strength ratios.

Liquidity Ratios

Liquidity ratios measure the ability of the firm to pay its bills as they come due. The liquidity ratios discussed in this chapter are current ratio, quick ratio, merchandise inventory turnover, and accounts receivable turnover.

Profitability Ratios

Profitability ratios measure how well the business is performing with earnings. The three discussed in this chapter are (1) the return on common stockholders' equity, (2) earnings per share of common stock, and (3) the price-earnings ratio.

Financial Strength Ratios

Financial strength ratios measure the ability of a business to pay its debts, maintain its credit standing, and borrow in the future. The three commonly used financial strength ratios are (1) the ratio of stockholders' equity to liabilities; (2) the ratio of property, plant, and equipment to long-term liabilities; and (3) equity per share.

Answers to Chapter Activities

Building Your Accounting Vocabulary

accounts receivable turnover Accounts receivable turnover is an indication of how quickly a company collects its average accounts receivable. It is the number of times per year that a company collects the average balance of Accounts Receivable.

base year The base year is the year being used for comparison.

common-size statements Common-size statements are those on which all items are reported as percentages of a key item and no dollar amounts are reported.

comparability Comparability refers to financial information that can be compared from one fiscal period to another or from one business to another.

current ratio The current ratio is the relationship between a company's current assets and its current liabilities.

earnings per share Earnings per share measures the amount of profit that could be assigned to each share of common stock.

equity per share Equity per share refers to the amount that would be paid on each share of stock if the corporation liquidated and the assets were sold for their book value.

horizontal analysis Horizontal analysis is comparing dollar amount changes and percentage changes for the same items on a company's financial statements for two or more periods.

merchandise inventory turnover Merchandise inventory turnover is the number of times a company's inventory is sold during a given year.

price-earnings ratio The price-earnings ratio is a measure commonly used to determine whether the market price of a corporation's stock is reasonable.

profitability Profitability refers to a company's ability to earn a reasonable profit on the owner's investment.

quick ratio The quick ratio is the relationship between short-term liquid assets and current liabilities.

ratio analysis Ratio analysis is the comparison of two amounts on a financial statement resulting in a percentage that shows the relationship between the two amounts.

vertical analysis With vertical analysis, every dollar amount reported on a financial statement is also stated as a percentage of a base amount reported on the same statement.

working capital Working capital is the amount by which current assets exceed current liabilities.

Reviewing Your Accounting Knowledge

1. The three techniques commonly used to analyze financial statement information are horizontal analysis, vertical analysis, and ratio analysis.
2. Percentages of increases or decreases are calculated on financial statements organized for horizontal analysis by dividing the dollar increase or decrease by the base year amount and multiplying by 100.
3. Horizontal analysis compares dollar amount changes and percentage changes for the same line item on a company's financial statement for two or more periods. With vertical analysis, every dollar amount reported on a financial statement is also stated as a percentage of a base amount reported on the same statement. Then the current year percentages are compared with the percentages of previous years or with the percentages of other businesses within the same industry.
4. When an income statement is prepared for vertical analysis, net sales is the base amount. On a comparative balance sheet

prepared for vertical analysis, the base amount is either total assets or total liabilities and stockholders' equity.

5. Changes on comparative financial statements are given in both dollar amounts and percentages because dollar amounts will indicate a volume change while a percentage represents relative differences.
6. If a firm has a gross profit percentage of 37%, this means that for every $1,000 in net sales, the company earned a gross profit of $370.
7. The quick ratio and current ratio differ because the quick ratio is the relationship between short-term liquid assets (those that can be converted to cash quickly) while the current ratio is the relationship between *all* current assets and current liabilities. The current ratio and quick ratio are similar in that both measure a company's ability to pay its bills and repay loans.
8. A company would want a high merchandise inventory turnover rate because it indicates a higher gross profit since more merchandise is being sold. It also means that the company has money tied up in inventory for shorter periods of time and that there is less chance that the inventory will spoil or become outdated.
9. Liquidity refers to the ease with which an asset can be converted to cash. Profitability refers to a company's ability to earn a reasonable profit on the investments of the owners.
10. The following ratios can be used to determine how well an investment is doing: earnings per share of stock, price-earnings ratio, and return on stockholders' equity.
11. Liquidity ratios include the current ratio, quick ratio, merchandise inventory turnover, and accounts receivable turnover. Profitability ratios include return on stockholders' equity, earnings per share of stock, and price-earnings ratio. Financial strength ratios include the ratio of stockholders' equity to liabilities; ratio of property, plant, and equipment to long-term liabilities; and equity per share.

Improving Your Math Skills

1. $38.35
2. $14.92
3. $27.73
4. $119.20
5. $6.05
6. $0.19
7. $1.28
8. $10.48
9. $5.58
10. $0.43
11. $83.33
12. $159.57

Chapter 13 Statement of Cash Flows

Teaching Suggestions

The purpose of this chapter is to introduce the fourth major financial statement that is now prepared by most businesses: the statement of cash flows.

The Statement of Cash Flows

The statement of cash flows presents information on why cash either increased or decreased during the accounting period.

Review the accrual basis of accounting using accrued salaries expense as the accrued expense example and accrued interest income as the accrued revenue example. Point out that the income statement is prepared by most businesses using the accrual basis of accounting; therefore, it reports revenue and expenses for an accounting period even though cash may not have been received or paid. Establish the need for converting the income statement from the accrual basis of accounting to the cash basis. This must be done to determine the change in the balance of the Cash in Bank account.

Remind students that the comparative balance sheet reports the change in the balance of Cash in Bank, but it does not provide the reason for the change. That is the reason for preparing the statement of cash flows.

Point out that the FASB *Statement of Financial Accounting Standards No. 95* states that the statement of cash flows must clearly show the amount of cash flows from (1) operating activities, (2) investing activities, and (3) financing activities. A company is also required to report noncash activities that do not directly affect cash flows of the current accounting period but will affect cash flows of future accounting periods.

Preparing the Statement of Cash Flows

Discuss how the income statement and the comparative balance sheet will be used in preparing the statement of cash flows. Point out that the general ledger accounts are used to analyze the balance changes in the balance sheet accounts.

The Cash Flows from Operating Activities

Point out that the income statement and comparative balance sheet must be used to determine cash flows from operating activities. Discuss the two parts of the cash flows from operating activities section. Note that cash receipts are taken from the net sales and other revenue sections of the income statement and that cash payments are taken from the cost of merchandise sold, operating expenses, and other expenses sections.

When reviewing the income statement, point out the related balance sheet account(s) needed to determine the cash flows from operating activities. Note that the Gain on Sale of Plant Assets account has no related balance sheet account. You might want to develop the following table as each cash flow is presented:

Income Statement Amount/Account	Related Balance Sheet Account(s)
Net Sales	Accounts Receivable
Cost of Mdse. Sold	Mdse. Inventory
Operating Expenses	Accounts Payable Prepaid Expenses Accrued Liabilities
Gain on Sale of Plant Assets	None
Interest Income	Interest Receivable
Interest Expense	Interest Payable
Federal Income Tax	Fed. Inc. Tax Payable

Point out why the net sales balance on the income statement represents both cash sales and sales on account. Explain why cash sales directly increase cash. Introduce the related balance sheet account that is used to determine the cash receipts from sales to customers.

Point out that the interest income reported on the income statement represents both cash receipts of interest and accrued interest. Identify the related balance sheet account that must be used to determine the cash receipts for interest income.

Point out the three amounts/accounts that must be used to determine the cash payments for purchases. Emphasize that to determine cash payments for purchases, a two-step procedure must be used: (1) Determine the cost of net purchases, and (2) determine the relationship between cost of net purchases and the change in the balance of the Accounts Payable account. Point out that merchandise can be purchased for cash or on account. Cash purchases directly decrease the cash flows.

Point out that operating expenses represent the cash spent or assets consumed to earn revenue during the accounting period. Discuss why the cash payments for operating expenses will not equal the operating expenses reported on the income statement if there are prepaid expenses, accrued liabilities, and depreciation expenses. Point out that cash payments for operating expenses is calculated in three steps: (1) Determine cash flows for prepaid expenses; (2) determine cash flows for accrued liabilities; and (3) determine cash flows for operating expenses that include depreciation expenses.

Illustrate the adjusting entry for the accrued expense for salaries earned but not yet paid. Show how the cash flow is not affected until the salaries are actually paid. Point out that the related balance sheet account is Accrued Liabilities.

Record in general journal form the adjusting entry for an accrued expense. Point out that the amount reported on the income statement includes the interest expense for which cash has not yet been paid.

Identify the related balance sheet account for Income Tax Expense. Discuss why the Income Tax Expense reported on the income statement does not represent the actual cash paid for income tax. Illustrate the adjusting entry for Income Tax Expense. Refer students to Figure 13-1 (page 359) to see how cash flows are reported in the operating activities section of the statement of cash flows.

The Cash Flows from Investing Activities Section

Illustrate in general journal form the entry to purchase marketable securities. Note that the credit to Cash in Bank directly affects the cash flow. Refer students to Figure 13-1. Point out that under the cash flows from investing activities section, changes in cash flows are listed separately to give complete information. Discuss the placement of parentheses around amounts that are cash outflows.

Illustrate in general journal form the purchase of a plant asset for cash. Note that the credit to the Cash in Bank account has a direct effect on the cash flow. Also illustrate in general journal form the sale of a plant asset for cash. Note that the debit to Cash in Bank also has a direct effect on the cash flow.

The Cash Flows from Financing Activities Section

Point out that when cash is borrowed using a note payable, a cash inflow results. When a payment is made on the note, there is a cash outflow. Use the T account illustrated on page 352.

Illustrate in general journal form the entries to record borrowing cash by issuing bonds and buying back bonds at a later time. Point out how these transactions directly affect cash flows. Discuss the transactions shown in the T account on page 352. Point out that the non-cash issue for $200,000 will be discussed later in the chapter.

Illustrate in general journal form the entry to issue capital stock for cash. Point out that this is a direct increase in cash flows. Refer students to the T accounts illustrated on page 353. Note that the cash inflow from issuing capital stock is $125,000 ($100,000 total par value + $25,000 excess).

Refer students to Figure 13-1 to see how cash flows from financing activities are reported on the statement of cash flows.

The Schedule of Noncash Investing and Financing Transactions

Point out the general ledger accounts affected by noncash investing and financing. Record in general journal form the issuing of bonds payable for plant assets. Discuss how although this transaction does not affect cash flows during the current accounting period, it will affect cash flows in future accounting periods. Refer students to Figure 13-1 to see how the schedule of noncash investing and financing transactions is included at the bottom of the statement of cash flows.

Answers to Chapter Activities

Building Your Accounting Vocabulary

cash equivalents Cash equivalents as defined by the Financial Accounting Standards Board are short-term, highly liquid investments. Examples of cash equivalents are U.S. Treasury bills and certificates of deposit.

cash flows from financing activities Cash flows from financing activities is the section of the statement of cash flows that includes transactions that affect certain liability and stockholders' equity accounts.

cash flows from investing activities Cash flows from investing activities is the section of the statement of cash flows that includes transactions that affect certain asset accounts—plant assets and marketable securities.

cash flows from operating activities Cash flows from operating activities is the section of the statement of cash flows that includes the cash transactions that are used to determine net income.

cash inflows Cash inflows are cash receipts. They represent increases in cash during the accounting period.

cash outflows Cash outflows are cash payments. They represent cash decreases during the accounting period.

noncash investing and financing activities Noncash investing and financing activities is a section of the statement of cash flows that includes transactions involving long-lived assets, long-term liabilities, or capital stock. Noncash investing and financing transactions do not involve cash.

statement of cash flows The statement of cash flows is a financial statement that is prepared at the end of a fiscal period to show how cash was affected by the operating, investing, and financing activities of a business during the accounting period. The statement explains why cash either increased or decreased during the accounting period.

Reviewing Your Accounting Knowledge

1. A statement of cash flows is prepared to explain why cash either increased or decreased during the accounting period.
2. The statement of cash flows is useful to business managers, investors, and creditors because they use the statement to determine the company's ability to pay liabilities and dividends and to determine the company's need for additional investing and financing.
3. The three classifications of cash flows reported on a statement of cash flows are (a) operating activities, (b) investing activities, and (c) financial activities.
4. The principal cash inflows for operating activities section of the statement of cash flows are cash receipts from sales and interest income. The principal cash outflows are cash payments for purchases of merchandise, operating expenses, interest expense, and federal income tax expense.
5. The income statement and comparative balance sheet are the two financial state-

ments that provide information needed to prepare a statement of cash flows.

6. Cash receipts from sales to customers are greater than the net sales reported on the income statement when the balance of Accounts Receivable decreases because cash receipts on account are greater than sales on account during the accounting period.
7. Interest Receivable is the balance sheet account used to determine cash receipts from interest income.
8. The two balance sheet accounts that are used to determine cash payments for purchases are (a) Merchandise Inventory and (b) Accounts Payable.
9. Depreciation expense reduces the cash flows for operating expenses because depreciation is an expense for which there is no cash payment.
10. A gain on the sale of a plant asset is not included on the statement of cash flows because it does not affect cash flows.
11. The Bonds Payable account is analyzed to determine the effects of cash flows from long-term borrowing.
12. Since noncash transactions do not affect cash flows for the current accounting period, they are not included in the statement of cash flows. However, the Financial Accounting Standards Board decided that a separate schedule of these noncash investing and financing transactions must be prepared because these transactions will affect future cash flows.

Improving Your Decision-Making Skills

If I do not understand what I am to do, I should stop the instructor and ask questions. I cannot assume that because no one asks questions everyone understands the instructor's comments. Other employees may be just as lost as I am. Some people will not ask questions because they do not want others to know they don't understand. Since the purpose of the training program is to learn procedures for the new computer system, I must be sure I take responsibility for getting what I need from the session.

UNIT 4 ACCOUNTING FOR OTHER FORMS OF ORGANIZATION

Chapter 14 Partnerships: Formation, Dissolution, and Liquidation

Teaching Suggestions

In this chapter, students will learn about the characteristics of a partnership, how partnerships are formed, and how they may be dissolved. Most business transactions are handled in the same manner, regardless of whether the business is a sole proprietorship, partnership, or corporation. Students will learn how to handle those transactions peculiar to the partnership form of business organization. They will learn how to record journal entries for partnership formation, dissolution, and liquidation.

Accounting for a Partnership

Of the three types of business organization, the partnership is the least common. Emphasize that partnerships are often found in professions such as law and medicine and in firms that stress personal service. Have students list businesses organized as partnerships in your local area or state. They may find very few true partnerships.

Characteristics of a Partnership

Discuss each characteristic of a partnership. Use examples with which students can readily identify.

Advantages of a Partnership

For each advantage, give a realistic example. Make the example one with which the students can easily identify. For example, suppose two people wish to form a partnership to operate a yarn store. One partner has experience in retail sales of yarns and accessories. The other partner has accounting and managerial skills. Their partnership offers the opportunity to pool their different skills to operate one business.

Disadvantages of a Partnership

Give examples for each disadvantage. You might also wish to point out to students that serious disagreements among the partners often lead to the dissolution of the partnership. Successful partners must therefore get along well and respect the rights and responsibilities of the other partners.

The Partnership Agreement

Emphasize the importance of the partnership agreement. This agreement should spell out what each partner is to do and how the assets are to be divided if the partnership is dissolved or liquidated. Ask students to imagine what might happen if some of the items listed on page 370 were not included in the partnership agreement. Also, ask what might happen if the partnership agreement did not exist at all.

Accounting for Partners' Equity

Use T accounts to illustrate a simple listing of accounts in the general ledger of a sole proprietorship. Next, introduce the fact that the only difference between accounting for a sole proprietorship and a partnership is the accounting for the changes in the owners' equity. Illustrate this difference by adding one capital account and one withdrawals account to the existing T accounts.

Stress the types of cash and noncash assets a partner may invest in a partnership. Discuss how the value of the noncash assets is determined. Use the examples in the table on page 371 to illustrate your points. After determining the value of the assets, explain the journal entry in Figure 14-2. Discuss with students why the previous accumulated depreciation is not recorded in the initial investment entry of the new partnership.

You might want to point out that if a partner withdraws a plant asset from the partnership, the asset's accumulated depreciation account must also be closed.

Dissolution of a Partnership

Use T accounts to illustrate the purchase of the interest of one of the partners by an outside party. Stress that the partnership's accountant is concerned only with removing the old partner from and placing the new partner in the accounting records.

Point out that investments of assets by a new partner will increase the owners' equity of the business. Total the capital in your T accounts to show the increase.

Discuss why the assets of a business are revaluated before a partner withdraws from the partnership. Give an example of what is meant by current market value. Stress why the partnership agreement should include a provision for an audit if a partner decides to withdraw. When the assets are revaluated, a journal entry is recorded.

Liquidation of a Partnership

Point out that the liquidation process may stretch over a long period of time. Compare a partnership liquidation to a current business that is advertising a "going-out-of-business sale." The transactions would be similar.

To illustrate a gain of the sale of assets, walk students through the four liquidation steps using T accounts. Point out that the gain from realization is allocated among the partners according to the method stated in the partnership agreement. Post each transaction shown in Figure 14-10 to the T accounts so that students can see how the various accounts of the partnership are closed. Before the last entry is posted, students should see that the amount recorded in the Cash in Bank account represents the total of the three partners' capital accounts. Each partner is entitled to receive cash equal to the balance recorded in his or her capital account.

Answers to Chapter Activities

Building Your Accounting Vocabulary

dissolution In the dissolution of a partnership, the original partnership is dissolved, but the business continues to operate. A change occurs in the personnel of the partnership.

liquidation In the liquidation of a partnership, both the partnership and business end.

mutual agency Mutual agency is the ability of any partner to enter into valid contracts in the name of the firm that are binding on the partnership.

partnership A partnership is an association of two or more persons to operate, as co-owners, a business for profit.

partnership agreement A partnership agreement is a written document that sets out the terms under which the partnership will operate.

realization Realization refers to the sale of the assets of a business for cash.

Reviewing Your Accounting Knowledge

1. Four characteristics of the partnership form of organization are (a) co-ownership of partnership property, (b) limited life, (c) unlimited liability, and (d) mutual agency.
2. Advantages of the partnership form of organization include the following: (a) an opportunity to pool the abilities, experiences, and resources of two or more persons; (b) ease of formation; (c) few legal restrictions; and (d) the fact that federal income taxes are not levied against the partnership as an entity. Disadvantages of the partnership form of organization include the following: (a) general partners—those who actively and publicly participate in the operations of the business—have unlimited liability; (b) the partnership has a limited life; (c) the actions of one partner are binding on the other partners; (d) raising large amounts of capital is difficult; and (e) it is difficult to transfer a partnership interest to another person.
3. Yes, the contract is binding. Because of the mutual agency concept, any partner can enter into valid, binding contracts for the purchase of goods or services for the business.
4. The partnership itself does not pay any federal income taxes. However, each partner must report and pay tax on his or her share of the partnership's net income, whether or not the share is withdrawn from the business.
5. Yes, it is possible for one owner to lose more than the amount he or she has invested. Each partner is personally liable for the debts of the partnership.
6. A partnership agreement usually includes the following items: (a) effective date of

the agreement; (b) names and addresses of the partners; (c) name, location, and nature of the business; (d) duration of the agreement; (e) investment of each partner; (f) duties, rights, and responsibilities of each partner; (g) withdrawals of capital to be allowed each partner; (h) agreement for sharing profits and losses; and (i) procedure for dividing assets when partnership is dissolved.

7. The assets are recorded on the books of the partnership at their current market values.
8. A partnership may be dissolved by any one of the following: the admission of a new partner, the withdrawal of a partner, and the death of a partner.
9. The new partner may be admitted by purchasing an interest from one or more of the original partners or by investing additional assets in the partnership.
10. In the dissolution of a partnership, the business continues to operate. When a partnership is liquidated, the business terminates its operations.
11. The four steps to liquidate a partnership are as follows: (a) The assets are sold for cash; (b) the total loss or gain is allocated among the partners; (c) liabilities are paid; and (d) the remaining cash is distributed to the partners.

Improving Your Analysis Skills

1. Sales were highest in 1986. Sales were lowest in 1980.
2. Sales were the same in 1983 and 1987.
3. Sales have been declining steadily since 1986.

Chapter 15 Partnerships: Division of Profits and Losses

Teaching Suggestions

At the end of the fiscal period, the partnership's net income or loss must be divided among the partners. In this chapter, students will learn about several methods that can be used to allocate partnership earnings. Students will also learn how to record the closing entries for the division of net income or loss and how to prepare the financial statements for a partnership.

Dividing Net Income or Net Loss

Emphasize that the partners can choose any method they wish to divide net income or net loss. You may wish to develop a handout for students that shows the effects of each of the five methods on the partners' capital accounts.

Dividing Net Income or Loss Equally

Since this method is the simplest, illustrate it first. Stress that, by law, this method is used if there is no clause in the partnership agreement as to how net income or loss is to be distributed. This method is often chosen when all partners contribute equally to the operation of the business.

Students should have little trouble with this method of dividing partnership earnings. Nevertheless, use T accounts to show the effect of this method (and the other methods) on the partners' capital accounts. You might also want to give students balances for the partners' withdrawals accounts. Then students can determine the total owners' equity of the partnership at the end of the period.

Throughout this textbook, a net income has been presented almost exclusively in the examples and problems. Therefore, you may wish to spend a little more time on the net loss assumptions in this chapter, since students are less familiar with them.

Dividing Net Income or Loss on a Fractional-Share Basis

Point out to students that the size of the fractions may be based on (1) the amount of each partner's investment and (2) the amount of time and expertise contributed by each partner.

Give students several other drills on ratios. For example:

$$3:2:1 = 3 + 2 + 1 = 6 = \frac{3}{6}, \frac{2}{6}, \text{ and } \frac{1}{6}$$

$$2:2:1 = 2 + 2 + 1 = 5 = \frac{2}{5}, \frac{2}{5}, \text{ and } \frac{1}{5}$$

$$1:4:2 = 1 + 4 + 2 = 7 = \frac{1}{7}, \frac{4}{7}, \text{ and } \frac{2}{7}$$

Point out that ratios usually follow the order in which the partners are listed in the partnership agreement. For example, if a partnership consists of three partners—Jones, Smith, and Tate—and the ratio is stated as 3:2:1, Jones will receive 3/6, Smith 2/6, and Tate 1/6.

Mention that the fractional-share ratios may be stated as percentages, for example, 60-40 or 40-30-30. It may be easier for students to work the calculations if the ratio is stated as a percentage.

Dividing Net Income or Loss Based on the Ratio of Capital Investments

When the partners' capital investment is more important than time devoted to the business or managerial talents, this method may be used to allocate profits and losses. The partnership agreement should specify which capital balances will determine the ratio (beginning, average, ending, and so on).

Dividing Net Income or Loss Based on Salary Allowances

Salary allowances are used to reward a partner who devotes more time to the business. The more time devoted to the business, the larger the salary allowance. The salary allowance method may also be used when the services of one partner are more valuable to the partnership than the services of another partner. For example, one partner may have a technical knowledge that is more valuable to the partnership than another person's sales ability.

Dividing Net Income or Loss Based on Interest Allowances

Salary allowances reward partners for the services they provide to the partnership. They do not, however, take into consideration the partners' capital investments. The interest allowance method further compensates the partner with the largest capital investment. Stress that an interest allowance provides an incentive for partners to leave their investments in the partnership.

If both the services contributed by the partners and the capital investments are unequal, the partners may choose to use both interest and salary allowances to allocate net income or loss.

Answers to Chapter Activities

Building Your Accounting Vocabulary

interest allowance An interest allowance is a method of distributing net income (or loss) that takes into account a partner's capital contribution.

salary allowance A salary allowance is an allocation of net income (or loss) used to recognize and reward differences in ability and time partners devote to the business.

statement of changes in partners' equity A statement of changes in partners' equity reports the changes in the balances of the partners' capital accounts.

Reviewing Your Accounting Knowledge

1. There are two differences between the closing entries for a partnership and those for a sole proprietorship.
   a. Instead of a single capital account and a single withdrawals account, in a partnership each partner has a capital account and a withdrawals account.
   b. In a partnership, Income Summary is closed into all of the partners' capital accounts by the amount of the net income (or loss). The partners' withdrawals accounts are closed into their respective capital accounts.
2. If no method is specified in the partnership agreement, net income or loss is allocated equally.
3. Five methods of dividing a partnership's net income or loss are as follows: (a) equally, (b) on a fractional-share basis, (c) based on a capital investments ratio, (d) based on salary allowances, and (e) based on interest allowances.
4. Partners may choose to divide net income or net loss equally if they all spend the same amount of time in the business, contribute equal amounts of capital, and have similar managerial talents.
5. When net income is divided on a fractional-share basis, two factors could be considered: (a) the amount of each partner's investment and (b) the value of each partner's services.
6. A salary allowance is an allocation of net income or loss. Salary expense is the wages paid to employees in return for their services.
7. The advantage to the partnership of providing an interest allowance on the partner's capital investments is that it provides an incentive for partners to not only leave their investments in the business but to increase them.
8. Hunt receives \$38,400 (\$64,000 × 3/5); Wright receives \$25,600 (\$64,000 × 2/5).
9. The three financial statements prepared for a partnership at the end of the fiscal period are an income statement, a state-

ment of changes in partners' equity, and a balance sheet.

10. A partnership must file an informational tax return (Form 1065), which reports how the year's net income or loss was allocated to each partner. A partnership itself does not pay income taxes. Partners must include their shares of the net income on their personal income tax returns. The total amount must be reported whether or not they withdrew that money.

Improving Your Human Relations Skills

Since Cathy and Latanya appear to be performing their work properly, it would probably be best not to talk with your supervisor at this time. Once the project has been started, however, you should talk with your supervisor if their feud appears to be jeopardizing the project.

You may want to discuss your concerns for the project with Cathy and Latanya and talk about the importance of teamwork.

Chapter 16 Not-for-Profit Organizations: Budgeting and Control

Teaching Suggestions

Although there are many businesses in the United States that operate to earn a profit, there are also organizations that operate for purposes other than earning a profit. These organizations are usually called not-for-profit organizations. Over 20% of the clerical and accounting workers in the United States are employed by not-for-profit organizations, the largest group being federal, state, and local government employees. It is therefore important for students who wish to study accounting to learn about accounting for not-for-profit organizations. The emphasis of this chapter is on the importance of budgeting and budget controls for a not-for-profit organization.

Characteristics of Not-for-Profit Organizations

Have students list a number of not-for-profit organizations in the local area. After students understand the difference between a profit-oriented and a not-for-profit business, have them compare the services or goods each provides.

Fund Accounting

Illustrate the funds your school's accounting personnel must account for. For example, the general fund, athletic fund, textbook fund, and lunch money fund are a few funds a school might manage. Stress that each fund must be accounted for separately, thus creating a need for fund accounting.

The Budgeting Process

Introduce students to budgeting by using a simple example. Ask each student how he or she would spend $100 a month if it were available. After students have prepared a list of ways to spend the $100, relate their planning and ways to spend the money to the basic principles involved in the budgeting process.

Lead students in understanding what a long-term goal is. Then use the swimming pool example for the Mountain View Recreation Center. You might have students outline some of their long-term goals.

Identify for students the meaning of a short-term goal. Explain that winning the district championship is a long-term goal, while winning each district game is a short-term goal.

Share with students an example of responsibility. Then relate this example to how individuals depend on one another to reach a goal. Use FBLA competition as an example. The goal could be to send the parliamentary procedures team to the national convention. Relate how each FBLA member can be a part of this goal by accepting a certain responsibility. After relating this example, review how a not-for-profit organization's budgeting process requires the cooperation of many people.

Mention that in preparing for a big competitive event, certain guidelines must be established. Certain deadlines must be met, information must be shared, and much planning and organizing must be done. This is also true for a not-for-profit organization. In the budgeting process, leaders must establish deadlines, information must be shared, and many individuals must work cooperatively with one another.

Stress that for a not-for-profit organization to operate efficiently, it must compare budgeted amounts to actual amounts. Lower revenue or higher expenditures than planned might require some type of budget adjustment.

Preparing a Budget

Emphasize that a budget—and its follow-up procedures—is one of the most important tools that a not-for-profit organization can use. Point out that profit-oriented businesses also use budgets to plan both their short- and long-term operations.

Emphasize that the revenue and expenditures projections are based in part on the previous year's budget and the actual results of the organization's operations.

Divide the class into four groups letting each group represent the budget committee of a not-for-profit organization. After discussing and illustrating the revenue projections for the Little League baseball program, have each group prepare the revenue projections for the not-for-profit organization in demonstration problem 16-1. Then have the groups complete Exercise 16-1.

After discussing and illustrating the expenditure projections for the Little League baseball program on page 417, have the four groups prepare the expenditure projections for the not-for-profit organization in demonstration problem 16-2. Then have the groups complete Exercise 16-2.

Zero-Base Budgeting

Emphasize that with zero-base budgeting, revenue projections are based on preparing an itemized listing of expected revenue from each source. Point out how the Mountain View Recreation Center established goals for each revenue source and then placed a dollar value on each goal. After discussing and illustrating the zero-base revenue projections on page 420, divide the class into four groups and prepare the revenue projections for demonstration problem 16-3. Then have the groups complete Exercise 16-3.

Lead students in developing zero-base expenditure projections using the illustration on page 421. Have the four groups determine the expenditure projections for demonstration problem 16-4. Then have the groups complete Exercise 16-4.

Summarizing the Program Budget Requests

Emphasize that once program budgets are prepared and approved, they are combined and summarized as a whole. The budget request summary shown in Figure 16-2 is an example of Mountain View Recreation Center's complete budget. It summarizes the budget of all of the center's programs: softball, baseball, basketball, crafts, swimming, and so on.

Budget Control

Emphasize that not-for-profit organizations (and profit-oriented businesses as well) must control their budgets; that is, they must continually monitor the actual amounts they are receiving or spending and make sure they stay within their projections. One way to do this is to prepare a budget summary report that compares the current year's budget and actual revenue and expenditure amounts with the previous year's actual revenue and expenditure amounts.

Use Figure 16-3 to show students how to determine the free balance amounts (column 3) and the over/under amounts (column 5). Point out that the numbers in parentheses under the column headings show what column combinations are used to determine the amounts in the column. For example, to determine the free balance, the amount in column 2 is subtracted from the amount in column 1.

Budget Adjustments

Point out that if revenue seems to be falling short of the estimated amounts, expenditures must be reduced. If expenditures are more than the estimated amount, either revenue must be increased or other expenditures must be reduced. On the other hand, if revenues are more than projections, the budget committee might consider either increasing certain expenditures or carrying over the surplus to the next budget period.

Answers to Chapter Activities

Building Your Accounting Vocabulary

budget A budget is a formal, written statement of expected revenue and expenditures for a future period of time.

budget adjustment A budget adjustment is a change made to a current budget amount because of decreased revenues or increased expenditures.

budget period The budget period is the future time period, usually 12 months, for which expected revenues and expenditures are planned.

budget summary report A budget summary report summarizes and compares the current year's budget and actual revenue and expenditure amounts with the previous year's actual revenue and expenditure amounts.

expenditure projections Expenditure projections are the estimates of the amounts to be paid out during a budget period.

free balance A free balance is the budgeted amount that remains to be collected or spent as of a specific date.

fund A fund is a set of accounts (asset, liability, equity, revenue, and expense) used to record the transactions for a particular activity of a not-for-profit organization.

fund accounting Fund accounting is the accounting system used by not-for-profit organizations to account for the transactions of their various funds.

not-for-profit organization A not-for-profit organization is one with goals other than earning a profit for its organizers. Its main goal is to provide services to its members or to the general public.

revenue projections Revenue projections are estimates of money to be received during a budget period.

surplus A surplus occurs when the revenue received for a budget period is more than the expenditures made.

zero-base budgeting Zero-base budgeting develops the coming year's budget projections as though they were being done for the first time without using previous years' actual revenue and expenditure figures.

Reviewing Your Accounting Knowledge

1. The main goal of a profit-oriented business is to earn a profit for its owners while the main goal of a not-for-profit organization is to provide services to its members or to the general public.
2. A budget is one of the most important financial tools a not-for-profit organization can use for the following reasons: (a) It forces the managers or directors of the organization to look closely at the organization's goals; (b) it requires the cooperation of everyone in the organization to work toward and carry out those goals; and (c) by comparing the budget with the actual results, the organization can evaluate its performance and, if necessary, revise its goals.
3. Five basic principles of budgeting are as follows: (a) Develop long-term goals, (b) develop short-term goals, (c) define budgeting responsibilities, (d) establish budgeting guidelines, and (e) establish follow-up procedures.
4. Long-term goals are like highway markers that point out the general directions that the organization can take while short-term goals are the specific "routes" an organization can take to meet its long-term goals.
5. It is important to develop follow-up procedures. Once a budget has been prepared and approved, it should be compared periodically with the actual revenue received and expenditures made to determine whether the budget or plans must be adjusted.
6. Estimates for revenues and expenditures must be made while preparing a budget.
7. Revenue and expenditure budget projections can be developed by using previous year's budgeted and actual amounts or by using zero-base budgeting without using the previous year's figures.
8. The purpose of a budget summary report is to summarize and compare the current year's budget and actual revenue and expenditure amounts with the previous year's actual revenue and expenditure amounts.
9. The free balance amount for an item is determined by subtracting the current year-to-date amount from the current budget amount.
10. It is sometimes necessary to adjust budget amounts if the budget amounts for certain items are not adequate.

Improving Your Communications Skills

1. source
2. occasionally, sometimes
3. few
4. depreciated
5. planning
6. may
7. benefit
8. priority
9. unique
10. when

Chapter 17 Not-for-Profit Organizations: Financial Reporting

Teaching Suggestions

The financial statements of a not-for-profit organization are much like those for a profit-oriented business; they summarize the financial activities of the organization. A not-for-profit organization's financial statements give financial information that evaluates the services provided as well as the organization's ability to continue to provide services. Groups outside the not-for-profit organization, such as creditors and contributors, are also interested in the financial statements. Students should understand not only how to prepare the statements but also how to interpret the accounting data.

End-of-Period Reporting for Not-for-Profit Organizations

Review the major financial statements prepared by a for-profit business. Then introduce the need for financial statements for a not-for-profit organization. Point out the major differences between a for-profit business's financial statements and the statements for a not-for-profit organization.

Statement of Revenue, Expenditures, and Changes in Fund Balance

The statement of revenue, expenditures, and changes in fund balance is prepared for each of a not-for-profit organization's funds in order to report revenue and expenditures for a budget period as well as the change in the fund balance.

When presenting the Sources of Revenue section, discuss and point out the differences among the three types of revenue (self-generated, support, and capital additions). Point out that the difference between support revenue and capital additions revenue is that capital additions revenue is restricted to a particular use by the contributor. Discuss the classification of the sources of revenue of the Merryville Memorial Library. You might also wish to return to the examples and problems in Chapter 16 and classify the revenue sources reported there.

Use Figure 17-2 to show how the total object expenditures are allocated to the various programs of the library. Use salaries as an example and prorate the salary cost to each program. Mention that one method of prorating salary expenditures is by the time a staff member spends on a program.

Balance Sheet

When introducing the balance sheet, point out that a not-for-profit organization would prepare a balance sheet for each of its funds. If it has ten different funds, it would prepare ten different balance sheets. Point out that a not-for-profit organization's balance sheet has three sections. Stress that the third section, Fund Balance, is the major difference between a not-for-profit and a for-profit organization. Fund Balance is used rather than owner's equity or stockholders' equity.

Introduce the general fund balance sheet. Compare the assets and liabilities reported on this balance sheet with those reported on the balance sheet of a profit-oriented business. Discuss the difference between a designated fund balance and an undesignated fund balance. Point out that a portion of the fund balance can be set aside for a specific purpose. All designations, however, must be approved by the organization's governing board.

Introduce the property, plant, and equipment fund balance sheet. Discuss the meaning of the term *capitalizing an expenditure*. Point out that in a not-for-profit organization, capital expenditures are first reported as object expenditures (under the Capital Additions heading) on the statement of revenue, expenditures, and changes in fund balance. Those expenditures are capitalized once a fiscal period, usually at the end of the period.

Notes to Financial Statements

This section discusses the importance of providing additional financial information that is used to support the financial statements of a not-for-profit organization. Remind students that this is one of the objectives of financial reporting. Be sure to make them aware that profit-oriented businesses also include footnotes on their financial statements. You may wish to have several annual reports of companies available for students to examine.

Answers to Chapter Activities

Building Your Accounting Vocabulary

capital additions revenue Capital additions revenue is the money a not-for-profit organization receives that is restricted to a particular use by the contributor.

deficit In a not-for-profit organization, a deficit occurs if expenditures exceed revenue. A deficit decreases the fund balance.

fund balance A fund balance is the difference

between the assets and the liabilities of a particular fund.

object expenditures Object expenditures are the expenditures of an organization classified according to the type of cost.

program expenditures Program expenditures are all of the expenditures made for a particular program of the organization.

self-generated revenue Self-generated revenue is the revenue a not-for-profit organization earns from delivering or producing goods, providing services, or from other activities.

statement of revenue, expenditures, and changes in fund balance A statement of revenue, expenditures, and changes in fund balance is the financial statement that reports a not-for-profit organization's revenue and expenditures for a budget period as well as the change in the fund balance.

support revenue Support revenue for a not-for-profit organization refers to the contributions received from individuals, businesses, or other organizations.

Reviewing Your Accounting Knowledge

1. A not-for-profit organization prepares financial statements to measure the performance of the organization and to plan for future activities.
2. Two groups that might be interested in a not-for-profit organization's financial statements: (a) management, contributors, and users of the organization and (b) creditors.
3. Two statements normally prepared by not-for-profit organizations are (a) a statement of revenue, expenditures, and changes in fund balance and (b) a balance sheet.
4. A general fund is a set of accounts that is not restricted to a specific purpose. The resources of the general fund can be used for any purpose designated by the director of the organization.
5. The three types of revenue for a not-for-profit organization are (a) self-generated revenue, (b) support revenue, and (c) capital additions revenue. Examples of self-generated revenue include membership dues; rental, entry, or tuition fees; taxes; interest on investments; and the money received from fund-raising projects or the sale of services. Examples of support revenue include gifts, donations, grants, money left to the organization in a will and the contribution of services or facilities. Examples of capital additions revenue include a gift that must be used to build a building or purchase property, plant, and equipment and money given to a college to be used for student loans.
6. Support revenue can be used for any purpose and is sometimes called *unrestricted funds*. Capital additions revenue can be used only for the specific purpose outlined by the person or group donating the money.
7. Two methods of classifying the expenditures of a not-for-profit organization are by program or by object.
8. The amount of the change in the fund balance for the budget period is determined by finding the difference between revenue and expenditures. The fund balance is increased if revenue exceeds expenditures (a surplus). The fund balance is decreased if expenditures exceed revenue (a deficit).
9. Capitalizing an expenditure is the process of transferring the general fund expenditures to the property, plant, and equipment fund.
10. The property, plant, and equipment fund balance sheet summarizes the long-lived assets of the organization. Because no liabilities are reported, the total assets amount equals the ending fund balance amount. The balance sheet for the general fund, however, includes liabilities. Therefore, the fund balance is equal to the difference between the assets and the liabilities.

Improving Your Problem-Solving Skills

The reimbursement request made by one of the branch managers for selling expenses that included receipts for a "night out" with his spouse is not an allowable business expense by the Internal Revenue Service. Your company's guidelines for reimbursable expenses should make this rule very clear. Therefore, you should return the reimbursement request to the branch manager along with an explanation and a copy of the company's guidelines. If the branch manager questions your interpretation of the guidelines, you should refer his protest to your supervisor.

UNIT 5 SPECIAL ACCOUNTING SYSTEMS

Chapter 18 Departmental Accounting Systems

Teaching Suggestions

In this chapter, students will learn about the accounting procedures followed by businesses that have organized their operations into departments. In introducing the chapter, ask students to name businesses in the local area that seem to be organized into departments. Then ask why those businesses would want to organize their operations into departments. Finally, ask students what type of information about the various departments would be useful to the managers of the business. Management would want to know whether the department is making or losing money. It might also want to know whether to expand a certain department, reduce it, or keep its operations the same.

Accounting by Departments

You may wish to point out that a business is likely to have departments that are cost centers and others that are profit centers. A cost center is a department that incurs expenses but does not generate revenues. The cost centers of a department store might be its head offices, accounting department, advertising department, and warehouse. A profit center is a department that incurs expenses *and* generates revenues. The selling departments of a department store are its profit centers. The manager of a cost center is judged on his or her ability to keep the department's costs within reason. The manager of a profit center is judged on his or her ability to generate earnings (revenues minus expenses). These departments could also be called service departments and productive departments.

More complete and reliable departmental accounting information has been made available in recent years because of the widespread use of computers. Input terminals located at customer checkout stations can capture sales and inventory information as they function as cash registers. The computer is capable of providing management with timely and reliable information concerning each department's performance. Information such as inventory turnover, gross profit calculations, the percentage of the total inventory invested in each individual item, sales by salesperson, pricing structures, and percentage comparisons among departments are now available to department managers and management of the business.

Allocating Operating Expenses

Emphasize that the cost allocation process is not an exact procedure. It can, however, be helpful when trying to decide upon the relative profitability of departments.

As you discuss the allocation of the various expenses with students, point out that not all companies use the same methods to allocate the same expenses among their departments. There is no hard-and-fast rule that says you must use net sales to allocate miscellaneous expenses, for example. The basis chosen should be appropriate. If net sales is the basis chosen, the expense to be allocated should vary with the level of sales. That is, if net sales increase, the expense should also increase.

Remind students that operating expenses are allocated before the work sheet and income statement are prepared. Many companies prepare departmental expense allocation sheets.

Net Income from Operations by Department

Remind students that departmental information for revenue and cost of merchandise sold would be taken from the separate departmental accounts or from departmental analysis sheets.

Preparing a Departmental Work Sheet

Go over the departmental work sheet in Figure 18-4 with students. Point out that there is no Adjusted Trial Balance section; there are separate Income Statement sections for each department. There is also a Nondepartmental

Income Statement section in which to enter the balances of other revenue and other expense account.

Remind students that the purpose of the work sheet is to organize the data needed to prepare the financial statements. Separate Income Statement sections are needed to organize the data for the departmentalized income statement.

Emphasize that the combined operating income is extended to the Nondepartmental Income Statement Credit column. This is done so that the total net income of the business can be calculated.

Reporting Operating Income by Departments

Go over the income statement in Figure 18-5 carefully with students. Point out that the data reported in each department's section are organized in much the same way as other income statements students have prepared. Since the income statement is departmentalized only through operating income, remind students to draw a double rule under each department's operating income.

Contribution Margin

Discuss with students whether it was "fair" to allocate all of the operating expenses of Custom Colors between the two departments. Discuss the concept of "direct" expenses and "indirect" expenses. Direct expenses are those costs over which a department head has control and can be held accountable. Indirect expenses are those costs over which a department head has no control. Contribution margin has also been defined as the difference between revenues and variable expenses, those expenses that are a direct result of revenue production.

Have students compare the income statements in Figures 18-5 and 18-6. The calculations are the same through gross profit on sales. From that gross profit, however, only those expenses over which the department heads have control (the direct expenses) are deducted.

Help students think in terms of "contributions" by individual departments. Departmental contributions are needed to cover indirect costs. Each department must make an "acceptable" contribution. Theoretically, any contribution above zero could add to the overall profit of the business. Be sure to point out that a department may not be eliminated simply because it has a loss.

Answers to Chapter Activities

Building Your Accounting Vocabulary

administrative expenses Administrative expenses are costs related to the management of the business such as office salaries and utilities expenses.

contribution margin Contribution margin is the contribution that a given department makes to the net income of a business.

departmental accounting system A departmental accounting system provides data for two or more departments.

direct expenses Direct expenses are expenses incurred for the sole benefit of a given department and thus are under the control of a department head.

indirect expenses Indirect expenses are expenses incurred for the business as a whole and not under the control of one department head.

selling expenses Selling expenses are those expenses incurred to sell or market the business's goods or services such as advertising and sales salaries.

Reviewing Your Accounting Knowledge

1. A company would departmentalize its records to determine how much of a contribution each department is making to the business's overall profit (or loss).
2. The two methods businesses can use to provide financial information by departments are as follows: (a) Keep separate revenue and cost of merchandise accounts in the general ledger for each department, and (b) keep only one general ledger account for each revenue and cost of merchandise account, but maintain supplementary records for each department.
3. A departmental analysis sheet itemizes revenues and costs for each department to calculate gross profit.
4. Two formats for preparing a departmentalized income statement are (a) reporting departmental data through gross profit on sales and (b) reporting departmental data through each department's operating income.
5. Rent expense is allocated on the basis of the floor space occupied by each department. Depreciation of store equipment is

allocated on the basis of the department listed in the plant asset subsidiary ledger. Salaries of office personnel are allocated on the basis of the amount of time the office personnel had to spend on each department. Property insurance expense is allocated on the basis of the value of the inventory and equipment held by each department, and liability insurance expense is allocated according to departmental sales.

6. A departmental work sheet differs from an ordinary work sheet in that on a departmental work sheet, there is an income statement section for each department and a nondepartmental income statement section; on an ordinary work sheet, there is only one income statement section.
7. The Nondepartmental Income Statement columns are used to record other revenue and other expense accounts.
8. Two examples of direct expenses are Sales Salaries Expense and Bad Debts Expense. Two examples of indirect expenses are Property Tax Expense and Office Salaries Expense.
9. Contribution margin is determined by subtracting direct expenses from gross profit on sales.
10. Contribution margin is useful to a business because (a) it holds the department manager responsible for expenses directly chargeable to that department and (b) management can use an income statement reporting contribution margin as a tool for planning and analyzing future operations.
11. Contribution margin is a more realistic way to report the profitability of a department because if the company eliminates a department, the company's net income will decrease by the amount of the department's contribution margin.

Improving Your Math Skills

1. $69.10 ($1,727.40 × .04)
2. $177.59 ($4,439.75 × .04)
3. $426.22 ($10,655.40 × .04)
4. $136.05 ($3,401.20 × .04)
5. $102.19 ($2,554.75 × .04)
6. Total bank card fee expense for the month is $911.15.

Chapter 19 Branch Accounting

Teaching Suggestions

Essentially, this chapter is a continuation of Chapter 18. Instead of dividing accounting activities into departments and delegating authority to departmental managers, accounting activities are divided by branches or stores, and authority is delegated to the store manager. The profitability and efficiency of each store is accounted for. Financial statements are prepared for the individual stores and for the combined operations of all stores. During the introduction to this chapter, be sure to give a few examples of multistore businesses in your area.

Multistore Businesses

If possible, give an example of a local business that has just expanded its operations by opening another store in a different location. Local TV, radio, and newspaper advertising can be helpful. Have students report on possible multistore businesses advertising on TV, on radio, or in the newspaper.

A multistore corporation may be the owner of several branches with each branch organized as a separate legal entity. An additional advantage of organizing each as a separate legal entity is to take advantage of current tax laws. You might wish to check to see whether or not this organizational structure is permitted in your state.

Some businesses expand by granting franchises. Franchises can operate as a multistore business. For example, an individual may purchase the franchise rights for several stores in an area and operate each as a separate entity but combine the operations of all stores.

Accounting Systems for Multistore Businesses

Point out that accounting procedures used may vary from one multistore business to another.

Decentralized Accounting System

Develop a chart of accounts that would be used by the two branches of a multistore business with the same owner. Point out that in a decentralized accounting system each branch would maintain its own accounting records (as any independent operation would). But each branch must use the same accounting procedures and chart of accounts. Ask students what problems might arise with such a system.

Centralized Accounting System

Discuss how a centralized accounting system can decrease expenses for a multistore business. Point out that even though the central accounting system performs all of the accounting functions, each branch must handle accounting-related tasks.

When developing a chart of accounts for a centralized accounting system, emphasize how each branch's accounts are identified. Also point out that the computer is the accounting tool that makes the centralized accounting system work. A branch may have the capability of entering its own accounting data and receiving accounting information from the computer located at the central accounting office.

Centralized accounting is sometimes referred to as *enterprise accounting.* Each branch or enterprise is considered to be a separate entity, and the general ledger can contain the accounts for all branches. However, the computer system must provide a means of breaking out each branch as a separate entity.

Journalizing Transactions in a Centralized Accounting System

The duties of the accounting clerks in the centralized accounting office will probably be specialized; that is, one accounting clerk may handle all the transactions of one branch. Or one accounting clerk may handle a certain type of transactions, such a sales on account.

Transferring Funds to the Cash in Bank—Payables Account

Point out that cash is usually transferred from the branch accounts to the Cash in Bank—Payables account at regular intervals, such as once a week. For example, on Tuesday an accounting clerk in the central office totals all bills that are due to be paid for each branch. The cash is transferred from the branches and the checks are written on Friday. The number of bills to be paid and the central accounting office's policy about taking advantage of cash discounts would determine how often checks are issued.

Interbranch Transactions

Develop the need for and use of a centralized warehouse for a multistore business. Point out that as a result of having a centralized warehouse, there will be interbranch transactions.

The branch accounting system includes procedures to clear the "Due from" and the "Due to" accounts. This is usually done once a month. Point out that the "Due from" and "Due to" accounts are offsetting. What is a "Due to" for one branch is a "Due from" for another branch.

The liability "Due to" must be paid by the branch that received the transferred merchandise. Once payment is made, the amount is no longer "Due to" the warehouse branch. Explain that once the payment is made to the warehouse branch, the "Due from" is satisfied.

End-of-Fiscal-Period Procedures

Ask students to explain why both individual branch financial statements and combined financial statements are prepared by a multistore business.

Combined Income Statement

Emphasize that when a combined income statement is prepared, neither revenue nor costs incurred from interbranch transactions should be recognized. Since they are offsetting, it is a simple matter to eliminate them. Emphasize that the normal balance of the interbranch cost of merchandise sold account Transfer Charges is a debit; thus, the account must be credited to be eliminated. The normal balance of the interbranch other revenue account Transfer Fees Earned is a credit; therefore, it must be debited to reduce its balance to zero. The debit and credit of the elimination are offsetting.

Combined Balance Sheet

Remind students that just as the results of interbranch transactions were eliminated from the combined income statement, the interbranch receivables and payables must be eliminated from the combined balance sheet. Emphasize that generally accepted accounting procedures for the combined financial statements of multistore businesses do not allow the reporting of amounts to be received from or paid to itself. Therefore, these amounts must be eliminated by subtracting the amounts from the individual statements. The amount to subtract from each individual statement will be the same.

Discuss the combined balance sheet in Figure 19-18. Point out that the normal balance of the "Due from" asset account is a debit; therefore, a credit eliminates its balance. The "Due to" liability account has a normal credit balance; therefore, a debit eliminates its balance. The debit and credit eliminations offset each other.

Emphasize that combining amounts on the combined balance sheet is similar to combining amounts entered in the Trial Balance and Adjustments sections of the work sheet. In other words, two debit balances would be added; two credit balances would be added; a debit balance and a credit balance on the same line would be subtracted and the new balance would be the larger of the two (or zero if they cancel each other).

Answers to Chapter Activities

Building Your Accounting Vocabulary

centralized accounting system In a centralized accounting system, a central accounting office keeps the accounting records and performs the accounting functions for all branches.

combined balance sheet A combined balance sheet reports the total balances of the asset, liability, and stockholders' equity accounts of all branches of a multistore business.

combined income statement A combined income statement reports the revenue, cost, and expenses of all the branches of a multistore business.

decentralized accounting system In a decentralized accounting system, each branch of the multistore business maintains its own accounting records.

franchise A franchise is a right, given by a company to an individual or another business, that allows another to use the company's name and to sell its goods or services in a specific area.

interbranch transaction An interbranch transaction is a transaction between branches of the same multistore business.

multistore business A multistore business is a business that has more than one store or branch.

Reviewing Your Accounting Knowledge

1. The advantages of incorporating the branches of a multistore business are as follows:
   a. Because each branch is a separate legal entity, the general liability of the multistore business is limited.
   b. Creditors generally cannot look beyond the assets of a branch to satisfy their claims.
   c. When one of the branches needs to borrow money, creditors can examine the combined financial statements of the multistore business.
   d. Within limits, each branch has its own organizational structure.
2. In a centralized accounting system, a central accounting office keeps the accounting records and performs the accounting functions for all branches. In a decentralized accounting system, each branch is an independent business with its own journals and ledgers.
3. A centralized accounting system can usually decrease expenses for a multistore business because an accounting office is not needed at each branch and the duplication of activities is eliminated. Therefore, it may be able to lower its salary and training costs, or it may require less equipment.
4. In a decentralized system, all branches use the same chart of accounts. In a centralized accounting system, there is one chart of accounts that includes a set of accounts for each branch. A branch's accounts can be identified by the last digit of the account number and the name of the branch after the account title.
5. A deposit verification report lists the sales and sales tax recorded at each cash register. It also lists deposits made by branches during the day. This report is used to verify the cash register report, the tapes, and the deposit slips. Also, the report is used as the source document for the journal entry to record a branch's cash sales.
6. In a centralized accounting system, all purchases must be authorized and placed by the central accounting office. Each branch prepares a purchase requisition for items it needs and sends it to the central accounting office. The purchasing agent decides what, when, and how many items are to be bought. The central office prepares purchase orders and sends them to appropriate suppliers.

7. The purpose of the Cash in Bank—Payables account is to keep a record of the transactions affecting the special checking account used by the central accounting office to make all of the cash payments.
8. When merchandise is shipped from one branch to another, the first entry records the transaction in the accounts of the branch shipping the merchandise. The second entry records the transaction in the accounts of the branch receiving the merchandise.
9. Cash in Bank—Payables is a current asset account. Transfer Fees Earned is an other revenue account. Transfer Charges is a cost of merchandise account. Due to Store 1 is a current liability account. Due from Store 2 is a current asset account.
10. The data for a combined income statement are taken from the individual branch income statements.
11. The Elimination columns are used to cancel the results of interbranch transactions.

Improving Your Decision-Making Skills

Following are some reasons for using the bank cards:

1. To increase sales.
2. To be more competitive with other clothing stores.
3. To avoid the expense of investigating a customer's credit.
4. To avoid maintaining a subsidiary ledger and collecting from customers.
5. To reduce possible loss from cash shortages if cash sales decrease.

Some reasons for not using bank cards are as follows:

1. The added costs involved in installing equipment to process bank card sales.
2. The bank card fee charged to a business for handling bank card sales.
3. The loss a business could suffer if a card is not valid and proper procedures are not followed in processing bank card sales.
4. The training of employees to use the equipment.
5. The additional time it takes to process a bank card sale.

Because Matt Cobb is near a college and is a local store owner, I would advise him not to issue his own single-purpose card but to use a bank card instead.

Following is some information I would need to know about his store before giving him any advice:

1. What is the amount of his annual sales?
2. What percentage of his business is from college students?
3. What is the estimated percentage of college students with bank cards?
4. What is the cost of the telephone line and equipment needed to operate a bank card system?
5. What is the charge to the business for the use of the bank card?

Chapter 20 The Voucher System of Accounting

Teaching Suggestions

In this chapter, students will learn about the voucher system of accounting. When introducing the chapter, point out that in a small business, the owner/manager has control over all aspects of the business: handling all purchases, keeping track of all receipts, making bank deposits, writing all checks. In essence, the owner/manager knows the "heartbeat" of the business.

As a business grows, it becomes increasingly more difficult for one person to handle all financial responsibilities. These responsibilities are therefore delegated to trusted employees. However, the accounting system must be modified such that the duties of one employee serve as a check on the responsibilities of another employee. The business therefore will develop a system of *internal controls*—procedures that protect its assets from waste, fraud, and theft. The voucher system is one example of an internal control procedure.

The Voucher System

Students should understand that the voucher system is not suitable for use by small businesses, for several reasons. In a small business, the owner/manager has control over all aspects of the business. Consequently, there is no need for further controls on purchases and cash payments. In addition, a small business normally does not have enough transactions to justify the extra paperwork and expense generated by the voucher system. The voucher system is, however, suitable for medium- to large-sized businesses, where numerous transactions occur on a daily basis and job responsibilities can be delegated to many people.

Vouchers

Perhaps the most important point students should understand about vouchers is that a voucher is prepared for every invoice or bill received. The voucher is prepared as soon as the liability is incurred, whether it is to be paid immediately or in the future.

Since the entire concept of vouchers is new to students, try to have sample vouchers available for students to examine. Use Figure 20-1 to point out the various features. Show students that this particular voucher must be approved by two different people.

Students should understand that when an invoice or bill is received, its pertinent data are entered immediately onto a prenumbered voucher. Mention that, before the voucher is prepared, several activities have already been performed by other employees. The incoming invoice has been verified against the purchase order and the receiving report. Prices and extensions on the invoice have also been checked for accuracy.

The Voucher Register

Emphasize that the voucher register, like the other journals, is a book of original entry. Take some time to point out the major difference between the voucher register and the purchases journal. All expenditures—whether for merchandise, equipment, or expenses such as rent or salaries and whether to be paid immediately or some time in the future—are recorded in the voucher register. Remind students that only purchases of merchandise and other items on account were recorded in the purchases journal.

Unpaid Vouchers File

Emphasize that because vouchers are filed according to their due dates, the possibility of missing the opportunity to take a cash discount is lessened. You might wish to compare this file with the tickler file often used with accounts payable.

Check Register

Emphasize that every transaction entered in the check register results in a debit to Vouchers Payable and a credit to Cash in Bank. Remind students that after a payment is recorded in the check register, the payment information is also entered in the Payment section of the voucher register.

Paid Vouchers File

Each paid voucher is a small packet of documents describing the purchase and its payment (a purchase order, invoice, receiving report, possibly a debit memo, and a copy of the voucher check).

Situations Requiring Special Treatment

You might wish to point out to students that if merchandise is returned to a supplier before the voucher is prepared and recorded, the purchases return is not recorded in the accounting records. Since the transaction has not yet been recorded as a debit to the Purchases account, there is no need to record the purchases return.

Students should realize that a voucher check is prepared only in payment of an approved, authorized voucher. If multiple payments are to be made on one invoice, a separate voucher must be prepared for each planned installment payment.

In your discussion of correcting an incorrect voucher, remind students that transactions affecting Vouchers Payable that are recorded in the general journal must also be noted in the voucher register.

The Voucher System as a Management Tool

Remind students that the voucher system is suitable for larger businesses that have a great many purchases and cash payments transactions. In such businesses, responsibilities are split among many individuals. The voucher system serves as a system of checks and balances on those individuals.

Answers to Chapter Activities

Building Your Accounting Vocabulary

check register The check register is a special journal that, in the voucher system, replaces the cash payments journal.

paid voucher file The paid voucher file contains all paid vouchers, filed in numerical order.

schedule of unpaid vouchers The schedule of unpaid vouchers lists the name of each creditor and the amount owed.

unpaid voucher file The unpaid voucher file contains all unpaid vouchers, filed according to their due dates.

voucher A voucher is a document that serves as written authorization for each cash payment.

voucher check A voucher check is a special check with an attached stub or a special area on the face of the check that is used to list the details of the cash payment.

voucher register The voucher register is a book of original entry in which all vouchers are recorded, in numerical order.

voucher system The voucher system is a system to control purchases and cash payments.

Reviewing Your Accounting Knowledge

1. The voucher system controls purchases and cash payments. The business's financial activities are delegated to various individuals or groups. One individual or group serves as a check on the other.
2. The seven components of the voucher system are vouchers, the voucher register, the unpaid voucher file, voucher checks, the check register, the paid voucher file, and the general journal.
3. The voucher system is more appropriate for medium- to large-sized businesses because it must have enough transactions to justify the extra paperwork it generates.
4. When a business uses the voucher system, vouchers are prepared for every cash payment transaction.
5. The voucher register expands upon and replaces the purchases journal. It differs from the purchases journal in that transactions recorded in the voucher register are credited to Vouchers Payable whereas transactions recorded in the purchases journal are credited to Accounts Payable.
6. The purpose of the unpaid voucher file is to maintain all unpaid vouchers according to their due dates to forecast how much cash is needed to pay bills and to ensure that bills are paid on time to take advantage of cash discounts.
7. No, when a voucher system is used, an accounts payable subsidiary ledger is not used because the unpaid voucher file takes the place of the accounts payable subsidiary ledger.
8. A business may prefer to use voucher checks rather than regular checks because a duplicate copy of the check that lists the details of the cash payment is kept by the business.
9. In the voucher system, the check register replaces the cash payments journal.
10. If a voucher has already been recorded in the voucher register, a purchases return transaction is recorded in the general journal as a debit to Vouchers Payable and a credit to Purchases Returns and Allowances. The purchases return is then noted in the voucher register.
11. In the voucher system, a separate voucher is prepared and recorded in the voucher register for each installment payment.
12. The voucher system serves as a management tool by providing the business with a systematic record of cash payments and aids in the efficient management of financial resources.

Improving Your Analysis Skills

1. B
2. A and E
3. D and B
4. 33

Chapter 21 Manufacturing Accounting

Teaching Suggestions

This chapter presents an overview of the cost flow in manufacturing operations. The concepts in the chapter are new and establish the foundation for understanding the cost accounting systems presented in Chapter 22. The chapter provides an introductory picture for manufacturing. Note, however, that manufacturing accounting does not require a special cost accounting system.

Manufacturing Operations

Students will probably have no trouble distinguishing between manufacturing businesses and merchandising businesses. Nevertheless, emphasize that manufacturing businesses make their products to sell to their customers. Merchandising businesses buy their products to resell to their customers.

If students have difficulty with the concept, compare a merchandiser and a manufacturer of shoes. The merchandiser—the shoe store—

buys shoes and sells them in the same form in which they were purchased. The manufacturer of shoes buys leather, glue, thread, cloth, nails, and dye and turns these items into salable shoes.

Elements of Manufacturing Costs

Point out that the main difference in accounting for a manufacturing business is in determining the cost of the goods that it produces and sells. Ask students to list the costs that go into manufacturing a pair of shoes. If they do not get beyond the list of raw materials mentioned above, refer them back to the definition of a manufacturing business.

Manufacturing Inventories

Develop the need for the three manufacturing inventory accounts with students. Remind them that a physical count is still needed for each inventory at the end of the fiscal period.

Point out that the raw materials inventory consists of the costs of the direct (raw) materials purchased and still unused at the end of the period. Emphasize that the work in process and finished goods inventories consist of all three manufacturing costs: direct materials, direct labor, and factory overhead. Ask students why this is so.

Manufacturing Accounts

Compare the partial chart of accounts presented in Figure 21-2 with that of a merchandising business—for example, the chart of accounts presented in Application Activity 1 on pages 60–61. Discuss the various accounts presented in the cost of goods section.

Since this chapter is presented using the periodic inventory system, year-end adjustments are required for the three manufacturing inventory accounts. Point out to students that the logic for the adjustments is the same as for a merchandising business except that because a manufacturing business has three inventory accounts, the procedure is repeated three times. Finished Goods Inventory is adjusted through Income Summary, while the other two inventory accounts are adjusted through Manufacturing Summary.

Determining the Cost of Manufacturing Inventories

You should present more than one way of calculating the factory overhead rate. Use machine hours as an example of another method of determining the factory overhead rate. For example,

$$\frac{\text{Factory Overhead}}{\text{Machine Hours}} = \frac{\$371{,}450}{11{,}500} = \begin{array}{l}\$32.30 \text{ per} \\ \text{machine hour}\end{array}$$

Automated plants generally use machine hours. Also, many firms calculate overhead rates based on direct labor *hours* because the labor rates may change, but the hours worked remain the same. Time may be more related to overhead than dollars.

Financial Statements for a Manufacturing Business

Point out the five financial statements prepared by a manufacturing business.

Schedule of Cost of Goods Manufactured

Three steps are required to complete the final goal of determining gross profit:

1. Calculate the cost of the direct materials used.
2. Calculate the cost of goods manufactured.
3. Calculate the cost of goods sold.

The logic of completing the three costs is about the same as for a merchandising firm except that you repeat the process three times and add labor and factory overhead to direct materials when calculating the cost of goods manufactured.

Make sure students understand the logic of the costs reported on this schedule rather than simply memorizing the accounts that appear there. Mention that some businesses prepare a second schedule for factory overhead costs. In that instance, only the balance of Factory Overhead Control is reported on the schedule of cost of goods manufactured.

Income Statement

Point out that only the balance of Finished Goods Inventory is reported on the income statement. The balances of the other two inventory accounts are part of the cost of goods manufactured amount.

Completing a Work Sheet for a Manufacturing Business

Point out that the work sheet in Figure 21-5 has a Cost of Goods Manufactured section and not an Adjusted Trial Balance section. Since a manufacturing business prepares a schedule of cost of goods manufactured, its work sheet should allow it to organize the data needed to prepare that schedule.

Work through the calculation of the cost of goods manufactured amount with students. Emphasize that this amount is then extended to the Income Statement Debit column. You might remind students that they did something similar on the departmentalized work sheet.

Answers to Chapter Activities

Building Your Accounting Vocabulary

direct labor Direct labor is the wages paid to those employees who actually work on a product, with either machinery or hand tools.

direct materials Direct materials are the raw materials used to make a product that can be easily traced to the completed product.

factory overhead Factory overhead refers to all manufacturing costs other than the costs of direct labor and direct materials. Factory overhead costs cannot be easily or directly traced to the product being manufactured.

factory supplies Factory supplies, often called *indirect materials,* are those other materials that do not become part of the finished product. Examples include oil and grease for machinery.

finished goods Finished goods are those products that have been completed and are available for sale.

indirect labor Indirect labor is the wages paid to the factory employees who do not physically work on a product.

manufacturing business A manufacturing business is one that transforms raw materials into a finished product through the use of labor and machinery.

schedule of cost of goods manufactured The schedule of cost of goods manufactured, which is prepared as a supporting document for the income statement, reports all the costs of the goods completed during the fiscal period.

work in process Work in process refers to those products that have not yet been completed at the end of the fiscal period.

Reviewing Your Accounting Knowledge

1. A manufacturing business buys raw materials and transforms those materials through the use of labor or machinery into finished products. A merchandising business purchases already completed products for resale to customers.
2. The three elements of manufacturing costs are (a) direct (or raw) materials, (b) direct labor, and (c) factory overhead.
3. Examples of factory overhead costs include indirect labor; factory supplies used; depreciation on factory equipment and factory buildings; salaries for factory supervisors; heat, light, and power for the factory; repairs and maintenance of factory equipment and buildings; insurance on factory equipment and buildings; property taxes on factory equipment and buildings; and the cost of small tools.
4. Direct labor is the wages paid to those employees who actually work on the product. Indirect labor is the wages paid to factory employees who do not physically work on the product.
5. A manufacturing business has these three inventory accounts: Raw Materials Inventory, Work in Process Inventory, and Finished Goods Inventory.
6. The Finished Goods Inventory account of a manufacturing business is similar to the Merchandise Inventory account of a merchandising business.
7. The Raw Materials Inventory, Work in Process Inventory, Direct Labor, and Factory Overhead accounts are summarized in the Manufacturing Summary account. The Manufacturing Summary account is then closed into the Income Summary account. The Finished Goods Inventory account and the revenue and operating expense accounts are summarized in the Income Summary account.
8. Factory overhead costs can be allocated to the Work in Process and Finished Goods Inventory accounts on the basis of a percentage of the direct labor costs assigned to the two inventories. The direct labor costs assigned to the two inventories are multiplied by the factory overhead rate (determined by dividing the factory overhead costs by the direct labor costs) to determine the amount of factory overhead costs to be allocated.
9. The five financial statements prepared by a manufacturing business at the end of a fiscal period are the schedule of cost of goods manufactured, the income statement, the statement of stockholders' equity, balance sheet, and the statement of cash flows.
10. The Raw Materials Inventory and Work in Process Inventory accounts appear on the schedule of cost of goods manufactured.

The Finished Goods Inventory account appears on the income statement.

11. The schedule of cost of goods manufactured is prepared before the income statement because the cost of goods manufactured amount must be included on the income statement.
12. The work sheet for a manufacturing business has a Cost of Goods Manufactured section. This section contains the balances of all accounts needed to prepare the schedule of cost of goods manufactured. The difference between the Debit and Credit columns in this section, which is the cost of goods manufactured, is transferred to the Income Statement Debit column.

Improving Your Human Relations Skills

This is a common human relations problem. If Paul Ford has performed well, he should be encouraged to continue this performance. He might be given additional responsibilities to recognize his quality work.

The issue of pay should be separated from performance. Mary Gordon needs to carefully explain that the small raise is a result of the company's financial situation, not Paul's performance. His future with the company looks bright, but monetary rewards will have to wait until the company performs better.

Chapter 22 Product Costing: Job and Process Accounting Systems

Teaching Suggestions

This chapter builds on the information presented in Chapter 21. In this chapter, students will learn about two cost accounting systems that can be used by manufacturing businesses.

Cost Accounting Systems

The information on manufacturing accounting in Chapter 21 was presented within the framework of a general accounting system; that is, there were no special procedures set up to account for the various manufacturing costs.

A cost accounting system is used when a business wants to determine the cost of manufacturing a specific product or batch of products. The information provided by a cost accounting system is used to determine ending inventory values, to control costs, to aid in planning future operations, and to set fair and competitive prices on the goods produced. Note, however, that not all manufacturing businesses use a cost accounting system.

Job Order Cost System

The job order cost system is most suitable where products differ in types of material and work performed. Each product is custom made according to the customer's specifications, and the price quoted is closely tied to estimated job costs.

For a job order cost system to function effectively, it must be possible to identify each job physically and separate its related costs. As a result, the profit or loss can be computed for each job, and the unit cost can be determined for purposes of inventory costing.

Source Documents Used in a Job Order System

Some discussion of the forms required in the job order cost system will help students understand how the system works. You may be able to get samples of forms from local manufacturing companies.

Remind students that the purpose of a job cost sheet is to keep track of direct materials, labor costs, and factory overhead applied for each job. Job cost sheets come in many shapes and sizes. Some, because of the size or complexity of the manufacturing process, are as large as work sheets.

Discuss with students the bottom portion of the job cost sheet in Figure 22-1. Point out that, since the costs are accumulated for each job as the product is being manufactured, the total cost of the product is known as soon as the production process is completed. As a result, the gross profit for the product can also be determined.

Journalizing Transactions in a Job Order System

Point out that in the job order cost system illustrated in this chapter, there is no Raw Materials Purchases account. When the business buys raw materials, the costs are debited directly to the Raw Materials Inventory account.

Stress that the purpose of a cost accounting system is to accumulate the total costs for a product or batch of products. Factory overhead is one of the three elements of manufacturing costs. Factory overhead costs are applied (allocated) to each job based on a predetermined factory overhead rate (the same rate is used throughout the year).

Once a job has been completed, the unit cost per product can be determined. For example, have students turn to the job cost sheet in Figure 22-1. Have them determine the unit cost per copy of the book ($9,500 ÷ 9,000 = $1.0555). Give students additional examples to calculate.

Process Cost Accounting System

Under a process cost system, costs are accumulated for a particular department, cost center, or production process. The unit cost for a day, week, month, or year is obtained by dividing the department costs by the number of units produced during the period. Put several additional examples on the board, and have students calculate the unit costs. Remind students that the unit cost is used to calculate the manufacturing costs that are to be transferred from one department's Work in Process Inventory account to another department's Work in Process Inventory account (or to the Finished Goods Inventory account).

A process cost accounting system requires procedures to

1. Accumulate materials, labor, and factory overhead costs by department.
2. Determine the unit cost for each department.
3. Transfer costs from one department to the next.
4. Assign costs to work in process.

Equivalent Units

Point out to students that a department's equivalent units must be calculated before the department's unit cost can be determined. Walk students through the calculations for converting partially completed units to whole units.

Journalizing Transactions in a Process Cost System

As you discuss and illustrate the transactions on pages 583–588, compare them to the transactions that were recorded in the job order cost system. Ask students to point out similarities and differences. Use demonstration problem 22-4 to show students how manufacturing costs are charged to the three Work in Process Inventory accounts.

You may wish to develop a flow chart that illustrates how costs flow through a process cost accounting system or use demonstration problem 22-5.

Cost of Production Report

It may be helpful for students to list on the board the five steps required to prepare a cost of production report. These steps include:

1. Summarize the physical units (units to be accounted for).
2. Compute output in terms of equivalent units.
3. Summarize the total costs to be accounted for (the amounts that have been debited to the work in process inventory account).
4. Compute the unit cost.
5. Compute the total costs for work completed and work in process.

Answers to Chapter Activities

Building Your Accounting Vocabulary

cost accounting system A cost accounting system is one in which the accounting records are organized to maintain accurate records of manufacturing costs.

cost of production report A cost of production report summarizes the units processed by the department and the costs charged to the department.

equivalent units Equivalent units are the number of units produced during a certain period of time, expressed in terms of fully completed units.

job cost sheet A job cost sheet is a form used in job order cost systems to record the various manufacturing costs (direct labor, direct materials, and factory overhead allocated) incurred for each job.

job order cost accounting A job order cost accounting system is one that is designed to accumulate manufacturing costs for each product or batch of products.

job order time card A job order time card is used to record the amount of time an employee spent on a particular job.

materials requisition A materials requisition authorizes the materials warehouse to transfer direct materials to the factory for use in the production process.

overapplied factory overhead Overapplied factory overhead occurs when the balance of the Factory Overhead Applied account is greater than the balance of the Factory Overhead Control account. In other words, more factory overhead costs were allocated than were actually incurred.

process cost accounting A process cost accounting system is one that is designed to accumulate costs for each manufacturing process or department rather than for a product or batch of products.

underapplied factory overhead Underapplied factory overhead occurs when the balance of the Factory Overhead Applied account is less than the balance of the Factory Overhead Control account. In other words, more factory overhead costs were incurred than were applied.

Reviewing Your Accounting Knowledge

1. The purpose of a cost accounting system is to maintain accurate records of manufacturing costs.
2. The job order cost accounting system accumulates manufacturing costs for each product or batch of products. The process cost accounting system accumulates manufacturing costs for each manufacturing process or department.
3. The Factory Overhead Control account is a controlling cost of goods account that summarizes all factory overhead costs. Separate factory overhead cost accounts are maintained in the factory overhead subsidiary ledger.
4. The three source documents used in the job order cost system are: the job cost sheet, the materials requisition, and the job order time card. The job cost sheet is a form used to record the various manufacturing costs incurred for a particular job. The materials requisition authorizes the materials warehouse to transfer direct (raw) materials to the factory for processing. The job order time card is used to record the amount of time an employee spent on a particular job.
5. When direct materials are purchased on account, Raw Materials Inventory is debited and Accounts Payable and the supplier's account are credited. When direct materials are requisitioned for the production process, Work in Process Inventory is debited and Raw Materials Inventory is credited.
6. In a job order cost system, direct labor costs are debited to the Work in Process Inventory account. Indirect labor costs are debited to the Factory Overhead Control account.
7. The predetermined factory overhead rate is calculated by dividing the estimated factory overhead costs by the estimated direct labor costs.
8. A business using a job order cost accounting system usually has either overapplied or underapplied factory overhead at the end of the fiscal period because the predetermined factory overhead rate is only an estimate.
9. To eliminate overapplied or underapplied factory overhead, the Factory Overhead Applied account and the Factory Overhead Control account are closed and the difference between the two accounts is transferred to the Cost of Goods Sold account at the end of the fiscal period.
10. When completed goods are sold, two journal entries are required. In the first entry, Cash in Bank or Accounts Receivable is debited and Sales is credited. In the second entry, Cost of Goods Sold is debited and Finished Goods Inventory is credited.
11. Equivalent units are the number of units produced in a period of time, expressed in terms of fully completed units. Partially completed units must be restated—either by estimating the stage of completion or by using the 50% rule—in terms of whole units. The number of completed and transferred units is added to the number of restated partially completed units to determine the equivalent units. The number of equivalent units is then used to determine the unit cost of the item being produced.
12. A cost of production report, prepared by each department, summarizes the units processed by the department and the costs charged to the department. The report also indicates the unit manufacturing cost by department.

Improving Your Communications Skills

The presentation to the fourth-grade class should be planned around a hands-on approach. Use one transaction, such as a sale on account, and actual documents, such as sales invoices, statements of account, checks, etc., to show all of the things you do to record the sale and the payment from the customer. Try to relate your comments to their experiences. Tell them about the importance of reading, writing, and arithmetic for all employees.

The presentation to the tenth-grade business math class should center around your responsibilities and the kinds of math calculations you have to make on the job. Explain the educational requirements for an entry-level position in the accounting department. Then explain the career paths available to an employee in this department. Discuss the requirements for job performance; for example, be on time, do a full day's work, contribute to the productivity of the business, etc.

Mini Practice Set: Application Activity 5 Preparing Financial Statements for a Manufacturing Business

In Application Activity 5, students are asked to prepare the end-of-period financial statements for a manufacturing business. Note that Express Manufacturing Company, Inc., uses a general accounting system rather than a cost accounting system.

The end-of-period trial balance has already been prepared and is included in the student working papers. Students must record the adjustments and complete the work sheet. Then they complete the rest of the end-of-period work. They prepare a schedule of cost of goods manufactured, income statement, statement of stockholders' equity, and balance sheet and journalize the adjusting and closing entries.

The accounting stationery needed to complete this activity is included in the student working papers. Most students should be able to complete this activity manually in two to three class periods.

UNIT 6

ACCOUNTING FOR BUSINESS DECISIONS

Chapter 23 Managerial Cost Control

Teaching Suggestions

In Chapter 21, students learned how to classify costs by function. In Chapter 22, they learned about product costs. In this chapter, students will learn how to separate and classify costs and expenses from the point of view of cost behavior. Students frequently become confused in their thinking about the behavior of costs. Therefore, a special effort must be made to help them think clearly about the concepts found in this chapter.

Cost Behavior

Explain that when accountants refer to cost behavior patterns, they generally mean the relationship between costs and various activities that cause the cost to be incurred. Point out that understanding cost behavior is the key to many decisions in an organization. The manager must be able to anticipate when a cost will rise or fall. If a cost is expected to change, the manager must know by how much. By understanding how costs behave, a manager can predict what a cost will be under various operating circumstances.

Stress the importance of classifying all costs as either variable or fixed. Introduce the total cost equation used to analyze total cost behavior.

Variable Costs

Point out that for a cost to be variable, it must be variable with something or an activity base. The activity base is referred to as a cost driver. In the hairbrush illustration in the chapter, the activity base that drives the cost is the number of units produced. The total variable cost changes as the number of units produced changes. Emphasize that the variable cost assigned to each unit does not change as the output (activity level) changes. Use the graph illustrated in Figure 23-1 and the table in Figure 23-2 to help students "see" how total variable costs behave.

Fixed Costs

Discuss with students the meaning of fixed costs. Emphasize that the total fixed cost does not change as the output (activity level) changes. Point out that the fixed cost assigned to each unit changes as the output changes. Use the graph illustrated in Figure 23-3 and the table in Figure 23-4 to help students understand how fixed costs behave.

After students have a basic understanding of the difference between the behavior of variable costs and fixed costs, use the following example to reinforce their learning.

Example: The Accounting Club sells trees each year to raise money to buy Christmas gifts for needy children. The trees cost $7.50 each. The parcel of land they use to store and sell them rents for $150.00. How do the variable and fixed cost behave? That is, do total costs vary with the activity level? If so, they are variable costs. If not, they are fixed.

	Total Cost	Unit Cost
1 tree	$ 7.50	$ 7.50
Rent	150.00	150.00
Totals	$157.50	$157.50
10 trees	$ 75.00	$ 7.50
Rent	150.00	15.00
Totals	$157.00	$ 22.50

Summary: As the (activity level) increases,

Total variable cost	*Increases*
Unit variable cost	*No change*
Total fixed cost	*No change*
Unit fixed cost	*Decreases*

Mixed Costs

The concept of mixed cost is important because mixed costs are common to a wide range of businesses. Like so many other efforts in accounting, the separation of mixed costs into their variable and fixed parts provides only an approximation of "true" cost. Using the truck rental example from the chapter simplifies the concept of mixed costs. Students can easily see the variable and fixed costs that are included in the total cost.

Introduce the high-low method for finding the variable and fixed parts of mixed costs. Point out that the fixed cost is the same for any month. Therefore, the amounts for any month could be used to determine the fixed costs.

Answers to Chapter Activities

Building Your Accounting Vocabulary

committed fixed costs Committed fixed costs are costs that cannot be eliminated very easily and are associated with long-range investments in plant, equipment, and the organization itself.

cost behavior Cost behavior refers to the way a cost changes in relation to a change in a business activity level.

discretionary fixed costs Discretionary fixed costs are costs that are usually based on decisions for a fiscal period and can be increased or decreased during the annual budgeting process.

fixed costs Fixed costs are costs that remain constant even though an activity level such as volume of production changes.

high-low method The high-low method is a widely used method for finding the variable and fixed parts of a mixed cost.

mixed costs Mixed costs are those costs that cannot be explained by a single cost behavior pattern.

relevant range The relevant range is a level of activity within which a cost behavior is valid.

variable costs Variable costs are costs that vary in direct proportion to an activity level such as volume of production.

Reviewing Your Accounting Knowledge

1. The owner makes decisions involving costs. Therefore, the owner needs to know how costs behave in relation to changes in a business activity and how profits will be affected.
2. A change in a business activity level may cause costs to increase, decrease, remain the same, or follow some other pattern of change.
3. The equation TC = FC + VC illustrates that total cost consists of two components: fixed costs and variable costs.
4. As output increases, the total variable cost increases.
5. As output increases, the variable cost assigned to each unit remains unchanged.
6. As output increases, the total fixed cost remains the same.
7. As output increases, the fixed cost assigned to each unit decreases.
8. A fixed cost is fixed only over a given range of activity. Therefore, managers must be aware of the relevant range of a fixed cost when they are considering a change, such as increasing the capacity of the assembly department. This change may not be possible without causing the fixed cost to jump up.
9. Committed fixed costs "lock" the owner or manager into a decision that cannot be changed for a long time. Therefore, a poor decision could affect the business for many years. Discretionary fixed costs, however, can be changed after a shorter period of time, usually a fiscal period. A poor decision, therefore, would affect the business only until the next annual budget is prepared.
10. Costs are mixed costs when they cannot be explained by a single cost behavior. Therefore, if the cost behavior pattern shows a change but a change other than in direct proportion to the activity level, the accountant would suspect that the cost data are mixed.
11. Examples of variable costs are direct materials, direct labor, and factory supplies expenses. Examples of fixed costs are depreciation, insurance and administrative salaries. Examples of mixed costs are truck rental charges, telephone charges, and copy machine leases.

Improving Your Problem-Solving Skills

The problem is one of business ethics. The accountant may try to influence the decision to award a contract based on a special favor, in this case a ham. Even though the accountant in no way acted in an unethical manner, taking the ham gives the appearance of unethical behavior. Unethical behavior in fact or even in appearance must be avoided.

Chapter 24 Cost-Volume-Profit Relationships

Teaching Suggestions

In Chapter 23, students learned to classify costs as either variable or fixed. In this chapter, they will learn how to use these classifications to analyze the relationship among costs, volume, and profit.

Cost-Volume-Profit Relationships

The understanding of cost-volume-profit (C-V-P) analysis is one of management's most vital tools for making decisions. Point out that in general C-V-P analysis involves a study of the relationship among costs (variable and fixed), volume (activity level, output), and profit (net income). Remind students that C-V-P analysis is a key factor in making decisions about introducing new products, pricing products, determining marketing strategy, and using production capacity. Be sure that through discussion and practice solving problems, students attain a basic level of understanding of C-V-P analysis. You may want to let them use the following list to practice C-V-P analysis.

1. TC = VC + FC
   Total Cost = Variable Cost + Fixed Cost
2. S = VC + FC + NI
   Sales = Variable Cost + Fixed Cost + Net Income (or Target Profit)
3. NI = S – VC – FC
   Net Income = Sales – Variable Cost – Fixed Cost
4. CM = S – VC
   Contribution Margin = Sales – Variable Cost
5. UCM = USP – UVC
   Unit Contribution Margin = Unit Selling Price – Unit Variable Cost
6. CMR = UCM ÷ USP or CMR = CM ÷ S
   Contribution Margin Ratio = Unit Contribution Margin ÷ Unit Selling Price or Contribution Margin Ratio = Contribution Margin ÷ Sales
7. BEP = FC ÷ UCM
   Break-Even Point (in units) = Fixed Costs ÷ Unit Contribution Margin
8. BES = FC ÷ CMR
   Break-Even Sales (in dollars) = Fixed Costs ÷ Contribution Margin Ratio

The Contribution Margin

Be sure students understand the difference between contribution margin and gross profit on sales. To calculate the contribution margin, variable manufacturing, variable administrative, and variable selling costs are subtracted from sales. Fixed manufacturing costs are not included in the calculation. To calculate the gross profit on sales, variable and fixed manufacturing costs are subtracted from sales. Administrative and selling costs are not included in the calculation. Use the discussion of Figure 24-1 to emphasize this point.

Be sure students understand how to calculate contribution margin, unit contribution margin, and contribution margin ratio. Point out that these amounts are used to calculate break-even point and target profit sales and to understand C-V-P analysis.

The Break-Even Point

C-V-P analysis begins with break-even calculations. Therefore, be sure students understand how to calculate the break-even point in both units and dollars. Discuss and illustrate the use of the break-even equation. Then show students how they can quickly calculate the break-even point in units by using the unit contribution margin.

Applying C-V-P Analysis

The use of "what if" questions by students is a very good introduction to what accountants call *sensitivity analysis*. "What if" questions are used to identify changes that might occur in projected data in relation to changes in other data. Be sure to discuss with students the analysis used to answer each "what if" situation illustrated in this section of the chapter. Emphasize the importance of this analysis to managers making business decisions.

Answers to Chapter Activities

Building Your Accounting Vocabulary

break-even point The break-even point is the point where total revenues are equal to total costs. There is neither a profit nor a loss.

contribution income statement The contribution income statement is an income statement on which all selling, administrative, and manufacturing costs are classified as either fixed costs or variable costs.

contribution margin The contribution margin is the contribution that a given product or department makes to paying for fixed costs and adding to the profit of a business. The contribution margin is calculated by subtracting total variable costs from total revenue.

contribution margin ratio The contribution margin ratio is the percentage of contribution margin to sales. The contribution margin ratio is calculated by dividing the amount of contribution margin by the amount of sales.

cost-volume-profit analysis Cost-volume-profit analysis uses cost to determine the effect of changes in volume on the profit that results.

margin of safety The margin of safety is the excess of target sales over break-even sales.

margin of safety ratio The margin of safety ratio is calculated by dividing the margin of safety by the target sales.

target profit The target profit is the net income goal of a business.

unit contribution margin The unit contribution margin is the difference between the unit selling price and the unit variable cost.

Reviewing Your Accounting Knowledge

1. For C-V-P analysis, all costs must be classified as either fixed or variable. Mixed costs must be separated into their fixed and variable parts.
2. The major difference between the format of a standard income statement and that of a contribution income statement is the way costs are classified. The standard income statement classifies costs by function—selling, administrative, or manufacturing. The contribution income statement classifies costs as either variable or fixed.
3. The contribution margin is the difference between revenues and total variable costs. The gross profit on sales is the difference between total revenues and cost of goods sold.
4. The unit contribution margin is expressed in unit dollar amounts. The contribution margin ratio is expressed as a percentage.
5. When the unit contribution margin is used to calculate the break-even point, the result is expressed in unit sales. When the contribution margin ratio is used, the result is expressed in dollar sales.
6. The target profit is part of management's way of planning and setting goals for the future. Management needs a target profit to work toward as a way to motivate employees.
7. A margin of safety of $6,500 means that the sales may decline by as much as $6,500 before the break-even point is reached and a loss occurs.
8. A margin of safety of 25% means that if sales fall more than 25%, the company will experience a loss.
9. C-V-P analysis is used to ask "what if" questions about what will happen to profits when volume, costs, or contribution margins change. The accountant is interested in the impact a decision made now will have on future profits.
10. a. If fixed costs increase, the break-even point increases.
    b. If the selling price decreases, the break-even point increases.
    c. If variable costs decrease, the break-even point decreases.

Improving Your Math Skills

1. $60.50 markdown; $49.50 selling price
2. $25.20 markdown; $44.79 selling price
3. $40.79 markdown; $199.16 selling price
4. $16.00 markdown; $63.99 selling price
5. $4.75 markdown; $14.24 selling price

Chapter 25 Using Cost Data for Pricing Decisions

Teaching Suggestions

This chapter covers the concepts needed to understand pricing. The setting of selling prices for goods and services is one of the most important decisions a manager must make. Pricing products or services is more extensive than many students will realize. It will be easy for them to visualize the need to price each item found in the department store or supermarket. Point out that all organizations that provide a service for a fee or sell a product must decide on the amount to charge for each service or item sold. For example, the construction firm must set a price to build a school and a dentist needs to know how much to charge to clean teeth. Once a selling price is set, it must be continuously evaluated in relation to current costs, market conditions, and competitors actions.

Major Influences on Pricing

Ask students to suggest what factors might influence the pricing of some products with which they are familiar. Ice skates could be one example for which they might respond with factors such as manufacturing costs, competition, season, market conditions, desired profit, and so on.

Common Pricing Methods

Discuss with students each of the common pricing methods described in this section. Additional pricing decisions and methods, such as for special orders, are not included here. The purpose of this chapter is to provide students with a straightforward approach to the concepts needed to understand the pricing of standard kinds of products.

Cost-Plus Pricing

Review with students the meaning of the term *markup*. Point out that the amount of markup is not etched in stone and can be altered to fit a particular pricing situation. A change may be made in response to the actions of competitors or customers. The pricing approaches in this section do not take into consideration the relationship between price and volume that was presented in Chapter 24. The price determined using a cost-plus approach is of great assistance to the manager, but it is usually only a target price that may be raised or lowered depending on volume or competition.

Labor and Materials Pricing

Point out the reasons for establishing a billing rate for labor and a materials loading charge. Ask students to list some local businesses that would probably use labor and materials pricing.

Answers to Chapter Activities

Building Your Accounting Vocabulary

billing rate for labor The billing rate for labor is a per hour amount charged customers that covers direct labor costs, benefits, and selling and administrative costs, and provides a profit.

cost variance Cost variance is the difference between a standard cost and an actual cost.

cost-plus pricing Cost-plus pricing is a pricing method in which a dollar amount or a percentage of the cost is added to the base cost to arrive at a selling price.

full cost-plus Full cost-plus is a pricing method that combines the product cost with the operating costs associated with the product to establish a full or total cost base.

materials loading charge The materials loading charge is the amount added to the purchase cost of parts and materials used on a job to determine the amount the customer will be billed.

pricing Pricing means assigning a selling price to a product or service.

product cost-plus Product cost-plus is a pricing method that adds a markup to the product cost.

standard cost-plus Standard cost-plus is a pricing method that uses predetermined costs for direct labor, direct materials, and factory overhead as the base for pricing.

variable cost-plus Variable cost-plus is a pricing method that uses just the variable costs that are assigned to the product as the base for pricing.

Reviewing Your Accounting Knowledge

1. The major influences on price are cost, competition, and economic conditions.
2. A farmer might not have to make pricing decisions because selling prices for farm products are usually the same and set by a national or international market and the government.
3. The purchase price is the price paid to a business for needed goods or services. The selling price is the price charged to customers for goods or services.
4. If it is a new business, it might seek library information about the markup percentages used by similar firms in the country. If it is an established business with a financial history, it would select a markup percentage based on experience, competition, and regulations.
5. A government contract allows a manufacturer to use full-cost pricing because many of the products needed by the government, like defense items, are so special and have such a limited market the seller would have difficulty setting a price that would allow for a profit.

6. Standard costs are established through the cooperative efforts of management, manufacturing, and the accountant.
7. Yes, you should expect standard and actual costs to differ. Standard costs are predetermined costs that are set before the actual costs are known.
8. Product cost-plus pricing uses the unit (product) manufacturing cost as the base for pricing. All manufacturing costs (fixed and variable) are used. Administrative and selling costs are not included. Variable cost-plus pricing uses just the variable costs assigned to the product as the base for pricing. The cost base is made up of the variable manufacturing, administrative, and selling costs. Fixed costs are not included.
9. The variable cost-plus pricing method provides a base cost that allows a company to apply the concepts of cost-volume-profit analysis.
10. A materials loading charge is added to cover the auto repair shop's overhead costs for ordering, handling, and storing the inventory and to provide a profit on the dollars invested in the inventory.
11. An accounting firm would set its billing rate to cover labor plus fringe benefits, overhead (supplies, rent, etc.), plus a profit to the owner of the firm.

Improving Your Decision-Making Skills

Following are some suggested responses. Students' answers will vary.

1. Should influence your decision. If you choose the higher salary, you may need to use some of your savings to pay for health care not covered by the benefit package.
2. Should influence your decision. Health care costs may be higher if you have small children, but a higher salary might provide more money for food, shelter, clothing, and entertainment.
3. Should influence your decision. If you know you will need to have dental work, for example, you may want to choose the better benefit package.
4. Should not influence your decision. Your decision should be based on your wants and needs.
5. Should influence your decision. If your car is in bad condition, you may need the higher salary to repair or replace your car.
6. Should influence your decision. If your spouse has good insurance, you may choose the higher salary and use your spouse's medical coverage.
7. Should influence your decision. The higher salary could help you qualify for a loan to buy a home or make home improvements.
8. Should influence your decision. As you get older, you may have more medical expenses and prefer the better health benefits.

Glencoe Accounting

ADVANCED COURSE
THIRD EDITION

CONCEPTS/PROCEDURES/APPLICATIONS

Donald J. Guerrieri
Norwin Senior High School
North Huntingdon, Pennsylvania

F. Barry Haber
Fayetteville State University
Fayetteville, North Carolina

William B. Hoyt
Wilton High School
Wilton, Connecticut

Robert E. Turner
McNeese State University
Lake Charles, Louisiana

GLENCOE
Macmillan/McGraw-Hill

New York, New York   Columbus, Ohio   Mission Hills, California   Peoria, Illinois

Donald J. Guerrieri is an accounting instructor at Norwin Senior High School, North Huntingdon, Pennsylvania. He has taught accounting at both the secondary and college levels. He also has experience working for a firm of certified public accountants. Dr. Guerrieri has written numerous articles on the teaching of accounting for a variety of educational journals. He is also a program speaker at business education seminars and conferences.

F. Barry Haber is Professor of Accounting at Fayetteville State University, Fayetteville, North Carolina. Dr. Haber is a certified public accountant and is active in the American Institute of Certified Public Accountants, where he has served on the AICPA Minority Doctoral Fellows Committee. In addition to teaching accounting principles, Dr. Haber has authored three other textbooks, as well as various articles and cases in accounting.

William B. Hoyt is head of the Business Education Department at Wilton High School, Wilton, Connecticut. In addition to teaching accounting, he has been active in the development of microcomputer usage in business education courses. In this endeavor, he has taken part in panel discussions, given workshops, and written on the use of microcomputers in the accounting instruction.

Robert E. Turner is the Vice President for Business Affairs at McNeese State University, Lake Charles, Louisiana. Mr. Turner has taught accounting and other business subjects at the high school and college levels. Mr. Turner has appeared on the programs of a number of business education conferences. He is also a frequent speaker at educational seminars around the country.

Send all inquiries to:
GLENCOE DIVISION
Macmillan/McGraw-Hill
936 Eastwind Drive
Westerville, OH 43081

ISBN: 0-02-803642-5 (Student's Edition)

Printed in the United States of America.

1 2 3 4 5 6 7 8 9 0 RRD-W 01 00 99 98 97 96 95 94

Contents

UNIT 3

UNIT 4

UNIT 5

UNIT 6

Preface

It has been said that "Accounting is the language of business." It might also be said that "The ability to *apply* accounting knowledge is critical to success in business." Mere knowledge of accounting terminology and principles is not enough to be effective in the business world; one must be able to *apply* that knowledge in planning, controlling, predicting, and evaluating. Furthermore, to be successful in today's competitive business environment, one should be able to utilize fully the potential of the computer in applying that knowledge.

Glencoe Accounting, Concepts/Procedures/Applications, Advanced Course, Third Edition, not only reconfirms and reinforces basic principles, procedures, and terminology learned in first year accounting, it also provides the opportunity to apply that knowledge in greater depth. This depth of application, coupled with a widening horizon of computer experience, will more nearly ensure that students have the tools to make the most of further study or to successfully enter the business world. It is a comprehensive program that continues to emphasize sound methodology, proven practices, and solid applications to help students succeed.

There are two basic reasons why students study a second year of accounting at the high school level. First, many students study advanced accounting because they plan to major in accounting or business in college and they want to be better prepared for their college courses. Second, high school graduates seeking employment immediately after high school will be more qualified for entry-level accounting jobs if they have completed two years of study in accounting.

Glencoe Accounting, Concepts/Procedures/Applications, Advanced Course, Third Edition, is designed to be used by the college-bound student as well as the vocational student. The textbook covers much of the same material that students will study in the beginning college accounting course, but at a level suitable for high school students. The coverage of practical accounting procedures—such as those for uncollectible accounts and plant assets—will help prepare students for the various tasks they will encounter on the job. The use of the computer will open students' eyes to its potential as a tool in accounting. Finally, the number and variety of problems and reinforcement activities will help students assimilate and apply the accounting principles and procedures in the textbook.

Course Objectives

Glencoe Accounting, Concepts/Procedures/Applications, Advanced Course, Third Edition is designed to be used in the second year of a complete two-year financial accounting course.

After studying this textbook and successfully completing activities in the textbook and the related working papers, students will be able to:

1. Explain both the basic and advanced principles and procedures that are applied to accounting records kept for profit-oriented businesses.
2. Use common techniques to analyze and interpret financial statements.
3. Describe the differences in accounting for the three types of business organizations: sole proprietorships, partnerships, and corporations.
4. Apply accounting procedures for not-for-profit organizations.
5. Describe the accounting systems used by departmentalized, branch, and manufacturing businesses.
6. Define the information required for the planning and control of business operations.

Organization of the Textbook

Glencoe Accounting, Concepts/Procedures/Applications, Advanced Course, Third Edition is organized in six units of twenty-five chapters. The first unit of the textbook reviews the basic principles and procedures that students learned in their first-year study of accounting. In Chapter 1, students review the first five steps of the accounting cycle as they analyze, journalize, and post various business transactions. In Chapter 2, students review the final five steps of the accounting cycle as they complete the end-of-fiscal-period activities for a merchandising business organized as a closely held corporation. This unit provides students with a solid base from which to expand their accounting knowledge.

Unit 2 elaborates upon transactions and procedures introduced in the first-year accounting course. The chapters within the unit are presented in the same order as the related accounts would appear on the balance sheet. In Chapter 3, students look at procedures that affect a corporation's cash, marketable securities, and accounts receivable. Chapter 4 discusses notes receivable. Merchandise inventory costs and investments are the topic of Chapter 5. The depreciation and disposal of plant assets, as well as a brief discussion of intangible assets, are covered in Chapter 6. Chapter 7 presents current liabilities, particularly notes payable. Long-term liabilities such as bonds are discussed in Chapter 8. In Chapter 9, students move on to stockholders' equity, specifically transactions involving the issuance of stock. Dividends, treasury stock, and the appropriation of retained earnings are covered in Chapter 10. Chapter 11 pulls the topics discussed in the unit together as students complete the end-of-period activities for a publicly held corporation.

Unit 3 introduces students to the uses of financial information for decision making. Chapter 12 presents several different methods and techniques that can be used to analyze and interpret the information presented in various financial statements. In Chapter 13, students learn how to prepare the fourth major financial statement prepared by businesses: the statement of cash flows.

The first two chapters of Unit 4 introduce students to the partnership form of business organization. Students learn how to account for the formation, dissolution, and liquidation of a partnership in Chapter 14 and how to divide partnership earnings in Chapter 15. The last two chapters in the unit focus on the accounting system used by not-for-profit organizations. In Chapter 16, students learn about the budgeting process, a major tool of a fund accounting system. Chapter 17 covers the financial statements prepared by a not-for-profit organization.

Unit 5 covers special accounting systems. In the first two chapters of the unit, students learn about the accounting systems and financial statements prepared by departmentalized businesses and businesses with branch operations. Chapter 18 presents the voucher system. The last two chapters in the unit introduce manufacturing businesses and procedures followed in a cost accounting system.

Unit 6 covers managerial and cost accounting and emphasizes those procedures used to make appropriate management decisions.

Special Features

Glencoe Accounting, Concepts/Procedures/Applications, Advanced Course, Third Edition uses full color to heighten student interest, emphasize key features, and illustrate important procedures. It continues the major features of the first-year textbook. These features are designed to promote student interest, involvement, and success.

Accounting cycle approach. The textbook uses a traditional accounting cycle approach to introduce students to new concepts and procedures. This step-by-step development gives students the guidance they look for and clearly demonstrates the continuity and interrelationships of the accounting process.

Chapter learning objectives. Clearly defined and stated objectives are included at the beginning of each chapter to help students know exactly what they are expected to learn. The mastery of these objectives is evaluated through end-of-chapter activities, applications, and examinations.

Vocabulary emphasis. The new accounting terms that are defined in each chapter are listed on the first page of the chapter. This list, which can be used to "preview" the meaning of each term, helps students achieve greater understanding and retention of the material in the chapter. End-of-chapter vocabulary reviews reinforce understanding of key terms.

Clear, conversational narrative. The textbook is written in a style that is appropriate for high school students. Simple analogies make concepts meaningful. Abundant, colorful illustrations and examples guide students through the preparation of accounting records.

Emphasis on transaction analysis. A solid review of the rules of debit and credit and the six-step method of analyzing transactions appears in the first unit of the textbook. Understanding the "why" of transaction analysis ensures that the "how" comes naturally.

Frequent learning reinforcement. "Check Your Learning" reinforcement activities follow major sections in every chapter to help students assume the responsibility for their own learning. "Remember" notes summarize key points and help cement important facts in students' minds. "Accounting Tips" at appropriate intervals remind students of essential practices and procedures. "Accounting Notes" inform students of interesting facts about business and the practice of accounting.

Chapter summaries. The key points in each chapter are presented in a numbered list format at the end of the narrative in each chapter.

Solid, end-of-chapter activities. Vocabulary reviews reinforce key accounting terms. Review questions help students expand their understanding of accounting concepts. Short activities encourage students to improve their skills in such important areas as decision making, communications, analysis, math, and human relations. A variety of exercises and problems, ranging from easy to challenging, gives students of all abilities the chance to gain practical accounting experience and to enjoy success.

Comprehensive application activities. These mini practice sets, at appropriate points in the textbook, require students to integrate new knowledge with learned procedures and to apply their cumulative skills.

Computer orientation. Information about computerized accounting systems is integrated into the chapter narrative, providing computer awareness and system comparisons for all students. Short vignettes, called "Focus on Computers," introduce specific aspects of computer technology. A broad range of computer activities is available on optional software: end-of-chapter problems and application activities; simulations; spreadsheets; and a microcomputer program for review, remediation and reinforcement of key accounting principles. All such activities are completely optional. While the computer integration is provided, the use of a computer is not required for successful completion of the course.

Ethics in business and accounting. Vignettes on ethical business and accounting situations, called "Focus on Ethics," are provided throughout the text. These ethical dilemmas illustrate the kinds of problems working professionals often encounter.

Complete learning package. A complete package of student and teacher materials is available for the advanced accounting course. This package includes the textbook, teacher's edition of the textbook, teacher's resource manual, teaching transparencies, student working papers, teacher's edition of the working papers, source documents for the text mini practice sets, tests, a business simulation, and software.

Acknowledgments

We wish to thank those individuals and companies that provided advice and assistance in the development of this program. We owe a debt of gratitude to thousands of teachers and students who used previous editions of the textbook and who offered encouragement, suggestions, and advice in making a good accounting program even better.

We especially wish to thank the Accounting Advisory Committee, composed of ten master accounting teachers from across the country, who provided excellent guidance and advice in the development and review of this program.

Finally, we wish to thank our families, colleagues, and friends who offered constant encouragement and support as we worked on the third edition.

Donald J. Guerrieri
F. Barry Haber
William B. Hoyt
Robert E. Turner

Educational Consultants and Reviewers

We wish to acknowledge the contributions of the following:

DeVon Allmaras
Longmont High School
Longmont, Colorado

Gail Blair
William Floyd High School
Mastic Beach, New York

Thelma H. Brooks
Southeast Career Center
Columbus, Ohio

Johnsie Crawford
Brandon Senior High School
Brandon, Florida

Jackie Dean
Washington High School
Washington, North Carolina

Gloria Farris
Seneca High School
Louisville, Kentucky

Trudy Formanek
Colstrip High School
Colstrip, Montana

Shirley A. Helwick
Western Hills High School
Fort Worth, Texas

Ruth Hennessy
Comeaux High School
Lafayette, Louisiana

Norma Hernandez
Galena Park I.S.D.
Galena Park, Texas

Mitch Hummel
Cocalico High School
Denver, Pennsylvania

Jerry Livingston
A.C. Jones High School
Beeville, Texas

Nancy Lord
Southeast Career Center
Columbus, Ohio

Ellen Lundeen
Grand Ledge High School
Grand Ledge, Michigan

Carolyn McGraw
Lakeland High School
Lakeland, Florida

David McDonald
Rincon High School
Tucson, Arizona

John Nigro
North Haven High School
North Haven, Connecticut

JoAnne Pamer
Burbank High School
Burbank, California

Nate Rosenberg
Palo Alto High School
Palo Alto, California

Debra Saffo
Southeast Career Center
Columbus, Ohio

Michael Sailes
Carver Area High School
Chicago, Illinois

Emma Jo Spiegelberg
Laramie High School
Laramie, Wyoming

Claudia Stuvland
Rogers High School
Puyallup, Washington

Sue Thomas
Norwood High School
Norwood, Massachusetts

Carl Wenzel
Geneva High School
Geneva, New York

Frank Wood
Arrowhead High School
Hartland, Wisconsin

Eleanor A. Young
Southeast Career Center
Columbus, Ohio

UNIT 1

THE ACCOUNTING CYCLE

In this unit, you will review the basic principles and procedures you learned during your first-year study of accounting. You will review the accounting equation and the effects of business transactions on assets, liabilities, and owner's equity. You will analyze various types of transactions for Campers Unlimited, a merchandising corporation. You will journalize the transactions in special journals and post the amounts to the general and subsidiary ledgers. You will then complete the end-of-period activities for the business.

By the time you finish studying the two chapters in this unit, you will have reviewed the complete accounting cycle.

CAMPERS UNLIMITED
Chart of Accounts

ASSETS	101	Cash in Bank
	105	Accounts Receivable
	110	Merchandise Inventory
	115	Supplies
	120	Prepaid Insurance
	150	Store Equipment
LIABILITIES	201	Accounts Payable
	205	Employees' Federal Income Tax Payable
	210	Employees' State Income Tax Payable
	215	Federal Income Tax Payable
	220	Federal Unemployment Tax Payable
	225	Social Security Tax Payable
	226	Medicare Tax Payable
	230	Insurance Premiums Payable
	235	Sales Tax Payable
	240	State Unemployment Tax Payable
STOCKHOLDERS' EQUITY	301	Capital Stock
	305	Retained Earnings
	310	Income Summary
REVENUE	401	Sales
	405	Sales Discounts
	410	Sales Returns and Allowances
COST OF MERCHANDISE	501	Purchases
	505	Transportation In
	510	Purchases Discounts
	515	Purchases Returns and Allowances
EXPENSES	601	Advertising Expense
	605	Bank Card Fees Expense
	610	Insurance Expense
	615	Miscellaneous Expense
	620	Payroll Tax Expense
	625	Rent Expense
	630	Salaries Expense
	635	Supplies Expense
	640	Utilities Expense
	650	Federal Income Tax Expense

Chapter 1

REVIEWING THE FIRST FIVE STEPS OF THE ACCOUNTING CYCLE

Accounting, you'll remember, is the process of recording and reporting financial events, or transactions. *Business transactions* are events that directly affect the operation of a business. Whenever a transaction occurs, the business's financial position changes. The purpose of an accounting system is to process the financial information and report it to interested users.

In this chapter, you will first review the basic accounting equation and the rules of debit and credit for the various types of accounts. Then you will review the first five steps of the accounting cycle, from analyzing transactions to preparing a trial balance.

Learning Objectives

When you have completed this chapter, you should be able to do the following:

1. Describe the effects of various business transactions on the basic accounting equation.
2. Record business transactions in special journals and in the general journal.
3. Post business transactions to the general and subsidiary ledger accounts.
4. Prove the accuracy of the subsidiary ledgers.
5. Prepare a trial balance.
6. Define the accounting terms presented in this chapter.

New Terms

assets
liabilities
stockholders' equity
basic accounting equation
double-entry accounting
debit
credit
fiscal period
revenue
cost of merchandise
expenses
general ledger
accounting cycle
source document
journal
sales journal
cash receipts journal
purchases journal
cash payments journal
general journal
contra account
correcting entry
posting
subsidiary ledger
controlling account
trial balance

Point out that property or items of value are assets of the business.

The Basic Accounting Equation

In your previous study of accounting, you learned that **assets** are items of value owned or controlled by a business. Cash, accounts receivable, supplies, equipment, buildings, and land are all examples of assets. The financial claims (property rights) to those assets are referred to as *equity*. In accounting, there are two types of equity. First, there are **liabilities,** the creditors' claims to the business's assets. Liabilities are the debts of the business. Second, there are the owner's claims to the assets. In a sole proprietorship, the owner's claims are known as *owner's equity*. In this unit, you will study the accounting records of Campers Unlimited, which is organized as a corporation. In a corporation, the owners' claims are known as **stockholders' equity**.

Remind students that liabilities are the creditors' claims to assets and that owner's equity is the owner's claim to assets.

In accounting, total assets are always equal to total equities. This relationship is set out in the **basic accounting equation:**

Assets = Liabilities + Stockholders' Equity

Double-Entry Accounting

As a business begins operations and records business transactions, its financial position changes. The business records these changes in the asset, liability, and stockholders' (or owner's) equity accounts. An **account** is a record of the increases and decreases in and the balance for a specific item, such as supplies.

Point out that this checks the accuracy of the entries.

In the **double-entry accounting** system, every business transaction affects the balance in at least two accounts. The increases and decreases in accounts caused by business transactions are recorded as debits and credits. A **debit** is an amount entered on the left side of an account. A **credit** is an amount entered on the right side of an account. Each transaction has a debit part and a credit part, and the total debit part must equal the total credit part. The basic accounting equation, therefore, always remains in balance.

Review these rules in detail. Use various examples.

The rules of debit and credit for asset, liability, and stockholders' equity accounts are as follows:

Assets		=	Liabilities		+	Stockholders' Equity	
Debit + Increase Side Balance Side	Credit – Decrease Side		Debit – Decrease Side	Credit + Increase Side Balance Side		Debit – Decrease Side	Credit + Increase Side Balance Side

R — E — M — E — M — B — E — R

The left side of an account is the debit side. The right side of an account is the credit side.

Have students name account titles in each category that they used during the first-year course.

Asset, liability, and stockholders' equity accounts are *permanent accounts*. Their balances are carried forward from one accounting period

See "ACCOUNTING NOTES . . ." below.

to the next. A business also has *temporary accounts*. Temporary accounts are used for one **fiscal period,** or the time covered by an accounting report. At the end of the period, the balances of the temporary accounts are transferred to the stockholders' equity account Retained Earnings.

Review these rules in detail.

For a merchandising business, temporary accounts include revenue, cost of merchandise, and expense accounts. **Revenue** is the income earned from the sale of goods and services. The **cost of merchandise** accounts record the actual cost to the business of the merchandise that will be resold to customers. **Expenses** are the amounts paid for goods and services used to operate the business. The rules of debit and credit for the temporary accounts are as follows:

Revenue		=	Cost of Merchandise		+	Expenses	
Debit – Decrease Side	Credit + Increase Side Balance Side		Debit + Increase Side Balance Side	Credit – Decrease Side		Debit + Increase Side Balance Side	Credit – Decrease Side

All of a business's accounts, whether kept manually or electronically, are referred to as the **general ledger**. A complete list of a business's accounts appears in the *chart of accounts*. A chart of accounts for Campers Unlimited appears on page 2. Take a moment to look at it. Notice that each account has a number and has been placed into one of the six classifications.

Have students complete Exercise 1-1 at this point.

The Steps in the Accounting Cycle

The **accounting cycle** refers to the activities a business completes within a fiscal period to keep its accounting records in order. The accounting cycle consists of ten steps:

Describe the process and reason for each step.

1. Collect source documents and verify the data on them.
2. Analyze business transactions.
3. Journalize business transactions.
4. Post each entry to the ledger accounts.
5. Prepare a trial balance.
6. Complete the work sheet.
7. Prepare the financial statements.
8. Journalize and post the adjusting entries.
9. Journalize and post the closing entries.
10. Prepare a post-closing trial balance.

In this chapter, you will review steps 1 through 5 of the accounting cycle. Chapter 2 will cover steps 6 through 10. In these two chapters, you will go through the complete accounting cycle for Campers Unlimited, a merchandising business organized as a corporation. Let's now look at the first step.

ACCOUNTING Notes

The word *fiscal* refers to financial matters. The fiscal period used by a business will vary from one company to another. One business may choose a six-month fiscal period while another may prefer a twelve-month period. A twelve-month fiscal period often does not coincide with the calendar year.

Collecting and Verifying Source Documents

As each business transaction occurs, the accounting clerk prepares a paper as evidence that the transaction took place. This paper is called a **source document**. Some common source documents are invoices, receipts, memorandums, check stubs, and sales slips. The accounting clerk begins the accounting cycle by collecting these source documents and checking the accuracy of the information and calculations contained on the documents.

Analyzing Business Transactions

Use demonstration problem 1-1 here.

After verifying a source document, the accounting clerk performs the second step in the accounting cycle: analyzing the information on the document to determine the debit and credit parts of the transaction.

To analyze a business transaction, you must determine the answers to these six questions:

Apply the six questions when reviewing transactions.

1. Which accounts are affected?
2. What is the classification of each account?
3. Is each account increased or decreased?
4. Which account is debited, and for what amount?
5. Which account is credited, and for what amount?
6. What is the complete entry?

R — E — M — E — M — B — E — R

The debit and credit parts of each transaction must be equal.

Before reading further, do the following activity to check your understanding of the material you have just studied.

Check Your Learning

The "Check Your Learning" activities are intended as short, self-check exercises for students. The answers to all of these activities are included at the back of the textbook.

Write your answers to these questions on a sheet of notebook paper.

1. In accounting, the two types of equity are __?__ and __?__.
2. Assets = Liabilities + Stockholders' Equity is referred to as the __?__.
3. The __?__ is a complete listing of a business's accounts.
4. Supplies is classified as a(n) __?__ account.
5. The revenue account Sales normally has a(n) __?__ balance.

Compare your answers to those in the answers section, which begins on page 676. Reread the preceding part of the chapter to find the correct answers to any questions you may have missed.

Journalizing Business Transactions

Review the term *chronological.* Equate it to a diary.

The third step in the accounting cycle is to record the debit and credit parts of each business transaction in a journal. A **journal** is a chronological record of a business's transactions.

Campers Unlimited has a large number of business transactions. To operate efficiently, it records those transactions in special journals. A *special journal* is a multicolumn journal that has columns reserved for recording specific types of transactions. Campers Unlimited uses four special journals: the sales journal, the cash receipts journal, the purchases journal, and the cash payments journal. Campers Unlimited also uses a general journal for transactions that cannot be entered in the special journals.

Let's see how Campers Unlimited records its business transactions in these journals. We'll begin with the sales journal.

Journalizing Sales on Account

Review the term *on account.* Remind students that cash sales would be recorded in the cash receipts journal.

The **sales journal** is a special journal used to record only sales of merchandise on account. The sales journal used by Campers Unlimited, shown in Figure 1-1, has three special amount columns: Sales Credit, Sales Tax Payable Credit, and Accounts Receivable Debit. These column headings indicate the general ledger accounts that are to be debited and credited. The source document for an entry in the sales journal is a sales slip.

SALES JOURNAL PAGE 19

	DATE		SALES SLIP NO.	CUSTOMER'S ACCOUNT DEBITED	POST. REF.	SALES CREDIT	SALES TAX PAYABLE CREDIT	ACCOUNTS RECEIVABLE DEBIT	
1	199- Dec.	1	92	Alex La Rosa		174 00	10 44	184 44	1
	1		2	3		4	5	6	

Figure 1-1 Journalizing a Sale on Account

Remind students to use the six-question approach to analyze this transaction.

Now let's look at a transaction and see how it is recorded in the sales journal. Remember to use the six-step method to analyze each part of this transaction.

December 1: *Sold merchandise on account to Alex LaRosa for $174.00 plus $10.44 sales tax, Sales Slip 92.*

Emphasize that journalizing is always done from left to right.

In this transaction, Sales is being increased, Sales Tax Payable is being increased, and Accounts Receivable is being increased. To journalize this transaction, follow these steps:

1. In the Date column of the sales journal, enter the date shown on the sales slip.
2. Enter the sales slip number in the Sales Slip Number column.
3. Enter the name of the charge customer in the Customer's Account Debited column.

4. Enter the total selling price of the merchandise in the Sales Credit column.
5. Enter the amount of sales tax in the Sales Tax Payable Credit column.
6. Enter the total amount to be received in the Accounts Receivable Debit column.

Use demonstration problem 1-2 here.

All sales of merchandise on account are journalized in this manner.

R — E — M — E — M — B — E — R

Always journalize from left to right.

Special journals simplify the journalizing and posting process. Special amount columns are provided to record debits and credits to frequently used accounts. As you saw in the preceding example, only one line was needed to record the December 1 entry in the sales journal. The totals of the special amount columns, rather than each individual entry, are posted to the general ledger accounts. The special journals, then, must be totaled, proved, and ruled at the end of each month. To do this, follow these steps:

Explain the process of proving a special journal to ensure that the total of the debit columns equals the total of the credit columns.

1. Draw a single rule across all amount columns.
2. Foot the amount columns (enter totals in small pencil figures immediately below the single rule).
3. Test for the equality of debits and credits. In the sales journal, the total of the two credit columns ($3,904.94) must equal the total of the debit column.
4. On the line below the single rule, enter the date the journal is being totaled in the Date column and the word *Totals* in the Customer's Account Debited column.
5. Enter the column totals just below the footings.
6. Double rule the amount columns.

$ 221.03
+3,683.91
$3,904.94

The same steps are followed for any special journal. Figure 1-2 shows the totaled and ruled sales journal.

SALES JOURNAL — PAGE 19

	DATE		SALES SLIP NO.	CUSTOMER'S ACCOUNT DEBITED	POST. REF.	SALES CREDIT	SALES TAX PAYABLE CREDIT	ACCOUNTS RECEIVABLE DEBIT	
1	199– Dec.	1	92	Alex La Rosa		174 00	10 44	184 44	1
2		2	93	Jason Cott		39 20	2 35	41 55	2
3		3	94	Juan Domingo		61 74	3 70	65 44	3
32		30	123	Kim Lockett		32 14	1 93	34 07	32
33		31	124	Debbie Low		70 81	4 25	75 06	33
34		31		Totals		3683 91	221 03	3904 94	34

Figure 1-2 Totaling and Ruling the Sales Journal

R — E — M — E — M — B — E — R

In the special journals, single and double rules are drawn across the amount columns only.

Journalizing Cash Receipts

Review the special amount columns.

The **cash receipts journal** is a special journal used to record all transactions in which cash is received. The number of special amount columns varies according to the business's needs. However, because every transaction recorded in this journal requires a debit to Cash in Bank, the cash receipts journal always has a Cash in Bank Debit column. In addition to the special amount columns, the cash receipts journal has a General Credit column. This column is used to record credits to general ledger accounts that cannot be entered in a special amount column. Figure 1-3 shows the cash receipts journal used by Campers Unlimited. The source documents for cash receipts journal entries include receipts and cash register tapes.

CASH RECEIPTS JOURNAL — PAGE 24

	DATE		DOC. NO.	ACCOUNT TITLE	POST. REF.	GENERAL CREDIT	SALES CREDIT	SALES TAX PAYABLE CREDIT	ACCOUNTS RECEIVABLE CREDIT	SALES DISCOUNTS DEBIT	CASH IN BANK DEBIT	
1	199- Dec.	2	R320	Store Equipment		35 00					35 00	1
2		3	R321	Scott Miller					50 00		50 00	2
3		5	T170	Cash Sales	✓		1 203 91	72 23			1 276 14	3
4		5	T170	Bank Card Sales	✓		587 63	35 26			622 89	4
5		8	R322	Paul Stetko					236 55	2 23	234 32	5
24		31	T174	Bank Card Sales	✓		487 25	29 24			516 49	24
25		31		Totals		1 163 19	14 831 60	889 90	3 206 80	181 40	19 910 09	25

Figure 1-3 The Cash Receipts Journal

Let's examine how several transactions are recorded in the journal.

December 2: *Received $35.00 cash from the Wentworth Company for an old calculator no longer being used, Receipt 320.*

Remind students that a merchandising business receives cash from many sources: cash received on account from charge customers, cash sales, bank card sales, and the sale of assets.

In this transaction, shown on line 1 of Figure 1-3, Campers sold an old calculator to another business for $35.00. Cash in Bank is being increased, and Store Equipment is being decreased. The date and number of the source document are entered in the first two columns. The name of the account being credited is written in the Account Title column. Since there is no special amount column for store equipment, the credit to Store Equipment is entered in the General Credit column. The amount of cash received is entered in the Cash in Bank Debit column.

December 3: *Received $50.00 on account from Scott Miller, Receipt 321.*

In this transaction, shown on line 2 of Figure 1-3, Campers Unlimited is receiving cash from a charge customer. Cash in Bank is being increased, and Accounts Receivable is being decreased. The customer's name is recorded in the Account Title column. The debit and credit amounts are entered in the special amount columns.

December 5: *Had cash sales of $1,203.91, plus sales tax of $72.23, Tape 170.*

In this transaction, shown on line 3 of Figure 1-3, Sales is being increased by $1,203.91 and Sales Tax Payable is being increased by $72.23. The total amount of cash received, $1,276.14, is debited to Cash in Bank. Notice that the words *Cash Sales* were written in the Account Title column and that a check mark was entered in the Posting Reference column of the cash receipts journal.

December 5: *Recorded bank card sales of $587.63, plus $35.26 sales tax, Tape 170.*

Discuss why bank card sales are considered cash sales.

Bank card sales are considered a form of cash sales. As you can see on line 4 of Figure 1-3, the transaction is recorded in much the same way cash sales are recorded. However, the words *Bank Card Sales* are written in the Account Title column.

December 8: *Received $234.32 from Paul Stetko in payment of Sales Slip 83 for $236.55, less a cash discount of $2.23, Receipt 322.*

Ask students why a business would offer a sales discount to its customers.

A *cash discount,* you'll remember, is a reduction in the amount owed given for prompt payment. Campers Unlimited allows some charge customers to take a 1% discount if they pay the amount owed within ten days. The original sale on account to Paul Stetko was for merchandise costing $223.16 plus sales tax of $13.39, for a total amount due of $236.55. Cash discounts can be taken only on the *total of the merchandise sold* ($223.16). The 1% discount is, therefore, $2.23. This transaction is illustrated on line 5 of Figure 1-3.

Use demonstration problem 1-3 here.

At the end of the month, the cash receipts journal is totaled, proved, and ruled as shown in Figure 1-3.

R — E — M — E — M — B — E — R

When a special journal is totaled, the total of the debit columns must equal the total of the credit columns.

Journalizing Purchases on Account

Point out that every transaction entered in the purchases journal will have a credit to Accounts Payable.

Remind students that only purchases of merchandise on account are recorded in the Purchases Debit column.

To operate, businesses need items such as supplies, equipment, merchandise, and furniture. When a business buys these items on account, it records the transactions in the **purchases journal.** Because each transaction involves buying something on account, Campers Unlimited's purchases journal has an Accounts Payable Credit column. The purchases journal also has a special amount column to record the purchase of merchandise on account. The General columns are used to record the purchase on account of all other items. Figure 1-4 illustrates Campers' purchases journal.

	PURCHASES JOURNAL								PAGE 25	
	DATE	INVOICE NO.	CREDITOR'S ACCOUNT CREDITED	POST. REF.	ACCOUNTS PAYABLE CREDIT	PURCHASES DEBIT	GENERAL ACCOUNT DEBITED	GENERAL POST. REF.	GENERAL DEBIT	
1	199- Dec. 3	1238	Star Tents		815 74	815 74				1
2	5	481	Oakdale Supply Co.		133 92		Supplies		133 92	2
18	30	1145	Arundel's, Inc.		363 00	363 00				18
19	31		Totals		8,893 10	7,914 81			978 29	19

Figure 1-4 The Purchases Journal

Let's now look at two transactions commonly recorded in the purchases journal.

December 3: *Received Invoice 1238 from Star Tents for merchandise purchased on account, $815.74.*

Use demonstration problem 1-4 here.

In this transaction, Campers is buying on account merchandise that it will later resell to customers. As shown on line 1 of Figure 1-4, Accounts Payable is being increased and is credited for $815.74. The Purchases account is being increased and is debited for $815.74. These amounts are recorded in the two special amount columns.

December 5: *Purchased $133.92 of supplies on account from Oakdale Supply Company, Invoice 481.*

Discuss the difference between merchandise and other items purchased to operate a business.

In this transaction, Campers is buying on account supplies it will use in its business operations. Accounts Payable is being increased and is credited for $133.92, as shown on line 2 of Figure 1-4. Supplies is being increased and is debited for $133.92. Since this is not a purchase of merchandise, the amount is entered in the General Debit column. The account title is entered in the General Account Debited column.

At the end of the month, the purchases journal is totaled, proved, and ruled as shown in Figure 1-4. Notice that only the amount columns are ruled.

Journalizing Cash Payments

All transactions in which cash is paid out or decreased are recorded in the **cash payments journal.** Every transaction entered in this journal involves a decrease to Cash in Bank. Therefore, there is always a Cash in Bank Credit column. In Campers Unlimited's journal, shown in Figure 1-5, special amount columns are also provided for debits to Accounts Payable and credits to Purchases Discounts. The journal also has a General Debit column and a General Credit column. The source documents for transactions recorded in the cash payments journal are check stubs and bank statements. Look at some common cash payments journal transactions.

Review the purpose of the General Debit and General Credit columns.

	DATE		DOC. NO.	ACCOUNT TITLE	POST. REF.	GENERAL DEBIT	GENERAL CREDIT	ACCOUNTS PAYABLE DEBIT	PURCHASES DISCOUNTS CREDIT	CASH IN BANK CREDIT	
1	199- Dec.	1	2932	Rent Expense		900 00				900 00	1
2		3	2933	T&D Corporation				761 21	7 61	753 60	2
3		5	2934	Purchases		683 40				683 40	3
7		12	2937	Salaries Expense		1584 00				1226 82	7
8				Emp. Fed. Inc. Tax Payable			144 00				8
9				Emp. State Inc. Tax Payable			71 00				9
10				Social Security Tax Payable			98 21				10
11				Medicare Tax Payable			22 97				11
12				Insurance Premiums Payable			21 00				12
23		31	—	Miscellaneous Expense		12 00				12 00	23
24		31	—	Bank Card Fees Expense		78 56				78 56	24
25		31		Totals		9314 19	583 41	6373 91	124 23	14980 46	25

CASH PAYMENTS JOURNAL — PAGE 29

Figure 1-5 The Cash Payments Journal

December 1: *Paid $900.00 to Gula Realty for the December rent, Check 2932.*

This transaction is illustrated on line 1 of Figure 1-5. Rent Expense is being increased; it is debited for $900.00. Since there is no special column, the amount is entered in the General Debit column. Cash in Bank is being decreased; it is credited for $900.00.

December 3: *Wrote Check 2933 for $753.60 to T & D Corporation for merchandise purchased on account, $761.21, less a discount of $7.61.*

Use demonstration problem 1-5 here.

In this transaction, which appears on line 2 of Figure 1-5, a payment is being made to one of Campers Unlimited's creditors. Accounts Payable is being decreased and is debited for $761.21, the amount of the original purchase on account. Because Campers is paying the invoice within the discount period, it may deduct a 1% discount of $7.61. That amount is entered in the Purchases Discounts Credit column. Cash in Bank is being decreased and is credited for $753.60, the total amount of cash actually paid out.

December 5: *Purchased merchandise from Arundel's, Inc., for $683.40 cash, Check 2934.*

This transaction, shown on line 3 of Figure 1-5, is recorded in the cash payments journal because it is a cash purchase of merchandise. (The purchases journal, remember, is for *credit* purchases.) The Purchases account is being increased and is debited for $683.40. Since there is no special column for purchases, the amount is entered in the General Debit column. Cash in Bank is credited for $683.40.

December 12: *Paid the payroll of $1,584.00 (gross earnings) for the pay period. Amounts withheld include employees' federal income tax, $144.00; employees' state income tax, $71.00; social security tax, $98.21 ($1,584 × .062 = $98.21); medicare tax, $22.97 ($1,584 × .0145 = $22.97); and insurance premiums, $21.00; Check 2937.*

This transaction is shown on lines 7 through 11 of Figure 1-5. The gross earnings amount is debited to Salaries Expense. Since it cannot be entered in a special column, the $1,584.00 is entered in the General Debit column. Cash in Bank is credited for the net pay of $1,226.82. *Net pay,* you'll remember, is the amount actually paid to employees. The amounts withheld from employees' pay become liabilities of the business. Each liability is recorded on a separate line, and the amounts are entered in the General Credit column.

December 31: *Recorded the bank service charge of $12.00, December bank statement.*

The bank automatically deducts the service charge from Campers Unlimited's checking account. Because the transaction results in a decrease to Cash in Bank, it is recorded in the cash payments journal. Bank service charges are summarized in the Miscellaneous Expense account; therefore, it is debited for $12.00. Cash in Bank is credited for $12.00. This transaction appears on line 23 of Figure 1-5. Notice that a dash was entered in the Document Number column. This indicates that a check was not written.

December 31: *Recorded the bank card fee of $78.56, December bank statement.*

Most banks charge a fee for handling a business's bank card sales, usually a certain percentage of the total bank card sales. As with the service charge, the bank automatically deducts the bank card fee from the business's checking account. This transaction is journalized much like the bank service charge transaction. As shown on line 24 of Figure 1-5, however, Bank Card Fees Expense is debited for $78.56. Cash in Bank is credited for the same amount.

At the end of the month, the cash payments journal is totaled, proved, and ruled as shown in Figure 1-5.

Journalizing General Journal Transactions

Explain the need for the general journal and the kinds of transactions that would be recorded there.

A business designs its special journals to handle particular kinds of transactions that occur frequently. Any transaction that cannot be recorded in a special journal is recorded in the general journal. The **general journal** is a two-column journal in which all types of transactions can be recorded. Examples of the transactions that Campers Unlimited records in its general journal include sales returns and allowances, purchases returns and allowances, employer's payroll taxes, and correcting entries.

All merchandising businesses, large or small, must have a system of recording financial transactions.

Let's examine some of these transactions. The entries for these transactions appear in Figure 1-6.

GENERAL JOURNAL — PAGE 13

	DATE		DESCRIPTION	POST. REF.	DEBIT	CREDIT	
1	199- Dec.	2	Sales Returns and Allowances		42 95		1
2			Sales Tax Payable		2 58		2
3			Accts. Receivable/Anita Sanchez	✓		45 53	3
4			Credit Memo 24				4
5		11	Accts. Pay./Abbott's Camp. Equip.	✓	73 18		5
6			Purchases Returns and Allow.			73 18	6
7			Debit Memo 27				7
8		12	Payroll Tax Expense		145 98		8
9			Social Security Tax Payable			98 21	9
10			Medicare Tax Payable			22 97	10
11			Fed. Unemploy. Tax Payable			3 20	11
12			State Unemploy. Tax Payable			21 60	12
13			Payroll Register 12/12				13
14		14	Supplies		65 00		14
15			Store Equipment			65 00	15
16			Memo 19				16

Figure 1-6 The General Journal

December 2: *Granted $45.53 credit to Anita Sanchez for the return of merchandise worth $42.95 plus sales tax of $2.58, Credit Memo 24.*

Discuss the purpose of a contra account.

Merchandising businesses use the Sales Returns and Allowances account to record the total amount of returned merchandise. Sales Returns and Allowances is a contra revenue account used to summarize the returns and allowances for damaged, defective, or unsatisfactory merchandise. A **contra account** is an account whose balance decreases another account's balance. The balance of Sales Returns and Allowances decreases the revenue account Sales; as a result, it has a normal debit balance. In this transaction it is debited for $42.95, the original sale price of the merchandise. Sales Tax Payable is debited for $2.58, because this amount is no longer owed to the state. Accounts Receivable and the account for Anita Sanchez are credited for $45.53, because Campers Unlimited no longer expects to receive this amount. The transaction appears on lines 1 through 4 of Figure 1-6. Notice that a diagonal line was entered in the Posting Reference column on line 3. This line indicates that the amount will be posted to *two* accounts.

Remind students to enter the diagonal line in the Posting Reference column of the general journal as they journalize the transaction.

December 11: *Issued Debit Memo 27 for $73.18 to Abbott's Camping Equipment for damaged merchandise returned to them.*

Like its customers, a business may return unacceptable merchandise to suppliers. Accounts Payable and the account for Abbott's Camping Equipment are being decreased; they are debited for $73.18. When a business returns merchandise, the cost of the merchandise is recorded in the contra cost of merchandise account Purchases Returns and Allowances, which has a normal credit balance. Since Campers Unlimited is returning merchandise, Purchases Returns and Allowances is credited for $73.18. This transaction appears on lines 5 through 7 of Figure 1-6.

Use demonstration problem 1-6 here to bring out the difference—and similarity—between a sales return and allowance and a purchases return and allowance.

December 12: *Recorded the employer's payroll taxes: social security taxes, $98.21; medicare taxes, $22.97; federal unemployment taxes, $3.20; and state unemployment taxes, $21.60; Payroll Register.*

Employers are required to pay taxes on their employees' wages. The employer must pay FICA taxes on total employee wages, using the same set percentage used by employees. (This text uses 7.65% of gross earnings. The rate—and the maximum taxable amount—can be changed at any time by Congress.) The FICA tax is divided into two parts: 6.2% for social security and 1.45% for medicare. The maximum taxable amounts set for 1994 are $57,600 for social security tax and $135,000 for medicare tax. The employer must also pay federal and state unemployment taxes. The federal unemployment tax rate is 0.8% of the first $7,000 of an employee's gross earnings; the state unemployment tax rate is 5.4% of the first $7,000 of an employee's gross earnings. Because this transaction occurs at the end of the year, most of Campers' employees have exceeded the $7,000 limit.

Remind students that these taxes are expenses of the employer, not the employee.

As shown on line 8 of Figure 1-6, Payroll Tax Expense is debited for the total of $145.98. The payroll taxes are liabilities, because they will be paid some time in the future. Each payroll liability account, then, is credited for the amounts shown in Figure 1-6.

December 14: *Discovered that $65.00 of supplies, bought for cash on November 19, had been incorrectly journalized and posted to the* Store Equipment *account, Memorandum 19.*

When an error in an entry is discovered after it has been posted to the general ledger, a **correcting entry** must be recorded in the general journal. In the November 19 entry, the debit should have been made to Supplies. To correct the entry, Supplies is now debited for $65.00 and Store

Use T accounts to assist students in analyzing correcting entries.

Equipment is credited for $65.00. This transaction appears on lines 13 through 15 of Figure 1-6.

Before reading further, do the following activity to check your understanding of journalizing business transactions.

Check Your Learning

Write your answers to these questions on a sheet of notebook paper.

1. What is the source document for a transaction recorded in the sales journal?
2. How do you prove the equality of debits and credits in a special journal?
3. If merchandise is purchased on account, which accounts are debited and which are credited?
4. When and how are the special journals ruled?
5. What are two types of transactions that would be recorded in the general journal?

Compare your answers to those in the answers section. Reread the preceding part of the chapter to find the correct answers to any questions you may have missed.

Have students complete Exercise 1-2 at this point.

Posting

The fourth step in the accounting cycle is posting. **Posting** is the process of transferring amounts from a journal to ledger accounts. In the accounting system used by Campers Unlimited, posting takes several forms:

1. Entries are posted from the special and general journals to the accounts in the subsidiary ledgers.
2. Entries in the general journal and amounts from the special journals that cannot be posted as part of a special amount column total are posted to the appropriate general ledger accounts.
3. The totals of the special amount columns of the special journals are posted to the general ledger accounts.

Posting to the Subsidiary Ledgers

A **subsidiary ledger** is a ledger (or book) that is summarized in a controlling account in the general ledger. A **controlling account** is an account whose balance must equal the total of all of the account balances in a subsidiary ledger. Campers Unlimited has two subsidiary ledgers. The *accounts receivable subsidiary ledger* contains accounts for all of its charge customers. Accounts Receivable is the controlling account for the accounts receivable subsidiary ledger. The *accounts payable subsidiary ledger* contains accounts for all of Campers' creditors. Accounts

Payable is the controlling account for the accounts payable subsidiary ledger.

Carefully review these posting procedures.

Entries are posted to the subsidiary ledgers daily. Figure 1-7 shows how a transaction in the sales journal is posted to an account in the accounts receivable subsidiary ledger. To post the December 1 transaction to Alex LaRosa's account, follow these steps:

1. Enter the date of the transaction listed in the journal in the Date column of the customer's account.
2. Enter the letter and page number of the journal on which the transaction was recorded in the Posting Reference column of the account. Use the letter *S* for the sales journal. (Use *CR* for the cash receipts journal, *P* for the purchases journal, *CP* for the cash payments journal, and *G* for the general journal.)
3. In the Debit column of the subsidiary ledger account, enter the amount recorded in the Accounts Receivable Debit column of the journal.
4. Compute the new balance and enter it in the Balance column.
5. Return to the sales journal and enter a check mark in the Posting Reference column.

$392.11
+184.44
$576.55

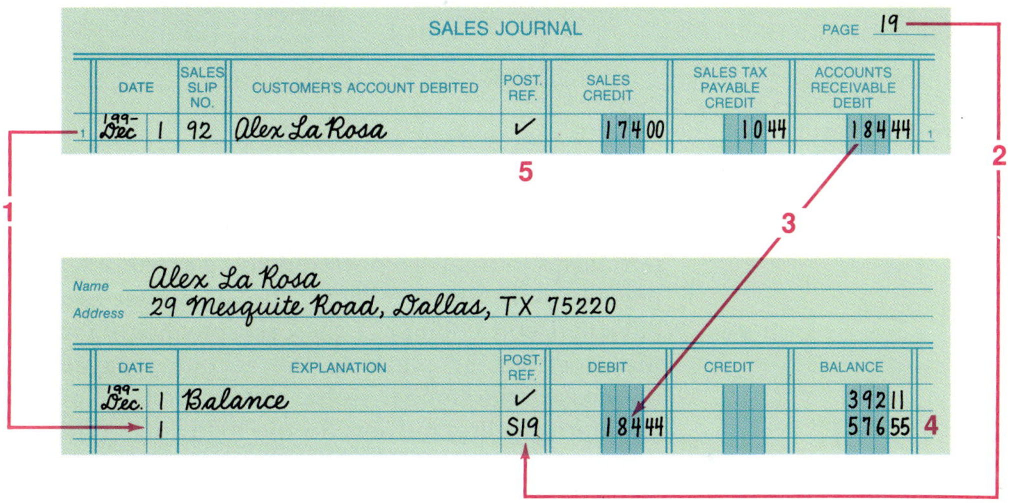

Figure 1-7 Posting a Sales Journal Entry to a Customer's Account in the Accounts Receivable Subsidiary Ledger

All posting from a special journal to a subsidiary ledger account is done in a similar manner.

R — E — M — E — M — B — E — R

Always post from left to right.

Use demonstration problem 1-7 here.

Transactions entered in the Accounts Receivable Credit column of the cash receipts journal are also posted to customers' accounts in the accounts receivable subsidiary ledger. For example, the December 8 cash receipt from Paul Stetko would be posted as shown in Figure 1-8. Notice that the same five steps are followed; however, the amount recorded in the Accounts Receivable Credit column is posted to the Credit column of the customer's account.

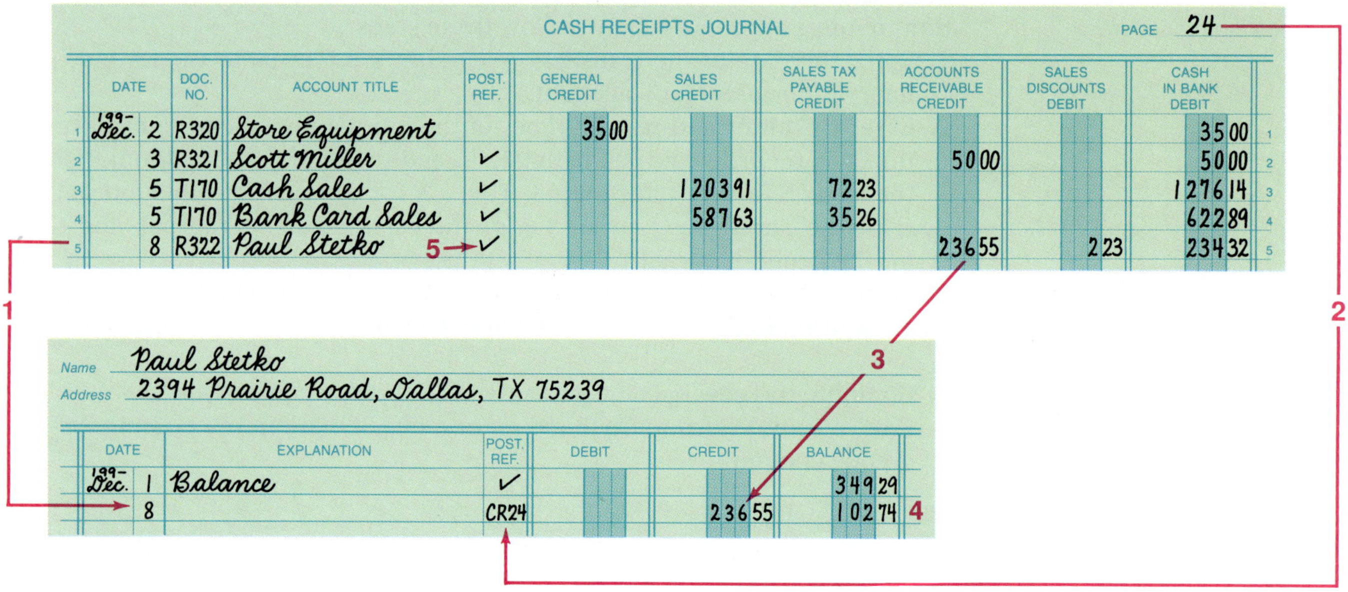

Figure 1-8 Posting from the Cash Receipts Journal to a Customer's Account in the Accounts Receivable Subsidiary Ledger

The amounts recorded in the Accounts Payable Credit column of the purchases journal are posted daily to creditors' accounts in the accounts payable subsidiary ledger. The amounts recorded in the Accounts Payable Debit column of the cash payments journal are posted daily to the creditors' accounts in the accounts payable subsidiary ledger. In both cases, the same five-step procedure is followed.

Before reading further, do the following activity to check your understanding of posting to the subsidiary ledger.

Check Your Learning

Write your answers to these questions on a sheet of notebook paper.

1. How often are amounts posted to the subsidiary ledgers?
2. What is the controlling account for the subsidiary ledger for charge customers' accounts?
3. To which subsidiary ledger would entries in the purchases journal be posted?

Compare your answers to those in the answers section. Reread the preceding part of the chapter to find the correct answers to any questions you may have missed.

Posting to the General Ledger

As mentioned earlier, amounts in the special journals that cannot be posted as part of a column total are posted individually to the general ledger accounts during the month. Such amounts are recorded in the General Debit and General Credit columns of the cash receipts, purchases, and cash payments journals. For example, in Figure 1-9 the first transaction recorded in the cash receipts journal must be posted to the Store Equipment account in the general ledger. To do this, follow these steps:

Point out the importance of the posting reference numbers that are placed in the journals to indicate that posting is complete.

1. Enter the date of the transaction listed in the journal in the Date column of the general ledger account.
2. Enter the letter and page number of the journal entry in the Posting Reference column of the account.
3. In the Credit column of the ledger account, enter the amount recorded in the General Credit column of the journal.
4. Compute and enter the new account balance.
5. Return to the journal and enter the general ledger account number in the Posting Reference column.

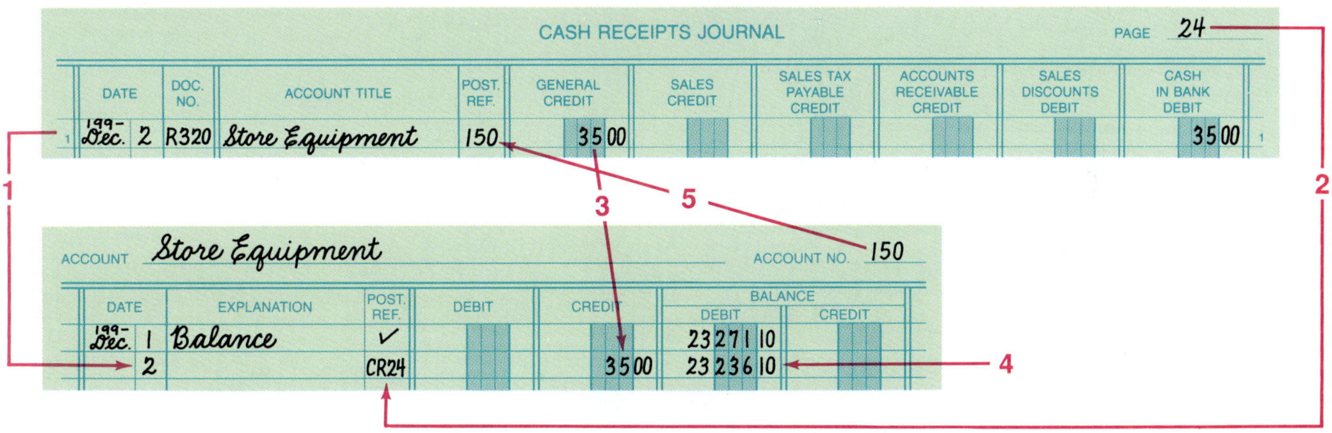

Figure 1-9 Posting from a Special Journal to an Account in the General Ledger

The same procedure should be followed when posting an amount from the General Debit or General Credit column of any special journal.

R — E — M — E — M — B — E — R

When computing a new account balance, debit amounts are added to accounts having a normal debit balance and credit amounts are subtracted from accounts with a normal debit balance. Likewise, credit amounts are added to and debit amounts subtracted from accounts with a normal credit balance.

Explain that this is posting the same amount to two different types of ledgers.

The general journal has no special amount columns. Each entry recorded in the general journal must be posted individually to the general ledger and to the subsidiary ledgers. For example, the December 2 entry recorded earlier is posted as shown in Figure 1-10. Notice that the $45.53 amount was posted to both the Accounts Receivable account and

Anita Sanchez's account in the accounts receivable subsidiary ledger. The Accounts Receivable account number and a check mark are placed on either side of the diagonal line in the Posting Reference column of the general journal.

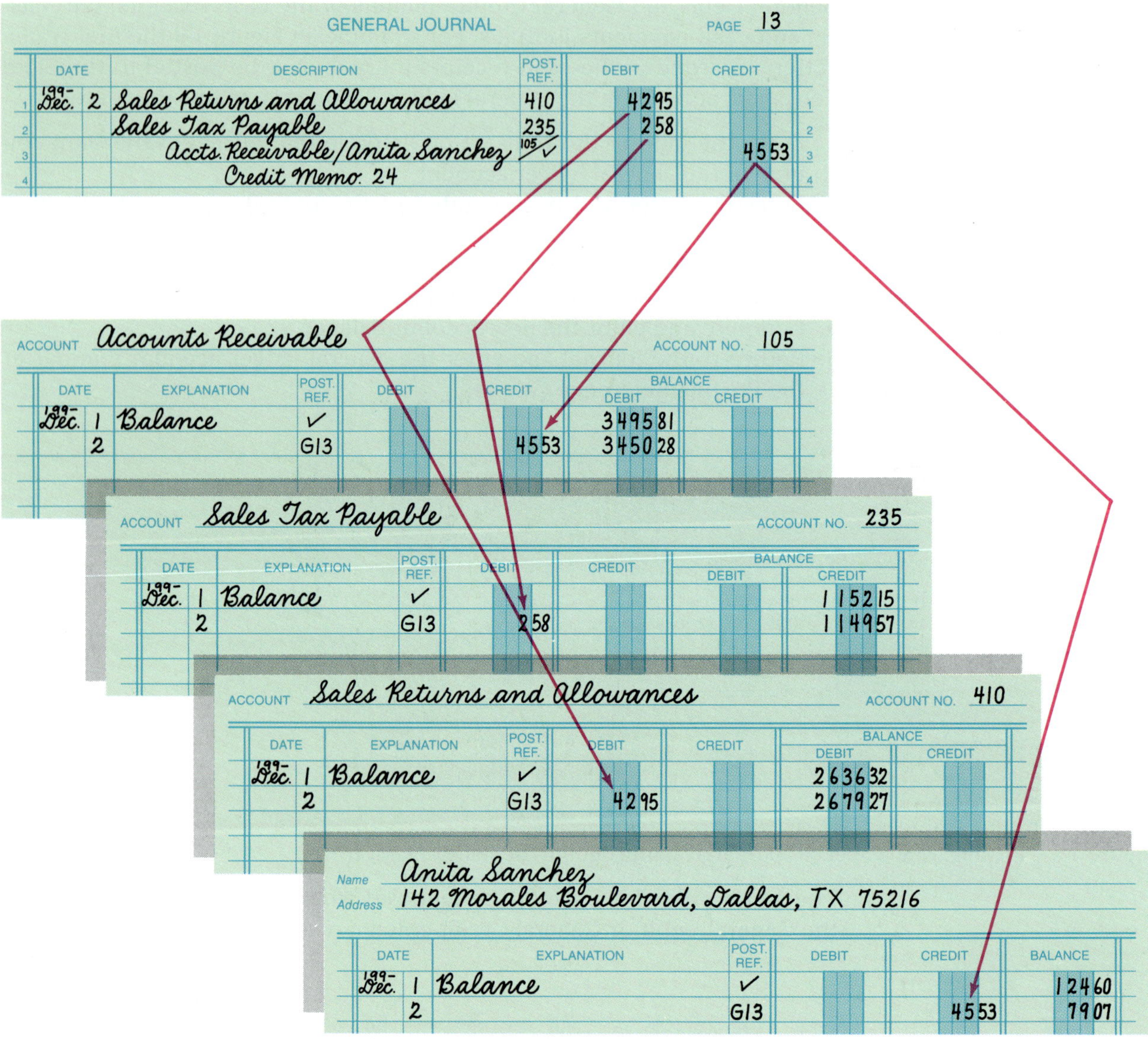

Figure 1-10 Posting from the General Journal to the General Ledger and Accounts Receivable Ledger

Posting Column Totals

Review why using special journals is more efficient.

As mentioned earlier, the special journals save time in posting. At the end of each month, the special journals are totaled, proved, and ruled. The *totals* of the special amount columns are then posted to the appropriate general ledger accounts. For example, to post the total of the Sales Credit column of the sales journal to the ledger account, follow the steps on page 21.

1. In the Date column of the Sales account, enter the date.
2. Enter the letter and page number of the journal in the Posting Reference column of the account.
3. In the Credit column of the account, enter the total from the Sales Credit column of the sales journal.
4. Compute the new balance and enter it in the correct Balance column.
5. Return to the journal and enter the number of the general ledger account—in parentheses—below the double rule in the column.

Figure 1-11 shows the posting of the column total. From the sales journal, column totals will also be posted to the Sales Tax Payable and Accounts Receivable accounts in the general ledger. The same procedure would be followed to post those column totals, as well as the column totals of any other special journal.

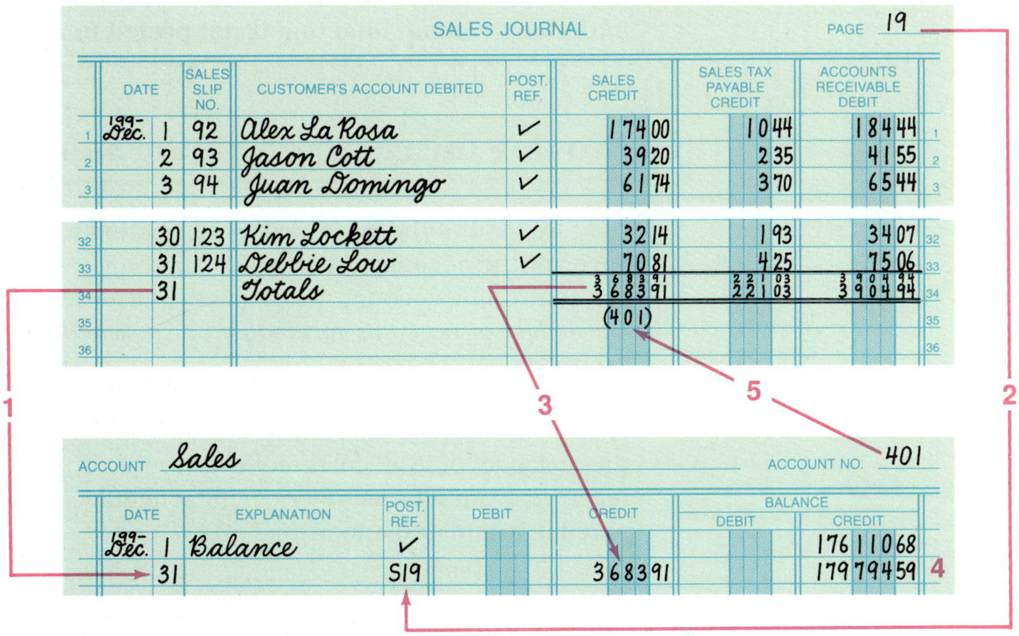

Figure 1-11 Posting Column Totals to the General Ledger

R — E — M — E — M — B — E — R

At the end of the month, the totals of the special amount columns of a special journal are posted to the general ledger accounts named in the column headings.

The entries in General Debit and General Credit columns of the special journals have already been posted individually to the ledger accounts. As a result, the totals of these columns are *not* posted. To indicate that these totals are not posted, place check marks, in parentheses, below the double rules in these columns. An example of this procedure is shown in the cash receipts journal in Figure 1-12.

Use demonstration problem 1-8 here.

CASH RECEIPTS JOURNAL — PAGE 24

	DATE	DOC. NO.	ACCOUNT TITLE	POST. REF.	GENERAL CREDIT	SALES CREDIT	SALES TAX PAYABLE CREDIT	ACCOUNTS RECEIVABLE CREDIT	SALES DISCOUNTS DEBIT	CASH IN BANK DEBIT	
	199-										
23	31	T174	Bank Card Sales	✓		487.25	29.24			516.49	23
24	31		Totals		1,163.19	14,831.60	889.90	3,206.80	181.40	19,910.09	24
25					(✓)	(401)	(235)	(105)	(405)	(105)	25

Figure 1-12 Posting References in the Cash Receipts Journal

R — E — M — E — M — B — E — R

After posting the total of a special amount column to a general ledger account, place the number of the account in parentheses below the double rule in the column. Place a check mark below the double rule under any column total that is not posted to a general ledger account.

Proving the Accuracy of the Subsidiary Ledgers

Review the purpose and importance of preparing these schedules.

At the end of the month, after all posting has been completed, the balances of the accounts in a subsidiary ledger should equal the balance of the controlling account. To prove the accuracy of the subsidiary ledgers, a *schedule of accounts receivable* and a *schedule of accounts payable* are prepared.

Campers Unlimited's schedule of accounts receivable for December appears in Figure 1-13. As you can see, the schedule lists each customer, the balance of the customer's account, and the total amount to be received from all customers. The schedule of accounts payable is prepared in a similar manner.

Campers Unlimited
Schedule of Accounts Receivable
December 31, 199-

Jason Cott	438.60	
Juan Domingo	174.51	
Alex La Rosa	883.45	
Kim Lockett	293.21	
Debbie Low	1,249.16	
Scott Miller	65.85	
Anita Sanchez	940.90	
Paul Stetko	102.74	
Total Accounts Receivable		4,148.42

ACCOUNT Accounts Receivable — ACCOUNT NO. 105

DATE		EXPLANATION	POST. REF.	DEBIT	CREDIT	BALANCE DEBIT	BALANCE CREDIT
199- Dec.	1	Balance	✓			3,495.81	
	2		G13		45.53	3,450.28	
	31		S19	3,904.94		7,355.22	
	31		CR24		3,206.80	4,148.42	

Figure 1-13 Schedule of Accounts Receivable

R — E — M — E — M — B — E — R

On the schedule of accounts receivable and the schedule of accounts payable, all accounts—even those with zero balances—are listed in alphabetical order.

Proving Cash

Proving cash is the process of determining whether the cash reported in the business's accounting records and in its checkbook agree. Ideally, a business should prove cash every day. When a business uses special journals, however, the Cash in Bank account is not updated until the end of the month. In many businesses, then, proving cash is done at the end of the month. The cash proof prepared by Campers Unlimited is shown in Figure 1-14.

Go through the steps for proving cash and emphasize the logical flow of what is being done.

Campers Unlimited
Cash Proof
December 31, 199-

Beginning Cash in Bank balance		11 853 52
Plus: Cash receipts for the month		19 910 09
Subtotal		31 763 61
Less: Cash payments for the month		14 980 46
Ending Cash in Bank balance		16 783 15
Check stub balance		16 783 15

Figure 1-14 Cash Proof

To prove cash, follow these steps:

1. Record the beginning balance of the Cash in Bank account.
2. Add the total cash received during the month. This is the total of the Cash in Bank Debit column of the cash receipts journal.
3. From the subtotal, subtract the total cash payments for the month. This is the total of the Cash in Bank Credit column of the cash payments journal.
4. Compare this figure against the balance shown on the last check stub in the checkbook. If the ending balance of Cash in Bank and the balance on the check stub match, cash is proved.

The ending balance of Cash in Bank is $16,783.15. Since the balance shown on the last check stub is also $16,783.15, cash has been proved.

Before reading further, do the following activity to check your understanding of the material you have just studied.

Check Your Learning

Write your answers to these questions on a sheet of notebook paper.

1. How do the special journals save time in posting?
2. How do you indicate that the total of a special amount column has been posted? How do you indicate that the total of a General Debit or General Credit column is not posted?
3. How is the accuracy of the subsidiary ledgers proved?
4. If the beginning Cash in Bank balance is $12,500, cash receipts for the month are $12,000, and cash payments for the month are $14,000, what is the ending Cash in Bank balance? Has cash been proved if the checkbook balance is $10,000?

Compare your answers to those in the answers section. Reread the preceding part of the chapter to find the correct answers to any questions you may have missed.

Have students complete Exercise 1-3 at this point.

Preparing the Trial Balance

Remind students that before a trial balance can be prepared, all amounts must be posted to the general ledger.

The fifth step in the accounting cycle is the preparation of the trial balance. A **trial balance** is prepared to prove the equality of debits and credits in the general ledger. It can be prepared at any time once posting has been completed.

At the end of a fiscal period, the trial balance is normally prepared in the first two amount columns of a work sheet. The accounts are listed in the trial balance in the order in which they appear in the chart of accounts. The balance of each account is entered in either the Trial Balance Debit or Credit column. Figure 1-15 shows the Trial Balance section of Campers Unlimited's work sheet for the year ended December 31. After all balances have been entered, the debit and credit columns are totaled, proved, and ruled. As you can see, both the Debit and Credit columns of the Trial Balance section of the work sheet total $253,609.95. The general ledger therefore is proved, and the first two amount columns are double ruled.

R — E — M — E — M — B — E — R

All general ledger accounts are listed in the trial balance, even if those accounts have a zero balance.

Campers Unlimited
Work Sheet
For the Year Ended December 31, 199-

ACCT. NO.	ACCOUNT NAME	TRIAL BALANCE DEBIT	TRIAL BALANCE CREDIT	ADJUSTMENTS DEBIT	ADJUSTMENTS CREDIT
101	Cash in Bank	16783 15			
105	Accounts Receivable	4148 42			
110	Merchandise Inventory	30376 95			
115	Supplies	3524 64			
120	Prepaid Insurance	1200 00			
150	Store Equipment	24106 90			
201	Accounts Payable		836 74		
205	Emp. Fed. Inc. Tax Pay.		288 00		
210	Emp. State Inc. Tax Pay.		297 32		
215	Fed. Inc. Tax Payable		—		
220	Fed. Unempl. Tax Pay.		38 40		
225	Social Security Tax Pay.		391 58		
226	Medicare Tax Payable		91 58		
230	Ins. Premiums Payable		42 00		
235	Sales Tax Payable		1110 93		
240	State Unempl Tax Pay.		126 50		
301	Capital Stock		20000 00		
305	Retained Earnings		33380 01		
310	Income Summary	—	—		
401	Sales		194626 19		
405	Sales Discounts	1036 81			
410	Sales Returns and Allow.	2808 17			
501	Purchases	98794 53			
505	Transportation In	4813 56			
510	Purchases Discounts		1449 27		
515	Purchases Ret. and Allow.		931 43		
601	Advertising Expense	9100 00			
605	Bank Card Fees Expense	1203 17			
610	Insurance Expense	—			
615	Miscellaneous Expense	1903 17			
620	Payroll Tax Expense	4313 24			
625	Rent Expense	10800 00			
630	Salaries Expense	30412 63			
635	Supplies Expense	—			
640	Utilities Expense	2284 61			
650	Federal Inc. Tax Expense	6000 00			
		253609 95	253609 95		

Figure 1-15 Preparing a Trial Balance on the Work Sheet

Summary of Key Points

1. The relationship between total assets and total equities is stated in the basic accounting equation: Assets = Liabilities + Stockholders' Equity. Assets are the items of value owned by a business. Liabilities are the debts of a business. Stockholders' equity is the owners' claims to the assets of a corporation.
2. In double-entry accounting, each business transaction affects at least two accounts.

3. The accounting cycle consists of the activities a business completes to keep its accounting records in an orderly fashion.
4. Special journals are multicolumn journals used to record specific types of business transactions. A sales journal is used to record all sales of merchandise on account. The cash receipts journal records all cash received by the business. The purchases journal records all items bought on account by the business. The cash payments journal records all transactions in which cash is paid out or decreased.
5. Transactions that cannot be recorded in the special journals are entered in the general journal.
6. The totals of the special amount columns of the special journals are posted at the end of the month to the general ledger accounts named in the column headings.
7. A subsidiary ledger is a ledger that is summarized in a controlling account in the general ledger. The accounts receivable subsidiary ledger contains accounts for the business's charge customers. The accounts payable subsidiary ledger contains accounts for the business's creditors.
8. At the end of the month, cash is proved by determining whether the balance of Cash in Bank according to the accounting records agrees with the balance shown in the checkbook.
9. A trial balance is prepared to prove the equality of debits and credits in the general ledger. The trial balance includes all accounts listed in the chart of accounts.

1 Review and Applications

Building Your Accounting Vocabulary

In your own words, write the definition of each of the following accounting terms. Use complete sentences for your definitions.

account
account cycle
assets
basic accounting equation
cash payments journal
cash receipts journal
contra account
controlling account
correcting entry
cost of merchandise
credit
debit
double-entry accounting
expenses
fiscal period
general journal
general ledger
journal
liabilities
posting
purchases journal
revenue
sales journal
source document
stockholders' equity
subsidiary ledger
trial balance

Reviewing Your Accounting Knowledge

1. Why are business transactions important?
2. What is the difference between a permanent account and a temporary account? Give three examples of each.
3. What are the six classifications of accounts found in a chart of accounts for a merchandising corporation?
4. What are the first five steps in the accounting cycle?
5. What six questions can be used to analyze business transactions?
6. Name and describe the use of the four special journals.
7. Why must a general journal be used with the special journals?
8. How is a cash discount calculated?
9. What are the two controlling accounts for the subsidiary ledgers?
10. Why is a schedule of accounts receivable prepared?
11. What are the steps followed to prove cash at the end of the month?
12. How are accounts listed on the trial balance?

Improving Your Decision-Making Skills

In the first-year course, you learned that the decision-making process can be followed when you must make a decision. The steps in this process are as follows:

1. Face the problem (recognize the need for a decision).
2. Get information about the problem.
3. List alternative ways of dealing with the problem.
4. Evaluate the alternatives.
5. Reach a decision.
6. Act on the decision.

Suppose you have completed your education and are ready to get a full-time job. Using the steps in the decision-making process, describe the actions you would take at each step. Be specific about information you would need and where you would get it.

Applying Accounting Procedures

Exercise 1-1 Classifying Accounts

Following is a list of accounts used by the Bargain Fence Company.

Accounts Payable
Accounts Receivable
Bank Card Fees Expense
Capital Stock
Cash in Bank
Federal Income Tax Expense
Social Security Tax Payable
Medicare Tax Payable
Merchandise Inventory
Prepaid Insurance
Purchases
Purchases Discounts
Retained Earnings
Salaries Expense
Sales
Sales Returns and Allowances
Sales Tax Payable
Store Equipment
Transportation In

Instructions: Use a form similar to the one that follows. For each general ledger account listed, indicate the classification of the account and its normal balance side.

Account	Classification	Normal Balance
Accounts Payable	Liability	Credit

Exercise 1-2 Identifying Special Journals

Instructions: Use a form similar to the one that follows. For each of the following transactions, identify the journal in which the transaction would be recorded by placing a check mark in the appropriate column. The first transaction is completed as an example.

Transactions	Sales Journal	Cash Receipts Journal	Purchases Journal	Cash Payments Journal	General Journal
1			√		

Transactions:

PJ 1. Bought office supplies on account.
GJ 2. Prepared a correcting entry.

CRJ 3. Sold merchandise for cash.
PJ 4. Bought merchandise on account.
SJ 5. Sold merchandise on credit.
PJ 6. Bought store equipment and agreed to pay for it later.
CRJ 7. Received a payment from a charge customer.
GJ 8. Sold office equipment on account.
CPJ 9. Paid for merchandise purchased on account.
CPJ 10. Bought merchandise for cash.
CPJ 11. Journalized the bank service charge.
GJ 12. Recorded the employer's payroll taxes.
CPJ 13. Paid freight charges on merchandise shipped from a supplier.

Exercise 1-3 Proving Cash

On June 30, the total of the Cash in Bank Debit column of the cash receipts journal is $20,125.45 and the total of the Cash in Bank Credit column of the cash payments journal is $22,520.42. The balance on check stub 3211 is $11,521.02.

Instructions: Use the form provided in the working papers. Prove cash for Pyramid Electronics for June. The balance of the Cash in Bank account on June 1 was $13,915.99.

Problem 1-1 Recording Transactions in Special Journals

The Tiger Music Shop uses special journals to record its transactions. The business had the following transactions during May.

Instructions:

(1) Record the following transactions in the sales journal, page 56; the cash receipts journal, page 42; the purchases journal, page 38; the cash payments journal, page 59; and the general journal, page 27.
(2) Total, prove, and rule the special journals.

SJ totals:
Sales, $391.89
Sales Tax Pay., $19.59
Accts. Rec., $411.48

CRJ totals:
Sales, $708.20
Sales Tax Pay., $35.41
Accts. Rec., $175.00
Cash in Bank, $918.61

PJ totals:
Accts. Pay., $420.49
Purchases, $295.49
General, $125.00

CPJ totals:
General Dr., $3,337.76
Accts. Pay., $549.26
Purch. Disc., $5.49
Cash in Bank, $3,881.53

Transactions:

May 1 Sold a compact disc player on account to Rodney Conway, $185.95 plus sales tax of $9.30, Sales Slip 1723.
2 Issued Check 2270 to Reale Associates for the monthly rent, $850.00.
4 Recorded cash sales of $437.82 plus $21.89 sales tax, Tape 385.
4 Recorded bank card sales of $270.38 plus sales tax of $13.52, Tape 385.
7 Purchased merchandise on account from Libby Company, $295.49, Invoice 9831.
10 Issued Credit Memo 28 for $33.34 to Ethel Ashby for the return of merchandise she purchased on account. The amount includes $31.75 of merchandise plus sales tax of $1.59.

13 Ron Zimmer sent a check for $175.00 to apply on account, Receipt 3456.

15 Purchased advertising on account from Radio Station WPDQ for $125.00, Invoice 384.

19 Carlos Munoz bought $29.95 of merchandise on account, plus sales tax of $1.49, Sales Slip 1724.

22 Discovered that $62.50 of supplies bought on account in April from K & D Supply was incorrectly journalized and posted to the Store Equipment account, Memorandum 24.

26 Purchased merchandise for cash, $2,384.99, Check 2271.

27 Sold a tape player on account to Amy Prys, $175.99 plus $8.80 sales tax, Sales Slip 1725.

29 Issued Check 2272 to CD Supply for $543.77, covering Invoice 4348 for $549.26, less a discount of $5.49.

30 Paid the telephone bill of $84.37, Check 2273.

31 Recorded the bank card fee from the May bank statement, $18.40.

COMPUTER PROBLEM

This element identifies a microcomputer problem.

Problem 1-2 Journalizing and Posting Business Transactions

The Oakdale Gift Shop uses special journals to record its business transactions. The general and subsidiary ledgers are included in the working papers that accompany this textbook. The account balances have already been entered.

Instructions:

SJ totals:
Sales, $61.80
Sales Tax Pay., $3.09
Accts. Rec., $23.05

CRJ totals:
General, $55.00
Sales, $3,139.97
Sales Tax Pay., $157.00
Accts. Rec., $150.00
Cash in Bank, $3,501.97

PJ totals:
Accts. Pay., $996.63
Purchases, $193.15
General, $803.48

CPJ totals:
General Dr., $5,684.75
General Cr., $497.84
Accts. Pay., $268.15
Purch. Disc., $3.86
Cash in Bank, $5,451.20

(1) Record the following transactions in the sales journal, page 17; the cash receipts journal, page 21; the purchases journal, page 18; the cash payments journal, page 26; and the general journal, page 9.

(2) Post transactions to the subsidiary ledgers on a daily basis.

(3) Post transactions in the General columns of the cash receipts, purchases, cash payments, and general journals to the general ledger on a daily basis.

(4) Total, prove, and rule the special journals.

(5) Post the column totals of the special journals to the general ledger accounts. Use the following order for posting: sales, cash receipts, purchases, cash payments.

Transactions:

Mar. 1 Issued Check 1734 to Housatonic Realty for the monthly rent, $950.00.

2 Sold merchandise on account to Ben Segal, $39.85 plus sales tax of $1.99, Sales Slip 1625.

6 Purchased merchandise on account from the L. J. Laine Company, $193.15, Invoice 2849, terms 2/10, n/30.

7 Issued Credit Memo 35 for $29.77 to Debbie Welsh, a charge customer, for the return of merchandise purchased on account. The amount includes $28.35 of merchandise and sales tax of $1.42.

10 A charge customer, Ben Segal, sent a check for $150.00 to apply on account, Receipt 1034.

12 Bought a half-page ad on account from *The Evening Sun,* $60.00, Invoice 355.

13 Recorded cash sales of $1,745.59 plus $87.28 sales tax, Tape 374.

13 Journalized the bank card sales of $1,394.38 plus sales tax of $69.72, Tape 374.

15 Issued Check 1735 for the cash purchase of merchandise, $1,290.49.

15 Paid the gross payroll of $1,847.69 with Check 1736. The amounts withheld include employees' federal income taxes, $217.00; employees' state income taxes, $94.49; social security taxes, $114.56; medicare taxes, $26.79, and insurance premiums, $45.00.

15 Recorded the employer's payroll taxes: social security taxes, $114.56; medicare taxes, $26.79; state unemployment taxes of 5.4% of gross earnings; and federal unemployment taxes of 0.8% of gross earnings.

16 Sent Check 1737 to the L. J. Laine Company, $189.29, in payment of Invoice 2849 for $193.15 less a discount of $3.86.

19 Discovered that $400.00 of office equipment bought on account in February from Fortune Supply had been incorrectly journalized and posted to the Display Equipment account, Memorandum 19.

21 Sold $21.95 of merchandise on account to Stan Garfield, sales tax $1.10, Sales Slip 1626.

23 Granted credit of $39.32 to Amy Gardner for the return of merchandise costing $37.45 plus $1.87 sales tax, Credit Memo 36.

24 Paid the telephone bill of $87.65, Check 1738.

25 Recorded the bank service charge of $9.50 and the bank card fee of $89.42 from the March bank statement.

27 Paid a $1,410.00 premium for a six-month insurance policy, Check 1739.

29 Sold display equipment to a neighboring business for $55.00 cash, Receipt 1035.

30 Received Invoice 2293 from Owens Company for display equipment bought on account, $743.48, terms n/30.

31 Sent Check 1740 for $75 to Bunnell Company to apply on account.

Problem 1-3 Proving the Subsidiary Ledgers and Cash

Use the journals and the general and subsidiary ledgers from Problem 1-2 to complete this problem.

Instructions:

Accts. Rec. bal. $780.21
Accts. Pay. bal. $1,713.48

(1) Prepare a schedule of accounts receivable and a schedule of accounts payable for the Oakdale Gift Shop. Use March 31 as the date. Compare the totals with the balances in the general ledger controlling accounts.

(2) Prove cash. The balance on check stub 1741 is $12,655.27.

TB totals, $72,968.97

Problem 1-4 Preparing a Trial Balance

Matthew's Office Supplies had the following balances in its general ledger accounts on October 31.

Instructions: Based on the account balances presented, prepare a trial balance for the month ended October 31, using the first two columns of a ten-column work sheet. Total, prove, and rule the columns.

101	Cash in Bank	$ 7,598.93
105	Accounts Receivable	2,370.29
110	Merchandise Inventory	31,282.32
115	Supplies	3,193.04
120	Prepaid Insurance	1,770.00
125	Store Equipment	7,960.46
130	Office Equipment	3,054.34
201	Accounts Payable	10,284.81
205	Employees' Federal Income Tax Payable	173.10
210	Employees' State Income Tax Payable	147.14
215	Federal Income Tax Payable	—
220	Social Security Taxes	93.52
221	Medicare Taxes	21.87
225	Sales Tax Payable	1,370.25
301	Capital Stock	25,000.00
302	Retained Earnings	12,771.75
303	Income Summary	—
401	Sales	22,829.45
405	Sales Discounts	289.41
410	Sales Returns and Allowances	305.39
501	Purchases	8,492.22
505	Transportation In	593.49
510	Purchases Discounts	94.87
515	Purchases Returns and Allowances	182.20
605	Advertising Expense	1,034.24
610	Bank Card Fees Expense	137.91
615	Insurance Expense	—
620	Maintenance Expense	211.29
625	Miscellaneous Expense	117.30
630	Payroll Tax Expense	262.10
635	Rent Expense	1,200.00
640	Salaries Expense	1,923.43
645	Supplies Expense	—
650	Utilities Expense	322.81
655	Federal Income Tax Expense	850.00

COMPUTER PROBLEM

Problem 1-5 Journalizing and Posting Transactions and Proving the Ledgers

The Kardos Marine Supply Store records its transactions in special journals. The general and subsidiary ledgers for the business are included in the working papers that accompany this textbook. The account balances have already been recorded.

Instructions:

SJ totals:
Sales, $222.19
Sales Tax Pay., $8.89
Accts. Rec., $231.08

(1) Record the November transactions in the special journals and the general journal. Use the following page numbers: sales journal, 28; cash receipts journal, 19; purchases journal, 16; cash payments journal, 26; general journal, 19.

CRJ totals:
General, $25.00
Sales, $8,515.32
Sales Tax Pay., $340.61
Accts. Rec., $157.60
Cash in Bank, $9,038.53

PJ totals:
Accts. Pay., $2,586.41
Purchases, $1,592.93
General, $993.48

CPJ totals:
General Dr., $4,725.82
General Cr., $788.69
Accts. Pay., $1,233.42
Purch. Disc., $23.26
Cash in Bank, $5,147.29

Accts. Rec. bal. $488.31
Accts. Pay. bal. $2,262.39

TB totals, $150,941.07

(2) Post the individual amounts from the five journals to the accounts receivable and the accounts payable subsidiary ledgers daily.
(3) Post the individual amounts from the General columns of the cash receipts, purchases, cash payments, and general journals daily.
(4) Total, prove, and rule the special journals.
(5) Post the special journals' column totals to the general ledger.
(6) Prepare a schedule of accounts receivable and a schedule of accounts payable.
(7) Prove cash. The balance on check stub 751 is $17,846.07.
(8) Prepare a trial balance for November in the first two columns of a work sheet.

Transactions:

Nov. 1 Paid the November rent of $945.00, Check 741.
2 Sold merchandise on account to Lisa Roberts, $122.29 plus sales tax of $4.89, Sales Slip 649.
2 Received a check for $80.00 from Vincent Lee to apply on account, Receipt 214.
3 Purchased an ad in the local newspaper for $94.00, Check 742.
4 Recorded the monthly bank card fees from the October 31 bank statement, $122.74.
4 Bought a new electronic typewriter on account from Topstone Office Equipment, Invoice 2392 for $795.00, terms n/30.
6 Paid the monthly telephone bill, $121.39, Check 743.
8 Issued Check 744 for $312.86 to Varga Corporation in payment of their Invoice 3867 for $319.24, less a discount of $6.38.
9 Bought supplies on account from Carol Supply, $198.48, Invoice 994, terms n/30.
11 Sent Credit Memo 82 to Jennifer Matthews for the return of merchandise costing $41.15 plus sales tax of $1.65.
13 Issued Check 745 for $70.19 to Carol Supply in payment of Invoice 949.
14 Sold an old office calculator for $25.00 cash, Receipt 215.
15 Cash sales for the period November 1–14 were $2,395.40 plus sales tax of $95.82, Tape 331.
15 Bank card sales for the first half of the month were $927.36 plus $37.09 sales tax, Tape 331.
17 Purchased a new display case for the store, $335.00, Check 746.
18 Returned defective merchandise purchased on account from Standard Automation, $94.50, Debit Memo 22.
20 Purchased $843.99 of merchandise on account from DeLucca Corporation, Invoice 391, dated November 18, terms 2/10, n/30.
22 Paid $183.03 for freight charges on merchandise bought from a supplier, Check 747.
24 Sold merchandise on account to Vincent Lee, $33.95 plus sales tax of $1.36, Sales Slip 650.
24 Purchased mechandise on account for $541.43 from Varga Corporation, Invoice 3896, dated November 21, terms 2/10, n/30.

25 Jeremy Hurth sent a check for $77.60 in payment of the amount owed, Receipt 216.

26 Issued Check 748 to DeLucca Corporation in payment of Invoice 391 totaling $843.99, less a discount of $16.88.

27 Discovered that an October purchase of supplies for $65.50 had been incorrectly journalized and posted as office equipment, Memorandum 24.

28 Prepared Check 749 for the gross payroll of $2,845.58. The amounts withheld were as follows: employees' federal income tax, $397.00; employees' state income tax, $129.00; social security tax, $176.43; medicare tax, $41.26; insurance premiums, $45.00.

28 Recorded the employer's tax liability for the payroll. The social security tax rate is 6.2%; the medicare tax rate is 1.45%; the federal unemployment tax rate is 0.8%; the state unemployment tax rate is 5.4%.

29 Sold a compass to Henry Peterson on account, $65.95 plus sales tax of $2.64, Sales Slip 651.

30 Paid the monthly electric bill, $79.08, Check 750.

30 Purchased merchandise on account from DeLucca Corp., $207.51, Invoice 774, dated November 28, terms 2/10, n/30.

30 Recorded cash sales of $3,065.46 plus sales tax of $122.62, Tape 332.

30 Bank card sales for November 15–30 were $2,127.10 plus $85.08 sales tax, Tape 332.

CHALLENGE PROBLEM

This element identifies a challenge problem.

Problem 1-6 Analyzing Errors

The bookkeeper for the Wilton Company made two errors while posting from the special and general journals.

Instructions: Answer the questions that follow the description of each error. Use plain paper or the space provided in the working papers that accompany this textbook.

(1) An entry in the Accounts Payable Debit column of the cash payments journal was not posted to the creditor's account in the subsidiary ledger.

(a) Will the general ledger accounts balance? If not, why not?
(b) Will the total debits and total credits in the cash payments journal prove equal? If not, why not?
(c) Will the schedule of accounts payable agree with the balance in the controlling account? If not, which balance will be greater?
(d) Will the balance in the Cash in Bank account be correct?
(e) When is this error likely to be caught?

(2) In the cash receipts journal, the cash sale of a typewriter for $100.00 was not posted to the Office Equipment account in the general ledger.

(a) Will the general ledger accounts balance? If not, why not?
(b) On the Trial Balance, will the total of the debit column or that of the credit column be larger?
(c) Will the net income be affected? If so, how?
(d) Will value of the office equipment be overstated or understated?
(e) Will the balance in the Cash in Bank account be correct?

Database Management: A Way to Organize and Find the Latest Information—Fast!

Imagine you are the manager of a car dealership. Recently, a manufacturer informed you that the 1994 model of a particular automobile has a defective gas gauge and a recall must be issued to all buyers. How would you go about issuing the recall?

The "traditional" way to handle such a task would be to have someone pull all the customer files and look through each file to find the buyers of the car in question. Then would come the task of typing a form letter and sending it to each owner. Just looking through all the customer files could take weeks. By using a computer and database management software, however, you could save thousands of dollars in time and labor.

In simple terms, database management is a means of locating specific information in an electronic filing system. The database—the collection of information records—can be anything: customer records, names and addresses of employees, invoices, accounts receivable, payables, tax records, payroll, budgets, résumés, marketing plans, projections, price lists, or inventory, among other information. Database management software allows a personal computer to store, sort, and retrieve any of the information contained in those records.

Databases allow you to locate information easily.

In the car dealership example, to put a recall in motion using database management software, you could instruct the computer, "List all customers who purchased 1994 model of car X." The computer could list the customers and their addresses and sort them according to ZIP code. It could also tell you which customers have already brought their cars in to have the gas gauge repaired.

Instead of having to rely on massive numbers of paper files in which information often remains buried, you can use a database management system to search, compare, combine, and manipulate data. Database management systems help to solve problems, make decisions, and project change—all important activities in today's competitive business world.

Chapter 2

REVIEWING THE FINAL FIVE STEPS OF THE ACCOUNTING CYCLE

In Chapter 1, you reviewed the first five steps of the accounting cycle. You analyzed various business transactions and journalized those transactions in the special and general journals. Then you posted the transactions to accounts in the general ledger and the subsidiary ledgers. Finally, you proved cash and the accuracy of the subsidiary ledgers and prepared a trial balance, using the first two columns of a ten-column work sheet.

In this chapter, you will review the last five steps of the accounting cycle, from preparing the work sheet to preparing the post-closing trial balance.

Learning Objectives

When you have completed this chapter, you should be able to do the following:

1. Determine which general ledger accounts must be adjusted and calculate the amounts of the adjustments.
2. Complete a ten-column work sheet.
3. Prepare the financial statements for a merchandising business: income statement, statement of retained earnings, and balance sheet.
4. Journalize and post the adjusting entries.
5. Journalize and post the closing entries.
6. Prepare a post-closing trial balance.
7. Define the accounting terms presented in this chapter.

New Terms

work sheet
adjustment
inventory
net income
net loss
income statement
net sales
cost of merchandise sold
net purchases
gross profit on sales
operating expenses
operating income
statement of retained earnings
balance sheet
adjusting entries
closing entries
post-closing trial balance

End-of-Fiscal-Period Work

Review the accounting assumption relating to time periods.

The balances of the general ledger accounts summarize the effects of business transactions for an accounting period. To evaluate a business's performance, however, managers, stockholders, and creditors need more than just a list of account totals. The information needed to make sound business decisions and to operate efficiently can be found in the end-of-period financial statements. These reports show the changes during the period and the financial position of the business. Before the reports are prepared, however, the accountant collects all the information on the work sheet.

Preparing a Ten-Column Work Sheet

The sixth step in the accounting cycle is to prepare a work sheet. A **work sheet** is a working paper used to collect information from the general ledger. The work sheet, then, contains the information needed to prepare the financial statements for the period.

In Chapter 1, you prepared a trial balance using the first two columns of the work sheet. This trial balance was prepared to prove the equality of debits and credits in the general ledger. If the trial balance does not prove equal, the errors must be found and corrected before the work sheet can be continued. Common errors that may occur include

Review in detail transposition and slide errors.

1. Addition or subtraction errors.
2. An omitted account.
3. An account balance entered in the wrong amount column.
4. A transposition error (reversing two digits).
5. A slide error (moving the decimal place).

Once the Trial Balance section of the work sheet is proved equal, the next section of the work sheet can be prepared.

Calculating Adjustments

Point out the accounting principle of matching revenue and expenses within a fiscal period.

Not all changes in account balances result from daily business transactions. Some changes result from the passage of time or from the internal operations of the business. As a result, the balances of some general ledger accounts must be brought up to date at the end of the fiscal period. The updating of accounts such as Supplies, Prepaid Insurance, and Merchandise Inventory is calculated on the work sheet through adjustments. An **adjustment** is an amount that is added to or subtracted from an account balance to bring that balance up to date. Accounts whose balances are not up to date *as of the last day of the fiscal period* must be adjusted.

The adjustments are entered in the Adjustments section of the work sheet. Once the work sheet reflects how the account balances must be brought up to date, the net income or loss for the period can be calculated and the financial statements prepared using the data on the work sheet.

R — E — M — E — M — B — E — R

If an account balance is not up to date as of the last day of the fiscal period, it must be adjusted.

Be sure students understand why the Merchandise Inventory account must be adjusted.

Review the importance of taking a physical inventory.

Adjusting the Merchandise Inventory Account For a merchandising business, the first adjustment that must be made is for Merchandise Inventory. The $30,376.95 balance for Merchandise Inventory entered in the Trial Balance section of the work sheet represents Campers Unlimited's beginning inventory. The **beginning inventory** is the merchandise on hand at the beginning of the fiscal period.

During the fiscal period, the balance of Merchandise Inventory does not change. Merchandise is bought and sold, but the transactions are recorded in the Purchases and Sales accounts. At the end of the period, a *physical inventory* (actual count) is taken of the merchandise on hand and still available for sale. Then the cost of the **ending inventory,** the merchandise on hand at the *end* of the period, is calculated.

Maintaining inventory records is part of the accounting process for businesses.

Review the adjustment using a larger and smaller ending inventory.

The cost of the ending inventory for Campers Unlimited is $31,274.81. To be brought up to date, the Merchandise Inventory account must be increased by $897.86 ($31,274.81 – $30,376.95). Merchandise Inventory has a normal debit balance. To increase the balance, Merchandise Inventory must be debited for $897.86. The amount is entered in the Adjustments Debit column of the work sheet, as shown in Figure 2-1. The Income Summary account is credited for the same amount. The $897.86 is entered in the Adjustments Credit column on the Income Summary line. Both amounts are labeled *(a)* so that they can be easily identified later when the adjusting entries are journalized.

Campers Unlimited
Work Sheet
For the Year Ended December 31, 199-

	ACCT. NO.	ACCOUNT NAME	TRIAL BALANCE DEBIT	TRIAL BALANCE CREDIT	ADJUSTMENTS DEBIT	ADJUSTMENTS CREDIT
1	101	Cash in Bank	16,783.15			
2	105	Accounts Receivable	4,148.42			
3	110	Merchandise Inventory	30,376.95		(a) 897.86	
18	310	Income Summary	—	—		(a) 897.86

Figure 2-1 Recording the Adjustment to Merchandise Inventory on the Work Sheet

R — E — M — E — M — B — E — R

If the ending inventory is greater than the beginning inventory, Merchandise Inventory is *debited* for the amount of the difference. If the ending inventory is less than the beginning inventory, Merchandise Inventory is *credited* for the amount of the difference.

Review what are considered supplies and have students name some.

Adjusting the Supplies Account As supplies are purchased during the fiscal period, the cost is debited to the asset account Supplies. During the normal operations of the business, many of these supplies are used up. Rather than crediting Supplies every time a sheet of paper or a pen is used, the accounting clerk makes an adjustment at the end of the period.

Remind students that all supplies purchased during the period are included in the balance of the Supplies account in the Trial Balance section.

For Campers Unlimited, the balance of the Supplies account reported in the Trial Balance section is $3,524.64. This amount represents the supplies on hand at the beginning of the year, plus the cost of all supplies purchased during the period.

At the end of the period, an accounting clerk at Campers took an inventory of the supplies. This inventory showed that $1,165.19 of supplies were still on hand. In other words, $2,359.45 of supplies was consumed during the period ($3,524.64 – $1,165.19).

Emphasize that the adjustment for Supplies represents the amount of supplies consumed during the period.

When the account is adjusted, Supplies is credited for $2,359.45, the amount of supplies consumed, and Supplies Expense is debited for the same amount. The two parts of the adjustment are labeled *(b)*, as shown in Figure 2-2.

Campers Unlimited
Work Sheet
For the Year Ended December 31, 199-

	ACCT. NO.	ACCOUNT NAME	TRIAL BALANCE DEBIT	TRIAL BALANCE CREDIT	ADJUSTMENTS DEBIT	ADJUSTMENTS CREDIT
4	115	Supplies	3,524.64			(b) 2,359.45
33	635	Supplies Expense	—		(b) 2,359.45	

Figure 2-2 Recording the Adjustment to Supplies on the Work Sheet

R — E — M — E — M — B — E — R

Each part of an adjustment is labeled with small letters in parentheses.

Discuss what is meant by a *prepaid* item. Point out why Prepaid Insurance is an asset and the expired portion of the premium is an expense.

Adjusting the Prepaid Insurance Account

On November 28, Campers Unlimited paid $1,200 for a six-month insurance policy. The cost of the premium was debited to the Prepaid Insurance account. At the end of the fiscal period, one month of the insurance coverage has expired. The Prepaid Insurance account must be credited for $200, the amount of the expired premium, to bring its balance up to date. The amount of the expired premium is an expense of doing business. Therefore, the Insurance Expense account is debited for $200. The two parts of the adjustment are labeled *(c),* as shown in Figure 2-3.

Campers Unlimited
Work Sheet
For the Year Ended December 31, 199-

	ACCT. NO.	ACCOUNT NAME	TRIAL BALANCE DEBIT	TRIAL BALANCE CREDIT	ADJUSTMENTS DEBIT	ADJUSTMENTS CREDIT
5	120	Prepaid Insurance	1 200 00			(c) 200 00
28	610	Insurance Expense	—		(c) 200 00	

Figure 2-3 Recording the Adjustment to Prepaid Insurance on the Work Sheet

Review the fact that a corporation estimates its net income and then determines its estimated taxes for the year. Once the actual amount is determined, an adjustment is made.

Adjusting the Federal Income Tax Expense Account

Campers Unlimited is organized as a corporation. As a result, it is required to pay federal income taxes on its net income. Campers Unlimited has already made quarterly payments totaling $6,000, an estimate of its tax liability for the year.

At the end of the period, Campers' accountant determined that the federal income tax for the year was $6,430. The balance in the Federal Income Tax Expense account must be increased to show the actual expense for the period. To adjust Federal Income Tax Expense, the accountant debits it for $430 and credits the liability account Federal Income Tax Payable for the same amount. This adjustment is labeled *(d),* as shown in Figure 2-4.

Campers Unlimited
Work Sheet
For the Year Ended December 31, 199-

	ACCT. NO.	ACCOUNT NAME	TRIAL BALANCE DEBIT	TRIAL BALANCE CREDIT	ADJUSTMENTS DEBIT	ADJUSTMENTS CREDIT
10	215	Fed. Inc. Tax Payable		—		(d) 430 00
35	650	Federal Inc. Tax Expense	6 000 00		(d) 430 00	

Figure 2-4 Recording the Adjustment to Federal Income Tax Expense on the Work Sheet

Use demonstration problem 2-1 here.

After all the adjustments have been entered on the work sheet, the Adjustments section is totaled, proved, and ruled. The total of the Debit column must equal the total of the Credit column.

R—E—M—E—M—B—E—R

The Adjustments section of the work sheet, like the Trial Balance section, must be proved before the work sheet can be continued.

Before reading further, do the following activity to check your understanding of adjustments.

Check Your Learning

Answer these questions on a sheet of notebook paper.

1. Merchandise Inventory has a balance of $16,309.12 in the Trial Balance section of the work sheet. The ending inventory is $18,721.05. What is the amount of the adjustment? Which account is debited? Which account is credited?
2. The Trial Balance section of the work sheet shows a balance of $3,206.69 for Supplies. The actual amount of supplies on hand at the end of the period is $1,286.42. What is the amount of the adjustment? Which account is debited? Which account is credited?
3. A company paid $5,850 for a six-month insurance policy on October 31. If its fiscal period ends on December 31, what is the amount of the adjustment? Which account is debited? Which account is credited?

Compare your answers to those in the answers section. Reread the preceding part of the chapter to find the correct answers to any questions you may have missed.

Completing the Adjusted Trial Balance Section

Be sure students understand that amounts in the Adjusted Trial Balance section are a result of combining amounts in the Trial Balance and Adjustments sections.

The Adjusted Trial Balance section of the work sheet shows the updated balances for all of the general ledger accounts. The section is completed by combining the balance of each account in the Trial Balance section with the adjustment, if any, in the Adjustments section. This section must also be totaled, proved, and ruled.

Figure 2-5 shows the Adjusted Trial balance section of Campers Unlimited's work sheet. Make sure you understand how all balances are determined before going on to the next section.

Campers Unlimited
Work Sheet
For the Year Ended December 31, 199-

ACCT. NO.	ACCOUNT NAME	TRIAL BALANCE DEBIT	TRIAL BALANCE CREDIT	ADJUSTMENTS DEBIT	ADJUSTMENTS CREDIT	ADJUSTED TRIAL BALANCE DEBIT	ADJUSTED TRIAL BALANCE CREDIT	INCOME STATEMENT DEBIT	INCOME STATEMENT CREDIT	BALANCE SHEET DEBIT	BALANCE SHEET CREDIT
101	Cash in Bank	16783 15				16783 15				16783 15	
105	Accounts Receivable	4148 42				4148 42				4148 42	
110	Merchandise Inventory	30376 95		(a) 897 86		31274 81				31274 81	
115	Supplies	3524 64			(b) 2359 45	1165 19				1165 19	
120	Prepaid Insurance	1200 00			(c) 200 00	1000 00				1000 00	
150	Store Equipment	24106 90				24106 90				24106 90	
201	Accounts Payable		836 74				836 74				836 74
205	Emp. Fed. Inc. Tax Pay.		288 00				288 00				288 00
210	Emp. State Inc. Tax Pay.		297 32				297 32				297 32
215	Fed. Inc. Tax Payable		—		(d) 430 00		430 00				430 00
220	Fed. Unempl. Tax Payable		38 40				38 40				38 40
225	Social Security Tax Pay.		391 58				391 58				391 58
226	Medicare Tax Payable		91 58				91 58				91 58
230	Ins. Premiums Payable		42 00				42 00				42 00
235	Sales Tax Payable		1110 93				1110 93				1110 93
240	State Unempl. Tax Pay.		126 50				126 50				126 50
301	Capital Stock		20000 00				20000 00				20000 00
305	Retained Earnings		33380 01				33380 01				33380 01
310	Income Summary	—	—		(a) 897 86		897 86		897 86		
401	Sales		194626 19				194626 19		194626 19		
405	Sales Discounts	1036 81				1036 81		1036 81			
410	Sales Returns and Allow.	2808 17				2808 17		2808 17			
501	Purchases	98794 53				98794 53		98794 53			
505	Transportation In	4813 56				4813 56		4813 56			
510	Purchases Discounts		1449 27				1449 27		1449 27		
515	Purch. Ret. and Allow.		931 43				931 43		931 43		
601	Advertising Expense	9100 00				9100 00		9100 00			
605	Bank Card Fees Expense	1203 17				1203 17		1203 17			
610	Insurance Expense	—		(c) 200 00		200 00		200 00			
615	Miscellaneous Expense	1903 17				1903 17		1903 17			
620	Payroll Tax Expense	4313 24				4313 24		4313 24			
625	Rent Expense	10800 00				10800 00		10800 00			
630	Salaries Expense	30412 63				30412 63		30412 63			
635	Supplies Expense	—		(b) 2359 45		2359 45		2359 45			
640	Utilities Expense	2284 61				2284 61		2284 61			
650	Federal Inc. Tax Expense	6000 00		(d) 430 00		6430 00		6430 00			
		253609 95	253609 95	3887 31	3887 31	254937 81	254937 81	176459 34	197904 75	78478 47	57033 06
	Net Inc. after Inc. Taxes							21445 41			21445 41
								197904 75	197904 75	78478 47	78478 47

Figure 2-5 Campers Unlimited's Completed Work Sheet

Extending Amounts to the Balance Sheet and Income Statement Sections

Remind students to begin at the top of the work sheet and extend all amounts in order.

Beginning with line 1, each account balance in the Adjusted Trial Balance section is extended to either the Balance Sheet section or the Income Statement section of the work sheet. The Balance Sheet section contains the balances of all the permanent general ledger accounts. The Income Statement section contains the balances of all the temporary general ledger accounts, including Income Summary. Examine the work sheet in Figure 2-5 to identify the accounts that are extended to each section.

R — E — M — E — M — B — E — R

Have students complete Exercise 2-1 at this point.

The balances of the permanent accounts are carried forward from one accounting period to the next. Each temporary account begins the fiscal period with a zero balance.

Completing the Work Sheet

After all of the balances have been extended, the last four amount columns are totaled and the net income (or net loss) for the period is calculated. **Net income** is the amount left after expenses for the period are subtracted from revenue. A **net loss** occurs when the expenses are greater than the gross profit on sales for the period. A net income amount is entered in the Income Statement Debit column *and* in the Balance Sheet Credit column. Campers Unlimited's net income, as shown on the work sheet in Figure 2-5, is $21,445.41.

Preparing the Financial Statements

Accounting assumption of time period.

Explain that this is the accounting characteristic of comparability.

The seventh step in the accounting cycle is to prepare financial statements. A business prepares various reports at the end of each fiscal period. These reports summarize the changes that have taken place during the period and describe the financial condition of the business at the end of the period. For these financial reports to be useful, the data must be presented in such a way that users will recognize similarities, differences, and trends from one period to another.

Using the information on the work sheet, Campers Unlimited prepares three end-of-period financial statements: the income statement, the statement of retained earnings, and the balance sheet. The first two statements report changes that have taken place over the fiscal period. The balance sheet reports the financial position of the business on a specific date—the last day of the fiscal period.

The Income Statement

Accounting assumption of time period.

The **income statement** reports net income or net loss of the business during the fiscal period. The income statement for a merchandising business contains five sections: (1) Revenue, (2) Cost of Merchandise Sold, (3) Gross Profit on Sales, (4) Operating Expenses, and (5) Net Income.

ACCOUNTING Tips The income statement shown in Figure 2-6 could be called a "multiple-step" income statement, since calculations are reported in each section to show how net income is determined.

All of the information needed to prepare the income statement appears in the work sheet, most of it in the Income Statement section. Figure 2-6 shows the completed income statement for Campers Unlimited. Review it as you read the following sections.

Campers Unlimited Income Statement For the Year Ended December 31, 199-				
Revenue:				
Sales			194626 19	
Less: Sales Discounts		1036 81		
Sales Ret. & Allow.		2808 17	3844 98	
Net Sales				190781 21
Cost of Merchandise Sold:				
Merch. Inv., Jan. 1, 199-			30376 95	
Purchases		98794 53		
Plus: Transportation In		4813 56		
Cost of Delivered Merch.		103608 09		
Less: Purch. Discounts	1449 27			
Purch. Ret. & Allow.	931 43	2380 70		
Net Purchases			101227 39	
Cost of Merch. Avail.			131604 34	
Merch. Inv., Dec. 31, 199-			31274 81	
Cost of Merch. Sold				100329 53
Gross Profit on Sales				90451 68
Operating Expenses:				
Advertising Expense			9100 00	
Bank Card Fees Expense			1203 17	
Insurance Expense			200 00	
Miscellaneous Expense			1903 17	
Payroll Tax Expense			4313 24	
Rent Expense			10800 00	
Salaries Expense			30412 63	
Supplies Expense			2359 45	
Utilities Expense			2284 61	
Total Operating Expenses				62576 27
Operating Income				27875 41
Less: Federal Inc. Tax				6430 00
Net Income				21445 41

Figure 2-6 Campers Unlimited's Income Statement

Review the role of contra accounts.

The Revenue Section

The revenue section reports the total revenue earned by the business during the period, less any deductions. It includes the Sales account and the contra revenue accounts Sales Discounts and Sales Returns and Allowances. Subtracting the balances of the two contra accounts from total sales gives the **net sales** for the period:

Sales
− Sales Discounts
− Sales Returns and Allowances
= Net Sales

Remind students that the cost of merchandise sold is the cost to the business of selling merchandise before operating expenses are deducted.

The Cost of Merchandise Sold Section

Before a merchandising business can calculate its gross profit, it must determine its cost of merchandise sold. The **cost of merchandise sold** is the actual cost to the business of the merchandise sold to customers. The cost of merchandise sold is calculated as follows:

Beginning Merchandise Inventory
+ Net Purchases During the Period
= Cost of Merchandise Available for Sale
– Ending Merchandise Inventory
= Cost of Merchandise Sold

Net purchases is the amount of all costs related to merchandise purchased during the period. It is calculated as follows:

Review why transportation costs increase net purchases.

Purchases
+ Transportation In
= Cost of Delivered Merchandise
– Purchases Discounts
– Purchases Returns and Allowances
= Net Purchases

R — E — M — E — M — B — E — R

Transportation costs increase net purchases. Purchases discounts, returns, and allowances decrease net purchases.

Use demonstration problem 2-2 here.

The Gross Profit on Sales Section The amount of profit earned during the period before expenses are deducted is the **gross profit on sales.** Gross profit on sales is found by subtracting the cost of merchandise sold from the net sales for the period:

Net Sales for the Period
– Cost of Merchandise Sold
= Gross Profit on Sales

Mention that cash expenditures are needed to earn revenue.

The Operating Expenses Section **Operating expenses** are the costs that expire or the costs that are incurred to earn revenue for the business. The titles and balances of all of the expense accounts *except* Federal Income Tax Expense are listed in the same order as on the work sheet. Federal Income Tax Expense is not an operating expense; it is considered cash paid out *as a result of* revenue earned rather than cash spent to earn revenue. On the income statement, the account balances are listed in the third amount column and the total operating expense amount is entered in the fourth amount column.

The Net Income Section The final section of the income statement reports the net income (or net loss) both before and after federal income taxes. The taxable income of a business, or the amount of income before federal income taxes, is called **operating income.**

Gross Profit on Sales
– Total Operating Expenses
= Operating Income
– Federal Income Taxes
= Net Income

Remind students that the net income or loss reported on the income statement must agree with the net income or loss shown on the work sheet.

The net income reported on the income statement must agree with the net income calculated on the work sheet.

Before reading further, do the following activity to check your understanding of the income statement.

Check Your Learning

Answer these questions on a sheet of notebook paper.

1. If purchases for the period are $9,495.30 and transportation costs are $483.61, what is the cost of delivered merchandise?
2. If net purchases are $17,301.40 and the beginning inventory is $36,817.49, what is the cost of merchandise available for sale?
3. If the cost of merchandise sold is $17,046.28 and net sales for the period are $36,501.96, what is the gross profit on sales?

Have students complete Exercise 2-2 at this point.

Compare your answers to those in the answers section. Reread the preceding part of the chapter to find the correct answers to any questions you may have missed.

The Statement of Retained Earnings

Campers Unlimited is organized as a corporation. Recall that in a corporation there are two stockholders' equity accounts: Capital Stock and Retained Earnings. The Capital Stock account summarizes the stockholders' investment in the corporation. The Retained Earnings account summarizes the profits kept by the corporation for future use.

The balance of the Capital Stock account changes only when the corporation issues more shares of stock. The **statement of retained earnings** is prepared to report the changes that have taken place in the Retained Earnings account during the fiscal period. The changes are the result of business operations (net income or net loss) or of the distribution of earnings. A net income increases the balance in Retained Earnings, while a net loss or a distribution of earnings decreases the balance in the account.

Point out that distribution of earnings is usually for dividends.

The statement of retained earnings serves as a supporting document for the balance sheet. The balance of the Retained Earnings account is used when preparing the balance sheet. The information needed to prepare the statement of retained earnings appears on the work sheet.

Figure 2-7 shows the statement of retained earnings for Campers Unlimited. Notice that the net income amount was added to the beginning balance of Retained Earnings. If there had been a net loss or a distribution of earnings to stockholders, the amounts would have been subtracted from the beginning balance. The ending balance of Retained Earnings calculated here ($54,825.42) is the amount reported on the balance sheet.

Campers Unlimited
Statement of Retained Earnings
For the Year Ended December 31, 199-

Retained Earnings, January 1, 199-		33 380 01
Net Income		21 445 41
Retained Earnings, December 31, 199-		54 825 42

Figure 2-7 Campers Unlimited's Statement of Retained Earnings

The Balance Sheet

Remind students that the balance sheet has a specific date.

Emphasize that two sources of information are used to prepare the balance sheet.

The **balance sheet** reports the final, updated balances of all asset, liability, and stockholders' equity accounts as of a specific date. It is prepared from information reported in the Balance Sheet section of the work sheet and in the statement of retained earnings.

Campers Unlimited's balance sheet is shown (in report form) in Figure 2-8. The balances for the asset and the liability sections and for Capital Stock are taken directly from the work sheet. The balance reported for Retained Earnings is the balance calculated on the statement of retained earnings. The total assets amount reported on the balance sheet must equal the total liabilities plus the stockholders' equity amount.

Campers Unlimited Balance Sheet December 31, 199–		
Assets		
Cash in Bank	16 783 15	
Accounts Receivable	4 148 42	
Merchandise Inventory	31 274 81	
Supplies	1 165 19	
Prepaid Insurance	1 000 00	
Store Equipment	24 106 90	
Total Assets		78 478 47
Liabilities		
Accounts Payable	836 74	
Employees' Federal Income Tax Payable	288 00	
Employees' State Income Tax Payable	297 32	
Federal Income Tax Payable	430 00	
Federal Unemployment Tax Payable	38 40	
Social Security Tax Payable	391 58	
Medicare Tax Payable	91 58	
Insurance Premiums Payable	42 00	
Sales Tax Payable	1 110 93	
State Unemployment Tax Payable	126 50	
Total Liabilities		3 653 05
Stockholders' Equity		
Capital Stock	20 000 00	
Retained Earnings	54 825 42	
Total Stockholders' Equity		74 825 42
Total Liabilities and Stockholders' Equity		78 478 47

Figure 2-8 Campers Unlimited's Balance Sheet

R — E — M — E — M — B — E — R

Total assets equal total liabilities plus total stockholders' equity.

Updating the General Ledger Accounts

Use T accounts to review the adjustments.

The eighth step in the accounting cycle is to journalize and post the adjusting entries. The adjustments recorded on the work sheet do *not* update the account balances in the general ledger. Accounts can be updated only through journal entries. The **adjusting entries** update the balances in all general ledger accounts affected by adjustments.

The work sheet is the source of the information used for journalizing the adjusting entries. The two parts (debit and credit) of each adjusting entry are found by matching the lettered amounts in the Adjustments section of the work sheet. The adjusting entries are recorded in the general journal. The debit part of the entry should be entered first.

Use demonstration problem 2-3 here.

In Figure 2-9, notice that the words *Adjusting Entries* are written in the Description column above the first entry.

GENERAL JOURNAL — PAGE 14

	DATE		DESCRIPTION	POST. REF.	DEBIT	CREDIT	
1			Adjusting Entries				1
2	199- Dec.	31	Merchandise Inventory		897 86		2
3			Income Summary			897 86	3
4		31	Supplies Expense		2,359 45		4
5			Supplies			2,359 45	5
6		31	Insurance Expense		200 00		6
7			Prepaid Insurance			200 00	7
8		31	Federal Income Tax Expense		430 00		8
9			Federal Income Tax Payable			430 00	9

Figure 2-9 Adjusting Entries for Campers Unlimited

Remind students that adjustments on the work sheet do not change the amounts in the general ledger until they are journalized and posted.

After the adjusting entries have been recorded in the general journal, they must be posted to the accounts in the general ledger. After the adjusting entries are posted, the balances of the general ledger accounts are the same as those reported on the financial statements—except for Retained Earnings. That account will be brought up to date when the closing entries are journalized and posted.

Emphasize the importance of the Posting Reference columns.

The first adjusting entry is posted (Figure 2-10). All other adjusting entries are posted in a similar manner. The posting reference should be recorded in both the general journal and the general ledger accounts.

GENERAL JOURNAL — PAGE 14

	DATE		DESCRIPTION	POST. REF.	DEBIT	CREDIT	
1			Adjusting Entries				1
2	199- Dec.	31	Merchandise Inventory	110	897 86		2
3			Income Summary	310		897 86	3

ACCOUNT Merchandise Inventory — ACCOUNT NO. 110

DATE		EXPLANATION	POST. REF.	DEBIT	CREDIT	BALANCE DEBIT	BALANCE CREDIT
199- Jan.	1	Balance	✓			30,376 95	
Dec.	31	Adjusting Entry	G14	897 86		31,274 81	

ACCOUNT Income Summary — ACCOUNT NO. 310

DATE		EXPLANATION	POST. REF.	DEBIT	CREDIT	BALANCE DEBIT	BALANCE CREDIT
199- Dec.	31	Adjusting Entry	G14		897 86		897 86

Figure 2-10 Posting the First Adjusting Entry to the General Ledger Accounts

Closing Entries

Review the need for closing entries.

The ninth step in the accounting cycle is to journalize and post the closing entries. **Closing entries** transfer the balances of the temporary accounts to a permanent general ledger account. After the closing entries are posted, all of the temporary accounts will have zero balances.

The Income Statement section of the work sheet is the source of information for the closing entries, which are recorded in the general journal. For a merchandising business organized as a corporation, three separate closing entries are made, as shown in Figure 2-11.

GENERAL JOURNAL — PAGE 14

Line	DATE		DESCRIPTION	POST. REF.	DEBIT	CREDIT	Line
11			Closing Entries				11
12	Dec.	31	Sales		194626 19		12
13			Purchases Discounts		1449 27		13
14			Purchases Returns and Allowances		931 43		14
15			Income Summary			197006 89	15
16		31	Income Summary		176459 34		16
17			Sales Discounts			1036 81	17
18			Sales Returns and Allowances			2808 17	18
19			Purchases			98794 53	19
20			Transportation In			4813 56	20
21			Advertising Expense			9100 00	21
22			Bank Card Fees Expense			1203 17	22
23			Insurance Expense			200 00	23
24			Miscellaneous Expense			1903 17	24
25			Payroll Tax Expense			4313 24	25
26			Rent Expense			10800 00	26
27			Salaries Expense			30412 63	27
28			Supplies Expense			2359 45	28
29			Utilities Expense			2284 61	29
30			Federal Income Tax Expense			6430 00	30
31		31	Income Summary		20545 41		31
32			Retained Earnings			20545 41	32

Figure 2-11 Campers Unlimited's Closing Entries

Use T accounts to outline the closing entries and demonstration problem 2-4 to review the actual entries. Discuss the reasons for each of the closing entries.

Review the purpose of the Income Summary account.

The first closing entry is made to close the accounts that have balances in the Income Statement *Credit* column of the work sheet. This entry, then, closes the revenue and contra cost accounts into Income Summary. The second closing entry is made to close into Income Summary the balances of the contra revenue, cost of merchandise, and expense accounts listed in the Income Statement *Debit* column. The third closing entry closes the balance of the Income Summary account into the Retained Earnings account. The balance transferred from Income Summary should be the net income (or loss) for the period.

R — E — M — E — M — B — E — R

The Income Summary account is used at the end of the fiscal period to summarize the revenue and expenses for the period.

After the three closing entries have been journalized, they must be posted to the general ledger. The first closing entry is posted as shown in Figure 2-12. The other closing entries are posted in a similar manner. After all posting is completed, the temporary accounts will have zero balances and the Retained Earnings account will be up to date.

GENERAL JOURNAL — PAGE 14

	DATE		DESCRIPTION	POST. REF.	DEBIT	CREDIT	
11			Closing Entries				11
12	Dec.	31	Sales	401	194626 19		12
13			Purchases Discounts	510	1449 27		13
14			Purchases Returns and Allowances	515	931 43		14
15			Income Summary	310		197006 89	15

ACCOUNT Income Summary — ACCOUNT NO. 310

DATE		EXPLANATION	POST. REF.	DEBIT	CREDIT	BALANCE DEBIT	BALANCE CREDIT
199- Dec.	31	Adjusting Entry	G14		897 86		897 86
	31	Closing Entry	G14		197006 89		197904 75

ACCOUNT Sales — ACCOUNT NO. 401

DATE		EXPLANATION	POST. REF.	DEBIT	CREDIT	BALANCE DEBIT	BALANCE CREDIT
199- Dec.	1	Balance	✓				176110 68
	31		S19		3683 91		179794 59
	31		CR24		14831 60		194626 19
	31	Closing Entry	G14	194626 19			—

ACCOUNT Purchases Discounts — ACCOUNT NO. 510

DATE		EXPLANATION	POST. REF.	DEBIT	CREDIT	BALANCE DEBIT	BALANCE CREDIT
199- Dec.	1	Balance	✓				1325 04
	31		CP29		124 23		1449 27
	31	Closing Entry	G14	1449 27			—

ACCOUNT Purchases Returns and Allowances — ACCOUNT NO. 515

DATE		EXPLANATION	POST. REF.	DEBIT	CREDIT	BALANCE DEBIT	BALANCE CREDIT
199- Dec.	1	Balance	✓				858 25
	11		G13		73 18		931 43
	31	Closing Entry	G14	931 43			—

Figure 2-12 Posting the First Closing Entry to the General Ledger

R—E—M—E—M—B—E—R

Be sure to write the words *Closing Entry* in the general ledger accounts.

Before reading further, do the following activity to check your understanding of adjusting and closing entries.

Check Your Learning

Write your answers to these questions on a sheet of notebook paper.

1. The ending balance of Retained Earnings is calculated on the ___?___.
2. The source of information for the adjusting entries is the ___?___.
3. For a corporation, there are ___?___ closing entries.
4. The purpose of the final closing entry is to close out the ___?___ account.

Compare your answers to those in the answers section. Reread the preceding part of the chapter to find the correct answers to any questions you may have missed.

You may want to use Exercise 2-3 at this point.

The Post-Closing Trial Balance

Review the purpose of preparing a post-closing trial balance. Point out that it includes only the balances of the permanent general ledger accounts.

At the end of the fiscal period, a **post-closing trial balance** is prepared to prove the equality of the debits and credits in the general ledger after the adjusting and closing entries have been posted. This is the tenth—and final—step in the accounting cycle. Figure 2-13 shows the post-closing trial balance for Campers Unlimited.

Campers Unlimited
Post-Closing Trial Balance
December 31, 199–

Account	Debit	Credit
Cash in Bank	16 783 15	
Accounts Receivable	4 148 42	
Merchandise Inventory	31 274 81	
Supplies	1 165 19	
Prepaid Insurance	1 000 00	
Store Equipment	24 106 90	
Accounts Payable		836 74
Employees' Federal Income Tax Payable		288 00
Employees' State Income Tax Payable		297 32
Federal Income Tax Payable		430 00
Federal Unemployment Tax Payable		38 40
Social Security Tax Payable		391 58
Medicare Tax Payable		91 58
Insurance Premiums Payable		42 00
Sales Tax Payable		1 110 93
State Unemployment Tax Payable		126 50
Capital Stock		20 000 00
Retained Earnings		54 825 42
Totals	78 478 47	78 478 47

Figure 2-13 Campers Unlimited's Post-Closing Trial Balance

The post-closing trial balance lists only the balances of the permanent general ledger accounts. The temporary accounts have zero balances and are not included on the post-closing trial balance.

The Accounting Cycle for a Merchandising Business

Review the ten steps in a class discussion.

You have now completed your review of the accounting cycle for a merchandising business organized as a corporation. To summarize, the steps in the accounting cycle are as follows:

1. Collect source documents and verify the data on them.
2. Analyze business transactions.
3. Journalize business transactions.
4. Post each entry to the ledgers.
5. Prepare a trial balance.
6. Complete the work sheet.
7. Prepare the financial statements.
8. Journalize and post the adjusting entries.
9. Journalize and post the closing entries.
10. Prepare a post-closing trial balance.

You may want to complete Exercise 2-4 at this point.

Remember: The basic steps in the accounting cycle are the same for all businesses regardless of how they are organized or the type of accounting system they use.

Summary of Key Points

1. A work sheet is prepared to organize all the data needed to update the ledger accounts and prepare the financial statements.
2. Changes in some accounts are not affected by daily business transactions. The end-of-fiscal-period adjustments to these accounts are planned and entered in the Adjustments section of the work sheet.
3. The net income (or net loss) for the period is first calculated on the work sheet.
4. A corporation prepares three financial statements: the income statement, the statement of retained earnings, and the balance sheet.
5. Adjusting entries are journalized and posted to bring the general ledger accounts up to date.
6. The closing entries are journalized and posted to close the balances of the temporary capital accounts into a permanent general ledger account. For a corporation, this is the Retained Earnings account.
7. After the closing entries have been posted, a post-closing trial balance is prepared.
8. The basic steps in the accounting cycle are the same for all businesses regardless of how they are organized or the type of accounting system they use.

2 Review and Applications

Building Your Accounting Vocabulary

In your own words, write the definition of each of the following accounting terms. Use complete sentences for your definitions.

adjusting entries
adjustment
balance sheet
beginning inventory
closing entries
cost of merchandise sold
ending inventory
gross profit on sales
income statement
net income
net loss
net purchases
net sales
operating expenses
operating income
post-closing trial balance
statement of retained earnings
work sheet

Reviewing Your Accounting Knowledge

1. Why is a work sheet prepared before the financial statements?
2. Why must certain general ledger accounts be updated at the end of the fiscal period?
3. Why must the Merchandise Inventory account be adjusted?
4. What is the purpose of the financial statements?
5. What three financial statements are usually prepared by a merchandising business organized as a corporation?
6. How is the cost of merchandise sold calculated?
7. Why is the income statement prepared before the statement of retained earnings?
8. What are the two stockholders' equity accounts of a corporation? What does each account summarize?
9. What is the reason for journalizing and posting closing entries?
10. Into which account are the balances of the temporary general ledger accounts closed?
11. How many steps are there in the accounting cycle?

Improving Your Analysis Skills

David Clune, an accounting clerk for Paterson Pet Store, prepared the end-of-period financial statements. In preparing the work sheet, David did not make an adjustment for Supplies. What effect will this omission have on the income statement and the balance sheet for the period?

Applying Accounting Procedures

Exercise 2-1 Identifying Amounts on the Work Sheet

Instructions: Use a form similar to the one that follows. For each numbered item, place a check mark in each section of the work sheet in which the amount would appear.

Items:

1. Ending merchandise inventory
2. Additional federal income taxes owed
3. Ending supplies inventory
4. Total supplies available during the period
5. Beginning merchandise inventory
6. Expired portion of the insurance premium
7. Supplies consumed during the period
8. Revenue for the period
9. Premiums paid for insurance coverage for the fiscal period
10. Estimated federal income taxes paid during the period

Number of Item	Trial Balance	Adjustments	Adjusted Trial Balance	Income Statement	Balance Sheet
1			√		√

1. $60,528.21
2. $46,170.27
3. $28,658.36
4. $31,240.04
5. $12,867.97
6. $18,100.48

Exercise 2-2 Calculating Amounts on the Income Statement

Instructions: For each group of figures that follows, determine the missing amount.

1.	Beginning merchandise inventory	$ 48,328.36
	Net purchases	12,199.85
	Cost of merchandise available for sale	?
2.	Net sales	$132,926.58
	Cost of merchandise sold	86,756.31
	Gross profit on sales	?
3.	Purchases	$ 25,869.58
	Transportation in	2,788.78
	Cost of delivered merchandise	?
4.	Cost of merchandise available for sale	$ 46,246.97
	Ending merchandise inventory	15,006.93
	Cost of merchandise sold	?
5.	Gross profit on sales	$ 36,810.95
	Operating expenses	23,942.98
	Operating income	?
6.	Operating income	$ 23,214.48
	Federal income tax	5,114.00
	Net income	?

Exercise 2-3 Identifying Accounts Affected by Adjusting and Closing Entries

The following account titles appear in the chart of accounts of the Seasonal Furniture Center, Inc.

Accounts Payable	Prepaid Insurance
Accounts Receivable	Purchases
Capital Stock	Purchases Discounts
Cash in Bank	Retained Earnings

Equipment
Federal Income Tax Expense
Federal Income Tax Payable
Income Summary
Insurance Expense
Merchandise Inventory
Miscellaneous Expense
Sales
Sales Returns and Allowances
Sales Tax Payable
Supplies
Supplies Expense
Transportation In
Utilities Expense

Instructions: Use a form similar to the one that follows to answer the following questions about each account.

1. Is the account affected by an adjusting entry?
2. Is the account affected by a closing entry?
3. Does the account appear on the post-closing trial balance?

Account Title	Is the account affected by an adjusting entry?	Is the account affected by a closing entry?	Does the account appear on the post-closing trial balance?
Accounts Payable	No	No	Yes

Exercise 2-4 Organizing the Steps in the Accounting Cycle

Instructions: Use the numbers 1–10 to place the following steps of the accounting cycle in their proper order.

2, 9 Analyze business transactions. — Journalize/post closing entries.
1, 4 Collect/verify source document data. — Post journal entries.
6, 7 Complete the work sheet. — Prepare financial statements.
3, 10 Journalize business transactions. — Prepare a post-closing trial balance.
8, 5 Journalize/post adjusting entries. — Prepare a trial balance.

Problem 2-1 Entering Adjustments on the Work Sheet

The Trial Balance section of the work sheet for Quincy Sports Center, Inc., has been completed. Following is a portion of that work sheet:

Quincy Sports Center, Inc.
Work Sheet
For the Year Ended December 31, 199–

	ACCT. NO.	ACCOUNT NAME	TRIAL BALANCE DEBIT	TRIAL BALANCE CREDIT	ADJUSTMENTS DEBIT	ADJUSTMENTS CREDIT
3	110	Merchandise Inventory	49 075 91			
4	115	Supplies	3 619 47			
5	120	Prepaid Insurance	1 710 00			
10	215	Fed. Income Tax Payable		—		
16	310	Income Summary	—	—		
23	605	Insurance Expense	—			
28	630	Supplies Expense	—			
29	635	Utilities Expense	1 835 29			
30	640	Fed. Income Tax Expense	800 00			
31			130 066 34	130 066 34		

Figure 2-14 Work Sheet for Problem 2-1

Adjustments:
(a) $2,751.34
(b) $2,145.98
(c) $235.00
(d) $152.00

Column totals:
Adj., $5,284.32

Instructions:

(1) Based on the following information, record the adjustments in the Adjustments section of the work sheet.
(a) The value of the ending merchandise inventory is $46,324.57.
(b) The supplies consumed during the year are valued at $2,145.98.
(c) The expired insurance premium for the year totals $235.00.
(d) Additional federal income taxes owed amount to $152.00.

(2) Total, prove, and rule the Adjustments section.

Problem 2-2 Preparing a Work Sheet

Adjustments:
(a) $5,172.05
(b) $2,013.01
(c) $336.00
(d) $300.00

Column totals:
TB, $109,012.73
Adj., $7,821.06
ATB, $114,484.78

Net income, $18,372.07

The December 31 balances of the general ledger accounts of the King Business Supply Company follow. Also listed is the information needed for the adjustments.

Instructions: Prepare a ten-column work sheet for the King Business Supply Company for the year ended December 31. (The account numbers and titles have already been entered on the work sheet.)

Cash in Bank	$11,796.54
Accounts Receivable	2,470.58
Merchandise Inventory	44,264.30
Supplies	5,289.41
Prepaid Insurance	2,016.00
Equipment	16,029.63
Accounts Payable	17,256.45
Employees' Federal Income Tax Payable	1,396.00
Employees' State Income Tax Payable	412.24
Federal Income Tax Payable	—
Federal Unemployment Tax Payable	339.56
Social Security Tax Payable	299.52
Medicare Tax Payable	70.05
Sales Tax Payable	3,275.40
State Unemployment Tax Payable	231.18
Capital Stock	25,000.00
Retained Earnings	17,737.03
Income Summary	—
Sales	42,456.59
Sales Discounts	207.93
Sales Returns and Allowances	692.37
Purchases	12,095.67
Transportation In	1,042.89
Purchases Discounts	153.31
Purchases Returns and Allowances	385.40
Advertising Expense	1,174.49
Bank Card Fees Expense	317.03
Insurance Expense	—
Miscellaneous Expense	364.86
Payroll Tax Expense	784.57
Rent Expense	1,300.00
Salaries Expense	6,483.48
Supplies Expense	—
Utilities Expense	882.98
Federal Income Tax Expense	1,800.00

Data for Adjustments

Ending merchandise inventory	$49,436.35
Supplies on hand, December 31	3,276.40
Insurance premium expired	336.00
Total federal income taxes for the year	2,100.00

Net sales, $41,556.29
COMS, $7,427.80
Gross profit, $34,128.49
Oper. exp., $13,656.42
Oper inc., $20,472.07

End. RE bal., $36,109.10

BS totals, $84,689.50

Problem 2-3 Preparing Financial Statements

Use the work sheet you prepared in Problem 2-2 to complete this problem.

Instructions:

(1) Prepare an income statement.
(2) Prepare a statement of retained earnings.
(3) Prepare a balance sheet.

Problem 2-4 Journalizing and Posting Adjusting and Closing Entries

Use the work sheet you prepared in Problem 2-2 to complete this problem.

Instructions:

(1) Journalize the adjusting entries on page 23 of the general journal. Post the entries to the ledger accounts that appear in the working papers.
(2) Journalize and post the closing entries.
(3) Prepare a post-closing trial balance.

P/C TB totals, $84,689.50

COMPUTER PROBLEM

Problem 2-5 Completing the End-of-Period Activities

The Hideaway is a gift shop that sells novelty gift items. The trial balance for the year ended December 31 has already been prepared and appears in the working papers.

Instructions:

Adjustments:
(a) $7,498.68
(b) $3,175.08
(c) $470.00
(d) $332.00

Net income, $8,672.58

Retained Earnings, $33,685.78

BS totals, $71,742.82

P/C TB totals, $71,742.82

(1) Complete the work sheet for The Hideaway. The information needed for the adjustments is as follows.
   (a) The cost of the ending inventory is $35,495.40.
   (b) Supplies on hand on December 31 are $2,830.37.
   (c) The insurance premium was paid on October 31 and was for a six-month period.
   (d) The actual federal income taxes owed the government are $1,532.00.
(2) Using the information on the work sheet, prepare an income statement.
(3) Prepare a statement of retained earnings.
(4) Prepare a balance sheet as of December 31.
(5) Journalize the adjusting entries on page 26 of the general journal. Post the entries to the ledger accounts.
(6) Journalize and post the closing entries.
(7) Prepare a post-closing trial balance.

CHALLENGE PROBLEM SPREADSHEET PROBLEM

Problem 2-6 Determining Missing Amounts on the Income Statement

Instructions: Following are the abbreviated income statements of three companies. Determine the missing amount for each question mark.

This element identifies a spreadsheet-application problem.

$79,764.55
$15,029.11
$83,194.21; $39,621.51
$2,434.06
$39,875.91
$983.93
$612.79
$39,155.61
$87,776.46
$34,291.81; $22,167.88
$56,481.06
$57,238.21; $35,967.27
$17,786.47
$18,943.76; $9,376.77

	Dalton Corp.	Bond, Inc.	Tynes Corp.
Net Sales	?	$121,295.70	$82,303.30
Merchandise Inventory, Jan. 1	$21,290.23	?	29,348.30
Purchases	65,405.45	?	?
Transportation In	?	2,302.29	254.40
Cost of Delivered Merchandise	67,839.51	85,496.50	?
Purchases Discounts	740.49	?	390.38
Purchases Returns and Allowances	?	1,192.38	329.92
Net Purchases	66,486.23	83,320.19	?
Cost of Merchandise Available	?	98,349.30	68,503.91
Merchandise Inventory, Dec. 31	31,295.40	?	?
Cost of Merchandise Sold	?	64,057.49	46,336.03
Gross Profit on Sales	23,283.49	?	?
Total Operating Expenses	?	38,294.45	26,590.50
Operating Income	5,497.02	?	?

FOCUS ON CAREERS

Accounting: A Dangerous Career

Although accountants deal with an often stressful, complex, and fast-paced business environment, it would be an exaggeration to describe the accounting field as particularly dangerous. There is one field of accounting, however, that combines a love of numbers with a love of law enforcement: the Drug Enforcement Agency (DEA).

Illegal drug trafficking has become a highly sophisticated industry, bringing incredible wealth and a high standard of living to those in charge of drug operations. With the passage of the Comprehensive Crime Control Act in 1984, it became possible for law enforcement officials to search for, seize, and dispose of assets bought with the proceeds of an illegal operation. Stopping drug traffickers by seizing their wealth helps take away their power. The catch is that officials must prove that these assets were bought with illegally gained money. Thus, the Drug Enforcement Agency has been actively recruiting accountants to become special agents.

Accountants working with the Drug Enforcement Agency track drug dealers who falsify records to hide their assets.

Accountants are needed as special agents because only they can make sense of the "paper trail" of falsified records that drug dealers use to help hide their assets. Accountants can also help trace "laundered" money—money that drug traffickers hide in foreign investments and accounts or money, property, possessions, and businesses that are made to appear as though they came from legitimate sources of income.

If you are interested in the DEA, you will be a special agent first and foremost and an accountant second. No matter what the background or the type of job desired, everyone must go through a 13-week intensive basic training course to learn self-defense techniques, use of firearms, criminology, investigation techniques, and drug identification. Once the course is completed, everyone starts out as a basic agent, working the streets. If you have a master's degree in accounting, however, you will start at a higher job classification, which translates into a higher salary.

Mini Practice Set

APPLICATION ACTIVITY 1

COMPUTER PROBLEM

A Complete Accounting Cycle for a Merchandising Business

In Unit 1, you reviewed the complete accounting cycle for a merchandising business organized as a corporation. Now you will have the opportunity to apply what you reviewed as you work through the complete accounting cycle for AquaLand, Inc.

When you have completed this activity, you will have done the following:

1. Analyzed business transactions.
2. Journalized business transactions in the four special journals and in the general journal.
3. Posted journal entries to the general ledger and to the accounts receivable and accounts payable subsidiary ledgers.
4. Posted the totals of the special journals to the general ledger.
5. Prepared a schedule of accounts receivable and a schedule of accounts payable.
6. Proved cash.
7. Prepared a work sheet.
8. Prepared financial statements.
9. Journalized and posted adjusting and closing entries.
10. Prepared a post-closing trial balance.

AquaLand, Inc.

AquaLand, Inc., is a retail tropical fish store that also sells a wide variety of related equipment and supplies. It is organized as a corporation. Because AquaLand has a large number of business transactions, it has chosen to record those transactions in special journals and in a general journal.

Chart of Accounts

The chart of accounts for AquaLand, Inc., appears below and at the top of the next page.

AQUALAND, INC.
Chart of Accounts

ASSETS	101	Cash in Bank
	105	Accounts Receivable
	110	Merchandise Inventory
	115	Supplies
	120	Prepaid Insurance
	150	Equipment

LIABILITIES	201	Accounts Payable
	205	Employees' Federal Income Tax Payable
	210	Employees' State Income Tax Payable
	215	Federal Income Tax Payable
	220	Federal Unemployment Tax Payable
	225	Social Security Tax Payable
	226	Medicare Tax Payable
	230	Insurance Premiums Payable
	235	Sales Tax Payable
	240	State Unemployment Tax Payable
STOCKHOLDERS' EQUITY	301	Capital Stock
	305	Retained Earnings
	310	Income Summary
REVENUE	401	Sales
	405	Sales Discounts
	410	Sales Returns and Allowances
COST OF MERCHANDISE	501	Purchases
	505	Transportation In
	510	Purchases Discounts
	515	Purchases Returns and Allowances
EXPENSES	601	Bank Card Fees Expense
	605	Insurance Expense
	610	Miscellaneous Expense
	615	Payroll Tax Expense
	620	Rent Expense
	625	Salaries Expense
	630	Supplies Expense
	635	Utilities Expense
	640	Federal Income Tax Expense

Accounts Receivable Subsidiary Ledger

815	Dan Cappel
818	Sally Chapin
822	Frank Dayton
840	Marcy Jackson
842	Robert Jacobs
880	Stratford High School

Accounts Payable Subsidiary Ledger

905	Blue Seas Unlimited
915	Fish World
925	International Pets, Inc.
940	K & M Supply
960	Nenje Company
990	Tropical Fish Corp.

Instructions: The forms for this application activity are included in the working papers that accompany this textbook.

SJ totals:
Sales, $527.60
Sales Tax Pay., $13.78
Accts. Rec., $541.38

CRJ totals:
Sales, $15,275.08
Sales Tax Pay., $610.99
Accts. Pay., 730.67
Cash in Bank, $16,616.74

(1) Record the December transactions in the special journals and in the general journal.

(2) Post the individual amounts from the five journals to the accounts receivable and accounts payable subsidiary ledgers daily.

(3) Post the individual amounts from the general journal and from the general columns of the cash receipts, purchases, and cash payments journals daily.

(4) Total, prove, and rule the special journals.

(5) Post the column totals from the special journals to the general ledger accounts. Use this order for posting: sales, cash receipts, purchases, cash payments.

PJ totals:
Accts. Pay., $1,860.76
Purchases, $1,764.25
General, $96.51

CPJ totals:
General Dr., $7,149.28
General Cr., $955.02
Accts. Pay., $1,938.81
Purch. Disc., $34.38
Cash in Bank, $8,098.69

AR bal., $1,358.84
AP bal., $3,407.77

TB totals, $193,328.27

Adjustments:
(a) $5,295.06
(b) $2,476.98
(c) $620.00
(d) $96.00

Net income, $14,065.91
Retained Earnings, $33,853.83

BS totals, $60,136.92

P/C TB totals, $60,136.92

(6) Prepare a schedule of accounts receivable and a schedule of accounts payable.
(7) Prove cash. The balance shown on check stub 1747 is $16,682.96.
(8) Prepare a trial balance on a ten-column work sheet.
(9) Complete the work sheet. Use the following information to enter the adjustments.
   (a) The ending merchandise inventory was $25,986.37.
   (b) The supplies inventory on December 31 was $1,294.45.
   (c) The one-year insurance policy was purchased on September 1.
   (d) Federal income taxes for the year total $3,096.00.
(10) Prepare an income statement.
(11) Prepare a statement of retained earnings.
(12) Prepare a balance sheet.
(13) Journalize and post the adjusting entries.
(14) Journalize and post the closing entries.
(15) Prepare a post-closing trial balance.

Transactions:

Dec. 2 Issued Check 1732 for $900.00 to Maxgate Realty for the December rent.
2 Sold merchandise on account to Dan Cappel, $32.95 plus sales tax of $1.32, Sales Slip 681.
3 Paid the monthly electric bill of $62.39, Check 1733.
4 Purchased fish (merchandise) on account from K & M Supply, $384.80, Invoice 2438 dated December 2, terms 2/10, n/30.
4 Wrote Check 1734 for $414.75 to Tropical Fish Corporation, payment for Invoice 9758 totaling $423.21 less a 2% discount of $8.46.
5 Received a $50.00 check from Marcy Jackson to apply on her account, Receipt 553.
6 Sent Check 1735 to First City Bank in full payment of the amounts withheld for employees' federal income taxes ($495.00); social security taxes ($386.38); and medicare taxes ($90.36).
6 Paid Blue Seas Unlimited $661.40 for Invoice 3416 totaling $674.90, less a $13.50 discount, Check 1736.
7 Sally Chapin bought merchandise on account, $82.65 plus sales tax of $3.31, Sales Slip 682.
7 Issued Credit Memo 175 to Frank Dayton for the return of merchandise costing $26.75, plus sales tax of $1.07.
9 Paid freight charges on merchandise bought from a supplier, Check 1737 for $116.69.
9 Purchased a new display case (equipment) for the store for $534.45, Check 1738.
9 Sent Check 1739 for $608.66 to K & M Supply to cover Invoice 2348 for $621.08, less a discount of $12.42.
10 Received Fish World's Invoice 328 (dated December 7, terms n/30) for merchandise purchased on account for $523.05.
10 Cash sales for December 1–10 totaled $3,205.58, plus $128.22 sales tax, Tape 198.

10 Bank card sales for December 1–10 were $901.74 plus sales tax of $36.07, Tape 198.

12 Sold on account to Sally Chapin merchandise costing $75.59 plus $3.02 sales tax, Sales Slip 683.

13 Received $125.00 from Dan Cappel to apply to his account, Receipt 554.

13 Sold to Stratford High School on account $183.23 of fish supplies, no sales tax, Sales Slip 684.

14 Had an outside step repaired (Miscellaneous Expense), $36.00, Check 1740.

14 Wrote Check 1741 for the total net pay due the employees. Gross earnings for the pay period were $3,652.68. The amounts withheld were: employees' federal income taxes, $447.90; social security taxes, $226.47; medicare taxes, $52.96; employees' state income taxes, $138.69; insurance premiums, $89.00.

14 Recorded the employer's payroll taxes. The payroll tax rates are as follows: social security, 6.2%; medicare, 1.45%; federal unemployment tax, 0.8%; state unemployment tax, 5.4%.

16 Paid the telephone bill of $72.93, Check 1742.

17 Robert Jacobs purchased $49.38 of merchandise on account, $1.98 sales tax, Sales Slip 685.

18 Bought office supplies on account from the Nenje Company, $96.51, Invoice 9333, dated December 15, terms n/30.

18 Prepared Receipt 555 for $455.67 received from Frank Dayton on account.

19 Sold Marcy Jackson a fish tank on account, $83.95 plus sales tax of $3.36, Sales Slip 686.

20 Discovered that a November purchase of $117.24 of equipment had been incorrectly journalized and posted to the Purchases account, Memo. 28.

20 December 11–20 cash sales amounted to $3,645.83 with sales taxes of $145.83, Tape 199.

20 Bank card sales totaled $1,202.31 for December 11–20, plus sales tax of $48.09, Tape 199.

21 Issued Check 1743 for $589.81 to the state for the sales taxes owed for November.

21 Sent Debit Memo 43 to International Pets, Inc., for full credit on damaged merchandise totaling $373.75 bought on account earlier.

23 Purchased a $25.00 roll of stamps for the office (Miscellaneous Expense), Check 1744.

23 Purchased $154.30 of merchandise on account from Blue Seas Unlimited, Invoice 3903 dated December 22, terms of 2/10, n/30.

23 Issued Check 1745 for $219.62 to the Nenje Company in payment of Invoice 9047 for the same amount.

24 Recorded the bank service charge of $12.00 and the bank card fee of $183.21, November bank statement.

26 Received Invoice 9958 (dated December 23, terms 2/10, n/30) from the Tropical Fish Corporation for merchandise purchased on account, $397.61.

27 Wrote Check 1746 to pay the monthly gas bill, $42.38.

28 Robert Jacobs bought fish supplies on account, $19.85 (sales tax $.79), Sales Slip 687.

29 Recorded Invoice 4113 totaling $304.49 for merchandise bought on account from Blue Seas Unlimited; the invoice was dated December 27 and had terms of 2/10, n/30.

30 Returned for full credit $122.28 of mechandise bought on account from the Tropical Fish Corporation, Debit Memo 44.

31 Recorded cash sales of $4,392.28 plus sales tax $175.69 for December 21–31, Tape 200.

31 Bank card sales for the period December 21–31 were $1,927.34, sales tax $77.09, Tape 200.

31 Received a check for $100.00 from Stratford High School on account, Receipt 556.

UNIT 2

ACCOUNTING FOR ASSETS, LIABILITIES, AND EQUITY

In Unit 1, you reviewed the steps in the accounting cycle and the procedures for recording and reporting the transactions of a merchandising business.

In this unit, you will look closely at several different types of business transactions that occur less often during the fiscal period. You'll learn how to account for bad debts, notes, inventories, plant assets, and depreciation. You'll look at transactions affecting a corporation's current and long-term liabilities. You'll also examine the ownership equity of a publicly held corporation.

MAYFAIRE, INC.
Chart of Accounts

ASSETS	101	Cash in Bank
	102	Change Fund
	103	Petty Cash Fund
	105	Marketable Securities
	110	Notes Receivable
	111	Notes Receivable Discounted
	112	Notes Receivable Past Due
	113	Interest Receivable
	115	Accounts Receivable
	117	Allowance for Uncollectible Accounts
	120	Merchandise Inventory
	125	Supplies
	130	Prepaid Insurance
	140	Bond Sinking Fund
	143	Sinking Fund Investments
	150	Office Equipment
	153	Accumulated Depreciation—Office Equipment
	155	Store Equipment
	157	Accumulated Depreciation—Store Equipment
	160	Delivery Equipment
	163	Accumulated Depreciation—Delivery Equipment
	165	Building
	167	Accumulated Depreciation—Building
	170	Land
LIABILITIES	201	Notes Payable
	203	Discount on Notes Payable
	205	Accounts Payable
	215	Dividends Payable—Preferred
	220	Dividends Payable—Common
	225	Employees' Federal Income Tax Payable
	230	Employees' State Income Tax Payable
	235	Federal Income Tax Payable
	240	Federal Unemployment Tax Payable
	245	Social Security Tax Payable
	246	Medicare Tax Payable
	250	Interest Payable
	255	Salaries Payable
	260	Sales Tax Payable
	265	State Unemployment Tax Payable
	270	Unearned Rent
	280	8% Bonds Payable

STOCKHOLDERS' EQUITY	301	Preferred 8% Stock
	305	Paid-in Capital in Excess of Par—Preferred
	310	Common Stock
	315	Paid-in Capital in Excess of Par—Common
	320	Retained Earnings
	325	Dividends—Preferred
	330	Dividends—Common
	335	Common Stock Dividend Distributable
	340	Treasury Stock
	343	Paid-in Capital from Sale of Treasury Stock
	350	Income Summary
REVENUE	401	Sales
	405	Sales Discounts
	410	Sales Returns and Allowances
COST OF MERCHANDISE	501	Purchases
	505	Transportation In
	510	Purchases Discounts
	515	Purchases Returns and Allowances
EXPENSES	601	Advertising Expense
	605	Bad Debts Expense
	610	Bank Card Fees Expense
	615	Cash Short and Over
	620	Delivery Expense
	625	Depreciation Expense—Building
	630	Depreciation Expense—Delivery Equipment
	635	Depreciation Expense—Office Equipment
	640	Depreciation Expense—Store Equipment
	645	Insurance Expense
	650	Miscellaneous Expense
	655	Payroll Tax Expense
	660	Salaries Expense
	665	Supplies Expense
	670	Utilities Expense
OTHER REVENUE	701	Gain on Disposal of Plant Assets
	705	Interest Income
	710	Rental Income
	715	Sinking Fund Income
	717	Gain on Sale of Sinking Fund Investments
OTHER EXPENSE	751	Bond Interest Expense
	753	Bonus to Employees
	755	Interest Expense
	760	Loss on Disposal of Plant Assets
	799	Income Tax Expense

Chapter 3

CASH, MARKETABLE SECURITIES, AND ACCOUNTS RECEIVABLE

One of the most important concerns for the management of any business is liquidity. *Liquidity* refers to the ease with which an asset can be converted to cash. A business with adequate liquidity has enough money on hand to (1) pay bills when they become due and (2) take care of unexpected needs for cash.

In this chapter, you will study the assets that are most closely associated with a business's liquidity. These assets include cash, short-term investments, and accounts receivable. You'll examine some internal control procedures that help businesses safeguard their cash. You'll learn about two cash funds that businesses use to make change and make small, incidental cash payments. You will also learn how to account for short-term investments. Finally, you will learn two methods of accounting for accounts receivable that are no longer collectible.

Learning Objectives

When you have completed this chapter, you should be able to do the following:

1. Account for cash and short-term investments.
2. Explain the difference between the direct write-off method and the allowance method of accounting for uncollectible accounts.
3. Record the adjusting entry for estimated uncollectible accounts.
4. Journalize the entries to write off uncollectible accounts receivable using both the direct write-off and allowance methods.
5. Journalize reinstatement of an account receivable that was written off.
6. Calculate the amount of the adjustment for bad debts expense using the percentage of net sales and the aging of accounts receivable methods.
7. Define the accounting terms presented in this chapter.

New Terms

publicly held corporation
change fund
petty cash fund
marketable securities
other revenue
uncollectible account
direct write-off method
matching principle
allowance method
book value of accounts receivable
percentage of net sales method
aging of accounts receivable method
installment sales

Accounting for Publicly Held Corporations

ACCOUNTING *Tips*
The names of accounts can be confusing when they use unfamiliar and technical words. An account title usually describes the kinds of transactions recorded in the account. When you see a new account title, think about how it is classified on the chart of accounts and try to relate the title to the transactions recorded in the account.

Throughout this unit, you will examine the transactions and accounting procedures of a merchandising business called Mayfaire, Inc. Mayfaire is a large retail business that sells a wide variety of consumer products, from sporting equipment to computers to appliances to kitchen and household items.

In Unit 1, you reviewed the business transactions of a family-owned, closely held corporation. Mayfaire, Inc., is organized as a publicly held corporation. A **publicly held corporation** is a corporation whose stock is widely held, has a large market, and is usually traded on a stock exchange such as the New York Stock Exchange. Many of the transactions discussed in this unit would be recorded in the same manner regardless of how the business is organized. The major difference lies in accounting for ownership equity. You'll learn more about the ownership of a publicly held corporation later in the unit. The chart of accounts for Mayfaire, Inc., appears on pages 66 and 67. Take a moment to look it over.

Accounting for Cash

Mention that stocks sold on a stock exchange have already been issued by a corporation.

Review the meaning of liquid assets.

Cash is a business's most liquid asset—the asset most quickly available for the payment of debts. The balance reported in the Cash in Bank account is generally considered to consist of coins and currency on hand, checks and money orders received from customers, and deposits in checking and savings accounts.

Because cash is so liquid, it is important to protect it from loss, waste, theft, forgery, and embezzlement. *Internal controls,* the procedures a business sets up to protect its cash and other assets, include the following:

1. Separate duties so that the person handling cash receipts and cash payments is not the same person who keeps the accounting records for amounts received and paid out.
2. Limit the number of employees who have access to cash. Those who do have access to cash should be insured (bonded).
3. Keep a minimum amount of cash on hand.
4. Make deposits daily.
5. Make all cash payments by check.
6. Record all cash payments and cash receipts promptly.
7. Use a safe or a cash register to physically protect the cash on hand.

The Change Fund

Explain the process a business goes through to establish the fund.

Many businesses need coins and currency to make change for customers. A **change fund** is a sum of money, consisting of varying denominations of bills and coins, that is used to make change in cash transactions. A change fund is established by writing a check for the amount of the fund, payable to the person who is to be in charge of the fund. That person cashes the check and places the bills and coins in the cash register drawer. Mayfaire, Inc., for example, has a change fund of $250.

When the check to establish the change fund is written, a new asset account is needed to record the amount of the fund. This asset account is usually called Change Fund. The Change Fund account appears in the chart of accounts immediately after Cash in Bank.

Change Fund is usually debited only once: when the business first establishes the fund. If the size of the fund needs to be increased later, the business writes a check for the amount of the increase. Change Fund then is debited for the amount of the increase, and Cash in Bank is credited.

Emphasize that this account has no normal balance.

Use demonstration problem 3-1 here.

Have students complete Exercise 3-1 at this point.

Occasionally, a sales clerk gives an incorrect amount of change to a customer. When this happens, the cash in the cash register, less the change fund, will not match the amount recorded on the cash register tapes. A cash shortage or overage thus occurs. Cash shortages or overages are recorded in the Cash Short and Over account. Cash Short and Over is an expense account. Cash shortages result in losses or expenses to the business; they are recorded as debits to Cash Short and Over. Cash overages represent gains or revenue to the business; they are recorded as credits to Cash Short and Over. Notice that Cash Short and Over does not have a normal balance side. If there are more cash shortages than overages, Cash Short and Over will have a debit balance. If there are more cash overages than shortages, the account will have a credit balance. At the end of the period, Cash Short and Over is closed into Income Summary.

Cash Short and Over	
Dr. Cash Shortages	Cr. Cash Overages

The Petty Cash Fund

Earlier we mentioned that a business should make all cash payments by check. However, writing checks for very small amounts is costly, time consuming, and impractical. Many businesses keep some cash on hand with which to make small cash payments. This cash on hand is called a **petty cash fund.** Some small cash payments that might be made from this fund include payments for postage stamps, small amounts of office or cleaning supplies, newspaper delivery, or messenger delivery charges.

Emphasize the need for a petty cash fund.

First, the business must decide on the maximum amount to be paid from petty cash and how much cash to place in the fund. Then a check for the amount of the fund is written, made payable to the *petty cashier*—the person responsible for the fund. The petty cashier places the cash in a petty cash box or drawer.

Point out that the Petty Cash Fund account is a current asset and is usually debited only once.

When the petty cash fund is established, the amount is recorded in an account titled Petty Cash Fund. Petty Cash Fund is an asset account and is listed in the chart of accounts immediately following Change Fund. The account is usually debited only once, when the fund is first established. Like Change Fund, it will be debited again only if the fund is increased.

Explain that Miscellaneous Expense is the account debited for this petty cash disbursement for postage.

Whenever a payment from the petty cash fund is made, a petty cash voucher is completed. A *petty cash voucher* is a receipt signed by both the petty cashier and the person who received the payment. The voucher, illustrated in Figure 3-1, is proof of payment from the fund. Paid vouchers are usually filed with the petty cash until the fund is replenished.

MAYFAIRE, INC.

Petty Cash Voucher **No. 744**

Date 10/12/-- **Amount** $2.90

For Postage due

Charge to Miscellaneous Expense

K. Conway — **Approved by**

R.L. Peters — **Received by**

Figure 3-1 Petty Cash Voucher

Review the use of the Cash Short and Over account. The concept is the same for the petty cash fund and the change fund.

Emphasize that the Petty Cash Fund account is not debited when petty cash is replenished.

Use demonstration problem 3-3 here.

At the end of the fiscal period, or when the fund becomes low, the petty cash fund is replenished to restore it to the original amount. First, the petty cashier adds all the petty cash vouchers. Then the cashier substracts this total from the original balance of the fund. The difference, called the *reconciled petty cash balance,* should agree with the amount of cash in the petty cash box. Occasionally, the amount of cash does not agree with the reconciled amount. When this occurs, there is a shortage or an overage, which is recorded in the Cash Short and Over account.

Next, the petty cashier sorts the petty cash vouchers according to the accounts in which they are to be recorded. Once this information is known, the replenishment check can be written and the journal entry prepared. For example, Mayfaire, Inc., has a petty cash fund of $75.00. At the end of December, the fund had a cash balance of $18.00 and petty cash vouchers as follows: supplies, $1.00; advertising expense, $29.40; delivery expense, $5.00; and miscellaneous expense, $23.60. There was a cash overage of $2.00. The entry to replenish the fund is shown in Figure 3-2.

CASH PAYMENTS JOURNAL PAGE 31

	DATE		DOC. NO.	ACCOUNT TITLE	POST. REF.	GENERAL DEBIT	GENERAL CREDIT	ACCOUNTS PAYABLE DEBIT	PURCHASES DISCOUNTS CREDIT	CASH IN BANK CREDIT	
1	199- Dec.	31	Ck 1473	Supplies		1 00				57 00	1
2				Advertising Expense		29 40					2
3				Delivery Expense		5 00					3
4				Miscellaneous Expense		23 60					4
5				Cash Short and Over			2 00				5

Figure 3-2 Journalizing the Entry to Replenish the Petty Cash Fund

Before reading further, do the following activity to check your understanding of how to account for cash.

Check Your Learning

Write your answers to these questions on a sheet of notebook paper.

1. The Factory Outlet has a change fund of $500. Sales for one day were $7,944. The amount of cash in the cash register drawer at the end of the day was $8,434. Is cash balanced, short, or over? If there is a shortage or overage, what is the amount?
2. The Topps Company has a petty cash fund of $65. At the end of the month, there was a cash balance of $7 and petty cash vouchers as follows: supplies, $21; advertising expense, $9; delivery expense, $16; and miscellaneous expense, $8. Which accounts are debited and which are credited when the fund is replenished? For what amounts?

Compare your answers to those in the answers section. Reread the preceding part of the chapter to find the correct answers to any questions you may have missed.

Marketable Securities

At certain times during the year, a business may find it has more cash on hand than it needs to pay current bills. That cash should not lie idle. Cash that is not needed for immediate operating needs is often invested in short-term investments called **marketable securities**. A business usually invests in marketable securities for a period of less than 12 months, or until the cash is needed to meet current operations. Marketable securities include government securities such as Treasury bills and the securities of large corporations. Treasury bills are the short-term debts of the U.S. government.

A record of a business's short-term investments is maintained in the account titled Marketable Securities. Marketable Securities is an asset account and usually follows Cash in Bank in the chart of accounts. The account is really a controlling account. The subsidiary ledger includes detailed information for each security owned: (1) type of security, (2) purchase date, (3) total cost, (4) maturity date, if applicable, and so on. The information contained in the subsidiary ledger will be needed when the securities are sold.

Point out that marketable securities are almost as liquid as cash because they are easily purchased or sold at quoted market prices on the various stock exchanges.

When a business purchases marketable securities, it records the securities at cost. For example, suppose that on June 1 Mayfaire, Inc., wanted to invest some excess cash.

June 1: *Bought U.S. Treasury bills,, at a cost of $9,750, Check 4834.*

Use demonstration problem 3-3 here.

In the transaction, the cost of the Treasury bills is debited to the Marketable Securities account. Cash in Bank is credited for $9,750.

Marketable Securities	
Dr.	Cr.
$9,750	

Cash in Bank	
Dr.	Cr.
	$9,750

The purchase of the Treasury bills is recorded as shown in Figure 3-3.

CASH PAYMENTS JOURNAL — PAGE 19

	DATE		DOC. NO.	ACCOUNT TITLE	POST. REF.	GENERAL DEBIT	GENERAL CREDIT	ACCOUNTS PAYABLE DEBIT	PURCHASES DISCOUNTS CREDIT	CASH IN BANK CREDIT	
1	199- June	1	C4834	Marketable Securities		9750 00				9750 00	1

Figure 3-3 Recording the Purchase of Marketable Securities

When the bills mature (come due) in 90 days, Mayfaire will receive $10,000. Income on marketable securities is recorded when it is received.

August 30: *Received $10,000 for the Treasury bills purchased on June 1, Receipt 1672.*

In this transaction, Cash in Bank is debited for $10,000, the amount of cash received, and Marketable Securities is credited for the cost of the securities, $9,750. The difference of $250 is interest and is credited to the Interest Income account. Interest Income is classified as an other revenue account. **Other revenue** is nonoperating revenue—revenue that a business receives or earns from activities outside its normal operations.

Cash in Bank	
Dr.	Cr.
$10,000	

Marketable Securities	
Dr.	Cr.
Bal. $9,750	$9,750

Interest Income	
Dr.	Cr.
	$250

Figure 3-4 shows the entry Mayfaire recorded on August 30.

CASH RECEIPTS JOURNAL — PAGE 24

	DATE		DOC. NO.	ACCOUNT TITLE	POST. REF.	GENERAL DEBIT	GENERAL CREDIT	SALES CREDIT	SALES TAX PAYABLE CREDIT	ACCOUNTS RECEIVABLE CREDIT	CASH IN BANK DEBIT	
	199-											
8	Aug.	30	R1672	Marketable Securities			9750 00				10000 00	8
9				Interest Income			250 00					9

Figure 3-4 Journalizing Interest Received on Marketable Securities

Accounting for Accounts Receivable

Another major type of liquid asset is Accounts Receivable. Today many businesses allow their customers to pay for merchandise a month or more after the date of the sale. However, businesses that sell goods or services on credit usually cannot collect all their accounts receivable. These unpaid accounts are losses and must eventually be removed from the accounting records. A business that grants credit should provide for any such anticipated losses in its accounting records.

Extending Credit

You may wish to ask a credit manager to speak to your class about credit and its use by business.

A business's credit department must keep a watchful eye on current customers. It must also evaluate the debt-paying ability of prospective customers and determine (1) whether to extend credit and (2) the maximum amount of credit to extend (called the *credit limit*). To do this, retail stores rely on reports from local retail credit bureaus. Wholesalers and manufacturers use wholesale credit bureaus, financial statements of prospective customers, and reports of national credit-rating institutions such as Dun and Bradstreet. Some businesses subscribe to credit bureaus or credit-rating agencies, which maintain credit files on charge customers, establish credit ratings, and conduct special investigations.

No matter how careful the credit department is, however, there will always be some charge customers who will not or cannot pay their bills. Accounts receivable that cannot be collected are known as **uncollectible accounts**, or *bad debts*. These uncollectible accounts become an expense to the business. They decrease ownership equity by decreasing the revenue earned.

Two methods of accounting for uncollectible accounts can be used: the direct write-off method and the allowance method.

Businesses often generate additional revenue by extending credit to their customers and allowing them a period of time to make payments on goods purchased.

The Direct Write-Off Method

The Accounts Receivable account should report only those accounts the business expects to collect. With the **direct write-off method**, the uncollectible amount is removed from the accounts receivable subsidiary ledger and the controlling account when the business determines the account will not be paid. This method is used primarily by small businesses with few charge customers and by professional enterprises.

Use T accounts to review the recording of the original sale on account.

Point out that businesses make every effort to collect amounts owed. They send notices of overdue bills and use collection agencies.

For example, on June 6 Baylor Flowers sold to John Case on account merchandise costing $60.00 plus sales tax of $4.20. The entry was recorded as a debit of $64.20 to Accounts Receivable, and Case's account, a credit of $60.00 to Sales, and a credit of $4.20 to Sales Tax Payable. Case failed to pay his bill when it came due. Finally, over one year later, Baylor decided Case was not going to pay the $64.20.

November 1: *Wrote off John Case's account as uncollectible, $64.20, Memorandum 115.*

Use the six-question approach to analyze this transaction.

In the transaction, Bad Debts Expense is debited for $64.20 because the uncollectible amount has become an expense. Notice that the amount written off includes the sales tax. The bad debts expense, therefore, also includes the expense of having to pay the sales tax. Accounts Receivable and Case's account in the accounts receivable subsidiary ledger are credited for $64.20, since the amount owed will not be received. In the subsidiary ledger account, an explanation notes that the account was written off as uncollectible.

GENERAL LEDGER

Bad Debts Expense

Dr.	Cr.
$64.20	

Accounts Receivable

Dr.	Cr.
Bal. $64.20	$64.20

SUBSIDIARY LEDGER

John Case

Dr.	Cr.
Bal. $64.20	$64.20

Figure 3-5 shows the journal entry for the transaction.

GENERAL JOURNAL — PAGE 24

	DATE		DESCRIPTION	POST. REF.	DEBIT	CREDIT	
1	199– Nov.	1	Bad Debts Expense		64 20		1
2			Accts. Receivable/John Case	✓		64 20	2
3			Memo. 115				3
4							4

Figure 3-5 Journalizing the Direct Write-Off of an Uncollectible Account

Reinstating an Account Previously Written Off

Use T accounts to review the entry to write off the account. Then use the same T accounts to analyze the entry to reinstate the account.

Sometimes the unexpected occurs and an account previously written off as uncollectible is collected. For example, suppose John Case suddenly decides to pay his account in full on December 15, after Baylor Flowers had written it off. Before the cash receipt can be recorded, Case's account must be *reinstated.* As Figure 3-6 illustrates, the entry to reinstate

Case's account is the exact opposite of the write-off entry. After this entry is posted, the cash receipt can be recorded.

GENERAL JOURNAL — PAGE 25

	DATE		DESCRIPTION	POST. REF.	DEBIT	CREDIT	
1	199- Dec.	15	Accounts Receivable/John Case	✓	64 20		1
2			Bad Debts Expense			64 20	2
3			Memo. 122				3
4							4

Figure 3-6 Journalizing the Reinstatement of an Account

Use demonstration problem 3-4 here.

The Tax Reform Act of 1986 made the direct write-off method the only method a business can use for income tax purposes. The direct write-off method is an accepted accounting procedure for businesses that have few uncollectible accounts. Businesses with many sales on credit, however, should use a method of accounting for uncollectible accounts that will match revenue with the expenses incurred in earning that revenue.

Before reading further, do the following activity to check your understanding of the direct write-off method.

Check Your Learning

The Bates Company uses the direct write-off method to account for uncollectible accounts. Record the following transactions in general journal form on a sheet of notebook paper.

June 10 Wrote off the account of Jason LeBleu as uncollectible, $200, Memorandum 44.

14 Received $98 as full payment from Sue Hicks, whose account had been written off as uncollectible last year, Memorandum 45/Receipt 1947.

Compare your answers to those in the answers section. Reread the preceding part of the chapter to find the correct entries for any items you may have missed.

Matching Bad Debts Losses with Sales

Review the matching principle.

The **matching principle** states that revenue for a fiscal period must be matched against the expenses incurred in earning that revenue during the period. This is the guiding principle behind adjusting entries. Recall that in adjusting for prepaid insurance, you debited Insurance Expense and credited Prepaid Insurance. In doing so, you allocated the insurance expense to the period in which the expense was incurred. Similarly, when a business sells merchandise on account to a customer who eventually fails to pay the amount owed, the business has incurred a bad debts expense that should be provided for in the year in which the sale was made.

Illustrate how a business does not know which accounts are uncollectible at the end of an accounting period.

When a business makes a sale on account, it doesn't know that the account may be uncollectible. In fact, the business will not be sure of the bad debts expense until it has repeatedly tried to collect the amount due and failed. The uncollectible amount will probably be written off several months after the sale, possibly during the next fiscal period. One way a business can match the bad debts expense against sales is to estimate how much of the sales for the period will be uncollectible in the future. Then an adjusting entry can be made at the end of the period to record the expense.

The Allowance Method

Explain why it is necessary to estimate bad debts expense when the allowance method is used.

Large businesses and businesses that sell mainly on a credit basis use the allowance method of accounting for uncollectible accounts. The **allowance method** matches potential bad debts expenses with the sales made during the same fiscal period. At the end of the period, the business estimates the amount of uncollectible accounts. (Various methods for determining the estimated uncollectible amount can be used. You'll learn about two such methods later in this chapter.) Next, the estimated uncollectible amount is recorded—first, as an adjustment on the work sheet and then, in an adjusting entry. The two accounts affected by the adjustment for the estimated uncollectible amount are Bad Debts Expense and Allowance for Uncollectible Accounts.

A business doesn't know for sure which accounts won't be collected. As a result, Accounts Receivable can't be credited directly for the estimated uncollectible amount. As you know, Accounts Receivable is a controlling account. Its balance must equal the total of the customer accounts in the accounts receivable subsidiary ledger. If a specific customer's account cannot be credited, neither can Accounts Receivable. You can compare this concept to a life insurance company that insures 1,000 newborn infants. The insurance company doesn't know who will be alive at age 21, but, based on past data, it can estimate how many will be alive at age 21.

Point out that other account titles that may be used are Allowance for Bad Debts and Allowance for Doubtful Accounts.

Be sure students understand why Allowance for Uncollectible Accounts is a contra account of Accounts Receivable and what is meant by the "book value of accounts receivable."

Because Accounts Receivable cannot be credited for the estimated uncollectible amount, another account, Allowance for Uncollectible Accounts, is used. Allowance for Uncollectible Accounts is a contra asset account. Its balance represents the business's total estimated uncollectible accounts. The account appears on the balance sheet as a deduction from Accounts Receivable. The difference between the two accounts is the book value of accounts receivable. The **book value of accounts receivable** is the amount the business can reasonably expect to receive from its charge customers.

Allowance for Uncollectible Accounts

Dr.	Cr.
Decrease Side	Increase Side Balance Side

Adjusting for Uncollectible Accounts

Based on past experience, a business can estimate the period's bad debts expense. For example, Mayfaire, Inc., uses the allowance method to account for uncollectible accounts. On December 31, it estimated that the bad debts expense for the period was $1,016.65.

Analyze the adjusting entry in T account form on the chalkboard.

In the adjustment, Bad Debts Expense is debited for $1,016.65, the estimated uncollectible amount for the period, and Allowance for Uncollectible Accounts is credited for $1,016.65, the amount of current accounts receivable that Mayfaire estimates to be uncollectible.

Bad Debts Expense	
Dr.	Cr.
Adj. $1,016.65	

Allowance for Uncollectible Accounts	
Dr.	Cr.
	Bal. $ 60.00
	Adj. 1,016.65

Review the procedures for recording an adjustment on the work sheet.

This adjustment is entered on the work sheet as shown in Figure 3-7. Notice that Bad Debts Expense had a zero balance before the adjustment. With the allowance method, Bad Debts Expense is used only at the end of the period, when it is increased by the adjusting entry. Allowance for Uncollectible Accounts is a permanent account; its balance is carried over from previous periods. In the Trial Balance section in Figure 3-7, Allowance for Uncollectible Accounts has a credit balance of $60.00. The $1,016.65 adjustment for the current period is added to the previous balance, resulting in an adjusted balance of $1,076.65.

Notice that on the work sheet Accounts Receivable has a debit balance of $28,667.00. When the balance of Allowance for Uncollectible Accounts is deducted from the balance of Accounts Receivable, the book value of accounts receivable is found to be $27,590.35.

R — E — M — E — M — B — E — R

Allowance for Uncollectible Accounts **is a contra asset account. It is reported on the balance sheet as a deduction from** Accounts Receivable. Accounts Receivable **minus** Allowance for Uncollectible Accounts **represents the book value of accounts receivable.**

Mayfaire,
Work
For the Year Ended

	ACCT. NO.	ACCOUNT NAME	TRIAL BALANCE DEBIT	TRIAL BALANCE CREDIT	ADJUSTMENTS DEBIT	ADJUSTMENTS CREDIT
7	115	Accounts Receivable	28 667 00			
8	117	Allow. for Uncoll. Accts.		60 00		(b) 1 016 65
33	605	Bad Debts Expense	—		(b) 1 016 65	

Figure 3-7 Recording the Adjustment for Bad Debts Expense

The adjusting entry for the estimated uncollectible amount for the period appears in Figure 3-8.

GENERAL JOURNAL — PAGE 25

	DATE		DESCRIPTION	POST. REF.	DEBIT	CREDIT	
1			Adjusting Entries				1
2	199- Dec.	31	Bad Debts Expense		1016 65		2
3			Allow. for Uncollectible Accts.			1016 65	3
4							4

Figure 3-8 Journalizing the Adjusting Entry for Bad Debts

Bad Debts Expense is closed, along with the other expense accounts, into Income Summary. Because Allowance for Uncollectible Accounts is a permanent account, it is not closed; its balance is carried over to the beginning of the next period.

Writing Off Uncollectible Accounts with the Allowance Method

Point out that businesses review receivables periodically to determine which specific accounts are uncollectible and should be written off.

Discuss why Allowance for Uncollectible Accounts is used rather than Bad Debts Expense.

Point out that the book value of accounts receivable does not change when an account is written off using the allowance method.

When a customer's account proves uncollectible, it is written off. With the direct write-off method, Bad Debts Expense is debited and Accounts Receivable and the customer's account are credited. With the allowance method, however, the Bad Debts Expense account cannot be used to write off a customer's account. Bad Debts Expense is used only at the end of the period, during the adjusting and closing process.

Instead, Allowance for Uncollectible Accounts is used to write off accounts. Allowance for Uncollectible Accounts is like a reservoir: It is "filled up" at the end of the year by the adjusting entry; then, the balance in the account is saved until it is needed. When a charge customer's account proves uncollectible, the business can dip into the reservoir to write off the account.

Let's look at an example. On January 23, after many attempts to collect the amount owed, Mayfaire, Inc., decided to write off the account of James C. Woods as uncollectible. The amount Woods owed was $80.00.

GENERAL LEDGER

Allowance for Uncollectible Accounts

Dr.	Cr
$80.00	Bal. $1,076.65

Accounts Receivable

Dr.	Cr.
Bal. $28,667.00	$80.00

SUBSIDIARY LEDGER

James C. Woods

Dr.	Cr.
Bal. $80.00	$80.00

Inc.
Sheet
December 31, 199-

ADJUSTED TRIAL BALANCE DEBIT	ADJUSTED TRIAL BALANCE CREDIT	INCOME STATEMENT DEBIT	INCOME STATEMENT CREDIT	BALANCE SHEET DEBIT	BALANCE SHEET CREDIT	
28667 00				28667 00		7
	1076 65				1076 65	8
1016 65		1016 65				33

Use demonstration problem 3-5 here.

Since Mayfaire no longer expects to receive payment, the amount must be removed from its books. In the transaction, Allowance for Uncollectible Accounts is debited for $80.00. The $80.00 is no longer part of the *estimated* bad debt; it *is* a bad debt. Allowance for Uncollectible Accounts is, therefore, decreased for the amount of the loss. Accounts Receivable and Woods' account in the accounts receivable subsidiary ledger are credited for $80.00. Figure 3-9 shows the journal entry to record the transaction.

GENERAL JOURNAL — PAGE 28

	DATE		DESCRIPTION	POST. REF.	DEBIT	CREDIT	
1	199- Jan.	23	Allowance for Uncollectible Accounts		80 00		1
2			Accts. Rec./James C. Woods	✓		80 00	2
3			Memo. 716				3
4							4

Figure 3-9 Journalizing the Write-Off of an Uncollectible Account with the Allowance Method

Notice that this entry does not involve an expense account. The expense was recorded as part of the previous year's adjusting entry. Notice, too, that the entry does not change the book value of accounts receivable.

	Balance Before Write-Off	Balance After Write-Off
Accounts Receivable	$28,667.00	$28,587.00
Less: Allowance for Uncollectible Accounts	1,076.65	996.65
Book value of accounts receivable	$27,590.35	$27,590.35

The total amount of accounts receivable written off during a fiscal period often does not agree with the uncollectible amount estimated at the end of the period. The written-off accounts usually turn out to be less than the estimated amount. As a result, there is a small credit balance in Allowance for Uncollectible Accounts at the end of the fiscal period. However, if the accounts written off exceed the estimated amount, Allowance for Uncollectible Accounts will temporarily have a debit balance. The debit balance will be eliminated by the adjusting entry at the end of the period.

Collecting an Account Previously Written Off

Explain that the account is first reinstated to show a complete record of what occurred.

An account written off as uncollectible with the allowance method may be paid later. When this happens, the charge customer's account must first be reinstated by an entry that is the exact opposite of the write-off entry.

Use demonstration problem 3-6 here.

For example, on March 2 Mayfaire received $80 from James C. Woods, whose account had been written off in January. Before the cash receipt can be recorded, Wood's account is reinstated by the journal entry shown in Figure 3-10. This entry is the exact opposite of the one shown in Figure 3-9. After the entry is posted, the cash receipt can be journalized.

GENERAL JOURNAL PAGE 30

	DATE		DESCRIPTION	POST. REF.	DEBIT	CREDIT	
1	199– Mar.	2	Accounts Receivable/James C. Woods	✓	80 00		1
2			Allow. for Uncollectible Accts.			80 00	2
3			Memo. 733				3
4							4

Figure 3-10 Journalizing the Reinstatement of an Account with the Allowance Method

Estimating Bad Debts Expense

Management, on the basis of its judgment and past experience, tries to make a reasonable estimate of the amount of its uncollectible accounts. Of course, any such estimate will be affected by economic conditions. In a period of prosperity and high employment, a business can expect fewer losses from uncollectible accounts than in a period of recession.

A business can use several methods to estimate the amount of the adjustment for uncollectible accounts for the period. We'll look at two of these methods.

The Percentage of Net Sales Method

Mention that the percentage of net sales method is used here because it is one of the easier methods.

The **percentage of net sales method** is a fairly simple method for estimating the amount of the adjustment for uncollectible accounts. With this method, the business assumes that a certain set percentage of the current period's net sales will be uncollectible. Net sales, you'll remember, is Sales less Sales Discounts and Sales Returns and Allowances. The estimated amount for the adjustment is calculated by multiplying the current year's net sales by a set percentage.

For example, over the past few years Mayfaire, Inc.'s actual bad debt losses from sales on account have averaged approximately 0.25% of net sales. Mayfaire will use this percentage to compute the current period's adjustment. For example, Mayfaire's net sales for the period are calculated as follows:

Sales		$412,750.00
Less: Sales Discounts	$2,063.00	
Sales Returns and Allowances	4,027.00	6,090.00
Net Sales		$406,660.00

Point out that the estimated bad debts amount for the period is added to the existing balance in the Allowance account.

Use demonstration problem 3-7 here.

The net sales amount is multiplied by the set percentage of 0.25% ($406,660.00 × .0025). Mayfaire's estimated bad debts expense for the period therefore is $1,016.65. This amount is used in the adjustment recorded on the work sheet in Figure 3-7. Notice that the amount of the adjustment is *added to* the previous balance of Allowance for Uncollectible Accounts. After the adjusting entry is journalized and posted, Allowance for Uncollectible Accounts will have a credit balance of $1,076.65.

Some businesses that make both cash and credit sales base their estimated bad debts expense on net *credit* sales rather than on net sales. For example, the Mason Furniture Company sells merchandise on both a cash and a credit basis. The charge sales for the year (as recorded in the sales journal) totaled $620,000. Sales Discounts and Sales Returns and Allowances on credit sales were $3,100 and $20,000, respectively. Mason's net credit sales are calculated as follows:

Credit Sales		$620,000.00
Less: Sales Discounts	$ 3,100.00	
Sales Returns and Allowances	20,000.00	23,100.00
Net Credit Sales		$596,900.00

Have students complete Exercise 3-2 at this point.

Mason Furniture estimates that its bad debts expense for the period will be 1.5% of its net credit sales. The amount of the company's adjustment for bad debts expense is, therefore, $8,953.50. The amount of the adjustment for bad debts is *added to* the previous balance of Allowance for Uncollectible Accounts ($220.00). After the adjusting entry is journalized and posted, Mason Furniture's Allowance for Uncollectible Accounts has a credit balance of $9,173.50.

$596,900.00
× .015
$ 8,953.50

Bad Debts Expense	
Dr.	Cr.
Adj. $8,953.50	

Allowance for Uncollectible Accounts	
Dr.	Cr.
	Bal. $ 220.00
	Adj. 8,953.50

R — E — M — E — M — B — E — R

When the estimated uncollectible amount is based on a set percentage of net sales or net credit sales, the total estimated uncollectible amount is added to the previous balance of Allowance for Uncollectible Accounts.

The Aging of Accounts Receivable Method

Stress what is meant by the term *aged* and how the uncollectible percentage is estimated for each group.

With the **aging of accounts receivable method**, each customer's account is examined and "aged" (classified according to its due date). The accounts are then separated into age groups: not yet due, 1–30 days past due, 31–60 days past due, and so on. Based on its past experience, the business can estimate what percentage of each age group will be uncollectible. Then the age group totals are multiplied by a certain percentage to determine the estimated uncollectible amount for each age group. The total of all the estimated uncollectible amounts represents the *end-of-period balance* of Allowance for Uncollectible Accounts. The adjustment made at the end of the fiscal period brings the balance of Allowance for Uncollectible Accounts *up to* the total estimated amount.

Point out that most large business computers are programmed to analyze accounts receivable by age and may include this information on the customer's account statement.

Let's look at an example. Evergreen Lawn Service estimates its bad debts expense by aging accounts receivable. At the end of the period, Evergreen examined its customer accounts and prepared an analysis of its accounts receivable. A portion of this analysis appears in Figure 3-11. As you can see, each customer's account was placed in a specific age group.

EVERGREEN LAWN SERVICE
Analysis of Accounts Receivable
December 31, 199-

Acc. No.	Customer Name	Total Amount Due	Not Yet Due	Days Past Due 1-30	31-60	61-90	Over 90
802	Alexander, F.	636.00	500.00	136.00			
804	Armstrong, P.	43.00	43.00				
810	Babick, C. E.	1,159.00					1,159.00
812	Beard, D.	114.00	100.00	20.00		80.00	
846	Wood, D.	220.00			220.00		
848	Wyatt, L.	306.50	298.00	8.50			
849	Young, J. B.	49.50			49.50		
	TOTALS	8,706.75	5,224.05	894.20	1,349.50	80.00	1,159.00

Figure 3-11 Analysis of Accounts Receivable

Next, the total for each age group is multiplied by the percentage the business estimates to be uncollectible. In Figure 3-12, for example, Evergreen estimates that 2% of the $5,224.05 of accounts receivable, or $104.48, will prove to be collectible. Of the $894.20 of accounts receivable 1–30 days past due, 4%, or $35.77, are estimated to be uncollectible. Using this method, Evergreen's total estimated uncollectible accounts receivable is $1,218.40.

EVERGREEN LAWN SERVICE
Aging of Accounts Receivable
Estimated Uncollectible Amount
December 31, 199-

Age Group	Amount	Estimated Percentage Uncollectible	Estimated Uncollectible Amount
Not yet due	$5,224.05	2%	$ 104.48
1-30 days past due	894.20	4%	35.77
31-60 days past due	1,349.50	10%	134.95
61-90 days past due	80.00	20%	16.00
Over 90 days past due	1,159.00	80%	927.20
TOTAL	$8,706.75		$1,218.40

Figure 3-12 Accounts Receivable Aging Schedule

Use demonstration problem 3-8 here.

Now an adjustment must be made to bring the balance of Allowance for Uncollectible Accounts up to the estimated amount of $1,218.40. On the

Have students complete Exercise 3-3 at this point.

work sheet, the balance of Allowance for Uncollectible Accounts is $210.00. The amount of the adjustment for bad debts expense is $1,008.40 ($1,218.40 – $210.00).

Bad Debts Expense	
Dr.	Cr.
Adj. $1,008.40	

Allowance for Uncollectible Accounts	
Dr.	Cr.
	Bal. $ 210.00
	Adj. 1,008.40
	Bal. $1,218.40

After the adjusting entry is journalized and posted, the balance of Allowance for Uncollectible Accounts will be $1,218.40, the total uncollectible amount determined by the aging procedure.

R — E — M — E — M — B — E — R

When the adjustment for bad debts expense is based on an aging of Accounts Receivable, Allowance for Uncollectible Accounts is adjusted to bring the balance up to the total estimated uncollectible amount.

Before reading further, do the following activity to check your understanding of the material you have just studied.

Check Your Learning

Write your answers to these questions on a sheet of notebook paper.

1. Bloomfield Galleries estimates that 3% of its net credit sales for the year will be uncollectible. If net credit sales are $21,490, what is the total estimated uncollectible amount?
2. The Shaw Company uses the percentage of net sales method to estimate its bad debts expense. Total Sales for the period were $75,400; Sales Discounts were $2,600; and Sales Returns and Allowances were $4,300. If Shaw estimates that 2% of its net sales will be uncollectible, what will be the amount of the adjustment?

Compare your answers to those in the answers section. Reread the preceding part of the chapter to find the correct answers to any questions you may have missed.

Installment Accounts Receivable

Show the students a simple installment sales contract that a local business uses.

Some businesses that sell goods or services allow customers to pay for their purchases over a period of time. Companies such as J. C. Penney and Sears and companies that sell items such as cars, furniture, and large appliances have millions of dollars in installment accounts receivable. With these **installment sales**, customers usually make a cash down payment and a series of equal monthly payments. The payment period may be a year or more. A minimum payment is due each month. This monthly payment includes a *finance charge* (interest) on the unpaid balance.

Point out that finance charges collected by the business are a source of revenue.

To provide more detailed information to management, businesses record installment sales in the two revenue accounts, Installment Sales and Finance Charges, and in the asset account Installment Accounts Receivable. Installment Accounts Receivable is a controlling account for the installment accounts receivable subsidiary ledger.

Let's look at a simple example of installment accounts receivable. On December 20, Landmark Appliance Center sold a $500.00 television set to Leigh Lewis. Since this was an installment sale, Lewis will also pay a finance charge of $47.28. The total cost is therefore $547.28. Lewis made a down payment of $50.00 and agreed to make 12 monthly payments of $41.44.

Use demonstration problem 3-9 here.

In the transaction, Cash in Bank is debited for $50.00, the amount of the down payment. Installment Accounts Receivable is debited for $497.28, the installment sale amount still to be paid. Installment Sales is credited for $500.00, the total of the merchandise sold on the installment plan. Finance Charges is credited for $47.28, the finance charge for this transaction.

Cash in Bank

Dr.	Cr.
$50.00	

Installment Accounts Receivable

Dr.	Cr.
$497.28	

Installment Sales

Dr.	Cr.
	$500.00

Finance Charges

Dr.	Cr.
	$47.28

The entry to record the installment sale appears in Figure 3-13.

CASH RECEIPTS JOURNAL — PAGE 72

	DATE		DOC. NO.	ACCOUNT TITLE	POST. REF.	GENERAL DEBIT	GENERAL CREDIT	INSTALLMENT SALES CREDIT	FINANCE CHARGES CREDIT	INSTALLMENT ACCTS. REC. DEBIT	CASH IN BANK DEBIT	
1	199- Sept.	14	IC 4166	Leigh Lewis				500 00	47 28	497 28	50 00	1

Figure 3-13 Journalizing an Installment Sale

When each monthly payment is received, Cash in Bank is debited and Installment Accounts Receivable is credited.

Summary of Key Points

1. A corporation whose ownership is confined to a small group of stockholders is called a privately held corporation. A corporation whose stock is traded on a stock exchange or over-the-counter is called a publicly held corporation.
2. Cash is the most liquid of all assets, and it is important to establish sound internal controls to protect it from loss, waste, theft, forgery, and embezzlement.
3. A change fund is an amount of money used to make change for cash transactions.
4. When errors in making change for cash customers occur, cash is said to be short or over. Shortages and overages are recorded in the account Cash Short and Over.
5. A petty cash fund is the cash a business has on hand for making small, incidental cash payments. A petty cash voucher must be prepared before a disbursement from the petty cash fund is made.
6. When a business has more cash in the bank than it needs to pay current bills, it may invest that cash in short-term investments called marketable securities. Income from marketable securities is recorded when it is received.
7. A business may account for bad debts using two methods: the direct write-off method and the allowance method.
8. The direct write-off method of accounting for uncollectible accounts is used primarily by businesses with few charge customers and by professional enterprises. When this method is used, Bad Debts Expense is debited and Accounts Receivable and the charge customer's account are credited.
9. The allowance method of accounting for uncollectible accounts matches the bad debts expense with the sales for the same fiscal period. An adjustment for the estimated amount of bad debts losses for the period is made at the end of the fiscal period. In the adjustment, Bad Debts Expense is debited and Allowance for Uncollectible Accounts is credited.
10. Allowance for Uncollectible Accounts is a contra asset account. It appears as a deduction from Accounts Receivable on the balance sheet. The difference between the balance of Accounts Receivable and that of Allowance for Uncollectible Accounts is the book value of accounts receivable. It is the amount the business can reasonably expect to receive from its charge customers.
11. To write off a charge account as uncollectible using the allowance method, the firm debits Allowance for Uncollectible Accounts and credits Accounts Receivable and the customer's account.
12. Several methods can be used to estimate the adjustment for uncollectible accounts, including (1) taking a set percentage of net sales or net credit sales and (2) aging Accounts Receivable.
13. When a business bases the estimate for bad debts expense on a percentage of net sales or net credit sales, the amount of the adjustment is added to the balance of Allowance for Uncollectible Accounts.

14. When a business ages its Accounts Receivable to estimate its bad debts expense, the balance of Allowance for Uncollectible Accounts is adjusted to bring it up to the total estimated amount.

15. Some businesses sell goods or services to customers and allow them to pay for their purchases over a period of time. With these installment sales, customers make a down payment and agree to make monthly payments. The monthly payment includes a finance charge on the unpaid balance, which represents revenue for the business.

3 Review and Applications

Building Your Accounting Vocabulary

In your own words, write the definition of each of the following accounting terms. Use complete sentences for your definitions.

aging of accounts receivable method
allowance method
book value of accounts receivable
change fund
direct write-off method
installment sales
marketable securities
matching principle
other revenue
percentage of net sales method
petty cash fund
publicly held corporation
uncollectible account

Reviewing Your Accounting Knowledge

1. What are internal controls? Why are they important?
2. Which accounts are debited and which are credited when a change fund is established?
3. How is Cash Short and Over classified? How is it used?
4. How often is Petty Cash Fund debited?
5. Why would a business invest in marketable securities?
6. Why are bad debts considered an expense for a business?
7. What two methods can be used to account for uncollectible accounts?
8. Why is the allowance method of handling uncollectible accounts considered more effective than the direct write-off method?
9. Why isn't Accounts Receivable credited for the estimated uncollectible amount when the allowance method is used?
10. How is Allowance for Uncollectible Accounts classified?
11. When an account is written off using the allowance method, why doesn't the book value of Accounts Receivable decrease?
12. Name two methods a business can use to estimate the uncollectible amount.

Improving Your Human Relations Skills

Rick Jaworski has been assigned to train Cynthia Van Dusen, a new accounting clerk. Cynthia comes to work five to ten minutes late almost every day, and Rick knows he has to teach her to be on time. However, Rick sometimes comes in a little late himself, but he feels justified in doing so because he works one to two hours of unpaid overtime every day. Should Rick change his habits to provide a good example for Cynthia, or should he explain that Cynthia has to "pay her dues" before she can adjust her work schedule? What would you do?

Applying Accounting Procedures

Exercise 3-1 Calculating Cash Short and Over

The Old Towne Café has a change fund of $60.00. The following table shows the daily cash sales and sales tax amounts for the week of April 10, as well as the cash in the cash drawer.

Instructions: Determine (1) the total sales amount, (2) the net amount of cash received, and (3) the amount of any cash shortage or overage. Use notebook paper or the form provided in the working papers.

Date	Cash Sales	Sales Tax	Cash in Drawer
Apr. 10	$513.40	$25.67	$600.07
11	497.30	24.87	582.17
12	356.15	17.81	438.96
13	502.70	25.14	588.09
14	624.80	31.24	714.89
15	827.10	41.36	939.46

Exercise 3-2 Estimating Bad Debts with the Percentage of Net Sales Method

The end-of-period account balances for several companies follow. Each company uses the percentage of net sales method to estimate its uncollectible accounts. The percentage each company uses is also listed.

Instructions: Calculate the amount of the adjustment for bad debts expense for each company. Use the form provided in the working papers.

		Sales	Sales Discounts	Sales Returns and Allowances	Percentage of Net Sales
$22,167.00	J&J Furniture Co.	$520,000	$9,400	$18,200	4.5%
1,160.50	Mendoza Bros., Inc.	44,400	500	1,700	2.75%
3,340.00	Greenwood Toy Center	175,000	3,100	4,900	2.0%
1,386.00	Nick's Office Supplies	97,000	1,100	3,500	1.5%
10,602.00	Sims Clothing Store	362,500	6,300	14,200	3.1%

SPREADSHEET PROBLEM

Exercise 3-3 Completing an Aging Schedule

The Brandon Corporation uses the allowance method of accounting for uncollectible accounts. It uses the aging of accounts receivable method to estimate its uncollectible amount.

Instructions: Complete the aging schedule, using the form included in the working papers.

	Age Group	Amount	Estimated Percentage Uncollectible	Estimated Uncollectible Amount
$ 494.00	Not yet due	$24,700	2%	
540.50	1–30 days past due	10,810	5%	
990.00	31–60 days past due	9,900	10%	
952.50	61–90 days past due	6,350	15%	
940.00	91–180 days past due	4,700	20%	
170.00	181–365 days past due	425	40%	
624.00	More than 1 year past due	780	80%	
$4,711.00	Totals	$57,665		

COMPUTER PROBLEM

Problem 3-1 Establishing and Replenishing a Petty Cash Fund

The Haggerty Newsstand established a petty cash fund for payments of $10 or less. The following transactions involve the fund.

Instructions: Record the following transactions on page 10 of the cash payments journal.

Transactions:

Feb.	1	Established a petty cash fund of $75.00, Check 1416.
	28	Issued Check 1443 for $70.35 to replenish the petty cash fund. Paid petty cash vouchers include office supplies, $6.15; advertising expenses, $15.65; delivery expenses, $22.75; and miscellaneous expenses, $24.80.

Problem 3-2 Journalizing Transactions for Marketable Securities

The Packard Corporation invests its extra cash in marketable securities.

Instructions: Record the following transactions in the cash receipts journal (page 18) and the cash payments journal (page 27).

Transactions:

Jan.	7	Purchased U.S. Treasury bills for $23,050, Check 812.
Apr.	7	Received $25,000 when the Treasury bills purchased in January matured, Receipt 361.

COMPUTER PROBLEM

Problem 3-3 Recording Transactions with the Direct Write-Off Method

Holiday Imports uses the direct write-off method to account for uncollectible accounts.

Instructions:

(1) Record the following transactions on page 29 of a general journal.

(2) Post the transactions to the accounts included in the working papers.

Transactions:

Jan.	17	Sold to Gail Buresh on account merchandise totaling $1,920, terms n/45, Sales Slip 302.
Mar.	2	Received $600 from Gail Buresh on account, Receipt 466.
Dec.	15	Wrote off the account of Gail Buresh as uncollectible, Memorandum 396.
	17	Received a check for $400 from Gail Buresh as part payment on the amount owed.Reinstated the account for the amount originally owed, Memorandum 399/Receipt 987.

Problem 3-4 Estimating and Journalizing the Adjusting Entry for Bad Debts Expense

The Owens Street Greenhouse uses the allowance method of accounting for uncollectible accounts. On December 31, the following balances appeared in the Trial Balance section of the company's work sheet.

Accounts Receivable	$ 11,352
Allowance for Uncollectible Accounts	207
Sales	199,014
Sales Discounts	2,189
Sales Returns and Allowances	7,754

Owens estimates that its bad debts losses will be 1.25% of net sales.

Instructions:

Adjustment, $2,363.39

(1) Determine the amount of the adjustment for bad debts.

(2) Record the adjusting entry on page 46 of the general journal.

(3) Post the adjusting entry to the Allowance for Uncollectible Accounts account.

Problem 3-5 Recording Transactions with the Allowance Method

The Janney Chemical Corporation uses the allowance method to account for uncollectible accounts. During the year, the company completed the transactions that follow.

Instructions:

(1) Record the entries on page 19 of a general journal.

(2) Post the entries to the general and subsidiary ledger accounts that appear in the working papers.

Transactions:

Feb. 23 Determined that the $1,500.00 account of John Graham was uncollectible and wrote it off, Memorandum 171.

Aug. 3 Collected 25% of the $3,462.80 owed by Levitt Bros., which has become bankrupt. Wrote off the remainder as uncollectible, Receipt 422/Memorandum 254.

Nov. 21 Received $500.00 from John Graham as part payment on the account written off in February, Memorandum 286/Receipt 649.

Dec. 31 Recorded the adjusting entry for estimated bad debts losses at 0.5% of net credit sales of $446,694.70.

31 Closed the Bad Debts Expense account.

COMPUTER PROBLEM

Problem 3-6 Recording Transactions with the Allowance Method

Westside Pool Supply uses the allowance method of accounting for uncollectible accounts. The following transactions are among those completed this year.

Instructions:

(1) Open the following accounts and record any January 1 balance.

117	Allowance for Uncollectible Accounts	$4,352.00
313	Income Summary	
610	Bad Debts Expense	

(2) Beginning on page 24 of a general journal, record the entries that follow. After each entry, post to the general ledger accounts you opened.

Book value, $91,226.68

(3) Determine the book value of accounts receivable.

Transactions:

Jan. 27 Sold merchandise on account to Kawas Athletic Club, $2,148.00 plus sales tax of $85.92, Sales Slip 216.

Feb. 13 Wrote off the account of Frank Burns, $340.08, Memorandum 131.

Apr. 2 Reinstated the account of Arnold Burke, which had been written off last year. Received $141.44 in full payment, Memorandum 149/Receipt 420.

Aug. 31 Received $319.28 unexpectedly from Celebrity Tennis, whose account had been written off last year. Reinstated the account for the original amount of $540.80 and recorded the $319.28 collection, Memorandum 190/Receipt 612.

Oct. 12 Received 25% of the $2,233.92 balance owed by Kawas Athletic Club, which went out of business. Wrote off the remainder as uncollectible, Receipt 703/Memorandum 206.

Dec. 28 Journalized a compound entry to write off the following accounts as uncollectible: Nathan Alexander, $71.76; Maxwell Fitness Center, $341.12; Sportsmed, $1,630.72; Susan Wilkins, $156.00; Memorandum 229.

31 By aging the $96,554.40 balance of Accounts Receivable, estimated that $5,327.72 of the accounts receivable will be uncollectible. Recorded the adjusting entry.

31 Recorded the closing entry for Bad Debts Expense.

COMPUTER PROBLEM

Problem 3-7 Aging Accounts Receivable

House of Carpets uses the accounts receivable aging method to estimate its uncollectible accounts. At the end of the fiscal period (December 31), a co-worker began to prepare the aging schedule. When that person became ill, you were asked to complete the schedule. The following customer accounts remain to be aged.

Account	Amount	Due Date
P. Vella	$ 983	Dec. 6
C. Webb	4,419	November 12, $1,902; Dec. 21, $2,517
R. Wood	120	Oct. 11
A. Yazbek	1,071	Sept. 14
Zamon Co.	562	Jan. 14 (next year)

Instructions:

(1) Complete the accounts receivable aging schedule included in the working papers.

(2) Calculate the total estimated uncollectible amount using the following percentages.

Not Yet Due	2%
1–30 Days Past Due	4%
31–60 Days Past Due	25%
61–90 Days Past Due	35%
Over 90 Days Past Due	55%

$ 854.70
947.20
2,415.50
1,330.00
2,118.05
$7,665.45

(3) Determine the amount of the adjustment if Allowance for Uncollectible Accounts has a credit balance of $354.

Adjustment, $7,311.45

CHALLENGE PROBLEM

Problem 3-8 Determining the Adjustment for Uncollectible Accounts

Barry Car Care Center opened for business four years ago. For the first three years, the company used the direct write-off method of accounting for uncollectible accounts. With net sales this year of $342,960, the Center decided to switch to the allowance method.

The company plans to use the percentage of net sales method to estimate the adjustment for bad debts expense. Accounting information for the first three years follows.

	Net Sales	Total Actual Bad Debts Losses
Year 1	$ 77,630	$ 932
Year 2	128,316	3,080
Year 3	242,938	4,130

Instructions:

2%
No
Adjustment, $6,859.20
Book value, $76,801.80

(1) Based on the figures for the first three years, what percentage of net sales would you suggest be used for the adjustment?

(2) Can Barry Car Care Center use the same accounts with the allowance method that it used with the direct write-off method? Why or why not?

(3) Using the percentage suggested in (1), what should be the amount of the adjustment?

(4) If Accounts Receivable has a year-end balance of $83,661, what is the book value of accounts receivable?

(5) Record the December 31 adjusting entry for bad debts expense on page 35 of a general journal.

FOCUS ON CAREERS

Taking Accounting to Court

When you hear the term *expert witness,* what comes to mind? Perhaps you picture a medical examiner in a whodunit movie who steps into the witness stand to testify that the deceased was a victim of murder rather than of death by natural causes. Believe it or not, accountants are other professionals who are called on to provide support to lawyers in courtroom settings.

Accountants who serve as expert witnesses, also known as *litigation support professionals,* know as much about working with lawyers as they do about auditing the books. They are often called in to assist with cases that involve fraud or commercial transactions.

Some examples of cases that benefit from accountants serving on the litigation team include embezzlement cases, hostile takeovers, class-action suits against companies filing bankruptcy, wrongful dismissal charges brought against corporations, and evaluations of wrongful business dealings. When lawyers enlist the aid of an accountant, they are first and foremost looking for someone to sort through all the information to locate what's important. Lawyers often need help pulling out the figures relevant to a case from the mountains of business data they have accumulated. Other valuable characteristics of a litigation support accountant include:

- Knowing how to crunch numbers.
- Being able to give objective advice.
- Knowing how the industry in question operates.
- Being able to explain accounting techniques to a jury.
- Being able to stand up well under cross-examination.

Accountants may serve as expert witnesses in court cases involving fraud or commercial transactions.

If being involved with law and litigation appeals to you, the best training you can obtain is a solid accounting foundation. As an expert witness, your credibility will be enhanced if you practice the work about which you testify.

Chapter 4
NOTES RECEIVABLE

Credit plays a very important role in the operation of most businesses. Many businesses grant credit on a charge-account basis, usually with payment due within 30 to 60 days. This type of credit involves the Accounts Receivable account.

Businesses may also grant credit on the basis of short-term, written agreements. These written agreements, called *promissory notes,* usually are used for credit transactions of more than 60 days. Most businesses use notes at one time or another, often by accepting them from customers.

In this chapter, you will learn how to record transactions involving promissory notes receivable.

Learning Objectives

When you have completed this chapter, you should be able to do the following:

1. Explain how businesses use promissory notes.
2. Determine the maturity date of a promissory note.
3. Determine the interest and maturity value of a promissory note.
4. Record journal entries for notes receivable.
5. Define the accounting terms presented in this chapter.

New Terms

promissory note
principal
face value
issue date
maturity date
term
payee
maker
interest
interest rate
maturity value
interest-bearing note
note receivable
dishonored note
discounting notes receivable
bank discount
proceeds
discount period
contingent liability
protest fee
accrual basis of accounting
accrued revenue
draft
trade acceptances

Mention that a promissory note is usually signed by both parties.

Promissory Notes

A **promissory note,** usually referred to simply as a *note,* is a written promise to pay a certain sum of money on demand or on a specified date. A promissory note is a formal legal document that serves as proof of a debt. To be enforceable, the note must contain certain information, as shown in Figure 4-1.

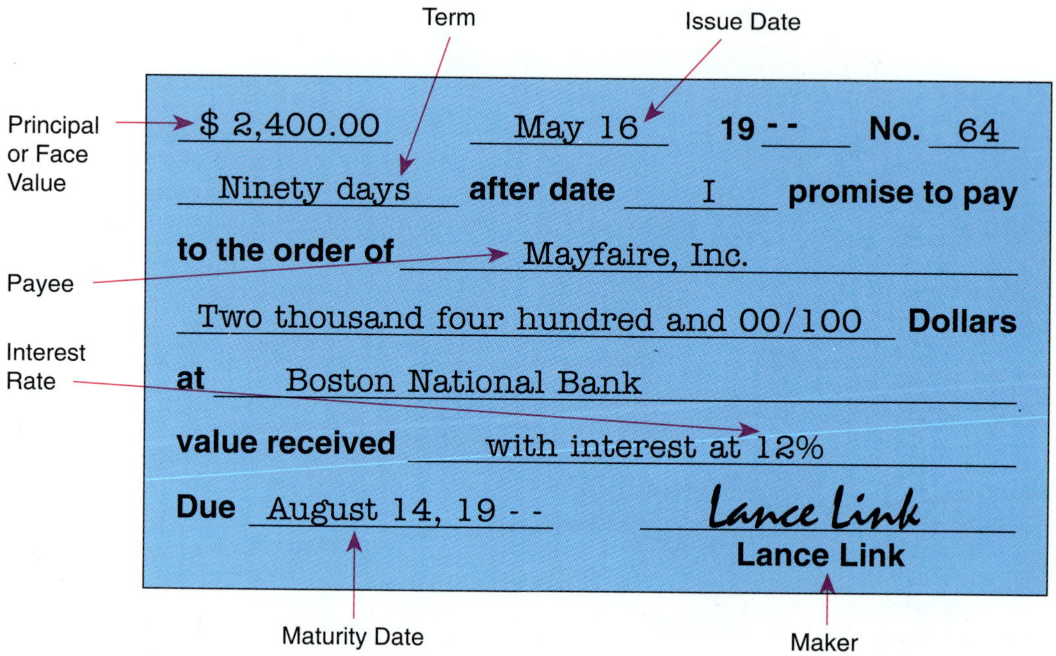

Figure 4-1 Promissory Note

The **principal** is the amount of money borrowed. The **face value** is the amount written on the "face" of the note. The principal and the face value are usually the same. The date the note is written is the **issue date.** The due date of the note is the **maturity date.** The amount of time between the issue date and the maturity date is the **term** of the note.

Call on individual students to identify each item on the note.

Like a check, a promissory note must be payable to the order of a particular person or company, known as the **payee.** It must also be signed by the **maker,** the person or firm making the promise. In the promissory note shown in Figure 4-1, Mayfaire, Inc., is the payee and Lance Link is the maker.

Determining the Maturity Date of a Note

The maker of a note must repay the note on a specified date. Once you know the issue date and the term of the note, you can easily determine the note's maturity date.

The term may be expressed in either days or months. If the term is expressed in months, the maturity date falls on the same day of the month as the issue date, plus, of course, the specified number of months. For example, a note issued on April 15 with a term of 3 months has a maturity date of July 15. If there is no day in the month of maturity that corresponds to the issue date, the maturity date becomes the last day of the month. For example, a 3-month note dated January 31 would be due on April 30.

Explain and illustrate how the maturity date (due date) of a note is determined.

Suppose the term of the note is expressed in days. Let's use the note in Figure 4-1 as an example. To determine the maturity date, follow these steps:

1. Determine the number of days left in the month of issue (May). In counting the number of days, begin counting with the day *after* the issue date, since the note states "after date."

31	Days in May
−16	Issue date
15	Days left in May

Subtract the date of the note from the number of days in the month. In our example, subtract 16 from 31, leaving 15 days in May. Remember that January, March, May, July, August, October, and December have 31 days; February has 28 days (29 in a leap year); and April, June, September, and November have 30 days.

90	Days in term
−15	Days left in May
75	Days left

2. Determine the number of days the note has left after the first month. To do this, subtract the days calculated in Step 1 from the term of the note.

75	Days left
−30	Days in June
45	Days left

3. Subtract the number of days in the second month (June) from the number of days left after Step 2. In our example, subtract the 30 days in June from 75.

45	Days left
−31	Days in July
14	Days left

4. Subtract the number of days in the third month (July) from the number of days left after Step 3. In our example, subtract the 31 days in July from 45.
5. Since there are 14 days left after subtracting the 31 days in July, the maturity date is 14 days into the next month. In other words, the maturity date for this particular note is August 14.

Businesses collect interest in return for letting customers borrow money or purchase goods on extended credit.

Use demonstration problem 4-1 here.

Review very carefully the time calendar in Figure 4-2.

Businesses and banks use time calendars to calculate the maturity dates of notes. Figure 4-2 shows a time calendar. The time calendar has two sets of days: (1) the day of the month (left and right sides) and (2) the day of the year by month.

Day of month	*Jan.*	*Feb.*	*Mar.*	*Apr.*	*May*	*June*	*July*	*Aug.*	*Sept.*	*Oct.*	*Nov.*	*Dec.*	*Day of month*
1	1	32	60	91	121	152	182	213	244	274	305	335	1
2	2	33	61	92	122	153	183	214	245	275	306	336	2
3	3	34	62	93	123	154	184	215	246	276	307	337	3
4	4	35	63	94	124	155	185	216	247	277	308	338	4
5	5	36	64	95	125	156	186	217	248	278	309	339	5
6	6	37	65	96	126	157	187	218	249	279	310	340	6
7	7	38	66	97	127	158	188	219	250	280	311	341	7
8	8	39	67	98	128	159	189	220	251	281	312	342	8
9	9	40	68	99	129	160	190	221	252	282	313	343	9
10	10	41	69	100	130	161	191	222	253	283	314	344	10
11	11	42	70	101	131	162	192	223	254	284	315	345	11
12	12	43	71	102	132	163	193	224	255	285	316	346	12
13	13	44	72	103	133	164	194	225	256	286	317	347	13
14	14	45	73	104	134	165	195	226	257	287	318	348	14
15	15	46	74	105	135	166	196	227	258	288	319	349	15
16	16	47	75	106	136	167	197	228	259	289	320	350	16
17	17	48	76	107	137	168	198	229	260	290	321	351	17
18	18	49	77	108	138	169	199	230	261	291	322	352	18
19	19	50	78	109	139	170	200	231	262	292	323	353	19
20	20	51	79	110	140	171	201	232	263	293	324	354	20
21	21	52	80	111	141	172	202	233	264	294	325	355	21
22	22	53	81	112	142	173	203	234	265	295	326	356	22
23	23	54	82	113	143	174	204	235	266	296	327	357	23
24	24	55	83	114	144	175	205	236	267	297	328	358	24
25	25	56	84	115	145	176	206	237	268	298	329	359	25
26	26	57	85	116	146	177	207	238	269	299	330	360	26
27	27	58	86	117	147	178	208	239	270	300	331	361	27
28	28	59	87	118	148	179	209	240	271	301	332	362	28
29	29	...	88	119	149	180	210	241	272	302	333	363	29
30	30	...	89	120	150	181	211	242	273	303	334	364	30
31	31	...	90	...	151	...	212	243	...	304	...	365	31

NOTE: For leap years, after February 28, the number of the day is one greater than that given in the table.

Figure 4-2 Time Calendar

To calculate the maturity date using the time calendar, follow these steps:

1. Locate the issue date (16, in our example) in the Day of Month column. Move across the day-of-the-year columns until you come to the issue month (May). In our example, May 16 is the 136th day of the year.
2. Add the number of days in the term of the note (90) to the day of the year. The sum of the two numbers in our example is 226.
3. Find the number 226 in the day-of-the-year columns. The date for the 226th day of the year is the maturity date of the note, August 14.

	136 Day of the year
+	90 Term
	226

Before reading further, do the following activity to check your understanding of how to determine the maturity date of a promissory note.

Check Your Learning

Determine the maturity dates for the following notes. Write your answers on a sheet of notebook paper. Use the manual method first; then check your answers using the time calendar.

	Date of Issue	Term
1.	October 16	60 days
2.	April 9	75 days
3.	February 17	90 days (leap year)
4.	June 10	120 days
5.	March 3	180 days

Compare your answers to those in the answers section. Reread the preceding part of the chapter to find the correct answers to any questions you may have missed.

Calculating Interest on a Note

ACCOUNTING Tips

One shortcut method of estimating interest is 60-days, 6%.

When a note is issued, the maker agrees to repay the principal with interest. **Interest** is a fee charged for the use of money. The **interest rate** is the amount of interest expressed as a percentage of the principal. For example, the interest rate for the note in Figure 4-1 is 12%. To the maker of the note, interest is an expense. To the payee, interest is revenue.

The equation for calculating interest is

$$\text{Interest} = \text{Principal} \times \text{Interest Rate} \times \text{Time}$$
$$(I = PRT)$$

Explain that because most banks and businesses use computers to calculate interest, they use the full year (365 days). Some businesses, however, use a 360-day year.

The principal is expressed in dollars, the interest rate is expressed as a percentage, and the time (the term of the note) is expressed in days or months. In the equation, time is always expressed as a fraction of one year.

Following are the time fractions for some common terms. Notice that 365 is the denominator of the time fraction when the term is expressed in days, and 12 is used when the term is expressed in months.

$$3 \text{ months} = \tfrac{3}{12} \quad 60 \text{ days} = \tfrac{60}{365}$$
$$6 \text{ months} = \tfrac{6}{12} \quad 90 \text{ days} = \tfrac{90}{365}$$

Look at Figure 4-1. In that note, the principal is $2,400, the interest rate is 12% (.12), and the term is 90 days ($\frac{90}{365}$). Let's calculate the interest on the note:

Principal	×	Interest Rate	×	Time	=	Interest
$2,400.00	×	.12	×	$\frac{90}{365}$	=	$71.01

The interest on the note is $71.01. If the term of this note were 3 months instead of 90 days, the interest would be calculated as follows:

Principal	×	Interest Rate	×	Time	=	Interest
$2,400.00	×	.12	×	$\frac{3}{12}$	=	$72.00

$2,400.00 Principal
\+ 71.01 Interest
$2,471.01 Maturity value

Use demonstration problem 4-2 here.

The **maturity value** is the principal plus the interest that must be repaid on the maturity date. The maturity value of this note is $2,471.01. A note that requires that the principal plus interest be repaid at maturity is called an **interest-bearing note.** The note in Figure 4-1, for example, is an interest-bearing note.

R — E — M — E — M — B — E — R

If the term of a note is less than 1 year, express the time as a fraction of 1 year, with a denominator of 12 (months) or 365 (days).

Spend some time discussing the interest table in Figure 4-3. Also, get interest tables from a bank or savings and loan to share with students.

Calculating Interest Using an Interest Table

To calculate interest, many businesses and banks use an interest table similar to the one in Figure 4-3.

SIMPLE INTEREST ON $100, 365 DAY BASIS

DAY	11.50 % INTEREST	DAY	11.75 % INTEREST	DAY	12.00 % INTEREST	DAY	12.25 % INTEREST	DAY	12.50 % INTEREST	DAY	12.75 % INTEREST
30	0.945205	30	0.965753	30	0.986301	30	1.006849	30	1.027397	30	1.047945
60	1.890411	60	1.931507	60	1.972603	60	2.013699	60	2.054795	60	2.095890
90	2.835616	90	2.897260	90	2.958904	90	3.020548	90	3.082192	90	3.143836
120	3.780822	120	3.863014	120	3.945205	120	4.027397	120	4.109589	120	4.191781
150	4.726027	150	4.828767	150	4.931507	150	5.034247	150	5.136986	150	5.239726
180	5.671233	180	5.794521	180	5.917808	180	6.041096	180	6.164384	180	6.287671
210	6.616438	210	6.760274	210	6.904110	210	7.047945	210	7.191781	210	7.335616
240	7.561644	240	7.726027	240	7.890411	240	8.054795	240	8.219178	240	8.383562
270	8.506849	270	8.691781	270	8.876712	270	9.061644	270	9.246575	270	9.431507
300	9.452055	300	9.657534	300	9.863014	300	10.068493	300	10.273973	300	10.479452
330	10.397260	330	10.623288	330	10.849315	330	11.075342	330	11.301370	330	11.527397
360	11.342466	360	11.589041	360	11.835616	360	12.082192	360	12.328767	360	12.575342
365	11.500000	365	11.750000	365	12.000000	365	12.250000	365	12.500000	365	12.750000
366	11.531507	366	11.782192	366	12.032877	366	12.283562	366	12.534247	366	12.784932

Figure 4-3 Interest Table

2.958904
× 24
11835616
5917808
71.013696 =
$71.01

Let's use the interest table to calculate the interest on the note in Figure 4-1. First, find the term of the note (90) in the Day column. Next, follow the row across until you reach the column for the interest rate (12.00%). The factor at which the column and row meet is 2.958904.

This interest table is for a principal amount of $100.00. Since the principal in our example is more than that, divide the principal ($2,400.00) by $100.00. Then multiply the answer, 24, by the factor 2.958904 to find the total interest. The interest calculated using the interest table is also $71.01. Since factors in an interest table are rounded off, there may be a few cents' difference from the interest calculated manually.

Calculating Interest Using a Computer

A computer can calculate the interest and maturity value of a note quickly and accurately. Using the appropriate software program, a business simply enters the principal, interest rate, and term of the note; the computer does the rest. The computer can also prepare a schedule to indicate when and how much the business can expect to receive from maturing notes. The use of a computer saves much time for businesses that receive many notes.

Before reading further, do the following activity to check your understanding of how to calculate interest.

Check Your Learning

Find the interest for each of the following notes. First, find the interest manually; then use the interest table in Figure 4-3 to check your answer.

	Principal	Interest Rate	Term
1.	$4,700	12.25%	30 days
2.	$3,500	11.50%	60 days
3.	$5,000	11.75%	90 days
4.	$8,000	12.00%	120 days
5.	$6,750	12.50%	180 days

Compare your answers to those in the answers section. Reread the preceding part of the chapter to find the correct answers for any items you may have missed.

You may want to complete Exercise 4-1 at this point.

Notes Receivable

A promissory note accepted by a person or business is called a **note receivable.** Businesses receive promissory notes for a variety of reasons. They often accept notes when charge customers ask for more time to pay their accounts. They may also ask for notes if they make loans to employees, preferred customers, or suppliers. In some business fields, the credit period is much longer than the normal 30-day period. As a result, transactions are often backed up by notes rather than by charge accounts. Farm machinery or construction equipment, for example, might be sold on a notes-receivable basis.

ACCOUNTING Notes

Companies that frequently accept promissory notes may choose to keep detailed information about notes receivable in a separate notes receivable register. Important information for each note is recorded on a single line.

Recording the Receipt of a Note Receivable

On May 3, Mayfaire sold to Tom Armour on account $500 of merchandise plus $20 sales tax. That transaction was recorded in Mayfaire's sales journal. On June 3, the following transaction occurred.

Emphasize that it is advantageous to the seller to accept a note receivable rather than extend credit to a charge customer.

June 3: *Received a $520, 30-day, 10% note (Note 419) from Tom Armour for the amount recorded as an account receivable.*

Point out that the money is still owed to the business but it is now entered in a different asset account.

The accounts affected by this transaction are Notes Receivable and Accounts Receivable in the general ledger and Tom Armour's account in the accounts receivable subsidiary ledger. Notes Receivable is a current asset account with a normal debit balance. Since it is being increased, Notes Receivable is debited for $520. The note replaces the amount recorded as an account receivable. As a result, Accounts Receivable and Tom Armour's account are being decreased and are credited for $520.

Notes Receivable	
Dr.	Cr.
$520.00	

Accounts Receivable	
Dr.	Cr.
Bal. $520.00	$520.00

Tom Armour	
Dr.	Cr.
Bal. $520.00	$520.00

Use demonstration problem 4-3 here.

This transaction is recorded in the general journal as shown in Figure 4-4.

GENERAL JOURNAL — PAGE 17

	DATE		DESCRIPTION	POST. REF.	DEBIT	CREDIT	
1	199- June	3	Notes Receivable		520 00		1
2			Accts. Receivable/Tom Armour	✓		520 00	2
3			Note 419				3

Figure 4-4 Journalizing the Receipt of a Note Receivable

Recording the Receipt of Cash for a Note Receivable

On July 3, Mayfaire received from Tom Armour the maturity value of the note.

July 3: *Received a check for $524.27 from Tom Armour for the principal ($520.00) plus interest ($520.00 × .10 × 30/365) due on the note, Receipt 1479.*

Discuss the new account Interest Income.

The accounts affected by this transaction are Cash in Bank, Notes Receivable, and Interest Income. Cash in Bank is debited for $524.27, the total amount of cash received. To decrease the asset, Notes Receivable is credited for $520.00. The interest Mayfaire received on the note receivable is considered to be revenue. Therefore, the amount received, $4.27, is credited to the other revenue account Interest Income.

Cash in Bank	
Dr.	Cr.
$524.27	

Notes Receivable	
Dr.	Cr.
Bal. $520.0	$520.00

Interest Income	
Dr.	Cr.
	$4.27

Mayfaire recorded the transaction as shown in Figure 4-5.

CASH RECEIPTS JOURNAL — PAGE 22

	DATE	DOC. NO.	ACCOUNT TITLE	POST. REF.	GENERAL DEBIT	GENERAL CREDIT	SALES CREDIT	SALES TAX PAYABLE CREDIT	ACCOUNTS RECEIVABLE CREDIT	CASH IN BANK DEBIT	
1	199- July 3	R1479	Notes Receivable			520 00				524 27	1
2			Interest Income			4 27					2

Figure 4-5 Journalizing the Receipt of Cash for a Note Receivable

Use demonstration problem 4-4 here.

Before reading further, do the following activity to check your understanding of how to record the collection of a note receivable.

Check Your Learning

Answer these questions on a sheet of notebook paper.

1. The Danbury Company received a 60-day, 8% note for $3,600, dated January 15, from Rick Rossi, a charge customer.
   a. Which accounts are debited and which are credited? For how much?
   b. What is the maturity date of the note? (This is *not* a leap year.)
2. On the maturity date, the Danbury Company received a check from Rossi in payment of the note.
   a. What was the amount of Rick Rossi's check?
   b. Which accounts are debited and which are credited? For how much?

Compare your answers to those in the answers section. Reread the preceding part of the chapter to find the correct answers to any questions you may have missed.

Dishonored Notes Receivable

Explain that when working with notes, the term *dishonor* means to fail to pay the note.

When the maker of a note fails to pay or renew the note at maturity, the note is called a **dishonored note.** The maker still owes the payee the maturity value of the note, and the payee should take legal steps to collect the debt. When a note is dishonored, it must be removed from the Notes Receivable account. The Notes Receivable account should be used only for those notes that have not yet matured. A note that has been dishonored is reported in a current asset account titled Notes Receivable Past Due. The amount entered in the account is the *maturity value* of the note (principal plus interest).

Point out that Notes Receivable Past Due is an asset account and is debited only when a note receivable is dishonored.

Mayfaire holds a $1,600.00, 9.5%, 60-day note dated May 13 from Graham Marsh. When Marsh failed to pay the note by the maturity date, the note was dishonored. Mayfaire must now remove the dishonored note from the Notes Receivable account.

July 12: *Graham Marsh dishonored his $1,600.00, 9.5%, 60-day note dated May 13, Memorandum 601.*

Use demonstration problem 4-5 here.

Marsh owes Mayfaire both the $1,600.00 principal and interest of $24.99 ($1{,}600.00 \times .095 \times \frac{60}{365}$). In the transaction, the Notes Receivable Past Due account is debited for $1,624.99, the total amount due on the note. Notes Receivable is credited for $1,600.00 to remove the dishonored note from the account. The Interest Income account is credited for $24.99 even though Marsh didn't pay the interest. As you know, revenue is recorded when it is earned rather than when it is received.

Notes Receivable Past Due	
Dr.	Cr.
$1,624.99	

Notes Receivable	
Dr.	Cr.
Bal. $1,600.00	$1,600.00

Interest Income	
Dr.	Cr.
	$24.99

This transaction is recorded in the general journal as shown in Figure 4-6.

GENERAL JOURNAL PAGE 18

	DATE		DESCRIPTION	POST. REF.	DEBIT	CREDIT	
1	199- July	12	Notes Receivable Past Due		1,624 99		1
2			Notes Receivable			1,600 00	2
3			Interest Income			24 99	3
4			Memo. 601				4

Figure 4-6 Journalizing a Dishonored Note Receivable

Mayfaire should continue to try to collect the amount due from Marsh. If Marsh eventually pays the dishonored note, the transaction will be recorded as a debit to Cash in Bank and a credit to Notes Receivable Past Due.

Use T accounts to analyze how to write off the past-due note that a company determines is uncollectible.

If Mayfaire determines that Marsh will not pay the note, it must write off the note as uncollectible. Most businesses record the transaction as a debit to Bad Debts Expense and a credit to Notes Receivable Past Due.

R — E — M — E — M — B — E — R

The Notes Receivable account is used to record notes that have not yet matured. The amount recorded in the Notes Receivable Past Due account is the maturity value of the dishonored note.

Discounting Notes Receivable

Emphasize the meaning of the terms *bank discount* and *proceeds.*

Review the formula for finding the proceeds.

Principal
+ Interest
Maturity Value
− Bank Discount
Proceeds

One advantage a business gets from accepting notes receivable is that it can sell the notes to a bank for cash rather than holding them until maturity. This practice is known as **discounting notes receivable.**

To discount a note, the business endorses the note and delivers it to the bank. The bank discounts the note by deducting its share of the interest in advance. Then the bank gives the remaining amount to the business. The amount deducted in advance is called the **bank discount.** The amount the business actually receives is called the **proceeds** —the maturity value minus the bank discount. The bank holds the note until the note becomes due and collects the maturity value directly from the maker of the note.

Recording a Discounted Note Receivable

On July 15, Mayfaire accepted a 10%, 60-day note for $1,800.00 from Tom Kite. It expects to receive $1,829.59, the $1,800.00 principal plus interest of $29.59 ($\$1{,}800.00 \times .10 \times \frac{60}{365}$), on the maturity date, September 13. However, on July 30 Mayfaire discounted the note to raise cash to buy additional merchandise.

July 30: *Discounted the Kite note receivable at the Paradise Valley Bank, discount rate 10.5%, Receipt 1563.*

Before the transaction can be recorded, the bank discount must be determined. The amount of the bank discount is based on the maturity value of the note and on the amount of time between the discount date and the maturity date of the note. This period of time is called the **discount period.** The discount period is determined by subtracting the number of days the business held the note from the number of days in the term of the note. As you can see in the following diagram, the discount period is 45 days (July 30 to September 13).

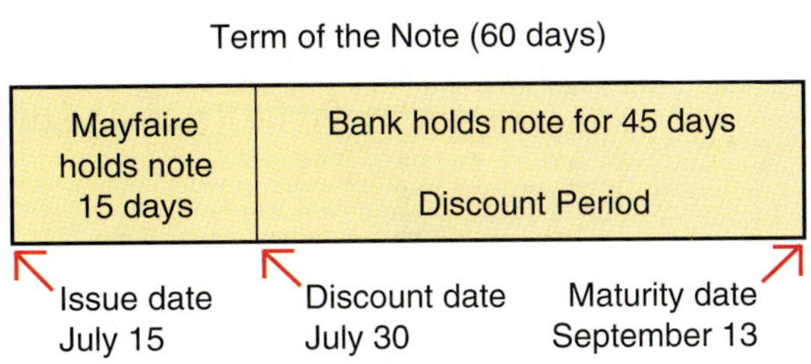

The amount of the bank discount is calculated in the same way as the interest; however, the maturity value of the note is the principal, the discount rate is the interest rate, and the discount period is used in the time fraction, as follows:

Maturity Value (Principal)	×	Discount Rate (Interest Rate)	×	Discount Period (Time)	=	Bank Discount (Interest)
$1,829.59	×	.105	×	$\frac{45}{365}$	=	$23.68

$1,829.59
– 23.68
$1,805.91

The amount of the proceeds is found by subtracting the bank discount from the maturity value. Mayfaire thus received $1,805.91 cash when it discounted the note. This transaction can now be journalized.

Cash in Bank	
Dr.	Cr.
$1,805.91	

Interest Income	
Dr.	Cr.
	$5.91

Notes Receivable Discounted	
Dr.	Cr.
	$1,800.00

Use demonstration problems 4-6 and 4-7 here.

Discuss why the Notes Receivable Discounted account is a contra asset account.

Stress the idea of book value of notes receivable.

Cash in Bank is debited for $1,805.91, the amount of the proceeds. Notice that the proceeds amount is greater than the face value of the note. The difference represents interest income to Mayfaire. The Interest Income account, therefore, is credited for $5.91. The face value of the note, $1,800.00, is credited to an account called Notes Receivable Discounted. Notes Receivable Discounted is a contra asset account and has a normal credit balance. It is used to report the face value of all discounted notes receivable. It is also used to determine the book value of notes receivable. It appears, therefore, on the balance sheet as a deduction from Notes Receivable. The transaction would be recorded as shown in Figure 4-7.

CASH RECEIPTS JOURNAL — PAGE 22

	DATE		DOC. NO.	ACCOUNT TITLE	POST. REF.	GENERAL DEBIT	GENERAL CREDIT	SALES CREDIT	SALES TAX PAYABLE CREDIT	ACCOUNTS RECEIVABLE CREDIT	CASH IN BANK DEBIT	
20	199– July	30	R1563	Notes Rec. Discounted			1 800 00				1 805 91	20
21				Interest Income			5 91					21

Figure 4-7 Journalizing a Discounted Note Receivable

As you just saw, if the proceeds are greater than the face value of the note, the difference represents interest *income*; if the proceeds are less than the face value, the difference represents interest *expense*. That expense would be debited to the Interest Expense account.

R — E — M — E — M — B — E — R

Notes Receivable Discounted is a contra asset account and has a normal credit balance.

Before reading further, do the following activity to check your understanding of discounting notes receivable.

Check Your Learning

On August 9, the Franklin Company received a 90-day, 10% note for $2,000, dated August 9, from Armco Metals. On September 8, Franklin discounted the note at its bank at 9.5%. Determine the following facts:

1. Number of days the Franklin Company held the note.
2. Number of days in the discount period.
3. Maturity value of the note.
4. Bank discount.
5. Proceeds.
6. Interest income or expense recorded by the Franklin Company.

Compare your answers to those in the answers section. Reread the preceding part of the chapter to find the correct answers for any items you may have missed.

Have students complete Exercise 4-2 at this point.

Contingent Liability

Explain that contingent means likely but not certain to occur.

Discuss the importance of endorsements and what they mean in business.

When Mayfaire discounted Tom Kite's note at the bank, it had to endorse the note. By that endorsement, Mayfaire agreed to pay the note when it became due if Tom Kite did not pay. Mayfaire's promise to pay the note is called a **contingent liability.** The liability of the endorser (Mayfaire) is contingent on (depends on) the possible dishonoring of the note by the maker (Kite). In other words, if Kite dishonors the note, Mayfaire is liable to the bank for the note's maturity value.

It is for this reason that accountants report discounted notes in the Notes Receivable Discounted account. A note cannot simply be removed from the Notes Receivable account when it is discounted. Because contingent liabilities may become actual liabilities, they affect the endorser's credit standing. Therefore, when a note is discounted, the contingent liability should appear in the accounts and on the endorser's balance sheet. By showing Notes Receivable Discounted on the balance sheet as a deduction from Notes Receivable, a reader of the balance sheet can see that contingent liability.

Ask students what the word *conservative* means.

This practice is an example of the accounting guideline of conservatism. **Conservatism** is one of the fundamental guidelines of accounting. To be conservative is to take the safe route. In reporting the financial position of a business, it is best to present amounts that are least likely to overstate income or assets.

When a discounted note receivable matures, the bank collects the maturity value directly from the maker. When the maker pays the bank, the endorser no longer has a contingent liability. The note, therefore, can be removed from the endorser's accounting records. In the Kite note example, Mayfaire would make an entry on September 13 debiting Notes Receivable Discounted for $1,800 and crediting Notes Receivable for $1,800, as shown in Figure 4-8.

GENERAL JOURNAL — PAGE 20

	DATE		DESCRIPTION	POST. REF.	DEBIT	CREDIT	
1	199– Sept.	13	Notes Receivable Discounted		1800 00		1
2			Notes Receivable			1800 00	2
3			Memo: 626				3

Figure 4-8 Removing a Paid Discounted Note Receivable from the Accounting Records

Dishonor of a Discounted Note Receivable

Suppose the maker dishonors (fails to pay) the discounted note. The bank can formally demand that the endorser pay the note because of the contingent liability. It does so by preparing and mailing to the endorser a *notice of dishonor and protest.* This notice identifies the note and states that the note was presented to the maker for payment and payment was refused. In addition to the maturity value, the endorser usually must pay a fee, known as a **protest fee.** A protest fee is similar to a bank charge for an NSF check.

Let's go back to the Kite note, which Mayfaire had discounted on July 31. Suppose Tom Kite dishonored the note. On September 13, the bank issued a notice of dishonor and protest and added a protest fee of $15.00. Mayfaire now owes the bank a total of $1,844.59 ($1,800.00 principal + $29.59 interest + $15.00 protest fee). Mayfaire is no longer *contingently* liable; it is *actually* liable.

Analyze the transactions using T accounts.

Two journal entries are required for the dishonored discounted note receivable. Since the note has been dishonored, it must be removed from the Notes Receivable Discounted account. The dishonored note must also be removed from the Notes Receivable account. See Figure 4-8.

Use demonstration problem 4-8 here.

In the second entry, the payment of the dishonored note receivable and protest fee is recorded and the note receivable is reclassified. In this entry, shown in Figure 4-9, the maturity value of the note, $1,829.59, is debited to the Notes Receivable Past Due account. Some businesses consider the protest fee charged by the bank as an administrative expense. Therefore, the $15.00 is debited to Miscellaneous Expense. Cash in Bank is credited for $1,844.59, the total amount paid out.

CASH PAYMENTS JOURNAL — PAGE 24

	DATE		DOC. NO.	ACCOUNT TITLE	POST. REF.	GENERAL DEBIT	GENERAL CREDIT	ACCOUNTS PAYABLE DEBIT	PURCHASES DISCOUNTS CREDIT	CASH IN BANK CREDIT	
	199–										
16	Sept.	13	C6472	Notes Receivable Past Due		1829 54				1844 59	16
17				Miscellaneous Expense		15 00					17

Figure 4-9 Journalizing the Payment of a Dishonored Discounted Note Receivable

The Accrual Basis of Accounting

A business's transactions don't always fit neatly within a fiscal period. Businesses buy merchandise when they need it; customers, in turn, buy merchandise when they want it. Sometimes these transactions extend from one fiscal period into the next. For example, a customer buys merchandise on account on December 20 but does not pay for it until January 20, during the next fiscal period. For a business's accounting records to be accurate, revenue should be reported when it is earned, regardless of when cash is received; expenses should be reported in the fiscal period in which they are incurred, regardless of when they are paid. Thus, most businesses use the accrual basis of accounting. The **accrual basis of accounting** recognizes revenue when it is earned and expenses when they are incurred. With this method, adjusting entries are used to account for transactions that affect more than one accounting period.

Explain that the word *accrue* means to increase, build up, or accumulate.

R — E — M — E — M — B — E — R

With the accrual basis of accounting, revenue is recorded when it is earned and expenses are recorded in the accounting period in which they are incurred.

Adjusting for Accrued Interest

You have learned that the payee of a promissory note receives interest, usually on the maturity date. To the payee, this interest is revenue. When a promissory note matures in the same fiscal period it is issued, there is no problem; the interest income is recorded in the period in which it is earned. A problem arises, however, when a promissory note is issued in one fiscal period but does not mature until the next fiscal period.

Let's look at an example. The fiscal period of Mayfaire, Inc., ends on December 31. On December 1, Mayfaire accepted a $500, 90-day, 9% note receivable from Paula Mays, a charge customer. The note was issued on December 1 and will mature on March 1. When the note was issued, it was recorded as a debit of $500 to Notes Receivable and a $500 credit to Accounts Receivable and Paula Mays' account in the subsidiary ledger.

TERM

- Issue date: December 1
- End of fiscal period: December 31
- Maturity date: March 1

On December 31 (the end of its fiscal period), Mayfaire has *earned* 30 days of interest on the note. In accounting, revenue that has been earned but not yet received and recorded is called **accrued revenue**. Mayfaire's accounting records should reflect this accrued interest. An adjusting entry must be made on December 31 to record the amount of interest income earned during the period. The amount of accrued interest is calculated as follows:

Principal	×	Interest Rate	×	Time	=	Interest
$500.00	×	.09	×	$\frac{30}{365}$	=	$3.70

Review how time was determined in these interest calculations.

In the adjusting entry, the $3.70 is debited to an asset account titled Interest Receivable. Interest Income is credited for $3.70, the amount of interest earned on the note in the current fiscal period.

Interest Receivable

Dr.	Cr.
Adj. $3.70	

Interest Income

Dr.	Cr.
	Bal. $285.17
	Adj. $3.70

Figure 4-10 shows the adjusting entry.

GENERAL JOURNAL — PAGE 21

	DATE		DESCRIPTION	POST. REF.	DEBIT	CREDIT	
1			Adjusting Entries				1
2	199- Dec.	31	Interest Receivable		3 70		2
3			Interest Income			3 70	3

Figure 4-10 Adjusting Entry for Accrued Interest Income

The accrued interest on the note receivable will be reported on the income statement as "other revenue." When the closing entries are made, Interest Income will be closed into Income Summary. The $3.70 reported in the Interest Receivable account will remain there until the note is paid on the maturity date.

You may want to complete Exercise 4-3 at this point.

R — E — M — E — M — B — E — R

An adjusting entry must be made at the end of the fiscal period for revenue that has accrued but has not yet been received and recorded.

Receiving Cash for Accrued Interest

On March 1, Mayfaire received a check from Paula Mays for the maturity value of the note. The maturity value is calculated as follows:

$$\text{Principal} \times \text{Interest Rate} \times \text{Time} = \text{Interest}$$
$$\$500.00 \times .09 \times \frac{90}{365} = \$11.10$$

The maturity value is, therefore, $511.10 ($500.00 + $11.10).

March 1: *Received a check for $511.10 from Paula Mays in full payment of the note dated December 1, Receipt 2110.*

In this transaction, Cash in Bank is debited for $511.10, the total amount of cash received. The collection of the note reduces the balance in the Notes Receivable account, so that account is credited for $500.00. The total amount of interest earned for 90 days is $11.10. However, $3.70 of that interest was earned and reported in the last fiscal period. The interest earned during the current fiscal period is $7.40 ($11.10 – $3.70). Interest Income is credited for $7.40. Because the accrued interest has now been collected, Interest Receivable is credited for $3.70.

Be sure students understand why only $7.40 was credited to Interest Income.

Cash in Bank

Dr.	Cr.
$511.10	

Interest Income

Dr.	Cr.
	$7.40

Interest Receivable

Dr.	Cr.
Adj. $3.70	$3.70

Notes Receivable

Dr.	Cr.
Bal. $500.00	$500.00

Figure 4-11 shows the entry to record the collection of the note.

CASH RECEIPTS JOURNAL PAGE 30

	DATE		DOC. NO.	ACCOUNT TITLE	POST. REF.	GENERAL DEBIT	GENERAL CREDIT	SALES CREDIT	SALES TAX PAYABLE CREDIT	ACCOUNTS RECEIVABLE CREDIT	CASH IN BANK DEBIT	
1	199- Mar.	1	R2110	Notes Receivable			500 00				511 10	1
2				Interest Receivable			3 70					2
3				Interest Income			7 40					3

Figure 4-11 Recording the Collection of Accrued Interest

Drafts and Trade Acceptances

Businesses use other documents that are similar to notes. These documents include drafts and trade acceptances. A **draft** is an order by one party (the drawer) to another party (the drawee) to pay a certain sum of money to a third party (the payee). A check is an example of a draft. In essence, a draft is a means of easily transferring money from one person or firm to another. Drafts are similar to notes in that they are normally negotiable.

For example, suppose a business sells merchandise to a customer it does not know well. The business can prepare a draft and attach it to a bill of lading for the merchandise. (A *bill of lading* is a document prepared by the transporting company, such as a trucking firm.) The customer can obtain the merchandise only by paying the draft, usually to a bank. Then the bank sends the amount collected to the business. The business can handle the transaction as a cash sale. It can also treat the transaction as a sale on account when the merchandise is shipped, followed by a cash receipt. The buyer records the transaction as a cash purchase.

When one party orders another to pay a certain sum of money at some later date and the second party agrees to do so in writing on the face of the instrument, that instrument in effect becomes a note. Documents of this type are known as **trade acceptances** and are accounted for in the same manner as notes. Normally, trade acceptances do not involve interest. If they are discounted, however, they are handled like non-interest-bearing notes.

Summary of Key Points

1. A promissory note is a written promise to pay a certain sum of money on demand or on a specified date.
2. Interest is the fee charged for the use of money. The equation for calculating interest is Interest = Principal × Interest Rate × Time. The interest rate is expressed as a percentage of the principal. Time is stated in terms of one year or a fraction of one year.

3. The maturity value of an interest-bearing note equals the principal plus the interest.
4. A note receivable is a promissory note accepted by a business. Notes Receivable is a current asset account.
5. A dishonored note is a note that is not paid or renewed at maturity. A dishonored note is removed from the Notes Receivable account and debited to the Notes Receivable Past Due account.
6. Notes receivable may be sold to a bank for cash; this procedure is known as discounting notes receivable. The bank discount is the amount deducted in advance by the bank. The amount of cash the business actually receives is called the proceeds.
7. Discounted notes are recorded in the Notes Receivable Discounted account, which is a contra asset account. It is reported on the balance sheet as a deduction from Notes Receivable.
8. The accrual basis of accounting recognizes revenue when it is earned and expenses when they are incurred.
9. Accrued revenue is revenue that has been earned but not yet received and recorded.

4 Review and Applications

Reviewing Your Accounting Vocabulary

In your own words, write the definition of each of the following accounting terms. Use complete sentences for your definitions.

accrual basis of accounting
accrued revenue
bank discount
conservatism
contingent liability
discount period
discounting notes receivable
dishonored note
draft
face value
interest
interest rate
interest-bearing note
issue date
maker
maturity date
maturity value
notes receivable
payee
principal
proceeds
promissory note
protest fee
term
trade acceptances

Reviewing Your Accounting Knowledge

1. Why is a promissory note more acceptable than a charge account?
2. How is interest calculated?
3. When might a business accept a note receivable?
4. What type of account is Notes Receivable Past Due? What amounts are entered in this account?
5. How are the proceeds calculated when a note receivable is discounted?
6. How is the Notes Receivable Discounted account classified? How and why is it reported on the balance sheet?
7. If the proceeds of a discounted note receivable are greater than the note's face value, what does the difference represent? In which account is the difference recorded?
8. Explain the contingent liability of the endorser of a note.
9. When a discounted note receivable is dishonored, what amount is recorded in the Notes Receivable Past Due account?
10. Why must an adjusting entry be made for interest that has accrued on a note receivable?

Improving Your Communications Skills

In business correspondence, it is always better to use specific rather than general terms. By being specific, you relay a stronger message and decrease the risk of misunderstandings. Rewrite the following phrases using more specific wording.

1. as soon as possible
2. some office furniture
3. sometime next month
4. at our branch office
5. this new employee
6. call Mr. Ramsay at his extension
7. comes in four colors
8. please contact me
9. business increased considerably
10. in business for a long time

Applying Accounting Procedures

SPREADSHEET PROBLEM

Exercise 4-1 Calculating Maturity Values

Instructions: Calculate the interest and the maturity value for each of the following notes.

$156.82; $10,756.82
$201.21; $5,301.21
$201.11; $7,451.11
$31.23; $1,931.23
$159.66; $3,859.66
$371.59; $7,221.59

	Principal	Interest Rate	Term
1.	$10,600	9%	60 days
2.	$ 5,100	12%	120 days
3.	$ 7,250	11.25%	90 days
4.	$ 1,900	8%	75 days
5.	$ 3,700	10.5%	150 days
6.	$ 6,850	11%	180 days

Exercise 4-2 Determining the Discount Period

Instructions: Determine the maturity date and the discount period for each of the following notes receivable. Assume February has 28 days.

Feb. 8; 88 days
Apr. 27; 73 days
Feb. 4 ; 33 days
May 17; 17 days
Feb. 27; 140 days
Nov. 25; 95 days

	Issue Date	Term	Discount Date
1.	October 11	120 days	November 12
2.	January 27	90 days	February 13
3.	December 6	60 days	January 2
4.	April 2	45 days	April 30
5.	August 31	180 days	October 10
6.	June 28	150 days	August 22

Exercise 4-3 Calculating Accrued Interest Income

Instructions: Determine the amount of the adjusting entry for accrued interest income on the following notes receivable. The fiscal period ends on December 31.

$ 14.05
167.81
15.04
11.84
29.11
463.62

	Principal	Interest Rate	Issue Date	Term
1.	$ 6,000	9.5%	December 22	90 days
2.	$12,500	10%	November 12	60 days
3.	$ 750	12%	October 31	120 days
4.	$ 1,300	8.75%	November 23	70 days
5.	$ 4,200	11%	December 8	45 days
6.	$16,350	9%	September 7	180 days

Problem 4-1 Journalizing the Issuance and Collection of a Note Receivable

The following transactions were among those completed by Murray Enterprises during the year.

Instructions: Record the transactions in the sales journal (page 13), cash receipts journal (page 19), and general journal (page 15).

Transactions:

Jan. 10 Sold merchandise on account to Bo-Jax Stores, $8,000, plus sales tax, $400. Sales Slip 1109.

Feb. 4 Received a 60-day, 10%, $8,400 note dated February 4 from Bo-Jax Stores to replace the amount recorded as an account receivable, Note 72.

Apr. 5 Received a $8,538.08 check from Bo-Jax Stores for the maturity value of the note issued February 4, Receipt 1155.

Problem 4-2 Accounting for a Dishonored Note Receivable

Jackson Lumber Center had the following transactions during the current year.

Instructions: Record the transactions on page 42 of a general journal.

Transactions:

Aug. 20 Accepted a 90-day, 8% note receivable (Note 103) for merchandise sold to Lynn Fredericks, $5,000 plus $250 sales tax.

Nov. 18 Lynn Fredericks dishonored the note receivable dated August 20, Memorandum 74.

Problem 4-3 Discounting a Note Receivable

Gateway Computer Systems had the following transactions during this fiscal period.

Instructions: Record the transactions on page 41 of a cash receipts journal and page 33 of a general journal.

Transactions:

June 20 Received a 90-day, 9.5%, $6,600 note dated June 20 from Roy & Company, CPAs (a charge customer) in payment of the amount recorded as an account receivable, Note 92.

July 16 Discounted the Roy & Company note at Dollar Bank at a discount rate of 11%, Receipt 180.

Sept. 2 Charge customer Boulder Glen Designs sent a $2,600 promissory note (Note 93) to replace its accounts receivable account. The term of the note was 120 days, and the interest rate was 9.25%.

18 Received notice from Dollar Bank that Roy & Company, CPAs, had paid the bank the maturity value of the note dated June 20. Removed the discounted note from the accounting records, Memorandum 260.

Oct. 27 Discounted Note 93 at Dollar Bank at a 10.75% discount rate, Receipt 219.

Problem 4-4 Accounting for a Dishonored Discounted Note Receivable

During the current year, Creative Productions completed the following transactions.

Instructions: Record the transactions in the cash receipts journal (page 36), cash payments journal (page 59), and general journal (page 47).

Transactions:

May 17 Accepted a 120-day, 8.75%, $3,400 note receivable, dated May 17, from Giles, Inc., in place of its accounts receivable amount, Note 23.

July 6 Discounted Note 23 at the Tri-County Bank at a 9.5% discount rate, Receipt 453.

Sept. 14 Received notice from Tri-County Bank that Giles, Inc., had dishonored its note on the maturity date. Tri-County charged Creative Productions a $25 protest fee. Removed the dishonored note receivable from the accounting records (Memorandum 92) and recorded the payment of the note plus the interest and the protest fee (Check 753).

Problem 4-5 Accounting for Accrued Interest Income

Dyna-Tech Computer Services accepted an 11.25%, 60-day note receivable, dated November 10, for $7,500 from Anderson Farm Products in return for Anderson's past-due account receivable.

Instructions: On cash receipts journal page 71 and general journal page 88,

(1) Record the receipt of the note on November 10 (Note 38).
(2) Record the December 31 adjusting entry for the accrued interest income on Note 38.
(3) Record the collection of Note 38 on the maturity date (Receipt 270).

COMPUTER PROBLEM

Problem 4-6 Journalizing Notes Receivable Transactions

Following are some of the transactions carried out by McKee Equipment Corporation this year.

Instructions: Record the transactions in the appropriate journals.

Transactions:

Jan. 12 Received word from Keystone Bank that Tim Norris had paid off his $3,000 note receivable, which had been discounted in December. Removed the note from the accounting records, Memorandum 21.

Mar. 17 Sold merchandise on account to Ken Still, $4,800 plus sales tax of $288, Sales Slip 302.

Apr. 4 Accepted a 90-day, 12% promissory note for $5,088 from Ken Still in place of his account receivable account, Note 12.

May 5 Discounted the Still note at the Keystone Bank at 14%, Receipt 412.

June 15 Sold merchandise to John Inman ($2,000 plus sales tax of $120) and received a 60-day, 11% note in return, Note 13.

July 3 Keystone Bank notified us that Ken Still dishonored his note (Note 12). The bank charged a $10 protest fee. Recorded the necessary entries, Memorandum 25/Check 441.

Aug.	1	Accepted a $1,500, 11%, 180-day note from Stevens Corporation for the amount recorded as an account receivable, Note 14.
	14	Received a check from John Inman for the maturity value of Note 13, Receipt 550.
Dec.	31	Recorded the accrued interest income on Note 14.

CHALLENGE PROBLEM

Problem 4-7 Accounting for Notes Receivable

You are the bookkeeper for Lamar Office Furniture Company. On March 17, Lamar sold merchandise totaling $8,250 to Benson Medical Center (Sales Slip 4116). The credit terms were 3/10, n/45, and there was a 5% sales tax. On May 15, Lamar accepted a 60-day, 13% note from Benson Medical Center in place of the past-due amount (Note 22). On May 30, Lamar discounted Benson's note at the Huntington Bank at 14.5% (Receipt 11351).

On July 15, Lamar received notice that Benson Medical Center had dishonored its note and the bank was charging a protest fee of $30 (Memorandum 978).

On December 28, Lamar determined that Benson would not pay its note. The note was therefore written off as uncollectible (Memorandum 1185).

Instructions: Record the transactions for March 17, May 15 and 30, July 15, and December 28 in the appropriate journals. Lamar uses the direct write-off method to account for uncollectible notes.

FOCUS ON ETHICS

Computers Point the Finger at Poor Credit Risks

Imagine this: You have a perfect driving record. You're careful. You don't take chances. Yet when you get your auto insurance bill, it's sky-high. Why? Insurers have to charge all drivers more to make up for the losses they suffer when bad drivers get into accidents.

Times are changing, though. It's now possible for insurers to identify bad drivers—even if those drivers have been in accidents in other states or while covered by other insurers—by a process known as *online sleuthing*.

Online sleuthing is the use of specialized databases to locate specific information about individuals. Various database services allow businesses like banks, insurance companies, and real estate firms, as well as individuals—detectives and government agents, for example—to find out information such as credit histories, financial profiles, driving records, medical histories, residence changes, and criminal and legal records.

The information gained from a database search can help banks decide who should get a loan, law firms determine whether potential partners are good risks, drug enforcement agencies track down drug traffickers, and insurance companies locate people with less-than-perfect driving records.

Although many people believe that such sleuthing is a breech of privacy, those who use the information argue that more good than harm comes from its use. To customers of any retail or wholesale business, for example, online sleuthing means not having to pay the bad debts expense created by others that is reflected in higher prices paid by the good-risk customers.

Database services allow businesses to identify potential good-risk customers.

Chapter 5

INVENTORIES AND INVESTMENTS

A merchandising business earns revenue by selling merchandise. In terms of dollars, Merchandise Inventory is usually a merchandising business's largest current asset. Also, because merchandise is continually being bought and sold, the cost of merchandise sold is the largest deduction from net sales. Accounting for merchandise, then, is extremely important.

In Unit 1, you saw how to account for the purchase and sale of merchandise. You also learned how to adjust Merchandise Inventory at the end of the fiscal period. In this chapter, you will learn how businesses determine the quantity of merchandise on hand and how they assign a cost value to the ending merchandise inventory.

Learning Objectives

When you have completed this chapter, you should be able to do the following:

1. Explain the importance of inventory valuation.
2. Explain the difference between a periodic and a perpetual inventory system.
3. Determine the cost of the ending merchandise inventory using the following methods: specific identification; first in, first out; last in, first out; and weighted average cost.
4. Assign a value to Merchandise Inventory using the lower-of-cost-or-market rule.
5. Explain why a business estimates its inventory.
6. Estimate the cost of the ending inventory using two common methods.
7. Define the accounting terms presented in this chapter.

New Terms

periodic inventory system
perpetual inventory system
specific identification method
first in, first out method (fifo)
last in, first out method (lifo)
weighted average cost method
market value
retail method
markup
gross profit method
investments

Merchandise Inventory

Briefly review the Purchases, Sales, and Merchandise Inventory accounts.

To provide a realistic financial picture, it is important for a business to determine the quantity and cost value of the merchandise it has on hand. Merchandise Inventory is the only account that appears on the two major financial statements—the balance sheet and the income statement. On the balance sheet, it appears in the Current Assets section. In many businesses, Merchandise Inventory is the current asset with the largest dollar amount. On the income statement, the beginning and ending inventories are used to determine the cost of merchandise sold. The cost of merchandise sold is usually the largest deduction from sales; therefore, the amounts reported for Merchandise Inventory affect the net income. Determining the quantity and cost of the inventory, then, is important in matching costs with revenue.

Managing the Inventory

Emphasize the importance of accurate inventory information for a business to operate efficiently and effectively.

To be successful, businesses must control the size and variety of their inventories. For efficient operation, a business needs to manage its inventory system to obtain information such as the amount of mechandise on hand at a given time, the cost of that merchandise, which items are selling (or not selling), and the proper amount of merchandise to have on hand.

An inventory that is too small or too large will cause problems for the business. If the inventory is too small, customers won't have enough variety and choice. They will go elsewhere, resulting in lost sales.

If the inventory is too large, different problems will arise. First, the business will have used a great deal of cash or credit power to purchase unneeded merchandise, leaving that cash or credit unavailable for other purposes. Second, the excess merchandise increases storage and insurance costs. Third, the surplus merchandise may lose its value when consumers turn to newer, better, or less expensive brands. To dispose of it, the business may have to sell it at a loss—and, if styles change, it may be difficult to sell the merchandise at all.

With the proper inventory control system, a business should be able to maintain an inventory sufficient to satisfy customers' needs. It should also be able to determine when and which items need to be reordered to prevent running out of them. The business will also be better able to take advantage of discounts and special sales offered by suppliers.

Determining the Quantity of Inventories

Businesses use two methods to determine the quantity of merchandise on hand: the periodic inventory system and the perpetual inventory system.

The Periodic Inventory System

Emphasize that this is a physical count.

Many merchandising businesses have no record of the exact quantity and cost of merchandise they have on hand at a given time. They do make spot checks from time to time as part of inventory control, but they can determine exact amounts only by physically counting the goods on hand. An inventory system in which the amount of goods on hand is determined by periodically counting them is known as the **periodic inventory system.**

Have students who have participated in a periodic inventory on a job to describe what they did.

A *physical inventory*—an actual count of the merchandise on hand—is usually taken when the amount of merchandise is at its lowest level. Many department stores, for example, take a physical inventory at the end of January, after the holiday rush and post-holiday sales. The inventory data is recorded on inventory sheets such as the one shown for Plaza Shoes in Figure 5-1.

PLAZA SHOES
Sporting Goods Department
Inventory Sheet

Page 1 Date 9/30/- - Clerk T. Maxwell

Stock No.	Item	Unit	Quantity	Unit Cost	Total Value	
K4312	L & T Low Cuts	Pr	15	19.50	292	50
M1149	King Mid-high Shoes	Pr	12	17.00	204	00
A9267	Speed Joggers	Pr	19	22.40	425	60
C1852	Kite Mid-highs	Pr	8	21.00	168	00

Figure 5-1 Inventory Sheet Used in a Periodic Inventory System

Ask students if they have seen or used these.

Today many businesses use electronic equipment when taking a physical inventory. The person taking the inventory simply enters the stock number of each item and the amount still on hand into a hand-held computer. When the physical count of all items in stock is completed, the computer prepares an up-to-date printout of the inventory items.

ACCOUNTING Notes
Accounting data stored on computer disks can easily be lost or destroyed. An employee can accidentally erase a file; an equipment failure can destroy a file. For security, businesses keep duplicate backup copies of disks locked in a separate file or vault.

The Perpetual Inventory System

The increasing use of computers has enabled many businesses to maintain a perpetual inventory system. In a **perpetual inventory system,** the business keeps a constant, up-to-date record of the amount of merchandise on hand. Let's look at an example.

In many stores today, each type of inventory item has a product code number. When an item is sold, the code number, quantity, and selling price of the item are entered into an electronic cash register. The cash register is *online* with (linked directly to) a computer. The computer updates the inventory information in its memory and determines the new balance on hand. Similarly, when merchandise items are purchased, the purchase information is entered into the computer and the inventory

Name businesses that could operate on a perpetual inventory system.

Ask students if they know of any local businesses that have cash registers online with a computer.

records are updated automatically. With all this information stored in the computer, the business can determine quantities and costs for any given item at any point in time. The computer can also list the balances of all the items in the inventory, in both units and dollars. Some businesses that have their own computers or employ an independent information processing firm receive such a listing or printout daily.

A business that sells large items with a high unit cost may use a manual perpetual inventory system. An appliance dealer, for example, could easily maintain an inventory card for each type of appliance in stock. The unit cost and the number of units purchased and sold would be recorded on the card continuously. Figure 5-2 illustrates an inventory card that could be used in a manual perpetual inventory system.

Item: Speed Joggers
Stock No. : A9267

Date		Received			Sold			Balance		
		Units	Cost	Total	Units	Cost	Total	Units	Cost	Total
199- Sept.	1							24	22.40	537.60
	5				7	22.40	156.80	17	22.40	380.80
	6	100	22.40	2,240.00				117	22.40	2,620.80
	16				29	22.40	649.60	88	22.40	1,971.20

Figure 5-2 Inventory Card Used in a Perpetual Inventory System

Discuss the need to perform a physical count at least once a year.

Even though inventory records are updated continuously, a business that uses the perpetual inventory system must take a physical inventory at least once a year. It does so to verify the balances shown on the inventory cards or in the computer records and to detect any losses due to breakage, spoilage, theft, or other causes.

By knowing the value of inventory, businesses can determine losses in the event of a natural disaster.

Before reading further, do the following activity to check your understanding of periodic and perpetual inventory systems.

Check Your Learning

Write the answers to these questions on a sheet of notebook paper.

1. The balance of the Merchandise Inventory account is reported on the income statement in the ___?___ section and on the balance sheet in the ___?___ section.
2. A(n) ___?___ is an actual count of the inventory items on hand.
3. A ___?___ inventory system maintains an up-to-date record of the amount of merchandise on hand.
4. A cash register that is directly linked to a computer is said to be ___?___.

Compare your answers to those in the answers section. Reread the preceding part of the chapter to find the correct answers to any questions you may have missed.

Assigning Costs to the Ending Inventory

Mention that the cost of the item may go down. Have students discuss why this might happen.

After the inventory items have been counted, unit costs are assigned and the total cost of the inventory is calculated. How do you determine the unit costs to assign? You might think this would be rather easy. Indeed, it would be if all purchases of an item had been made for the same unit cost. Then you'd need only to look at one invoice, check the unit cost, and multiply it by the number of items on hand. Unfortunately, nothing is ever that simple. A business usually makes several purchases of a given item during the fiscal period, and the unit cost often varies from one purchase to another. A can of spray paint that costs $.90 in January may cost $.94 in March. So, which unit cost should be assigned to the merchandise on hand?

There are four commonly accepted methods of assigning costs to the merchandise in the ending inventory: (1) specific identification; (2) first in, first out; (3) last in, first out; and (4) weighted average cost.

The Specific Identification Costing Method

Point out that exact costs are the most accurate.

When a firm sells "big-ticket" items such as cars, appliances, or furniture, it can keep track of the cost of each individual item fairly easily. With the **specific identification method**, the actual cost of each item in the ending inventory is determined and assigned to the item. To determine the actual cost of an item, the business simply checks the purchase invoice. Let's look at an example.

Mayfaire, Inc., began the period with a beginning inventory of 22 pairs of Wallace Jogging Shoes. It had purchased those 22 pairs at a cost of $27 a pair. During the year, Mayfaire purchased 184 more pairs at the following prices:

Beginning inventory (January 1)	22 pairs @ $27.00 a pair =	$ 594.00
Purchased March 12	60 pairs @ $28.00 a pair =	1,680.00
Purchased July 26	75 pairs @ $32.00 a pair =	2,400.00
Purchased November 10	49 pairs @ $35.00 a pair =	1,715.00
Total pairs available	206 pairs	$6,389.00

Have students name different types of businesses that could use this method successfully.

When it took a physical inventory at the end of the year, Mayfaire found that it had 26 pairs left in stock. Of these 26 pairs, 12 had been bought in November, 10 in July, and 4 back in March. Using the specific identification method, Mayfaire could assign a cost to the ending inventory as follows:

4 pairs @ $28.00 a pair =	$112.00
10 pairs @ $32.00 a pair =	320.00
12 pairs @ $35.00 a pair =	420.00
26 pairs	$852.00

The cost of Mayfaire's ending inventory of Wallace Jogging Shoes, then, is $852.00. Mayfaire can determine the cost of merchandise sold by subtracting the cost of the ending inventory from the cost of the merchandise available for sale:

Total pairs available (206 pairs)	$6,389.00
Less ending inventory (26 pairs)	– 852.00
Cost of merchandise sold (180 pairs)	$5,537.00

R — E — M — E — M — B — E — R

The cost of merchandise sold is determined by subtracting the cost of the ending inventory from the cost of merchandise available for sale. The cost of merchandise available for sale is the value of the beginning inventory plus net purchases.

Have students complete Exercise 5-1 at this point.

The First In, First Out Costing Method

Mention that the acronym *fifo* is usually used when describing this method.

The **first in, first out method (fifo)** is based on the assumption that the first items purchased (first in) were the first items sold (first out). The items in the ending inventory, then, are those that were purchased last. First in, first out is a logical way for a firm to rotate its stock of merchandise. For example, think of the milk sold in a grocery store. Because milk will sour, the grocer puts the milk that was purchased first in the front of the shelves and places later purchases of milk behind the earlier purchases. At the end of the week, the inventory consists of the milk that was purchased most recently.

Let's apply the fifo method to the jogging shoes example. As you know, 206 pairs were available for sale during the year.

Beginning inventory (January 1)	22 pairs @ $27.00 a pair =	$ 594.00
Purchased March 12	60 pairs @ $28.00 a pair =	1,680.00
Purchased July 26	75 pairs @ $32.00 a pair =	2,400.00
Purchased November 10	49 pairs @ $35.00 a pair =	1,715.00
Total pairs available	206 pairs	$6,389.00

Point out that in this example, fifo yields an ending inventory amount higher than specific identification.

Mayfaire has 26 pairs on hand in the ending inventory. Using the fifo method, the ending inventory consists of the pairs purchased most recently. The 26 pairs on hand, then, were part of the November purchase. The cost of the ending inventory is calculated as follows:

26 pairs @ $35.00 a pair = $910.00

With an ending inventory of $910.00, the cost of merchandise sold under the fifo method is as follows:

Total pairs available (206 pairs)	$6,389.00
Less ending inventory (26 pairs)	– 910.00
Cost of merchandise sold (180 pairs)	$5,479.00

R — E — M — E — M — B — E — R

When assigning a cost to the inventory using the fifo method, the accountant assumes that the ending inventory consists of those items purchased most recently.

Have students complete Exercise 5-2 at this point.

Emphasize that in periods of rising costs, the lifo method will usually yield a lower ending inventory amount that the fifo method.

The Last In, First Out Costing Method

The **last in, first out method (lifo)** is based on the assumption that the most recently purchased articles are sold first. The articles in the ending inventory are those that were purchased first. Think of a business that sells coal. When the company buys coal from its supplier, the new coal is added to the top of the pile. When the company sells coal to its customers, coal is taken off the top of the pile. The ending inventory consists of those first few tons at the bottom of the pile.

Let's go back to the 26 pairs of Wallace Jogging Shoes in the ending inventory. Using the lifo method, the items in the ending inventory consist of 22 pairs that were in the beginning inventory and 4 of the pairs purchased in March. The cost of the ending inventory is calculated as follows:

22 pairs @ $27.00 a pair =	$594.00
4 pairs @ $28.00 a pair =	112.00
26 pairs	$706.00

The cost of mechandise sold using the lifo method is as follows:

Total pairs available (206 pairs)	$6,389.00
Less ending inventory (26 pairs)	– 706.00
Cost of merchandise sold (180 pairs)	$5,683.00

R — E — M — E — M — B — E — R

You may want to complete Exercise 5-3 at this point.

When costing inventory with the lifo method, the accountant assumes that the ending inventory consists of those items purchased first.

The Weighted Average Cost Method

Discuss the concept of average cost.

An alternative to keeping track of the cost of each item purchased is to use the weighted average cost method. With the **weighted average cost method,** the cost of the ending inventory is determined by assigning an average unit cost to all like items in the ending inventory. The weighted average cost method is often used by companies that deal in fluids such as oil. It makes sense to average the costs because separate purchases are usually mixed together.

Let's see how an average unit cost is calculated using the jogging shoes example. First, Mayfaire determines the total cost of the Wallace Jogging Shoes it had available for sale during the year:

22 pairs	@ $27.00 a pair =	$ 594.00
60 pairs	@ $28.00 a pair =	1,680.00
75 pairs	@ $32.00 a pair =	2,400.00
49 pairs	@ $35.00 a pair =	1,715.00
206 pairs		$6,389.00

Explain that the weighted average cost method usually yields an amount between the lifo and fifo amounts.

Next, Mayfaire calculates the average cost per pair by dividing the total cost of mechandise available for sale by the total pairs available for sale:

$$\frac{\$6{,}389.00}{206 \text{ pairs}} = \$31.02 \text{ (average cost per pair)}$$

To find the value of the ending inventory, Mayfaire multiplies the average cost per pair of $31.01 by the number of pairs in the ending inventory as follows:

$$26 \text{ pairs} \times \$31.02 = \$806.52$$

The cost of merchandise sold using the weighted average cost method is determined as follows:

Total pairs available (206 pairs)	$6,389.00
Less ending inventory (26 pairs)	– 806.52
Cost of merchandise sold (180 pairs)	$5,582.48

Have students complete Exercise 5-4 here.

When this method is used, the cost of the ending inventory is affected by the number of units purchased at each price. In other words, the more units purchased at one price, the more influence—or weight—that purchase price has on the average cost.

Before reading further, do the following activity to check your understanding of how to calculate inventory costs.

Check Your Learning

Use demonstration problem 5-1 here to compare and contrast the fifo, lifo, and weighted average methods.

The Ling Company's beginning inventory of pens on July 1 consisted of 28 units purchased at $4.00 each. Purchases and sales during July were as follows:

July	2	Sold 13 units
	8	Purchased 10 units @ $4.08
	13	Sold 19 units
	20	Purchased 24 units @ $4.15
	29	Sold 11 units

1. How many units are in the ending inventory?
2. Determine the cost of the ending inventory using the specific identification method. Of the units on hand at the end of the month, 4 were purchased on July 8, 6 were purchased on July 20, and the remaining units were included in the beginning inventory.
3. Calculate the cost of the ending inventory of pens using the fifo and lifo methods.

Compare your answers to those in the answers section. Reread the preceding part of the chapter to find the correct answers to any questions you may have missed.

Comparing Inventory Methods

If prices don't change very much, all four inventory costing methods give just about the same results. In a market in which prices are constantly rising and falling, however, each method yields different amounts. The following table compares the gross profit on the sale of the jogging shoes using the four methods.

	Specific Identification	First In, First Out	Last In, First Out	Weighted Average Cost
Sales (@ $55.00 a pair)	$9,900.00	$9,900.00	$9,900.00	$9,900.00
Cost of Merchandise Sold	5,537.00	5,479.00	5,683.00	5,582.74
Gross Profit on Sales	$4,363.00	$4,421.00	$4,217.00	$4,317.26

The effects of the four methods are as follows:

Discuss each of these effects to be sure students understand.

1. Because the actual cost is determined for each item in the ending inventory, the specific identification method matches costs exactly with revenue.
2. Fifo is the most realistic method for determining the value of ending inventory, because inventory is valued at the most recent costs.
3. In a period of rising prices, lifo yields the smallest gross profit and, therefore, the smallest taxable income. This is a definite tax advantage for many businesses because prices are generally rising. If prices fell, lifo would become a disadvantage.

4. Weighted average cost is a compromise between lifo and fifo, both for the amount of the ending inventory and for the cost of merchandise sold. This method does not always reflect the current market costs because the costs are averaged.

Have students discuss what might happen if businesses could switch methods whenever they wanted.

All four methods of determining inventory costs are acceptable. A business may use any of the four methods, but it must use the chosen method consistently. The consistent use of an inventory costing method helps stockholders and creditors compare financial reports from one period to another. Although a business may change its method of assigning inventory costs, it may not change back and forth repeatedly and must, in fact, get permission from the IRS. Changes in costing methods must also be disclosed in the financial statements.

When deciding which costing method to use, the owner or manager compares the four methods and selects the one likely to be most beneficial for the business. Current economic conditions and the future economic outlook should also be considered.

Reporting Inventory Using the Lower-of-Cost-or-Market Rule

Once the cost of the inventory has been calculated using one of the four costing methods, it is reported on the financial statements. When reporting the cost of the ending inventory, the business may value the inventory at the calculated cost or at market value, whichever is lower. **Market value** refers to the current price that is being charged for similar items in the marketplace. It is the price at which the items could be replaced. Even if prices are mostly rising, the market value of a given item may be less than the original cost.

Point out the importance of using market value on the financial statements, when it is lower than the actual cost.

Under the *lower-of-cost-or-market rule,* if the market value is lower than the calculated cost, the inventory is reported at its market value on the financial statements. For example, suppose Mayfaire uses the lifo method to assign costs to its inventory. With this method, the cost of the ending inventory of 26 Wallace Jogging Shoes was determined to be $706.00. Now assume the market value of the shoes is $19.50. The market value of the ending inventory, then, is $507.00. Since the market value of the inventory is less than the calculated cost, Mayfaire would report the cost of the inventory on the financial statements at $507.00.

Estimating the Value of Inventories

For a business to function efficiently, management must have interim financial reports prepared monthly or quarterly. Merchandise inventory figures are an important part of those financial statements. Taking a physical inventory, however, is both time consuming and expensive. Many businesses, therefore, estimate the value of the ending inventories for interim financial statements.

Explain that estimated inventories can assist a business in getting an indication of how it is doing.

There may be other reasons for estimating the value of an inventory. Natural disasters, such as fire or flood, may destroy a business's inventory, making a physical count impossible. The inventory must be estimated to determine the value of damaged or destroyed merchandise for insurance and tax purposes. Let's look at the two most frequently used methods of estimating the value of inventories: the retail method and the gross profit method.

The Retail Method of Estimating Inventories

As the name implies, the **retail method** is widely used by retail businesses, particularly department stores, to estimate the value of their inventories. When a business uses the retail method to estimate its inventory, it first calculates the cost of merchandise available for sale at cost *and* at retail. *At retail* refers to the selling (retail) price of the inventory items. A retailer buys merchandise at cost and adds a certain dollar amount or a percentage of the cost to arrive at the selling price. This added amount is referred to as the **markup.**

Mayfaire takes a physical inventory at the end of each year. For its monthly financial statements, however, Mayfaire uses the retail method to estimate the value of its inventory. The following table shows how it makes this estimate:

	At Cost	At Retail
Merchandise Inventory (beginning)	$ 41,200	$ 68,600
Net Purchases	78,800	131,400
Merchandise Available for Sale	$120,000	$200,000

Cost ratio: $\frac{\$120,000}{\$200,000} = 60\%$

Deduct retail sales	142,000
Retail value of ending inventory	$ 58,000

Estimated cost of ending inventory: $58,000 × 60% = $ 34,800

Point out that the percentage used in the calculations is that portion of the retail price that is the cost of the merchandise. It is not the markup percentage.

When a business uses the retail method to estimate its inventory, the beginning inventory and net purchases must be recorded at both their cost and retail values. As you can see, Mayfaire's total merchandise available for sale has a cost of $120,000 and a retail value of $200,000. Next, the cost ratio, the ratio of cost to retail price, is calculated. This ratio provides an estimate of how much of the retail value of the merchandise is cost rather than markup. The cost of Mayfaire's inventory is an estimated 60% of the selling price. Then, the total sales for the period are subtracted from the retail price of the goods available for sale to find the *retail* value of the ending inventory. Since Mayfaire's total retail sales for the month were $142,000, the retail value of the ending inventory is $58,000. Finally, the estimated cost of the ending inventory is found by multiplying the retail value of the ending inventory by the cost ratio: $58,000 × 60% = $34,800.

Use demonstration problem 5-2 here.

The Gross Profit Method of Estimating Inventories

Sometimes a business finds that the retail prices of its beginning inventory and net purchases aren't readily available. In such cases, the business can use the gross profit method to estimate the value of its ending inventory. As the name implies, the **gross profit method** uses the percentage of gross profit the business earned over a given period of time to estimate the value of the inventory. The gross profit percentage is found by dividing the gross profit by the net sales for the period. This is usually done by examining past financial statements.

Once the gross profit percentage is known, net sales can be divided into its two parts: gross profit and cost of merchandise sold. From there, it's a matter of working backward through an income statement. The cost of merchandise sold is deducted from the merchandise available for sale to determine the estimated ending inventory. Let's look at an example.

On the night of April 29, the inventory of the Midtown Leather Shop was destroyed by fire. The company's accounting records, however, were saved. For insurance purposes, the owner must estimate the value of the inventory using the gross profit method. By looking at past income statements, the owner learned that the average gross profit percentage for the past five years was 39%. Using the information in the accounting records, the owner can prepare a partial income statement. This income statement is shown in Figure 5-3.

Midtown Leather Shop
Income Statement
For Period January 1, 199- through April 29, 199-

Net Sales		250 000 00
Cost of Merchandise Sold:		
Merchandise Inventory, Jan. 1, 199-	53 000 00	
Net Purchases	146 000 00	
Merchandise Available for Sale	199 000 00	
Less Merchandise Inventory, Apr. 29, 199-		
Cost of Merchandise Sold		
Gross Profit (39% of net sales)		

Figure 5-3 Partial Income Statement

When presenting the steps, put the partial income statement on the board and have students discuss each step in determining the ending inventory amount.

To find the value of the ending inventory, it is now necessary to work backward. The gross profit is estimated by multiplying the amount of net sales by the gross profit percentage: $250,000 × .39 = $97,500. The cost of merchandise sold is determined by subtracting the estimated gross profit from net sales:

Net sales	$250,000
Estimated gross profit	– 97,500
Cost of merchandise sold	$152,500

The value of the ending merchandise inventory is the difference between the value of the merchandise available for sale and the cost of merchandise sold:

Use demonstration problem 5-3 here.

Merchandise available for sale	$199,000
Cost of merchandise sold	–152,500
Estimated ending inventory	$ 46,500

The income statement can now be completed as shown in Figure 5-4.

Midtown Leather Shop Income Statement For Period January 1, 199- through April 29, 199-		
Net Sales		250 000 00
Cost of Merchandise Sold:		
Merchandise Inventory, Jan. 1, 199-	53 000 00	
Net Purchases	146 000 00	
Merchandise Available for Sale	199 000 00	
Less Merchandise Inventory, Apr. 29, 199-	46 500 00	
Cost of Merchandise Sold		152 500 00
Gross Profit (39% of net sales)		97 500 00

Figure 5-4 Completed Portion of Income Statement

Before reading further, do the following activity to check your understanding of estimating inventory values.

Check Your Learning

Write your answers to these questions on a sheet of notebook paper.

1. ___?___ is the amount or percentage added to the cost of an item to determine its selling price.
2. With the ___?___ method of estimating the value of inventories, records of the beginning inventory and purchases are maintained both at cost and at selling price.
3. With the ___?___ method of estimating the value of inventories, the cost of the ending inventory is found by working backward through an income statement.

Compare your answers to those in the answers section. Reread the preceding part of the chapter to find the correct answers to any questions you may have missed.

Inventory Valuation and the Financial Statements

Stress the importance of accurate inventory amounts.

As you learned earlier, Merchandise Inventory is the only general ledger account that appears on both the income statement and the balance sheet. A mistake made in determining the cost of the ending inventory, then, results in the reporting of incorrect amounts on the two statements.

An error in determining the cost of the ending merchandise inventory has a dramatic effect on net income. For example, suppose a business had a beginning merchandise inventory of $82,000. Net sales for the period were $260,000, net purchases totaled $180,000, and the cost of the ending merchandise inventory is $96,000. The net income for the period would be determined as follows:

Year 1 (With Correct Ending Inventory)

Net Sales		$260,000
Cost of Merchandise Sold:		
Beginning Merchandise Inventory	$ 82,000	
Net Purchases	180,000	
Cost of Merchandise Available	$262,000	
Less Ending Merchandise Inventory	96,000	
Cost of Merchandise Sold		166,000
Gross Profit on Sales		$ 94,000
Total Operating Expenses		30,000
Net Income		$ 64,000

Now assume the cost of the ending merchandise inventory had been understated by $10,000, that is, the ending merchandise inventory had been incorrectly calculated at $86,000 instead of $96,000. The error would result in a $10,000 decrease in net income:

Year 1 (With Incorrect Ending Inventory)

Net Sales		$260,000
Cost of Merchandise Sold:		
Beginning Merchandise Inventory	$ 82,000	
Net Purchases	180,000	
Cost of Merchandise Available	$262,000	
Less Ending Merchandise Inventory	86,000	
Cost of Merchandise Sold		176,000
Gross Profit on Sales		$ 84,000
Total Operating Expenses		30,000
Net Income		$ 54,000

You can see that if the ending merchandise inventory is understated, the net income will be understated by the same amount, and the two amounts will be directly proportional to each other. Similarly, if the ending merchandise inventory is overstated, net income will be overstated.

Something else must be taken into account. Since the ending inventory of one year becomes the beginning inventory of the following year, the net income of the following year is also affected, but in the *opposite* way. To see this, let's continue our illustration into Year 2. The correct ($96,000) ending inventory of Year 1 becomes the beginning inventory of Year 2:

Year 1 (With Correct Beginning Inventory)

Net Sales		$296,000
Cost of Merchandise Sold:		
Beginning Merchandise Inventory	$ 96,000	
Net Purchases	194,000	
Cost of Merchandise Available	$290,000	
Less Ending Merchandise Inventory	100,000	
Cost of Merchandise Sold		190,000
Gross Profit on Sales		$106,000
Total Operating Expenses		35,000
Net Income		$ 71,000

If, however, the incorrect ending inventory—$86,000—from Year 1 becomes the beginning inventory for Year 2, the following income statement will result:

Year 1 (With Incorrect Beginning Inventory)

Net Sales		$296,000
Cost of Merchandise Sold:		
Beginning Merchandise Inventory	$ 86,000	
Net Purchases	194,000	
Cost of Merchandise Available	$280,000	
Less Ending Merchandise Inventory	100,000	
Cost of Merchandise Sold		180,000
Gross Profit on Sales		$116,000
Total Operating Expenses		35,000
Net Income		$ 81,000

From this example, you can see that if the beginning merchandise inventory is understated by $10,000, the net income will be overstated by $10,000. These two amounts are indirectly proportional to each other. Similarly, if the beginning merchandise inventory is understated, net income will be overstated.

Notice, however, that over the two-year period, the two incorrect net income amounts will offset each other. The understatement of the first year will be canceled out by the overstatement of the following year:

Year	Correct Ending Inventory ($96,000)	Incorrect Ending Inventory ($86,000)
1	$ 64,000	$ 54,000
2	71,000	81,000
Total	$135,000	$135,000

Go through these four points using the previous examples.

The effect of an error in determining the cost of the ending inventory on the income statement can be summarized as follows:

1. If the ending inventory is overstated, net income for the period will be overstated.
2. If the ending inventory is understated, net income for the period will be understated.
3. If the beginning inventory is overstated, net income for the period will be understated.
4. If the beginning inventory is understated, net income for the period will be overstated.

Investments

This is a good time to discuss effective and efficient management.

Proper inventory control is essential for efficient business operation. If the inventory is too small, variety and choice for the customer are limited. If the inventory is too large, cash is being wasted on unnecessary items. Proper investment of cash is also essential for efficiency.

In Chapter 3, you learned that when a business has excess cash, it may choose to invest that cash in short-term marketable securities. When cash is available for a longer period of time—usually one year or more—long-term investments can be made. **Investments** are long-term assets that are not intended to be converted to cash or to be used in the normal business operations within the next accounting period. Real estate, both land and buildings, are considered investments if they are not used in the normal business operations. The stocks and bonds of other corporations are also considered investments. Companies often purchase such assets with the expectation of earning dividends or interest.

Emphasize the importance of sound investments.

When investments are purchased, they are recorded in the accounting records at their *cost*. For example, suppose Mayfaire bought 500 shares of stock in Schoenle Data Systems as an investment. Mayfaire paid a total of $11,750 for the stock. The transaction would be recorded as an $11,750 debit to the investments account Schoenle Data Systems Stock and an $11,750 credit to Cash in Bank.

During the time Mayfaire holds the Schoenle stock, it will receive dividends as a return on the investment. (You'll learn more about dividends in Chapter 10.) Mayfaire also hopes that the price of the stock will increase. If that happens, Mayfaire could sell the stock and make a profit on the transaction.

A business must watch its investments carefully. Investments may need to be adjusted if the business's operations or market conditions change.

Summary of Key Points

1. Correct valuation of inventory is important—it affects a business's net income and the Current Assets section of the balance sheet.
2. The two inventory control systems businesses use are the periodic inventory system and the perpetual inventory system.
3. There are four methods of calculating the cost of the ending inventory: specific identification; first in, first out (fifo); last in, first out (lifo); and weighted average cost.
4. Gross profit, net income, and income tax obligations are affected by the method used to determine the cost of ending inventory.
5. Under the lower-of-cost-or-market rule, the ending inventory is reported on the financial statements at cost or at its market value, whichever is lower.
6. Market value is the current price that is being charged for similar inventory items in the marketplace. It is the price at which inventory items could be replaced.
7. Businesses often estimate the value of their ending inventories. Two methods of estimating the value of inventories are the retail method and the gross profit method.
8. Markup is the amount or percentage of the cost of an item that is added to the cost price to arrive at the selling price.
9. An error in the ending inventory will affect the income statement and balance sheet for the current period and for the next period.
10. Investments are assets—generally long term—that are not intended to be converted to cash or to be used in the business's normal operations within the next accounting period.

5 Review and Applications

Building Your Accounting Vocabulary

In your own words, write the definition of each of the following accounting terms. Use complete sentences for your definitions.

- first in, first out method (fifo)
- gross profit method
- investments
- last in, first out method (lifo)
- market value
- markup
- periodic inventory system
- perpetual inventory system
- retail method
- specific identification method
- weighted average cost method

Reviewing Your Accounting Knowledge

1. Why is it important to determine the cost value of Merchandise Inventory?
2. Name two ways in which a business benefits by having effective inventory management procedures.
3. What is the difference between the periodic inventory system and the perpetual inventory system?
4. Why do businesses that use a perpetual inventory system still take a periodic inventory at least once a year?
5. Why is the specific identification method the most realistic method for determining inventory costs?
6. What does the term *weighted* mean in relation to the weighted average cost method?
7. Name one advantage and one disadvantage of the lifo method of valuing inventories.
8. Under what market conditions is the lower-of-cost-or-market rule applied?
9. Why might a firm estimate the value of its inventory rather than take a physical inventory?
10. Under what circumstances would the gross profit method be used instead of the retail method to estimate the value of the ending inventory?
11. What is the effect on net income if the beginning inventory is understated?
12. What is the difference between short-term and long-term investments?

Improving Your Problem-Solving Skills

You are the payroll clerk for a small business. Your good friend Lisa Waters works for the same company. You and Lisa usually take coffee breaks together and often have lunch together.

At lunch one day, Lisa told you about her career plans. She was very interested in her supervisor's job responsibilities and salary rate. Lisa knows that you handle the payroll information, and she hoped you would volunteer the information. You didn't. Finally, Lisa's curiosity got the best of her. She asked you what her supervisor's salary is.

How should you respond to Lisa's question? Why? What types of information do you believe should remain confidential in the office? Why?

Applying Accounting Procedures

Exercise 5-1 Costing Inventory with the Specific Identification Method

Delsey's Home Appliances made the following purchases of Maxim dishwashers during the year.

February 13	14 dishwashers @ $179.50 each
April 2	30 dishwashers @ $183.00 each
July 2	18 dishwashers @ $191.00 each
September 14	12 dishwashers @ $196.00 each
November 3	24 dishwashers @ $203.50 each

$2,341.00

Instructions: Of the 12 dishwashers still on hand, 2 were purchased in April, 3 in July, 3 in September, and 4 in November. Calculate the cost of the ending inventory using the specific identification method. Use the form provided in the working papers.

Exercise 5-2 Costing Inventory with the Fifo Method

During the first six months of the year, Bentsen's had the following Blow Easy hair dryers for sale.

Beginning inventory	32 hair dryers @ $7.07 each
Purchased January 27	84 hair dryers @ $7.05 each
Purchased March 2	48 hair dryers @ $7.19 each
Purchased April 2	72 hair dryers @ $7.56 each
Purchased June 14	42 hair dryers @ $7.60 each

$349.44

Instructions: Calculate the cost of the ending inventory of 46 hair dryers using the fifo method. Use the form provided in the working papers.

Exercise 5-3 Costing Inventory with the Lifo Method

Racine Communications had the following beginning inventory and purchases of Channel cordless telephones during the year.

Beginning inventory	24 telephones @ $81.49 each
Purchased March 1	49 telephones @ $82.69 each
Purchased June 14	144 telephones @ $82.49 each
Purchased September 28	36 telephones @ $84.25 each
Purchased November 19	36 telephones @ $86.60 each

$6,749.98

Instructions: Calculate the cost of the ending inventory of 82 telephones using the lifo method. Use the form provided in the working papers.

Exercise 5-4 Costing Inventory with the Weighted Average Cost Method

The Bath House had the following beginning inventory and purchases of bath towels during the year.

Beginning inventory	34 bath towels @ $2.35 each
Purchased February 8	24 bath towels @ $2.79 each
Purchased April 8	72 bath towels @ $2.84 each
Purchased June 28	60 bath towels @ $2.99 each
Purchased September 10	24 bath towels @ $2.92 each
Purchased December 3	48 bath towels @ $2.90 each

$76.14

Instructions: Calculate the cost of the ending inventory of 27 bath towels using the weighted average cost method. Use the form provided in the working papers.

Problem 5-1 Maintaining an Inventory Card

The Sound Machine uses a perpetual inventory system and determines the cost of its inventory using the fifo method.

Instructions: Use a form similar to the one that follows. For each of the following transactions, determine:

(1) The total cost of the units purchased or sold.
(2) The balance of units on hand. If necessary, determine the number of units on hand at the various unit costs.
(3) The cost of the units on hand at the various unit costs.
(4) The total cost of the inventory of #107A cassette players. The beginning inventory has already been entered on the inventory card.

Transactions:

Jan.	6	Sold 18 units
Feb.	2	Purchased 20 units @ $54 each
	14	Sold 16 units
Mar.	1	Sold 10 units
	17	Purchased 16 units @ $56 each

Item: Cassette Player, #107A

Date	Received			Sold			Balance		
	Units	Cost	Total	Units	Cost	Total	Units	Cost	Total
Jan. 1							30	$53	$1,590

Figure 5-5 Inventory Card for Probem 5-1

Problem 5-2 Determining Gross Profit

The Picture Frame uses the periodic inventory system. On December 31 (the end of the fiscal period), the accounting records provided the following amounts.

Merchandise inventory, Jan. 1	$113,000
Net purchases	135,000
Net sales	207,000

A physical inventory revealed that the ending inventory was $104,000.

COMS, $144,000.00
Gross profit, $63,000.00

Instructions: Determine the cost of merchandise sold and the gross profit for the year ended December 31. Show your results in income statement form.

COMPUTER PROBLEM

Problem 5-3 Assigning Costs to the Ending Inventory

The Complete Computer uses the periodic inventory system. Data (beginning inventory, purchases, and ending inventory) for three models of computers on hand follows.

Instructions:

(1) Assign a cost to the December 31 ending inventory using the specific identification method.
  (a) For Model CL311: Of the 11 units on hand, 9 were purchased in November, 1 in August, and 1 in June.
  (b) For Model DE243: Of the 6 units on hand, 2 were purchased in August, 3 were purchased in June, and 1 was part of the beginning inventory.
  (c) For Model 6X16: Of the 28 units on hand, 18 were purchased in November, 4 in August, and 6 in March.

(2) Assign a cost to the December 31 ending inventory using the fifo method.

(3) Assign a cost to the December 31 ending inventory using the lifo method.

(4) Assign a cost to the December 31 ending inventory using the weighted average cost method. Round the unit cost to the nearest dollar.

	CL311	DE243	6X16
Beginning inventory	8 @ $432	1 @ $779	17 @ $318
Purchased March 6	14 @ $450	5 @ $782	24 @ $322
Purchased June 28	19 @ $451	7 @ $788	26 @ $322
Purchased August 31	13 @ $452	4 @ $789	28 @ $324
Purchased November 20	9 @ $455		23 @ $327
Ending inventory	11	6	28

Problem 5-4 Assigning Inventory Costs and Determining Gross Profit

The Bustelos Company uses the periodic inventory system. On January 1, the company's inventory of Product AL6 was 14,000 gallons, which was bought at a cost of $.68 per gallon. Bustelos made the following purchases shown on page 139.

Date	Quantity (gallons)	Cost per Gallon	Total Cost
Jan. 23	10,000	$.72	$ 7,200
Feb. 5	12,000	.74	8,880
22	9,000	.74	6,660
Mar. 6	19,000	.73	13,870
29	8,000	.75	6,000
Apr. 17	9,000	.76	6,840
May 19	6,000	.76	4,560
June 18	4,000	.78	3,120
	77,000		$57,130

On June 30, the company had 11,000 gallons on hand. During this six-month period, all of the Product AL6 sales were made at $.88 per gallon.

Instructions:

(1) Assign a cost to the ending inventory using each of the following methods: weighted average cost, fifo, and lifo.

(2) Determine the cost of merchandise sold for each method.

(3) Determine the amount of the gross profit for each method.

SPREADSHEET PROBLEM

Problem 5-5 Determining Inventory Cost with the Lower-of-Cost-or-Market Rule

The Mountaineer Shop assigns a value to its ending inventory using the lower-of-cost-or-market rule. A partial inventory record follows; the complete record is included in the working papers.

Instructions: Complete the inventory record, using the following steps.

(1) Select the lower of the cost or the market value. Enter that amount in the Price to Be Used column.

(2) Calculate the total cost of each item by multiplying the quantity in the ending inventory by the price to be used.

Total cost, $27,418.60

(3) Determine the total cost for this page of the inventory record.

THE MOUNTAINEER SHOP
Inventory Record Page 1

Item No.	Item	Ending Inventory	Cost per Unit	Current Market Value	Price to be Used	Total Cost
1152	Sleeping bag	30	$95.00	$105.00	$95.00	$2,850.00

Figure 5-6 Inventory Record for Problem 5-5

Problem 5-6 Estimating Inventory Using the Retail Method

On December 31, the end of the fiscal period, the accounting records of the Gold Star Gift Shop provided the following information.

	At Cost	At Retail
Beginning inventory	$ 46,781	$ 77,189
Net purchases	124,916	206,112
Net sales		185,318

Instructions:

Cost of end. inv., $59,770

Loss, $4,181

(1) Use the retail method to estimate the cost of the ending inventory.

(2) At the end of the fiscal period, Gold Star Gift Shop took a physical inventory and found that the total retail value of its inventory was $91,130. The difference between the estimated and actual ending inventory may have been due to shoplifting. Convert the retail value of the physical inventory into its cost value and determine the amount of the loss.

Problem 5-7 Estimating Inventory with the Gross Profit Method

On the morning of May 17, the manager of the Arcadia Fur Salon discovered that a large portion of the merchandise had been stolen over the weekend. The accounting records, including the information for the period January 1 through May 17, were not disturbed. These records showed that over the past four years, the store's gross profit averaged 34% of net sales. Additional data from the accounting records is as follows.

Merchandise inventory, Jan. 1	$164,889
Net purchases through May 17	375,609
Net sales through May 17	516,739

Instructions:

Mdse. inv., May 17, $199,450.00

Loss, $125,267.00

(1) Use the gross profit method to estimate the cost of the May 17 inventory. Show your calculations in income statement form.

(2) A physical inventory was taken, and the cost of the remaining inventory was determined to be $74,183. What is the amount of the loss?

CHALLENGE PROBLEM

Problem 5-8 Estimating Inventories, Cost of Merchandise Sold, and Gross Profit

For its interim financial reports, the Puritan Auto Center decided to estimate the value of its ending inventory. The company's accounting records provided the following information.

Net sales	$243,000
Beginning inventory at cost	181,000
Beginning inventory at retail	278,400
Net purchases at cost	85,900
Net purchases at retail	132,200
Gross profit as a percentage of net sales	33%

Instructions:

$108,940
$104,090
GP method ($162,810)
Retail method ($85,040)

(1) Use the retail method to estimate the cost of the ending inventory. Use plain paper or the form provided in the working papers.

(2) Use gross profit method to estimate the cost of ending inventory.

(3) Which method would yield a higher cost of merchandise sold?

(4) Which method would yield a higher gross profit?

FOCUS ON CAREERS

Computer Consultant: Two Careers in One

As more and more businesses rely on computers to keep track of their correspondence, finances, and inventory, the demand for computer consultants continues to rise. Computer consultants are specialists who work with clients to help them use computers to achieve specific goals. These consultants recommend hardware and software packages that can help clients meet those goals.

Accountants who work as computer consultants are hybrid specialists—they are experts in two fields. These consultants assess a client's accounting needs, such as managing day-to-day operations, preparing taxes, controlling inventory, and generating reports. Then, they recommend, or sometimes design, the necessary hardware and software packages that can achieve the results the client is seeking.

Recommending and designing such problem-solving systems may not be the only service provided by a computer consultant. Some consultants are responsible for training a client's staff to use a newly implemented system. Other consultants actually sell the hardware and software packages they recommend.

Many computer consultants work as part of a larger firm; for example, some CPA firms have a consulting division. Other consultants choose to go into business for themselves. In either setting, computer consultants must have a thorough knowledge of the features and functions of an accounting system, understand the fundamentals of a microcomputer, and have a detailed grasp of applications software. Other qualities that are important in this field are good communication skills and the ability to work well under pressure.

Computer consultants help their clients determine what hardware and software packages they need.

If you enjoy accounting and computers and would like to use your skills to solve problems, computer consulting may be for you. As you develop expertise in both areas, you may gain the competitive advantage you need to start a successful business.

Chapter 6

PROPERTY, PLANT, AND EQUIPMENT ASSETS AND INTANGIBLE ASSETS

Most businesses use many different assets in their operations. Cash, supplies, equipment, buildings, land, and merchandise are all familiar types of assets. Since the business will use them to produce benefits for a number of years, some of these assets require special treatment in the accounting records. This group includes assets such as equipment, furniture, and buildings.

As assets are used up in the business's operations, their costs are converted to expenses and matched against the revenue for the same period. In this chapter, you will learn how the costs of long-lived assets such as the cost of equipment, are allocated (spread) over the assets' lives. You will also learn how to account for the disposal of long-lived assets.

Learning Objectives

When you have completed this chapter, you should be able to do the following:

1. Identify property, plant, and equipment assets and record their initial costs.
2. Calculate the annual estimated depreciation expense for a plant asset using four common methods.
3. Calculate depreciation for a partial year.
4. Determine the book value of a plant asset.
5. Journalize the adjusting entries for depreciation.
6. Record the entries for the disposal of a plant asset.
7. Define the accounting terms presented in this chapter.

New Terms

current assets
property, plant, and equipment
appraisal value
depreciation
salvage value
depreciable cost
straight-line method
units-of-production method
double-declining-balance method
book value
accumulated depreciation
sum-of-the-years'-digits method
intangible assets

Property, Plant, and Equipment Assets

Most of a business's assets can be classified as either current assets or property, plant, and equipment assets. **Current assets** are assets that are either used up or converted to cash during the normal operating cycle of the business—usually one year. Cash, notes and accounts receivable, supplies, prepaid insurance, and merchandise inventory are all examples of current assets. **Property, plant, and equipment** are long-lived assets that are used in the production or sale of other assets or services and benefit the business for several accounting periods. These assets, often simply called *plant assets,* are purchased for use in the business rather than for resale. Plant assets include land, buildings, office furniture and equipment, vehicles, and tools. Separate accounts are maintained for each type of property, plant, and equipment asset.

Point out that plant assets are also called long-term or fixed assets.

R — E — M — E — M — B — E — R

Property, plant, and equipment assets are expected to benefit a business for more than one accounting period. Current assets are expected to be consumed or converted to cash in one accounting period.

Mention that the first issue in accounting for long-lived assets is to determine their initial cost.

Determining the Cost of Property, Plant, and Equipment

Property, plant, and equipment require special treatment in a business's accounting records. The first step in accounting for long-lived assets is to determine and record their initial cost.

Equipment

The cost of equipment includes all normal costs necessary for acquiring and installing it. Let's assume that the Olympia Flower Shop purchased a new cash register. The price of the cash register was $850.00, plus $42.50 sales tax. Olympia journalized the purchase as a debit of $892.50 to Store Equipment and a credit for the same amount to Cash in Bank. Notice that the amount debited to Store Equipment included not only the unit price but the sales tax amount. The cost of the cash register could also have included freight charges, insurance costs incurred while it was being transported, and the costs of unpacking and assembling it. Had Olympia taken advantage of a discount, the discount amount would have decreased the total amount paid. The discount would have been *credited* to the Store Equipment account.

Have students name some other examples of costs or expenses that would not be considered normal and necessary.

Only normal and necessary preparation costs are debited to the asset account. Amounts paid out as a result of carelessness, vandalism, or other unusual causes cannot be included. For example, suppose the employee who was unpacking the cash register dropped it. The repair cost would be charged to an expense account, such as Repair Expense.

The repair cost is an expense because the repair does not *add to* the usefulness of the cash register; it *restores* it.

Land

Discuss some other costs that would be debited to the Building account.

The cost of land includes the amount paid for the land, plus other charges connected with the sale: real estate agent's commission, legal fees, and certain other costs incurred while preparing the land for use. For example, Speedy Dry Cleaners bought land for a building. Speedy plans to tear down the building that stands on the land. It debits the cost of the building—as well as the cost of tearing it down—to the Land account.

Buildings

The cost of an existing building that will be used in the business is debited to the Building account. The cost of constructing a building would also be debited to the Building account. The construction cost includes not only money spent for labor and materials but also costs such as architectural and engineering fees, premiums for insurance during construction, and other necessary and normal expenditures for the project.

Be sure students understand why these values must be separated.

A building and land are usually bought together for one price. That one price must be divided between the Land account and the Building account. When a business is considering buying property, it wants to know whether the price being quoted is appropriate. The business usually hires a qualified person to determine the property's **appraisal value**, that is, its estimated worth. For example, suppose the Sport Shoe pays $400,000 for property that includes land and a building. An appraiser values the property at $500,000—$100,000 for the land and $400,000 for the building. The value of the land is 20% of the appraisal value ($100,000 ÷ $500,000). The value of the building is 80% of the appraisal value ($400,000 ÷ $500,000). These percentages are then used to determine the amounts allocated to the Land and Building accounts. The amount debited to Land is $80,000 ($400,000 × .20); the amount debited to Building is $320,000 ($400,000 × .80).

R — E — M — E — M — B — E — R

When land and a building are purchased for one price, the value of the land must be separated from the value of the building.

Land Improvements

Ask students to name other examples of land improvements.

Land improvements are amounts paid out for improvements that are (1) not as permanent as the land or (2) not directly associated with a building. Land improvements include the cost of items such as driveways, parking lots, trees and shrubs, fences, and outdoor lighting systems. For accounting purposes, the cost of land improvements must be separated from the cost of land or buildings.

Before reading further, do the following activity to check your understanding of how to determine the cost of long-lived assets.

Check Your Learning

Write your answers to these questions on a sheet of notebook paper.

1. Clinton Publications bought a new printing press for $68,000, with credit terms of 2/10, n/30. Clinton paid the invoice within the discount period, along with $710 in transportation charges. Clinton also paid $990 to install the press and $832 to make the power connections. How much should Clinton debit to the Equipment account?
2. The Frame Hut purchased land and a building for $270,000. The property was appraised for $300,000—30% for the land and 70% for the building. What amount should the company debit to the Land account? To the Building account?

Compare your answers to those in the answers section. Reread the preceding part of the chapter to find the correct accounting principles for any questions you may have missed.

Allocating the Cost of Plant Assets

Discuss the matching principle.

An item of supplies may be bought and used up in one fiscal period. Its cost is charged as an expense to that fiscal period. A plant asset, on the other hand, is used over several fiscal periods. Its usefulness, however, decreases over time owing to use, inadequacy, and obsolescence. To follow the matching principle, the cost of the plant asset must be spread out over those accounting periods in which it is used.

Point out that depreciation describes the gradual conversion of the cost of a plant asset into an expense.

Depreciation is a systematic procedure for allocating (spreading) the cost of plant assets to the accounting periods in which the business receives service from those assets. The amount by which a plant asset depreciates in each fiscal period is charged as an expense to that fiscal period. All plant assets except land depreciate. Land is considered to have an unlimited life—it does not wear out. As a result, its cost is not written off over a number of years.

Stress the fact that depreciation is an estimate.

It is difficult to predict accurately how many years a plant asset can be used. Any method of calculating depreciation provides only an *estimate* of how quickly a plant asset is used up or loses its value. To determine a plant asset's depreciation for an accounting period, three factors must be considered: (1) the depreciable cost, (2) the estimated useful life of the asset, and (3) the method of depreciation used.

R — E — M — E — M — B — E — R

Land has an unlimited useful life. Its cost is not written off as an expense.

Depreciable Cost

Point out that the salvage value could be zero in some cases.

A plant asset eventually becomes used up or worn out and needs to be replaced or discarded. This usually happens while the asset still has some value. The estimated value of a plant asset at the time of its disposal is called the asset's **salvage value**, or *disposal value*. When a business buys a plant asset, it's hard to predict its salvage, or disposal, value. Many businesses estimate the salvage value based on their own experience or on data supplied by trade associations or government agencies. Often, if a business expects the salvage value to be small relative to the cost of the asset, the salvage value is set at zero.

$16,000
− 1,500
$14,500

Give students an opportunity to determine the depreciable cost of plant assets by listing on the board the original cost and salvage value of several different plant assets.

The **depreciable cost** of an asset is the estimated amount to be depreciated: the original cost less any salvage value. For example, suppose Mayfaire, Inc., purchased a delivery truck for $16,000. The truck has an estimated salvage value of $1,500. The depreciable cost of the truck, therefore, is $14,500. It is the depreciable cost of a plant asset that is *expensed,* or allocated, over a number of fiscal periods.

R—E—M—E—M—B—E—R

The depreciable cost of a plant asset is the asset's cost minus any salvage value.

Useful Life

Give examples of technology such as microcomputers that become outdated before they wear out.

For accounting purposes, the *useful life* of a plant asset is based on the asset's expected use. The length of a plant asset's useful life is affected not only by physical wear and tear but also by technological change and innovation. A car, for example, may have an average useful life of five years. To offer customers the latest models, however, a car rental company may replace its cars every year. A company that has a fleet of cars for its sales force may replace the cars every three years. The useful life of a computer is most often determined by advances in technology. Computers usually operate effectively for several years. Before they physically wear out, computers become obsolete and are replaced by more advanced models.

Methods of Calculating Depreciation

Depreciation provides for the systematic allocation of the cost of a plant asset over the asset's useful life. Several methods can be used to calculate the depreciation amounts. A business need not use the same method to calculate the depreciation for all of its assets.

The four most common methods of calculating depreciation are (1) the straight-line method, (2) the units-of-production method, (3) the double-declining-balance method, and (4) the sum-of-the-years'-digits method.

The Straight-Line Method

Mention that the straight-line method is common due to its ease of calculation.

The **straight-line method** is based on the assumption that depreciation depends only on the passage of time. Repairs and maintenance costs are assumed to be about the same every year. With this method of calculating depreciation, the business charges (converts to an expense) an equal amount of depreciation during each year of the plant asset's useful life. The annual depreciation expense amount is found by dividing the asset's depreciable cost by the estimated number of years in the asset's useful life.

Let's look at an example. On January 6, Mayfaire, Inc., bought a delivery truck for $16,000. The truck has an estimated useful life of 5 years and an estimated salvage value of $1,500. The depreciable cost, therefore, is $14,500 ($16,000 – $1,500). The annual depreciation expense is found as follows:

Depreciable Cost	÷	Useful Life (in Years)	=	Depreciation Expense per Year
$14,500	÷	5	=	$2,900

Use demonstration problem 6-1 here.

When expressed as a percentage, the annual straight-line depreciation is 20% ($2,900 ÷ $14,500 *or* 1 year of 5 = 1/5 = 20%). In other words, 20% of the depreciable cost of the truck is depreciated in each year of the asset's useful life.

The Units-of-Production Method

Ask students to name common plant assets that would be appropriate for this method.

In some types of businesses, the use of a plant asset varies greatly from one accounting period to another. For example, a building contractor may use a certain piece of construction equipment only two months during a year. The **units-of-production method** of calculating depreciation is based on the idea that depreciation is the result of use rather than of time. The useful life of the asset may be expressed in miles driven, hours used, or units produced, whichever is most appropriate.

To find the annual depreciation, first the depreciable cost is divided by the total estimated units of production. Then the resulting depreciation per unit is multiplied by the units of production for that year.

Let's use the truck example again. Suppose the truck, which has a depreciable cost of $14,500, has an estimated useful life of 125,000 miles. The depreciation per mile would be as follows:

Depreciable Cost	÷	Estimated Units of Production	=	Depreciation Expense per Unit
$14,500	÷	125,000 miles	=	$0.116 per mile

Let's also assume that the truck was driven 30,000 miles during the first year. The depreciation expense for that year would be calculated as follows:

Depreciation Expense per Unit	×	Units of Production for the Year	=	Depreciation Expense per Year
$0.116	×	30,000	=	$3,480

Use demonstration problem 6-2 here.

The depreciation expense for the remaining years of the truck's useful life will depend on the number of miles the truck is driven in each year. For example, if the truck were driven only 20,000 miles in the second year, the depreciation expense for that year would be $2,320 (20,000 miles × $0.116 per mile).

The Double-Declining-Balance Method

The **double-declining-balance method** is an accelerated method of depreciation. It allows larger amounts of depreciation to be taken during the early years of an asset's useful life. This method is based on the assumption that an asset operates most efficiently during the first few years and requires increased repair and maintenance in later years. The depreciation expense, therefore, should be greater during the earlier years to offset the higher repair and maintenance expenses later. In this way, the total annual expenses of the asset are spread out fairly evenly over the asset's life.

With the double-declining-balance method, the salvage value and depreciable cost are *not* used to determine the depreciation. The amount of depreciation is calculated using the asset's current book value. The **book value** of an asset is the asset's value according to the records (books) of the business. The book value of an asset is the asset's original cost minus the accumulated depreciation. **Accumulated depreciation** is the total amount of depreciation that has been recorded up to a specific point in time.

Emphasize that the straight-line rate is calculated but the method is not used.

With the double-declining-balance method, the annual depreciation expense is calculated by multiplying the asset's book value by the double-declining-balance rate. To find the double-declining-balance rate, follow these steps:

1. Determine the annual straight-line depreciation rate.
2. Multiply the annual straight-line depreciation rate by 2. The result is the double-declining-balance depreciation rate.

Then the double-declining-balance rate is multiplied by the plant asset's book value to determine the depreciation. The double-declining-balance rate stays the same for each year the plant asset is depreciated. The book value—the amount on which the depreciation expense is based—decreases each year. The amount of depreciation, therefore, also decreases each year.

Use several examples to be sure students understand the calculation.

Let's use the double-declining-balance method to calculate the depreciation expense for the truck used in our earlier examples. The straight-line depreciation rate, calculated earlier, is 20%. Double the straight-line depreciation rate is 40% (20% × 2). The book value of the truck at the beginning of the first year is $16,000, which is also the truck's cost. The first year's depreciation expense is calculated as follows:

Book Value	×	Double-Declining-Balance Rate	=	Depreciation Expense First Year
$16,000	×	.40	=	$6,400

Use demonstration problem 6-3 here.

The depreciation expense for later years is determined in the same way. Remember, however, that the book value of the asset decreases each year. At the beginning of the second year, the book value of the truck is $9,600 ($16,000 – $6,400 accumulated depreciation). The depreciation expense for the second year is calculated as shown on the next page.

Book Value	×	Double-Declining-Balance Rate	=	Depreciation Expense
$9,600	×	.40	=	$3,840

The following table shows the book value, annual depreciation expense, and accumulated depreciation of the truck for its estimated useful life with the double-declining-balance method:

Year	Book Value	Depreciation Rate	Annual Depreciation Expense	Accumulated Depreciation
1	$16,000	40%	$6,400	$ 6,400
2	9,600	40%	3,840	10,240
3	5,760	40%	2,304	12,544
4	3,456	40%	1,382	13,926
5	2,074		574	14,500

This could be confusing for students; therefore, review and give other examples.

Notice that the amount of depreciation expense in the fifth year is $574 rather than $830 (40% of the book value of $2,074). With the double-declining-balance method, the salvage value of the asset is not considered *until* the last year of the asset's useful life. In the last year, the depreciation expense is limited to the amount that will reduce the asset's book value to its estimated salvage value. Since the salvage value is estimated at $1,500, the depreciation expense for the year is $574 ($2,074 – $1,500). The asset cannot be depreciated below its salvage value.

R — E — M — E — M — B — E — R

The book value of a plant asset is the asset's cost minus the accumulated depreciation.

The Sum-of-the-Years'-Digits Method

The **sum-of-the-years'-digits method** is also an accelerated method of depreciation. It uses fractions based on the number of years in the plant asset's estimated useful life to determine the depreciation expense. Like the double-declining-balance method, this method allows higher amounts of depreciation expense to be taken during the early years of an asset's estimated useful life. Unike the double-declining-balance method, the asset's salvage value is considered in the calculations.

The annual depreciation expense amount is calculated by multiplying the asset's depreciable cost by the yearly fraction. Before you can calculate the depreciation expense with this method, you must find the years' fractions. To do this, follow these steps:

Demonstrate other examples using 4, 6, and 8 years.

1. Determine the number of years in the asset's useful life. For example, our truck has an estimated useful life of 5 years.

2. Find the sum of the years' digits by adding the digits (numbers) of the years in the asset's useful life. The calculation for the truck's useful years is as follows:

$$1 + 2 + 3 + 4 + 5 = 15$$

In this case, the sum of the years' digits is 15. This number becomes the denominator of the fractions used with this method.

3. List the fractions, *in descending order,* using the year as the numerator and the sum of the year's digits as the denominator. For example,

$$\frac{5}{15} \quad \frac{4}{15} \quad \frac{3}{15} \quad \frac{2}{15} \quad \frac{1}{15}$$

Use demonstration problem 6-4 here.

To find the annual depreciation expense, the depreciable cost is multiplied by the year's fraction. The 5/15 fraction is used to determine the first year's depreciation expense, the 4/15 fraction is used in the second year, the 3/15 fraction is used in the third year, and so on. In the truck example, the depreciation expense for the first year is calculated as follows:

Depreciable Cost	×	Year's Fraction	=	Depreciation Expense First Year
$14,500	×	5/15	=	$4,833

The following table shows the annual depreciation expense and the accumulated depreciation of the truck using the sum-of-the-years'-digits method:

Year	Depreciable Cost	Year's Fraction	Annual Depreciation Expense	Accumulated Depreciation
1	$14,500	5/15	$4,833	$ 4,833
2	14,500	4/15	3,867	8,700
3	14,500	3/15	2,900	11,600
4	14,500	2/15	1,933	13,533
5	14,500	1/15	967	14,500

Comparing the Four Depreciation Methods

The table that follows compares the four depreciation methods, using the truck as the plant asset being depreciated. With the straight-line method, the amount of depreciation is the same for each year of the asset's useful life. The accumulated depreciation increases evenly, while the book value decreases evenly until it reaches the disposal value. The annual depreciation using the units-of-production method may vary widely, depending on how much the asset is used. The double-declining-balance method and the sum-of-the-years'-digits method are accelerated methods of depreciation. They result in larger depreciation amounts during the early years of the plant asset's useful life and smaller amounts in later years.

	Straight-Line Method	Units-of-Production Method	Double-Declining-Balance Method	Sum-of-the-Years'-Digits Method
Year 1				
Beginning Book Value	$16,000	$16,000	$16,000	$16,000
Depreciation Expense	2,900	3,480	6,400	4,833
Accumulated Depreciation	2,900	3,480	6,400	4,833
Year 2				
Beginning Book Value	$13,100	$12,520	$ 9,600	$11,167
Depreciation Expense	2,900	2,900	3,840	3,867
Accumulated Depreciation	5,800	6,380	10,240	8,700
Year 3				
Beginning Book Value	$10,200	$ 9,620	$ 5,760	$ 7,300
Depreciation Expense	2,900	3,132	2,304	2,900
Accumulated Depreciation	8,700	9,512	12,544	11,600
Year 4				
Beginning Book Value	$ 7,300	$ 6,488	$ 3,456	$ 4,400
Depreciation Expense	2,900	2,438	1,382	1,933
Accumulated Depreciation	11,600	11,950	13,926	13,533
Year 5				
Beginning Book Value	$ 4,400	$ 4,050	$ 2,074	$ 2,467
Depreciation Expense	2,900	2,550	574	967
Accumulated Depreciation	14,500	14,500	14,500	14,500

Before reading further, do the following activity to check your understanding of how to calculate the annual depreciation expense.

Check Your Learning

Write your answers to these questions on a sheet of notebook paper.

At the beginning of the year, Harvest Home, a restaurant, bought cooking equipment for $13,400. The equipment has an estimated disposal value of $840 and an estimated useful life of 4 years. Determine the amount of depreciation for the first year using each of the following methods.

1. Straight-line method.
2. Units-of-production method assuming the equipment has a useful life of 14,000 hours and was used 3,700 hours during the first year (round the depreciation expense per unit to two decimal places).
3. Double-declining-balance method.
4. Sum-of-the-years'-digits method.

Have students complete Exercise 6-2 at this point.

Compare your answers to those in the answers section. Reread the preceding part of the chapter to find the correct answers to any questions you may have missed.

Calculating Depreciation for Less Than One Year

So far, we've assumed that the plant assets were bought at the beginning of the fiscal period. However, this rarely happens in real life. Businesses buy plant assets during the year whenever they're needed. As a result, it is often necessary to calculate the depreciation for that part of the year during which the asset was actually owned. For example, if a business owned a plant asset for only 4 months of the fiscal period, the depreciation would be calculated on 4/12 of a full year's depreciation.

Mention the matching principle.

The time period is usually rounded off to the nearest whole month. In other words, if a business owns an asset for *less than* half a month, that month is not counted when calculating the depreciation expense. If the business owns the asset for more than half of a month, the whole month is counted.

For example, suppose a plant asset is purchased on June 11. The depreciation is computed from June 1, counting the entire month. Had the asset been purchased on June 17, the depreciation would be calculated from July 1; the month of June would not be counted.

The following table shows additional examples; the fiscal period is assumed to end on December 31.

Give some additional dates to be sure students understand this procedure.

Date Acquired	Cost	Salvage Value	Depreciation Method	Useful Life	Depreciation Expense for First Year
Apr. 12	\$9,000	\$1,000	Straight-line	5 yrs.	$\frac{\$8,000}{5}$ = \$1,600 per year \$1,600 × 9/12 = \$1,200
Oct. 19	\$6,000	\$200	Double-declining-balance	8 yrs.	\$6,000 × .25 = \$1,500 per year \$1,500 × 2/12 = \$250
Aug. 8	\$6,800	\$500	Sum-of-the-years'-digits	6 yrs.	\$6,300 × 6/21 = \$1,800 per year \$1,800 × 5/12 = \$750

Recording Depreciation Expense

At the end of the fiscal period, an adjusting entry to record the depreciation expense is made. The depreciation amount is debited to an expense account titled Depreciation Expense. The depreciation amount cannot be credited to a plant asset account because the amount of depreciation is only an estimate. Instead, a contra plant asset account, Accumu-

Review the purpose of a contra account.

Emphasize that the Accumulated Depreciation accounts will be carried from period to period.

lated Depreciation, is used to record the total amount of depreciation allocated to a plant asset. The balance of a contra account, you'll remember, decreases the balance of that account's related account. In this case, the related account is a plant asset account. If a business has several types of plant assets, it will have several expense and contra asset accounts, for example, Accumulated Depreciation—Equipment and Accumulated Depreciation—Building. Now let's look at an example of how depreciation expense is recorded.

On January 6, Mayfaire, Inc., bought a delivery truck for $16,000. The truck has an estimated useful life of 5 years and a disposal value of $1,500. The depreciable cost is, therefore, $14,500. On December 31 Mayfaire must make an adjustment, entered first on the work sheet, for the annual depreciation expense on the truck. Mayfaire uses the straight-line method of calculating depreciation. The annual depreciation expense, calculated on page 147, is $2,900.

The two accounts affected by the adjustment are Depreciation Expense—Delivery Equipment and Accumulated Depreciation—Delivery Equipment. Depreciation Expense—Delivery Equipment is debited for $2,900, that part of the cost of the truck that is being allocated as an expense for this fiscal period. The contra plant asset account Accumulated Depreciation—Delivery Equipment is credited for $2,900, because that account is used to record the total amount of depreciation allocated.

Depreciation Expense—Delivery Equipment	
Dr.	Cr.
Adj. $2,900	

Accumulated Depreciation—Delivery Equipment	
Dr.	Cr.
	Adj. $2,900

Figure 6-1 shows the adjusting entry to record the first year's depreciation expense.

GENERAL JOURNAL — PAGE 25

	DATE		DESCRIPTION	POST. REF.	DEBIT	CREDIT	
1	199-		Adjusting Entries				1
18	Dec.	31	Deprec. Exp.-Delivery Equipment		2900 00		18
19			Accum. Deprec.-Delivery Equip.			2900 00	19

Figure 6-1 Recording the Adjusting Entry for Depreciation Expense

Remind students that the data for this adjusting entry is taken from the Adjustments section of the work sheet.

The accumulated depreciation accounts are listed in the Property, Plant, and Equipment section of the balance sheet, immediately below their related asset accounts. A portion of Mayfaire's balance sheet showing the Property, Plant and Equipnment section appears in Figure 6-2. The balances entered in the second (middle) amount column represent the book value for each type of property, plant, and equipment asset. As you can see, the balance of each contra asset account is subtracted from its related asset account to show the asset's book value.

Mayfaire, Inc. Balance Sheet December 31, 199-			
Property, Plant, and Equipment			
Office Equipment	12 000 00		
Less: Accum. Depreciation	6 000 00	6 000 00	
Store Equipment	43 000 00		
Less: Accum. Depreciation	18 000 00	25 000 00	
Delivery Equipment	30 000 00		
Less: Accum. Depreciation	21 000 00	9 000 00	
Building	60 000 00		
Less: Accum. Depreciation	28 000 00	32 000 00	
Land		30 000 00	
Total Prop., Plant, and Equipment			102 000 00

Figure 6-2 Property, Plant, and Equipment Section of a Balance Sheet

Depreciation and Income Tax Reporting

Students may be confused thinking this is a questionable procedure.

You have seen that depreciation is recorded as a business expense. Expenses, as you know, are deducted from gross profit to determine the business's net (taxable) income. The depreciation method a business uses, therefore, can have an effect on net income. Businesses often use one depreciation method for financial accounting purposes and another method for income tax purposes.

Many businesses use the straight-line method when preparing financial statements at the end of the fiscal period. The straight-line method allocates less depreciation expense for the period and results in the reporting of higher earnings on the financial statements. When preparing the tax returns for the year, however, most businesses use an accelerated method of depreciation. An accelerated method allocates greater amounts of depreciation in the early years and results in the reporting of a lower net income.

In 1981, Congress passed a law that substituted a new depreciation method called the *Accelerated Cost Recovery System (ACRS)*. ACRS was a mandatory system that *for tax purposes* ignored the concepts of estimated useful life and salvage value. Instead, depreciation was computed (1) on the asset's unadjusted cost (rather than on its depreciable cost) and (2) over a period of years set by law. With ACRS, depreciation was calculated by multiplying the asset's cost by certain set percentages. Subsequently, Congress revised the tax laws when it passed the Tax Reform Act of 1986. The new *Modified Accelerated Cost Recovery System (MACRS)* kept the basic ACRS concepts but increased the number of years over which depreciation can be calculated.

Emphasize that the purpose of allowing two methods of reporting depreciation is to encourage businesses to invest in new equipment.

Explain that the accelerated methods (ACRS and MACRS) allow businesses to write off the cost in a more rapid manner.

The intent of Congress was to encourage businesses to invest in new plant and equipment by allowing them to write off the costs of the assets quickly. Both ACRS and MACRS accelerate the write-off of plant assets in two ways. First, they allow businesses to write off the cost of plant assets over shorter periods of time. Second, they permit businesses to write off most of the cost in the assets' early years. Tax methods of depreciation such as ACRS and MACRS, however, are not acceptable for financial reporting under generally accepted accounting principles.

Plant Asset Records

Most businesses maintain records for the plant assets they purchase. A business can use these *plant asset records* to keep track of the accumulated depreciation and book value for each asset, as well as to determine the amount of the adjusting entry for depreciation. A plant asset record also contains information such as the date the asset was purchased, the original cost, the estimated useful life, and so on. A plant asset record is also helpful if a business has to prepare a claim for an insured loss. Figure 6-3 shows the plant asset record for Mayfaire's delivery truck.

PLANT ASSET RECORD

ITEM Delivery Truck — GENERAL LEDGER ACCOUNT Delivery Equipment

SERIAL NUMBER 19347-295823 — MANUFACTURER Heavy Duty Trucks, Inc.

PURCHASED FROM Steele Motors — EST. SALVAGE VALUE $1,500

ESTIMATED LIFE 5 Years — LOCATION Company Garage

DEPRECIATION METHOD Straight-line — DEPRECIATION PER YEAR $2,900 — RATE OF DEPRECIATION 20%

Date	Explanation	Asset			Accumulated Depreciation			Book Value
		Debit	Credit	Balance	Debit	Credit	Balance	
1/6/92	Purchased	$16,000		$16,000				$16,000
12/31/92						$2,900	$2,900	13,000
12/31/93						2,900	5,800	10,200
12/31/94						2,900	8,700	7,300
12/31/95						2,900	11,600	4,400
12/31/96						2,900	14,500	1,500

Figure 6-3 Plant Asset Record

Discuss the fact that each plant asset account (such as Office Equipment) is a controlling account, similar to Accounts Receivable.

Plant assets are divided according to type; for example, store equipment includes items such as display cases, cash registers, counters, storage shelves, and so on. To account for the depreciation of each item, a separate record card is kept for each plant asset. Store Equipment then becomes a controlling account, and the store equipment plant asset records become a subsidiary ledger. This relationship is similar to that of Accounts Receivable, which is also a controlling account.

Before reading further, do the following activity to check your understanding of the material you have just studied.

Plant assets include equipment purchased to operate a business.

Check Your Learning

On May 12, the RMM Company purchased new office equipment costing $3,000. The equipment has an estimated useful life of four years and a salvage value of $500. RMM uses the straight-line method to calculate the estimated depreciation on this equipment. The company's fiscal period ends on December 31.

Answer these questions on a sheet of notebook paper.

1. What is the annual depreciation on this equipment?
2. What is the amount of the adjusting entry to record the depreciation on this equipment at the end of the first year?
3. In the adjusting entry, which account is debited? Which account is credited?

Compare your answers to those in the answers section. Reread the preceding part of the chapter to find the correct answers to any questions you may have missed.

Disposing of Plant Assets

Sooner or later, a business disposes of its plant assets by (1) discarding them, (2) selling them, or (3) trading them in for other assets. When a business disposes of a plant asset, it must first record the depreciation up to the date of the disposal. Then it can remove the asset from the accounting records. Let's look at some examples.

Discarding Plant Assets

When plant assets are no longer useful to the business and have no disposal value, they are discarded.

Emphasize that the Accumulated Depreciation account must be closed when the plant asset account is closed.

Discarding an Asset with No Book Value On August 23, Mayfaire discarded a display case that originally cost $1,300. The display case had no salvage value and had already been fully depreciated. An asset is fully depreciated when its book value is zero. A fully depreciated asset is kept on the accounting records for as long as it is still being used; however, the company cannot take any additional depreciation on it.

Since the display case is fully depreciated, it is not necessary to record any additional depreciation. To remove the display case from the accounting records, Mayfaire debits Accumulated Depreciation—Store Equipment for $1,300 and credits Store Equipment for the same amount. This entry reduces the balances of both accounts to zero.

Accumulated Depreciation—Store Equipment	
Dr.	Cr.
$1,300	Bal. $1,300

Store Equipment	
Dr.	Cr.
Bal. $1,300	$1,300

Figure 6-4 shows the journal entry to record the disposal of the display.

GENERAL JOURNAL — PAGE 19

	DATE		DESCRIPTION	POST. REF.	DEBIT	CREDIT	
1	199– Aug.	23	Accum. Deprec.–Store Equipment		1300 00		1
2			Store Equipment			1300 00	2
3			Memo. 616				3

Figure 6-4 Journalizing the Disposal of a Fully Depreciated Plant Asset

Discarding an Asset with a Book Value On October 4, Mayfaire discarded a time clock that cost $1,620. The time clock had an estimated useful life of 9 years and a disposal value of zero. Annual depreciation expense is, therefore, $180 ($1,620 ÷ 9). The accumulated depreciation as of December 31 of the previous year was $1,440. Before the disposal of the time clock can be recorded, the depreciation expense for the current year must be recorded. This step is necessary because the time clock was used until October 1 and, under the matching principle, a portion of its cost must be allocated to the accounting periods in which the asset was used. The depreciation expense for the period from January 1 to September 30 is $135 ($180 × 9/12). That amount is debited to Depreciation Expense—Office Equipment and credited to Accumulated Depreciation—Office Equipment.

Depreciation Expense—Office Equipment	
Dr.	Cr.
$135	

Accumulated Depreciation—Office Equipment	
Dr.	Cr.
	Bal. $1,440
	135

The general journal entry to record the depreciation expense appears on lines 1 through 3 of Figure 6-5.

GENERAL JOURNAL — PAGE 21

	DATE		DESCRIPTION	POST. REF.	DEBIT	CREDIT	
1	199- Oct.	4	Deprec. Expense—Office Equipment		135 00		1
2			Accum. Deprec.—Office Equip.			135 00	2
3			Memo: 632				3
4		4	Accum. Deprec.—Office Equipment		1575 00		4
5			Loss on Disposal of Plant Assets		45 00		5
6			Office Equipment			1620 00	6
7			Memo: 632				7

Figure 6-5 Recording the Discarding of a Plant Asset with a Book Value

Use demonstration problem 6-5 here.

Mention that Loss on Disposal of Plant Assets is another expense account.

The book value of the time clock is now $45 ($1,620 – $1,575 accumulated depreciation). Mayfaire is discarding an asset that has a book value of $45. It, therefore, has a *loss,* which must be shown in the accounting records. This loss is recorded as an expense. The amount of the loss is debited to an other expense account titled Loss on Disposal of Plant Assets. In the entry, Accumulated Depreciation—Office Equipment is debited for $1,575, Loss on Disposal of Plant Assets is debited for $45, and Office Equipment is credited for $1,620.

Accumulated Depreciation—Office Equipment	
Dr.	Cr.
$1,575	Bal. $1,575

Loss on Disposal of Plant Assets	
Dr.	Cr.
$45	

Office Equipment	
Dr.	Cr.
Bal. $1,620	$1,620

The entry to record the disposal of the time clock is shown on lines 4 through 7 of Figure 6-5.

R—E—M—E—M—B—E—R

Before the disposal of a plant asset can be recorded, the depreciation expense up to the date of disposal must be recorded.

Selling Plant Assets

It's very difficult to estimate the exact disposal value of a plant asset. It's likely, therefore, that when a business sells a plant asset, the selling price will not be the same as the asset's book value. The difference between the book value and the selling price will determine whether the business has a gain or a loss on the sale.

▲ Selling an Asset at a Loss On August 21, Mayfaire sold a desk for $190. The desk originally cost $1,600, and the accumulated depreciation as of the end of the previous year was $1,248. The annual depreciation expense is $156.

First, the depreciation expense for the current year must be recorded. Depreciation for the current year is \$104 (\$156 × 8/12). The total accumulated depreciation, then, is \$1,352, as shown in the following T accounts:

Depreciation Expense— Office Equipment

Dr.	Cr.
\$104	

Accumulated Depreciation— Office Equipment

Dr.	Cr.
	Bal. \$1,248
	104

Emphasize that the business is incurring a loss even though it is receiving some cash on the sale of the plant asset.

Use demonstration problem 6-6 here.

The book value of the desk is \$248 (\$1,600 – \$1,352). However, Mayfaire is receiving only \$190 from the sale. It has therefore incurred a loss of \$58 (\$248 – \$190). This loss is debited to the Loss on Disposal of Plant Assets account. The complete transaction is shown in the following T accounts:

Cash in Bank

Dr.	Cr.
\$190	

Accumulated Depreciation— Office Equipment

Dr.	Cr.
\$1,352	Bal. \$1,352

Loss on Disposal of Plant Assets

Dr.	Cr.
\$58	

Office Equipment

Dr.	Cr.
Bal. \$1,600	\$1,600

Figure 6-6 shows the entry to record the sale of the desk.

CASH RECEIPTS JOURNAL — PAGE 23

	DATE	DOC. NO.	ACCOUNT TITLE	POST. REF.	GENERAL DEBIT	GENERAL CREDIT	SALES CREDIT	SALES TAX PAYABLE CREDIT	ACCOUNTS RECEIVABLE CREDIT	CASH IN BANK DEBIT	
	199–										
8	Aug. 21	1602	Accum. Depr.-Off. Equip.		1 352 00					190 00	8
9			Loss on Disp. of Pl. Assets		58 00						9
10			Office Equipment			1 600 00					10

Figure 6-6 Journalizing the Sale of a Plant Asset at a Loss

▲ **Selling an Asset at a Gain** On January 10, Mayfaire sold some display shelves for \$250. The shelves had originally cost \$4,200; accumulated depreciation to date is \$4,060. The book value of the display equipment is \$140 (\$4,200 – \$4,060). Since Mayfaire is receiving \$250, it has a gain of \$110 (\$250 – \$140 book value). This gain is recorded in the Gain on Disposal of Plant Assets account. Gain on Disposal of Plant Assets is classified as an other revenue account. The T accounts on page 160 show the transaction.

Use demonstration problem 6-7 here.

Cash in Bank	
Dr.	Cr.
$250	

Accumulated Depreciation—Store Equipment	
Dr.	Cr.
$4,060	Bal. $4,060

Store Equipment	
Dr.	Cr.
Bal. $4,200	$4,200

Gain on Disposal of Plant Assets	
Dr.	Cr.
	$110

The entry to record the sale of the equipment appears in Figure 6-7.

CASH RECEIPTS JOURNAL — PAGE 17

	DATE		DOC. NO.	ACCOUNT TITLE	POST. REF.	GENERAL DEBIT	GENERAL CREDIT	SALES CREDIT	SALES TAX PAYABLE CREDIT	ACCOUNTS RECEIVABLE CREDIT	CASH IN BANK DEBIT	
	199–											
6	Jan.	10	892	Accum. Depr.–St. Equip.		4 060 00					250 00	6
7				Store Equipment			4 200 00					7
8				Gain on Disp. of Pl. Assets			110 00					8

Figure 6-7 Journalizing the Sale of a Plant Asset at a Gain

Before reading further, do the following activity to check your understanding of the material you have just studied.

Check Your Learning

On a sheet of notebook paper, indicate whether the following statements are true or false.

1. When a plant asset is disposed of, the business must first record the depreciation up to the date of the disposal.
2. When a plant asset is fully depreciated, it is discarded.
3. The book value of a plant asset is not considered when the plant asset is sold.
4. If a company discards a plant asset that still has some book value, it has incurred a loss.

Compare your answers to those in the answers section. Reread the preceding part of the chapter to find the correct answers to any questions you may have missed.

Have students complete Exercise 6-3 at this point.

Exchanging Plant Assets

A business often trades in (exchanges) one plant asset for another, similar asset. Usually the business receives a *trade-in allowance* on the old asset and pays the balance owed in cash. The trade-in allowance is normally different from the book value of the old asset. If the trade-in allowance is *greater* than the book value, the business has a gain; if it is *less* than the book value, the business has a loss.

The gains and losses on the exchange of similar plant assets, however, are handled differently than the gains and losses on the sale of plant assets. In the accounting records, when one plant asset is exchanged for a similar asset, (1) a loss is recognized but (2) a gain is not recognized. When gains are not recognized, the recorded value of the new asset equals what the business gave up to acquire it. In other words, the recorded value of the new asset should equal the book value of the old asset plus any cash paid out. Let's look at some examples.

This section may be difficult for students; therefore, work through all the calculations with students.

R — E — M — E — M — B — E — R

When a plant asset is exchanged for a similar asset, losses are recognized in the accounting records but gains are not recognized.

Loss Recognized on the Exchange of Plant Assets

Mayfaire, Inc., owns a delivery truck that originally cost $30,000. The accumulated depreciation recorded to date is $21,000. The truck therefore has a book value of $9,000 ($30,000 – $21,000).

Now let's assume the following transaction took place.

January 12: *Traded in the old truck for a new, smaller truck costing $11,000. Received a trade-in allowance of $7,000 for the old truck and paid $4,000 cash, Check 2537.*

In this case, Mayfaire has a loss on the transaction. While it has acquired an asset valued at $11,000, it has given up assets totaling $13,000 ($4,000 cash and a truck with a book value of $9,000). Mayfaire, therefore, has a loss of $2,000 on the transaction. Since this loss must be recognized in the accounting records, it is debited to the Loss on Disposal of Plant Assets account.

$13,000
–11,000
$ 2,000 loss

Use demonstration problem 6-8 here.

The transaction is illustrated in the T accounts that follow and in Figure 6-8. Note that the recorded value of the new truck is the list price of $11,000.

CASH PAYMENTS JOURNAL — PAGE 15

	DATE	DOC. NO.	ACCOUNT TITLE	POST. REF.	GENERAL DEBIT	GENERAL CREDIT	ACCOUNTS PAYABLE DEBIT	PURCHASES DISCOUNTS CREDIT	CASH IN BANK CREDIT	
	199-									
6	Jan. 12	Ck 2537	Delivery Equipment (new truck)		11 000 00				4 000 00	6
7			Accum. Deprec.-Delivery Equipment		21 000 00					7
8			Loss on Disposal of Plant Assets		2 000 00					8
9			Delivery Equipment (old truck)			30 000 00				9

Figure 6-8 Recognizing a Loss on the Exchange of Plant Assets

ACCOUNTING Notes
According to the accounting guideline of conservatism, accountants should take the "safe route"—the one that is least likely to overstate income. Losses on the exchange of a plant asset, therefore, are recognized in the accounting records.

Delivery Equipment

Dr.	Cr.
Bal. $30,000	$30,000 (old truck)
11,000 (new truck)	

Accumulated Depreciation—Delivery Equipment

Dr.	Cr.
$21,000	Bal. $21,000

Loss on Disposal of Plant Assets

Dr.	Cr.
$2,000	

Cash in Bank

Dr.	Cr.
	$4,000

Gain Not Recognized on the Exchange of Plant Assets

Earlier we mentioned that losses on the exchange of plant assets are recognized, but gains are not. For example, suppose that when Mayfaire traded in the old truck, it received a trade-in allowance of $11,000. In other words, the dealer agreed to accept the old truck (book value $9,000) in full payment for the new one.

$11,000
– 9,000
$ 2,000 gain

In this case, Mayfaire has a gain of $2,000. It is acquiring an asset with a list price of $11,000 while giving up an asset with a book value of $9,000. This gain, however, is not recognized in the accounting records. You'll remember that the recorded value of the new asset should equal the book value of the old asset, plus any cash paid out. Since there was no cash involved in this transaction, Mayfaire records the value of the new truck in the Delivery Equipment account as $9,000 (the book value of the old truck). This transaction is illustrated in the following T accounts and in Figure 6-9.

Use demonstration problem 6-9 here.

GENERAL JOURNAL — PAGE 12

	DATE		DESCRIPTION	POST. REF.	DEBIT	CREDIT	
1	199– Jan.	12	Delivery Equipment (new truck)		9 000 00		1
2			Accum. Deprec.–Delivery Equipment		21 000 00		2
3			Delivery Equipment			30 000 00	3
4			Memo: 523				4

Figure 6-9 Journalizing the Exchange of Plant Assets with a Gain (Example 1)

Delivery Equipment

Dr.	Cr.
Bal. $30,000	$30,000 (old truck)
9,000 (new truck)	

Accumulated Depreciation—Delivery Equipment

Dr.	Cr.
$21,000	Bal. $21,000

$11,000
–10,000
$ 1,000 gain

Now suppose Mayfaire received a trade-in allowance of $10,000 and paid $1,000 cash. Mayfaire has acquired an asset worth $11,000 while giving up assets (the old truck worth $9,000 and $1,000 cash) of $10,000. Mayfaire still has a gain on the transaction, but the gain is now $1,000.

Since the gain should not be recognized on the accounting records, the recorded value of the new truck is $10,000, the book value of the old truck plus the amount of cash paid out. This transaction is illustrated in the following T accounts and in Figure 6-10.

CASH PAYMENTS JOURNAL — PAGE 15

	DATE	DOC. NO.	ACCOUNT DEBITED	POST. REF.	GENERAL DEBIT	ACCOUNTS PAYABLE DEBIT	PURCHASES DISCOUNTS CREDIT	CASH IN BANK CREDIT	
	199-								
6	Jan. 12	Ck 2537	Delivery Equipment (new truck)		10 000 00			1 000 00	6
7			Accum. Deprec.–Delivery Equipment		21 000 00				7
8			Delivery Equipment (old truck)			30 000 00			8

Figure 6-10 Journalizing the Exchange of Plant Assets with a Gain (Example 2)

Delivery Equipment	
Dr.	Cr.
Bal. $30,000	$30,000
10,000	

Accumulated Depreciation— Delivery Equipment	
Dr.	Cr.
$21,000	Bal. $21,000

Cash in Bank	
Dr.	Cr.
	$1,000

R — E — M — E — M — B — E — R

When gains are not recognized, the recorded value of the new asset is equal to what the business gave up to acquire the asset.

Other Assets

Emphasize that most businesses have some intangible assets. In some businesses, such as music and publishing, the intangible assets are a major aspect of the total assets of the business.

Discuss the concept of "goodwill" and give some examples, both local and national.

In addition to the assets you've studied thus far, businesses often have other forms of assets that are more difficult to visualize. These assets are referred to as *intangible assets.* **Intangible assets** are long-lived assets that have no physical substance; that is, they are invisible to the eye. These assets usually have to do with legal rights or advantages that have a value for the business. Intangible assets include items such as organization costs, goodwill, copyrights, trademarks, patents, and franchises.

Organization costs refer to the costs directly related to establishing a corporation. These may include various state fees, attorneys' fees, printing costs, and accountants' fees. You'll learn more about organization costs in Chapter 9. *Goodwill* generally refers to the good reputation of a business. From an accounting standpoint, goodwill exists when a buyer pays more for a business than the current market value of the business's assets. Since the buyer has paid more than the current market value of the tangible assets, the additional money is attributed to goodwill, an intangible asset. *Patents* and *copyrights* are exclusive rights granted by the federal government. Patents are given for particular products or processes, while copyrights are issued for literary, musical, or artistic materials. A *trademark* is a registered symbol or name identifying a certain product

Have students complete Exercise 6-1 at this point.

or service. A *franchise* is a right to conduct business under a contracted name, such as McDonald's. The cost of these assets is written off, or *amortized,* over the periods during which the business receives benefits. The maximum time periods range from 17 years for patents to 40 years for goodwill and copyrights.

Summary of Key Points

1. Property, plant, and equipment assets are long-lived assets that are expected to benefit the business for a number of years.
2. The original cost of a property, plant, and equipment asset includes all the normal costs necessary for acquiring and installing it.
3. All property, plant, and equipment assets, with the exception of land, are depreciable; that is, their costs are charged as expenses over their useful lives. Depreciation is a procedure for allocating the cost of a plant asset to the periods in which the business receives service from the asset.
4. Land has an unlimited life and is not depreciated. The value of land must be separated from the value of buildings when the two have been purchased as one package.
5. There are four methods of determining depreciation: the straight-line method, the units-of-production method, the double-declining-balance method, and the sum-of-the-years'-digits method.
6. The book value of a plant asset is equal to the asset's cost minus the accumulated depreciation.
7. Depreciation is recorded at the end of the fiscal period in an adjusting entry as a debit to the asset's Depreciation Expense account and a credit to the asset's Accumulated Depreciation account.
8. A plant asset record is often kept for each plant asset. This record usually lists the date acquired, cost, and depreciation taken to date.
9. A business may dispose of its plant assets by (1) discarding them, (2) selling them, or (3) trading them in for other assets.
10. Before the disposal of a plant asset can be recorded, the depreciation expense up to the date of disposal must be recorded.
11. If a business incurs a loss when it discards or sells a plant asset, it records the loss in the other expense account Loss on Disposal of Plant Assets. If the business has a gain when it discards or sells a plant asset, it records the gain in the other revenue account Gain on Disposal of Plant Assets.
12. When a business exchanges (trades) a plant asset for a similar plant asset, losses are recognized in the accounting records, but gains are not recognized. When a gain occurs, the recorded value of the new asset is the book value of the old asset plus any cash given.
13. Intangible assets are long-lived assets with no physical substance. Their cost is written off over their useful lives.

6 Review and Applications

Building Your Accounting Vocabulary

In your own words, write the definition of each of the following accounting terms. Use complete sentences for your definitions.

accumulated depreciation
appraisal value
book value
current assets
depreciable cost
depreciation
double-declining-balance method
intangible assets
property, plant, and equipment
salvage value
straight-line method
sum-of-the-years'-digits method
units-of-production method

Reviewing Your Accounting Knowledge

1. What is the difference between current assets and property, plant, and equipment assets?
2. What types of costs are included in the initial cost of a property, plant, and equipment asset?
3. Why is land handled differently than other property, plant, and equipment assets?
4. Are land improvements depreciable? What kinds of expenditures are considered land improvements?
5. Why is depreciation considered to be an estimate?
6. What three factors must be known before a plant asset's depreciation expense can be calculated?
7. What is the advantage of using an accelerated depreciation method? Which two methods are considered to be accelerated depreciation methods?
8. Which two accounts are involved when recording the adjusting entry for the depreciation of a plant asset?
9. Why might a business use one method of depreciation for financial statements and another method for tax reporting?
10. Describe the use and operation of the plant asset ledger. What information is usually listed on each plant asset record?
11. Why are gains or losses on the sale of plant assets not listed in the Revenue or Operating Expenses sections of the income statement?
12. How are gains and losses on the exchange of similar plant assets handled in the accounting records?

Improving Your Math Skills

It is important for accounting workers to know how to change fractions to decimals. For example, fractions cannot be entered into a calculator unless they are first changed to decimal form. Change the following fractions to decimals. Round the decimals to four decimal places.

1. $\frac{1}{2}$
2. $\frac{7}{8}$
3. $\frac{5}{9}$
4. $\frac{1}{4}$
5. $\frac{3}{11}$
6. $\frac{5}{8}$
7. $\frac{5}{12}$
8. $\frac{2}{25}$
9. $\frac{3}{20}$
10. $\frac{6}{7}$

Applying Accounting Procedures

Exercise 6-1 Classifying Asset Accounts

Following are some assets of the Waterbury Company.

Accounts Receivable
Building
Cash in Bank
Delivery Equipment
Land
Land Improvements
Machinery
Office Equipment
Organization Costs
Prepaid Insurance
Supplies
Trademarks

Instructions: Use a form similar to the one that follows. For each asset, indicate whether it is a current asset; a property, plant, and equipment asset; or an intangible asset. Place a check mark in the correct column.

Asset	Current Asset	Property, Plant, & Equipment Asset	Intangible Asset
Accounts Receivable	√		

COMPUTER PROBLEM

Exercise 6-2 Determining Depreciation Expense, Accumulated Depreciation, and Book Value

On January 1, the Precision Tool Corporation bought a machine costing $56,000. The machine has an estimated useful life of 5 years and an estimated salvage value of $2,000.

Instructions: For each year of the machine's useful life, determine (1) the annual depreciation expense, (2) the accumulated depreciation, and (3) the book value. Use the form provided in the working papers to calculate the amounts using each of the following methods. Round your answers to the nearest whole dollar.

(1) Straight-line method
(2) Double-declining-balance method
(3) Sum-of-the-years'-digits method

	Straight-Line Method			Double-Declining-Balance Method			Sum-of-the-Years'-Digits Method		
Year	Depr. Exp.	Accum. Depr.	Book Value	Depr. Exp.	Accum. Depr.	Book Value	Depr. Exp.	Accum. Depr.	Book Value
1									

Exercise 6-3 Disposing of Plant Assets

Follett Dental Clinic owns a piece of equipment that originally cost $23,500. Annual depreciation is $2,250, and the accumulated depreciation as of January 1 (the first day of the fiscal period) is $14,625. Follett disposed of the equipment on October 20.

Instructions: Answer the following questions. Use plain paper or the space provided in the working papers.

$1,875
$16,500
$7,000
Yes, $7,000 loss
Gain, $650
Loss, $800

1. What is the depreciation for the current year (up to the disposal date)?
2. What is the accumulated depreciation as of October 20?
3. What is the book value as of October 20?
4. If Follett discards the equipment as having no value, is there a loss? If so, how much?
5. If Follett sells the equipment for $7,650, is there a gain or a loss? For how much?
6. Suppose Follett trades in the equipment for a newer model costing $27,600. Follett receives a $6,200 trade-in allowance and pays the balance in cash. Is there a gain or a loss on the transaction? For what amount?

Problem 6-1 Recording Estimated Annual Depreciation

On May 12, the Oakdale Service Company purchased an industrial vacuum cleaner for $4,900. The vacuum cleaner has an estimated useful life of 5 years and a salvage value of $250. Oakdale uses the straight-line method of calculating depreciation.

Deprec. Exp., $620.00

Instructions: On page 42 of a general journal, record the December 31 adjusting entry for the estimated depreciation on the vacuum cleaner (Equipment).

Problem 6-2 Using the Units-of-Production Method

On August 23, the Color Production Corporation purchased new photographic equipment (Photo Equipment) costing $14,595. The equipment has a salvage value of $150 and an estimated useful life of 45,000 hours. The current fiscal period ended on December 31. During the period, the equipment operated approximately 950 hours.

Instructions:

Deprec. Exp., $305.00

(1) Use the units-of-production method to calculate the depreciation for the fiscal period. Round your answer to the nearest whole dollar.
(2) Record the depreciation on page 85 of a general journal.

Problem 6-3 Discarding a Plant Asset

J & M Enterprises owns a word processor (Office Equipment) that originally cost $8,900. The accumulated depreciation as of January 1 (the first day of the fiscal period) is $6,563; the annual depreciation is $1,250. On July 22, the company discarded the word processor.

Instructions: On general journal page 23,

Deprec. Exp., $729.00

(1) Prepare the entry to record the depreciation up to July 22. Round the depreciation amount to the nearest whole dollar. Use Memorandum 42 as the source document.

(2) Record the entry to discard the word processor. Use Memorandum 42 as the source document.

COMPUTER PROBLEM

Problem 6-4 Selling Plant Assets

On April 4, Frank's Catch of the Day sold four display cases for $1,600 cash. The following details are from the plant asset records: cost, $8,172; accumulated depreciation as of the previous December 31, $6,478; annual depreciation, $984.

Instructions:

Deprec. Exp., $246.00

(1) On general journal page 16, record the entry to bring the depreciation up to date. Use Memorandum 137 as the source document.

(2) On page 21 of a cash receipts journal, record the sale of the display cases. Use Receipt 759 as the source document.

Problem 6-5 Exchanging a Plant Asset

On August 21, the Buckley Manufacturing Company traded in a finishing machine (Equipment) on a newer model costing $9,250. Buckley received a trade-in allowance of $1,700 on the old machine and issued Check 8492 for $7,550. The plant asset records show that the original cost of the old finishing machine was $7,375, the accumulated depreciation as of December 31 of last year was $5,860, and the annual depreciation is $846.

Instructions:

Deprec. Exp., $564.00

(1) On general journal page 36, record the current year's depreciation. Use Memorandum 994 as the source document.

(2) Record the entry for the exchange of the two machines on page 45 of the cash payments journal.

Problem 6-6 Recording Plant Asset Transactions

During a three-year period, the Wilton Appliance Company completed the following transactions related to its delivery truck.

Instructions:

(1) Open these general ledger accounts: Delivery Equipment, account no. 135; Accumulated Depreciation—Delivery Equipment, account no. 136; Depreciation Expense—Delivery Equipment, account no. 640; Truck Repair Expense, account no. 645.

(2) Record the transactions in the cash payments journal (page 27) and general journal (page 17).

(3) Post the transactions to the accounts opened in (1).

Transactions:

Year 1

Jan. 7 Bought a new delivery truck for $23,550, Check 2843.

Oct. 27 Issued Check 3046 for $497 in repairs to the truck.

Dec. 31 Recorded the adjusting entry for depreciation for the fiscal year. The truck has an estimated useful life of 4 years and an estimated salvage value of $1,050. Wilton uses the sum-of-the-years'-digits method to estimate depreciation.

31 Closed the appropriate accounts into Income Summary.

Year 2

May 17 Paid $284 to replace a windshield on the truck, Check 3896.

Dec. 31 Recorded the depreciation for the fiscal year.

31 Closed the appropriate accounts into the Income Summary account.

Year 3

Apr. 14 Bought new headlights for the truck, paying $174, Check 4385.

Sept. 29 Traded in the old truck for a new one costing $28,400. Received a trade-in allowance of $4,000 and issued Check 4605 for the difference. Recorded the entry for the year-to-date depreciation on the truck (Memorandum 1743) and the entry for the exchange of the trucks.

Dec. 31 Recorded the depreciation on the new truck for the partial year. The estimated useful life of the truck is 4 years; it has a salvage value of $1,200.

31 Closed the appropriate accounts into Income Summary.

CHALLENGE PROBLEM

COMPUTER PROBLEM

Problem 6-7 Evaluating Depreciation Methods

You are the accountant for Small Tools, Inc., a company that manufactures hand tools. The company plans to purchase a new tooling machine at a cost of $13,000. The machine has an estimated disposal value of $325 and an estimated useful life of 5 years. You have been asked to supply management with some information.

Instructions:

(1) Determine the annual depreciation, accumulated depreciation, and book value of the machine for the first three years using the straight-line method, the double-declining-balance method, and the sum-of-the-years'-digits method. Use plain paper or the table provided in the working papers.

(2) Answer the following questions.

(a) Which depreciation method would yield the highest book value after three years?

(b) Which depreciation method would allow the maximum amount of depreciation over the three years?

(3) Assume that at the end of three years, Small Tools, Inc., can sell the machine for $3,500. Answer the following questions.

(a) Would any of the depreciation methods provide for a gain on the sale of the machine? If so, which method(s) and how much of a gain?

(b) Would any of the methods result in a loss on the sale? If so, which method(s) and how much of a loss.

FOCUS ON

COMPUTERS

Online Accountants: Using Computers to Keep Current

Online data banks provide access to the latest information on tax laws and accounting practices.

In addition to working with company ledgers, accountants must keep up to date with changing tax laws and accounting practices. Before computers became common office additions, accountants spent hours on the phone and in the library trying to locate the information they needed. With computers, accountants can get this information quickly and easily through access to online communication services.

All an accountant needs to access huge data banks, such as the IRS's online information service, is an electronic modem device connected to a microcomputer. Modems translate electronic signals from a computer into pulses of sound that are carried across phone lines to other computers. Information coming from the data banks of an online service are translated by the accountant's modem into words and numbers that appear on the computer screen or are printed out directly.

Online data banks contain a library's worth of information without the library. The IRS's online information service contains information found in 70 taxpayer information publications, plus miscellaneous forms and tax tips and aids for doing computer research. Other online services provide daily summaries and updates of all developments and court decisions concerning federal and state tax laws.

Legal services also are available online. Libraries of legal statutes, regulations, and the complete IRS tax code are available through a single phone call.

Other data banks contain information such as detailed financial statements of many companies; the complete text of articles from *The Wall Street Journal, Barron's,* and the Dow Jones News Service before they are published; and economic and marketing forecasts.

Of course, using a data bank isn't free. The cost is assessed by monthly subscription, amount of time used, or both. A telephone call can cost anywhere from about $20 to well over $100, depending on whether or not it is made during prime business hours. Most users of online services, however, find that the time and effort saved is well worth the cost.

Mini Practice Set

APPLICATION ACTIVITY 2

Accounting for Current and Long-Term Assets

In the last four chapters, you learned the procedures to account for current assets and plant assets. Now you will have the opportunity to review and apply what you learned by completing the work sheet for Fast Gifts.

When you have completed this activity, you will have done the following:

COMPUTER PROBLEM

1. Calculated the estimated amount of uncollectible accounts.
2. Calculated the amount of accrued interest income on notes receivable.
3. Determined the value of the ending merchandise inventory.
4. Calculated the annual depreciation expense for plant assets.
5. Entered all adjustments on the Adjustments section of the work sheet.
6. Completed the work sheet.
7. Prepared a balance sheet.

Fast Gifts

Fast Gifts is a retail merchandising business that sells a wide variety of gift items. Fast Gifts is organized as a closely held corporation. The manager and sole stockholder is Lynn Fast.

The Trial Balance section of the work sheet for the year ended December 31 has been completed and is included in the working papers that accompany this textbook.

Instructions:

Adjustments:
(a) $1,396.42
(b) $65.58
(c) $8,327.45
(d) $2,523.20
(e) $450.00
(f) $1,723.17
(g) $1,570.12
(h) $350.00

Column totals:
Adj., $16,405.94
ATB, $334,002.19

Net income, $22,601.57

BS totals, $139,823.42

(1) Based on the information that follows, calculate the amounts for the end-of-period adjustments and enter those adjustments in the Adjustments section of the work sheet.
(2) Complete the work sheet, determining the amount of the net income or loss.
(3) Prepare the end-of-period balance sheet for Fast Gifts.

Adjustment Information:

1. **Adjustment for uncollectible accounts:** Fast Gifts uses the percentage of net sales method to estimate its bad debts expense. After examining the accounts receivable records for the past five years, the company's auditor estimated that approximately 0.75% of net sales will not be collected.
2. **Adjustment for accrued interest on notes receivable:** Fast Gifts holds

two notes receivable that have not been discounted and mature during the next fiscal period.

Principal	Issue Date	Term	Interest Rate
$2,500	September 28	120 days	9.5%
390	November 15	90 days	9%

3. **Adjustment for merchandise inventory:** Fast Gifts uses the fifo method to assign costs to its inventory items. After a physical inventory, it was determined that the cost of the inventory items is $61,294.75. Unfortunately, Item 7844, small table lamps, was accidentally left off the inventory list. That omission was just discovered. The inventory records for the small table lamps are as follows.

Beginning inventory	12 units @ $21.85
Purchased February 19	15 units @ $22.50
Purchased April 26	10 units @ $22.65
Purchased June 3	20 units @ $22.93
Purchased September 16	12 units @ $23.18
Purchased November 18	10 units @ $23.42

   A physical count indicates that 28 units are still on hand on December 31.

   Determine the total cost of the ending inventory, and enter the adjustment on the work sheet.
4. **Adjustment for store supplies:** An inventory count revealed that $630.80 of supplies are on hand on December 31.
5. **Adjustment for prepaid insurance:** The insurance premium of $1,350.00 was paid on November 2 and covered a six-month policy.
6. **Adjustment for the depreciation of store equipment:** Fast Gifts uses the sum-of-the-years'-digits method to determine annual depreciation for store equipment. The depreciation has been calculated for all of the store equipment except the cash register. That depreciation expense totals $1,294.00.

   The cash register was purchased on March 2 of this year for $1,595.00. It has a salvage value of $50.00 and an estimated useful life of 5 years.

   Determine the total depreciation expense for store equipment for the period, and enter that amount on the work sheet.
7. **Adjustment for the depreciation of display equipment:** Fast Gifts uses the straight-line method to determine the depreciation for its display equipment. Most of the equipment was purchased three years ago; its estimated annual depreciation is $1,544.50.

   Fast Gifts purchased a new display rack on December 3 of this year. The rack cost $2,459.00. Its useful life is estimated to be 8 years, and there is no salvage value.

   Determine the total depreciation expense for display equipment for the period, and enter that amount on the work sheet.
8. **Adjustment for federal income tax:** The actual taxes for the year total $3,950.00.

Chapter 7

ACCOUNTS PAYABLE, NOTES PAYABLE, AND OTHER CURRENT LIABILITIES

In the earlier chapters of this unit, you learned how to account for various types of assets, from cash funds to plant assets. In the next two chapters, you'll look at another component of the balance sheet: liabilities.

As you know, liabilities are the debts or obligations of a business. Businesses incur liabilities to pay expenses, purchase merchandise and other items, or expand their operations. These liabilities can be classified as either current liabilities or long-term liabilities. You are already familiar with many current liabilities: Accounts Payable, Sales Tax Payable, and so on. In this chapter, you will learn how to account for several other current liabilities, including Notes Payable.

Learning Objectives

When you have completed this chapter, you should be able to do the following:

1. Distinguish between current and long-term liabilities.
2. Explain the process of recording invoices at their net amounts.
3. Explain the difference between interest-bearing and non-interest-bearing notes payable.
4. Journalize transactions involving current liabilities.
5. Record adjusting entries for accrued and prepaid interest expense.
6. Define the accounting terms presented in this chapter.

New Terms

current liabilities
long-term liabilities
net amount method
note payable
accrued expense
discounting a note payable
non-interest-bearing note payable
prepaid expense
unearned revenue

Types of Liabilities

Remind students that most liability accounts have the word *payable* in the account title.

A business normally has several kinds of liabilities, which are classified as either current or long-term. **Current liabilities** are the debts or obligations that a business expects to pay off in one year or within its normal operating cycle, whichever is longer. In most cases, current liabilities are paid out of current assets or by incurring another short-term liability. Accounts payable, notes payable, salaries payable, payroll and other taxes payable, and unearned revenue are examples of current liabilities. Liabilities that are *not* due during the next fiscal period or operating cycle are called **long-term liabilities.** Examples of long-term liabilities include bonds payable and mortgage notes payable.

Throughout the rest of this chapter, you'll look at the accounting procedures for various current liabilities, particularly notes payable. Chapter 8 discusses long-term liabilities in more detail.

Accounts Payable

Early in your study of accounting, you learned that accounts payable are the amounts owed to suppliers for goods and services bought on account. A business that makes many purchases on account usually maintains an accounts payable subsidiary ledger. The balance of the Accounts Payable account in the general ledger equals the total of the individual accounts in this subsidiary ledger.

Ask students how it is advantageous for the seller to offer cash discounts.

You have seen that in accounting for accounts payable, many businesses take advantage of the cash discounts their suppliers offer. A business can save a considerable amount of money over a fiscal period if it takes advantage of these cash discounts. In fact, it's poor management *not* to take advantage of cash discounts. Unfortunately, with the accounting procedure you have been using, management doesn't know when discounts are not taken. The Purchases Discounts account tells management only about discounts that *are* taken.

To overcome this disadvantage, many accountants prefer to use the net amount method of recording invoices. The **net amount method** assumes that the business *always* takes advantage of cash discounts. As a result, invoices are recorded in the accounting records at the net amount (the total amount less the cash discount). The Purchases Discounts account is, therefore, not needed.

Let's suppose that Mayfaire, Inc., uses the net amount method and that it had the following transaction:

March 1: *Purchased merchandise on account from Alonzo Products, Inc., $5,000; terms 2/10, n/30; Invoice 4712 dated March 1.*

Be sure students understand how to calculate the net amount of an invoice.

Invoices, remember, are recorded at the net amount. The net amount of this invoice is calculated as shown on the next page.

ACCOUNTING Notes

An offer of a 2% reduction in price for payment 20 days early—in 10 days rather than 30—amounts to an annual interest rate of 36%.

$5,000 invoice total	$5,000 invoice total
× .02 discount rate	− 100 cash discount
$ 100 cash discount	$4,900 net amount

The transaction is then recorded in the purchases journal as a debit of $4,900 to Purchases and a credit of $4,900 to Accounts Payable and the subsidiary ledger account of Alonzo Products, Inc.

GENERAL LEDGER

Purchases		Accounts Payable		Alonzo Products, Inc. (SUBSIDIARY LEDGER)	
Dr.	Cr.	Dr.	Cr.	Dr.	Cr.
$4,900			$4,900		$4,900

If Mayfaire pays the invoice within the discount period (by March 11), the transaction will be recorded as a debit of $4,900 to Accounts Payable and the creditor's account and a credit of $4,900 to Cash in Bank.

GENERAL LEDGER

Accounts Payable		Cash in Bank		Alonzo Products, Inc. (SUBSIDIARY LEDGER)	
Dr.	Cr.	Dr.	Cr.	Dr.	Cr.
$4,900	Bal. $4,900		$4,900	$4,900	Bal. $4,900

If, however, Mayfaire pays the invoice *after* March 11, it can no longer take advantage of the cash discount. In other words, it will have lost the cash discount. As a result, Mayfaire must pay the total amount of the invoice, $5,000. This total is larger than the amount recorded in the accounting records ($4,900). With the net amount method, the cash discount amount of $100 that Mayfaire did not take advantage of is debited to an account titled Discounts Lost.

Introduce the new Discount Lost account and discuss when it is used.

Discounts Lost is classified as an expense account and has a normal debit balance. It appears on the income statement in the Operating Expenses section. Ideally, the balance of this account should be zero or very low. An increase in the balance of the account indicates that accounting procedures are not being followed. Management will want to take steps to correct the situation.

Let's see how the payment transaction would be recorded if Mayfaire paid the invoice after the discount period.

March 31: *Issued Check 3802 for $5,000 in payment of Invoice 4712 from Alonzo Products, Inc.*

Use T accounts to illustrate this transaction.

In the transaction, Accounts Payable and the creditor's account are debited for $4,900. Recall that this is the amount at which the invoice was originally recorded. The amount of the cash discount not taken, $100, is debited to the Discounts Lost account. Cash in Bank is credited for $5,000.

GENERAL LEDGER

Accounts Payable		Discounts Lost		Cash in Bank	
Dr.	Cr.	Dr.	Cr.	Dr.	Cr.
$4,900	Bal. $4,900	$100			$5,000

SUBSIDIARY LEDGER

Alonzo Products, Inc.	
Dr.	Cr.
$4,900	Bal. $4,900

Have students complete Exercise 7-1 at this point.

The transaction would be recorded in the cash payments journal as illustrated in Figure 7-1. Notice that this cash payments journal contains a special Discounts Lost Debit column.

CASH PAYMENTS JOURNAL — PAGE 14

	DATE		DOC. NO.	ACCOUNT TITLE	POST. REF.	GENERAL DEBIT	GENERAL CREDIT	ACCOUNTS PAYABLE DEBIT	DISCOUNTS LOST DEBIT	CASH IN BANK CREDIT	
1	199– Mar.	31	C3802	Alonzo Products, Inc.				4 900 00	100 00	5 000 00	1

Figure 7-1 Recording the Payment of an Invoice after the Discount Period

Notes Payable

In Chapter 4, you learned that a promissory note is a written promise to pay on demand a certain sum of money on a specific date. In that chapter, you studied the accounting procedures for notes receivable—promissory notes accepted by a person or business. A **note payable** is a promissory note issued by a person or a business. A business may issue a note payable (1) when it purchases merchandise or other assets, (2) to gain more time to pay an account payable, and (3) when the business borrows money. Notes payable can be either interest-bearing or non-interest-bearing.

Discuss when a business might issue a note payable.

Interest-Bearing Notes Payable

Point out that the principal and the face value of an interest-bearing note are the same. The maturity value includes the interest charge.

An *interest-bearing note,* you'll remember, is a note that requires the face value (the principal) plus interest to be paid on maturity. With an interest-bearing note payable, the face value and the principal are the same. The maturity value of a note is calculated as follows:

Principal (Face Value of Note) + Interest = Maturity Value

▲ Recording the Issuance of an Interest-Bearing Note Payable On August 20, Mayfaire, Inc., purchased $800 of merchandise on account from Colonial, Inc. The credit terms were n/30. Mayfaire recorded that transaction in its purchases journal as a debit to Purchases for $800 and a credit to Accounts Payable and to Colonial, Inc.'s account, for $800. On September 20 (the due date), Mayfaire asked Colonial to accept a note for the amount of the account payable. Colonial agreed.

September 20: *Issued a 90-day, 10% note payable for $800 to Colonial, Inc., in place of the amount recorded as an account payable, Note 17.*

The accounts affected by this transaction are Accounts Payable and Notes Payable in the general ledger and the Colonial, Inc., account in the accounts payable subsidiary ledger. Since a note is being issued in place of the amount recorded as an account payable, the $800 must be removed from the Accounts Payable account. Accounts Payable and Colonial's account are, therefore, debited for $800. Notes Payable is a current liability account and has a normal credit balance. It is credited for $800 to show the increase in the liability.

GENERAL LEDGER

Accounts Payable	
Dr.	Cr.
$800	Bal. $800

Notes Payable	
Dr.	Cr.
	$800

SUBSIDIARY LEDGER

Colonial, Inc.	
Dr.	Cr.
$800	Bal. $800

Stress the fact that the money is still owed.

In this transaction, Notes Payable is substituted for Accounts Payable. The note does not pay the debt; it merely reclassifies the amount owed from Accounts Payable to Notes Payable. Colonial prefers the note because the note is written evidence of the amount owed. In addition, Colonial will earn interest of 10%. Figure 7-2 shows the general journal entry for this transaction.

GENERAL JOURNAL — PAGE 37

	DATE		DESCRIPTION	POST. REF.	DEBIT	CREDIT	
1	199– Sept.	20	Accts. Payable/Colonial, Inc.	✓	800 00		1
2			Notes Payable			800 00	2
3			Note 17				3

Figure 7-2 Journalizing the Issuance of an Interest-Bearing Note Payable

Review how to calculate interest.

Recording the Payment of an Interest-Bearing Note Payable

When the interest-bearing note payable falls due, Mayfaire prepares a check for the maturity value (principal plus interest). The interest amount is calculated as follows:

Principal	×	Interest Rate	×	Time	=	Interest
$800.00	×	.10	×	90/365	=	$19.73

$800.00
+ 19.73
$819.73

December 19: *Issued Check 7967 to Colonial, Inc., for $819.73, the maturity value of Note 17 issued on September 20.*

In this transaction, Notes Payable is debited for $800.00 because Mayfaire no longer owes the liability. The interest amount, $19.73, is debited to the other expense account Interest Expense. Cash in Bank is credited for $819.73, the amount of the check.

Notes Payable	
Dr.	Cr.
$800.00	Bal. $800.00

Interest Expense	
Dr.	Cr.
$19.73	

Cash in Bank	
Dr.	Cr.
	$819.73

Use demonstration problem 7-1 here.

The transaction is recorded in the cash payments journal as shown in Figure 7-3.

CASH PAYMENTS JOURNAL — PAGE 30

	DATE		DOC. NO.	ACCOUNT TITLE	POST. REF.	GENERAL DEBIT	GENERAL CREDIT	ACCOUNTS PAYABLE DEBIT	PURCHASES DISCOUNTS CREDIT	CASH IN BANK CREDIT	
1	199- Dec.	19	C7967	Notes Payable		800 00				819 73	1
2				Interest Expense		19 73					2

Figure 7-3 Journalizing the Payment of an Interest-Bearing Note Payable

By signing a promissory note, customers agree to repay a specific amount of borrowed money plus interest to a lending company.

Before reading further, do the following activity to check your understanding of interest-bearing notes payable.

Check Your Learning

Write your answers to these questions on a sheet of notebook paper.

1. The Craft Corporation issued a 60-day, 10% note (Note 12) dated October 1 to Frontier, Inc., in place of a $3,000 account payable.
   a. Which account(s) are debited? For what amount?
   b. Which account(s) are credited? For what amount?

2. On November 30, the Craft Corporation issued Check 161 to Frontier, Inc., in payment of Note 12.
   a. Which account(s) are debited? For what amount?
   b. Which account(s) are credited? For what amount?

Compare your answers to those in the answers section. Reread the preceding part of the chapter to find the correct answers to any questions you may have missed.

TERM
- Issue Date December 24
- End of Fiscal Period December 31
- Maturity Date February 22

Be sure students understand why an adjusting entry must be made for the accrued interest expense.

Adjusting for Accrued Interest Expense In Chapter 4, you learned that a promissory note that is issued in one fiscal period may not mature until the next fiscal period. For example, Mayfaire's fiscal period ends on December 31. On December 24, the company issued a 60-day, 9%, $1,800 note payable (Note 19). That note will not mature until February 22 of the *next* fiscal period. On that date, Mayfaire will repay the principal plus interest.

On December 31, however, Mayfaire has incurred an expense for 7 days' interest (from December 24 to December 31). An expense incurred in one fiscal period but not paid until a later fiscal period is called an **accrued expense.** An adjusting entry to recognize the accrued expense must be made at the end of the fiscal period.

The accrued interest is calculated as follows:

Principal	×	Interest Rate	×	Time	=	Interest
$1,800.00	×	.09	×	7/365	=	$3.11

Discuss how the accrued interest is calculated.

In the adjusting entry, Interest Expense is debited for $3.11, the amount of the accrued interest chargeable to the *current* fiscal period. Interest Payable, a current liability account, is credited for $3.11.

Interest Expense

Dr.	Cr.
Adj. $3.11	

Interest Payable

Dr.	Cr.
	Adj. $3.11

Figure 7-4 shows the adjusting entry.

GENERAL JOURNAL					PAGE 25
DATE		DESCRIPTION	POST. REF.	DEBIT	CREDIT
		Adjusting Entries			
Dec.	31	Interest Expense		3 11	
		Interest Payable			3 11

Figure 7-4 Adjusting for Accrued Interest Expense

The accrued interest on the note payable will be reported on the income statement in the Other Expenses section.

On February 22, Mayfaire issued a check for the maturity value of the note.

February 22: *Issued Check 9002 for $1,826.63 to Valley National Bank in payment of the note payable issued December 24.*

Use demonstration problem 7-2 here.

In this transaction, Notes Payable is debited for $1,800.00 to decrease the liability. The total interest expense on the note is $26.63. Of this amount, $3.11 was incurred and reported in the *previous* fiscal period through an adjusting entry. Because the interest is now being paid, the $3.11 must be removed from the Interest Payable account. The account is, therefore, debited for that amount. The remaining interest amount of $23.52 is an expense of the *current* fiscal period. Interest Expense is, therefore, debited for $23.52. Cash in Bank is credited for the total amount paid out, $1,826.63.

$$\begin{array}{r} \$26.63 \\ -\ 3.11 \\ \hline \$23.52 \end{array}$$

Notes Payable	
Dr.	Cr.
$1,800.00	Bal. $1,800.00

Interest Payable	
Dr.	Cr.
$3.11	Bal. $3.11

Interest Expense	
Dr.	Cr.
$23.52	

Cash in Bank	
Dr.	Cr.
	$1,826.63

The entry to record this transaction appears in Figure 7-5.

CASH PAYMENTS JOURNAL									PAGE 32
DATE		DOC. NO.	ACCOUNT TITLE	POST. REF.	GENERAL DEBIT	GENERAL CREDIT	ACCOUNTS PAYABLE DEBIT	PURCHASES DISCOUNTS CREDIT	CASH IN BANK CREDIT
199-									
Feb.	22	C9002	Notes Payable		1 800 00				1 826 63
			Interest Payable		3 11				
			Interest Expense		23 52				

Figure 7-5 Recording the Payment of a Note Payable

Non-Interest-Bearing Notes Payable

Point out that the maturity value and the face value of a non-interest-bearing note are the same.

Businesses often borrow money from banks and issue notes payable as proof of the debt. Sometimes the bank requires the borrower to pay the interest on the note payable at the time the note is issued rather than on the maturity date. The bank deducts the interest from the face value of the note and gives the difference to the borrower. This process is called **discounting a note payable**. A note payable from which the interest has been deducted in advance is called a **non-interest-bearing note payable**, because no interest rate is stated on the note itself. On a non-interest-bearing note payable, the face value and the maturity value are the same. In Chapter 4, you learned that an interest charge deducted in advance is called the *bank discount* and the amount of cash the borrower actually receives is called the *proceeds*. The proceeds equals the face value of the note minus the bank discount.

R — E — M — E — M — B — E — R

On interest-bearing notes, the face value is equal to the principal. On non-interest-bearing notes, the face value equals the maturity value.

Recording the Issuance of a Non-Interest-Bearing Note Payable

Let's see how a non-interest-bearing note payable would be recorded in the accounting records. Mayfaire had the following transaction.

September 10: *Issued a $4,000, 60-day, non-interest-bearing note payable to Valley National Bank that was discounted at 12%, Note 16.*

The first step is to calculate the amount of the bank discount. The bank discount, you'll remember, is calculated in the same way as the interest on an interest-bearing note payable. The bank's discount rate is the interest rate used in the calculation.

Face Value (Maturity Value)	×	Discount Rate (Interest Rate)	×	Time	=	Bank Discount (Interest)
$4,000.00	×	.12	×	60/365	=	$78.90

Have students complete Exercise 7-2 at this point.

The bank discount is deducted from the face value of the note to determine the proceeds: $4,000.00 – $78.90 = $3,921.10.

The accounts involved in this transaction are Cash in Bank, Discount on Notes Payable, and Notes Payable. Cash in Bank is debited for $3,921.10, the amount of cash received.

The face value of a non-interest-bearing note payable includes (1) the amount actually borrowed ($3,921.10) and (2) the bank discount ($78.90). Recall that the bank discount is the interest charge on the note. Since it has already been deducted, it cannot be recorded in a liability account. The $78.90 could be recorded in an expense account. The company, however, has not yet *incurred* the expense. Instead, the $78.90 is recorded in

Introduce the new contra liability account and discuss how it is used.

an account called Discount on Notes Payable. Discount on Notes Payable is a contra liability account and has a normal debit balance. In this transaction, it is debited for the $78.90. Notes Payable is credited for $4,000.00, the face value of the note.

Cash in Bank	
Dr.	Cr.
$3,921.10	

Discount on Notes Payable	
Dr.	Cr.
$78.90	

Notes Payable	
Dr.	Cr.
	$4,000.00

This transaction is recorded in the cash receipts journal as shown in Figure 7-6.

CASH RECEIPTS JOURNAL — PAGE 24

	DATE	DOC. NO.	ACCOUNT TITLE	POST. REF.	GENERAL DEBIT	GENERAL CREDIT	SALES CREDIT	SALES TAX PAYABLE CREDIT	ACCOUNTS RECEIVABLE CREDIT	CASH IN BANK DEBIT	
	199-										
6	Sept. 10	N16	Discount on Notes Pay.		78 90					3 921 10	6
7			Notes Payable			4 000 00					7
8											8

Figure 7-6 Journalizing the Issuance of a Non-Interest-Bearing Note Payable

Discount on Notes Payable is reported on the balance sheet as a deduction from Notes Payable. The difference between the two accounts is referred to as the *book value of notes payable.*

R — E — M — E — M — B — E — R

Discount on Notes Payable **is a contra liability account and has a normal debit balance. The balance of the account is a deduction from the** Notes Payable **account.**

▲ Recording the Payment of a Non-Interest-Bearing Note Payable

When a non-interest-bearing note payable matures, a check is written for the maturity value of the note. With a non-interest-bearing note payable, the maturity value is the same as the face value. At the same time, the bank discount amount must be recognized as an expense. To do this, the bank discount amount is transferred from the Discount on Notes Payable account to the Interest Expense account.

Discuss why the amount in the Discount on Notes Payable account becomes an expense.

November 9: *Issued Check 7292 for $4,000.00 to Valley National Bank in payment of Note 16 issued on September 10.*

To remove the note payable from Mayfaire's accounting records, Notes Payable is debited for $4,000.00. Cash in Bank is credited for $4,000.00, the maturity value of the note. To show that the bank discount has now become an expense, Interest Expense is debited for $78.90 and Discount on Notes Payable is credited for $78.90.

Notes Payable	
Dr.	Cr.
$4,000.00	Bal. $4,000.00

Cash in Bank	
Dr.	Cr.
	$4,000.00

Interest Expense	
Dr.	Cr.
$78.90	

Discount on Notes Payable	
Dr.	Cr.
Bal. $78.90	$78.90

Review the use of a compound entry.

This transaction is recorded in the cash payments journal as shown in Figure 7-7. Two separate entries could be used to record (1) the payment of the non-interest-bearing note payable and (2) the interest expense. It is much simpler, however, to use one compound entry.

CASH PAYMENTS JOURNAL — PAGE 29

	DATE		DOC. NO.	ACCOUNT TITLE	POST. REF.	GENERAL DEBIT	GENERAL CREDIT	ACCOUNTS PAYABLE DEBIT	PURCHASES DISCOUNTS CREDIT	CASH IN BANK CREDIT	
	199–										
11	Nov.	9	C7292	Notes Payable		4000 00				4000 00	11
12				Interest Expense		78 90					12
13				Discount on Notes Payable			78 90				13

Figure 7-7 Journalizing the Payment of a Non-Interest-Bearing Note Payable

Before reading further, do the following activity to check your understanding of non-interest-bearing notes payable.

Check Your Learning

Write your answers to these questions on a sheet of notebook paper.

1. On January 15, the Craft Corporation borrowed $6,000 from Paradise National Bank by issuing a 90-day non-interest-bearing note (Note 15) that was discounted at 9%.
   a. Which account(s) are debited? For what amount?
   b. Which account(s) are credited? For what amount?
2. On April 15, the Craft Corporation issued Check 219 to Paradise National Bank in payment of Note 15.
   a. Which account(s) are debited? For what amount?
   b. Which account(s) are credited? For what amount?

Compare your answers to those in the answers section. Reread the preceding part of the chapter to find the correct answers to any questions you may have missed.

Mention that *prepaid* means to pay in advance.

▲ **Adjusting for Prepaid Interest Expense** As you just learned, the bank discount on a non-interest-bearing note payable is the interest expense deducted in advance. In accounting, an expense paid in advance is called a **prepaid expense**. When the note is paid on the maturity date, the interest charge is recognized as an expense and transferred from the Discount on Notes Payable account to the Interest Expense account.

There is no problem from an accounting standpoint when a note matures in the same fiscal period in which it was issued. Businesses, however, often issue non-interest-bearing notes payable in one fiscal period that do not mature until the next fiscal period. When this happens, an adjusting entry must be made at the end of the fiscal period to record the portion of the prepaid interest that is an expense of the current fiscal period. Let's look at an example.

Place these T accounts on the chalkboard and keep them there as you discuss and record the adjusting entry for prepaid interest expense and the payment of the note.

On December 16, Mayfaire borrowed $1,000.00 from the National Bank of Commerce by issuing a 45-day non-interest-bearing note payable (Note 18) that was discounted at 10%. As the following T accounts show, Cash in Bank was debited for $987.67, the amount of the proceeds. Discount on Notes Payable was debited for $12.33, the amount of the bank discount. Notes Payable was credited for $1,000.00, the face value of the note.

Cash in Bank

Dr.	Cr.
$987.67	

Discount on Notes Payable

Dr.	Cr.
$12.33	

Notes Payable

Dr.	Cr.
	$1,000.00

By December 31, a portion of the $12.33 bank discount has become an expense. An adjusting entry to recognize the expense in this fiscal period must be made. The amount of the interest expense (from December 16 to December 31) is calculated as follows:

Principal	×	Interest Rate	×	Time	=	Interest
$1,000.00	×	.10	×	15/365	=	$4.11

In the adjusting entry, Interest Expense is debited for $4.11, the portion of the bank discount that has become an expense. Discount on Notes Payable is credited for $4.11 to remove the actual amount of interest expense for the period. Discount on Notes Payable now has a balance of $8.22. Figure 7-8 shows the adjusting entry for this transaction.

Interest Expense

Dr.	Cr.
Adj. $4.11	

Discount on Notes Payable

Dr.	Cr.
Bal. $12.33	Adj. $4.11

GENERAL JOURNAL				PAGE 25
DATE	DESCRIPTION	POST. REF.	DEBIT	CREDIT
199-	Adjusting Entries			
Dec. 31	Interest Expense		4 11	
	Discount on Notes Payable			4 11

Figure 7-8 Adjusting Entry for Prepaid Interest Expense

Use demonstration problem 7-3 here.

On the maturity date (January 30), Mayfaire will issue a check to the National Bank of Commerce for $1,000.00 (the face value of the note). The transaction will be recorded as a debit of $1,000.00 to Notes Payable and a credit of $1,000.00 to Cash in Bank. At the same time, the amount remaining in the Discount on Notes Payable account is transferred to Interest Expense. Discount on Notes Payable, therefore, is credited for $8.22 and Interest Expense is debited for $8.22. Figure 7-9 shows this journal entry.

Interest Expense	
Dr.	Cr.
$8.22	

Discount on Notes Payable	
Dr.	Cr.
Bal. $8.22	8.22

Notes Payable	
Dr.	Cr.
$1,000.00	Bal. $1,000.00

Cash in Bank	
Dr.	Cr.
	$1,000.00

CASH PAYMENTS JOURNAL								PAGE 31
DATE	DOC. NO.	ACCOUNT TITLE	POST. REF.	GENERAL DEBIT	GENERAL CREDIT	ACCOUNTS PAYABLE DEBIT	PURCHASES DISCOUNTS CREDIT	CASH IN BANK CREDIT
199-								
Jan. 30	C8617	Notes Payable		1 000 00				1 000 00
		Interest Expense		8 22				
		Discount on Notes Payable			8 22			

Figure 7-9 Recording the Payment of a Non-Interest-Bearing Note Payable

R — E — M — E — M — B — E — R

At the end of a fiscal period, an adjusting entry must be prepared to recognize that portion of a prepaid expense that has become an expense during the period.

Renewing an Interest-Bearing Note Payable at Maturity

Discuss why the interest rate is higher.

Occasionally the maker of a note cannot pay the note in full at maturity. When this happens, the maker may arrange to renew all or part of the note. Usually the maker pays the interest on the old note and issues a new note at a higher interest rate. The interest rate is higher on the second note because the risk that the maker won't honor the note is higher.

For example, suppose Mayfaire issued a 60-day, 10%, \$2,000 note to Jay-Max, Inc., on April 15 (Note 13). That transaction was recorded as a debit of \$2,000 to Accounts Payable and to Jay-Max's account and a credit of \$2,000 to Notes Payable.

On the maturity date, Jay-Max allowed Mayfaire to renew the note. Mayfaire first had to pay the interest due on the existing note, which is calculated as follows:

Principal	×	Interest Rate	×	Time	=	Interest
\$2,000.00	×	.10	×	60/365	=	\$32.88

Use demonstration problem 7-4 here.

Then an entry is made to record the payment of the interest on the existing note and the issuance of the new note (Note 14). The term of the new note is 30 days, and the new interest rate is 11%. Figure 7-10 shows the compound entry.

CASH PAYMENTS JOURNAL PAGE 19

	DATE	DOC. NO.	ACCOUNT TITLE	POST. REF.	GENERAL DEBIT	GENERAL CREDIT	ACCOUNTS PAYABLE DEBIT	PURCHASES DISCOUNTS CREDIT	CASH IN BANK CREDIT	
	199-									
21	June 14	C5059 N14	Notes Payable (Note 13)		2000 00				32 88	21
22			Interest Expense		32 88					22
23			Notes Payable (Note 14)			2000 00				23

Figure 7-10 Journalizing the Renewal of an Interest-Bearing Note at Maturity

Dividends Payable

Dividends are a distribution of the earnings of a corporation made to the corporation's stockholders. (You'll look at dividends in more detail in Chapter 10.) The corporation's board of directors decides whether a dividend will be paid. When the board declares (votes to pay) a dividend, a liability is created. The corporation has an obligation to pay the amount of the dividend to its stockholders. There is usually a short period of time between the date the dividend is declared and the date the dividend is paid. During that time, the declared dividend is a current liability of the corporation. The liability is recorded in the Dividends Payable account.

Federal Income Tax Payable

As you know, the income of a corporation is taxed by the federal government, most state governments, and some cities and towns. The corporation estimates the amount of its federal income taxes for the year and then pays the estimated amount in four equal installments during that year. The installments are due on the 15th day of April, June, September, and December. The amount paid in each installment is debited to the Income Tax Expense account.

At the end of the fiscal period, the corporation calculates its net income and the actual amount of the income tax. If the estimated income

You may want to get a copy of the current tax rate tables to discuss with the class.

tax amount exceeds the actual tax amount for the year, the corporation has made an overpayment. Usually, however, the estimated amount is less than the actual income tax expense amount. An adjusting entry to recognize the additional taxes owed is recorded. As you know, the credit part of that adjusting entry is posted to the current liability account Federal Income Tax Payable. (The Internal Revenue Service provides income tax rate tables that corporations can use to determine both their estimated and actual income tax liabilities. The federal income tax rates for corporations in effect at the time this text was written were used to calculate the federal income taxes in the text.)

Payroll Liabilities

Many current liabilities are associated with payroll. As you learned in the first-year course, a business withholds various amounts from its employees' paychecks. These withheld amounts include mandatory deductions for federal income taxes, FICA taxes (which include social security and medicare taxes), state income taxes, and voluntary deductions such as union dues and health insurance. The business itself is also liable for certain payroll taxes: FICA taxes, federal unemployment taxes, and state unemployment taxes. Until the business pays the withheld amounts to the appropriate government agency or business, the amounts are considered current liabilities.

Salaries Payable

Discuss why some of the salaries liability is an expense of the current period.

DECEMBER						
S	M	T	W	T	F	S
	1	2	3	4	5	6
7	8	9	10	11	12	13
14	15	16	17	18	19	20
21	22	23	24	25	26	27
28	29	30	31			

The end of a business's fiscal period rarely corresponds to the end of a payroll period. At the end of the fiscal period, therefore, expenses for employees' salaries may have accrued (accumulated) but not yet been paid. To recognize all expenses for the fiscal period, an adjusting entry must be made at the end of the period to record any accrued salaries.

Mayfaire pays its employees weekly. At the end of the current fiscal period, Mayfaire owes its employees $960 for salaries earned on December 29–31. Although Mayfaire has incurred the $960 expense during this fiscal period, it will not pay the employees until January 2, during the *next* fiscal period. For Mayfaire's accounting records to show the correct salaries expense for the period, an adjusting entry must be made on December 31.

The accounts affected by this adjusting entry are Salaries Expense and Salaries Payable, a current liability account. Salaries Expense is debited for $960, the amount of the accrued salaries expense for the current fiscal period. Salaries Payable is credited for $960, the amount owed to employees for this fiscal period.

Salaries Expense	
Dr.	Cr.
Bal. $82,500	
Adj. 960	

Salaries Payable	
Dr.	Cr.
	Adj. $960

Figure 7-11 shows the adjusting entry.

GENERAL JOURNAL — PAGE 25

	DATE		DESCRIPTION	POST. REF.	DEBIT	CREDIT	
1	199-		Adjusting Entries				1
24	Dec.	31	Salaries Expense		960 00		24
25			Salaries Payable			960 00	25
26							26

Figure 7-11 Adjusting Entry for Accrued Salaries Expense

R — E — M — E — M — B — E — R

An adjusting entry must be made at the end of the fiscal period for expenses that have accrued but have not yet been recorded.

On January 2, Mayfaire prepares the weekly payroll of $1,600.00.

January 2: *Issued Check 8192 to the Payroll Bank Account for $1,314.40. Payroll deductions include $134.40 for employees' federal income taxes, $99.20 for social security taxes, $23.20 for medicare taxes, and $28.80 for employees' state income taxes.*

Have students complete Exercise 7-3 at this point.

Of the $1,600.00 salaries expense amount, $960.00 is an expense charged to the previous fiscal period and $640.00 is an expense charged to the current fiscal period. Salaries Expense is, therefore, debited for $640.00, the amount of the expense for the current accounting period. Salaries Payable is debited for $960.00 to show the decrease in the liability. The various payroll liability accounts are credited for the amounts withheld. Cash in Bank is credited for $1,314.40, the total of the check written for the weekly payroll.

Salaries Expense	
Dr.	Cr.
$640.00	

Salaries Payable	
Dr.	Cr.
$960.00	Bal. $960.00

Cash in Bank	
Dr.	Cr.
	$1,314.40

Employees' Federal Income Tax Payable	
Dr.	Cr.
	$134.40

Social Security Tax Payable	
Dr.	Cr.
	$99.20

Medicare Tax Payable	
Dr.	Cr.
	$23.00

Employees' State Income Tax Payable	
Dr.	Cr.
	$28.00

Figure 7-12 shows the entry to record this transaction.

CASH PAYMENTS JOURNAL — PAGE 31

	DATE	DOC. NO.	ACCOUNT DEBITED	POST. REF.	GENERAL DEBIT	GENERAL CREDIT	ACCOUNTS PAYABLE DEBIT	PURCHASES DISCOUNTS CREDIT	CASH IN BANK CREDIT	
1	199- Jan. 2	C8192	Salaries Expense		640 00				1314 40	1
2			Salaries Payable		960 00					2
3			Emp. Fed. Inc. Tax Payable			134 40				3
4			Social Security Tax Payable			99 20				4
5			Medicare Tax Payable			23 20				5
6			Emp. State Inc. Tax Payable			28 80				6

Figure 7-12 Recording the Payment of the Weekly Payroll

Sales Tax Payable

As you know, most states and many cities levy a sales tax on retail transactions. The business collects the sales taxes from customers and periodically pays those taxes to the government agency. Until the taxes that have been collected are paid to the government, they are a current liability of the business. Those taxes are recorded in the Sales Tax Payable account.

Unearned Revenue

Give examples of revenue received in advance.

Businesses often receive revenue before it is earned. Publishing companies, for example, usually require that magazine subscriptions be paid for in full before the first issue is sent out. Other examples of revenue received in advance include cash received in advance for rental properties, season tickets to sports and theatrical series, advertising campaigns, insurance premiums, and work to be completed in the future. Revenue received in advance but not yet earned is referred to as **unearned revenue**. When revenues are received in advance, the business has an obligation to deliver the goods or perform the services. These unearned revenues, therefore, represent a current liability to the business. As the business delivers the merchandise or performs the service, it earns a part of the advance payment. Then the earned portion is transferred from the current liability account to a revenue account. This is done through an adjusting entry at the end of the fiscal period.

Let's look at an example. Mayfaire is a merchandising business; its main source of revenue is from the sale of merchandise. It has, however, an additional source of revenue. Mayfaire owns the land and building in which it operates. Since the building is large, Mayfaire rents office space to another business for an annual rent of $12,000 ($1,000 a month). According to the lease agreement, the rent must be paid in advance. On May 1, Mayfaire had the following transaction.

May 1: *Received $12,000 for the rental of office space for one year, Receipt 1261.*

Point out that unearned in an account title implies it is a liability account.

The accounts affected by this transaction are Cash in Bank and Unearned Rent. Cash in Bank is debited for $12,000, the amount of cash received. Since the $12,000 has not yet been earned, it should not be credited to a revenue account. When Mayfaire received the cash, it incurred an obligation to provide the office space for one year. The $12,000 is therefore credited to a current liability account titled Unearned Rent.

Cash in Bank	
Dr.	Cr.
$12,000	

Unearned Rent	
Dr.	Cr.
	$12,000

This transaction is recorded in the cash receipts journal as shown in Figure 7-13.

CASH RECEIPTS JOURNAL — PAGE 15

	DATE		DOC. NO.	ACCOUNT TITLE	POST. REF.	GENERAL DEBIT	GENERAL CREDIT	SALES CREDIT	SALES TAX PAYABLE CREDIT	ACCOUNTS RECEIVABLE CREDIT	CASH IN BANK DEBIT	
1	199- May	1	R1261	Unearned Rent			12000 00				12000 00	1

Figure 7-13 Recording the Entry for Unearned Rent

Have students complete Exercise 7-4 at this point.

On December 31, Mayfaire has earned 8/12 of the rent received in advance. An adjusting entry to transfer that amount from the Unearned Rent account to a revenue account is made. In the adjusting entry, Unearned Rent is debited for $8,000 ($1,000 × 8). The same amount is credited to the Rental Income account.

Unearned Rent	
Dr.	Cr.
Adj. $8,000	Bal. $12,000

Rental Income	
Dr.	Cr.
	Adj. $8,000

This adjusting entry appears in Figure 7-14.

GENERAL JOURNAL — PAGE 25

	DATE		DESCRIPTION	POST. REF.	DEBIT	CREDIT	
1	199-		Adjusting Entries				1
26	Dec.	31	Unearned Rent		8000 00		26
27			Rental Income			8000 00	27

Figure 7-14 Adjusting Entry for Unearned Rent

After the adjusting entry is posted, Unearned Rent has a balance of $4,000. This amount is the rent for the remaining four months of the lease agreement.

R — E — M — E — M — B — E — R

Unearned revenue is a liability of the business.

Summary of Key Points

1. Liabilities can be classified as either current or long term. Current liabilities are those the business expects to pay within one year. Long-term liabilities are those that are due more than one year in the future.
2. A business can choose to record its invoices using the net amount method. With this method, invoices are recorded at their net amount. Discounts that are not taken are recorded in Discounts Lost, which is classified as an expense account.
3. A promissory note issued by a person or business is called a note payable. Notes Payable is a current liability account.
4. On the maturity date of an interest-bearing note payable, the maker must repay the principal plus interest.
5. A non-interest-bearing note payable is a note from which the interest has been deducted in advance. The amount deducted in advance is called the bank discount. The amount the borrower actually receives is called the proceeds. On the maturity date, a check is written for the face value of the note.
6. The maker of a note may decide to renew the note at maturity. Usually the maker pays the interest owed on the old note and issues a new note, often at a higher interest rate.
7. At the end of the fiscal period, a business must prepare an adjusting entry for any interest expense that is chargeable to the fiscal period. The interest expense may be either an accrued expense (on an interest-bearing note) or a prepaid expense (on a non-interest-bearing note).
8. At the end of the period, when the business knows the exact amount of its net income, an adjusting entry is made either for the amount of additional federal income tax owed or for the amount of federal income tax overpaid.
9. Unearned revenue is revenue that has been received but not yet earned. It is recorded as a current liability.

7 Review and Applications

Building Your Accounting Vocabulary

In your own words, write the definition for each of the following accounting terms. Use complete sentences for your definitions.

accrued expense
current liabilities
discounting a note payable
long-term liabilities
net amount method
non-interest-bearing note payable
note payable
prepaid expense
unearned revenue

Reviewing Your Accounting Knowledge

1. Indicate whether the following are current or long-term liabilities: Accounts Payable, Bonds Payable, Dividends Payable, Notes Payable, Salaries Payable, Unearned Rent.
2. Why would a business choose to record its invoices at the net amount?
3. On the maturity date, what amount must the maker repay for an interest-bearing note payable? For a non-interest-bearing note payable?
4. How are the proceeds for a non-interest-bearing note payable calculated?
5. How is the book value of notes payable determined?
6. Why must an adjusting entry be recorded for accrued interest expense?
7. What is the difference between an accrued expense and a prepaid expense?
8. Classify the following accounts: Discounts Lost, Interest Expense, Discount on Notes Payable, Salaries Payable, Rental Income.
9. If a business makes an adjusting entry for accrued salaries, which accounts are debited? Which are credited?
10. How are unearned revenues reported on the balance sheet?

Improving Your Decision-Making Skills

You have just been hired as an accounting clerk. Several people in the office dress very casually for work even though the company encourages appropriate business dress. It is tempting to wear casual clothes on some days, and you think you could probably get away with it since some of the others do. What should you do?

Applying Accounting Procedures

Exercise 7-1 Using the Net Amount Method of Recording Invoices

The Wright Bicycle Company records invoices at their net amount. The company recently received the following invoices.

Invoice Total	Invoice Date	Terms	Date Paid
$1,470	January 4	2/10, n/30	January 12
$1,350	January 12	2/10, n/30	January 20
$6,500	January 22	3/15, n/45	March 1
$4,200	February 7	3/10, n/45	February 28
$1,250	February 14	1/10, n/30	February 28

Instructions: Use the form provided in the working papers that accompany the textbook. For each invoice, indicate

1. The amount debited to the Purchases account
2. Whether the invoice was paid within the discount period
3. Any amount debited to Discounts Lost and the amount credited to Cash in Bank on the date of payment

SPREADSHEET PROBLEM

Exercise 7-2 Computing the Bank Discount and Proceeds on Non-Interest-Bearing Notes Payable

Instructions: Compute the amount of the bank discount and proceeds for the following non-interest-bearing notes. Use the form provided in the working papers.

$24.66; $2,475.34
$59.45; $3,160.55
$111.78; $7,888.22
$28.05; $1,371.95
$813.70; $14,186.30

	Face Value	Discount Rate	Term of Note
1.	$ 2,500	12.00%	30 days
2.	$ 3,200	10.00%	45 days
3.	$ 8,000	8.50%	60 days
4.	$ 1,400	9.75%	75 days
5.	$15,000	11.00%	180 days

Exercise 7-3 Calculating Accrued Salaries

The Rollins Camera Company pays its employees weekly. The weekly payroll (five workdays) is $1,500. On December 31, the end of Rollins' fiscal period, salaries have accrued for December 28–31.

Instructions: Use the space provided in the working papers to answer the following questions.

1. $1,200.00

3. $300.00

1. What is the total accrued salaries expense as of December 31?
2. In the adjusting entry, which accounts will be debited? Which will be credited?
3. When Rollins next pays its employees their weekly salaries, what amount will be debited to Salaries Expense?

Exercise 7-4 Analyzing Transactions for Unearned Revenue

The Happer Corporation publishes a gardening magazine called *The Green Thumb*. Subscriptions to the magazine must be paid in advance.

Instructions: Answer the following questions. Use plain paper or the space provided in the working papers.

1. During the week ended January 7, Happer received $12,000 from customers for subscriptions to *The Green Thumb*. Which accounts will be debited in the journal entry? Which will be credited?

2. By the end of the fiscal period, the Happer Corporation has received a total of $624,500 for subscriptions to *The Green Thumb*. Of that amount, $374,700 represents revenue earned during the current fiscal period. The remaining amount represents unearned revenue for future fiscal periods.
   a. Which accounts will be debited and which accounts credited in the adjusting entry to record the revenue earned during the fiscal period?
   b. What is the amount of the adjustment?

Adj., $374,700

Problem 7-1 Recording Invoices at Their Net Amount

The Gilbert Company records its purchases on account using the net amount method.

Instructions: Record the following transactions in the purchases journal (page 16) and in the cash payments journal (page 23).

Transactions:

Sept.	1	Purchased merchandise on account from Dotson Manufacturing, $5,600, terms 3/15, n/45, Invoice 4058.
	3	Received Invoice 511 from Archer Electronics for merchandise totaling $1,440 purchased on account; terms 2/10, n/30.
	14	Issued Check 593 to Dotson Manufacturing in payment of Invoice 4058 dated September 1.
	14	Paid Invoice 511 from Archer Electronics by preparing Check 594.

Problem 7-2 Issuing and Paying an Interest-Bearing Note Payable

Jet Star Systems carried out the transactions that follow.

Instructions: Record these transactions in a cash payments journal (page 12) and a general journal (page 9).

Transactions:

Oct.	1	Issued a $1,400.00, 45-day, 8.5% note payable to Compu-Tech, Inc., as an extension on an amount recorded as an account payable, Note 20.
	5	Purchased a fax machine (Office Equipment) for $2,000.00 from Fax Enterprises by issuing a 30-day, 8% note payable, Note 21.
Nov.	4	Wrote Check 318 for $2,013.15 payable to Fax Enterprises for the principal ($2,000.00) and interest ($13.15) due on Note 21.
	15	Issued Check 327 to Compu-Tech, Inc., for the principal ($1,400.00) and interest ($14.67) due on Note 20.

Problem 7-3 Issuing and Paying a Non-Interest-Bearing Note Payable

Corporate Jets, Inc., borrowed $40,000 from the American Federal Bank, issuing a 90-day, non-interest-bearing note payable that the bank discounted at 8.5%.

Instructions: Use a cash receipts journal (page 6) and a cash payments journal (page 9) to prepare the entries for the following transactions.

1. The issuance of the note payable (Note 37) on May 17 (Receipt 318)
2. The payment of Note 37 on the maturity date (Check 419)

Problem 7-4 Renewing an Interest-Bearing Note Payable at Maturity

Gym Pac, Inc., had the transactions that follow.

Instructions: Record the transactions in a cash receipts journal (page 17) and a cash payments journal (page 20).

Transactions:

July 10 Borrowed $5,000 from the Walnut Creek Bank by issuing a 60-day, 9% interest-bearing note payable, Note 10 and Receipt 369.

Sept. 8 Issued Check 473 to Walnut Creek Bank for the interest due on Note 10, plus a $1,000 part payment on the principal. Renewed the note by issuing a 45-day, 10%, $4,000 note payable (Note 11).

Oct. 23 Issued Check 612 to the Walnut Creek Bank in full payment of the principal and interest due on Note 11.

COMPUTER PROBLEM

Problem 7-5 Journalizing Accounts and Notes Payable Transactions

Metro Car Leasing had the following transactions involving its accounts payable and notes payable. Metro records all invoices at the net amount.

Instructions: Record the following transactions in a cash receipts journal (page 13), purchases journal (page 12), cash payments journal (page 18), and general journal (page 16).

Transactions:

Year 1

Nov. 14 Purchased $3,000 of office furniture on account from The Office Outlet, terms 2/10, n/30, Invoice 495.

20 Borrowed $8,000 from City Bank by issuing a 30-day, 11% interest-bearing note payable, Note 5.

22 Borrowed $4,500 from Tri-Rivers Bank by issuing a 30-day, non-interest-bearing note discounted at 11.5%, Note 6.

24 Issued Check 516 to The Office Outlet for the amount due on Invoice 495.

Dec. 14 Issued a 60-day, 10%, $1,000 interest-bearing note payable (Note 7) to West, Inc., in place of the amount recorded as an account payable.

20 Wrote Check 577 to City Bank in payment of Note 5 plus interest.

22 Issued Check 581 to Tri-Rivers Bank in payment of Note 6.

31 Recorded the adjusting entry for the interest that has accrued on Note 7.

Year 2

Feb. 12 Paid West, Inc., the amount owed on Note 7 by issuing Check 630.

CHALLENGE PROBLEM

Problem 7-6 Journalizing Transactions Involving Current Liabilities

Following are some of the transactions carried out by Americana Studios. Americana uses the net amount method for recording invoices.

Instructions: Record these transactions in the appropriate journals.

Transactions:

Year 1

Nov.	1	Rented office space to Duncan Myers and received a year's rent of $5,400.00 in advance, Receipt 793.
	16	Purchased on account from Franklin Bros. store equipment totaling $4,000.00, terms 3/15, n/30, Invoice 853.
	16	Purchased merchandise on account from Bradley Products, $3,600.00, terms 2/10, n/30, Invoice 205.
Dec.	2	Issued an 11%, 30-day note payable (Note 12) to Franklin Bros. in place of the amount recorded as an account payable.
	15	Borrowed $2,500.00 from the Ohio National Bank by issuing a 60-day, non-interest-bearing note payable that was discounted at 12%, Note 13.
	15	Prepared Check 488 for $1,312.50 as the fourth installment for estimated federal corporate income taxes.
	16	Paid the amount owed on Invoice 205 from Bradley Products, Check 493.
	31	Paid Franklin Bros. the amount owed on Note 12, Check 501.
	31	Recorded the adjusting entry for the prepaid interest on Note 13.
	31	Recorded the adjusting entry for rental income earned during the fiscal period.
	31	Recorded the adjusting entry for federal income taxes. Taxable income is $39,550.00, and the income tax rate is 15%. Estimated income taxes paid during the year total $5,250.00.
	31	Recorded the adjusting entry for salaries that have accrued for December 30–31. The biweekly salary expense is $3,125.00.

Year 2

Jan.	10	Paid the biweekly payroll of $3,125.00. Amounts withheld include federal income taxes, $278.13; state income taxes, $118.75; social security taxes, $193.75; and medicare taxes, $45.31; Check 516.
Feb.	13	Issued Check 549 to the Ohio National Bank for the amount owed on Note 13.

Inside Trading

John has been an accountant for a large manufacturing firm for a number of years. He enjoys working for a large corporation, and he has learned quite a bit about how the business world functions as a whole. Recently, for example, he has been following with interest certain activities in his department that could indicate a company takeover. Just yesterday his group was asked to evaluate the assets and liabilities of a major competitor. Within his company's "rumor mill," John has heard that his company plans to acquire the competitor within the year.

John has been telling his good friend Karen, in a general way, about the things he is learning, but is careful and guarded about giving out any specific information. His company"s formal code of ethics forbids revealing information about confidential company actions, and John knows that telling Karen about the probable takeover is against the law as well.

Then, one day, Karen asks for John's advice about her financial difficulties. She is struggling to pay off several school loans and some other personal debts, and she is afraid that she will never be able to make ends meet. She asks John to take a look at her budget and financial records and give her some pointers. John agrees to help her. While looking over her records, John finds that she owns stock in the company his firm is planning to acquire.

What is the ethical dilemma that John now faces? He realizes that if Karen were to find out about the upcoming takeover, she could certainly make some financial gains by wisely handling her stocks. If he gave her this information, however, he would be breaking the law. On the other hand, he rationalizes, what difference would it make if Karen knew? Her holdings certainly were not large enough to upset his company's proceedings, and she certainly would not tell anyone. She was completely trustworthy. If he told Karen, though, could he consider himself completely trustworthy? Could his company?

Ethical dilemmas often result when a large company policy is brought down to an individual scale. For example, while John knew that inside trading by major stockholders could seriously hamper or even halt his company's plans, it did not seem that Karen's activities could do that much harm. Often, it helps to decide such situations by determining the worst-case scenario. For instance, what if Karen, in strict confidence, told her stockbroker why she was buying and selling her stock? Then, her broker passed along this information to his closest friends and family, and a few of his largest clients, who then told others. Resolving ethical situations often requires a look into the future to see who will be affected, either positively or negatively.

Chapter 8

LONG-TERM LIABILITIES

Corporations use several sources of funds to finance their operations. They acquire cash and other assets by selling stock to investors and by earning profits and retaining them in the business. They can also borrow the funds needed. Corporations often borrow money on a short-term basis by issuing notes payable. You learned about those forms of current liabilities in Chapter 7. Corporations may also borrow money on a long-term basis.

In this chapter, you will learn about two kinds of long-term liabilities: mortgage notes and bonds payable. You will learn how to journalize transactions involving these long-term liabilities.

Learning Objectives

When you have completed this chapter, you should be able to do the following:

1. Distinguish between mortgage notes and bonds payable.
2. Journalize transactions involving mortgage notes.
3. Identify the various types of bonds.
4. Journalize transactions for the issuance of bonds.
5. Explain the purpose of a bond sinking fund.
6. Journalize transactions involving a bond sinking fund.
7. Define the accounting terms presented in this chapter.

New Terms

mortgage
bond
bond issue
underwriter
bond certificate
bond indenture
leverage
term bond
serial bond
registered bond
coupon bond
secured bond
unsecured bond
contract rate
market interest rate
face value
premium
discount
carrying value
amortize
callable bond
call price
sinking fund

Acquiring Funds

Businesses need money to continue their normal operations, to expand their operations, and to purchase merchandise and other assets. As you've seen, businesses can borrow the money they need by issuing short-term notes payable. Businesses can also issue notes for somewhat longer periods of time, such as two to five years. Usually when a business issues a note payable for this length of time, it pays the interest periodically during the term of the note rather than on the maturity date. Businesses can also borrow funds by issuing mortgage notes or bonds. Let's look first at mortgage notes.

Mortgage Notes

Compare a business mortgage and a homeowner mortgage.

When a business wants to purchase a plant asset such as land, buildings, or equipment, it often borrows the money from a financial institution and signs a mortgage. A **mortgage** is a formal, legal agreement in which the borrower agrees to repay the amount owed plus interest over a 5- to 30-year period. The borrower, or *mortgagor,* agrees to make regular payments of interest and principal over the term of the note, usually monthly. The mortgage contract typically gives the lending institution, called the *mortgagee,* the right to foreclose, or *repossess,* the mortgaged assets if the borrower fails to repay the note.

Issuing a Mortgage Note

The owners of the Meadow Link Golf Club want to expand their current 9-hole golf course to 18 holes. They estimate that it will cost $192,000 to complete the project. Since the owners do not have all the cash they need, they decide to borrow the amount needed and mortgage the land.

September 1: *Signed a 15-year mortgage note with the Paradise Bank to borrow $150,000 at 9% interest, Receipt 511.*

Introduce the Mortgage Payable account.

In this entry, Cash in Bank is debited for $150,000, the amount of cash borrowed and received. The Mortgage Payable account is credited for the same amount. Mortgage Payable is a long-term liability account and has a normal credit balance. Figure 8-1 shows the entry to record the receipt of cash from the mortgage loan.

CASH RECEIPTS JOURNAL — PAGE 41

	DATE		DOC. NO.	ACCOUNT TITLE	POST. REF.	GENERAL DEBIT	GENERAL CREDIT	SALES CREDIT	SALES TAX PAYABLE CREDIT	ACCOUNTS RECEIVABLE CREDIT	CASH IN BANK DEBIT	
1	19-- Sept.	1	R511	Mortgage Payable			150 000 00				150 000 00	1

Figure 8-1 Journalizing the Issuance of a Mortgage Note

Businesses can borrow money to expand their facilities and make their property more valuable.

Recording Mortgage Payments

According to the terms of the mortgage, Meadow Link Golf Club will repay the loan over 15 years by making monthly payments of $1,500. A portion of this amount is the interest charge on the unpaid principal; a portion of the payment is used to reduce the principal amount. In the early years of a mortgage, the interest portion is larger than the portion used to decrease the principal. For example, on October 1 Meadow Link made the first payment.

October 1: *Wrote Check 4410 to the Paradise Bank for $1,500 as payment of interest ($1,125) and principal ($375).*

In this transaction, Mortgage Payable is debited for $375, that portion of the monthly payment used to decrease the principal. Interest Expense is debited for $1,125, one month's interest on the unpaid balance ($150,000 × .09 × 1/12). Cash in Bank is credited for $1,500, the total amount being paid out.

Mortgage Payable		Interest Expense		Cash in Bank	
Dr.	Cr.	Dr.	Cr.	Dr.	Cr.
$375	Bal. $150,000	$1,125			$1,500

Use demonstration problem 8-1 here.

The cash payments journal entry appears in Figure 8-2. After this payment is recorded, the unpaid balance of the mortgage is $149,625 ($150,000 – $375).

	DATE		DOC. NO.	ACCOUNT TITLE	POST. REF.	GENERAL DEBIT	GENERAL CREDIT	ACCOUNTS PAYABLE DEBIT	PURCHASES DISCOUNTS CREDIT	CASH IN BANK CREDIT	
1	19-- Oct.	1	Ck. 4410	Mortgage Payable		375 00					1
2				Interest Expense		1 125 00				1 500 00	2

CASH PAYMENTS JOURNAL — PAGE 63

Figure 8-2 Recording a Mortgage Payment of Interest and Principal

Borrowing Money by Issuing Bonds

Briefly discuss U.S. Savings Bonds and explain how all bonds become a liability of the issuer.

Often, when a corporation wishes to borrow a large sum of money over a long period of time, it issues bonds. A **bond** is similar to a long-term promissory note. It is a promise to repay a certain amount (the principal) at a specified date and to pay interest at set times. The corporation pays interest to bondholders at a fixed rate and usually pays that interest semiannually (twice a year). Bonds are issued for terms of five years or longer. Bonds are also issued by the federal government. Municipal bonds are issued by governmental units such as cities, states, and local school districts. In this chapter, however, we will discuss only bonds issued by corporations.

Be sure to emphasize this new terminology.

Frequently a corporation sells an entire **bond issue**—the total amount of bonds issued at the same time—to an investment firm known as an **underwriter.** The underwriter, in turn, sells the bonds to the general public, usually in denominations of $1,000 or $10,000. For example, a $1,000,000 bond issue may consist of a thousand $1,000 bonds. Each bondholder receives a **bond certificate** as evidence of the corporation's debt.

To protect the bondholders' investment, the corporation must select a trustee, usually a large bank. The *trustee* makes certain that the corporation fulfills all of its responsibilities to the bondholders. These responsibilities include paying interest to the bondholders on specific dates and paying the bond issue when it becomes due.

The corporation also prepares a contract called a bond indenture. The **bond indenture** is a binding agreement between the corporation and the bondholders that defines the bondholders' rights, privileges, and limitations. This document also describes items such as the bond interest rate, maturity date of the bonds, interest payment dates, and characteristics of the bonds.

Advantages of Issuing Bonds

Raising funds by issuing bonds offers a corporation certain advantages including the following:

Discuss advantages and disadvantages of issuing bonds.

1. The bond-issuing corporation may be able to earn a greater return on the money it raises than it has to pay out in interest. This advantage is known as **leverage.** For example, suppose Mayfaire, Inc., issues $200,000 of bonds with an interest rate of 7%. Mayfaire must pay the bondholders a total of $14,000 each year in interest ($200,000 × .07). Now suppose Mayfaire can use the $200,000 in the business to

increase its net income by $30,000 a year. The extra $16,000 ($30,000 – $14,000) available each year can be used for other purposes.

2. Interest payments to bondholders are tax-deductible expenses.
3. Bondholders are creditors of the corporation. They have no say over the corporation's operations. Stockholders, therefore, can retain control of the corporation.

Disadvantages of Issuing Bonds

As you might expect, raising needed cash by issuing bonds also has certain disadvantages:

1. Since bondholders are creditors, bond interest payments are fixed expenses; that is, the interest payments must be made year after year, according to the terms of the bond indenture.
2. The corporation must eventually repay the principal of the bonds it issues.

R — E — M — E — M — B — E — R

A bondholder is a creditor of a corporation. A bondholder receives semiannual interest payments and, on the maturity date, the repaid principal amount.

Types of Bonds

You may want to have a guest speaker from an investment company talk to your class about bonds in general.

To attract the greatest number of buyers, an automobile manufacturer offers different models of cars with various combinations of accessories and at different prices. To appeal to many investors, corporations have created a variety of bonds, each with slightly different combinations of characteristics.

ACCOUNTING Notes
Bondholders are creditors of a corporation; therefore, they would receive payments from remaining assets before stockholders if the company goes bankrupt.

Term and Serial Bonds

When all the bonds within a bond issue have the same term (when they all become due at the same time), they are called **term bonds**. For example, all of the bonds in a 10-year bond issue dated January 1, 1992, mature on January 1, 2002.

If a bond issue has a series of maturity dates, the bonds are called **serial bonds**. For example, $1,000,000 of serial bonds issued April 1, 1992, may mature as follows:

$100,000 on April 1, 1997	$100,000 on April 1, 2002
$100,000 on April 1, 1998	$100,000 on April 1, 2003
$100,000 on April 1, 1999	$100,000 on April 1, 2004
$100,000 on April 1, 2000	$100,000 on April 1, 2005
$100,000 on April 1, 2001	$100,000 on April 1, 2006

Registered and Coupon Bonds

Point out that most bonds that are issued today are registered bonds.

Most bonds issued today are **registered bonds**. When bonds are registered, the names of the owners are recorded in the issuing corporation's records. This procedure offers the bondholder greater protection against theft. It also lets the corporation know who owns its bonds and is entitled to interest payments. If the bondholder wishes to sell the bond before it matures, the corporation will cancel the bond certificate surrendered by the original bondholder and issue a new certificate to the new bondholder. The corporation may maintain a subsidiary ledger for its registered bondholders.

Coupon bonds get their name from the interest coupons attached to each bond certificate. Coupon bonds are sometimes called *bearer bonds,* because the interest coupons are payable to the bearer or holder of the coupon. When the bond interest is due, the owner of the bond clips the coupon and deposits it with a commercial bank for collection. Coupon bonds are rarely issued today because they offer no protection for bondholders and because the corporation must document the amount of interest paid to each bondholder for the IRS.

Discuss the difference between secured and unsecured bonds.

Secured and Unsecured Bonds

A bond that is covered or backed up by corporate assets, such as buildings or equipment, is called a **secured bond**. These bonds are also called *mortgage bonds* or *equipment trust bonds*. If the corporation *defaults* (does not pay the principal or interest), the bondholders, acting through a trustee, may take over the pledged assets.

An **unsecured bond** or *debenture* is a bond that is issued on the corporation's credit standing; it is not backed up by the assets of the corporation. Unsecured bonds usually succeed only when issued by financially strong firms.

A bond may have characteristics from all three classifications. For example, 20-year mortgage bonds with interest coupons are term bonds, coupon bonds, and secured bonds.

Before reading further, do the following activity to check your understanding of bonds.

Check Your Learning

On a sheet of notebook paper, indicate whether these statements are true or false.

1. Bonds are issued only by corporations.
2. Bonds are usually issued for short periods of time.
3. The total amount of bonds sold at one time is called the bond issue.
4. Bondholders, like stockholders, are owners of the corporation.
5. A debenture is a bond backed up by certain assets of the corporation.

Compare your answers to those in the answers section. Reread the preceding part of the chapter to find the correct answers to any questions you may have missed.

Accounting for Bonds Payable

Introduce the Bonds Payable account.

Discuss how bond issues are reported on the balance sheet of the corporation.

When a corporation issues bonds, it records the transaction in the Bonds Payable account. Bonds Payable is classified as a long-term liability account. If there is more than one bond issue, the company maintains a separate account for each bond issue. On the balance sheet, each bond issue is identified by its interest rate and due date. There are three possible ways a corporation will issue bonds: (1) at face value, (2) at a premium, or (3) at a discount.

R — E — M — E — M — B — E — R

Bonds Payable **is a long-term liability account. It has a normal credit balance.**

Bond Interest Rates

When a corporation issues bonds, it specifies a certain rate of interest it will pay. This rate of interest is called the **contract rate,** because it is stated in the bond indenture. The contract rate will not change over the term of the bond issue.

Interest rates, however, change from day to day. The amount a corporation receives when it issues bonds and the actual amount of interest it will pay out depend on the market rate of interest. The **market interest rate** is the rate a borrower (the corporation) is willing to pay and lenders (investors) are willing to accept for the use of their money.

Explain that the bond market works like an auction in which bonds are bought and sold to the highest bidder.

The market interest rate on bond interest changes from day to day. It depends mainly on the interest rate offered by other investment options, including bonds being issued by other corporations. Suppose Mayfaire, Inc., plans to issue $200,000 of 8%, 10-year bonds in denominations of $1,000. Mayfaire will receive the $1,000 for its bonds *only* if the market interest rate is 8%, or very close to 8%. If the current rate of interest for other, similar bonds has gone up to 9%, potential investors probably will not buy Mayfaire's bonds. Wise investors would not pay Mayfaire $1,000 for an 8% bond that pays only $80 interest a year ($1,000 × .08) if they could earn 9%, or $90, interest a year ($1,000 × .09) elsewhere. Since there would be little demand for its bonds, Mayfaire would have to accept less than $1,000. If the market interest rate dropped to 7%, Mayfaire's 8% bonds would become very popular. Investors would be willing to pay *more* than $1,000 because they would earn more interest per year with the Mayfaire bonds than they would with other, similar bonds.

When issuing bonds, most corporations try to set the contract rate as close as possible to the market interest rate. When the contract rate and the market rate are the same, bonds are said to be issued at **face value**. It takes time, however, to notify various regulatory agencies, advertise the bond issue, and print the bond certificates. Often the market rate and the contract rate differ on the date the bonds are issued. The issue price of the bonds (the price investors are willing to pay on the date of issue) may not equal the face value. If the issue price is more than the face value, the bonds are said to be issued at a **premium**. If the issue price is less than the face value, the bonds are said to be issued at a **discount**.

R — E — M — E — M — B — E — R

The contract rate is the interest rate stated on the bond. The market interest rate is the interest rate borrowers (corporations) are willing to pay and investors are willing to accept for the use of their money.

Issuing Bonds at Face Value

Face value of a bond is equal to 100%.

The board of directors of Mayfaire, Inc., authorized the issuance of \$200,000 of 8%, 10-year bonds (face value \$1,000). Interest on the bonds will be paid semiannually (twice a year), on June 30 and December 31. The bonds were sold on January 2 for their face value.

January 2: *Received \$200,000 cash for 200 8%, 10-year bonds, face value \$1,000, Receipt 862.*

Discuss and illustrate the journal entry required when bonds are issued at face value.

In this transaction, Cash in Bank is debited for \$200,000, the total amount of cash received, and 8% Bonds Payable is credited for \$200,000 to show the increase in the liability. The entry for this transaction is recorded in the cash receipts journal as shown in Figure 8-3.

CASH RECEIPTS JOURNAL — PAGE 17

	DATE	DOC. NO.	ACCOUNT TITLE	POST. REF.	GENERAL DEBIT	GENERAL CREDIT	SALES CREDIT	SALES TAX PAYABLE CREDIT	ACCOUNTS RECEIVABLE CREDIT	CASH IN BANK DEBIT	
1	19-- Jan. 2	R862	8% Bonds Payable			200 000 00				200 000 00	1

Figure 8-3 Journalizing the Issuance of Bonds Payable

Recording the Interest on Bonds Payable

Point out that the entry to record bond interest is the same each time an interest payment is made by the corporation.

Interest on the bonds issued by Mayfaire is paid semiannually, on June 30 and December 31 of each year. Interest is calculated using the same formula as that for the interest on notes. The interest to be paid on June 30 is determined as follows:

$$\text{Principal} \times \text{Interest Rate} \times \text{Time} = \text{Interest}$$
$$\$200{,}000 \times .08 \times \frac{6}{12} = \$8{,}000$$

June 30: *Issued Check 5250 for \$8,000 in payment of the semiannual interest on bonds payable.*

The amount of the interest, \$8,000, is debited to the Bond Interest Expense account. Bond Interest Expense is classified as an other expense account and has a normal debit balance. Cash in Bank is credited for \$8,000. The entry to record the June 30 interest payment appears in Figure 8-4, page 206.

Use demonstration problem 8-2 here.

CASH PAYMENTS JOURNAL — PAGE 20

	DATE		DOC. NO.	ACCOUNT DEBITED	POST. REF.	GENERAL DEBIT	GENERAL CREDIT	ACCOUNTS PAYABLE DEBIT	PURCHASES DISCOUNTS CREDIT	CASH IN BANK CREDIT	
	19--										
22	June	30	C5250	Bond Interest Expense		8 000 00				8 000 00	22

Figure 8-4 Journalizing the Payment of Bond Interest

Usually a separate checking account for the bond interest is set up. Payments to individual bondholders would be made from this account.

Issuing Bonds at a Premium

Point out that to issue bonds at a premium is to issue bonds at a price greater than face value (100%).

If the contract rate of interest on a bond issue is higher than the market rate, investors may be willing to pay a premium for the bonds. For example, on January 2, Jay-Jax Enterprises issued $250,000 of 10-year bonds with a contract rate of 10%. The current market interest rate is 9%. Since the contract rate is greater than the market rate, Jay-Jax was able to issue the bonds at 104. The figure *104* refers to the price of the bonds. It means that investors are willing to pay an amount equal to 104% of the face value of the bonds.

R — E — M — E — M — B — E — R

If the contract rate of interest on bonds is greater than the market rate, bonds can be issued at more than their face value, or at a premium.

January 2: *Received $260,000 for $250,000, 10%, 10-year bonds, face value $1,000, Receipt 509.*

In this transaction, Cash in Bank is debited for $260,000, the total amount of cash received ($250,000 × 1.04). 10% Bonds Payable is credited for $250,000, the total face value of the bond issue. The additional $10,000 is credited to an account called Premium on Bonds Payable. Premium on Bonds Payable is classified as a long-term liability account with a normal credit balance. The Premium on Bonds Payable account is used to record any amount received in excess of the bonds' face value. Figure 8-5 shows the journal entry to record the issuance of the bonds at a premium.

Use T accounts to analyze the journal entry that is associated with issuing bonds at a premium.

CASH RECEIPTS JOURNAL — PAGE 23

	DATE		DOC. NO.	ACCOUNT TITLE	POST. REF.	GENERAL DEBIT	GENERAL CREDIT	SALES CREDIT	SALES TAX PAYABLE CREDIT	ACCOUNTS RECEIVABLE CREDIT	CASH IN BANK DEBIT	
1	19-- Jan.	2	R509	10% Bonds Payable			250 000 00				260 000 00	1
2				Prem. on Bonds Payable			10 000 00					2

Figure 8-5 Journalizing the Issuance of Bonds at a Premium

If a balance sheet were prepared right after this transaction was recorded, the accounts would appear as shown on the next page.

Long-Term Liabilities:		
10% Bonds Payable, due 1/1/Year 10	$250,000	
Plus Premium on Bonds Payable	10,000	$260,000

Emphasize that face value *plus* premium *equals* carrying value.

As you can see, Premium on Bonds Payable appears immediately below 10% Bonds Payable in the Long-Term Liabilities section. The premium of $10,000 is added to the face value of $250,000 to arrive at the carrying value. The **carrying value** is the amount at which the corporation is "carrying" the bond issue on the corporate records. In other words, it is the present value of the bond issue, in this case, $260,000.

R — E — M — E — M — B — E — R

Premium on Bonds Payable **is used to record the amount of cash received in excess of the face value of the bonds.**

Make sure students understand why a premium reduces the corporation's total interest expense.

Point out that, since the actual annual interest cost is $24,000, the Bond Interest Expense account must be adjusted at the end of the fiscal period.

When bonds are issued at a premium, the interest expense incurred by the corporation over the life of the bond issue will be less than the contract rate. The premium offsets the interest expense paid out. For example, the following table shows the total cost to Jay-Jax Enterprises of the bonds issued at a premium. Notice that the $10,000 premium actually *decreases* the total interest cost. Instead of a yearly interest cost of $25,000 ($250,000 ÷ 10 years), the annual interest cost is only $24,000 ($240,000 ÷ 10 years).

Cash to be paid to bondholders:	
Face value of the bonds at maturity	$250,000
Interest payments ($250,000 × .10 × 10 yrs.)	+250,000
Total cash to be paid to bondholders	$500,000
Less cash received from bondholders on issue date	–260,000
Total interest expense for 10 years	$240,000

The Bond Interest Expense account must be adjusted to reflect the actual annual interest cost. To do this, the corporation writes off, or **amortizes,** a portion of the Premium on Bonds Payable account each year. The amortization is made through an adjusting entry. For example, Jay-Jax uses the straight-line method to calculate the amount of the bond premium amortization. The $10,000 bond premium therefore is amortized in equal installments of $1,000 over 10 years ($10,000 ÷ 10 years). This is very similar to computing depreciation using the straight-line method. Figure 8-6 shows the adjusting entry.

GENERAL JOURNAL — PAGE 13

	DATE		DESCRIPTION	POST. REF.	DEBIT	CREDIT	
1			Adjusting Entry				1
2	Year1 Dec.	31	Premium on Bonds Payable		1 000 00		2
3			Bond Interest Expense			1 000 00	3

Figure 8-6 Adjusting Entry to Amortize a Bond Premium

Now let's look at Jay-Jax's Bond Interest Expense account. The two $12,500 debits represent the interest paid to bondholders on June 30 and

December 31. After the adjusting entry is posted, the balance of the Bond Interest Expense account is reduced to $24,000, the actual bond interest expense for the year.

Bond Interest Expense	
Dr.	Cr.
$12,500	Adj. $1,000
12,500	

Premium on Bonds Payable	
Dr.	Cr.
Adj. $1,000	Bal. $10,000

Use demonstration problem 8-3 here.

The balance of the Premium on Bonds Payable account is now $9,000. Over the life of the bond issue (in this case, 10 years), the Premium on Bonds Payable account will gradually decrease. At the end of the 10th year, the balance in the account will be zero. When the bonds mature, the carrying value of Bonds Payable will be $250,000, which is also the maturity value.

R — E — M — E — M — B — E — R

A bond premium reduces the corporation's total interest expense over the life of the bond issue.

Issuing Bonds at a Discount

Emphasize that to issue bonds at a discount is to issue bonds for less than face value (100%).

A corporation may issue bonds with a contract interest rate that is less than the market interest rate. Such bonds usually sell for *less* than their face value. For example, on January 2 Tri-Valley Industries issued $300,000 of 8%, 20-year bonds. Since the market interest rate was 8.5%, Tri-Valley was able to issue the bonds at only 98; that is, investors were willing to pay only 98% of the bonds' face value.

January 2: *Tri-Valley Industries received $294,000 cash for $300,000 of 8%, 20-year bonds, face value $1,000, Receipt 857.*

Use T accounts to illustrate the journal entry for issuing bonds at a discount.

In this transaction, Cash in Bank is debited for $294,000, the total amount of cash received. The account 8% Bonds Payable is credited for $300,000, the face value of the bond issue. The difference between the face value of the bonds and the cash actually received ($6,000) is debited to an account called Discount on Bonds Payable. Discount on Bonds Payable is classified as a contra long-term liability account and has a normal debit balance. The transaction appears in Figure 8-7.

CASH RECEIPTS JOURNAL — PAGE 47

	DATE	DOC. NO.	ACCOUNT TITLE	POST. REF.	GENERAL DEBIT	GENERAL CREDIT	SALES CREDIT	SALES TAX PAYABLE CREDIT	ACCOUNTS RECEIVABLE CREDIT	CASH IN BANK DEBIT	
1	Year 1 Jan. 2	R857	Discount on Bonds Pay.		6 000 00					294 000 00	1
2			8% Bonds Payable			300 000 00					2

Figure 8-7 Journalizing the Issuance of Bonds at a Discount

Have students complete Exercise 8-1 at this point.

The Discount on Bonds Payable account appears in the Long-Term Liabilities section of the balance sheet as a deduction from 8% Bonds Payable. As you can see, the carrying value of Tri-Valley's bonds is only $294,000.

Long-Term Liabilities:		
8% Bonds Payable, due 1/1/Year 20	$300,000	
Less Discount on Bonds Payable	6,000	$294,000

R — E — M — E — M — B — E — R

The carrying value is the face value of the bond issue plus any premium or minus any discount. When the bonds mature, the carrying value will be the same as the maturity value.

Make sure students understand why the discount increases the corporation's total interest expense over the term of the bond.

When bonds are issued at a discount, the corporation actually pays out *more* interest over the term than that stated in the contract rate. Tri-Valley's actual interest cost is the total interest paid to bondholders over the life of the bond issue *plus* the amount of the bond discount. Notice in the following table that the $6,000 discount *increases* the total interest cost. Instead of a yearly interest cost of $24,000 ($480,000 ÷ 20 years), the annual interest cost is $24,300 ($486,000 ÷ 20 years).

Cash to be paid to bondholders:	
Face value of the bonds at maturity	$300,000
Interest payments ($300,000 × .08 × 20 yrs.)	+ 480,000
Total cash to be paid to bondholders	$780,000
Less cash received from bondholders on issue date	– 294,000
Total interest expense over 20 years	$486,000

R — E — M — E — M — B — E — R

A bond discount increases the corporation's total interest expense over the life of the bond issue.

To adjust the Bond Interest Expense account to show the actual interest cost, the corporation amortizes the balance of the Discount on Bonds Payable account over the life of the bond issue. Using the straight-line method, the $6,000 discount is amortized in equal annual installments of $300 ($6,000 ÷ 20 years). Figure 8-8 shows the adjusting entry made at the end of each fiscal period.

GENERAL JOURNAL — PAGE 28

	DATE		DESCRIPTION	POST. REF.	DEBIT	CREDIT	
1			Adjusting Entries				1
2	Year1 Dec.	31	Bond Interest Expense		300 00		2
3			Discount on Bonds Payable			300 00	3

Figure 8-8 Adjusting Entry to Amortize a Bond Discount

Use demonstration problem 8-4 here.

If you look at Tri-Valley's Bond Interest Expense account, you'll see two $12,000 debits: the interest paid to bondholders on June 30 and on December 31. After the adjusting entry is posted, the balance of the Bond Interest Expense account is $24,300, the actual bond interest expense for the year. The Discount on Bonds Payable account now has a balance of $5,700. When the bonds mature, Discount on Bonds Payable will be fully amortized. The carrying value of the bonds will then be $300,000, the maturity value.

Bond Interest Expense

Dr.	Cr.
$12,000	
12,000	
Adj. 300	

Discount on Bonds Payable

Dr.	Cr.
$6,000	Adj. $300

R — E — M — E — M — B — E — R

Bond premiums and bond discounts must be amortized, or written off, over the life of the bonds. This is done through an adjusting entry at the end of each fiscal period.

Before reading further, do the following activity to check your understanding of the material you have just studied.

Check Your Learning

On January 1, Lann Enterprises issued $600,000 of 8%, 5-year bonds at 103 with interest paid semiannually, on June 30 and December 31. Write your answers to the following questions on a sheet of notebook paper.

1. Were these bonds issued at face value, at a premium, or at a discount?
2. On January 1, which accounts were debited and which credited? For what amounts?
3. What is the amount of the semiannual interest payment?
4. a. Must an adjusting entry be made at the end of the fiscal period?
b. If so, which accounts are debited and which are credited? For what amounts?

Compare your answers to those in the answers section. Reread the preceding part of the chapter to find the correct answers to any questions you may have missed.

Accrued Bond Interest

A corporation often issues bonds with interest payment dates that do not coincide with the end of its fiscal year. For example, Lone Star Enterprises' fiscal period ends on December 31. On April 1, Lone Star issued $2,000,000 of 15-year, 10% bonds at face value. Interest is payable on September 30 and March 31.

On September 30, a journal entry is made to record the semiannual interest payment of $100,000 ($2,000,000 × .10 × 6/12). In the entry, Bond Interest Expense is debited for $100,000 and Cash in Bank is credited for the same amount. The next semiannual interest payment will not be made until March 31. By December 31, however, interest expense will have accrued for the three months of October, November, and December. This interest expense must be recorded. The accrued interest expense totals $50,000 ($2,000,000 × .10 × 3/12). Lone Star records the accrued interest expense in an adjusting entry. Bond Interest Expense is debited for $50,000, the amount of the accrued interest expense. The accrued interest is a liability that will be paid during the next fiscal period. The amount is, therefore, credited to a current liability account titled Bond Interest Payable. The adjusting entry appears in Figure 8-9.

Use T accounts to illustrate the adjusting entry for accrued bond interest.

GENERAL JOURNAL PAGE 37

	DATE		DESCRIPTION	POST. REF.	DEBIT	CREDIT	
1			Adjusting Entry				1
2	Year 1 Dec.	31	Bond Interest Expense		50 000 00		2
3			Bond Interest Payable			50 000 00	3

Figure 8-9 Adjusting Entry to Record Accrued Bond Interest

After the entry is posted, the two bond interest accounts have the following balances:

Bond Interest Expense	
Dr.	Cr.
Bal. $100,000	
Adj. 50,000	

Bond Interest Payable	
Dr.	Cr.
	Adj. $50,000

On March 31, Lone Star makes the next semiannual interest payment to the bondholders. The total amount to be paid is $100,000. Of this amount, $50,000 was an expense in the previous fiscal period and $50,000 is an expense for the current fiscal period. Since the liability owed to bondholders from the previous year is now being paid, Bond Interest Payable is debited for $50,000. Bond Interest Expense is debited for $50,000, the interest expense for the current fiscal period. Cash in Bank is credited for $100,000, the total amount of cash paid out.

Use demonstration problem 8-5 here.

Bond Interest Expense		Bond Interest Payable		Cash in Bank	
Dr.	Cr.	Dr.	Cr.	Dr.	Cr.
$50,000		$50,000	Bal. $50,000		$100,000

The cash payments journal entry appears in Figure 8-10.

CASH PAYMENTS JOURNAL — PAGE 47

	DATE	DOC. NO.	ACCOUNT TITLE	POST. REF.	GENERAL DEBIT	GENERAL CREDIT	ACCOUNTS PAYABLE DEBIT	PURCHASES DISCOUNTS CREDIT	CASH IN BANK CREDIT	
1	Year 2 Mar. 31	3203	Bond Interest Expense		50 000 00				100 000 00	1
2			Bond Interest Payable		50 000 00					2

Figure 8-10 Journalizing the Semiannual Interest Payment to Bondholders

R — E — M — E — M — B — E — R

If the interest payment dates do not correspond to the end of the corporation's fiscal period, an adjusting entry to record the accrued bond interest expense must be made at the end of the fiscal period.

Before reading further, do the following activity to check your understanding of bond interest.

Check Your Learning

On April 1, Churma Industries issued $1,000,000 of 6%, 10-year bonds at 96, with interest payable semiannually, on March 31 and September 30. Answer these questions on a sheet of notebook paper.

1. What was the total amount of cash received on April 1?
2. What is the amount of the adjusting entry to amortize the bond discount on December 31?
3. What is the amount of the adjusting entry to record the accrued bond interest expense on December 31?

Compare your answers to those in the answers section. Reread the preceding part of the chapter to find the correct answers to any questions you may have missed.

Redemption of Bonds

Many corporations issue bonds that they can buy back, or *redeem,* at a later time. A bond that a corporation has the option to redeem is referred to as a **callable bond**. The amount the corporation agrees to pay for

Point out that most bonds today are issued with a call feature.

the bond is the **call price**. The call price is usually higher than the face value.

Issuing callable bonds lets a corporation take advantage of changes in the market interest rate. A corporation could redeem a bond issue with a high contract interest rate and replace it with a bond issue with a lower contract interest rate. For example, four years ago the Newberry Chemical Corporation issued $3,000,000 of 12%, 25-year callable bonds with a call price of 102. The yearly interest expense on these bonds is $360,000. Today, because the market interest rate is much lower, Newberry could issue similar bonds with a contract rate of 9%. The annual interest expense on these bonds would be $270,000. Newberry could save $90,000 a year with the lower interest rate. If Newberry redeemed the bonds, however, it would have to pay out $3,060,000 ($3,000,000 × 1.02 call price).

Make sure students understand why it would be advantageous for Newberry Chemical Corp. to call in its current bond issue and issue new bonds with a lower interest rate.

When a corporation redeems its bonds at a price that is less than the bonds' carrying value, it realizes a gain. If it redeems its bonds at a price that is more than their carrying value, it incurs a loss.

Redeeming Bonds at a Loss

Mid-Atlantic Industries has $750,000 of callable 9% bonds outstanding with a call price of 102. There is an unamortized discount of $2,000. The carrying value of Mid-Atlantic's bonds, therefore, is $748,000 ($750,000 – $2,000). After making the December 31 interest payment, Mid-Atlantic exercises its option and redeems the bonds on the same date.

December 31: *Redeemed the complete $750,000 bond issue at the call price of 102, Check 1643.*

In this transaction, 9% Bonds Payable is debited for $750,000, the face value of the bond issue being redeemed. Cash in Bank is credited for $765,000, the amount of cash paid out at the call price ($750,000 × 1.02). Since the bond issue is being redeemed, the discount must be removed from the accounting records. Discount on Bonds Payable, therefore, is credited for $2,000, the amount of the unamortized discount. The difference between the carrying value ($748,000) and the cash paid ($765,000) represents a loss of $17,000 on the transaction. This amount is debited to an account called Loss on Redemption of Bonds. This account is classified as an other expense account and has a normal debit balance.

Use demonstration problem 8-6 here.

Cash in Bank	
Dr.	Cr.
	$765,000

9% Bonds Payable	
Dr.	Cr.
$750,000	Bal. $750,000

Discount on Bonds Payable	
Dr.	Cr.
Bal. $2,000	$2,000

Loss on Redemption of Bonds	
Dr.	Cr.
$17,000	

Figure 8-11 shows the entry to record this transaction.

CASH PAYMENTS JOURNAL — PAGE 33

	DATE		DOC. NO.	ACCOUNT TITLE	POST. REF.	GENERAL DEBIT	GENERAL CREDIT	ACCOUNTS PAYABLE DEBIT	PURCHASES DISCOUNTS CREDIT	CASH IN BANK CREDIT	
1	199– Dec.	31	CK 1643	9% Bonds Payable		750 000 00				765 000 00	1
2				Loss on Redemption of Bonds		17 000 00					2
3				Discount on Bonds Payable			2 000 00				3

Figure 8-11 Journalizing the Redemption of Bonds at a Loss

R — E — M — E — M — B — E — R

When a bond issue is redeemed, the amount of cash paid out is the face value of the bond issue multiplied by the call price.

Redeeming Bonds at a Gain

Not all bonds that are issued are callable. A corporation, nevertheless, can buy back as many of its bonds as it can find on the open market. For example, Greengate Mall Corporation has $2,000,000 of 8% coupon bonds outstanding with an unamortized premium of $10,000. The carrying value of the bond issue is $2,010,000 ($2,000,000 + $10,000). On January 1, Greengate had the following transaction:

January 1: *Bought $200,000 of own bonds (one-tenth of the original issue) in the open market at 99, Check 4671.*

Stress the importance of the unamortized premium or discount when a portion of the bond issue is purchased on the open market.

In this transaction, 8% Bonds Payable is debited for $200,000, the face value of the bonds being redeemed. Since one-tenth of the bond issue is being redeemed, one-tenth of the unamortized premium must be removed from the accounting records. Premium on Bonds Payable is debited for $1,000 ($10,000 × .1). Cash in Bank is credited for $198,000, the amount of cash paid for the bonds ($200,000 × .99).

Use demonstration problem 8-7 here.

The carrying value of the bonds being redeemed is $201,000 ($200,000 + $1,000 premium). When the carrying value is greater than the cash being paid out, the corporation has a gain on the transaction. The amount of the difference, $3,000, is credited to an account called Gain on Redemption of Bonds. Gain on Redemption of Bonds is classified as an other revenue account and has a normal credit balance.

Cash in Bank	
Dr.	Cr.
	$198,000

8% Bonds Payable	
Dr.	Cr.
$200,000	Bal. $2,000,000

Premium on Bonds Payable	
Dr.	Cr.
$1,000	Bal. $10,000

Gain on Redemption of Bonds	
Dr.	Cr.
	$3,000

The entry for this transaction appears in Figure 8-12.

CASH PAYMENTS JOURNAL — PAGE 62

	DATE		DOC. NO.	ACCOUNT TITLE	POST. REF.	GENERAL DEBIT	GENERAL CREDIT	ACCOUNTS PAYABLE DEBIT	PURCHASES DISCOUNTS CREDIT	CASH IN BANK CREDIT	
1	199- Jan.	1	CK 4671	8% Bonds Payable		200 000 00				198 000 00	1
2				Premium on Bonds Payable		1 000 00					2
3				Gain on Redemption of Bonds			3 000 00				3

Figure 8-12 Journalizing the Redemption of Bonds at a Gain

Have students complete Exercise 8-2 at this point.

R — E — M — E — M — B — E — R

If the carrying value is greater than the amount being paid out for a bond issue, the corporation has a gain on the transaction. If the amount being paid out is greater than the carrying value, it has a loss on the transaction.

Bond Sinking Fund

Stress that the liability for a bond issue must be paid off when the bonds mature.

When a bond issue matures, the corporation must pay the bondholders the full maturity value. To be able to do that, many corporations set up sinking funds. A **sinking fund** is a special fund used to pay off the bond issue when it comes due. A bond sinking fund provides greater security for bondholders because it tries to ensure that there is enough cash on hand to pay off the bond issue.

The corporation usually makes annual deposits of cash to the sinking fund. The cash is invested in income-producing securities. When a bond issue matures, the total of the annual cash deposits plus the earnings on the investments should approximately equal the bonds' maturity value. The sinking fund may be controlled by either the corporation or a trustee, usually a bank.

Emphasize that most bond indentures require that annual deposits be made to a special fund so sufficient cash will be available when the bonds mature.

For example, Mayfaire, Inc., has issued $200,000 of 8%, 10-year bonds dated January 2. The bond indenture states that at the end of each of the 10 years, Mayfaire must make equal annual deposits in a sinking fund. Mayfaire, which manages its own sinking fund, plans to invest the money in marketable securities that will yield approximately 8% per year. The money earned from the investments plus the annual $15,000 deposit should equal approximately $200,000 in 10 years.

During the 10-year period, Mayfaire makes a number of transactions that affect the sinking fund. Figure 8-13 illustrates some of these entries.

GENERAL JOURNAL PAGE 10

	DATE		DESCRIPTION	POST. REF.	DEBIT	CREDIT	
1	Year 1 Dec.	31	Bond Sinking Fund		15 000 00		1
2			Cash in Bank			15 000 00	2
3			Check 2287				3
6	Year 2 Feb.	1	Sinking Fund Investments		9 900 00		6
7			Bond Sinking Fund			9 900 00	7
8			Check 100				8
11	Year 2 Aug.	3	Bond Sinking Fund		400 00		11
12			Sinking Fund Income			400 00	12
13			Receipt 101				13
23	Year 5 May	5	Bond Sinking Fund		10 250 00		23
24			Sinking Fund Investments			9 900 00	24
25			Gain on Sale of Sink. Fund Invest.			350 00	25
26			Receipt 175				26
36	Year 10 Dec.	31	Bonds Payable		200 000 00		36
37			Bond Sinking Fund			200 000 00	37
38			Check 315				38

Figure 8-13 Journalizing Bond Sinking Fund Transactions

Year 1
December 31: *Made the annual deposit of $15,000 to the bond sinking fund, Check 2287.*

In this transaction, the amount of the deposit is debited to Bond Sinking Fund and credited to Cash in Bank. Bond Sinking Fund is classified as an investments account. *Investments,* you'll remember, are assets, generally long-term, that are not intended for use in the business's normal operations. A separate checking account is usually set up for the bond sinking fund. The entry for this transaction is shown in general journal form on lines 1 through 3 of Figure 8-13. (This entry would normally be recorded in Mayfaire's cash payments journal.)

Year 2
February 1: *Bought $10,000 of Superior Steel 8%, 10-year bonds at 99, Check 100.*

In this transaction, Mayfaire was willing to buy Superior Steel's bonds at 99% of their face value. The actual cash paid out was, therefore, $9,900 ($10,000 × .99). When Mayfaire invests the sinking fund cash, the transaction will be recorded as a debit to an account titled Sinking Fund Investments. Sinking Fund Investments is also classified as an investments account. Bond Sinking Fund is credited. The journal entry is shown on lines 6 through 8 of Figure 8-13.

Year 2
August 3: *Received $400 interest from Superior Steel for sinking fund investments, Receipt 101.*

When Mayfaire receives interest or dividend income for its sinking fund investments, it debits Bond Sinking Fund and credits the Sinking Fund

Income account. Sinking Fund Income is classified as an other revenue account. This transaction is illustrated on lines 11–13 of Figure 8-13.

Year 5
May 5: *Received $10,250 from the sale of sinking fund investments that were originally purchased for $9,900, Receipt 175.*

Occasionally a business decides to sell a particular investment to reinvest the money in something else. In this transaction, Mayfaire has decided to sell the Superior Steel 8% bonds it bought in Year 2. Bond Sinking Fund is debited for $10,250, the total cash received from the sale of the investment. Sinking Fund Investments is credited for $9,900, the original amount invested. The difference of $350 ($10,250 – $9,900) represents a profit on the investment. That amount is credited to an other revenue account titled Gain on Sale of Sinking Fund Investments. The transaction is shown on lines 23 through 26 of Figure 8-13.

Year 10
December 31: *Issued bond sinking fund Check 315 for $200,000 to retire the bond issue.*

Use demonstration problem 8-8 here.

When a bond issue matures, the business sells all of its sinking fund investments. The cash received from the sale of the sinking fund investments, plus the last annual deposit, should equal $200,000. The entry to record the payment of the bond issue is shown on lines 36–38, Figure 8-13.

R — E — M — E — M — B — E — R

Bond Sinking Fund and Sinking Fund Investments are long-term investment accounts. Sinking Fund Income and Gain on Sale of Sinking Fund Investments are other revenue accounts.

Before reading further, do the following activity to check your understanding of bond sinking funds.

Check Your Learning

Have students complete Exercise 8-3 at this point.

Orchard Hill Furniture issued $500,000 of 5-year, 9% bonds. The company also set up a bond sinking fund and plans to invest all of the money placed in the fund. At the beginning of the fifth year of the bond issue, the balance of the company's Sinking Fund Investments account is $450,000. On a sheet of notebook paper, prepare the entries in general journal form to record the following.

1. The sale of the investments for $460,000 on July 27, Receipt 660.
2. The final deposit in the sinking fund on July 31, bringing the balance of the account up to $500,000, Check 997.
3. The payment of the bonds on August 1, Check 498.

Compare your answers to those in the answers section. Reread the preceding part of the chapter to find the correct entries for any items you may have missed.

Summary of Key Points

1. A mortgage note is a long-term liability. It is often issued when a business needs a large sum of money to purchase plant assets such as land, buildings, or equipment. The mortgage contract usually gives the creditor the right to repossess the mortgage assets if the borrower fails to repay the mortgage note.
2. A bond is a long-term liability, much like a promissory note. The issuing corporation promises to repay the borrowed amount at a set time and to pay interest at specified times, usually semiannually.
3. Bondholders are creditors of the corporation.
4. The market interest rate, the rate that borrowers are willing to pay and lenders are willing to accept for the use of money, affects the issue price of bonds.
5. Bonds are issued at a premium when the issue price is higher than the face value. Bonds are issued at a discount when the issue price is lower than the face value. The carrying value of a bond issue is the face value plus any premium or minus any discount.
6. A corporation amortizes (writes off) the premium or the discount on bonds payable over the life of the bond issue. The amortization is recorded through an adjusting entry.
7. A corporation redeems its bonds when it wishes to eliminate the debt or to refinance the debt at a lower rate of interest.
8. A bond sinking fund may be established to accumulate assets to repay the principal of a bond issue at maturity.

8 Review and Applications

Building Your Accounting Vocabulary

In your own words, write the definition of each of the following accounting terms. Use complete sentences for your definitions.

amortize	contract rate	registered bond
bond	coupon bond	secured bond
bond certificate	discount	serial bond
bond indenture	face value	sinking fund
bond issue	leverage	term bond
callable bond	market interest rate	underwriter
call price	mortgage	unsecured bond
carrying value	premium	

Reviewing Your Accounting Knowledge

1. When would a company choose to issue a mortgage note?
2. Is a bondholder an owner of a corporation? Why or why not?
3. What are the duties of an underwriter? A trustee?
4. What information is included in a bond indenture?
5. Name two advantages and two disadvantages of issuing bonds.
6. Which type of bonds are considered "bearer" bonds? Why?
7. How does the market interest rate affect the issue price of bonds?
8. If a corporation sells its bonds at a price of 103, have the bonds been sold at face value, at a premium, or at a discount? Explain.
9. How is the carrying value of a bond issue calculated?
10. Why does the amortization of a bond discount increase the total interest expense to a corporation? Why does the amortization of a bond premium decrease the total interest expense to a corporation?
11. When might a corporation have to record an adjusting entry for accrued interest expense?
12. Why would a corporation want to call its bonds when it can wait to pay off the debt?

Improving Your Analysis Skills

José was examining the past two years' financial statements of The Music Box, a store that sells records, tapes, and CDs. He noticed that sales for the business had increased 17% during the past year. He also noticed that during the same period, net income had *decreased* 5%. Suggest as many reasons as you can why sales increased but net income decreased.

Applying Accounting Procedures

SPREADSHEET PROBLEM

Exercise 8-1 Computing the Carrying Value of Bonds Payable

Instructions: Calculate the carrying values of the following bond issues. Use the space provided in the working papers.

1. $100,000 of 12% bonds issued at 104 — $104,000
2. $150,000 of 6% bonds issued at 96 — $144,000
3. $200,000 of 10% bonds issued at 101 — $202,000
4. $175,000 of 7.5% bonds issued at 98 — $171,500

SPREADSHEET PROBLEM

Exercise 8-2 Computing Losses and Gains on the Redemption of Bonds

Details about several different bond issues follow. All or a portion of these bond issues were recently redeemed.

Total Face Value	Unamortized Premium/Discount	Amount Redeemed	Purchase/Call Price
$400,000	$ 2,000 discount	$400,000	103
$250,000	$ 2,500 premium	$250,000	99
$350,000	$ 3,000 premium	$350,000	98
$700,000	none	$500,000	101
$800,000	$21,000 discount	$200,000	104
$500,000	$20,000 premium	$400,000	102

Instructions: For each bond issue, determine (1) the carrying value of the portion being redeemed, (2) the total cash paid, and (3) the gain or loss on the redemption. Use the form provided in the working papers.

Exercise 8-3 Classifying Bond Accounts

Following are several of the accounts introduced in this chapter.

Bond Interest Expense	Gain on Sale of Sinking Fund Investments
Bond Interest Payable	Loss on Redemption of Bonds
Bond Sinking Fund	Premium on Bonds Payable
Bonds Payable	Sinking Fund Income
Discount on Bonds Payable	Sinking Fund Investments
Gain on Redemption of Bonds	

Instructions: For each account, indicate its classification and normal balance side (dr. or cr.). Use the form provided in the working papers.

Problem 8-1 Journalizing Transactions for Mortgage Notes

The Beacon Communications Company purchased land and a building for its new offices. The company signed a 15-year, 9% mortgage note for $75,000 for a portion of the purchase price.

Instructions: Record the following transactions in a cash payments journal, page 43.

Transactions:

Oct. 1 Purchased land and a building by issuing Check 4633 for $25,000.00 and signing a $75,000.00 mortgage note for the remainder of the purchase price. The cost of the land was 30% of the total price paid.

Nov. 1 Made the first mortgage payment of $760.70 (Check 4680). Of this amount, $562.50 was interest and $198.20 was a payment on principal.

Dec. 1 Made the second mortgage payment: interest, $561.01; principal, $199.69 (Check 4730).

Problem 8-2 Issuing Bonds at Face Value

On January 5, the board of directors of the Allegheny Equipment Company authorized the issuance of $1,000,000 of 8.5%, 15-year bonds, with interest payable on June 30 and December 31.

Instructions: Record the following transactions in the cash receipts journal (page 19) and cash payments journal (page 26).

Transactions:

Jan. 5 Issued $1,000,000 of 8.5%, 15-year bonds at face value, Receipt 305.

June 30 Paid the semiannual interest on the bonds, Check 558 for $42,500.

Dec. 31 Wrote Check 707 in payment of the $42,500 semiannual bond interest.

COMPUTER PROBLEM

Problem 8-3 Issuing Bonds at a Premium

On January 2, Lakewood Enterprises issued $750,000 of 9%, 10-year bonds with interest payable on June 30 and December 31.

Instructions: Record the following transactions in the cash receipts journal (page 16), cash payments journal (page 27), and general journal (page 18).

Transactions:

Jan. 2 Issued $750,000 of 10-year, 9% bonds at 102 (face value, $1,000), Receipt 487.

June 30 Paid the semiannual bond interest, issuing Check 603.

Dec. 31 Issued Check 998 in payment of the semiannual bond interest.

31 Recorded the adjusting entry for the amortization of the bond premium.

31 Closed the Bond Interest Expense account.

COMPUTER PROBLEM

Problem 8-4 Issuing Bonds at a Discount

The board of directors of Seaview Mobile Communications authorized the issuance of $900,000 of 7%, 20-year bonds with interest payable on June 30 and December 31.

Instructions:

(1) Record the following transactions in the cash receipts journal (page 34), the cash payments journal (page 49), and the general journal (page 27).

(2) Post the transactions to the Discount on Bonds Payable and the Bond Interest Expense accounts.

Transactions:

Jan. 6 Issued $900,000 of 7%, 20-year bonds at 99% of their face value of $1,000, Receipt 406.

June 30 Wrote Check 778 for the semiannual interest payment.

Dec. 31 Issued Check 1012 as payment of the semiannual bond interest.

31 Recorded the adjusting entry to amortize the bond discount.

31 Closed the Bond Interest Expense account.

Problem 8-5 Accounting for Accrued Bond Interest

Bon-Air Fresheners, Inc., is authorized to issue $800,000 of 10-year, 8% bonds dated May 1, with interest payable on October 31 and April 30.

Instructions: Record the following transactions in a cash receipts journal (page 5), cash payments journal (page 68), and general journal (page 49).

Transactions:

Year 1

May 1 Issued $800,000 of bonds at 103, Receipt 758.

Oct. 31 Issued Check 1232 for the semiannual bond interest payment.

Dec. 31 Recorded the adjusting entry for accrued bond interest expense.

31 Amortized the bond premium through an adjusting entry.

31 Closed the Bond Interest Expense account.

Year 2

Apr. 30 Paid the semiannual bond interest, Check 1801.

Problem 8-6 Redeeming a Bond Issue

Five years ago, the Wellington Corporation issued $600,000 of 10-year, 9% callable bonds, call price 101. Interest is payable on March 31 and September 30.

Instructions: Record the following transactions in the cash receipts journal (page 47), the cash payments journal (page 52), and the general journal (page 30).

Transactions:

Year 1

Sept. 30 Issued Check 315 in payment of the semiannual bond interest.

Oct. 1 Redeemed the complete bond issue at the call price, Check 316. There was no unamortized premium or discount.

Dec. 1 Issued $600,000 of 7.5%, 5-year bonds at 102, Receipt 210. Interest is payable on May 31 and November 30.

31 Recorded the adjusting entry for accrued bond interest.

31 Recorded the adjusting entry for the unamortized bond premium.

31 Closed the Bond Interest Expense account.

Year 2
May 31 Issued Check 362 for the interest expense on the new bond issue.

Problem 8-7 Recording Bond Sinking Fund Transactions

Five years ago, Delta Laser, Inc., issued $500,000 of 9.5%, 15-year bonds, receiving $515,000 cash. The interest on the bonds is paid on June 30 and December 31. There is an unamortized premium of $10,000. The company has a bond sinking fund to which it makes annual deposits.

Instructions:

(1) Record the following transactions in the cash payments journal (page 61) and the general journal (page 44).

(2) Post the transactions to the Bond Sinking Fund, Sinking Fund Investments, Premium on Bonds Payable, Sinking Fund Income, and Bond Interest Expense accounts.

Transactions:

Year 1
Jan. 5 Deposited $20,000 in the bond sinking fund, Check 810.
30 Used $19,000 from the bond sinking fund to purchase various securities, Check 125.
June 30 Paid the semiannual bond interest, Check 890.
Dec. 2 Received $10,790 in interest and dividends from sinking fund investments, Receipt 130.
12 Received $95,562 from the sale of various sinking fund investments that originally cost $85,900, Receipt 131.
31 Issued Check 1437 for the semiannual bond interest payment.
31 Recorded the adjusting entry for the amortization of the bond premium.
31 Closed the Sinking Fund Income and Bond Interest Expense accounts.

Year 2
Jan. 1 Made the annual deposit of $20,000 to the bond sinking fund, Check 1440.
1 Used the bond sinking fund to buy one-quarter of the 9.5% bond issue on the open market at a price of 98, Check 126.

CHALLENGE PROBLEM

Problem 8-8 Evaluating a Bond Issue

$2,856,250
$8,568,750
$5,250,000
$193,750 loss
$7,875,000
$693,750
$500,000

Five years ago, the Graphics Effects Corporation issued $5,000,000 of 11.5%, 20-year bonds with a call price of 105. Semiannual interest payments have been made each June and December for the past five years. There is an unamortized bond premium of $56,250. The company is considering redeeming the 11.5% bonds and issuing $5,000,000 of 10.5%, 15-year bonds.

Instructions: Answer the following questions.

1. How much interest expense has Graphics Effects paid out over the past five years? Include the amortized premium in your calculations. The bonds were originally issued at 101.5.

2. Over the next 15 years, how much interest would be paid on the 11.5% bond issue?
3. How much would it cost Graphics Effects to redeem the original bond issue?
4. Would Graphics Effects have a gain or a loss on the redemption? What amount?
5. How much interest would be paid over the next 15 years for a 10.5% bond issue?
6. How much interest expense would Graphics Effects save over the next 15 years if it redeemed the old bonds and issued the new bonds at face value?
7. Considering the premium the company would have to pay for redeeming the existing bonds, how much would Graphics Effects save over the next 15 years?

Astronomically Advanced Computers

Have you ever looked into the sky on a clear night, far away from city lights, and tried to count the stars? When you are far away from artificial lights, you can see stars behind stars behind stars, and the job of keeping track of them becomes impossible. In fact, you would need a computer! Astronomers—scientists who study stars, planets, and other objects in the universe—use computers to locate and track stars and many other things.

For both professional and casual observers, studying the stars is fascinating and raises many questions: How did these objects form? How old are they? How long will they last? Many of these questions could not be even remotely answered until the advent of supercomputers.

Since most of the objects we see in the sky are many light-years away, it is impossible, through direct observation, to gather firsthand information about a celestial object, either by travel or by satellite. Knowing, however, what scientists know about the physical and chemical processes of the universe, astronomers can use computers to test hypotheses and form theories. Computers can also help make sense of data that are gathered through direct observation.

Some of the ways computers are used in the field of astronomy include

- Aiding telescopes so they can provide the astronomer with information about the object he or she is viewing or can locate an object that the astronomer enters in the computer.
- Unscrambling information gathered by space telescopes when atmospheric movements distort the image.
- Devising simulations of galaxy formation, star formation, and black hole formation and behavior.
- Computing past, present, and future planetary movements.

Astronomers use computers to gather information while studying the stars, planets, and other objects in the universe.

Even with the incredible advances in the computer industry, many of the discoveries made by astronomers will remain unverified. As technology increases, however, more and more hypotheses can be tested to obtain more precise answers.

Mini Practice Set

APPLICATION ACTIVITY 3

COMPUTER PROBLEM

Accounting for Liabilities

In Chapters 7 and 8, you learned how to record a variety of transactions that affect current and long-term liabilities, such as notes payable, bonds, and sinking funds. You will now have the opportunity to review and apply what you have learned by recording selected transactions for Metro Sports World, Inc.

When you have completed this activity, you will have done the following:

1. Calculated the maturity value of interest-bearing notes payable.
2. Calculated the discount and proceeds of non-interest-bearing notes payable.
3. Recorded transactions for notes payable.
4. Determined the amount of bond interest expense.
5. Recorded transactions for bonds payable.
6. Journalized transactions involving a bond sinking fund.
7. Recorded transactions involving mortgage notes.
8. Posted transactions involving liabilities to the general ledger accounts.
9. Prepared a trial balance at the end of the year.
10. Entered adjustments involving liabilities on a work sheet.
11. Recorded adjusting entries affecting liabilities.

Metro Sports World, Inc.

Metro Sports World, Inc., is a retail merchandising business that sells sporting and athletic equipment. The business is organized as a publicly held corporation. It has a large number of stockholders, and its stock is traded on a major stock exchange.

Chart of Accounts

A partial chart of accounts for Metro Sports World, Inc., follows. Most of these accounts have been opened in the general ledger.

METRO SPORTS WORLD
Chart of Accounts (Partial)

ASSETS	101	Cash in Bank
	140	Bond Sinking Fund
	143	Sinking Fund Investments
	155	Store Equipment
	165	Building
	170	Land

LIABILITIES	201	Notes Payable
	203	Discount on Notes Payable
	210	Bond Interest Payable
	215	Federal Income Tax Payable
	220	Interest Payable
	270	12% Bonds Payable
	273	Premium on Bonds Payable
	275	9% Bonds Payable
	278	Discount on Bonds Payable
	290	Mortgage Payable
OTHER INCOME	701	Sinking Fund Income
	710	Gain on Sale of Sinking Fund Investments
OTHER EXPENSES	751	Bond Interest Expense
	755	Interest Expense
	760	Loss on Redemption of Bonds
	799	Income Tax Expense

Business Transactions

Transactions affecting Metro's liability accounts that took place during the fiscal period follow. Metro maintains a bond sinking fund and has a separate checking account for the fund.

Instructions: **(1)** Record the transactions in the appropriate journals. Begin recording the transactions on page 49 of the cash receipts journal, page 55 of the cash payments journal, and page 61 of the general journal. **(2)** Post the transactions to the general ledger accounts included in the working papers.

Transactions:

Jan. 1 Received $12,000 from sinking fund investments, Receipt 279.

1 Sold for $130,500 various sinking fund investments that had been purchased for $100,000, Receipt 280.

1 Used the bond sinking fund to redeem the entire 12% bond issue, plus the unamortized bond premium, at the call price of 104 (Check 104).

Mar. 2 Purchased store equipment from Sierra Equipment Company for $12,000 by issuing a 120-day, 10% note payable, Note 32.

Apr. 1 Issued $300,000 of 9%, 10-year bonds at 98, Receipt 2375. Interest is payable semiannually on October 1 and April 1.

May 5 Borrowed $6,000 from the Dollar Bank for 90 days by issuing a non-interest-bearing note (Note 33) that the bank discounted at 11% (Receipt 2751).

June 30 Issued Check 5102 to the Sierra Equipment Company in payment of the principal and interest due on Note 32.

Aug. 3 Paid to the Dollar Bank the amount owed on Note 33 (Check 5613) and recorded the interest expense.

Sept. 13 Issued a $10,000, 60-day, 10.5% note payable (Note 34) to the Dollar Bank (Receipt 4176).

Oct. 1 Signed a 20-year, $8\frac{1}{2}\%$ mortgage note for $150,000 to purchase land and a building for a new store (Memorandum 4163). The cost of the land was 40% of the total price.

1 Issued Check 6463 for the semiannual interest on the bonds issued April 1.

3 Deposited $45,000 in the bond sinking fund by issuing Check 6483.

Nov. 1 Made the first mortgage payment of $1,700 (Check 6801). Of this amount, $1,062 was interest and $638 was a payment on principal.

12 Paid the interest due on Note 34 (Check 6922) and renewed the note by issuing a 60-day, $10,000, 11% note payable (Note 35).

15 Purchased various securities with sinking fund cash, $40,000, Check 301.

Dec. 1 Wrote Check 7172 for the second mortgage payment: principal, $642; interest, $1,058.

TB totals, $2,457,889.00

31 Received $475 from sinking fund investments, Receipt 281.

Handling End-of-Period Activities

(1) Prepare a trial balance, using the first two columns of a work sheet. The account numbers and titles have already been entered on the work sheet. Use the balances of the accounts included in the working papers and the balances that follow to complete the trial balance.

Account	Debit	Credit
Cash in Bank	$256,394.14	
Accounts Receivable	216,050	
Allowance for Uncollectible Accounts		$ 256
Merchandise Inventory	324,500	
Supplies	23,690	
Prepaid Insurance	9,500	
Accumulated Depreciation—Store Equipment		5,250
Accumulated Depreciation—Building		—
Accounts Payable		33,750
Federal Income Tax Payable		—
Sales Tax Payable		7,813
Common Stock		300,000
Paid-in Capital in Excess of Par		30,000
Retained Earnings		129,750
Income Summary		—
Sales		1,432,500
Sales Returns and Allowances	34,000	
Purchases	843,750	
Purchases Discounts		16,875
Bad Debts Expense	—	
Depreciation Expense—Store Equipment	—	
Depreciation Expense—Building	—	
Insurance Expense	—	
Miscellaneous Expense	16,510	
Rent Expense	30,000	
Salaries Expense	183,420	
Supplies Expense	—	
Utilities Expense	54,000	

Adjustments:
(a) $6,750.00
(b) $10,008.00
(c) $147.67
(d) $450.00

(2) Enter the adjustments affecting current and long-term liabilities on the work sheet.

(a) Three months of bond interest expense have accrued on the $300,000, 9% bond issue.

(b) Total federal income taxes for the year are $110,008.

(c) Interest expense has accrued for Note 35, which was issued November 12.

(d) The discount incurred on the 9% bonds payable must be amortized.

(3) Record the adjusting entries for these adjustments in the general journal.

(4) Post the adjusting entries to the appropriate accounts in the general ledger.

Chapter 9

STOCKHOLDERS' EQUITY: CONTRIBUTED CAPITAL

Although corporations are fewer in number than sole proprietorships and partnerships, they account for more business activity than the other two forms combined. Often, a company begins as a sole proprietorship or a partnership. As it grows and prospers, it usually needs more investment capital. To raise that additional capital, the business incorporates, which allows it to sell stock.

In this chapter, you will learn about the characteristics, advantages, and disadvantages of corporations. You will also learn how corporations raise capital and how they journalize transactions for the issuance of stock.

Learning Objectives

When you have completed this chapter, you should be able to do the following:

1. Define a corporation and list some of its advantages and disadvantages.
2. Describe the organization and management of a corporation.
3. Describe the different types of capital stock.
4. Journalize transactions for the issuance of par-value and no-par stock.
5. Record transactions for stock subscriptions.
6. Define the accounting terms presented in this chapter.

New Terms

corporation
stockholder
stock
stock certificate
double taxation
articles of incorporation
charter
board of directors
pre-emptive right
authorized capital stock
issued shares
outstanding stock
common stock
par-value stock
no-par stock
preferred stock
stockholders' ledger
legal capital
stated value
stock subscription

The Nature of a Corporation

Emphasize that a corporation is a separate legal entity.

In 1819, John Marshall, Chief Justice of the U.S. Supreme Court, defined a corporation as "an artificial being, invisible, intangible, and existing only in contemplation of the law." This means that a **corporation** is an artificial legal entity that has rights and responsibilities of its own. It may own property, enter into contracts, sue and be sued in the courts, and so forth. In every respect, it is a separate legal entity that has a continuous existence separate from that of its owners. The owners of a corporation are called **stockholders**.

Chief Justice John Marshall helped to define the legal requirements of corporations.

Advantages of a Corporation

Discuss the advantages of a corporation over a sole proprietorship or partnership.

The corporation has several advantages over the sole proprietorship and the partnership forms of organization:

1. *Limited liability.* As a separate legal entity, a corporation is responsible for its own debts. All that stockholders (owners) can lose is the amount of their investment. This is the most important advantage for stockholders. The owners of sole proprietorships and partnerships, you'll remember, can be held personally liable for the debts of the business.
2. *Ease of raising capital.* Since a corporation can sell stock, it can raise greater amounts of investment capital than a sole proprietorship or partnership can. Sole proprietorships and partnerships are limited to the investments of their individual owners. Some corporations have more than one million stockholders.

3. *Ease of transferring ownership.* **Stock,** the shares of ownership in a corporation, can easily be transferred from one person to another without the permission of other stockholders. All that is required for transfer of ownership is to transfer the **stock certificate,** a document that shows how many shares of corporation stock a particular shareholder owns. In a partnership, the other partners must approve changes in ownership for the business to continue.
4. *Continuous existence.* The length of life of a corporation is set out in its charter. When the charter expires, it may be renewed. The death, incapacity, or withdrawal of a stockholder does not affect the life of the corporation. Such a circumstance would end a partnership.
5. *Professional management.* Large corporations are owned by many stockholders who do not usually participate in its day-to-day operations. The corporation, through the board of directors, is free to employ professional managers who have the ability to direct and operate the business.

Explain that since a corporation has many owners who do not participate in the day-to-day operations, it is free to hire the best talent available to manage the business.

Disadvantages of a Corporation

Discuss the disadvantages of a corporation over a sole proprietorship or partnership.

The corporation also has a number of disadvantages:

1. *Taxation.* In addition to the usual property and payroll taxes, corporations must pay income taxes and charter fees. Since a corporation is a separate legal entity, its earnings are subject to federal and state income taxes. Part of the corporation's after-tax profits may be distributed to stockholders in the form of dividends. These dividends are then taxed as personal income to the stockholders. This procedure is known as the **double taxation** of corporations. Many consider double taxation the major disadvantage of the corporate form. In addition, a corporation must pay a fee to the state in return for the issuance of a charter or a license to operate. These charter fees may be considered additional taxes.
2. *Government regulation.* States create corporations by granting charters. As a result, states can exercise closer control and supervision over corporations than over sole proprietorships or partnerships. States may even regulate the amount of net income that a corporation must keep in the business, the extent to which it may buy back its own stock, and the amount of real estate it may own. In contrast, states do not impose further regulations on sole proprietorships and partnerships; they need only have legal purposes.

Emphasize that a charter is granted in the state where a corporation will primarily operate and must be obtained before business can begin.

Forming a Corporation

Point out that forming a corporation is more involved than forming a sole proprietorship or partnership.

To organize a corporation, a person or persons must submit an application to the appropriate official (usually the corporation commissioner or secretary of state) of the state in which the company is to be incorporated. The application is called the **articles of incorporation.** Generally, the application must include these items.

- Name and address of the corporation.
- Nature of the business to be conducted.
- Amount and description of the capital stock to be issued.
- Names and addresses of the subscribers (people who are going to buy stocks) and the amount of stock subscribed by each.
- Names of the promoters (or temporary officers) who will serve until the first meeting of the stockholders is held.

The articles of incorporation must be signed by the promoters and must be accompanied by a charter fee.

When the state officials approve them, the articles of incorporation become the **charter** of the corporation. Shortly after receiving the charter, the stock subscribers hold a meeting to elect an acting board of directors and to develop bylaws. The charter and the bylaws provide the basic rules for operating the corporation. The **board of directors** govern and are responsible for the affairs of the corporation. The directors in turn appoint the officers, who serve as the managers of the business. The corporation then issues stock certificates to the subscribers who have paid in full. At this point, stockholders actually exist; they can now elect a permanent board of directors.

Emphasize that many corporations are privately held.

The size of the corporation may vary in the number of stockholders and amounts of investment. It may be a small corporation with only a few stockholders and an investment of only $1,000. It may also be a giant corporation, with more than a million stockholders and an investment of more than $1 billion dollars. In the small corporation, those few stockholders may also be the directors and the officers. A corporation whose ownership is confined to a small group of stockholders, you'll remember, is called a closely held corporation. A corporation whose stock is publicly traded on a stock exchange or over the counter is called a publicly held corporation.

Organization Costs

Stress that organization costs refer only to those costs the corporation incurred during its formation.

Let's suppose Mayfaire, Inc., is just forming. The organizers hire an accountant to set up the books. One of the things the accountant must determine is the costs of organizing the corporation. The costs include such items as fees paid to the state, attorney's fees, promotional costs, travel expenses, charges for printing stock certificates, and so on. The total cost of organizing the corporation is debited to an account called Organization Costs. As you learned in Chapter 6, this account is classified as an intangible asset. Organization costs benefit the corporation throughout its entire life. Since the life of a corporation is unknown, the organization costs are amortized (written off as an expense) over a period of years.

Point out that these costs are usually written off over a five-year period.

R — E — M — E — M — B — E — R

Organization Costs **is an intangible asset. The amount debited to the account will be written off as an expense over a number of years.**

Stock Certificates

Remind students that a stock certificate is evidence of ownership in a corporation.

Stock certificates are proof of ownership in a corporation. A corporation issues stock certificates only when the stock has been paid for in full. In a small corporation, the certificates often have stubs attached. The certificates and stubs are bound in a stock certificate book, much like a checkbook. Each certificate must list the name of the stockholder, the number of shares issued, and the date of issuance. The stub must also show the name and address of the stockholder, the number of shares listed on the stock certificate, and the date of issuance. Both certificates and stubs are numbered consecutively. Figure 9-1 shows an example of a stock certificate.

If possible, bring in sample stock certificates for students to examine.

Figure 9-1 Stock Certificate

When a stockholder transfers ownership of stock, he or she surrenders the stock certificate to the corporation. The corporation cancels the certificate and the matching stub. It then issues one or more new stock certificates. In this way, the corporation can maintain an up-to-date record of its stockholders and the number of shares owned by each.

Large, publicly held corporations usually have independent registrars and transfer agents to maintain their stockholder records. The registrars and transfer agents are usually banks and trust companies.

ACCOUNTING Notes

In Japan as well as in some other countries, stock certificates are no longer issued to stockholders. Accounting records indicate stock ownership. U.S. corporations have been slow to adopt this procedure.

Management of a Corporation

Stockholders are the owners of a corporation. They delegate authority to the board of directors, who oversee the corporation's affairs. Often, the directors are also stockholders, although this is not always the case.

Review and discuss the responsibilities of each level.

The board of directors, in turn, delegates authority to the officers and managers, who actually run the business. The officers themselves may be members of the board of directors. Figure 9-2 shows a typical organization chart for a corporation.

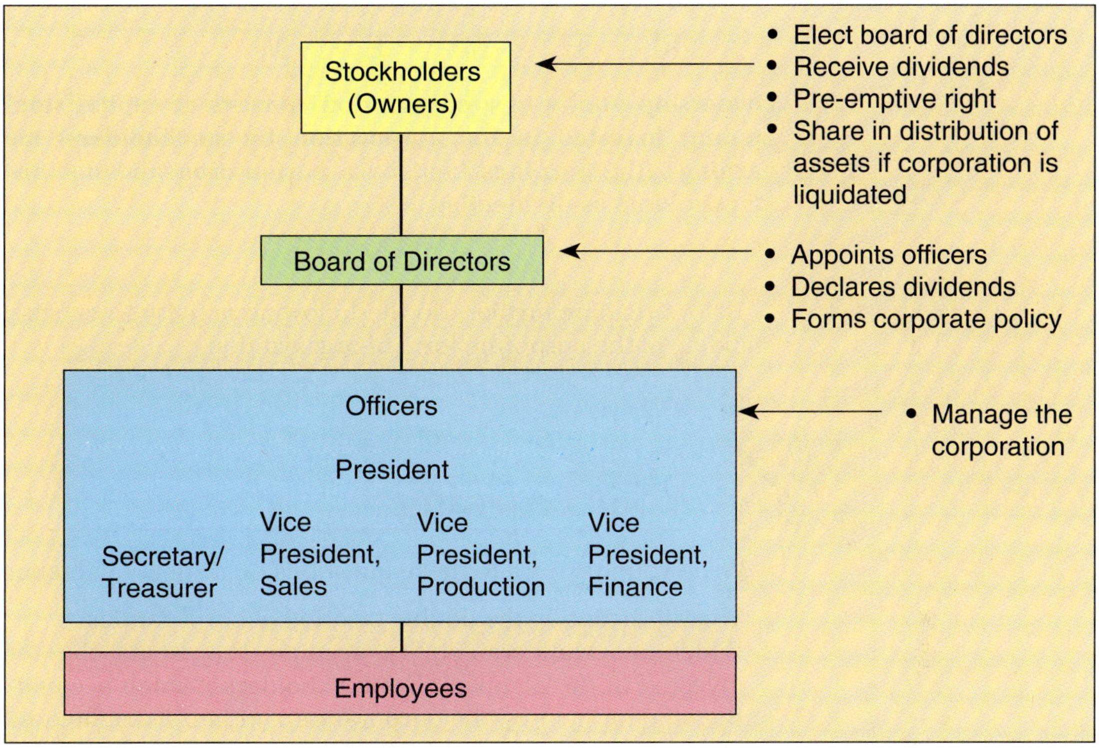

Figure 9-2 Corporation Organization Chart

Stockholders' Equity

Be sure students realize that the total ownership equity of a corporation is referred to as "stockholders' equity."

As you know, ownership equity in a corporation is called *stockholders' equity*. Stockholders' equity represents the value of the owners' (stockholders') claims to the assets of the business. Corporations must report stockholders' equity in two parts: (1) the equity that has been paid into the corporation by stockholders and (2) the equity earned by the corporation and retained in the business. The capital stock account(s) summarizes the owners' investment. The Retained Earnings account is used to summarize earnings held by the business and not distributed as dividends.

Emphasize that all profits do not have to be distributed in dividends.

Dividends are shares of a corporation's earnings distributed to stockholders. The sources of the earnings are the current year's net income after income taxes and the retained earnings of prior years. Dividends are determined by the board of directors and are always issued at a specific amount per share. For example, the board of directors may declare a dividend of $1.20 per share. You'll learn more about dividends in Chapter 10.

Explain that pre-emptive right goes with common stock.

If Mayfaire, Inc., decides to issue additional shares of stock, each original stockholder has the right to subscribe to, or purchase, additional shares in proportion to her or his present holding. This is known as the stockholders' **pre-emptive right**. For example, assume Mayfaire decides to issue 1,000 more shares. In addition, assume the number of shares of stock originally issued was 10,000 shares, of which Jan Hunt owns 2,000. She currently owns one-fifth (2,000 ÷ 10,000) of the total number of shares issued. She has the right, therefore, to subscribe to 200 shares (1,000 shares × 1/5) of the new issue.

R — E — M — E — M — B — E — R

Ownership equity in a corporation consists of capital stock (the total amount invested in the corporation by stockholders) and retained earnings (the earnings kept by a corporation and not distributed to stockholders as dividends).

Before reading further, do the following activity to check your understanding of the corporate form of organization.

Check Your Learning

Write your answers to these questions on a sheet of notebook paper.

1. What is meant by the double taxation of corporations?
2. Which stockholders' equity account represents the total amount invested in the company by stockholders? Which account represents the amount held by the corporation and not distributed to stockholders as dividends?
3. Joanne Hamill owns 500 shares of stock in the Bricker Corporation, which has already issued 10,000 shares. The company plans to issue 5,000 more shares. How many shares of stock does Joanne Hamill have the right to subscribe to?

Compare your answers to those in the answers section. Reread the preceding part of the chapter to find the correct answers to any questions you may have missed.

Capital Stock

Point out that the maximum number of shares a corporation is permitted to issue is set out in the corporation's charter.

The shares of ownership in a corporation are referred to as *capital stock*. **Authorized capital stock** is the maximum number of shares of stock a corporation may issue, as set out in its charter. **Issued shares** are those shares that have been sold to the stockholders. Stock that is actually in the hands of stockholders is called **outstanding stock**.

To appeal to as many investors as possible, a corporation may issue more than one kind of capital stock. The two main types of capital stock are common and preferred.

Common Stock

Mention that all corporations issue common stock.

When a corporation issues only one type of stock, that stock is called **common stock.** Holders of common stock have all of the rights listed in Figure 9-2. In addition, common stockholders may vote on issues at the corporation's annual meetings. They are allowed one vote for each share of stock owned.

Explain that stock is not usually sold for par-value.

Common stock may be either par-value or no-par stock. **Par-value stock** is stock that has a specific value printed on the stock certificate. The share of stock illustrated in Figure 9-1 has a par value of $1. **No-par stock** is stock that does not have a value printed on the stock certificate.

Preferred Stock

As the name implies, **preferred stock** has certain preferences over common stock. The most common preferences are that (1) the corporation pays dividends to preferred stockholders before it pays them to common stockholders and (2) it pays them at a uniform, stated rate. The dividend on preferred stock is stated as a percentage of the par value of the stock, for example, 8%. The stock itself is then referred to as *Preferred 8% Stock.* If the corporation goes out of business, holders of preferred stock receive their share of the corporation's assets before holders of common stock. Holders of preferred stock, however, usually cannot vote at the corporation's annual meetings. Preferred stock is generally par-value stock. There are several specific types of preferred stock.

Emphasize nonvoting privileges.

Cumulative and Noncumulative Preferred Stock Suppose a corporation has had a bad year and finds that it cannot pay the dividend on its preferred stock (that is, it must "pass a dividend"). Stockholders who own *cumulative preferred stock* accumulate any dividends passed in previous years. The corporation must pay the passed dividends in full before it can pay any dividends to common stockholders. Holders of *noncumulative preferred stock* do not accumulate any passed dividends. In other words, if the corporation passes a dividend, the dividend is gone forever. Since preferred stockholders naturally want a regular dividend, most preferred stock is cumulative.

Point out that most preferred stock is cumulative.

Participating and Nonparticipating Preferred Stock As mentioned earlier, the dividend on preferred stock is set at a certain percentage of the stock's par value. Some preferred stock, however, provides for dividends that exceed this set amount. This kind of preferred stock is called *participating preferred stock.* Holders of participating preferred stock first receive their regular dividend. Next, the corporation allocates a certain amount to holders of its common stock. Then the holders of participating preferred stock are allowed to participate, or share, in any further distributions. The dividends of *nonparticipating preferred stock,* on the other hand, are limited to the regular rate. Most preferred stock is nonparticipating.

Explain that since most corporations want to regulate or control the dividends paid to stockholders, most preferred stock is nonparticipating.

R — E — M — E — M — B — E — R

The capital stock of a corporation may consist of both common stock and preferred stock.

Issuing Stock

Remind students that separate stockholders' equity accounts are set up for each different type of stock.

Stock is issued when the buyer has paid for it in full or when the corporation has received noncash assets in exchange for the stock. Let's first discuss the issuance of par-value stock and then the issuance of no-par stock.

Issuing Stock at Par for Cash

A separate general ledger account is maintained for each class of stock, such as Common Stock and Preferred 8% Stock. The capital stock accounts summarize the par value of the stock issued. When stock is sold at par for cash, the transaction is recorded as a debit to Cash in Bank and a credit to the appropriate stock account. Remember that par value is the face value printed on each stock certificate.

Remind students of the difference between authorized and issued shares.

For example, Mayfaire, Inc., was organized with authorized capital of 10,000 shares of $50-par preferred 8% stock and 50,000 shares of $25-par common stock. Just after it was organized, Mayfaire had the following transaction.

August 1: *Issued 2,500 shares of preferred 8% stock at par and 20,000 shares of common stock at par, Receipt 1.*

Make sure students understand that when stock is issued at par, the amount credited to the capital stock account(s) is the total par value of the stock.

Use demonstration problem 9-1 here.

In this transaction, Mayfaire received a total of $625,000 cash in return for the shares of stock. When stock is issued at its par value, the amount credited to the capital stock account is determined by multiplying the number of shares issued by the stock's par value. In this transaction, therefore, Preferred 8% Stock was credited for $125,000 (2,500 shares × $50) and Common Stock was credited for $500,000 (20,000 shares × $25). Cash in Bank was debited for $625,000, the total amount of cash received. This transaction is shown in Figure 9-3.

Cash in Bank	
Dr.	Cr.
$625,000	

Preferred 8% Stock	
Dr.	Cr.
	$125,000

Common Stock	
Dr.	Cr.
	$500,000

CASH RECEIPTS JOURNAL — PAGE 1

	DATE		DOC. NO.	ACCOUNT TITLE	POST. REF.	GENERAL DEBIT	GENERAL CREDIT	SALES CREDIT	SALES TAX PAYABLE CREDIT	ACCOUNTS RECEIVABLE CREDIT	CASH IN BANK DEBIT	
1	199– Aug.	1	R1	Preferred 8% Stock			125000 00				625000 00	1
2				Common Stock			500000 00					2

Figure 9-3 Journalizing the Issuance of Stock at Par Value

Point out that the capital stock accounts are really controlling accounts.

The capital stock accounts (Preferred 8% Stock and Common Stock) are actually controlling accounts. The subsidiary ledger for each account may be the stock certificate book. It may also be a supplementary record showing the name and address of each stockholder and the number of shares owned. This ledger is known as a **stockholders' ledger**.

General Ledger Controlling Account	Subsidiary Ledger
Preferred 8% Stock	Preferred 8% Stockholders' Ledger
Common Stock	Common Stockholders' Ledger

R — E — M — E — M — B — E — R

The amount credited to the capital stock account is the par value of the stock issued.

Issuing Stock at Par for Noncash Assets

Corporations often accept assets other than cash in exchange for their stock. For example, Mayfaire, Inc., received equipment, a building, and land from stockholders, in exchange for common stock.

August 1: *Issued 3,840 shares of common stock in exchange for office equipment valued at $6,000; a building valued at $60,000; and land valued at $30,000; Memorandum 5.*

Explain that the number of shares issued in exchange for the noncash assets depends on the fair market value of the assets—not the other way around.

When a corporation accepts an asset other than cash, the asset is recorded at its fair market value. The market value in turn determines the number of shares of stock that are issued at par. In the transaction, the total market value of the noncash assets is $96,000 ($6,000 + $60,000 + $30,000). That total is then divided by the par value of the stock to determine the number of shares issued ($96,000 ÷ $25 = 3,840 shares). Figure 9-4 shows the journal entry.

GENERAL JOURNAL PAGE 1

	DATE		DESCRIPTION	POST. REF.	DEBIT	CREDIT	
1	19– Aug.	1	Office Equipment		6 000 00		1
2			Building		60 000 00		2
3			Land		30 000 00		3
4			Common Stock			96 000 00	4
5			Memo. 5				5

Figure 9-4 Journalizing the Issuance of Stock for Noncash Assets

Use demonstration problem 9-2 here.

A corporation may give shares of its stock to its organizers in exchange for their services during the organization. When this happens, the corporation debits the value of the services to the intangible asset account Organization Costs. Suppose Mayfaire, Inc., issued 500 shares of common stock to its organizers. The journal entry to record this transaction appears in Figure 9-5.

GENERAL JOURNAL — PAGE ____

	DATE		DESCRIPTION	POST. REF.	DEBIT	CREDIT	
	199-						
6	Aug.	1	Organization Costs		12 500 00		6
7			Common Stock			12 500 00	7
8			Memo: 6				8

Have students complete Exercise 9-1 at this point.

Figure 9-5 Journalizing the Issuance of Common Stock to Organizers

Issuing Stock in Excess of Par Value

A corporation such as Mayfaire, Inc., generally issues its stock at a price other than par value. The price at which stock can be issued usually depends on the following factors:

1. The corporation's earnings record, financial condition, and dividend record.
2. The potential for growth in the corporation's earnings.
3. The supply of and demand for money for investment purposes in the economy.
4. General business conditions and prospects for the future.

Mention that the two states are California and Delaware.

Issuing stock at a discount (at a price below its par value) is illegal in most states and rarely occurs. (Only two states still allow corporations to issue stock below par.) This topic, therefore, will not be discussed in this chapter.

When a corporation issues stock at a price above its par value, the stock is said to be issued "in excess of par." This higher price may be a result of the corporation's past success and its good prospects for growth in the future.

Emphasize that Paid-in Capital in Excess of Par is classified as a stockholders' equity account.

Explain that the amounts recorded in the account do not represent profits to the corporation, but rather an additional investment by stockholders.

When a corporation issues stock at a price above its par value, Cash in Bank is debited for the amount of cash received. The capital stock account is credited for the total par value of the stock issued. Any difference between the amount of cash received and the total par value of the shares is credited to an account called Paid-in Capital in Excess of Par. Paid-in Capital in Excess of Par is a stockholders' equity account with a normal credit balance. The amounts recorded in this account represent a part of the stockholders' investment; it does *not* represent a profit to the corporation. On the balance sheet, the paid-in capital account appears immediately below its related capital stock account. A separate paid-in account is kept for each type of stock. The balance of the paid-in account is added to the balance of its related capital stock account to determine the total paid-in capital.

R E M E M B E R

The Paid-in Capital in Excess of Par **account is used to record the difference between the total amount received from stockholders and the par value of the stock issued.**

Mayfaire, Inc., had the following transaction.

October 1: *Issued 2,000 shares of $25-par common stock at $29, Receipt 68.*

Make sure students understand how to calculate the amount credited to the paid-in capital account.

In this transaction, Mayfaire received $58,000 for 2,000 shares of common stock (2,000 shares × $29). Before the transaction can be journalized, the corporation must determine how much of the $58,000 should be credited to Common Stock and how much should be credited to the paid-in capital account. Since the par value of the stock is $25, Mayfaire received an extra $4 for each share, or $8,000.

Common Stock, 2,000 shares @ $25 par	=	$50,000
Excess, 2,000 shares @ $4.00 per share	=	8,000
Total received, 2,000 shares @ $29		$58,000

Use demonstration problem 9-3 here.

In this transaction, Cash in Bank is debited for $58,000, the total amount of cash received. Common Stock is credited for $50,000, the par value of the 2,000 shares issued. Paid-in Capital in Excess of Par—Common is credited for $8,000, the amount of the difference between the cash received and the par value of the stock being issued. The transaction is illustrated in Figure 9-6.

Cash in Bank		Common Stock		Paid-in Capital in Excess of Par—Common	
Dr.	Cr.	Dr.	Cr.	Dr.	Cr.
$58,000			Bal. $596,000		$8,000
			50,000		

CASH RECEIPTS JOURNAL — PAGE 3

	DATE		DOC. NO.	ACCOUNT TITLE	POST. REF.	GENERAL DEBIT	GENERAL CREDIT	SALES CREDIT	SALES TAX PAYABLE CREDIT	ACCOUNTS RECEIVABLE CREDIT	CASH IN BANK DEBIT	
1	199- Oct.	1	R68	Common Stock			50 000 00				58 000 00	1
2				Paid-in Cap. in Exc. of								2
3				Par-Common			8 000 00					3

Figure 9-6 Journalizing the Issuance of Common Stock in Excess of Par Value

Preferred stock issued at a price above its par value would be recorded in a similar manner. The difference between the total amount of cash received and the total par value of the shares issued would be credited to the Paid-in Capital in Excess of Par—Preferred account.

R — E — M — E — M — B — E — R

For par-value stock, the capital stock account is credited for the total par value of the stock issued.

Before reading further, do the following activity to check your understanding of how to record transactions involving the sale of par-value stock.

Check Your Learning

On a sheet of notebook paper, record the following transactions of the United Print Company in general journal form.

Apr. 2	Issued 4,000 shares of $50-par common stock at par, Receipt 101.
6	Issued 1,000 shares of $50-par common stock to J. Zimmer for services rendered in setting up the accounting records of the corporation, Memorandum 3.
June 5	Issued 2,000 shares of $50-par common stock at $51.50, Receipt 226.

Compare your answers to those in the answers section. Reread the preceding part of the chapter to find the correct entries for any items you may have missed.

No-Par Stock

Explain that no-par stock avoids confusion as to par value and market value.

No-par stock, as you recall, does not have a specific par value printed on the stock certificates. At one time all stock had to have a par value. Today corporations in all 50 states can issue no-par stock. Some of the advantages claimed for no-par stock are as follows:

1. No-par stock may be issued at any price because it does not have a par value.
2. No-par stock prevents confusion on the part of stockholders about the value of the stock. For example, some investors may believe that par-value stock is worth the amount printed on the face of the stock certificate.
3. With no-par stock, more realistic values are placed on the noncash assets acquired by the corporation in exchange for the stock. As you remember, the business records the noncash assets at their current market values. A corporation's directors determine the values of the noncash assets. Using no-par stock greatly reduces the possibility of placing an inflated (overestimated) value on the noncash assets.

Emphasize that stockholders are liable for the debts of a corporation only up to the amount of their investments.

▲ **Stated Value** Stockholders have limited liability, therefore, the creditors of a corporation have no claim against the personal assets of stockholders. The creditors can look only to the assets of the corporation. To give some protection to creditors, states require corporations to keep in the business a minimum amount of the capital contributed by the stockholders. This amount is called the **legal capital**. Legal capital varies among the states, but it is usually the par value of the shares of capital stock issued. A corporation's legal capital, then, is the amount recorded in its capital stock accounts.

When states began to pass laws to permit corporations to issue no-par stock, they tried to continue to protect creditors by requiring that all or part of the amount the corporation received for its no-par shares be held by the corporation. To make it easier to do this, the board of directors of a corporation may set a stated value on its no-par stock. **Stated value** is simply the value assigned to a share of no-par stock by the board of directors. The board of directors may set whatever stated value it chooses, provided it meets the state's legal capital requirements.

Although par value and stated value seem similar, they are definitely different. The corporation's charter sets the par value of its stock. The corporation can change the par value only with the approval of the state. On the other hand, the board of directors of a corporation can change the stated value of its no-par stock by simply passing a resolution.

If a corporation issues no-par stock with a stated value, it may (1) record the total amount received in the Common Stock account or (2) record any amount received over the stated value in a separate paid-in capital account. If the second method is chosen, the journal entries are very similar to those for par-value common stock issued in excess of par.

R — E — M — E — M — B — E — R

The stated value of no-par stock is the value the board of directors has assigned to the stock.

Point out that the paid-in capital account is not used if there is no stated or par value.

Issuing No-Par Stock without a Stated Value

If a corporation issues no-par stock without a stated value, the entire amount the corporation receives for the stock is credited to the capital stock account.

Use demonstration problem 9-4 here.

For example, the Minon Corporation is authorized to issue 20,000 shares of no-par stock without a stated value. On May 1, the Minon Corporation issued 1,000 shares of no-par stock at $40 per share. On May 15, it issued another 1,000 shares at $42 per share. In both transactions, the total amount the corporation received for its stock was credited to the Common Stock account. These two transactions are illustrated in the following T accounts and in Figure 9-7.

CASH RECEIPTS JOURNAL — PAGE 4

	DATE		DOC. NO.	ACCOUNT TITLE	POST. REF.	GENERAL DEBIT	GENERAL CREDIT	SALES CREDIT	SALES TAX PAYABLE CREDIT	ACCOUNTS RECEIVABLE CREDIT	CASH IN BANK DEBIT	
1	199- May	1	R67	Common Stock			40 000 00				40 000 00	1
15		15	R79	Common Stock			42 000 00				42 000 00	15

Figure 9-7 Journalizing the Issuance of No-par Stock Without a Stated Value

Cash in Bank

Dr.	Cr.
5/1 $40,000	
5/15 42,000	

Common Stock

Dr.	Cr.
	5/1 $40,000 (1,000 shares @ $40)
	5/15 42,000 (1,000 shares @ $42)

Issuing No-Par Stock in Excess of Stated Value Fairfield Campers is authorized to issue 50,000 shares of no-par stock. Fairfield's board of directors chose to set a stated value of $25 per share for its no-par common stock. The corporation has also decided to record any amount received over the stated value in a separate paid-in capital account. Fairfield Campers had the following stock transactions.

June 1: *Issued 4,000 shares of no-par common stock (stated value $25) at $28 per share, receiving cash, Receipt 102.*

September 1: *Issued 2,000 shares of no-par common stock at $30 per share, receiving cash, Receipt 156.*

Explain how these transactions are similar to those for par-value stock.

These transactions are similar to those for par-value stock issued in excess of par. Just as for par-value stock, the excess is credited to a paid-in capital account, Paid-in Capital in Excess of Stated Value. For example, in the June 1 transaction Cash in Bank is debited for $112,000, the total amount of cash received (4,000 shares × $28). The Common Stock account is credited for the stated value of the shares issued, $100,000 (4,000 shares × $25). The amount received in excess of the stated value, $12,000 ($3 per share), is credited to Paid-in Capital in Excess of Stated Value. The September 1 transaction is handled in the same way, as shown in the following T accounts. The entries to record these transactions appear in Figure 9-8.

Use demonstration problem 9-5 here.

Cash in Bank		Common Stock		Paid-in Capital in Excess of Stated Value	
Dr.	Cr.	Dr.	Cr.	Dr.	Cr.
6/1 $112,000			6/l $100,000		6/1 $12,000
9/1 60,000			9/1 50,000		9/1 10,000

CASH RECEIPTS JOURNAL — PAGE 4

	DATE		DOC. NO.	ACCOUNT TITLE	POST. REF.	GENERAL DEBIT	GENERAL CREDIT	SALES CREDIT	SALES TAX PAYABLE CREDIT	ACCOUNTS RECEIVABLE CREDIT	CASH IN BANK DEBIT	
1	199- June	1	R102	Common Stock			100 000 00				112 000 00	1
2				Paid-in Cap. in Exc. of								2
3				Stated Value			12 000 00					3
23	Sept.	1	R156	Common Stock			50 000 00				60 000 00	23
24				Paid-in Cap. in Exc. of								24
25				Stated Value			10 000 00					25

Figure 9-8 Journalizing the Issuance of No-par Stock in Excess of Stated Value

R — E — M — E — M — B — E — R

The Paid-in Capital in Excess of Stated Value account may be used to record the difference between the total amount received from stockholders and the stated value of the no-par stock issued.

Before reading further, do the following activity to check your understanding of the material you have just studied.

Check Your Learning

The Spangler Corporation is authorized to issue 100,000 shares of no-par stock. On September 14, the company issued 4,000 shares of stock at $12 a share.

1. How much cash did the company receive for the 4,000 shares of stock?
2. If the stock has no stated value, which accounts were debited and which were credited for the September 14 transaction? For what amounts?
3. If the stock has a stated value of $10, which accounts were debited and which were credited for the September 14 transaction? For what amounts?

Compare your answers to those in the answers section. Reread the preceding part of the chapter to find the correct answers to any questions you may have missed.

Stock Subscriptions

Compare stock subscriptions to buying a product on lay-away. Point out that the store will only give you the product when it is paid for in full.

Some investors may wish to purchase a corporation's stock but be unable to pay for the stock right away. To accommodate these investors, a corporation may sell its stock on an installment basis. With this procedure, known as a **stock subscription**, the investor (subscriber) enters into a contract with the corporation. The subscriber promises to pay at a later date for a certain number of shares at an agreed price. The corporation promises to issue the shares when the investor has finished paying for them in full.

Emphasize that the Subscriptions Receivable account is a current asset.

The amount of the stock subscription represents an asset to the corporation: cash that will be received in the future. The amount of the subscription, therefore, is debited to a current asset account called Subscriptions Receivable. The total par or stated value of the stock is credited to Common Stock Subscribed, a temporary stockholders' equity account. This account represents the par or stated value of the stock not yet fully paid for and therefore not yet issued. Any difference between the subscription price and the par value or stated value is recorded in a paid-in capital account.

As the subscriber sends in payments, these amounts are debited to Cash in Bank and credited to Subscriptions Receivable. When the subscriber finishes paying for all the shares in full, the stock is issued. At that time, Common Stock Subscribed is debited and the capital stock account is credited for the par or stated value of the stock issued. When corporations have subscriptions for both common and preferred stock, separate accounts are kept for each class of stock, for example, Common

Stock Subscribed and Subscriptions Receivable—Preferred. Let's look at some transactions involving stock subscriptions.

R — E — M — E — M — B — E — R

The Common Stock Subscribed account is a temporary stockholders' equity account. It is used to record the par or stated value of the stock subscribed to but not yet issued.

Subscription Transactions for No-Par Stock

The Santos Manufacturing Corporation, a newly organized company, had the following stock subscription transactions.

May 1: *Received subscriptions to 10,000 shares of no-par common stock (stated value $10) at $14 per share, with a down payment of 50% of the subscription price, Memorandum 27 and Receipt 201.*

Use T accounts on the chalkboard to analyze the subscription transactions for no-par stock.

Two journal entries are required to record the May 1 transaction. The first entry records the total stock subscription. The second entry records the receipt of one-half of the subscription price from the subscribers. Figure 9-9 shows these entries.

GENERAL JOURNAL — PAGE 2

	DATE		DESCRIPTION	POST. REF.	DEBIT	CREDIT	
1	199– May	1	Sub. Rec.-Common		140 000 00		1
2			Common Stock Subscribed			100 000 00	2
3			Paid-in Cap. in Exc. of Stated Value			40 000 00	3
4			Memo. 27				4

CASH RECEIPTS JOURNAL — PAGE 2

	DATE		DOC. NO.	ACCOUNT TITLE	POST. REF.	GENERAL DEBIT	GENERAL CREDIT	SALES CREDIT	SALES TAX PAYABLE CREDIT	ACCOUNTS RECEIVABLE CREDIT	CASH IN BANK DEBIT	
1	199– May	1	R201	Sub. Rec.-Common			70 000 00				70 000 00	1

Figure 9-9 Journalizing a Subscription for No-Par Stock

On June 1, Santos received an additional $28,000 (20% of the subscription price) from subscribers. This cash receipt was recorded in the same way as the May 1 cash receipt. Finally, in July, Santos received the balance of the subscription price due from all of the subscribers. Only when the stock has been completely paid for will the corporation issue the stock.

July 1: *Received the final 30% of the subscription price from all subscribers; issued 10,000 shares of no-par stock, Receipt 275 and Memorandum 43.*

Use demonstration problem 9-6 here.

Again two journal entries are required to record this transaction. In the first entry, the receipt of the final payment of $42,000 due from subscribers is recorded. In the second entry, the issuance of the 10,000 shares of no-par stock by the corporation is recorded. These entries appear in Figure 9-10.

CASH RECEIPTS JOURNAL — PAGE 4

	DATE	DOC. NO.	ACCOUNT TITLE	POST. REF.	GENERAL DEBIT	GENERAL CREDIT	SALES CREDIT	SALES TAX PAYABLE CREDIT	ACCOUNTS RECEIVABLE CREDIT	CASH IN BANK DEBIT	
1	199– July 1	R275	Sub. Rec.–Common			42 000 00				42 000 00	1

GENERAL JOURNAL — PAGE 4

	DATE	DESCRIPTION	POST. REF.	DEBIT	CREDIT	
	199–					
4	July 1	Common Stock Subscribed		100 000 00		4
5		Common Stock			100 000 00	5
6		Memo. 43				6

Figure 9-10 Journalizing the Final Payment on a Stock Subscription and the Issuance of the Stock

The effects of this transaction, as well as the effects of the earlier stock subscription transactions, are shown in the following T accounts:

Cash in Bank

Dr.	Cr.
5/1 $70,000	
6/1 28,000	
7/1 42,000	

Subscriptions Receivable—Common

Dr.	Cr.
5/1 $140,000	5/1 $70,000
	6/1 28,000
	7/1 42,000

Common Stock

Dr.	Cr.
	7/1 $100,000

Common Stock Subscribed

Dr.	Cr.
7/1 $100,000	5/1 $100,000

Paid-in Capital in Excess of Stated Value

Dr.	Cr.
	5/1 $40,000

Common Stock Subscribed represents the total par value of the shares subscribed. It is used to record the shares that have been subscribed for, but not yet paid for in full. When the investors have completely paid for all of the shares, the firm records the issuing of the stock by debiting the Common Stock Subscribed account and crediting the Common Stock account.

Subscription Transactions for Par-Value Stock

The Beazley Corporation, a newly organized company, had the following subscription transactions involving its preferred stock.

June 15: *Received subscriptions for 2,500 shares of preferred 9% stock ($100 par value) at $104 per share, with a down payment of 40% of the subscription price, Memorandum 32 and Receipt 161.*

July 1: *Received 30% of the subscription price from all subscribers (2,500 shares), Receipt 183.*

July 15: *Received 30% of the subscription price from subscribers to 500 shares; issued 500 shares of preferred 9% stock, Receipt 200 and Memorandum 41.*

These entries appear in the cash receipts journal and general journal as shown in Figure 9-11.

GENERAL JOURNAL — PAGE 5

DATE		DESCRIPTION	POST. REF.	DEBIT	CREDIT
199– June	15	Sub. Rec.–Preferred		260 000 00	
		Preferred 9% Stock Subscribed			250 000 00
		Paid-in Cap. in Exc. of Par–Preferred			10 000 00
		Memo. 32			
July	15	Preferred 9% Stock Subscribed		50 000 00	
		Preferred 9% Stock			50 000 00
		Memo. 41			

CASH RECEIPTS JOURNAL — PAGE 2

DATE		DOC. NO.	ACCOUNT TITLE	POST. REF.	GENERAL DEBIT	GENERAL CREDIT	SALES CREDIT	SALES TAX PAYABLE CREDIT	ACCOUNTS RECEIVABLE CREDIT	CASH IN BANK DEBIT
199– June	15	R161	Sub. Rec.–Preferred			104 000 00				104 000 00
July	1	R183	Sub. Rec.–Preferred			78 000 00				78 000 00
	15	R200	Sub. Rec.–Preferred			15 600 00				15 600 00

Figure 9-11 Journalizing Transactions for Preferred Stock Subscriptions

The effect of all these transactions is illustrated in the T accounts that follow:

Cash in Bank

Dr.	Cr.
6/15 $104,000	
7/1 78,000	
7/15 15,600	

Subscriptions Receivable—Preferred

Dr.	Cr.
6/15 $260,000	6/15 $104,000
	7/1 78,000
	7/15 15,600

Preferred 9% Stock

Dr.	Cr.
	7/15 $50,000

Preferred 9% Stock Subscribed

Dr.	Cr.
7/15 $50,000	6/15 $250,000

Paid-in Capital in Excess of Par—Preferred

Dr.	Cr.
	6/15 $10,000

Emphasize that the stock is not issued until it is paid for in full.

As you can see, the Preferred 9% Stock Subscribed account represents the total par value of the shares subscribed. Earlier we mentioned that a corporation does not issue stock until the subscriber has paid for it in full. Because only 500 shares had been paid for in full, Beazley issued only 500 shares.

Use demonstration problem 9-7 here.

Since investors may finish paying for subscriptions at varying times, the company has to maintain an account for each subscriber. The Subscriptions Receivable accounts then become controlling accounts, as follows:

General Ledger Controlling Account	**Subsidiary Ledger**
Subscriptions Receivable—Preferred	Preferred 9% Stock Subscribers' Ledger
Subscriptions Receivable—Common	Common Stock Subscribers' Ledger

Have students complete Exercises 9-2 and 9-3 at this point.

Before reading further, do the following activity to check your understanding of how to record transactions involving stock subscriptions.

Check Your Learning

On a sheet of notebook paper, describe the five transactions recorded in the following T accounts of Celestial Foods, Inc. Match the numbers in parentheses to determine the complete transaction.

Cash in Bank

Dr.	Cr.
(1) $16,000	
(3) 9,500	
(4) 12,500	

Subscriptions Receivable—Common

Dr.	Cr.
(2) $22,000	**(3)** $ 9,500
	(4) 12,500

Common Stock

Dr.	Cr.
	(1) $12,000
	(5) 20,000

Common Stock Subscribed

Dr.	Cr.
(5) $20,000	**(2)** $20,000

Paid-in Capital in Excess of Stated Value

Dr.	Cr.
	(1) $4,000
	(2) 2,000

Compare your answers to those in the answers section. Reread the preceding part of the chapter to find the correct answers to any questions you may have missed.

Summary of Key Points

1. A corporation is defined as "an artificial being, invisible, intangible, and existing only in contemplation of the law."
2. As a form of business organization, the corporation has the following advantages: limited liability of stockholders, ease of raising capital, ease of transferring ownership rights, continuous existence, and professional management. The disadvantages of a corporation are additional taxation and increased government regulation.
3. In a corporation, the stockholders (the owners of the corporation) elect the board of directors. The board of directors, in turn, appoints the officers to manage the corporation.
4. Ownership equity in a corporation is called stockholders' equity. Stockholders' equity consists of capital stock (the amount invested in the corporation by stockholders, including additional paid-in capital) and retained earnings (the earnings held by the corporation and not distributed to stockholders as dividends).
5. There are two types of capital stock: common stock and preferred stock. Preferred stock has a preference over common stock in receiving dividends. Preferred stockholders, however, usually do not have voting privileges.
6. Par-value stock is stock that has a certain value printed on the stock certificate. No-par stock does not have a value printed on the stock certificate. No-par stock may or may not have a stated value, a value assigned by the corporation's board of directors.
7. When stock is issued at a price above its par or stated value, the difference between the total amount received and the par or stated value of the stock is credited to a paid-in capital account.
8. Corporations may issue stock to investors on an installment basis. The amount to be received from subscribers is debited to the Subscriptions Receivable account.
9. A corporation does not issue stock until the stock has been paid for in full.
10. Separate general ledger accounts are maintained for the different classes of capital stock and for their related paid-in capital and subscription accounts.

9 Review and Applications

Building Your Accounting Vocabulary

In your own words, write the definition of each of the following accounting terms. Use complete sentences for your definitions.

- articles of incorporation
- authorized capital stock
- board of directors
- charter
- common stock
- corporation
- double taxation
- issued shares
- legal capital
- no-par stock
- outstanding stock
- par-value stock
- pre-emptive right
- preferred stock
- stated value
- stock
- stock certificate
- stockholder
- stockholders' ledger
- stock subscription

Reviewing Your Accounting Knowledge

1. Why is a corporation called a "separate legal entity"?
2. List at least two advantages and two disadvantages of the corporate form of business organization. In your opinion, which is the greater advantage and which is the greater disadvantage?
3. Name three types of organization costs. How is Organization Costs classified? What eventually happens to the Organization Costs account?
4. What is the difference between capital stock and retained earnings?
5. What rights do common stockholders generally have?
6. What advantages do preferred stockholders have over common stockholders? What disadvantages do they have?
7. What does the balance of the capital stock account represent?
8. If a corporation issues its stock at a price above par, has it earned a profit on the sale of the stock?
9. What is the difference between par value and stated value?
10. Why might a corporation issue stock on a subscription basis?
11. What is the purpose of the Common Stock Subscribed account? What happens to that account?

Improving Your Human Relations Skills

Gail and Jeff are two of your co-workers. From the time they arrive until the time they leave, Gail and Jeff spend most of the day complaining—about the company, your supervisors, work space, the tasks they've been asked to do, poor communications, and so on. You've tried to overlook their complaints, but their negativism is starting to get to you. What should you do?

Applying Accounting Procedures

Exercise 9-1 Determining the Stock to Be Issued to Incorporators

Sally Martin, Raymond O'Connell, and Heather Williams have formed a corporation called The Magic Pan. The new corporation is authorized to issue 5,000 shares of no-par common stock with a stated value of $20. The three incorporators are to receive shares of stock in exchange for assets they are contributing to the corporation. Martin is contributing $19,000 of merchandise. O'Connell is contributing store equipment valued at $14,000 and $1,000 in supplies. Williams is contributing $9,000 of office equipment. Williams has also agreed to pay the organization costs of $2,200 in return for shares of stock.

Martin, 950
O'Connell, 750
Williams, 560

Instructions: Based on this information, determine the amount of stock that should be issued to each person.

Exercise 9-2 Classifying Corporate Accounts

The following accounts are among those in the Dylan Corporation's general ledger.

Common Stock
Common Stock Subscribed
Organization Costs
Paid-in Capital in Excess of Par—Preferred
Preferred 9% Stock
Retained Earnings
Subscriptions Receivable—Common

Instructions: Classify each account listed and indicate whether it has a normal debit or credit balance. Use a sheet of notebook paper or the form provided in the working papers.

Exercise 9-3 Determining Paid-in Capital

The balance sheet of Lindt Home Improvements, Inc., included the following amounts.

Preferred 10% Stock, $50 Par	$ 177,250
Paid-in Capital in Excess of Par—Preferred	10,635
Common Stock, $20 Stated Value	2,535,000
Paid-in Capital in Excess of Stated Value	443,620
Common Stock Subscribed	465,000

Instructions: Answer the following questions. Use notebook paper or the space provided in the working papers.

3,545 **1.** How many shares of preferred 10% stock have been issued?
126,750 **2.** How many shares of common stock have been issued?
23,250 **3.** How many shares of common stock have investors subscribed for?
$3,166,505 **4.** What is the total paid-in capital?

Problem 9-1 Issuing Capital Stock at Par

The Zapata Corporation was organized on March 10 of this year. It was authorized to issue 500 shares of $65-par cumulative preferred 8% stock and 10,000 shares of $25-par common stock. The following transactions were completed during the first year of operation.

Instructions: Record these transactions in the cash receipts journal (page 1) and the general journal (page 1).

Transactions:

Mar. 13 Received cash for 4,000 shares of common stock issued at $25 per share, Receipt 101 for $100,000.

13 Issued 100 shares of common stock to accountant J. Dumser for accounting services during the incorporation of the business, Memorandum 103.

July 8 Investors paid $65 a share for 200 shares of preferred stock; received $13,000 cash, Receipt 238.

Sept. 26 Received display equipment valued at $7,500 in exchange for 300 shares of common stock, Memorandum 294.

Problem 9-2 Issuing Stock at a Premium

The LaRosa Dental Corporation has authorized capital of 2,000 shares of $50-par preferred 9% stock and 15,000 shares of $20-par common stock. During the first year of operation, LaRosa's completed the following transactions affecting stockholders' equity.

Instructions: Record the transactions on page 2 of a cash receipts journal, page 1 of a cash payments journal, and page 2 of a general journal.

Transactions:

May 3 Issued 320 shares of common stock in exchange for store equipment valued at $6,400, Memorandum 104.

4 Received $21 a share for 4,500 shares of common stock, Receipt 1.

5 Wrote Check 101 for $1,500 and issued 175 shares of common stock to the attorney for $5,000 in legal and charter fees in forming the corporation, Memorandum 112.

June 19 Received $15,000 cash for 300 shares of preferred 9% stock issued at $50 per share, Receipt 132.

July 14 Investors paid $53 per share for 600 shares of preferred 9% stock, Receipt 173.

26 Received $15,400 for 700 shares of common stock, Receipt 189.

Problem 9-3 Recording Transactions for Stock Subscriptions

The Westport Equipment Leasing Company is authorized to issue 10,000 shares of $100-par preferred 8% stock and 50,000 shares of $25-par common stock.

Instructions: Record the following transactions concerning stock subscriptions in a cash receipts journal (page 13) and a general journal (page 18).

Compare stock subscriptions to buying a product on lay-away. Point out that the store will only give you the product when it is paid for in full.

Emphasize that the Subscriptions Receivable account is a current asset.

Transactions:

July 7 Received subscriptions to 15,000 shares of common stock at $25 per share, Memorandum 173; collected 50% of the subscription price, Receipt 466.

Aug. 6 Subscribers to 15,000 shares of common stock paid an additional 30% of the subscription price, Receipt 517.

Sept. 6 Investors subscribed to 700 shares of preferred 8% stock at $104 per share, Memorandum 223; received 40% of the subscription price, Receipt 602.

8 The final 20% of the subscription price was received from the subscribers to the common stock; issued the stock certificates, Receipt 610 and Memorandum 229.

Oct. 18 Received subscriptions to 9,000 shares of common stock at $27 per share; at this time, the subscribers paid 50% of the subscription price, Memorandum 284 and Receipt 688.

COMPUTER PROBLEM

Problem 9-4 Handling Capital Stock Transactions

The Cummings Bake Shop was incorporated on August 1. It is authorized to issue 25,000 shares of no-par common stock with a stated value of $15 and 3,000 shares of $50-par, nonparticipating, preferred 9% stock. The company has also chosen to record any amount received over the stated value in a separate paid-in capital account. Following are some of the accounts used by Cummings Bake Shop.

130	Subscriptions Receivable—Common
133	Subscriptions Receivable—Preferred
150	Store Equipment
170	Organization Costs
301	Preferred 9% Stock
303	Paid-in Capital in Excess of Par—Preferred
305	Common Stock
308	Paid-in Capital in Excess of Stated Value
350	Preferred 9% Stock Subscribed
353	Common Stock Subscribed

Instructions: Record the following transactions in the appropriate journals.

Transactions:

Aug. 2 Received subscriptions to 7,000 shares of no-par common stock at $18 per share, collecting 40% of the subscription price from all subscribers, Memorandum 112 and Receipt 102.

2 Acquired store equipment valued at $6,480 in exchange for 432 shares of no-par common stock, Memorandum 113.

16 The subscribers to 7,000 shares of no-par common stock paid an additional 30% of the subscription price, Receipt 104.

19 Issued 210 shares of no-par common stock in return for $3,150 in legal services for the incorporation, Memorandum 139.

21 Investors agreed to pay $52 a share for 800 shares of preferred 9% stock, Memorandum 143; collected 50% of the subscription price, Receipt 117.

22 Paid an accountant $850 for accounting services needed for incorporating the business, Check 1009.

29 The common stock subscribers paid the remaining 30% of the subscription price, Receipt 136. The 7,000 shares were issued to the subscribers, Memorandum 169.

Sept. 8 Received $20 per share subscriptions to 4,000 shares of no-par common stock, Memorandum 182; collected 50% of the subscription price, Receipt 149.

13 Received an additional 30% of the subscription price from the subscribers to 800 shares of preferred 9% stock, Receipt 162.

18 Issued 300 shares of preferred 9% stock at $53 per share, Receipt 176.

27 Prepared Receipt 191 when subscribers to 2,000 shares of no-par common stock paid the remaining 50% of the subscription price. The stock was issued to the subscribers, Memorandum 211.

29 Subscribers to 800 shares of preferred 9% stock paid the remaining 20% of the subscription price, Receipt 195. Issued the stock to the subscribers, Memorandum 219.

Problem 9-5 Determining Stockholders' Equity Information

Tom's Ski Shop, Inc., has authorized capital of 2,000 shares of $50-par preferred 8% stock and 100,000 shares of no-par common stock with a stated value of $5. The following account balances were taken from the Balance Sheet section of the work sheet for the fiscal year ended December 31.

Subscriptions Receivable—Preferred	$ 2,862
Subscriptions Receivable—Common	8,464
Preferred 8% Stock	49,250
Paid-in Capital in Excess of Par—Preferred	405
Common Stock	292,000
Paid-in Capital in Excess of Stated Value	22,080
Preferred 8% Stock Subscribed	6,750
Common Stock Subscribed	36,800

Instructions: Based on this information, answer the following questions.

985
135
$53.00
40%
58,400
7,360
85.6%
$407,285

1. How many shares of preferred 8% stock have been issued?
2. How many shares of preferred 8% stock are presently in subscription?
3. If the preferred stock that has already been issued was issued at par, what was the subscription price for a share of the preferred stock in question 2?
4. What percentage of the total subscription price for the preferred stock remains to be paid?
5. How many shares of common stock have been issued?
6. How many shares of common stock have been subscribed for but not yet issued?
7. If the original subscription price of the common stock was $8 per share, what percentage of the common stock subscription has been paid to date? Round your answer to the nearest tenth of a percent.
8. What is the total paid-in capital amount?

CHALLENGE PROBLEM

Problem 9-6 Identifying Errors in Stock Subscription Entries

The Butterworth Corporation is authorized to issue 10,000 shares of \$50-par preferred 9% stock and 50,000 shares of no-par common stock with a stated value of \$20. The following account balances appeared in the general ledger as of July 1.

Subscriptions Receivable—Common	3,000
Subscriptions Receivable—Preferred	1,000
Preferred 9% Stock	200,000
Paid-in Capital in Excess of Par—Preferred	3,500
Common Stock	600,000
Paid-in Capital in Excess of Stated Value	28,384
Retained Earnings	193,000
Preferred 9% Stock Subscribed	10,000
Common Stock Subscribed	30,000

On July 8, the Butterworth Corporation received subscriptions to 3,000 shares of preferred 9% stock at \$53.50 per share. A down payment of 25% of the subscription price was made at the same time. The journal entries that were recorded and posted appear in the working papers.

Instructions:

(1) Answer the following questions.
- (a) What error(s) was made in recording the July 8 transaction?
- (b) What effect will the error(s) have on the Preferred 9% Stock account? Explain.
- (c) What effect will the error(s) have on the Subscriptions Receivable—Preferred account? Explain.
- (d) What effect will the error(s) have on total stockholders' equity on the July 31 balance sheet? Explain.

(2) On the same general journal page, prepare a correcting entry for the error(s) that were made on July 8. Use July 11 as the date of the entry and Memorandum 207 as the source document.

Computers: Helping Make April 15 Less Taxing

Accountants use software programs to prepare income tax forms accurately.

As all taxpayers bemoan every April, tax laws are complicated and changing constantly. For CPAs specializing in tax preparation, keeping up with the changing law, IRS codes, and tax rulings is essential. By helping people track all these changes as well as compute their taxes, computers can help make the complex field of tax accounting simpler for both taxpayers and accountants.

In general, computers can make it easier to keep up with, and to figure out, different tax changes and procedures. For example, for the individual taxpayer trying to translate his or her 50-page tax forms, simple income-tax software programs give step-by-step instructions on what data to input. The program then organizes the data and instructs the user on where to put the information on the tax forms. Many programs link forms and schedules so that once a form such as Schedule A ("Itemized Deductions") is completed on the computer, the needed figures are automatically transferred to the appropriate line on a computerized Form 1040.

Accountants specializing in tax preparation use computers to help them perform a variety of tasks, such as setting up record-keeping systems, performing audits, preparing financial reports, and helping clients with tax-planning decisions. Computers can also assist accountants in managing information throughout the year; at the year's end, an accountant can print out summaries of operations with only a few keystrokes.

Accountants also need to track changes in the tax code—which has swelled to three times the number of words it contained in 1959—and in tax rulings. Imagine trying to keep on top of this information when the IRS alone issues a new ruling every two hours of every workday! With a computer and special online data banks, however, accountants have access to daily updates in tax law changes and court decisions.

Although no one looks forward to tax time, computers can help make the process of figuring taxes easier to deal with and even more interesting. And remember: The cost of the software is tax deductible!

Chapter 10

STOCKHOLDERS' EQUITY: EARNINGS AND DISTRIBUTIONS

In Chapter 9, you learned how corporations are organized and some of the legal requirements that must be met to start a corporation. You also learned that ownership in a corporation is represented by shares of stock. Then, you saw how to record transactions for the issuance of common and preferred stock.

In this chapter, you will continue your study of the stockholders' equity of a corporation. First, you will see how a corporation distributes its earnings to stockholders. You will also learn how a corporation acquires and reissues shares of its own stock and how it sets aside its retained earnings for future use.

Learning Objectives

When you have completed this chapter, you should be able to do the following:

1. Explain the difference between a cash dividend and a stock dividend.
2. Record journal entries for the declaration and payment of dividends.
3. Record journal entries involving treasury stock.
4. Journalize entries for the appropriation of retained earnings.
5. Define the accounting terms presented in this chapter.

New Terms

dividend
cash dividend
stock dividend
stock split
treasury stock
appropriating retained earnings

Dividends

Describe distribution of earnings as the income paid for using the money invested in stock. Show how it is similar to interest paid by a bank.

People invest in the stock of corporations for a number of reasons. Some people buy stock and hope to benefit from its increasing market value. Others buy stock expecting to share in the profits earned by the corporation. These shared profits come in the form of dividends. A **dividend** is a distribution of earnings—in the form of either cash or shares of stock—that a corporation makes to its stockholders. The dividend a stockholder receives depends on the number of shares of stock he or she owns and whether the stock is preferred or common.

Point out that the board of directors is under no legal obligation to declare dividends.

A dividend may be declared (authorized) only by the corporation's board of directors. The directors, however, are not required to declare a dividend. Once a dividend has been declared, the board of directors must arrange to pay it. Three dates are important in the declaration and payment of a dividend:

1. The *date of declaration* is the date on which the board of directors declares, or votes to pay, a dividend. Dividends are declared separately for each class of stock.
2. The *date of record* is the date as of which the ownership of shares is set. People who own stock on this date are eligible for dividends. The date of record is ordinarily about one to two weeks after the date of declaration.
3. The *date of payment* is the date on which the dividend is actually paid.

Journal entries must be made on the date of declaration and the date of payment. No entry is required on the date of record. Now let's look at two types of dividends: cash dividends and stock dividends.

Cash Dividends

Most dividends are cash dividends. **Cash dividends** are distributions in the form of cash paid by the corporation to stockholders as a reward for their investment. A cash dividend is expressed as a specific amount per share, such as $1.12 per share. A stockholder who owns 100 shares of stock would thus receive $112 ($1.12 × 100 shares). Most publicly held corporations pay dividends on a quarterly basis.

Emphasize that although a cash dividend is expressed as a specific amount per share, the amount of the dividend on preferred stock is usually stated as a percentage of the stock's par value.

The dividend for preferred stock is usually stated as a percentage of the stock's par value. Mayfaire, for example, is authorized to issue $50-par 8% preferred stock. The annual dividend on the preferred stock is, therefore, $4 ($50 par value × .08). If dividends are declared and paid quarterly, a stockholder will receive $1 each quarter for each share of preferred stock.

Before a corporation can pay a cash dividend, three things are required:

1. *Retained earnings.* Retained earnings, as you know, are the profits the corporation has kept and not distributed to stockholders. The company must have a sufficient balance in the Retained Earnings account against which to charge the cash dividend.
2. *An adequate amount of cash.* A corporation may have a large balance in its Retained Earnings account but may lack enough cash. The past

Stress that a corporation must have cash to pay a cash dividend.

earnings of the corporation may have been invested in equipment or merchandise or may be in the form of accounts receivable. The balance of the Cash in Bank account must be large enough to cover the total cash dividend paid out.

3. *Formal declaration by the board of directors.* The payment of dividends is not automatic. Some corporations declare dividends regularly, while others seldom, if ever, pay dividends.

The board of directors must pass the declaration in the form of a motion, which is recorded in a minute book. The *minute book* is a written, narrative record of all actions taken at official meetings. A corporation's minute book usually contains all details relating to the purchase of plant and equipment, bank loans, officers' salaries, and so on.

On January 20, the board of directors of Mayfaire, Inc., declared a quarterly cash dividend for its preferred stockholders. (Preferred stockholders, you'll remember, are entitled to receive dividends before common stockholders.)

January 20: *Declared a quarterly cash dividend of $1 per share (on 2,500 shares of preferred stock outstanding) to all the stockholders of record as of February 11, payable on March 2, Minute Book p. 380.*

Explain that the Dividends account is a temporary contra stockholders' equity account.

The amount of the dividend could be debited directly to the Retained Earnings account. Most corporations, however, prefer to use a separate account so that the dividend amounts can be easily determined. When a dividend is declared, the total amount of the dividend is debited to an account titled Dividends. Dividends is a temporary contra stockholders' equity account. It is used to summarize the dividends declared by the corporation during the fiscal period. At the end of the fiscal period, the balance of the Dividends account is closed into the Retained Earnings account. In this way, it is very similar to a sole proprietor's or partner's withdrawals account. If a corporation is authorized to issue two types of stock, a separate dividends account is set up for each type of account. Mayfaire, Inc., therefore has a Dividends—Preferred account and a Dividends—Common account.

Use T accounts to illustrate the entry for recording the declaration of a cash dividend and the payment of the cash dividend.

The total amount of the dividend declared on January 20 is \$2,500 (2,500 shares × \$1). In the transaction, Dividends is debited for \$2,500. Since the dividend will not be paid until March 2, Dividends Payable—Preferred, a current liability account, is credited for \$2,500, as illustrated below. The general journal entry for this transaction appears in Figure 10-1.

Dividends	
Dr. Increase Side Balance Side	Cr. Decrease Side

Dividends—Preferred	
Dr.	Cr.
$2,500	

Dividends Payable—Preferred	
Dr.	Cr.
	$2,500

GENERAL JOURNAL — PAGE 12

	DATE		DESCRIPTION	POST. REF.	DEBIT	CREDIT	
	199-						
11	Jan.	20	Dividends—Preferred		2500 00		11
12			Dividends Payable—Preferred			2500 00	12
13			Minute Book, p. 380				13

Figure 10-1 Recording the Declaration of a Cash Dividend

Remember: A journal entry is not necessary on February 11, the date of record. An entry *is* necessary on the date of payment.

March 2: *Issued a check for $2,500 in payment of the dividend declared on January 20, Check 3331.*

When the dividend is actually paid, Dividends Payable—Preferred is debited for $2,500 since the liability is being decreased. Cash in Bank is credited for the same amount:

Dividends Payable—Preferred	
Dr.	Cr.
$2,500	Bal. $2,500

Cash in Bank	
Dr.	Cr.
	$2,500

Figure 10-2 shows the cash payments journal entry for this transaction.

CASH PAYMENTS JOURNAL — PAGE 17

	DATE		DOC. NO.	ACCOUNT TITLE	POST. REF.	GENERAL DEBIT	GENERAL CREDIT	ACCOUNTS PAYABLE DEBIT	PURCHASES DISCOUNTS CREDIT	CASH IN BANK CREDIT	
	199-										
1	Mar.	2	C3331	Dividends Payable—Preferred		2500 00				2500 00	1

Figure 10-2 Journalizing the Payment of a Cash Dividend

Mayfaire opened a separate checking account from which it pays cash dividends. Check 3331 is deposited in this account. A separate check is prepared for each stockholder eligible to receive a cash dividend. A cash dividend for common stockholders would be handled in a similar manner.

Use demonstration problem 10-1 here.

The total amount available for a common stock dividend may depend on the amount paid to preferred stockholders. Suppose that on January 20, Mayfaire's board of directors had declared a total quarterly cash dividend of $7,668. Preferred stockholders, you will remember, are entitled to receive dividends before common stockholders. The amount available for common stockholders would be $5,168 ($7,668 – $2,500).

At the end of the fiscal period, the Dividends accounts are closed into Retained Earnings. A cash dividend thus decreases a corporation's assets (cash) and its total stockholders' equity (retained earnings).

Before reading further, do the following activity to check your understanding of cash dividends.

Check Your Learning

The Ajax Shoe Company was incorporated with authorized capital of 50,000 shares of $25-par common stock. To date, 6,000 shares have been issued. On January 12, the board of directors voted to declare a cash dividend of $.75 a share (Minute Book, p. 505) to stockholders of record as of January 31, payable on February 20 (Check 1834). Write your answers to the following questions on a sheet of notebook paper.

1. What is the total amount of the cash dividend?
2. If Paula Mott owns 500 shares of the Ajax Shoe Company stock, what is the amount of the cash dividend she will receive?
3. On which dates must journal entries be recorded?
4. In general journal form, record the journal entries required.

Compare your answers to those in the answers section. Reread the preceding part of the chapter to find the correct answers to any questions you may have missed.

Have students complete Exercise 10-1 at this point.

Stock Dividends

Explain why a corporation may give its stockholders a stock dividend rather than a cash dividend.

Occasionally a corporation wishes to give its stockholders some return on their investment but does not wish to distribute cash or other assets that are needed to finance future expansion. The corporation may choose to make a stock dividend. A **stock dividend** is a distribution of shares of its own stock that a corporation makes to its stockholders. In other words, the dividend distributed to stockholders consists of shares of stock rather than cash.

Point out that a stock dividend does not decrease the corporation's assets.

A stock dividend does not decrease the corporation's assets as a cash dividend does. It merely transfers a dollar amount from Retained Earnings to the paid-in capital accounts. The amount transferred is the fair market value (usually the current market price) of the additional shares of stock issued.

Let's look at an example. On October 11, Mayfaire, Inc., had the following balances in its stockholders' equity accounts:

Preferred Stock, $50 par, 2,500 shares outstanding	$125,000
Common Stock, $25 par, 25,840 shares outstanding	646,000
Paid-in Capital in Excess of Par—Common	8,000
Retained Earnings	193,889
Dividends—Preferred	(10,000)
Total Stockholders' Equity	$962,889

October 11: *The board of directors declared a 10% common stock dividend of 2,584 shares (25,840 × .10) to common stockholders of record as of November 1, payable on November 16. The present market value of the stock is $28 per share.*

A corporation acquires and issues shares of its own stock.

Explain the importance of knowing the market value of stock when recording the declaration of a stock dividend.

Introduce the two new accounts needed to record the declaration of a stock dividend.

The effect of a stock dividend, you will remember, is to transfer an amount equal to the market value of the stock from Retained Earnings to the paid-in capital accounts and to increase the number of outstanding shares. Since the market value of the stock is \$28, the total amount of the stock dividend is \$72,352 (2,584 shares × \$28). Retained Earnings is debited for this amount. The total par value of the stock being issued is \$64,600 (2,584 shares × \$25 par value). This amount is credited to an account called Common Stock Dividend Distributable. This account is a temporary stockholders' equity account, *not* a liability account. There is no obligation to distribute cash or other assets; the obligation is to distribute additional shares of stock. It appears on the balance sheet in the Paid-in Capital section, below the Common Stock account. Finally, when the market value of the stock is more than the par value, the difference is recorded in the Paid-in Capital in Excess of Par account. This account is, therefore, credited for \$7,752 (\$72,352 – \$64,600).

Retained Earnings	
Dr.	Cr.
\$72,352	Bal. \$193,889

Common Stock Dividend Distributable	
Dr.	Cr.
	\$64,600

Paid-in Capital in Excess of Par—Common	
Dr.	Cr.
	Bal. \$8,000
	7,752

Figure 10-3 shows the journal entry for the October 11 transaction.

GENERAL JOURNAL — PAGE 21

DATE		DESCRIPTION	POST. REF.	DEBIT	CREDIT
199-					
Oct.	11	Retained Earnings		72 352 00	
		Common Stock Div. Distributable			64 600 00
		Paid-in Cap. in Exc. of Par-Common			7 752 00
		Minute Book, p. 407			

Figure 10-3 Journalizing the Declaration of a Stock Dividend

R — E — M — E — M — B — E — R

The Common Stock account is used to record the par value of the stock issued in a stock dividend. Any excess must be credited to Paid-in Capital in Excess of Par—Common.

Point out that total stockholders' equity is unchanged by this transaction.

After this transaction is posted, the balances of the stockholders' equity accounts are as follows. Notice that total stockholders' equity is unchanged, although the balances of the individual accounts have changed.

Preferred Stock, $50 par, 2,500 shares	$125,000
Common Stock, $25 par, 25,840 shares outstanding	646,000
Common Stock Dividend Distributable, 2,584 shares	64,600
Paid-in Capital in Excess of Par—Common	15,752
Retained Earnings	121,537
Dividends—Preferred	(10,000)
Total Stockholders' Equity	$962,889

Use T accounts to illustrate the distribution of a stock dividend transaction.

As with cash dividends, no journal entry is required on November 1. On November 16, the stock dividend is distributed to the common stockholders. Common Stock Dividend Distributable is debited for $64,600 to show that the stock due the stockholders has now been issued. Common Stock is credited for $64,600, the par value of the additional shares being issued.

Common Stock Dividend Distributable

Dr.	Cr.
$64,600	Bal. $64,600

Common Stock

Dr.	Cr.
	Bal. $646,000
	64,600

The journal entry for the transaction appears in Figure 10-4.

GENERAL JOURNAL PAGE 22

	DATE		DESCRIPTION	POST. REF.	DEBIT	CREDIT	
1	199- Nov.	16	Common Stock Dividend Distributable		64 600 00		1
2			Common Stock			64 600 00	2
3			Minute Book, p. 407				3

Figure 10-4 Journalizing the Distribution of a Stock Dividend

R — E — M — E — M — B — E — R

The Common Stock Dividend Distributable account is used to record the par value of a stock dividend declared but not yet paid to stockholders.

The total stockholders' equity for the corporation is still unchanged. After this transaction is posted, the stockholders' equity accounts have the following balances shown on the next page.

Preferred Stock, $50 par, 2,500 shares	$125,000
Common Stock, $25 par, 28,424 shares outstanding	710,600
Paid-in Capital in Excess of Par—Common	15,752
Retained Earnings	121,537
Dividends—Preferred	(10,000)
Total Stockholders' Equity	$962,889

Use the first two transactions of demonstration problem 10-2 here to illustrate the declaration and distribution of a stock dividend.

Have students complete Exercise 10-2 at this point.

The stock dividend has no effect on the proportionate share of ownership of an individual stockholder. For example, Jan Hunt owned 2,000 shares of Mayfaire's stock. This represented a 8% share in the corporation (2,000 shares owned ÷ 25,840 shares outstanding). When the corporation declared a 10% stock dividend, she received 258 shares (10% of 2,584 shares). Her total stock now amounts to 2,258 shares; the corporation's total stock outstanding is now 28,424 shares. Jan still has a 8% share in the ownership (2,258 shares owned ÷ 28,424 shares outstanding).

Discuss the reasons for issuing a stock dividend.

Since a stockholder's proportionate share in a company does not change when the company issues a stock dividend, you may wonder why a corporation issues stock dividends. Here are a few reasons:

1. Stock dividends assure stockholders that they are receiving a return on their investments. The corporation, in turn, does not have to take cash or other assets out of the business.
2. The board of directors may wish to keep assets permanently in the business. By issuing a stock dividend, the corporation increases its permanent paid-in capital accounts (Common Stock and Paid-in Capital in Excess of Par) and decreases the balance of Retained Earnings, against which cash dividends are charged.
3. Stock dividends are not considered income. Stockholders, therefore, don't have to pay income taxes on them.

R — E — M — E — M — B — E — R

A stock dividend has no effect on a corporation's total assets or its total stockholders' equity.

Stock Split

A **stock split** is a deliberate split in the par or stated value of a corporation's stock and the issuance of a proportionate number of additional shares. For example, a corporation with 10,000 shares of $50-par common stock outstanding reduces the par value to $25 and increases the number of outstanding shares to 20,000. In this case, the corporation is doubling the number of outstanding shares (making what is called a *2-for-1 split*). If you owned 200 shares before the split, you would own 400 shares after it. This 2-for-1 stock split reduces the market price per share by about half. It also increases the stock's salability, because the stock now costs less.

ACCOUNTING Notes

Stocks can split in any combination e.g., 2-for-1, 5-for-2, 8-for-1. A reverse split also could occur. In a reverse split, a stockholder exchanges two old shares for one new share worth twice as much as the old shares.

The company may accomplish the stock split by calling in all the old shares and issuing new stock certificates on a 2-for-1 basis. It may also issue an additional share for each old share. The journal entry to record

Discuss why a corporation splits its stock.

this stock split appears in Figure 10-5. (The par values are listed only as an explanation.)

GENERAL JOURNAL — PAGE 62

	DATE		DESCRIPTION	POST. REF.	DEBIT	CREDIT	
1	199- Nov.	15	Common Stock ($50 par value)		500 000 00		1
2			Common Stock ($25 par value)			500 000 00	2
3			Minute Book, p. 1117				3

Figure 10-5 Recording a Stock Split

Complete demonstration problem 10-2 here to illustrate a stock split entry.

Point out that a stock split does not change the total dollar amount in stockholders' equity.

A stock split does not change the balances of the stockholders' equity accounts. The headings of the capital stock accounts in the ledger are changed to show the new par or stated value per share. The stockholders' ledger is also revised to show the new distribution of shares. (In practice, almost all accountants record stock splits with a memorandum entry.)

Treasury Stock

Discuss the meaning of treasury stock. Give students several reasons why a corporation would buy back its own stock.

Treasury stock is stock that has been issued by the corporation and then reacquired and held. A corporation often reacquires shares of its own stock through donations from stockholders or by buying them back in the open market. The corporation may hold treasury stock indefinitely or may reissue it to stockholders at a later time.

There are several reasons why a corporation buys back its own stock:

1. To have stock available to reissue to officers and employees under a bonus plan or employee stock-purchase plan.
2. To support the market price of the stock if it is unusually low.
3. To have shares available for exchanges of stock if the company acquires other companies.

When Mayfaire buys back its own stock, it records the transaction in the Treasury Stock account. The Treasury Stock account is not an investment account. Technically, a corporation cannot own a part of itself. It is a contra stockholders' equity account and has a normal debit balance. It appears on the balance sheet as a deduction from the total paid-in capital and retained earnings.

Treasury Stock

Dr.	Cr.
Increase Side	Decrease Side
Balance Side	

R — E — M — E — M — B — E — R

Treasury Stock **is a contra stockholders' equity account. It is used to record the cost of a company's own stock that is reacquired and held.**

Treasury stock does not affect the number of shares of issued stock. It does, however, reduce the number of shares of stock outstanding. Although treasury stock is not entitled to cash dividends, it does participate in stock dividends and stock splits. Treasury stock can be reissued at a price below its par or stated value with no contingent liability. That is, the holders of reissued treasury stock cannot be held liable for the difference between the par value of the stock and the discounted price at which it was reissued. In other respects, it is similar to unissued stock. Treasury stock has no voting rights, no pre-emptive right to share in new stock issues, and no right to share in the assets if the corporation should be liquidated.

Purchasing Treasury Stock

Let's look at some transactions involving treasury stock. Mayfaire, Inc., had the following transaction.

November 16: *Bought 2,000 shares of own stock at $29 per share, Check 7386.*

Emphasize that the price paid for the reacquired stock is the amount debited to Treasury Stock.

In accounting for the purchase of treasury stock, the par or stated value of the stock is ignored. The total price paid for the reacquired stock, $58,000 (2,000 shares × $29) is debited to the Treasury Stock account. Cash in Bank is credited for $58,000.

Treasury Stock	
Dr.	Cr.
$58,000	

Cash in Bank	
Dr.	Cr.
	$58,000

Figure 10-6 illustrates this transaction.

CASH PAYMENTS JOURNAL — PAGE 22

	DATE 199–		DOC. NO.	ACCOUNT TITLE	POST. REF.	GENERAL DEBIT	GENERAL CREDIT	ACCOUNTS PAYABLE DEBIT	PURCHASES DISCOUNTS CREDIT	CASH IN BANK CREDIT	
20	Nov.	16	C7386	Treasury Stock		58 000 00				58 000 00	20

Figure 10-6 Recording the Purchase of Treasury Stock

Selling Treasury Stock

The shares of treasury stock may be sold at cost, below cost, or above cost. Mayfaire had the following transaction.

November 30: *Sold 100 shares of treasury stock at $30 per share, Receipt 2017.*

Introduce the new account Paid-in Capital from the Sale of Treasury Stock.

When the company resells its treasury stock at a price above its cost, the difference between the cost and the selling price is credited to a stockholders' equity account titled Paid-in Capital from Sale of Treasury Stock. This account appears in the Paid-in Capital section of the balance sheet, below the other capital stock accounts.

In this transaction Cash in Bank is debited for $3,000, the total amount of cash received on the sale of the treasury stock. Treasury Stock is credited for $2,900, the *cost* of the stock being reissued (100 shares × $29). Paid-in Capital from Sale of Treasury Stock is credited for $100, the amount of the difference between the cost and the selling price.

Cash in Bank		Treasury Stock		Paid-in Capital from Sale of Treasury Stock	
Dr.	Cr.	Dr.	Cr.	Dr.	Cr.
$3,000		Bal. $58,000	$2,900		$100

The cash receipts journal entry appears in Figure 10-7.

CASH RECEIPTS JOURNAL — PAGE 26

	DATE 199–		DOC. NO.	ACCOUNT TITLE	POST. REF.	GENERAL DEBIT	GENERAL CREDIT	SALES CREDIT	SALES TAX PAYABLE CREDIT	ACCOUNTS RECEIVABLE CREDIT	CASH IN BANK DEBIT	
13	Nov.	30	R2017	Treasury Stock			2900 00				3000 00	13
14				Pd-in Cap. fr. Sale of Treas. Stk.			100 00					14

Figure 10-7 Recording the Sale of Treasury Stock at More Than Its Cost

December 15: *Sold 100 shares of treasury stock at $28 per share, Receipt 2067.*

In this transaction, the stock was sold for less than its cost. As a result, Paid-in Capital from Sale of Treasury Stock is debited rather than credited.

Cash in Bank		Treasury Stock		Paid-in Capital from Sale of Treasury Stock	
Dr.	Cr.	Dr.	Cr.	Dr.	Cr.
$2,800		Bal. $55,100	$2,900	$100	Bal. $100

The entry for this transaction appears in Figure 10-8.

CASH RECEIPTS JOURNAL — PAGE 27

	DATE 199–		DOC. NO.	ACCOUNT TITLE	POST. REF.	GENERAL DEBIT	GENERAL CREDIT	SALES CREDIT	SALES TAX PAYABLE CREDIT	ACCOUNTS RECEIVABLE CREDIT	CASH IN BANK DEBIT	
16	Dec.	15	R2067	Pd-in Cap. fr. Sale of Treas. Stk.		100 00					2800 00	16
17				Treasury Stock			2900 00					17

Figure 10-8 Recording the Sale of Treasury Stock at Less Than Its Cost

R — E — M — E — M — B — E — R

Paid-in Capital from Sale of Treasury Stock **is debited when treasury stock is sold for less than its cost and credited when treasury stock is sold for more than its cost.**

Point out that occasionally a corporation will issue shares of its stock to its employees.

Occasionally, a corporation issues shares of its treasury stock to its employees.

December 27: *Reissued 200 shares of treasury stock as a bonus to employees, Memorandum 668.*

Introduce the new other expense account, Bonus to Employees.

In this transaction, the other expense account Bonus to Employees is debited for $5,800, the total cost of the stock being issued. Treasury Stock is credited for the same amount.

Bonus to Employees	
Dr.	Cr.
$5,800	

Treasury Stock	
Dr.	Cr.
Bal. $52,200	$5,800

Use demonstration problem 10-3 here.

Figure 10-9 shows the general journal entry for this transaction.

GENERAL JOURNAL PAGE 24

	DATE		DESCRIPTION	POST. REF.	DEBIT	CREDIT	
1	199– Dec.	27	Bonus to Employees		5 800 00		1
2			Treasury Stock			5 800 00	2
3			Memo. 668				3

Figure 10-9 Issuing Treasury Stock as a Bonus to Employees

Before reading further, do the following activity to check your understanding of transactions involving treasury stock.

Check Your Learning

Write your answers to the questions that follow on a sheet of notebook paper. The Crabtree Corporation has 122,500 shares of its $10-par common stock outstanding. Over several months, the following transactions took place.

Jan. 16 Bought 15,000 shares of own stock at $14.00 per share, Check 5411.

Mar. 19 Sold 2,500 shares of treasury stock at $12.50 per share, Receipt 1631.

June 8 Sold 3,000 shares of treasury stock for $16.00 per share, Receipt 2710.

15 Reissued 4,000 shares of treasury stock as a bonus to employees, Memorandum 29.

After these transactions are posted,

1. How many shares of stock are outstanding?
2. How many shares of treasury stock is the Crabtree Corporation holding?
3. Does the Paid-in Capital from Sale of Treasury Stock have a debit or a credit balance?

Compare your answers to those in the answers section. Reread the preceding part of the chapter to find the correct answers to any questions you may have missed.

Have students complete Exercise 10-3 at this point.

Appropriating Retained Earnings

Earlier in the chapter, we stated that a corporation must have an adequate balance in its Retained Earnings account before declaring a cash dividend. This is because the Dividends account is closed into Retained Earnings at the end of the period. The balance of the Retained Earnings account, however, need not be used only for cash or stock dividends. The board of directors may wish to earmark part of retained earnings for some specific purpose. Suppose the directors decide they want to provide for future expansion. The board may do so by **appropriating retained earnings**. When retained earnings are appropriated, the board passes a resolution (which is recorded in the minute book) restricting a certain amount of retained earnings for a specific purpose. Some reasons for appropriating retained earnings include the following:

Discuss the various reasons for appropriating retained earnings.

- For plant expansion.
- For bond indebtedness—to provide for bond interest payments or principal repayment.
- For self-insurance—to provide for potential casualty losses.
- For inventory losses—to provide for possible decreases in the value of merchandise.
- For contingencies—to provide for unexpected events.

A separate account is set up for each appropriation and labeled "Retained Earnings Appropriated for (purpose)." The balance of the Retained Earnings account, then, represents unappropriated retained earnings.

For example, the Littel Communications Company plans to build or buy a separate building for its offices. To finance the project, the board of directors decided to restrict $25,000 of retained earnings each year for ten years, for a total appropriation of $250,000. At the end of each of those ten years, the accountant makes the closing entry shown in Figure 10-10. (This entry is usually made after the other closing entries.)

GENERAL JOURNAL PAGE 41

	DATE		DESCRIPTION	POST. REF.	DEBIT	CREDIT	
1			Closing Entries (Cont.d)				1
2	199- Dec.	31	Retained Earnings		25 000 00		2
3			Retained Earn. Appro. for Building			25 000 00	3

Figure 10-10 Recording the Appropriation of Retained Earnings

Use T accounts to show the moving of retained earnings to an appropriation account.

This appropriation decreases by $25,000 each year the amount of retained earnings available to pay dividends. If Littel cannot declare and pay out dividends, the company is preserving its net assets—mostly cash. This appropriation, however, does *not* represent a separate cash fund.

At the end of the 10-year period, although there is not an actual $250,000 cash fund, there *is* an additional $250,000 accumulated in net assets (assets minus liabilities). Littel can now make plans to convert the

Use demonstration problem 10-4 here.

$250,000 increase in net assets into cash to put a down payment on the building.

When the objective—buying or constructing the building—has been accomplished, the corporation no longer has to restrict Retained Earnings. The accountant can then make the entry shown in Figure 10-11, which reverses the ten previous entries.

GENERAL JOURNAL PAGE 162

	DATE		DESCRIPTION	POST. REF.	DEBIT	CREDIT	
1	199– Jan.	18	Retained Earn. Appro. for Building		250 000 00		1
2			Retained Earnings			250 000 00	2
3			Memo. 4166				3

Have students complete Exercise 10-4 at this point.

Figure 10-11 Reversing the Appropriation of Retained Earnings

Summary of Key Points

1. A dividend is a distribution a corporation makes to its stockholders as a return on their investment. Dividends may be in the form of cash or shares of stock.
2. The total amount of a cash dividend is debited to the Dividends account. Dividends is a temporary contra stockholders' equity account, which is eventually closed into Retained Earnings. A separate Dividends account is set up for each type of stock.
3. Dividends—either cash dividends or stock dividends—decrease the Retained Earnings account. Cash dividends decrease both a corporation's assets and its retained earnings. Stock dividends affect neither the corporation's total assets nor its total stockholders' equity.
4. A stock split, which is a reduction in the par or stated value of a stock accompanied by the issuance of a proportional amount of new stock, reduces the market price per share and increases the stock's salability.
5. Treasury stock is a corporation's own stock that has been issued and is later reacquired by the corporation. Treasury Stock is a contra stockholders' equity account. Stock reacquired by the corporation is recorded in the account at cost.
6. A corporation may wish to divide the Retained Earnings account into two parts: appropriated and unappropriated retained earnings.

10 Review and Applications

Building Your Accounting Vocabulary

In your own words, write the definition of each of the following accounting terms. Use complete sentences for your definitions.

appropriating retained earnings
cash dividend
dividend
stock dividend
stock split
treasury stock

Reviewing Your Accounting Knowledge

1. Name and explain the three dates that are important in the dividend process.
2. On which dates must journal entries be made for dividends?
3. What is a minute book? Why is it important?
4. What are the three requirements that must be met before a corporation can pay a cash dividend?
5. What type of account is Dividends? How does it affect the Retained Earnings account?
6. What is the difference between a cash dividend and a stock dividend?
7. What effect does a cash dividend have on the total stockholders' equity of a corporation? What effect does a stock dividend have?
8. Why might a corporation choose to make a stock dividend?
9. What is the difference between a stock dividend and a stock split?
10. Give two reasons why a corporation buys back its own stock.
11. Classify the following accounts: Dividends Payable, Common Stock Dividend Distributable, Treasury Stock, Paid-in Capital from Sale of Treasury Stock, Bonus to Employees.
12. How are retained earnings appropriated?

Improving Your Communications Skills

Your writing will be more effective if you use the active voice of a verb whenever possible. In the active voice, the subject of the sentence performs the action. In the passive voice, the subject is acted upon. In a sentence, passive voice is indicated by a form of the verb "to be" (such as *was*) and the word *by*. On a sheet of notebook paper, change each of the following sentences from passive to active voice.

1. The task was completed by John by the end of the day.
2. Everything that was done by us that day was a waste of time.
3. The case was accepted by the attorney.
4. A discount has been offered by the store.
5. The computer was serviced by the new technician.
6. The letter was dictated and signed by the sales manager.
7. The interview was canceled by the applicant.

8. The office copier was repaired by the copy center.
9. The report was reviewed in draft form by about a dozen people.
10. The stack of papers was thrown into the wastebasket by Helen.

COMPUTER PROBLEM

Applying Accounting Procedures

Exercise 10-1 Calculating Cash Dividends

The Phillips Company is authorized to issue 15,000 shares of preferred 7% stock ($60 par) and 100,000 shares of $10-par common stock. The board of directors recently declared the regular quarterly dividend for preferred stockholders and a cash dividend of $.25 per share for common stockholders. At the time the dividend was declared, the company had 2,000 shares of preferred stock and 49,000 shares of common stock outstanding.

Instructions: Calculate

$1.05; $0.25 1. The quarterly dividend per share for preferred stock and for common stock
$2,100; $12,250 2. The total dividend for each class of stock
$14,350 3. The amount of the total cash dividend

Exercise 10-2 Calculating a Stock Dividend

On June 30, the stockholders' equity of the Northam Chemical Company, Inc., is as follows.

Paid-in Capital:	
Common Stock, $60-par, 250,000 shares authorized, 75,000 shares issued	$4,500,000
Paid-in Capital in Excess of Par	70,000
Retained Earnings	500,000

On July 26, when the stock was selling for $84 per share, the board of directors voted a 5% stock dividend, distributed on August 15 to stockholders of record on July 31.

Instructions: Answer the following questions. Use the space provided in the working papers.

3,750 1. How many shares of stock is this stock dividend?
$315,000 2. What is the amount debited to the Retained Earnings account?
$4,725 3. If a stockholder owns 4,500 shares before the stock dividend, how many does he or she own after the stock dividend is distributed?

Exercise 10-3 Analyzing Treasury Stock Transactions

The Zohn Company is authorized to issue 500,000 shares of $5-par common stock.

Instructions:

(1) Record the following transactions in the T accounts provided in the working papers. Identify the transactions by number.

(a) 500
(b) credit, $2,375

(2) Use the space provided to answer the following questions. After the transactions have been recorded,
   (a) How many shares of treasury stock remain?
   (b) Does the Paid-in Capital from Sale of Treasury Stock have a debit or a credit balance? What is the amount?

Transactions:

1. Purchased 24,000 shares of own common stock for $7.00 per share.
2. Sold 4,250 shares of the treasury stock for $6.00 per share.
3. Sold 1,000 shares of the treasury stock for $6.50 per share.
4. Received $7.75 per share for 9,500 shares of the treasury stock.
5. Reissued 8,750 shares of the treasury stock as a bonus to employees.

Exercise 10-4 Analyzing Stockholders' Equity Transactions

Instructions: Indicate the effect of each of the following transactions on the Common Stock, Dividends, Treasury Stock, and Retained Earnings accounts. Indicate increases with a plus sign (+), decreases with a minus sign (–), and no effect with a zero (0). Use the form provided in the working papers.

Transactions:

1. A cash dividend is declared.
2. A stock dividend is distributed.
3. A 2-for-1 stock split is distributed.
4. A company buys 5,000 of its own shares.
5. Retained earnings is appropriated $50,000 per year for 10 years to provide for plant expansion.
6. Closed the Dividends account at the end of the period.

Problem 10-1 Recording Cash Dividend Transactions

The following information appeared on the December 31 balance sheet of the Oliver Corporation.

Preferred 8% Stock, $100 par, 500 shares authorized, 300 shares issued	$ 30,000
Common Stock, $75-par, 10,000 shares authorized, 6,000 shares issued	450,000
Paid-in Capital in Excess of Par—Common	48,000
Retained Earnings	100,000

Instructions: Record the following transactions in a general journal and a cash payments journal.

Transactions:

Apr. 4 The board of directors of the Oliver Corporation declared a semiannual cash dividend to preferred stockholders and a $1.50 cash dividend to common stockholders, Minute Book, page 999.

May 14 Paid the cash dividend declared on April 4, Check 1688.

Problem 10-2 Handling Stock Dividends

On March 9, stockholders' equity of the Caldwell Home Improvement Corporation was as follows.

Common Stock, $10 par, 100,000 shares authorized, 60,000 shares issued	$600,000
Paid-in Capital in Excess of Par	48,000
Retained Earnings	90,000

On that date, when the stock was selling at $14 per share, the corporation's directors voted a 5% stock dividend distributable on April 1 to the March 15 stockholders of record.

Instructions: On general journal page 44, record the entries for the declaration and distribution of the dividend. The declaration of the dividend was entered on page 163 of the corporation's minute book.

Problem 10-3 Recording Treasury Stock Transactions

The capital stock of Ridgeway Engineering, Inc., on January 1 is as follows.

Common Stock, $10 par, 1,000,000 shares authorized, 400,000 shares issued	$4,000,000
Paid-in Capital in Excess of Par	5,000,000

Instructions:

(1) Record the following transactions in a cash receipts journal (page 21) and a cash payments journal (page 34).

(2) Post the entries to the Treasury Stock and Paid-in Capital from Sale of Treasury Stock accounts provided in the working papers.

Transactions:

Feb. 10 Purchased 3,000 shares of own common stock for $12.50 per share, Check 1166 for $37,500.

Mar. 1 Issued Check 1201 for the purchase of 10,000 shares of own common stock at $12.00 per share.

June 19 Sold the 3,000 shares purchased on February 10 for $12.00 per share, Receipt 967.

Oct. 2 Recorded the sale of 4,000 of the shares purchased on March 1 for $15.00 per share, Receipt 1332.

Problem 10-4 Journalizing Dividend and Treasury Stock Transactions

The following information appeared on the December 31 balance sheet of the Haller Transportation Corporation.

Common Stock, $50 par, 20,000 shares authorized, 16,000 shares issued	$800,000
Paid-in Capital in Excess of Par	64,000
Retained Earnings	105,000

Instructions: Record the following transactions on page 57 of the cash receipts journal, page 72 of the cash payments journal, and page 88 of the general journal.

Transactions:

Jan.	1	The board of directors declared a semiannual cash dividend of $1 per share on 16,000 shares outstanding, payable on February 7 to stockholders of record on January 16, Minute Book page 844.
Feb.	7	Paid the cash dividend, Check 7124.
May	15	Purchased 1,500 shares of own common stock at $58 per share, Check 7349.
July	1	The board of directors declared a semiannual cash dividend of $1 per share on 14,500 shares outstanding to stockholders of record on July 20, payable on August 3, Minute Book page 946.
Aug.	3	Paid the cash dividend, Check 9444.
Oct.	15	Sold 500 shares of treasury stock at $65, Receipt 8284.
Nov.	29	Received $60 per share for 700 shares of treasury stock, Receipt 9001.

Problem 10-5 Recording Transactions for Stock Splits, Dividends, and Treasury Stock

The following balances appeared in the general ledger accounts of Sweet, Inc., on January 1.

Common Stock, $30 par, 75,000 shares authorized, 20,000 shares issued	$600,000
Paid-in Capital in Excess of Par	25,000
Retained Earnings	500,000

The following transactions took place during the first few months of the fiscal period.

Instructions: Record these transactions in the appropriate journals.

Transactions:

Jan.	15	Declared a cash dividend of $0.75 per share on 20,000 shares outstanding to stockholders of record as of January 30, payable on February 10, Minute Book page 442.
Feb.	10	Paid the cash dividend, Check 941.
Mar.	20	The board of directors declared and distributed a 2-for-1 stock split, Minute Book page 501.
Apr.	30	Purchased 3,000 shares of own common stock at $14 per share, Check 1141.
July	15	Declared a cash dividend of $0.40 per share to stockholders of record as of July 30, payable on August 10, Minute Book page 516.
Aug.	10	Issued Check 1341 in payment of the cash dividend.
	15	Reissued 1,500 shares of own common stock as a bonus for employees, Memorandum 641.

COMPUTER PROBLEM

Problem 10-6 Recording Stockholders' Equity Transactions

Spinner Textiles, Inc., has the following stockholders' equity accounts on January 1.

Preferred 8% Stock, $50 par, 25,000 shares authorized, 12,000 shares issued	$600,000
Paid-in Capital in Excess of Par—Preferred	50,000
Common Stock, $10 par, 100,000 shares authorized, 30,000 shares issued, 25,000 outstanding	300,000
Paid-in Capital in Excess of Par—Common	245,000
Retained Earnings	555,000
Treasury Stock (5,000 shares at cost)	62,500

Instructions: Record the following transactions in the appropriate journals.

Transactions:

Jan.	5	The board of directors declared the regular quarterly cash dividend for preferred stockholders and a cash dividend of $0.20 per share for common stockholders of record on January 15, payable on February 5, Minute Book page 342.
Feb.	5	Wrote Check 785 for the cash dividend declared January 5.
	21	Sold 3,000 shares of the treasury stock for $15.00 per share, Receipt 602.
Apr.	5	Voted the regular quarterly cash dividend for preferred stockholders of record on April 15, payable on May 5, Minute Book page 412.
May	5	Wrote Check 1098 for the cash dividend declared April 5.
June	8	Recorded Receipt 819 for $6,250.00 for the sale of 500 shares of the treasury stock.
July	5	Declared the regular quarterly cash dividend for preferred stockholders of record on July 15, payable on August 5, Minute Book page 428.
Aug.	5	Wrote Check 1472 for the cash dividend declared July 5.
Sept.	7	Sold the remaining shares of treasury stock for $12.00 per share, Receipt 1064.
Oct.	5	Voted the fourth quarter cash dividend for preferred stockholders of record on October 15, payable on November 6, Minute Book page 476.
	5	Declared a 20% stock dividend to common stockholders of record on October 15, distributable on November 1, Minute Book page 476. The market price of the stock on October 5 is $11.75 per share.
Nov.	1	Distributed the stock dividend declared on October 5, Minute Book page 476.
	6	Paid the cash dividend for preferred stockholders, Check 1829.
Dec.	31	The board of directors voted to appropriate $50,000 of retained earnings each year for five years to provide for the purchase of new equipment. Recorded the closing entry for the appropriation.

CHALLENGE PROBLEM

Problem 10-7 Calculating Corporate Dividends

The Burke Corporation has outstanding 1,000 shares of $100-par preferred 12% stock and 10,000 shares of $50-par common stock. Over the past three years, the board of directors has voted cash dividends totaling $5,000 in Year 1, $12,000 in Year 2, and $81,000 in Year 3.

Instructions: Compute the dividend per share and the total dividend paid to preferred stockholders and to common stockholders each year under each of the following situations.

Total dividend:
$12,000; $69,000
$19,000; $62,000
$16,500; $64,500

1. The preferred stock is noncumulative and nonparticipating.
2. The preferred stock is cumulative and nonparticipating.
3. The preferred stock is participating and noncumulative. The terms for the participating preferred stock are as follows. In any one year, the regular 12% dividend is paid to preferred stockholders. Then common stockholders are paid a 12% dividend. Finally, any remaining dividend amount is divided equally between the preferred stock and the common stock. The stockholders in each class share that remaining amount equally.

FOCUS ON CAREERS

Financial Planners: Helping Clients Reach Their Goals

One of the fastest-growing professions today is that of the financial planner. A financial planner helps individuals and businesses use their resources to achieve their financial objectives.

Although an accounting degree is not mandatory for becoming a financial planner, accountants make up one of the fastest-growing segments of this field. Both accountants and financial planners have many characteristics in common. They must be methodical, analytical, and good with numbers. In addition, public accountants have an easy time building up a clientele. They have already earned the trust of many clients, so it is not difficult to advise those people in other areas.

Financial planners must be well versed in economics, computer technology, real estate analysis, and actuarial science. They must also work well with people, have excellent written and oral communication skills, and demonstrate an ability to solve problems.

Helping people plan for retirement and plan their estates is a large part of financial planning. In doing so, interpersonal skills are just as important as technical knowledge. Since every client is different, the financial planner must discover how the client works with money, how he or she feels about money, and what goals he or she wants to accomplish. Only when these factors are understood can the financial planner successfully develop, implement, and monitor a financial plan.

The future for financial planners is bright. Those who want to maximize their chances of success become a Certified Financial Planner (CFP) or a Chartered Financial Consultant (ChFC) or both. To become accredited, a person must complete six to ten college-level courses, usually available through correspondence study. Employment situations vary: Financial planners may be self-employed or employed by a bank, an accounting firm, or a brokerage firm.

With the many demands our fast-paced society has placed on people's money, financial planners can help clients find ways to save and use their money to its best advantage.

Financial planners give advice to their clients on how to use financial resources to receive the best advantage.

Chapter 11

WORK SHEET AND FINANCIAL STATEMENTS

In this unit, you have learned a number of procedures for the accounts that appear on a corporation's balance sheet. You learned how to analyze and record transactions affecting uncollectible accounts; notes; inventories; property, plant, and equipment; short- and long-term liabilities; stocks; dividends; and retained earnings. Each of these procedures was presented as a separate accounting activity. Each accounting procedure, however, plays a vital part in the total operation of the business.

In this chapter, you will pull together all the accounting data for these procedures onto the work sheet. Then, you'll use that work sheet as a tool to prepare a corporation's financial statements.

Learning Objectives

When you have completed this chapter, you should be able to do the following:

1. Determine which general ledger accounts must be adjusted.
2. Prepare an eight-column work sheet for a merchandising corporation.
3. Prepare an income statement for a merchandising corporation.
4. Prepare a statement of stockholders' equity for a merchandising corporation.
5. Prepare a balance sheet for a merchandising corporation.
6. Explain the purpose of notes to the financial statements.
7. Define the accounting terms presented in this chapter.

New Terms

accrual
deferral
statement of stockholders' equity
notes to financial statements

The Eight-Column Work Sheet

ACCOUNTING Notes
The work sheet is not published in the corporation's annual report because it has little meaning for managers, stockholders, and creditors. The work sheet is the accountant's tool for assembling financial data necessary for preparing financial statements.

The general ledger accounts summarize the changes caused by business transactions during an accounting period. They do not, however, summarize the overall performance of a company. To evaluate a business's performance, managers, stockholders, and creditors need more than a list of account balances. They need to know the net income, the value of stockholders' equity, and the company's financial strength. This information is reported on the financial statements. The purpose of the work sheet is to assemble all the financial data needed to prepare the end-of-period financial statements and journal entries.

Previously, you learned how to assemble the accounting data on a ten-column work sheet. To save time preparing the work sheet, however, some businesses omit the Adjusted Trial Balance section. Mayfaire, Inc., uses an eight-column work sheet.

Emphasize why an eight-column work sheet is now being used.

The Trial Balance Section

Stress that preparation of the work sheet cannot proceed until the debit and credit totals of the trial balance are equal.

At the end of the fiscal period, a trial balance is prepared using the first two columns of the work sheet. The trial balance, as you know, is prepared to prove the equality of debits and credits in the general ledger. The account number, account title, and balance of each general ledger account are entered on the work sheet. The Debit and Credit columns are then totaled, proved, and ruled.

Point out that account balances are totaled on the last line of each page and carried forward to the first line of the next page.

The completed work sheet for Mayfaire, Inc., appears in Figure 11-1 on pages 282–284. As you can see, every general ledger account is listed in the Trial Balance section, even those with zero balances. Notice also that the account balances are totaled on the *last* line of each page of the work sheet. The words *Carried Forward* are written in the Account Name column. The totals are then entered on the first line of the next page. These totals are identified by the words *Brought Forward* written in the Account Name column.

The Adjustments Section

Most businesses have certain accounts that do not show up-to-date balances at the end of the accounting period. Adjustments must be made to those accounts to bring them up to date. In Chapter 2, you planned and recorded the adjustments for merchandise inventory, supplies used during the period, and the part of the prepaid insurance premium that had expired. Although they are included on the work sheet, we will not discuss these adjustments in this chapter. If necessary, review pages 37–41 in Chapter 2 for the discussion of these adjustments.

Mention that the term *accrue* means to accumulate.

Mayfaire, Inc., has other accounts that must be adjusted at the end of the accounting period. Most of these adjustments involve accruals and deferrals. The accrual basis of accounting recognizes revenue when it is earned and expenses when they are incurred. An **accrual**, then, is the recognition of revenue or expenses that have gradually increased over time but that have not yet been recorded. Examples of accruals include the interest on a note receivable that matures during the next fiscal period and the salary expense incurred during the current fiscal period but

Mayfaire, Inc.
Work Sheet
For the Year Ended December 31, 199-

ACCT. NO.	ACCOUNT NAME	TRIAL BALANCE DEBIT	TRIAL BALANCE CREDIT	ADJUSTMENTS DEBIT	ADJUSTMENTS CREDIT	INCOME STATEMENT DEBIT	INCOME STATEMENT CREDIT	BALANCE SHEET DEBIT	BALANCE SHEET CREDIT
101	Cash in Bank	397,117.24						397,117.24	
102	Change Fund	250.00						250.00	
103	Petty Cash Fund	75.00						75.00	
105	Marketable Securities	205,000.00						205,000.00	
110	Notes Receivable	500.00						500.00	
111	Notes Receivable Discounted	—						—	
112	Notes Receivable Past Due	1,624.99						1,624.99	
113	Interest Receivable	—		(a) 3.70				3.70	
115	Accounts Receivable	28,667.00						28,667.00	
117	Allowance for Uncollectible Accounts		60.00		(b) 1,016.65				1,076.65
120	Merchandise Inventory	92,470.25		(c) 18,056.05				110,526.30	
125	Supplies	5,210.00			(d) 3,600.00			1,610.00	
130	Prepaid Insurance	3,600.00			(e) 1,200.00			2,400.00	
140	Bond Sinking Fund	25,000.00						25,000.00	
143	Sinking Fund Investments	25,000.00						25,000.00	
150	Office Equipment	112,000.00						112,000.00	
153	Accumulated Depreciation-Office Equip.		5,200.00		(f) 800.00				6,000.00
155	Store Equipment	143,000.00						143,000.00	
157	Accumulated Depreciation-Store Equipment		16,500.00		(g) 1,500.00				18,000.00
160	Delivery Equipment	130,000.00						130,000.00	
163	Accumulated Depreciation-Delivery Equip.		18,100.00		(h) 2,900.00				21,000.00
165	Building	60,000.00						60,000.00	
167	Accumulated Depreciation-Building		25,000.00		(i) 3,000.00				28,000.00
170	Land	30,000.00						30,000.00	
201	Notes Payable		2,800.00						2,800.00
203	Discount on Notes Payable	12.33			(j) 4.11			8.22	
205	Accounts Payable		6,350.00						6,350.00
215	Dividends Payable-Common		—						—
220	Dividends Payable-Preferred		—						—
225	Employees' Federal Income Tax Payable		134.40						134.40
230	Employees' State Income Tax Payable		28.80						28.80
235	Federal Income Tax Payable		—		(n) 5,690.00				5,690.00
240	Federal Unemployment Tax Payable		12.80						12.80
245	Social Security Tax Payable		198.40						198.40
246	Medicare Tax Payable		46.40						46.40
250	Interest Payable		—		(k) 3.11				3.11
255	Salaries Payable		—		(l) 960.00				960.00
260	Sales Tax Payable		1,362.41						1,362.41
	Carried Forward	1,259,526.81	75,793.21	18,059.75	20,673.89	—	—	1,272,782.45	91,662.97

Figure 11-1 Completed Work Sheet

Mayfaire, Inc.
Work Sheet (Continued)
For the Year Ended December 31, 199-

ACCT. NO.	ACCOUNT NAME	TRIAL BALANCE DEBIT	TRIAL BALANCE CREDIT	ADJUSTMENTS DEBIT	ADJUSTMENTS CREDIT	INCOME STATEMENT DEBIT	INCOME STATEMENT CREDIT	BALANCE SHEET DEBIT	BALANCE SHEET CREDIT
	Brought Forward	1,259,526.81	75,793.21	18,059.75	20,673.87	—	—	1,272,782.45	91,662.97
265	State Unemployment Tax Payable		86.40						86.40
270	Unearned Rent		12,000.00	(m) 8,000.00					4,000.00
280	8% Bonds Payable		200,000.00						200,000.00
301	Preferred 8% Stock		125,000.00						125,000.00
305	Paid-in Capital in Excess of Par-Preferred		—						—
310	Common Stock		710,600.00						710,600.00
315	Paid-in Capital in Excess of Par-Common		15,752.00						15,752.00
320	Retained Earnings		121,537.00						121,537.00
325	Dividends-Preferred	10,000.00						10,000.00	
330	Dividends-Common	—						—	
335	Common Stock Dividend Distributable	—						—	
340	Treasury Stock	46,400.00						46,400.00	
343	Paid-in Capital from Sale of Treasury Stock		—						—
350	Income Summary	—	—		(c) 18,056.05		18,056.05		
401	Sales		412,750.00				412,750.00		
405	Sales Discounts	2,063.00				2,063.00			
410	Sales Returns and Allowances	4,027.00				4,027.00			
501	Purchases	194,379.50				194,379.50			
505	Transportation In	5,720.50				5,720.50			
510	Purchases Discounts		2,175.00				2,175.00		
515	Purchases Returns and Allowances		1,650.00				1,650.00		
601	Advertising Expense	2,361.50				2,361.50			
605	Bad Debts Expense	—		(b) 1,016.65		1,016.65			
610	Bank Card Fees Expense	1,788.10				1,788.10			
615	Cash Short and Over	13.50				13.50			
620	Delivery Expense	601.95				601.95			
625	Depreciation Expense-Building	—		(i) 3,000.00		3,000.00			
630	Depreciation Expense-Delivery Equip.	—		(h) 2,900.00		2,900.00			
635	Depreciation Expense-Office Equipment	—		(f) 800.00		800.00			
640	Depreciation Expense-Store Equipment	—		(g) 1,500.00		1,500.00			
645	Insurance Expense	—		(e) 1,200.00		1,200.00			
650	Miscellaneous Expense	125.00				125.00			
655	Payroll Tax Expense	11,426.25				11,426.25			
660	Salaries Expense	82,500.00		(l) 960.00		83,460.00			
665	Supplies Expense	—		(d) 3,600.00		3,600.00			
670	Utilities Expense	9,635.00				9,635.00			
	Carried Forward	1,630,568.11	1,677,343.61	41,036.40	38,729.92	329,617.95	434,631.05	1,329,182.45	1,268,638.37

Figure 11-1 Completed Work Sheet *(Continued)*

Mayfaire, Inc.
Work Sheet (Continued)
For the Year Ended December 31, 199-

ACCT. NO.	ACCOUNT NAME	TRIAL BALANCE		ADJUSTMENTS		INCOME STATEMENT		BALANCE SHEET	
		DEBIT	CREDIT	DEBIT	CREDIT	DEBIT	CREDIT	DEBIT	CREDIT
	Brought Forward	1,630 568 11	1,677 343 61	41 036 40	38 729 92	329 617 95	434 631 05	1,329 182 45	1,268 638 37
701	Gain on Disposal of Plant Assets		110 00				110 00		
705	Interest Income		285 17		(a) 3 70		288 87		
710	Rental Income		—		(m) 8 000 00		8 000 00		
715	Sinking Fund Income		400 00				400 00		
717	Gain on Sale of Sinking Fund Investments		—				—		
751	Bond Interest Expense	16 000 00				16 000 00			
753	Bonus to Employees	5 800 00				5 800 00			
755	Interest Expense	167 67		(j) 4 11		174 89			
				(k) 3 11					
760	Loss on Disposal of Plant Assets	103 00				103 00			
799	Income Tax Expense	25 500 00		(n) 5 690 00		31 190 00			
		1,678 138 78	1,678 138 78	46 733 62	46 733 62	382 885 84	443 429 92	1,329 182 45	1,268 638 37
	Net Income					60 544 08			60 544 08
						443 429 92	443 429 92	1,329 182 45	1,329 182 45

Figure 11-1 Completed Work Sheet *(Concluded)*

Explain that the term *defer* means to delay.

not paid until the next period. A **deferral** is a delay in recognizing revenue for cash already received or an expense for a bill already paid. Examples of deferrals include prepaid expenses, such as insurance, and unearned revenue, such as rent received in advance.

Mayfaire's adjustments include those for accrued interest income on notes receivable, estimated bad debts, depreciation of plant assets, prepaid interest expense on notes payable, accrued interest expense on notes payable, accrued salaries, deferred rental income, and federal corporate income taxes.

Review the calculations to determine interest.

Adjustment for Accrued Interest Income On December 1, Mayfaire accepted a $500.00, 9%, 90-day note receivable from a charge customer. Even though the note will not mature until March 1, interest has accrued and must be reported as income in this fiscal period. The amount of the accrued interest income is determined as follows:

Principal	×	Interest Rate	×	Time	=	Interest
$500.00	×	.09	×	$\frac{30}{365}$	=	$3.70

Use T accounts on the chalkboard to analyze the adjusting entries presented in the chapter.

In the adjustment, Interest Receivable is debited for $3.70, the amount of interest earned but not yet received as of December 31. Interest Receivable is a current asset account. The same amount is credited to the Interest Income account. The adjustment for accrued interest income is labeled *(a)* on the work sheet in Figure 11-1.

Interest Receivable

Dr.	Cr.
Adj. $3.70	

Interest Income

Dr.	Cr.
	Bal. $285.17
	Adj. $3.70

Adjustment for Estimated Bad Debt Losses In Chapter 3, you learned that not all charge customers can or will pay their bills. An account receivable that cannot be collected becomes an expense to the business. To match its potential bad debt losses with revenue earned, Mayfaire uses the allowance method to account for uncollectible accounts. To estimate the adjustment for uncollectible accounts, Mayfaire uses the percentage of net sales method. Based on its past experience, Mayfaire estimates that 1/4% of net sales will become uncollectible.

Point out that the decimal equivalent of 1/4 of 1% is .0025.

At the end of the fiscal period, Mayfaire's net sales are $406,660.00. Multiplying this amount by 1/4%, Mayfaire determined that the estimated bad debts expense is $1,016.65. In the adjustment, Bad Debts Expense is debited for $1,016.65 and Allowance for Uncollectible Accounts is credited for the same amount. This adjustment is labeled *(b)* on the work sheet in Figure 11-1.

Bad Debts Expense

Dr.	Cr.
Adj. $1,016.65	

Allowance for Uncollectible Accounts

Dr.	Cr.
	Bal. $60.00
	Adj. $1,016.65

R — E — M — E — M — B — E — R

When the adjustment for bad debts expense is based on a percentage of net sales, the total estimated uncollectible amount is added to the previous balance of Allowance for Uncollectible Accounts.

Adjustments for Depreciation In Chapter 6, you learned that all plant, property, and equipment assets except land are depreciated; that is, their costs are spread out over the accounting periods in which they are used. There are several methods of calculating the amount of depreciation. Whichever method is used, an adjusting entry is made at the end of the fiscal period to record the depreciation expense. Let's look at one adjustment for depreciation.

Review the straight-line method of depreciation.

Mayfaire uses the straight-line method of calculating depreciation. The balance of the Building account in the Trial Balance section of the work sheet is $60,000. This amount, you remember, represents the *cost* of the building. The balance of the Accumulated Depreciation—Building account is $28,000. This amount represents the total amount of depreciation taken on the building in previous fiscal periods. Mayfaire has determined that the annual estimated depreciation on the building is $3,000. An adjustment for this amount must be recorded on the work sheet.

Ask students why letters and not numbers are used to label the adjusting entries.

In the adjustment, Depreciation Expense—Building is debited for $3,000, the amount of depreciation expense for the current fiscal period. Accumulated Depreciation—Building is credited for $3,000. This adjustment is labeled *(i)* in Figure 11-1. After the adjusting entry is posted, the accumulated depreciation account will have a balance of $31,000.

Depreciation Expense—Building

Dr.	Cr.
Adj. $3,000	

Accumulated Depreciation—Building

Dr.	Cr.
	Bal. $28,000
	Adj. 3,000

Mayfaire also makes adjustments for the depreciation of its office equipment *(f)*, store equipment *(g)*, and delivery equipment *(h)*.

Adjustment for Prepaid Interest Expense On December 16, Mayfaire borrowed $1,000.00 from the National Bank of Commerce by issuing a 45-day, non-interest-bearing note payable. The $1,000.00 is included in the balance for Notes Payable in the Trial Balance section of the work sheet. The bank discounted the note at 10%, deducting $12.33 in advance. The bank discount was recorded in the contra liability account Discount on Notes Payable. Although the note will not mature until the next fiscal period (on January 30), a portion of the prepaid interest expense must be charged as an expense to the current fiscal period.

Remind students that Discount on Notes Payable is a contra liability account.

The amount of the interest expense for the current period is determined as follows:

The costs for equipment are spread out over the accounting periods in which the equipment is used.

Review why 15 days is used to determine the interest expense.

$$\text{Principal} \times \text{Discount Rate} \times \text{Time} = \text{Interest}$$
$$\$1{,}000.00 \times .10 \times \frac{15}{365} = \$4.11$$

Interest Expense is debited for $4.11, the amount of interest expense chargeable to the current accounting period. Discount on Notes Payable is credited for the same amount. After the adjusting entry is journalized and posted, Discount on Notes Payable will have a debit balance of $8.22. This amount is the prepaid interest expense chargeable to the next fiscal period. The adjustment for prepaid interest expense is labeled *(j)* in Figure 11-1.

Interest Expense	
Dr.	Cr.
Bal. $167.67	
Adj. $4.11	

Discount on Notes Payable	
Dr.	Cr.
Bal. $12.33	Adj. $4.11

Adjustment for Accrued Interest Expense

On December 24, Mayfaire issued a 60-day, 9%, $1,800.00 note payable. The note will mature on February 22 of the next fiscal period. As of December 31, however, Mayfaire has accrued interest expense on this note for 7 days. This accrued interest must be recorded as an expense for this fiscal period. The amount of the accrued interest is calculated as follows:

Review how to calculate the maturity date of a note payable.

$$\text{Principal} \times \text{Interest Rate} \times \text{Time} = \text{Interest}$$
$$\$1{,}800.00 \times .09 \times \frac{7}{365} = \$3.11$$

In the adjustment, Interest Expense is debited for $3.11, the amount of the accrued interest for this fiscal period. The same amount is credited to Interest Payable. This adjustment is labeled *(k)* on the work sheet in Figure 11-1.

Interest Expense	
Dr.	Cr.
Bal. $171.78	
Adj. 3.11	

Interest Payable	
Dr.	Cr.
	Adj. $3.11

Remind students that accrued salaries have been earned but not yet paid.

Adjustment for Accrued Salaries

Adjustment for Accrued Salaries In the Trial Balance section of Mayfaire's work sheet, the Salaries Expense account has a balance of $82,500. This is the total amount of employees' salaries paid during the fiscal period. By December 31, however, an additional $960 in salaries have accrued (for December 29–31) and must be recorded; that is, salaries have been earned by employees but have not yet been paid. In the adjustment, Salaries Expense is debited for $960, the salaries expense that has accrued for December 29–31. Since the salaries have not yet been paid, they represent a liability. Salaries Payable, therefore, is credited for $960. The adjustment for accrued salaries expense is labeled *(l)* in Figure 11-1.

Salaries Expense	
Dr.	Cr.
Bal. $82,500	
Adj. 960	

Salaries Payable	
Dr.	Cr.
	Adj. $960

Adjustment for Unearned Rental Income

Adjustment for Unearned Rental Income Since Mayfaire is a merchandising business, its main source of revenue is the sale of merchandise. It has, however, another source of revenue. Mayfaire owns the land and building in which it operates. Because the building is large, Mayfaire leases office space to another business for an annual rent of $12,000 ($1,000 a month). According to the lease agreement, the rent must be paid in advance. Mayfaire received the $12,000 on May 1. It recorded the transaction in the liability account Unearned Rent. That amount appears as a credit in the Trial Balance section of Mayfaire's work sheet.

Ask students why the rent received on May 1 was recorded in a liability account and not in the Rent Income account.

At the end of the accounting period, eight months of the lease have expired. Mayfaire has, therefore, earned $8,000 of the rent received in advance ($1,000 × 8). That amount must be transferred from the liability account to a revenue account. In the adjustment, Unearned Rent is debited for $8,000. Rental Income is credited for $8,000, the amount of rent earned during the accounting period. The adjustment for earned rental income is labeled *(m)* on the work sheet in Figure 11-1.

Unearned Rent	
Dr.	Cr.
Adj. $8,000	Bal. $12,000

Rental Income	
Dr.	Cr.
	Adj. $8,000

Walk students through the steps to determine the adjustment for income taxes.

Adjustment for Federal Income Taxes At the end of the year, a work sheet is prepared to organize the adjustments and determine the net income for the year. Up to this point, you have been given the total amount of the income taxes for the year. Knowing that amount, you were able to enter the adjustment on the work sheet along with the other adjustments.

Usually, however, the adjustment for income taxes is determined as the work sheet is being prepared. Look again at Mayfaire's work sheet in Figure 11-1. To determine the adjustment for income taxes and complete the work sheet, you would follow these steps:

1. Make sure all of the adjustments have been recorded *except* the adjustment for corporate income taxes. Do *not* total the Adjustments columns.
2. Extend all account balances *except* that of Income Tax Expense into the Balance Sheet and Income Statement sections.
3. On a separate sheet of paper, total the amounts listed in the Income Statement Debit and Credit columns. Then tentatively determine the net income before taxes by subtracting the Income Statement Debit total from the Income Statement Credit total. (The objective is to determine the net income in advance and then calculate the exact amount of the income tax.)

Income Statement Credit	$443,429.92
Income Statement Debit	–351,695.84
Net income before taxes	$ 91,734.08

$31,190
–25,500
$ 5,690

4. Determine the federal income tax on the net income. By using the IRS tax rate tables, Mayfaire found that its total federal income taxes for the year were $31,190. Since Mayfaire has already paid $25,500 during the year, it now owes $5,690.

5. Record the adjustment for federal income taxes in the Adjustments section of the work sheet. The adjustment is recorded as a debit of $5,690 to Income Tax Expense and a $5,690 credit to Federal Income Tax Payable. In Figure 11-1, this adjustment is labeled *(n)*.

Income Tax Expense	
Dr.	Cr.
Bal. $25,500	
Adj. 5,690	

Federal Income Tax Payable	
Dr.	Cr.
	Adj. $5,690

Use demonstration problem 11-1 here.

R — E — M — E — M — B — E — R

At the end of the fiscal period, the adjustment for additional income taxes owed is recorded on the work sheet as a debit to Income Tax Expense and a credit to Federal Income Tax Payable.

In this discussion, we've been assuming that Mayfaire determined its income tax by multiplying its net income for the year by the tax rate. The corporation's net income was also its taxable income. In Chapter 7, you learned that taxable income is the amount on which taxes are assessed.

Taxable income for a corporation is usually sales less various exemptions and deductions specified by law and the IRS.

Discuss why the net income on the income statement may differ from the corporation's taxable income.

The net income shown on a corporation's income statement, however, may differ from its taxable income. Here are some reasons why:

1. The corporation may use one depreciation method for financial accounting purposes and another depreciation method for income tax purposes. For example, the company might use the straight-line method of depreciation when preparing financial statements, but MACRS for income tax purposes.
2. A company may include certain types of revenue on its income statement, but not on its tax return. For example, the interest or dividends received on some investments is not taxable. And some revenues, such as gains on the sale of property, are taxed at different rates.
3. A corporation may record certain types of expenditures as assets and, therefore, not include them on the income statement. The same expenditures may be listed on a tax return as expenses. Expenditures for research and development are an example of this.

Before reading further, do the following activity to check your understanding of the material you have just studied.

Check Your Learning

Write your answers to these questions on a sheet of notebook paper.

1. Software City Enterprises made equal quarterly tax payments of $750. At the end of the period, its tax liability was determined to be $3,200. What is the amount of the adjustment? The adjustment is entered as a debit to __?__ and a credit to __?__.
2. The annual depreciation on office equipment is $1,800. The adjustment is recorded as a debit to __?__ and a credit to __?__.
3. The accrued interest on a note receivable is $150. The adjustment is entered as a debit to __?__ and a credit to __?__.
4. The prepaid interest on a non-interest-bearing note payable is $90. The adjustment is entered as a debit to __?__ and a credit to __?__.
5. Cardello Electric Supply Company's fiscal period ends on December 31. On April 1, it received $7,200 in advance for office space it rented out for 12 months. If the business defers revenue received in advance, how much has been earned by December 31? The adjustment is recorded as a debit to __?__ and a credit to __?__.

Compare your answers to those in the answers section. Reread the preceding part of the chapter to find the correct answers to any questions you may have missed.

Have students complete Exercises 11-1 and 11-2 at this point.

Completing the Adjustments Section After the adjustment for federal income taxes has been determined and entered on the work sheet, the Adjustments section is totaled and ruled. Since each adjustment has an equal debit and credit, the total of the Adjustments Debit and Credit columns should be the same.

R — E — M — E — M — B — E — R

The Adjustments section of the work sheet, like the Trial Balance section, must balance before the work sheet can be completed.

Point out that if the total of the Income Statement Credit column is larger than the total of the Income Statement Debit column, the business has a net income. If the total of the Income Statement Debit column is larger, the business has a net loss.

Completing the Work Sheet

After the Adjustments section has been totaled, the Federal Income Tax Payable balance is extended to the Balance Sheet Credit column and the Income Tax Expense balance is extended to the Income Statement Debit column. The last four columns of the work sheet are then totaled. The net income (or loss) for the fiscal period is calculated and recorded and the work sheet is then completed. As you can see, Mayfaire had a net income of $60,544.08.

R — E — M — E — M — B — E — R

The net income or net loss amount calculated in the Income Statement section must agree with the amount calculated in the Balance Sheet section.

Preparing End-of-Period Financial Statements

As you know, the work sheet is used to prepare a business's financial statements. These statements are useful to management, creditors, and governmental agencies. Management uses the financial statements to evaluate past performance and to help make future business decisions. Since creditors have a vested interest in the business, they want to know whether Mayfaire will be able to pay its debts. In addition, government agencies, employees, and consumer groups are also interested in the financial strength of the business.

Mayfaire prepares three financial statements: the income statement, the statement of stockholders' equity, and the balance sheet.

The Income Statement

Since the income statement reports the financial progress of the business, it is the first financial statement a business prepares. The work sheet contains all the data needed to prepare the income statement. Mayfaire's income statement appears in Figure 11-2.

As you know, a merchandising business earns revenue by selling merchandise to customers. The cash spent or assets consumed to earn that revenue are referred to as *operating expenses.* Some businesses earn revenue and have certain expenses that are not related to their normal operations. Such revenue and expenses are called *other revenue* and *other expenses.*

Mayfaire, Inc.
Income Statement
For the Year Ended December 31, 199-

Revenue:				
Sales			412750 00	
Less: Sales Discounts		2063 00		
Sales Ret. + Allow.		4027 00	6090 00	
Net Sales				406660 00
Cost of Merchandise Sold:				
Merch. Inv., Jan. 1, 199-			92470 25	
Purchases	194379 50			
Transportation In	5720 50			
Cost of Delivered Merch.		200100 00		
Less: Purch. Discounts	2175 00			
Purch. Ret. + Allow.	1650 00	3825 00		
Net Purchases			196275 00	
Cost of Merch. Avail.			288745 25	
Merch. Inv., Dec. 31, 199-			110526 30	
Cost of Merch. Sold				178218 95
Gross Profit from Sales				228441 05
Operating Expenses:				
Advertising Expense			2361 50	
Bad Debts Expense			1016 65	
Bank Card Fees Expense			1788 10	
Cash Short and Over			13 50	
Delivery Expense			601 95	
Deprec. Exp.–Building			3000 00	
Deprec. Exp.–Del. Eq.			2900 00	
Deprec. Exp.–Off. Eq.			800 00	
Deprec. Exp.–Store Eq.			1500 00	
Insurance Expense			1200 00	
Miscellaneous Exp.			125 00	
Payroll Tax Expense			11426 25	
Salaries Expense			83460 00	
Supplies Expense			3600 00	
Utilities Expense			9635 00	
Total Operating Exp.				123427 95
Operating Income				105013 10
Other Revenue:				
Gain on Disp. of Pl. Assets		110 00		
Interest Income		288 87		
Rental Income		8000 00		
Sinking Fund Income		400 00		
Gain on Sale of Sk. Fd. Inv.		—	8798 87	
Other Expenses:				
Bond Interest Expense		16000 00		
Bonus to Employees		5800 00		
Interest Expense		174 89		
Loss on Disp. of Pl. Assets		103 00	22077 89	
Net Deduction				13279 02
Net Income before Inc. Tax				91734 08
Federal Income Tax				31190 00
Net Income				60544 08

Figure 11-2 Income Statement

Review which accounts are reported as other revenue and which are other expenses.

Since other revenue and other expenses are not related to a business's normal operations, they are reported separately on the business's income statement. Look at Mayfaire's income statement. Just below the

Operating Income line, there is an Other Revenue section. Reported in this section are income from rental property, interest, and the bond sinking fund, as well as gains from the disposal of plant assets and sinking fund investments. The Other Expenses section that follows includes Bond Interest Expense, Bonus to Employees, Interest Expense, and Loss on Disposal of Plant Assets.

$ 8,798.87
−22,077.89
($13,279.02)

The difference between the total other revenue and the total other expenses is either a net addition to or a net deduction from income. Since Mayfaire's other expenses are greater than its other revenue, there is a net deduction of $13,279.02.

Use demonstration problem 11-2 here.

Notice, also, that the federal income tax amount is listed separately. Although income taxes are a normal expense for a corporation, they are not included with the operating expenses. In this way, the amount of taxable income is more easily seen on the income statement.

R — E — M — E — M — B — E — R

The net income reported on the income statement must agree with the net income calculated on the work sheet.

The Statement of Stockholders' Equity

So far, you have prepared a statement of retained earnings for closely held corporations. That statement reported the changes that had taken place in the Retained Earnings account during the fiscal period. The statement was very simple, reporting the beginning balance of Retained Earnings, the net income or loss, and the ending balance of Retained Earnings.

Discuss the types of information reported on this financial statement.

Today many corporations prepare a statement of stockholders' equity instead of a statement of retained earnings. The **statement of stockholders' equity** reports changes that have taken place in *all* of the stockholders' equity accounts during the period. This statement reveals much more about the transactions that affected stockholders' equity during the period. The types of information reported on the statement of stockholders' equity include

1. The number of any shares of stock issued during the period and the total amount received for those shares.
2. Treasury stock transactions.
3. Net income for the period.
4. Any dividends declared during the period (cash or stock).

The statement of stockholders' equity prepared by Mayfaire, Inc., appears in Figure 11-3. The information needed to prepare the statement is taken from the work sheet and from the general ledger accounts. Notice there are specific columns for preferred stock, common stock, treasury stock, and retained earnings. There is also *one* column in which to record the additional paid-in capital for all three stock accounts. In addition, there is a Total column, which summarizes all of the other columns.

Mayfaire, Inc.
Statement of Stockholders' Equity
For the Year Ended December 31, 199-

	$50 Par Preferred 8% Stock	$25 Par Common Stock	Treasury Stock	Paid-in Capital	Retained Earnings	Total
Balance, January 1, 199-	125 000 00	596 000 00	—	—	193 889 00	914 889 00
Issued 2,000 sh. of common stock		50 000 00		8 000 00		58 000 00
Treasury Stock:						
Purchased 2,000 sh. of common stk.			<58 000 00>			<58 000 00>
Sold 100 shares			2 900 00	100 00		3 000 00
Sold 100 shares			2 900 00	<100 00>		2 800 00
Issued 200 shares as bonus			5 800 00			5 800 00
Net Income					60 544 08	60 544 08
Dividends:						
Preferred Stock cash dividend					<10 000 00>	<10 000 00>
Common Stock stk. dividend		64 600 00		7 752 00	<72 352 00>	—
Balance, December 31, 199-	125 000 00	710 600 00	<46 400 00>	15 752 00	172 081 08	977 033 08

Figure 11-3 Statement of Stockholders' Equity

Point out that the common stock issued, treasury stock transactions, and stock dividends for the year are reported separately on this statement.

The first line in Figure 11-3 shows the balance in the accounts at the beginning of the fiscal period. Transactions that took place during the period and that affect the stockholders' equity accounts are described in the left column. The increase or decrease amounts are recorded in the individual amount columns and in the Total column.

For example, the second line on the statement indicates that Mayfaire issued 2,000 shares of common stock during the period. The issuance of the common stock increased the balance of the Common Stock account by $50,000. Since the stock was issued at a price above par, the Paid-in Capital account was increased by $8,000.

The next five lines describe the treasury stock transactions that took place during the period. Remember, Treasury Stock has a normal debit balance. On the statement of stockholders' equity, any debit balances or any amounts that decrease account balances are enclosed in parentheses. The $58,000 debit balance for Treasury Stock, for example, is enclosed in parentheses.

The net income earned by a corporation increases Retained Earnings. Any dividends declared by a corporation decrease Retained Earnings. On the statement, the dividends for preferred stock and for common stock are reported separately. Look at how the stock dividend for common stockholders was reported. A stock dividend, remember, does not affect total stockholders' equity. It simply transfers an amount from Retained Earnings to the paid-in capital accounts.

The balance for Retained Earnings calculated on the statement of stockholders' equity is used to prepare the corporation's balance sheet.

R — E — M — E — M — B — E — R

A net income increases the balance of the Retained Earnings account. A net loss and any dividends paid decrease the balance of the Retained Earnings account.

The Balance Sheet

Ask students to identify the two sources of the data needed to prepare the balance sheet.

As you know, the balance sheet reports the updated balances of all asset, liability, and stockholders' equity accounts. The information needed to prepare the balance sheet is taken from two different sources. The balances of the asset, liability, and paid-in capital accounts are taken from the Balance Sheet section of the work sheet. The balance of the Retained Earnings account is taken from the statement of stockholders' equity.

ACCOUNTING **Tips**

Current assets are listed in order of liquidity on the balance sheet.

Point out that this is a classified balance sheet.

Mayfaire's balance sheet appears in Figure 11-4. This is a classified balance sheet; that is, the accounts are reported by their classifications. The Assets section, for example, is divided into three classifications. The first classification lists the business's current assets, the second reports the company's investments accounts, and the third lists the property, plant, and equipment assets. This balance sheet also reports the book value of notes receivable, accounts receivable, and each type of plant asset. The various contra accounts are reported on the balance sheet as deductions from their related asset accounts.

Point out that this balance sheet reports the book values of notes receivable, accounts receivable, and each type of plant asset.

Mayfaire, Inc.
Balance Sheet
December 31, 199-

Assets			
Current Assets:			
Cash in Bank		397117 24	
Change Fund		250 00	
Petty Cash Fund		75 00	
Marketable Securities		205000 00	
Notes Receivable	500 00		
Less: Notes Receivable Discounted	—	500 00	
Notes Receivable Past Due		1624 99	
Interest Receivable		3 70	
Accounts Receivable	28667 00		
Less: Allow. for Uncoll. Accts.	1076 65	27590 35	
Merchandise Inventory		110526 30	
Supplies		1610 00	
Prepaid Insurance		2400 00	
Total Current Assets			746697 58
Investments:			
Bond Sinking Fund		25000 00	
Sinking Fund Investments		25000 00	
Total Investments			50000 00
Property, Plant, and Equipment			
Office Equipment	112000 00		
Less: Accum. Deprec.–Off. Equip.	6000 00	106000 00	
Store Equipment	143000 00		
Less: Accum. Deprec.–Store Equip.	18000 00	125000 00	
Delivery Equipment	130000 00		
Less: Accum. Deprec.–Deliv. Equip.	21000 00	109000 00	
Building	60000 00		
Less: Accum. Deprec.–Building	28000 00	32000 00	
Land		30000 00	
Total Property, Plant, & Equipment			402000 00
Total Assets			1,198697 58

Figure 11-4 Balance Sheet

Mayfaire, Inc. Balance Sheet (Continued) December 31, 199–			
Liabilities			
Current Liabilities:			
Notes Payable	2800 00		
Less: Discount on Notes Pay.	8 22	2791 78	
Accounts Payable		6350 00	
Dividends Payable-Common		—	
Dividends Payable-Preferred		—	
Emp. Fed. Income Tax Payable		134 40	
Emp. State Income Tax Payable		28 80	
Federal Income Tax Payable		5690 00	
Fed. Unemployment Tax Payable		12 80	
Social Security Tax Payable		198 40	
Medicare Tax Payable		46 40	
Interest Payable		3 11	
Salaries Payable		960 00	
Sales Tax Payable		1362 41	
State Unemployment Tax Payable		86 40	
Unearned Rent		4000 00	
Total Current Liabilities			21664 50
Long-Term Liabilities:			
8% Bonds Payable			200000 00
Total Liabilities			221664 50
Stockholders' Equity			
Paid-in Capital:			
Preferred 8% Stock, $50 par, 10,000 sh. authorized, 2,500 sh. issued		125000 00	
Common Stock, $25 par, 50,000 shares authorized, 28,424 sh. issued	710600 00		
Paid-in Cap. in Exc. of Par-Common	15752 00	726352 00	
Total Paid-in Capital		851352 00	
Retained Earnings		172081 08	
Total Paid-in Capital + Ret. Earnings		1,023433 08	
Less: Treas. Stock (1,600 sh. at cost)		46400 00	
Total Stockholders' Equity			977033 08
Total Liabilities + Stockholders' Equity			1,198697 58

Figure 11-4 Balance Sheet *(Concluded)*

Accounts in the Liabilities section are reported as either current liabilities or long-term liabilities. The Stockholders' Equity section is classified into paid-in capital and retained earnings.

The Stockholders' Equity section of the balance sheet for a publicly held corporation is more detailed than that of a closely held corporation. As you can see, each permanent capital stock account is listed separately under the heading "Paid-in Capital." Each listing describes the par value, the number of shares authorized, and the number of shares issued. Preferred stock is always listed before common stock. Notice, also, that the Dividends accounts are *not* listed on the balance sheet. The Dividends accounts are closed into Retained Earnings at the end of the fiscal period. The balance of Retained Earnings shown on the balance sheet reflects the dividends declared during the period.

Use demonstration problem 11-3 here.

Treasury stock is reported on the balance sheet as a deduction from the total paid-in capital and retained earnings amount. The number of shares of treasury stock being held is also reported.

R — E — M — E — M — B — E — R

When preparing the balance sheet, the amount reported for Retained Earnings is taken from the statement of stockholders'equity, not the work sheet.

Before reading further, do the following activity to check your understanding of the material you have just studied.

Check Your Learning

Write the answers to these questions on a sheet of notebook paper.

1. The data needed to prepare the income statement are taken from the __?__.
2. Rental Income and Interest Income would be listed in the __?__ section of the income statement.
3. On the income statement, if other revenue is greater than other expenses, there is a __?__ for income.
4. Dividends declared during the fiscal period are reported on the __?__.
5. The statement of stockholders' equity is prepared as a supporting document for the __?__.
6. The balance of the Retained Earnings account reported on the balance sheet is taken from the __?__.
7. The book value of notes receivable is reported in the __?__ section of the balance sheet.

Compare your answers to those in the answers section. Reread the preceding part of the chapter to find the correct answers to any questions you may have missed.

Notes to Financial Statements

Provide several examples of actual annual reports that include notes to financial statements for students to look at.

The financial statements of a publicly held corporation present a great deal of information. For a user to have a good understanding of the business's financial position and the results of its operations, he or she must have more information than the financial statements present. Some of that information can be found in the notes to financial statements. The **notes to financial statements** contain additional information that explains significant matters not disclosed in the financial statements and the accounting policies followed by the organization. These notes are an important part of a business's reporting system. A portion of the notes to financial statements for Mayfaire, Inc., appears in Figure 11-5.

Mayfaire, Inc.

Mayfaire, Inc.
Notes to Financial Statements
For the Year Ended December 31, 199-

Note A: Summary of Significant Accounting Policies

1. The financial statements of Mayfaire, Inc., have been prepared on the accrual basis.
2. Marketable securities are reported at the lower of their cost or their market value.
3. The cost of inventories is calculated using the last in, first out method. Inventories are reported at the lower of cost or market value.
4. Property, plant, and equipment are reported at cost, less depreciation. Depreciation is calculated using the straight-line method.
5. Earnings per share are computed based on the average number of shares of common stock outstanding.

Note B: Marketable Securities and Investments

1. Marketable securities consist of U.S. Treasury bills.
2. Sinking fund investments are composed of certificates of deposit. A listing appears below.

Lake City National Bank (10.5%)	$10,000
National Bank of Commerce (9.0%)	15,000
Total	$25,000

Note C: Pension Plan

The company withholds FICA taxes and contributes the employer's share as required by law. No other pension plan is in effect.

Figure 11-5 Notes to Financial Statements

Completing the Accounting Cycle

After the financial statements have been prepared, the work sheet is used as the source document for journalizing the adjusting and closing entries. The data for the adjusting entries are taken from the Adjustments section of the work sheet.

Most of the information needed for the closing entries can be found in the Income Statement section of the work sheet. A publicly held corporation prepares four closing entries. The first three closing entries are the same as those prepared for a closely held corporation. In the fourth closing entry, the balances of the Dividends accounts are closed into Retained Earnings. Figure 11-6 illustrates this closing entry.

GENERAL JOURNAL — PAGE 29

	DATE		DESCRIPTION	POST. REF.	DEBIT	CREDIT	
1	199-		Closing Entries				1
29	Dec.	31	Retained Earnings		10 000 00		29
30			Dividends—Preferred			10 000 00	30

Figure 11-6 Journalizing the Closing Entry for the Dividends Accounts

Be sure students understand that only permanent balance sheet accounts are listed on the post-closing trial balance. All temporary accounts have been closed and have zero balances.

After the adjusting and closing entries have been posted, a post-closing trial balance is prepared. Mayfaire's post-closing trial balance appears in Figure 11-7.

Mayfaire, Inc. Post-Closing Trial Balance December 31, 199-		
Cash in Bank	397,117.24	
Change Fund	250.00	
Petty Cash Fund	75.00	
Marketable Securities	205,000.00	
Notes Receivable	500.00	
Notes Receivable Past Due	1,624.99	
Interest Receivable	3.70	
Accounts Receivable	28,667.00	
Allowance for Uncollectible Accounts		1,076.65
Merchandise Inventory	110,526.30	
Supplies	1,610.00	
Prepaid Insurance	2,400.00	
Bond Sinking Fund	25,000.00	
Sinking Fund Investments	25,000.00	
Office Equipment	112,000.00	
Accumulated Depreciation-Office Equipment		6,000.00
Store Equipment	143,000.00	
Accumulated Depreciation-Store Equipment		18,000.00
Delivery Equipment	130,000.00	
Accumulated Depreciation-Delivery Equipment		21,000.00
Building	60,000.00	
Accumulated Depreciation-Building		28,000.00
Land	30,000.00	
Notes Payable		2,800.00
Discount on Notes Payable	8.22	
Accounts Payable		6,350.00
Employees' Federal Income Tax Payable		134.40
Employees' State Income Tax Payable		28.80
Federal Income Tax Payable		5,690.00
Federal Unemployment Tax Payable		12.80
Social Security Tax Payable		198.40
Medicare Tax Payable		46.40
Interest Payable		3.11
Salaries Payable		960.00
Sales Tax Payable		1,362.41
State Unemployment Tax Payable		86.40
Unearned Rent		4,000.00
8% Bonds Payable		200,000.00
Preferred 8% Stock		125,000.00
Common Stock		710,600.00
Paid-in Capital in Excess of Par-Common		15,752.00
Retained Earnings		172,081.08
Treasury Stock	46,400.00	
	1,319,182.45	1,319,182.45

Figure 11-7 Post-Closing Trial Balance

Summary of Key Points

1. The work sheet is prepared to organize all the data needed to update the general ledger accounts, to prepare financial statements, and to record the adjusting and closing entries.

2. Adjustments recorded on the work sheet may include those for estimated bad debts, depreciation, accrued interest, deferred revenue, accrued salaries, and corporate income taxes.
3. The three financial statements prepared by a merchandising business organized as a publicly held corporation are the income statement, the statement of stockholders' equity, and the balance sheet.
4. Other revenue and other expenses are reported in a separate section of the income statement. The difference between total other revenue and total other expenses is either a net addition to or a net deduction from income.
5. On the income statement, the federal income tax amount is listed separately so that taxable income can be recognized more easily.
6. The statement of stockholders' equity reports the changes that have taken place in all of the stockholders' equity accounts during the fiscal period. The balance for Retained Earnings calculated on this statement is reported on the balance sheet.
7. A classified financial statement is one on which information is reported in categories.
8. Notes to financial statements report additional information useful for understanding the financial statements.
9. At the end of the fiscal period, the balances of the Dividends accounts are closed into Retained Earnings.

11 Review and Applications

Building Your Accounting Vocabulary

In your own words, write the definition for each of the following accounting terms. Use complete sentences for your definitions.

- accrual
- deferrals
- notes to financial statements
- statement of stockholders' equity

Reviewing Your Accounting Knowledge

1. Why must most businesses make adjusting entries at the end of the accounting period?
2. What is the difference between an accrual and a deferral? Give an example of each.
3. List four adjustments normally made by a merchandising corporation at the end of its fiscal period.
4. On the work sheet, which accounts are debited and which are credited in the adjustment for accrued interest income for the fiscal period?
5. If a business uses the allowance method of accounting for uncollectible accounts, which accounts are affected by an adjustment for the period's estimated uncollectible amount?
6. Which account is credited for the annual depreciation on a plant asset?
7. What does the balance in the Discount on Notes Payable account represent?
8. What is the classification of the Unearned Rent account?
9. Why might a corporation's taxable income differ from the net income reported on its income statement?
10. What three financial statements does a merchandising corporation prepare at the end of a fiscal period?
11. What information is reported on the statement of stockholders' equity?
12. What happens to a corporation's Dividends account at the end of the period?
13. Why are notes to financial statements prepared?

Improving Your Problem-Solving Skills

A co-worker with whom you are friendly manages the petty cash fund. A couple of times each month, she borrows small amounts of money from the fund, usually when she has forgotten to cash a check or is running short of cash. She always leaves an IOU and always repays the money before the fund has to be replenished.

In your opinion, is this honest? Explain. What do you think might happen to your friend if a supervisor found the petty cash fund short?

Applying Your Accounting Knowledge

Exercise 11-1 Identifying Accruals and Deferrals

Instructions: Use a form similar to the one that follows. For each of the following items, indicate whether the item is an accrual or a deferral.

Deferral
Accrual
Accrual
Deferral
Deferral
Accrual
Deferral
Accrual
Deferral
Accrual

1. A three-year premium paid on an insurance policy
2. Salaries owed but not yet paid
3. Property taxes incurred for the last two months of the fiscal period
4. Cash received for season tickets to a concert series
5. The bank discount deducted in advance for a non-interest-bearing note
6. Additional corporate federal income taxes owed
7. Office supplies on hand
8. Interest on a note receivable that is not yet due
9. Tuition collected in advance by a school
10. Interest on an interest-bearing note payable due in the next fiscal period

Item	Accrual	Deferral
1		√

Exercise 11-2 Analyzing Adjustments

Instructions: Each of the following account titles represents one-half of an adjustment recorded on the work sheet. Use a form similar to the one shown. For each item, indicate the title of the account that would appear in the other half of the adjustment.

1. Merchandise Inventory is credited.
2. Depreciation Expense—Store Equipment is debited.
3. Bad Debts Expense is debited.
4. Interest Income is credited.
5. Interest Expense is debited.
6. Salaries Payable is credited.
7. Rental Income is credited.
8. Federal Income Tax Expense is debited.
9. Supplies Expense is debited.
10. Prepaid Insurance is credited.

Item	Account Debited	Account Credited
1	Income Summary	Merchandise Inventory

Problem 11-1 Preparing a Work Sheet

Lone Star Enterprises, Inc., is a publicly held corporation with authorized capital of 50,000 shares of $10-par common stock. The company's December 31 trial balance has been completed and appears on the work sheet in the working papers. The data needed for the adjustments follow.

Adjustments:
(a) $59.18
(b) $1,440.00
(c) $7,836.00
(d) $945.00
(e) $1,100.00
(f) $1,500.00
(g) $110.00
(h) $1,008.00
(i) $3,200.00
(j) $1,160.00

Net income, $38,473.78

1. The accrued interest on the note receivable is $59.18.
2. The estimated uncollectible accounts receivable total $1,440.00.
3. The ending merchandise inventory is $90,440.00.
4. The ending office supplies inventory is $375.00.
5. The expired portion of the insurance premium totals $1,100.00.
6. The estimated depreciation of the store equipment is $1,500.00.
7. The portion of the discount on the note payable that is interest expense for this fiscal period is $110.00.
8. Accrued salaries total $1,008.00.
9. Rental income totaling $3,200.00 has been earned in this period.
10. The company owes an additional $1,160.00 for federal income tax.

Instructions: Complete the eight-column work sheet for Lone Star Enterprises for the year ended December 31.

Problem 11-2 Preparing Financial Statements for a Merchandising Business

Retained Earnings, $47,599.68

Total stock. equity, $131,349.68

BS totals, $145,901.80

Instructions: Use the work sheet you prepared in Problem 11-1 to complete this problem.

(1) Prepare an income statement.
(2) Prepare a statement of stockholders' equity. Lone Star Enterprises issued no stock during the fiscal period.
(3) Prepare a classified balance sheet.

Problem 11-3 Journalizing Adjusting Entries

Instructions: Using the work sheet that you prepared in Problem 11-1, journalize Lone Star Enterprises' adjusting entries. Use general journal page 23.

COMPUTER PROBLEM

Problem 11-4 Preparing a Work Sheet and Financial Statements

Executone, Inc., is a publicly held merchandising corporation that specializes in business phones and fax machines. The company is authorized to issue 4,000 shares of $50-par preferred 8% stock and 50,000 shares of $5-par common stock. The balances of the company's general ledger accounts as of December 31 follow.

Cash in Bank	$ 75,650.78
Notes Receivable	6,000.00
Interest Receivable	0.00
Accounts Receivable	28,485.60
Allowance for Uncollectible Accounts	64.87
Merchandise Inventory	53,695.00

Supplies	3,270.00
Prepaid Insurance	2,400.00
Prepaid Rent	9,600.00
Furniture and Fixtures	34,500.00
Accum. Deprec.—Furniture & Fixtures	6,935.00
Store Equipment	58,000.00
Accum. Deprec.—Store Equipment	9,200.00
Notes Payable	10,000.00
Accounts Payable	4,600.00
Employees' Federal Income Tax Payable	147.00
Employees' State Income Tax Payable	54.00
Federal Income Tax Payable	0.00
Federal Unemployment Tax Payable	12.00
Social Security Tax Payable	186.00
Medicare Tax Payable	43.50
Interest Payable	0.00
Salaries Payable	0.00
State Unemployment Tax Payable	81.00
9% Bonds Payable	100,000.00
Discount on Bonds Payable	2,000.00
Preferred 8% Stock	25,000.00
Common Stock	49,000.00
Paid-in Capital in Excess of Par—Common	8,750.00
Retained Earnings	21,400.00
Dividends—Preferred	2,000.00
Dividends—Common	12,250.00
Income Summary	0.00
Sales	239,802.32
Sales Returns & Allowances	13,178.67
Purchases	68,440.00
Purchases Discounts	820.00
Purchases Returns & Allowances	1,368.80
Advertising Expense	2,500.00
Bad Debts Expense	0.00
Deprec. Exp.—Furniture & Fixtures	0.00
Deprec. Exp.—Store Equipment	0.00
Insurance Expense	0.00
Payroll Tax Expense	10,803.00
Rent Expense	0.00
Salaries Expense	78,000.00
Supplies Expense	0.00
Utilities Expense	3,325.00
Interest Income	0.00
Bond Interest Expense	9,000.00
Interest Expense	166.44
Income Tax Expense	4,200.00

Adjustments:
(a) $51.78
(b) $554.50
(c) $6,095.00
(d) $1,200.00
(e) $1,400.00
(f) $2,400.00
(g) $1,400.00
(h) $1,900.00
(i) $164.38
(j) $250.00
(k) $400.00
(l) $2,000.00

Net income, $34,665.91

Retained Earnings, $41,815.91

Total stock. equity, $124,565.91

BS totals, $240,503.79

Instructions:

(1) Prepare an eight-column work sheet for Executone, Inc., for the year ended December 31. The account numbers and titles have already been entered on the work sheet. Data for the adjustments includes the following.

(a) Executone accepted a $6,000.00, 10.5%, 90-day note receivable from a charge customer on December 1.

(b) By aging its accounts receivable, Executone estimates its uncollectible accounts to be $554.50.

(c) The cost assigned to the ending merchandise inventory is $47,600.00.
(d) The ending store supplies inventory is $2,070.00.
(e) On June 1, Executone paid $2,400.00 for a one-year fire insurance policy.
(f) On October 1, Executone signed a one-year lease on the building for its store and offices. The company paid the full year's rent in advance.
(g) The estimated depreciation on the company's furniture and fixtures is $1,400.00.
(h) Estimated depreciation for the company's store equipment is $1,900.00.
(i) On November 1, Executone borrowed $10,000.00 from the Commercial Bank, issuing a 120-day, 10% interest-bearing note payable.
(j) Executone's weekly (6-day) payroll is $1,500.00. Salaries have accrued for 1 day (December 31).
(k) The $100,000, 5-year, 9% bonds were issued on January 1 of this year at 98. The bond discount is amortized over the 5-year period using the straight-line method.
(l) Executone's total federal income tax expense for the year is $6,200.00.

(2) Prepare an income statement.

(3) Prepare a statement of stockholders' equity. During the period, Executone issued 3,000 shares of common stock at $6.75 per share.

(4) Prepare a classified balance sheet. Place the Assets section on one page and the Liabilities and Stockholders' Equity sections on the second page.

CHALLENGE PROBLEM

Problem 11-5 Analyzing Errors on the Work Sheet

Errors made while calculating or recording adjustments on the work sheet may affect the amounts reported on the financial statements. The following list includes several types of errors.

Instructions: Indicate the effect each error will have on the amounts reported on the financial statements using the chart provided in the working papers. Enter an O for "overstated," a U for "understated," and an N for "no effect."

Errors:

1. The ending merchandise inventory was overstated by $5,000.
2. Uncollectible accounts are estimated at 2% of net sales. When the adjustment was calculated, a net sales amount of $321,986 was used rather than the correct amount of $221,986.
3. The amount of supplies used during the period was calculated at $1,988; the correct amount was $2,188.
4. The adjustment for the additional $1,116 owed in corporate federal income taxes was omitted.

5. On November 30, the company accepted a 90-day, 9.75% note receivable. When the accrued interest income for the period was calculated, a 9% interest rate was used.
6. The adjustment for the portion of the prepaid insurance premium that had expired was omitted.
7. When the adjustment for other income was made, Unearned Rent was credited and Rental Income was debited.
8. The adjustment to amortize the bond premium was omitted.
9. When the adjustment for depreciation was recorded, the Equipment account rather than the Depreciation Expense—Equipment account was debited.
10. Uncollectible accounts are estimated by aging the Accounts Receivable accounts. The $645 estimated uncollectible amount was added to the $113 credit balance of Allowance for Uncollectible Accounts.

Accounting on the Go

Like many of today's professionals, accountants often work in different places. Traveling from one place to another, whether from a central office to a client's office or from one state to another, can be a bother if important tools must be left behind. Today, these tools—a computer and software—are often taken along for the ride—and the work.

When laptop computers were first introduced in the 1980s, they were remarkable but not very functional. The most recent laptop computers, however, have the same capabilities as larger desktop models, except that laptops can be comfortably carried in a briefcase or held on your lap.

To be considered a laptop, a computer must be a fully capable personal computer that weighs 15 pounds or less. Other than fulfilling that common definition, laptop computers vary in their characteristics. Some laptop computers run on batteries, while others require a power cord. Their processing power also varies depending on the kind of processor chips, math coprocessors, hard drives, and disk drives the system supports. The display screens vary in visual detail, and the keyboards range from full-size ones to models with calculator-size keys.

Accountants find laptops very useful because these computers are now able to process and store a lot of data. Since many laptops can use spreadsheet and word processing software, accountants can take their computers to clients' offices to use in balancing the books, completing an audit, or writing a financial report. Now, instead of going back to the office to do some work, accountants can take their offices with them.

With laptop computers, accountants can process data for their clients almost anywhere and at anytime.

Mini Practice Set
APPLICATION ACTIVITY 4

Accounting for a Publicly Held Corporation

In the last three chapters, you learned how to record various stockholders' equity transactions for a publicly held corporation. In addition, you learned how to prepare an eight-column work sheet and the financial statements for a publicly held corporation. Now you will have the opportunity to apply what you have learned by completing various accounting activities for Jet Star Products, Inc.

When you have completed this activity, you will have done the following:

COMPUTER PROBLEM

1. Recorded adjustments and prepared an eight-column work sheet.
2. Prepared an income statement.
3. Prepared a statement of stockholders' equity.
4. Prepared a balance sheet.
5. Analyzed business transactions affecting stockholders' equity.
6. Journalized stockholders' equity transactions.

Jet Star Products, Inc.

Jet Star Products, Inc., is a publicly held retail merchandising corporation that sells a wide variety of office automation equipment. Some of its products include desktop computers, electronic typewriters, text-editing systems, and intelligent telephones. The company was incorporated several years ago with authorized capital of 10,000 shares of $50-par preferred 10% stock and 100,000 shares of $20-par common stock.

Chart of Accounts

The chart of accounts for Jet Star Products, Inc., appears below and on the next page.

JET STAR PRODUCTS, INC.
Chart of Accounts

	101	Cash in Bank
	105	Accounts Receivable
	110	Allowance for Uncollectible Accounts
	115	Subscriptions Receivable—Preferred
	120	Subscriptions Receivable—Common
ASSETS	125	Merchandise Inventory
	130	Store Supplies
	140	Bond Sinking Fund
	145	Sinking Fund Investments
	150	Office Equipment
	155	Accumulated Depreciation—Office Equipment

	160	Store Equipment
	165	Accumulated Depreciation—Store Equipment
	170	Land
	201	Accounts Payable
	205	Corporate Income Tax Payable
	210	Dividends Payable—Preferred
LIABILITIES	215	Dividends Payable—Common
	251	10% Bonds Payable
	255	Premium on Bonds Payable
	301	Preferred 10% Stock
	305	Preferred 10% Stock Subscribed
	310	Paid-in Capital in Excess of Par—Preferred
	315	Common Stock
STOCKHOLDERS'	320	Common Stock Subscribed
EQUITY	325	Paid-in Capital in Excess of Par—Common
	330	Retained Earnings
	335	Dividends—Preferred
	340	Dividends—Common
	345	Common Stock Dividend Distributable
	350	Treasury Stock
	355	Paid-in Capital from Sale of Treasury Stock
	390	Income Summary
	401	Sales
REVENUE	405	Sales Discounts
	410	Sales Returns and Allowances
	501	Purchases
COST OF	505	Transportation In
MERCHANDISE	510	Purchases Discounts
	515	Purchases Returns and Allowances
	601	Advertising Expense
	605	Bad Debts Expense
	610	Depreciation Expense—Office Equipment
	615	Depreciation Expense—Store Equipment
EXPENSES	620	Miscellaneous Expense
	625	Rent Expense
	630	Salaries Expense
	635	Store Supplies Expense
	640	Utilities Expense
OTHER REVENUE	701	Sinking Fund Income
OTHER EXPENSES	751	Bond Interest Expense
	790	Income Tax Expense

Preparing End-of-Period Financial Statements

You began working for Jet Star Products, Inc., at the end of the company's fiscal period. The trial balance has already been entered on the work sheet by another accounting clerk. This work sheet appears in the working papers that accompany this textbook.

Instructions:

Adjustments:
(a) \$9,457.50
(b) \$125,000.00
(c) \$2,400.00
(d) \$1,350.00
(e) \$7,650.00
(f) \$600.00
(g) \$3,206.00

Net income, \$54,533.50

Retained Earnings, \$120,791.50

Total stock. equity, \$1,174,791.50

BS totals, \$1,370,960.00

(1) Complete the eight-column work sheet for Jet Star Products, Inc., for the year ended December 31. The information needed for the adjustments is as follows.
- (a) Bad debt expenses are estimated to be 1.5% of net credit sales of \$630,500.
- (b) The cost of the ending merchandising inventory was \$325,000.
- (c) At the end of the period, there were \$800 of store supplies on hand.
- (d) The annual depreciation on Jet Star's office equipment is \$1,350.
- (e) The annual depreciation of the store equiment is \$7,650.
- (f) The bonds were issued at 106 five years ago. The bond premium is amortized using the straight-line method over the ten-year life of the bonds.
- (g) Jet Star's total federal income taxes for the fiscal period are \$31,206.

(2) Prepare an income statement.

(3) Prepare a statement of stockholders' equity. During the period, Jet Star issued 1,000 shares of preferred 10% stock at \$54 a share. The company also bought 320 shares of its own common stock on the open market for \$25 a share.

(4) Prepare a classified balance sheet. Place the Assets section on the first page and the Liabilities and Stockholders' Equity sections on the second page.

(5) Journalize the adjusting and closing entries, beginning on page 22 of a general journal.

Recording Business Transactions

The following transactions affecting stockholders' equity took place during the first four months of the next fiscal year.

Instructions:

(1) Record these transactions in a cash receipts journal (page 51), cash payments journal (page 63), and general journal (page 24).

(2) A portion of Jet Star's general ledger is included in the working papers. The balances shown are as of January 1. Post the transactions to those accounts provided.

Transactions:

Jan. 3 Issued 1,500 shares of \$20-par common stock in exchange for land with a fair market value of \$30,000, Memorandum 19.

5 Bought back 50 shares of common stock from a stockholder at \$21 a share, Check 1399.

10 Issued 500 shares of \$50-par preferred 10% stock at \$51, Receipt 1226.

15 Wrote Check 1419 for the dividend owed to preferred stockholders.

20 Issued 3,000 shares of \$20-par common stock at \$22, Receipt 1267.

30 Paid common stockholders the dividend declared during the last fiscal period, Check 1450.

Feb. 1 Received subscriptions for 5,000 shares of common stock at $22 per share (Memorandum 34); received a down payment of 50% of the subscription price from all subscribers (Receipt 1311).

10 Received subscriptions for 200 shares of $50-par preferred 10% stock at $52, Memorandum 39.

28 Sold 100 shares of treasury stock at $22 per share, Receipt 1422. The stock had originally been purchased at $25 per share.

Mar. 1 Subscribers to the 5,000 shares of common stock paid an additional 25% of the subscription price, Receipt 1423.

15 The board of directors voted to pay the quarterly cash dividend of $1.25 per share to all preferred stockholders of record as of March 22, payable on April 15, Minute Book, page 250.

15 The board of directors declared a 5% stock dividend for common stockholders of record as of March 22, distributable on April 15, Minute Book, page 251. The present market value of the stock is $24 per share.

24 Received the full amount due from the subscribers to 200 shares of preferred 10% stock, Receipt 1515. Issued the stock to the subscribers, Memorandum 56.

Apr. 1 Subscribers to the 5,000 shares of common stock paid the final 25% of the subscription price, Receipt 1547; issued the common stock to subscribers, Memorandum 64.

15 Issued Check 1759 for $3,206 to the Internal Revenue Service for the federal corporate income tax owed for the previous year.

15 Issued Check 1760 in payment of the cash dividend for preferred stockholders declared on March 15.

15 Distributed to common stockholders the stock dividend declared on March 15, Minute Book, page 261.

30 Sold 220 shares of treasury stock at $25 per share, Receipt 1663. The stock was purchased last year at $25 per share.

HERITAGE HOME CENTER

A Comprehensive Accounting Simulation

Heritage Home Center, Inc., is a business simulation based on a retail home furnishings store located in Columbus, Ohio. The company is organized as a publicly held corporation.

Heritage Home Center, Inc., has a large volume of business transactions. The business, therefore, uses special journals and the general journal to record its business transactions. This simulation is available from the publisher and can be completed manually and/or on the microcomputer.

When you have completed this simulation, you will have done the following:

1. Analyzed business transactions from source documents.
2. Maintained the business checking account by writing checks, making deposits, and reconciling the bank statement.
3. Journalized business transactions in the four special journals and in the general journal.
4. Posted journal entries to the general ledger and to the accounts receivable and accounts payable subsidiary ledgers.
5. Posted the totals of the special journals to the general ledger.
6. Proved cash.
7. Prepared a schedule of accounts receivable and a schedule of accounts payable.
8. Prepared a trial balance and an eight-column worksheet with adjustments.
9. Prepared financial statements.
10. Journalized and posted adjusting and closing entries.
11. Prepared a post-closing trial balance.

UNIT 3

UNDERSTANDING BUSINESS INFORMATION

The financial statements a business prepares are of interest to a variety of groups. People both inside and outside the business use the information provided on the statements to help them make decisions. For these statements to be useful, people must be able to find information that shows important relationships and helps them make comparisons from year to year and from company to company. In this unit, you will first learn techniques for interpreting information contained on financial statements. Then, you will learn about a fourth financial statement that most businesses prepare today.

Chapter 12

ANALYZING AND INTERPRETING FINANCIAL STATEMENTS

Up to this point in your study of accounting, you have focused on analyzing and summarizing business transactions and reporting the results on financial statements. The information presented on the financial statements enables management to make more informed business decisions and stockholders and creditors to evaluate the company's operations. But just how do you analyze and interpret the financial data on the financial statements?

In this chapter, you will learn about comparative financial statements and some of the methods used to analyze and interpret financial data.

Learning Objectives

When you have completed this chapter, you should be able to do the following:

1. Prepare a comparative income statement and balance sheet for horizontal analysis.
2. Prepare a comparative income statement and balance sheet for vertical analysis.
3. Calculate commonly used ratios.
4. Use ratios to analyze the performance of a business.
5. Define the accounting terms presented in this chapter.

New Terms

horizontal analysis
comparability
base year
vertical analysis
common-size statements
working capital
ratio analysis
current ratio
quick ratio
merchandise inventory turnover
accounts receivable turnover
profitability
earnings per share
price-earnings ratio
equity per share

Interpreting Financial Data

In this "information age," we are constantly bombarded with facts. A given set of facts by itself, however, is not significant. To interpret any facts, you must have something with which to compare them. For example, suppose you are told that a certain corporation had a net income of $510,000 during the past year. What exactly does this mean? Does this net income amount indicate a successful year or a poor year? How does that amount compare with other years? Does it represent a reasonable return on investment? How does that net income amount compare with the net income of other firms in the same industry?

Point out that relationships are the key to statement analysis.

As you can see, numbers by themselves generally don't mean very much. It is their relationship to other numbers or their change from one period to another that is more revealing. The techniques of financial analysis are intended to show these relationships and changes. Three common techniques used to evaluate the information presented on financial statements are horizontal analysis, vertical analysis, and ratio analysis.

Horizontal Analysis

Horizontal analysis is the comparison of dollar amount changes and percentage changes for the same items on a company's financial statements for two or more periods. As we study horizontal analysis, we'll look at the income statement of Hillside Office Equipment, Inc., shown in Figure 12-1. As you can see, this income statement combines and compares the financial information for two fiscal periods. As a result, it is

Business managers use data from financial statements to make informed business decisions.

Mention that many firms make four- or five-year comparisons.

called a *comparative income statement*. An important accounting characteristic, **comparability** refers to financial information that can be compared from one fiscal period to another or from one business to another. Comparable data are presented in such a way that the user can recognize similarities, differences, and trends.

Hillside Office Equipment, Inc.
Comparative Income Statement
For the Years Ended December 31, 1993 and 1992

			Increase (Decrease) (1993 over 1992)	
	1993	1992	Amount	Percentage
Revenue:				
Net Sales	$ 968,900	$850,500	$118,400	13.92%
Cost of Merchandise Sold:				
Merchandise Inventory, Jan. 1	208,700	140,200	68,500	48.86%
Purchases	812,200	639,000	173,200	27.10%
Mdse. Available for Sale	1,020,900	779,200	241,700	31.02%
Less: Merch. Inv., Dec. 31	359,700	208,700	151,000	72.35%
Cost of Merchandise Sold	661,200	570,500	90,700	15.90%
Gross Profit on Sales	307,700	280,000	27,700	9.89%
Operating Expenses:				
Selling Expenses	149,700	130,600	19,100	14.62%
Administrative Expenses	58,800	57,300	1,500	2.62%
Total Operating Expenses	208,500	187,900	20,600	10.96%
Operating Income	99,200	92,100	7,100	7.71%
Other Expenses:				
Interest Expense	9,000	8,400	600	7.14%
Net Income before Income Taxes	90,200	83,700	6,500	7.77%
Federal Income Taxes	30,668	28,458	2,210	7.77%
Net Income	$ 59,532	$ 55,242	$ 4,290	7.77%

Figure 12-1 Comparative Income Statement Showing Horizontal Analysis

Calculate the net sales line for the students.

The first two columns present the dollar amounts for the current year (1993) and for the previous year (1992). The last two columns show the increases or decreases for 1993 over 1992, which are expressed first in dollars and then in percentages. Any decreases are indicated by enclosing the amounts and percentages in parentheses.

Look at the first line, net sales. Net sales for 1992 were $850,500; net sales for 1993 were $968,900. By subtracting the 1992 net sales from the 1993 net sales, you can see that there was an increase of $118,400.

$968,900	Net Sales for 1993
–850,500	Net Sales for 1992
$118,400	1993 Increase over 1992

To calculate the percentage of increase in net sales, divide the dollar increase ($118,400) by the net sales amount during the base year and multiply by 100. The **base year** is the year being used for comparison.

In this case, 1993 figures are being compared to those from 1992; thus, the base year is 1992. As the following calculation shows, net sales in 1993 increased 13.92% over 1992 net sales:

$$\frac{\$118,400}{\$850,500} = .1392 \times 100 = 13.92\%$$

R — E — M — E — M — B — E — R

To calculate the percentage of increase in net sales, divide the dollar increase by the base year amount and multiply by 100.

When analyzing an income statement, people often compare all of the percentage changes with the percentage change in net sales. Hillside's net sales increased 13.92% from 1992 to 1993. The other percentage changes on the income statement should also be approximately 13.92%. If they vary considerably from 13.92%, they may be out of line and the reasons for the differences should be investigated.

Let's look at the main items on the income statement.

Item	Percentage Change
Net Sales	13.92%
Cost of Merchandise Sold	15.90%
Gross Profit on Sales	9.89%
Total Operating Expenses	10.96%
Net Income	7.77%

You can see that gross profit on sales and net income vary considerably from the 13.92% increase in net sales. Since gross profit on sales is determined by subtracting the cost of merchandise sold from net sales, the entire Cost of Merchandise Sold section of the income statement should be investigated. This is a starting point in determining why there was a rather small percentage increase in net income (7.77%). The percentage changes for the items in the Cost of Merchandise Sold section are as follows:

Item	Percentage Change
Merchandise Inventory, Jan. 1	48.86%
Net Purchases	27.10%
Merchandise Inventory, Dec. 31	72.35%

Use demonstration problem 12-1 here.

The merchandise inventory of January 1 was a carry-over from 1992. Why was there such a large increase in net purchases (27.10%)? Notice too that the 1993 ending merchandise inventory was 72.35% larger than in 1992. To purchase that quantity of merchandise requires a great deal of cash. To justify such a large increase in merchandise inventory, there should have been a larger increase in net sales.

Have students complete Exercise 12-1 at this point.

Vertical Analysis

Point out that the base amounts used depend on the financial statement.

Another tool used to analyze financial statements is vertical analysis. With **vertical analysis**, every dollar amount reported on a financial statement is also stated as a percentage of a base amount reported on the same statement. Then the current year percentages are compared with the percentages of previous years or with the percentages of other businesses within the same industry. The percentages can also be used to prepare future budgets.

Calculate the current assets percentages for 1993 with the students.

On the income statement, each amount is reported as a percentage of net sales. On a comparative balance sheet, as shown in Figure 12-2, each individual asset is expressed as a percentage of total assets. The individual liabilities and equities are reported as a percentage of the total liabilities and stockholders' equity amount.

Let's look first at Cash in Bank. The percentages are calculated as follows:

	1993	1992
$\frac{\text{Cash in Bank}}{\text{Total Assets}}$	$\frac{\$\ 20{,}700}{\$886{,}500} = 2.33\%$	$\frac{\$\ 34{,}850}{\$776{,}750} = 4.49\%$

Since Merchandise Inventory was a problem on the previous financial statement, let's also look at those percentages:

	1993	1992
$\frac{\text{Merchandise Inventory}}{\text{Total Assets}}$	$\frac{\$359{,}700}{\$886{,}500} = 40.57\%$	$\frac{\$208{,}700}{\$776{,}750} = 26.87\%$

Use demonstration problem 12-2 here.

Have students complete Exercise 12-2 at this point.

These percentages point out Hillside's poor position with respect to Cash in Bank and Merchandise Inventory. The changes in the balances of other related accounts should also be examined. For example, the fact that Cash in Bank decreased while Accounts Payable increased may indicate a pending financial crisis. To be able to meet its bills, Hillside may be forced to sell off some of its merchandise at cost, or even below cost.

R — E — M — E — M — B — E — R

On an income statement arranged for vertical analysis, each dollar amount is expressed as a percentage of net sales. On a balance sheet arranged for vertical analysis, each dollar amount is expressed as a percentage of total assets or of total liabilities and stockholders' equity.

Have students complete Exercise 12-3 at this point.

The financial statements can also be prepared as common-size statements. **Common-size statements** are statements in which all items are reported as percentages of a key item on the statement. On these statements, no dollar amounts are reported. Common-size statements, then, would be like the statements prepared for vertical analysis—but without the amount columns. Common-size statements are most useful in comparing two companies that differ in size.

Before reading further, do the following activity to check your understanding of horizontal and vertical analysis.

Hillside Office Equipment, Inc.
Comparative Balance Sheet
For the Years Ended December 31, 1993 and 1992

	1993		1992	
	Dollars	Percentage	Dollars	Percentage
Assets				
Current Assets:				
Cash in Bank	$ 20,700	2.33%	$ 34,850	4.49%
Marketable Securities	120,000	13.53%	116,000	14.93%
Accounts Receivable (Net)	83,300	9.40%	84,600	10.89%
Subscriptions Receivable	10,000	1.13%	0	0.00%
Merchandise Inventory	359,700	40.57%	208,700	26.87%
Prepaid Expenses	4,800	0.54%	4,600	0.59%
Total Current Assets	$598,500	67.51%	$448,750	57.77%
Property, Plant, and Equipment:				
Equipment (Net)	60,000	6.77%	75,000	9.66%
Building (Net)	168,000	18.95%	192,000	24.72%
Land	54,000	6.09%	54,000	6.95%
Total Prop., Plant, and Equip.	$282,000	31.81%	$321,000	41.33%
Intangible Assets:				
Organization Costs	6,000	0.68%	7,000	0.90%
Total Assets	$886,500	100.00%	$776,750	100.00%
Liabilities				
Current Liabilities:				
Accounts Payable	$ 72,000	8.12%	$ 33,600	4.32%
Dividends Payable	12,000	1.35%	9,000	1.16%
Federal Income Tax Payable	3,100	0.35%	2,800	0.36%
Salaries Payable	6,000	0.68%	5,400	0.70%
Total Current Liabilities	$ 93,100	10.50%	$ 50,800	6.54%
Long-Term Liabilities:				
8% Bonds Payable (Net)	196,000	22.11%	196,000	25.23%
Total Liabilities	$289,100	32.61%	$246,800	31.77%
Stockholders' Equity				
Paid-in Capital:				
Common Stock, $100 Par (4,000 shares authorized, 3,000 shares issued)	300,000	33.84%	300,000	38.62%
Common Stock Subscribed	10,000	1.13%	0	0.00%
Paid-in Capital in Excess of Par	86,000	9.70%	86,000	11.07%
Total Paid-in Capital	$396,000	44.67%	$386,000	49.69%
Retained Earnings	201,400	22.72%	143,950	18.54%
Total Stockholders' Equity	$597,400	67.39%	$529,950	68.23%
Total Liabilities and Stockholders' Equity	$886,500	100.00%	$776,750	100.00%

Figure 12-2 Comparative Balance Sheet Showing Vertical Analysis

Check Your Learning

On a sheet of notebook paper, calculate the percentage of increase or decrease for the following items.

	1993	1992
Cash in Bank	$ 30,200	$ 19,400
Notes Receivable	26,000	31,000
Equipment (Net)	102,600	108,600
Retained Earnings	70,000	61,000

Compare your answers to those in the answers section. Reread the preceding part of the chapter to find the correct answers for any items you may have missed.

ACCOUNTING Notes
Publicly held corporations include their financial statements in the annual reports to stockholders. Annual reports of large corporations are usually very comprehensive and long—50 pages or more.

Working Capital

Discuss the importance of working capital to the success of a business.

The amount by which current assets exceed current liabilities is known as a company's **working capital**. Working capital is an important measure of a company's liquidity. Since current liabilities are usually paid out of current assets, working capital represents the excess assets available to continue operations, purchase inventory, obtain credit, or expand operations. Lack of working capital can lead to the failure of the business.

Using amounts from the comparative balance sheet, the working capital for Hillside Office Equipment, Inc., is calculated as follows:

	1993	1992
Current Assets	$598,500	$448,750
– Current Liabilities	– 93,100	– 50,800
Working Capital	$505,400	$397,950

Working capital is useful when analyzing one company's financial statements. It is difficult, however, to compare one company's working capital with another company's. For example, working capital of $50,000 may be adequate for a small grocery store but totally unacceptable for a large grocery chain.

R—E—M—E—M—B—E—R

Working capital is current assets less current liabilities.

Ratio Analysis

Point out that computer software can be used to calculate liquidity, profitability, and financial strength ratios.

A ratio is a relationship between two numbers. **Ratio analysis** is the comparison of two amounts on a financial statement resulting in a percentage that shows the relationship between the two amounts. Ratio analysis is generally used to evaluate a company's liquidity, profitability, and financial strength.

Liquidity Ratios

Earlier you learned that *liquidity* refers to the ease with which an asset can be converted to cash. A *liquidity ratio* is a measure of a business's ability to pay its current debts and provide for unexpected needs for cash. Let's look at several liquidity ratios.

Explain that the current ratio is a test for solvency.

Current Ratio The relationship between a company's current assets and its current liabilities is known as its **current ratio.** A firm's current ratio indicates whether it can pay its bills and repay loans. The current ratio is calculated by dividing the dollar amount of current assets by the dollar amount of current liabilities. Using amounts from Figure 12-2, Hillside's current ratios are calculated as follows:

	1993	1992
$\frac{\text{Current Assets}}{\text{Current Liabilities}}$	$\frac{\$598{,}500}{\$\ 93{,}100} = 6.43{:}1$	$\frac{\$448{,}750}{\$\ 50{,}800} = 8.83{:}1$

Point out that the use of a colon in a ratio means "to". In these examples, it shows the relationship to the number "1".

Hillside's 1993 current ratio of 6.43:1 (or 6.43 to 1) indicates that it has over $6 of current assets for every $1 of current liabilities. In 1992, however, the ratio was higher. The company had almost $9 of current assets for every $1 in current liabilities.

Generally, a ratio of 2:1 is considered adequate for most businesses. What is considered an adequate current ratio, however, varies from industry to industry and even from business to business within an industry.

Explain that the quick ratio is a more stringent test of solvency since it includes only the most liquid assets and computes a new ratio.

Quick Ratio Although the current ratio is an indicator of a firm's ability to meet its current debts, it is based on total current assets. Current assets, as you know, include merchandise inventory and prepaid expenses such as supplies and insurance. It usually takes time to convert inventory into cash, and prepaid items are consumed during normal operations. A business with a satisfactory current ratio may actually be in a poorer position in terms of liquidity when the inventory makes up a large part of the current assets amount.

Mention that the quick ratio is often called the "acid test" ratio.

A ratio that measures a company's short-term liquidity is the quick ratio. The **quick ratio** is the relationship between short-term liquid assets and current liabilities. Short-term liquid assets—those that can be converted to cash quickly—are cash, net receivables, and marketable securities (short-term investments). The quick ratio is determined by dividing a company's quick assets by its current liabilities. Following are Hillside's quick assets:

	1993	1992
Cash in Bank	$ 20,700	$ 34,850
Marketable Securities	120,000	116,000
Accounts Receivable (Net)	83,300	84,600
Subscriptions Receivable	10,000	0
Total Quick Assets	$234,000	$235,450

Use demonstration problem 12-3 here.

The quick ratio is calculated as follows:

	1993	1992
Quick Assets / Current Liabilities	$234,000 / $ 93,100 = 2.51:1	$235,450 / $ 50,800 = 4.63:1

Have students complete Exercise 12-4 at this point.

A quick ratio of at least 1:1 is normally considered satisfactory. Hillside's 1993 quick ratio indicates that it had $2.51 in quick assets for every $1.00 in current liabilities. While the company's ratio is well above the norm, it decreased considerably from the 1992 ratio of 4.63:1.

Mention that the merchandise inventory turnover is sometimes called the "cost of sale/inventory" ratio. Merchandise inventory turnover is a measure of activity; it measures the speed with which inventory is converted to cash.

Merchandise Inventory Turnover The number of times a business's inventory is sold during a given year is the company's **merchandise inventory turnover**. This ratio is calculated by dividing the cost of merchandise sold by the average merchandise inventory. The average merchandise inventory is found by adding the beginning and ending inventory amounts and dividing that total by 2. Here are the calculations for Hillside:

	1993	1992
Merchandise Inventory, Jan. 1	$208,700	$140,200
Merchandise Inventory, Dec. 31	359,700	208,700
	$568,400	$348,900
Average Merchandise Inventory	$568,400 / 2 = $284,200	$348,900 / 2 = $174,450
Cost of Merchandise Sold / Average Merchandise Inventory	$661,200 / $284,200 = 2.33 times/year	$570,500 / $174,450 = 3.27 times/year

Use demonstration problem 12-4 here.

In general, a higher merchandise inventory turnover rate indicates a higher gross profit since more merchandise is being sold. It also means the business has money tied up in inventory for shorter periods of time. As a result, storage and insurance costs are lower. A higher turnover rate also means there is less chance that the inventory will spoil (if it is perishable) or become out of date.

The merchandise inventory turnover for one business can be compared with figures for the rest of the industry as a test of the company's merchandising efficiency. You can see there has been a serious decrease in Hillside's merchandise inventory turnover rate. The lower rate may mean sales were lower than expected or the merchandise was inappropriate. Management should investigate the reasons behind the low turnover rate.

The merchandise inventory turnover can also be used to determine the number of days the merchandise was kept in stock. This is calculated by dividing 365 days by the turnover figure:

	1993	1992
$\frac{365}{\text{Turnover Rate}}$	$\frac{365}{2.33 \text{ times/year}} = 157$ days	$\frac{365}{3.27 \text{ times/year}} = 112$ days

This ratio shows that Hillside's merchandise remained in stock 45 days more in 1993 than it did in 1992. The company should investigate its sales and purchasing practices to improve the inventory turnover rate.

Point out that accounts receivable turnover is a measure of activity. It measures the speed with which accounts receivable are converted to cash.

Accounts Receivable Turnover A business should try to collect its accounts receivable as quickly as possible. As you learned in Chapter 3, the "older" an account, the more likely it is to become uncollectible. **Accounts receivable turnover** is an indication of how quickly a business collects its average accounts receivable. It is the number of times per year that the business collects the average balance of Accounts Receivable. This ratio is calculated by dividing net credit sales by average net accounts receivable. The net credit sales were $820,100 for 1993 and $684,300 for 1992. The January 1 net accounts receivable amount for 1992 (which appeared on the 1991 balance sheet) was $64,400. Hillside's accounts receivable turnover is calculated as follows:

	1993	1992
Net Accounts Receivable, Jan. 1	$ 84,600	$ 64,400
Net Accounts Receivable, Dec. 31	83,300	84,600
	$167,900	$149,000
Average Net Accounts Receivable	$\frac{\$167,900}{2} = \$83,950$	$\frac{\$149,000}{2} = \$74,500$
$\frac{\text{Net Credit Sales}}{\text{Average Net Accounts Receivable}}$	$\frac{\$820,100}{\$\ 83,950} = 9.77$ times/year	$\frac{\$684,300}{\$\ 74,500} = 9.18$ times/year

Explain that the accounts receivable turnover ratio is more meaningful to accountants when it is analyzed in terms of the number of days a year the receivables were on the books.

The accounts receivable turnover rate is more meaningful when looked at in terms of the number of days the receivables were on the books. This rate can be determined by dividing 365 days by the turnover figure. The following illustration shows Hillside's calculations:

	1993	1992
$\frac{365}{\text{Turnover Rate}}$	$\frac{365}{9.77 \text{ times/year}} = 37$ days	$\frac{365}{9.18 \text{ times/year}} = 40$ days

Use demonstration problem 12-5 here.

In 1993, Hillside took 37 days to collect its accounts receivable, an improvement of 3 days over 1992. Since Hillside's credit terms are net 30 days, however, these accounts receivable were 7 days past due in 1993 and 10 days past due in 1992. Hillside should take steps to reduce the number of days accounts receivable remain on the books. The company might try to improve billing procedures or look at its credit granting requirements.

Before reading further, do the following activity to check your understanding of the material you have just studied.

Check Your Learning

The following information appeared on the comparative income statement of the Blendon Company. On a sheet of notebook paper, compute the merchandise inventory turnover rate for 1993 and 1992. In addition, determine the number of days the merchandise was kept in stock.

	1993	1992
Merchandise Inventory, Jan. 1	$132,000	$140,000
Merchandise Inventory, Dec. 31	120,600	132,000
Cost of Merchandise Sold	$740,800	$720,200

Compare your answers to those in the answers section. Reread the preceding part of the chapter to find the correct answers for any items you may have missed.

Have students complete Exercise 12-5 at this point.

Profitability Ratios

Profitability refers to the business's ability to earn a reasonable profit on the owners' investment. *Profitability ratios*, then, are used to evaluate the earnings performance of the business during the accounting period. A business's earning power is an important measure of its ability to grow and continue to earn revenue. In this section, we'll look at three profitability ratios.

Point out that this ratio measures how effectively management is using the investments of stockholders.

Return on Common Stockholders' Equity Stockholders are naturally very interested in the net income earned by corporations in which they have invested. They want to know whether their investments are being used properly and whether they can expect a reasonable return. The *return on common stockholders' equity* measures how well a business has used the resources provided by stockholders. Since Hillside has only one class of stock, this ratio is calculated by dividing the net income by the average value of stockholders' equity. (If Hillside also had preferred stock, the preferred stock dividends for the period would have been subtracted from the net income amount and the balances of the preferred stock accounts subtracted from the stockholders' equity amounts.) The calculations for Hillside follow. The beginning stockholders' equity for 1992 was $487,300.

Go over these calculations carefully with students.

	1993	1992
Stockholders' Equity, Jan. 1	$ 529,950	$ 487,300
Stockholders' Equity, Dec. 31	597,400	529,950
	$1,127,350	$1,017,250

	1993	1992
Average Stockholders' Equity	$\frac{\$1,127,350}{2} = \$563,675$	$\frac{\$1,017,250}{2} = \$508,625$
$\frac{\text{Net Income}}{\text{Average Stockholders' Equity}}$	$\frac{\$59,532}{\$563,675} = 10.56\%$	$\frac{\$55,242}{\$508,625} = 10.86\%$

Explain that comparison should be made with the industry average to gain further insight into the degree of risk involved.

As you can see, the ratio shows that in 1993 Hillside earned $10.56 for each $100.00 invested by stockholders. This ratio declined slightly from 1992 to 1993. Past ratios probably should be examined to make sure the decrease is not a trend.

Point out that this ratio is used to judge the performance of a company and to compare its performance with the performance of other similar companies.

Earnings per Share of Common Stock Earnings per share of common stock is one of the most frequently reported financial measures. **Earnings per share** measures the amount of profit that can be assigned to each share of common stock. Stockholders and potential investors use this ratio to judge a company's performance and compare one company's performance with those of other businesses. Since it is such a widely used ratio, earnings per share is usually reported on the income statement, just below the net income amount.

If a corporation has only one class of capital stock, earnings per share is computed by dividing net income by the number of outstanding shares of common stock. If the company also has preferred stock, any dividends on preferred stock must first be deducted from net income. (Dividends on preferred stock, you'll remember, are paid before those on common stock.) Here are the calculations for Hillside:

	1993	1992
$\frac{\text{Net Income}}{\text{Outstanding Common Stock}}$	$\frac{\$59,532}{3,000 \text{ shares}} = \$19.84$	$\frac{\$55,242}{3,000 \text{ shares}} = \$18.41$

Obviously, any change in the number of shares outstanding during the year has an effect on the earnings per share. That's why a company must disclose any stock dividends or stock splits on its financial statements.

Emphasize that the market price per share is used to calculate this ratio. Stock exchange information can be used to determine market price.

Price-Earnings Ratio A measure commonly used to determine whether the market price of a corporation's stock is reasonable is the **price-earnings ratio.** The price-earnings ratio of a company's stock is calculated by dividing the market price per share by the earnings per share. At the end of 1993, the market price of a share of Hillside's common stock was $130.00; at the end of 1992, it had been $125.00. Hillside's price-earnings ratio is calculated as follows:

	1993	1992
$\frac{\text{Market Price per Share}}{\text{Earnings per Share}}$	$\frac{\$130.00}{\$\ 19.84} = 6.55:1$	$\frac{\$125.00}{\$\ 18.41} = 6.79:1$

Use demonstration problem 12-6 here.

Have students complete Exercise 12-6 at this point.

The price-earnings ratio indicates how investors feel about the future earnings of the company and how much they are willing to pay for every $1 of a company's earnings per share. What is considered a "reasonable" price-earnings ratio varies from one industry to another. In some industries, a 15:1 price-earnings ratio is normal. In other industries, an acceptable ratio may be more than 30:1.

Financial Strength Ratios

The equity of a corporation is composed of creditors' claims and stockholders' investments. Creditors are concerned with a company's ability to pay its debts. If a company is unable to repay its obligations, creditors have first claim to the assets of the company. Such a claim takes precedence over claims of stockholders. Management is also concerned with its company's ability to pay its debts, maintain its credit standing, and borrow in the future.

Discuss why this ratio is so important to creditors of a company and why a high ratio is a good indicator.

▲ **Ratio of Stockholders' Equity to Liabilities** One ratio both creditors and management look at is the *ratio of stockholders' equity to liabilities*. This ratio indicates to creditors how "safe" their loans to the company are and how well the business can absorb losses. This ratio is found by dividing total stockholders' equity by total liabilities. Following are the calculations for Hillside:

	1993	1992
$\frac{\text{Total Stockholders' Equity}}{\text{Total Liabilities}}$	$\frac{\$597,400}{\$289,100} = 2.07:1$	$\frac{\$529,950}{\$246,800} = 2.15:1$

This ratio indicates that in 1993, stockholders were providing $2.07 of equity for every $1.00 provided by creditors. Creditors like to see a high ratio, because stockholders' equity can be used to absorb losses. In addition, if their investment is large, owners will think twice about assuming sizable risks.

Mention that this ratio measures the degree of indebtedness to property, plant, and equipment.

▲ **Ratio of Property, Plant, and Equipment to Long-Term Liabilities** Property, plant, and equipment assets are often used as security when a company borrows money on a long-term basis. As a result, creditors are very interested in the *ratio of property, plant, and equipment to long-term liabilities*. This ratio also indicates the company's ability to borrow more money on a long-term basis in the future. It is determined by dividing the book value of property, plant, and equipment assets by total long-term liabilities. Hillside's calculations are as follows:

	1993	1992
$\frac{\text{Book Value of Property, Plant, and Equipment}}{\text{Long-Term Liabilities}}$	$\frac{\$282,000}{\$196,000} = 1.44:1$	$\frac{\$321,000}{\$196,000} = 1.64:1$

In 1993, Hillside had $1.44 in property, plant, and equipment assets for every $1.00 of long-term liabilities. This was a slight decrease from the 1992 figures. Both figures, however, would be acceptable to long-term creditors.

Point out that this ratio assumes that a corporation will liquidate its assets at their book value.

Equity per Share Among the techniques used to determine the financial strength of a business is equity per share. **Equity per share** refers to the amount that would be paid on each share of stock if the corporation liquidated and the assets were sold for their book value.

If a corporation has only one class of stock, equity per share is determined by dividing the total stockholders' equity by the number of shares of common stock outstanding. Hillside's equity per share is calculated as follows:

Use demonstration problem 12-7 here.

	1993	1992
$\frac{\text{Total Stockholders' Equity}}{\text{Common Stock Outstanding}}$	$\frac{\$597{,}400}{3{,}000 \text{ shrs}} = \$199.13/\text{shr}$	$\frac{\$529{,}950}{3{,}000 \text{ shrs}} = \$176.65/\text{shr}$

Have students complete Exercise 12-7 at this point.

Equity per share increases as a business retains net income. You'll notice that Hillside's equity per share increased in 1993 by $22.48 in one year. This indicates that Hillside is retaining net income.

Summary of Key Points

1. Three techniques used to analyze and interpret financial statements are horizontal analysis, vertical analysis, and ratio analysis.
2. Comparative financial statements compare financial data over two or more years.
3. Horizontal analysis involves comparing dollar amount changes and percentage changes for the same item on a company's financial statements for two or more periods.
4. With vertical analysis, every dollar amount on the financial statement is also stated as a percentage of a base amount on the same statement. On the income statement, the base amount is net sales. On the balance sheet, the base amount is total assets or total liabilities and stockholders' equity.
5. Ratio analysis is a means of showing the relationship between two items on a financial statement. Ratio analysis is used to evaluate a company's liquidity, profitability, and financial strength.
6. Liquidity ratios include the current ratio, quick ratio, merchandise inventory turnover, and accounts receivable turnover. Profitability ratios include the return on common stockholders' equity, earnings per share, and the price-earnings ratio. Ratios used to evaluate a company's financial strength include the ratio of stockholders' equity to liabilities, the ratio of property, plant, and equipment to long-term liabilities, and equity per share.

12 Review and Applications

Building Your Accounting Vocabulary

In your own words, write the definition of each of the following accounting terms. Use complete sentences for your definitions.

- accounts receivable turnover
- base year
- common-size statements
- comparability
- current ratio
- earnings per share
- equity per share
- horizontal analysis
- merchandise inventory turnover
- price-earnings ratio
- profitability
- quick ratio
- ratio analysis
- vertical analysis
- working capital

Reviewing Your Accounting Knowledge

1. Name three techniques commonly used to analyze financial statement information.
2. How are percentages of increase or decrease calculated on financial statements organized for horizontal analysis?
3. How does horizontal analysis differ from vertical analysis?
4. When an income statement is prepared for vertical analysis, what is the base amount? What is the base amount on a balance sheet prepared for vertical analysis?
5. Why are changes given in both dollar amounts and percentages on comparative financial statements?
6. A business has a gross profit percentage of 37%. What does this mean?
7. How does the quick ratio differ from the current ratio? How are they similar?
8. Why would a business want a high merchandise inventory turnover rate?
9. What is the difference between liquidity and profitability?
10. Which ratio can stockholders use to help determine how well their investments are doing?
11. Of the ratios presented in this chapter, which measure a company's liquidity? Its profitability? Its financial strength?

Improving Your Math Skills

Mathematical accuracy is very important in accounting, but sometimes the solutions to mathematical problems are carried out to more decimal places than accountants need. When this happens with amounts of money, most businesses round off the amount to the nearest cent. Round off the following dollar amounts to the nearest cent.

1. $38.345
2. $14.9153
3. $27.732
4. $119.195632
5. $6.049
6. $0.1925
7. $1.2768
8. $10.481
9. $5.5819
10. $0.42857
11. $83.3333
12. $159.574468

Applying Accounting Procedures

Exercise 12-1 Preparing a Horizontal Analysis

The following amounts appeared on the comparative balance sheet of the Higgins Heating Company, Inc.

$15,000; 11.54%
($12,900); (9.09%)
$2,100; 0.77%
($4,500); (4.48%)
$6,600; 3.85%
$2,100; 0.77%

	1993	1992
Current Assets	$145,000	$130,000
Property, Plant, and Equipment	129,000	141,900
Total Assets	$274,000	$271,900
Liabilities	$ 96,000	$100,500
Stockholders' Equity	178,000	171,400
Total Liabilities and Stockholders' Equity	$274,000	$271,900

Instructions: Calculate the amount and percentage of increase or decrease for each item. Use the form provided in the working papers. Round percentages to two decimal places.

Exercise 12-2 Preparing a Vertical Analysis

Following are the amounts that appeared on the income statement of Cox Electronics.

100.00%; 100.00%
75.00%; 72.92%
25.00%; 27.08%
17.27%; 17.19%
7.73%; 9.90%
1.93%; 2.47%
5.80%; 7.42%

	1993	1992
Net Sales	$1,100,000	$960,000
Cost of Merchandise Sold	825,000	700,000
Gross Profit on Sales	$ 275,000	$260,000
Operating Expenses	190,000	165,000
Operating Income	$ 85,000	$ 95,000
Income Taxes	21,250	23,750
Net Income	$ 63,750	$ 71,250

Instructions: Prepare a comparative income statement showing vertical analysis. Use the form provided in the working papers, and round all percentages to two decimal places.

Exercise 12-3 Preparing a Common-Size Statement

The following amounts appeared on a comparative income statement for Monroe Craft Centers.

100.00%; 100.00%
56.37%; 57.21%
43.63%; 42.79%
33.30%; 33.93%
10.33%; 8.86%
1.61%; 1.33%
8.71%; 7.54%

	1993	1992
Net Sales	$514,100	$504,300
Cost of Merchandise Sold	289,800	288,500
Gross Profit on Sales	$224,300	$215,800
Operating Expenses	171,200	171,100
Operating Income	$ 53,100	$ 44,700
Income Taxes	8,300	6,700
Net Income	$ 44,800	$ 38,000

Instructions: Prepare a common-size income statement using net sales as the base amount. Round percentages to two decimal places.

Exercise 12-4 Calculating Liquidity Ratios

The following data were taken from the balance sheet of the Gunther Company.

Cash in Bank	$149,000
Marketable Securities	73,000
Accounts Receivable (Net)	480,000
Merchandise Inventory	171,000
Prepaid Expenses	8,000
Accounts Payable	250,000
Notes Payable	25,000
Salaries Payable	5,000

Instructions: Using the preceding information,

$601,000
3.15:1
2.51:1

(1) Determine the company's working capital.
(2) Calculate the current ratio.
(3) Calculate the quick ratio.

Exercise 12-5 Calculating Accounts Receivable Turnover Rates

The following data were taken from the financial statements of the Conner Company.

Accounts Receivable (Net), Jan. 1	$ 150,000
Accounts Receivable (Net), Dec. 31	180,000
Net credit sales	1,200,000

Instructions: Using the preceding information,

7.27
50.21

(1) Calculate the accounts receivable turnover rate.
(2) Determine the number of days it took Conner to collect its accounts receivable.

Exercise 12-6 Calculating Profitability Ratios

The Stockholders' Equity section of the balance sheet for the Hicks Health Services Corporation follows. The beginning stockholders' equity amount was $2,940,000. Net income for the year was $150,000. The current market price of the stock is $63 per share.

Paid-in Capital:	
Common Stock, $50 par (50,000 shares authorized, 40,000 shares issued	$2,000,000
Paid-in Capital in Excess of Par	400,000
Total Paid-in Capital	$2,400,000
Retained Earnings	690,000
Total Stockholders' Equity	$3,090,000

Instructions: Using the preceding information,

4.98% (1) Calculate the return on common stockholders' equity.
$3.75 (2) Calculate the earnings per share.
16.80:1 (3) Determine the price-earnings ratio.

Exercise 12-7 Calculating Financial Strength Ratios

The following data were taken from the financial statements of the Simmons Corporation.

Property, Plant, and Equipment (Net)	$565,000
Current Liabilities	110,000
Long-Term Liabilities	278,000
Stockholders' Equity	422,000
Shares of common stock outstanding	9,500 shares

Instructions: Using the preceding information,

1.09:1 (1) Determine the ratio of stockholders' equity to liabilities.
2.03:1 (2) Determine the ratio of property, plant, and equipment to long-term liabilities.
$44.42 (3) Calculate the equity per share.

SPREADSHEET PROBLEM

Problem 12-1 Preparing a Horizontal Analysis of an Income Statement

A portion of the comparative income statement for Watts House of Sports for the fiscal years ended December 31, 1992 and 1993 appears in Figure 12-3. During 1993, the company held a sales promotion campaign that cost $20,000 more than the store usually spent for advertising.

Watts House of Sports
Comparative Income Statement
For the Years Ended December 31, 1993 and 1992

	1993	1992
Revenue:		
Net Sales	$450,000	$325,000
Cost of Merchandise Sold:		
Merchandise Inventory, Jan. 1	$ 25,000	$ 23,000
Net Purchases	250,000	198,000
Merchandise Available for Sale	$275,000	$221,000
Less: Merchandise Inventory, Dec. 31	34,000	25,000
Cost of Merchandise Sold	$241,000	$196,000
Gross Profit on Sales	$209,000	$129,000
Operating Expenses:		
Selling Expenses	$ 71,100	$ 52,000
Administrative Expenses	24,000	22,000
Total Operating Expenses	95,100	74,000
Operating Income	$113,900	$ 55,000
Other Expenses:		
Interest Expense	1,000	800
Net Income before Income Taxes	$112,900	$ 54,200
Federal Income Taxes	28,225	13,550
Net Income	$ 84,675	$ 40,650

Figure 12-3 Comparative Income Statement for Problem 12-1.

Instructions: Using horizontal analysis, prepare a comparative income statement for the two-year period. Round off percentages to two decimal places. Use the form provided in the working papers.

SPREADSHEET PROBLEM

Problem 12-2 Preparing a Vertical Analysis of a Balance Sheet

The partial comparative balance sheet for Watts House of Sports appears in Figure 12-4.

Watts House of Sports
Comparative Balance Sheet
December 31, 1993 and 1992

	1993	1992
Assets		
Current Assets:		
Cash in Bank	$ 26,000	$100,000
Marketable Securities	76,000	141,000
Accounts Receivable (Net)	74,000	70,000
Merchandise Inventory	34,000	25,000
Prepaid Expenses	6,000	7,000
Total Current Assets	$216,000	$343,000

Property, Plant, and Equipment:		
Equipment (Net)	95,000	90,000
Building (Net)	382,000	100,000
Land	75,000	25,000
Total Property, Plant, and Equipment	$552,000	$215,000
Total Assets	$768,000	$558,000
Liabilities		
Current Liabilities:		
Accounts Payable	$ 45,000	$ 50,000
Salaries Payable	6,000	6,600
Sales Tax Payable	2,200	2,800
Total Current Liabilities	$ 53,200	$ 59,400
Long-Term Liabilities:		
Mortgage Payable	200,000	25,000
Total Liabilities	$253,200	$ 84,400
Stockholders' Equity		
Paid-in Capital:		
Common Stock, $25 Par (20,000 shares authorized, 15,000 shares issued)	$375,000	$375,000
Paid-in Capital in Excess of Par	30,000	30,000
Total Paid-in Capital	$405,000	$405,000
Retained Earnings	109,800	68,600
Total Stockholders' Equity	$514,800	$473,600
Total Liabilities and Stockholders' Equity	$768,000	$558,000

Figure 12-4 Comparative Balance Sheet for Problem 12-2

Instructions: Using vertical analysis, prepare a comparative balance sheet for the two-year period. Round off the percentages to two decimal places. Use the form provided in the working papers.

Problem 12-3 Preparing Comparative Financial Statements

The partially completed comparative financial statements of the Corley Distribution Company, Inc., are included in the working papers.

Instructions: Complete the income statement and the balance sheet using both horizontal analysis and vertical analysis. Use the forms provided in the working papers. Round off all percentages to two decimal places.

COMPUTER PROBLEM

Problem 12-4 Using Ratio Analysis on Financial Statements

You will need the comparative financial statements for the Corley Distribution Company, Inc., that were prepared in Problem 12-3 to complete this problem.

Instructions: Determine the following ratios for Corley Distribution for 1993. If necessary, use a separate sheet of paper for your calculations.

$292,450 **1.** Working capital
9.30:1 **2.** Current ratio

5.78:1 **3.** Quick ratio
3.95 **4.** Merchandise inventory turnover
92 **5.** Number of days merchandise was kept in stock
7.58 **6.** Accounts receivable turnover (net credit sales for 1993 were $625,000)
48 **7.** Number of days receivables were on the books
9.43% **8.** Return on common stockholders' equity
$1.26 **9.** Earnings per share (Corley has issued 30,000 shares of common stock)
12.10:1 **10.** Price-earnings ratio (the present market price of the stock is $15.25 per share)
2.00:1 **11.** Ratio of stockholders' equity to liabilities
1.69:1 **12.** Ratio of property, plant, and equipment to long-term liabilities
$13.67 **13.** Equity per share

CHALLENGE PROBLEM

Problem 12-5 Interpreting Financial Data

Thompson Casuals sells both men's and women's clothing. You are interested in purchasing a large number of shares of the company's stock for investment purposes. To allow you to make a thorough financial analysis of the business, the following information covering the past three years has been supplied.

	1991	1992	1993
Current assets	$600,000	$690,000	$700,000
Total liabilities	$280,000	$290,000	$300,000
Current ratio	5:1	5.4:1	5.9:1
Quick ratio	1.25:1	1.75:1	2:1
Ratio of stockholders' equity to liabilities	4:1	4.25:1	4.5:1

Instructions: Based on this information, answer the following questions. Use plain paper or the form provided in the working papers. Round your answers to the nearest whole dollar.

1. What are the current liabilities for each of the three years?
2. What are the quick assets for each of the three years?
3. What are the long-term liabilities for each of the three years?
4. What is the total stockholders' equity for each of the three years?
(6) $87,288 **5.** What is the working capital for each of the three years?
(7) $101,356 **6.** By what amount did the quick assets increase from 1991 to 1993?
7. By what amount did working capital increase from 1991 to 1993?

FOCUS ON CAREERS

International Accounting: The Best of Many Worlds

More and more accountants are moving into the glamorous—and lucrative—field of international accounting. It's become such an expanded career opportunity because the possibilites in international business are growing so rapidly. Today, many U.S. corporations own companies overseas, and foreign investments in U.S. companies are over $200 billion. Accountants working for these corporations may be preparing financial reports for readers both inside and outside the United States.

You might think that accounting is accounting no matter where you go. That's not the case, however. In Australia, the accounting methods recommended for use tend to significantly overstate earnings. British accounting is flexible: Some companies overstate earnings, while others understate them. British companies also do not defer taxes, whereas U.S. businesses always do so for book versus tax-time differences. German accounting includes hidden cash reserves that are difficult to uncover, making some prosperous companies look poor.

All these differences mean that an accountant trained in methods accepted in the United States must also understand how methods used overseas work, as well as how to "translate" the figures from one country to another.

If international accounting appeals to you, knowing a second, and maybe even a third, language is helpful. It also helps if you like to travel—you could be doing lots of it!

To work with international businesses, an acountant must understand the similarities and differences of accounting procedures in other countries.

Chapter 13

THE STATEMENT OF CASH FLOWS

So far in your study of accounting, you have prepared three financial statements at the end of a fiscal period. The income statement reports the results of a business's operations during a fiscal period. The statement of changes in stockholders' equity reports the changes that have taken place in stockholders' equity during the period. The balance sheet reports the financial position of a business at the end of the fiscal period. None of these financial statements, however, show why and how the cash position of the business changed during the period.

In this chapter, you will learn about a fourth financial statement that shows the sources and uses of cash during the accounting period.

Learning Objectives

When you have completed this chapter, you should be able to do the following:

1. Explain the purpose of the statement of cash flows.
2. Identify the classifications of cash flows reported on the statement of cash flows.
3. Analyze the income statement and balance sheet information needed to prepare the statement of cash flows.
4. Determine cash flows from operating activities using the direct method.
5. Determine cash flows from investing activities.
6. Determine cash flows from financing activities.
7. Prepare a statement of cash flows.
8. Prepare a schedule of noncash investing and financing transactions.
9. Define the accounting terms presented in this chapter.

New Terms

statement of cash flows
cash inflows
cash outflows
cash equivalents
cash flows from operating activities
cash flows from investing activities
cash flows from financing activities
noncash investing and financing transactions

The Statement of Cash Flows

Discuss the purpose of the statement of cash flows.

The **statement of cash flows** is prepared at the end of a fiscal period to show how cash was affected by the business's operating, investing, and financing activities during the accounting period. The statement explains why cash either increased or decreased during the accounting period. Cash flows include both inflows and outflows. **Cash inflows** are cash receipts. **Cash outflows** are cash payments.

Review the accrual basis of accounting and explain why the income statement must be converted from the accrual basis to the cash basis of accounting.

When the accrual basis of accounting is used, revenue is recorded when it is earned and expenses are recorded when they are actually incurred. The income statement reports the revenues and expenses for the accounting period even if cash has not been received from charge customers and payments have not been made to creditors. The amounts on the income statement, therefore, must be converted to cash basis accounting to determine the cash inflows and outflows for the accounting period. These cash inflows and outflows change the balance of the Cash in Bank account. The comparative balance sheet for the current accounting period reports the change in the balance of Cash in Bank, but it does not provide the reasons for the change. These details are reported on the statement of cash flows.

Be sure students understand that both cash and cash equivalents are reported on the statement of cash flows.

Cash reported on the statement of cash flows includes both cash and cash equivalents. **Cash equivalents** as defined by the Financial Accounting Standards Board, are short-term, highly liquid investments. Examples of cash equivalents are U.S. Treasury bills and certificates of deposit. A business invests in cash equivalents to earn interest when it has more cash on hand than it needs to pay current bills.

The statement of cash flows is useful to business managers, investors, and creditors. These individuals use the statement to evaluate the company's ability to pay liabilities and dividends and to determine its need for additional investing and financing.

Discuss and illustrate the kinds of transactions included in each of the three sections of the statement of cash flows.

The Financial Accounting Standards Board requires that the statement of cash flows be divided into sections that will show separately those cash flows related to (1) operating activities, (2) investing activities, and (3) financing activities. Let's look at these three classifications of cash flows.

Cash flows from operating activities include the cash transactions used to determine net income. These transactions are either cash inflows (receipts) or cash outflows (payments). The Johnson Corporation's inflows are cash receipts from sales and interest income. Its outflows are cash payments for purchases of merchandise, operating expenses, interest expense, and federal income tax expense. Interest income and interest expense are listed as other revenue and other expenses on the income statement. The Financial Accounting Standards Board, however, has decided that interest income and interest expense should be classified as cash flows from operating activities.

Cash flows from investing activities include transactions that affect certain asset accounts. These transactions are either cash inflows (receipts) or cash outflows (payments). The Johnson Corporation's inflows are cash receipts from sales of plant assets. Its outflows are cash payments for purchases of marketable securities and plant assets.

Cash flows from financing activities include transactions that affect certain liability and stockholders' equity accounts. These transactions are either cash inflows (receipts) or cash outflows (payments). The Johnson Corporation's inflows are cash receipts from issuing notes payable, bonds payable, and capital stock. Its outflows are cash payments for repaying notes payable, redeeming bonds payable, and paying cash dividends to stockholders.

A business's sources and uses of cash must be recorded for each fiscal period. The statement of cash flows reports a business's operating activities from cash receipts and cash payments for the entire accounting period.

Preparing the Statement of Cash Flows

Point out that the increases or decreases in balance sheet accounts, other than Cash in Bank, are used to determine the effect on cash flows.

The statement of cash flows shown in Figure 13-1 contains five sections: (1) the heading, (2) the cash flows from operating activities, (3) the cash flows for investing activities, (4) the cash flows for financing activities, and (5) the schedule of noncash investing and financing transactions. Much of the information needed to complete the statement of cash flows is taken from the income statement and comparative balance sheet shown in Figures 13-2 and 13-3 on pages 340 and 341. You will be referred to these illustrations as you read the procedures for preparing the statement of cash flows.

ACCOUNTING Notes

Under the Tax Reform Act of 1986, a corporation with over $5 million gross sales must use accrual basis accounting.

Johnson Corporation
Statement of Cash Flows
For the Year Ended December 31, 199-

Cash Flows From Operating Activities		
Cash Receipts From:		
Sales to Customers	$971,000	
Interest Income	6,700	
Total Cash Receipts From Operating Activities		$977,700
Cash Payments for:		
Purchases	$(715,000)	
Operating Expenses	(150,000)	
Interest Expense	(5,700)	
Income Tax Expense	(31,500)	
Total Cash Payments for Operating Activities		(902,200)
Net Cash Flows From Operating Activities		$ 75,500
Cash Flows From Investing Activities		
Purchases of Marketable Securities	$(90,000)	
Purchases of Plant Assets	(50,000)	
Sales of Plant Assets	15,000	
Net Cash Flows From Investing Activities		(125,000)
Cash Flows From Financing Activities		
Cash Receipts From Issuing Notes Payable	$150,000	
Cash Payments of Notes Payable	(200,000)	
Cash Receipts From Issuing Bonds Payable	100,000	
Cash Payments of Bonds Payable	(50,000)	
Cash Receipts From Issuing Capital Stock	125,000	
Cash Payments of Dividends to Stockholders	(20,000)	
Net Cash Flows From Financing Activities		105,000
Net Increase in Cash		$ 55,500

Schedule of Noncash Investing and Financing Transactions	
Issue of Bonds Payable for Plant Assets	$200,000

Figure 13-1 Statement of Cash Flows

The Heading

The statement of cash flows reports the activities for the entire accounting period. The Johnson Corporation's accounting period is one year. The date for the statement of cash flows, therefore, is written "For the Year Ended December 31, 199-."

The Cash Flows From Operating Activities Section

Review why the income statement must be converted from the accrual basis to the cash basis of accounting.

The cash flows from operating activities section is divided into two parts: (1) cash receipts and (2) cash payments. The Johnson Corporation uses the direct method to convert the income statement from the accrual basis to the cash basis. The specific cash receipts and cash payments are listed separately. Then the amount of net cash flows from operating activities is calculated. Look at Figure 13-1 to review the cash inflows and outflows that are included in this section. Notice that parentheses are placed around amounts that represent cash outflows.

Explain the transactions that directly increase cash flows and those that result in a delay in recognizing cash inflows and outflows.

Cash Receipts From Sales to Customers The amount of net sales reported on the income statement represents income from both cash sales and sales on account. Cash sales directly increase cash flows during the accounting period because Cash in Bank is debited immediately for the amount of the sale. Sales on account, however, are debited to Accounts Receivable at the time of the sale. Cash in Bank is not debited until cash is received on account, which may or may not occur during the same accounting period as the sale. The net sales amount on the income statement and the change in the Accounts Receivable account on the balance sheet, therefore, are used to calculate cash inflows from cash receipts from sales to customers.

If the balance of Accounts Receivable decreases, cash receipts from sales to customers are greater than the net sales reported on the income statement. This is so because cash receipts on account are greater than sales on account during the accounting period.

Illustrate how the change in the balance of the Accounts Receivable account affects the cash receipts from sales to customers.

On the income statement in Figure 13-2, the amount of net sales is $964,000. On the balance sheet in Figure 13-3, the balance of Accounts Receivable decreased by $7,000. The activity in the Accounts Receivable account that caused this decrease is shown in the following T account. The account balance decreased from $59,000 to $52,000 during the year. The amount of cash receipts on account is $7,000 more than the amount of sales on account.

Accounts Receivable

Debit	Credit
Bal. $59,000	Rec. $515,000
Sales 508,000	
Bal. 52,000	

Johnson Corporation
Income Statement
For the Year Ended December 31, 199-

Net Sales			$964,000
Cost of Merchandise Sold			700,000
Gross Profit on Sales			$264,000
Operating Expenses (includes Depreciation of $42,000)			204,000
Operating Income			$ 60,000
Other Revenue:			
Gain on Sale of Plant Assets	$3,000		
Interest Income	8,000		
Total Other Revenue		$11,000	
Other Expenses:			
Interest Expense		5,200	
Net Addition			5,800
Net Income before Income Tax			$ 65,800
Federal Income Tax			29,800
Net Income			$ 36,000

Figure 13-2 Abbreviated Income Statement

Johnson Corporation
Comparative Balance Sheet
December 31, 1993 and 1992

	1993	1992	Increase (Decrease)
Assets			
Current Assets:			
Cash in Bank	$ 218,300	$ 162,800	$ 55,500
Marketable Securities	250,000	160,000	90,000
Interest Receivable	6,300	5,000	1,300
Accounts Receivable (net)	52,000	59,000	(7,000)
Merchandise Inventory	160,000	135,000	25,000
Prepaid Expenses	6,000	5,000	1,000
Total Current Assets	$ 692,600	$ 526,800	$165,800
Plant Assets:			
Plant Assets	$1,005,000	$ 775,000	$230,000
Less: Accumulated Depreciation	132,000	98,000	34,000
Total Plant Assets	$ 873,000	$ 677,000	$196,000
Total Assets	$1,565,600	$1,203,800	$361,800
Liabilities			
Current Liabilities:			
Notes Payable	$ 125,000	$ 175,000	$ (50,000)
Accounts Payable	80,000	70,000	10,000
Accrued Liabilities	39,300	26,300	13,000
Interest Payable	2,000	2,500	(500)
Federal Income Tax Payable	5,300	7,000	(1,700)
Total Current Liabilities	$ 251,600	$ 280,800	$ (29,200)
Long-Term Liabilities:			
Bonds Payable	500,000	250,000	250,000
Total Liabilities	$ 751,600	$ 530,800	$220,800
Stockholders' Equity			
Capital Stock, $100 Par	$ 600,000	$ 500,000	$100,000
Paid-in Capital in Excess of Par	100,000	75,000	25,000
Retained Earnings	114,000	98,000	16,000
Total Stockholders' Equity	$ 814,000	$ 673,000	$141,000
Total Liabilities and Stockholders' Equity	$1,565,600	$1,203,800	$361,800

Figure 13-3 Comparative Balance Sheet

When the balance of Accounts Receivable decreases, cash receipts from sales to customers are calculated as shown on next page.

Net Sales (from income statement)	$964,000
+ Decrease in Accounts Receivable (from balance sheet)	+ 7,000
Cash receipts from sales to customers	$971,000

Use demonstration problem 13-1 here.

If the balance of Accounts Receivable increases, cash receipts from sales to customers are less than the net sales amount reported on the income statement. This is because cash receipts on account are less than sales on account during the year. When the balance of Accounts Receivable increases, cash receipts from sales to customers are calculated as follows:

You may want to have students complete Exercise 13-1 at this point.

Net Sales (from income statement)
− Increase in Accounts Receivable (from balance sheet)
Cash receipts from sales to customers

Cash Receipts from Interest Income The amount of interest income reported on the income statement represents both cash receipts of interest and accrued interest. The accrued interest has been earned but not yet received. Cash in Bank is not debited until cash for the interest is received. The interest income amount on the income statement and the change in the Interest Receivable account on the balance sheet, therefore, are used to calculate cash inflows from cash receipts from interest income.

Illustrate how the change in the balance of the Interest Receivable account affects the cash receipts from interest income.

If the balance of Interest Receivable increases, cash receipts from interest income are less than the interest income reported on the income statement. On the income statement in Figure 13-2, the amount of interest income is $8,000. On the balance sheet in Figure 13-3, the balance of Interest Receivable increased by $1,300. When the balance of Interest Receivable increases, cash receipts from interest income are calculated as follows:

Interest Income (from income statement)	$8,000
Increase in Interest Receivable (from balance sheet)	−1,300
Cash receipts from interest income	$6,700

Use demonstration problem 13-2 here.

If the balance of Interest Receivable decreases, cash receipts from interest income are greater than the interest income reported on the income statement. When the balance of Interest Receivable decreases, cash receipts from interest income are calculated as follows:

Interest Income (from income statement)
+ Decrease in Interest Receivable (from balance sheet)
Cash receipts from interest income

Before reading further, do the following activity to check your understanding of how to calculate cash receipts from sales to customers and cash receipts from interest income.

Check Your Learning

Write your answers to these questions on a sheet of notebook paper. Indicate whether cash flows increase or decrease.

1. What is the amount of cash receipts from sales to customers if the income statement reports net sales of $200,000 and Accounts Receivable on the balance sheet increased $25,000 during the current year?
2. What is the amount of cash receipts from sales to customers if the income statement reports net sales of $245,000 and Accounts Receivable on the balance sheet decreased $4,000 during the current year?
3. What is the amount of cash receipts from interest income if the income statement reports interest income of $4,500 and Interest Receivable on the balance sheet decreased $300 during the current year?
4. What is the amount of cash receipts from interest income if the income statement reports interest income of $6,200 and Interest Receivable on the balance sheet increased $700 during the current year?

You may want to have students complete Exercise 13-2 at this point.

Compare your answers to those in the answers section. Reread the preceding part of the chapter to find the correct answers to any questions you may have missed.

Emphasize the two-step procedure.

Cash Payments for Purchases The cost of merchandise sold amount reported on the income statement and the changes in the Merchandise Inventory and Accounts Payable accounts on the balance sheet are used to calculate cash flows from cash payments for purchases. Let's look at the two steps used to compute this amount.

Step 1: Determine the cost of net purchases. If the balance of Merchandise Inventory increases, the cost of net purchases is greater than the cost of merchandise sold reported on the income statement. This is so because more merchandise is bought than is sold during the year.

Illustrate the effects that increases and decreases in merchandise inventory have on the cost of net purchases. Be sure students understand the *why* behind each illustration.

On the income statement in Figure 13-2, the amount of cost of merchandise sold is $700,000. On the balance sheet in Figure 13-3, the balance of Merchandise Inventory increased by $25,000. When the balance of Merchandise Inventory increases, the cost of net purchases is calculated as follows:

Cost of Merchandise Sold (from income statement)	$700,000
+ Increase in Merchandise Inventory (from balance sheet)	+ 25,000
Cost of net purchases	$725,000

If the balance of Merchandise Inventory decreases, the cost of net purchases is less than the cost of merchandise sold reported on the income statement. This is because more merchandise is sold than is bought during the year. When the balance of Merchandise Inventory decreases, the cost of net purchases is calculated as follows:

Cost of Merchandise Sold (from income statement)
− Decrease in Merchandise Inventory (from balance sheet)
Cost of net purchases

Step 2: Determine the relationship between the cost of net purchases and the change in the balance of the Accounts Payable **account.** During the accounting period, purchases of merchandise can be made either for cash or on account. Purchases of merchandise for cash directly decrease cash flows because Cash in Bank is credited immediately for the amount of the purchase. Purchases of merchandise on account, however, are credited to Accounts Payable at the time of the purchase. Cash in Bank is not credited until a payment is made on account, which may or may not occur during the same accounting period as the purchase. The cost of net purchases and the change in the balance of Accounts Payable, therefore, are used to calculate the cash outflows from cash payments for purchases made during the accounting period.

Illustrate how the change in the balance of the Accounts Payable account affects the cash payments for purchases.

If the balance of Accounts Payable increases, cash payments for purchases are less than the cost of net purchases. This is so because cash payments on account are less than the purchases on account during the accounting period. On the balance sheet in Figure 13-3, the balance of Accounts Payable increased by $10,000. The activity that caused this increase is shown in the following T account:

Accounts Payable

Dr.	Cr.
Pay. $715,000	Bal. $70,000
	Pur. 725,000
	Bal. 80,000

When the balance of Accounts Payable increases, cash payments for purchases are calculated as follows:

Cost of net purchases	$725,000
− Increase in Accounts Payable (from balance sheet)	− 10,000
Cash payments for purchases	$715,000

Use demonstration problem 13-3 here.

If the balance of Accounts Payable decreases, cash payments for purchases are greater than the cost of net purchases. This is because cash payments on account are greater than purchases on account during the accounting period. When the balance of Accounts Payable decreases, cash payments for purchases are calculated as follows:

Cost of net purchases
+ Decrease in Accounts Payable (from balance sheet)
Cash payments for purchases

R — E — M — E — M — B — E — R

Two steps are used to calculate cash flows from cash payments for purchases:

1. Cost of Merchandise Sold	+ -	**Increase in Merchandise Inventory** **or** **Decrease in Merchandise Inventory**	=	**Cost of net purchases**
2. Cost of net purchases	+ -	**Decreases in Accounts Payable** **or** **Increase in Accounts Payable**	=	**Cash payments for purchases**

Before reading further, do the following activity to check your understanding of how to calculate cash payments for purchases.

Check Your Learning

Write your answers to these questions on a sheet of notebook paper. Indicate whether cash flows increase or decrease.

1. What is the cost of net purchases if the income statement reports cost of merchandise sold as $600,000 and Merchandise Inventory on the balance sheet increased $70,000 during the current year?
2. What is the cost of net purchases if the income statement reports cost of merchandise sold as $600,000 and Merchandise Inventory on the balance sheet decreased $40,000 during the current year?
3. What is the amount of cash payments for purchases if the cost of net purchases is $248,000 and Accounts Payable on the balance sheet decreased $7,000 during the current year?
4. What is the amount of cash payments for purchases if the cost of net purchases is $390,000 and Accounts Payable on the balance sheet increased $20,000 during the current year?
5. What is the amount of cash payments for purchases if the income statement reports cost of merchandise sold as $790,000, Merchandise Inventory on the balance sheet decreased $28,000, and Accounts Payable on the balance sheet decreased $40,000 during the current year?

You may want to have students complete Exercise 13-3 at this point.

Compare your answers to those in the answers section. Reread the preceding part of the chapter to find the correct answers to any questions you may have missed.

Cash Payments for Operating Expenses Operating expenses on the income statement represent the cash spent or assets consumed to earn revenue during the accounting period. The amount of cash paid for operating expenses during the accounting period will not equal the operating expenses reported on the income statement if there are pre-

Emphasize the three-step procedure.

paid expenses, accrued liabilities, and depreciation expenses. Let's look at three steps used to compute cash payments for operating expenses.

Step 1: Determine cash flows for prepaid expenses. A *prepaid expense* is an expense paid in advance and usually recorded initially as an asset. An example is prepaid insurance. The initial transaction is recorded as a debit to Prepaid Expenses and a credit to Cash in Bank. The transaction directly affects cash flows. Only the portion of the asset used up during the accounting period is an expense for that period. The amount of operating expenses reported on the income statement, therefore, may not include all cash payments for prepaid expenses.

Illustrate how the change in the Prepaid Expense account balance affects the cash flows for operating expenses.

If the balance of Prepaid Expenses increases, cash payments for operating expenses are greater than the amount of operating expenses reported on the income statement. On the income statement in Figure 13-2, the amount of operating expenses is $204,000. On the balance sheet in Figure 13-3, the balance of Prepaid Expenses increased by $1,000. When the balance of Prepaid Expenses increases, operating expenses after cash flows for prepaid expenses are calculated as follows:

Operating Expenses (from income statement)	$204,000
+ Increase in Prepaid Expenses (from balance sheet)	+ 1,000
Operating expenses after cash flows for prepaid expenses	$205,000

You may want to break demonstration problem 13-4 into three sections and use the cash flows for prepaid expenses section here.

If the balance of Prepaid Expenses decreases, cash payments for operating expenses are less than the amount of operating expenses reported on the income statement. When the balance of Prepaid Expenses decreases, operating expenses after cash flows for prepaid expenses are calculated as follows:

Operating Expenses (from income statement)
– Decrease in Prepaid Expenses (from balance sheet)
Operating expenses after cash flows for prepaid expenses

Step 2: Determine cash flows for accrued liabilities. Expenses that build up daily but are not recorded until the end of the fiscal period are accrued expenses. An example is salaries earned by employees but not yet paid to them. The adjusting entry for an accrued expense is recorded as a debit to the expense account and a credit to the related accrued liability account, such as Salaries Payable. Cash flows are not affected until the salaries are actually paid.

Illustrate how the change in the Accrued Liabilities account balance affects the cash flows for operating expenses.

If the balance of Accrued Liabilities increases, cash payments for operating expenses are less than the amount of operating expenses reported on the income statement. This is because the actual cash payment for this expense will not occur during the current accounting period. On the balance sheet in Figure 13-3, Accrued Liabilities increased by $13,000. When the balance of Accrued Liabilities increases, operating expenses after cash flows for accrued liabilities are calculated as follows:

Operating expenses after cash flows for prepaid expenses	$205,000
– Increase in Accrued Liabilities (from balance sheet)	– 13,000
Operating expenses after cash flows for accrued liabilities	$192,000

You may wish to have students complete the cash flow for accrued liabilities section of demonstration problem 13-4 here.

If the balance of Accrued Liabilities decreases, cash payments for operating expenses are greater than the amount of operating expenses reported on the income statement. When the balance of Accrued Liabilities decreases, operating expenses after cash flows for accrued liabilities are calculated as follows:

Operating expenses after cash flows for prepaid expenses
\+ Decrease in Accrued Liabilities (from balance sheet)
Operating expenses after cash flows for accrued liabilities

Point out why depreciation expense requires no cash payment.

Complete demonstration problem 13-4 here.

Step 3: Determine cash flows for operating expenses that include depreciation expenses. Depreciation is an expense for which there is no cash payment. When depreciation is recorded, a depreciation expense account is debited and an accumulated depreciation account is credited. Cash flows are not affected by this transaction. Cash payments for operating expenses, therefore, are less than the amount of operating expenses reported on the income statement if there are depreciation expenses. The income statement in Figure 13-2 indicates that the Johnson Corporation recorded $42,000 of depreciation expenses during the current accounting period. The final step in calculating cash payments for operating expenses is to subtract the amount of depreciation expenses, as follows:

Operating expenses after cash flows for accrued liabilities	$192,000
– Depreciation Expenses	– 42,000
Cash payments for operating expenses	$150,000

R — E — M — E — M — B — E — R

Three steps are used to calculate cash flows for operating expenses:

	1.	2.	3.	
Operating Expenses	**+ Increase in Prepaid Expenses** or **– Decrease in Prepaid Expenses**	**+ Decrease in Accrued Liabilities** or **– Increase in Accrued Liabilities**	**– Depreciation Expenses**	**= Cash Payments for Operatings Expenses**

You may want to have students complete Exercise 13-4 at this point.

Cash Payments for Interest Expense Interest incurred for unpaid notes is an accrued expense. Cash payments for the interest are not made until the maturity date of the note. Cash flows are not affected until the cash payment occurs. When the adjusting entry for the accrued expense is recorded, Interest Expense is debited and the related liability account Interest Payable is credited.

Illustrate how the change in the Interest Payable account balance affects the cash payments for interest expense.

If the balance of Interest Payable decreases, cash payments for interest expense are greater than the amount of interest expense reported on the income statement. On the income statement in Figure 13-2, the amount of interest expense is $5,200. On the balance sheet in Figure 13-3, the balance of Interest Payable decreased by $500. When the balance of Interest Payable decreases, cash payments for interest expense are calculated as follows:

Interest Expense (from income statement)	$5,200
+ Decrease in Interest Payable (from balance sheet)	+ 500
Cash payments for interest expense	$5,700

Use Instruction 1 of demonstration problem 13-5 here.

If the balance of Interest Payable increases, cash payments for interest expense are less than the amount of interest expense reported on the income statement. When the balance of Interest Payable increases, cash payments for interest expense are calculated as follows:

Interest Expense (from income statement)
− Increase in Interest Payable (from balance sheet)
Cash payments for interest expense

Cash Payments for Income Tax Expense The amount of income tax expense reported on the income statement seldom equals the amount of income tax actually paid during the year. One reason for the difference is that the final payment of the income tax for the current year is not due until the following year.

Illustrate how the change in the liability account Federal Income Tax Payable affects the cash flow.

If the balance of Federal Income Tax Payable decreases, cash payments for income tax expense are greater than the amount of income tax reported on the income statement. In Figure 13-2, the amount of federal income tax is $29,800. In Figure 13-3, the balance of Federal Income Tax Payable decreased by $1,700. When the balance of Federal Income Tax Payable decreases, cash payments for income tax expense are calculated as follows:

Federal Income Tax (from income statement)	$29,800
+ Decrease in Federal Income Tax Payable (from balance sheet)	+ 1,700
Cash payments for income tax expense	$31,500

If the balance of Federal Income Tax Payable increases, cash payments for income tax expense are less than the amount of income tax reported

Use Instruction 2 of demonstration problem 13-5 here.

on the income statement. When the balance of Federal Income Tax Payable increases, cash payments for income tax expense are calculated as follows:

Federal Income Tax (from income statement)
– Increase in Federal Income Tax Payable (from balance sheet)
Cash payments for income tax expense

Before reading further, do the following activity to check your understanding of how to calculate cash payments for operating expenses, interest expense, and income tax expense.

Check Your Learning

Write your answers to these questions on a sheet of notebook paper. Indicate whether cash flows increase or decrease.

1. What is the amount of cash payments for operating expenses if the income statement reports operating expenses of $200,000, Prepaid Expenses on the balance sheet decreased $1,500, Accrued Liabilities increased $15,000, and the amount of Depreciation Expenses reported was $18,000?
2. What is the amount of cash payments for interest expense if the income statement reports interest expense of $3,200 and Interest Payable decreased $400?
3. What is the amount of cash payments from income tax expense if the income statement reports income tax expense of $10,490 and Federal Income Tax Payable increased $720?

You may want to have students complete Exercise 13-5 at this point.

Compare your answers to those in the answers section. Reread the preceding part of the chapter to find the correct answers to any questions you may have missed.

The Cash Flows From Investing Activities Section

Identify the general ledger accounts that are used to determine the cash flows from investing activities.

The cash flows from investing activities section of the statement of cash flows reports changes that occur in long-lived asset accounts and short-term investment accounts during the accounting period. As you learned earlier, long-lived assets are called *plant assets* and short-term investments are called *marketable securities.*

Point out that purchases of marketable securities are cash outflows.

Purchases of Marketable Securities When marketable securities are purchased, the Marketable Securities account is debited and the Cash in Bank account is credited. This transaction directly affects the cash flows. During the current accounting period, the Johnson Corpora-

Explain that changes in cash flows in this section are reported separately to give complete information.

tion purchased marketable securities for $90,000. The increase in the balance of the Marketable Securities account created by this purchase appears on the balance sheet in Figure 13-3.

Look at the cash flows from investing activities section of the statement of cash flows in Figure 13-1. In this section of the statement, changes in cash flows are listed separately to give complete information. Since net amounts are not calculated, parentheses are placed around amounts that are cash outflows. Purchases of marketable securities are outflows. The $90,000, therefore, is placed in parentheses.

Discuss how the purchase of a plant asset for cash affects the cash flow.

Purchases and Sales of Plant Assets When a plant asset is purchased for cash, the Plant Assets account is debited and the Cash in Bank account is credited. This transaction directly affects the cash flows. During the current accounting period, the Johnson Corporation purchased plant assets for $50,000 cash.

When a plant asset is sold (disposed of) for cash, the Cash in Bank account is debited for the amount of cash receipts for the sale. This transaction directly affects the cash flows. The following additional accounts are affected by sales of plant assets transactions: Accumulated Depreciation, Plant Assets, and Gain (or Loss) on Sale of Plant Assets. Let's look at an example of a sale of a plant asset for cash transaction.

During the current year, the Johnson Corporation sold a plant asset for $15,000 cash. The plant asset originally cost $20,000 and had accumulated depreciation of $8,000. This transaction resulted in a gain on the sale. The following T accounts show the transaction:

Cash in Bank

Dr.	Cr.
$15,000	

Accumulated Depreciation—

Dr.	Cr.
$8,000	

Plant Assets

Dr.	Cr.
	$20,000

Gain on Sale of Plant Assets

Dr.	Cr.
	$3,000

Discuss why the gain (or loss) on the sale of a plant asset is not reported on the statement of cash flows.

The gain (or loss) on the sale of plant assets is determined by the amount of cash received at the time of the sale. The gain (or loss) on the sale of plant assets does not affect cash flows. Therefore, the gain on sale of plant assets amount reported on the income statement in Figure 13-2 is not included on the statement of cash flows.

The Johnson Corporation's purchases and sales of plant assets are listed separately on the statement of cash flows as shown in Figure 13-1.

Use demonstration problem 13-6 here.

Before reading further, do the following activity to check your understanding of how to prepare the cash flows from investing activities section of the statement of cash flows.

Check Your Learning

Write the answers to these questions on a sheet of notebook paper.

1. If marketable securities are purchased for $50,000 cash, do cash flows increase or decrease?
2. A plant asset that was sold for $21,000 cash originally cost $40,000 and had accumulated depreciation of $24,000. The gain on the sale was $5,000. Which amounts affect cash flows and are reported on the statement of cash flows?
3. If a plant asset is purchased for $70,000 cash, do cash flows increase or decrease?
4. Why are parentheses placed around some of the amounts listed in the cash flows from investing activities section of the statement of cash flows?

Compare your answers to those in the answers section. Reread the preceding part of the chapter to find the correct answers to any questions you may have missed.

You may want to have students complete Exercise 13-6 at this point.

The Cash Flows From Financing Activities Section

Identify the general ledger accounts that are used to determine cash flows from financing activities.

The cash flows from financing activities section reports the inflows and outflows that change the balances of the short-term liability account Notes Payable, the long-term liability account Bonds Payable, and the stockholders' equity accounts. Notes payable issued to replace accounts payable are considered operating activities and are not included in the financing activities section.

Illustrate the cash outflows and inflows from notes payable transactions.

Note that the cash payment for interest expense is reported in the operating activities section.

Cash Flows From Short-Term Borrowing A business may borrow cash by issuing a short-term note payable to a bank. Cash in Bank is debited and Notes Payable is credited for the amount borrowed. This transaction directly affects the cash flows. When it is time to repay the amount borrowed, Cash in Bank is credited and Notes Payable is debited. This transaction also directly affects the cash flows.

The Notes Payable account is analyzed to determine which cash inflows and outflows affected this account during the accounting period. The effects of the Johnson Corporation's short-term borrowing transactions are shown in the T account that follows. The $150,000 credit represents a cash inflow, because cash was received when the note was issued. The $200,000 debit represents a cash outflow, because cash was used to repay the note.

Notes Payable	
Dr.	Cr.
Pay. $200,000	Bal. $175,000
	Issue 150,000
	Bal. 125,000

Look at the cash flows from financing activities section of the statement of cash flows in Figure 13-1 on page 339. In this section, changes in cash flows are listed separately to give complete information. Since net amounts are not calculated, parentheses are placed around amounts that are cash outflows.

Ask students to determine whether issuing bonds and then redeeming bonds are cash inflows or outflows.

Cash Flows From Long-Term Borrowing A company may borrow cash over a long period of time and issue bonds. When bonds are issued, Cash in Bank is debited for the amount of cash received and Bonds Payable is credited. Issuing bonds for cash directly affects cash flows. When the business buys back (redeems) the bonds at a later time, Cash in Bank is credited for the amount of cash paid out and Bonds Payable is debited. Redeeming bonds directly affects cash flows.

The Bonds Payable account is analyzed to determine the effects of cash flows during the accounting period. The Johnson Corporation's Bonds Payable account appears in the following T account. The $100,000 credit represents a cash inflow, because cash was received when the bonds were issued. The $200,000 credit was recorded when bonds were issued to acquire a plant asset without paying cash. This noncash transaction will be discussed later in the chapter. The $50,000 debit represents a cash outflow, because cash was paid to redeem the bonds. The $100,000 cash inflow and the $50,000 cash outflow are reported separately on the statement of cash flows in Figure 13-1 on page 339.

Review why the cash payment for interest expense is reported in the operating activities section.

Bonds Payable	
Dr.	Cr.
Redeem $50,000	Bal. $250,000
	Cash
	Issue 100,000
	Noncash
	Issue 200,000
	Bal. 500,000

Cash Receipts From Issuing Capital Stock A corporation may issue capital stock to increase cash flows during the accounting period. When stock is sold at a price above its par value, the Cash in Bank account is debited for the amount of cash received, the Capital Stock account is credited for the total par value, and the Paid-in Capital in Excess of Par account is credited for the excess.

The Capital Stock and Paid-in Capital in Excess of Par accounts are analyzed to determine the cash inflows during the accounting period. The Johnson Corporation's Capital Stock and Paid-in Capital in Excess of Par accounts are shown in the T accounts that follow. Capital Stock was credited for $100,000 and Paid-in Capital in Excess of Par was credited for $25,000, for a total credit of $125,000. This $125,000 represents the cash inflow that occurred when the Johnson Corporation issued 1,000 shares of $100-par capital stock at $125. The $125,000 cash inflow is reported on the statement of cash flows in Figure 13-1.

Identify the two general ledger accounts that are analyzed to determine the cash flows from issuing capital stock.

Point out that the excess is a cash inflow.

Capital Stock

Dr.	Cr.
	Bal. $500,000
	Issue 100,000
	Bal. 600,000

Paid-in Capital in Excess of Par

Dr.	Cr.
	Bal. $75,000
	Issue 25,000
	Bal. 100,000

Cash Dividend Payments to Stockholders A corporation usually declares and pays a cash dividend to stockholders during a fiscal period. When a cash dividend is declared, the Dividends account is debited and the Dividends Payable account is credited. When a cash dividend is paid, the Dividends Payable account is debited and the Cash in Bank account is credited. A cash outflow occurs when the dividend is actually paid.

Review the entries to record the declaration and payment of a dividend.

At the end of the year, the Dividends account is closed to the Retained Earnings account. The Retained Earnings and Dividends Payable accounts, therefore, are analyzed to determine the cash outflows during the year. The Johnson Corporation's Retained Earnings and Dividends Payable accounts appear in the T accounts that follow. The Johnson Corporation's board of directors declared a $20,000 cash dividend that was later paid to the stockholders. The $20,000 cash outflow is reported on the statement of cash flows in Figure 13-1.

Remind students that a cash outflow occurs when a cash dividend is actually paid, not when the dividend is declared.

Retained Earnings

Dr.	Cr.
Dividend Decl. $20,000	Bal. $98,000
	Net Income 36,000
	Bal. 114,000

Dividends Payable

Dr.	Cr.
Dividend Paid $20,000	Dividend Decl. $20,000

Use demonstration problem 13-7 here.

Before reading further, do the following activity to check your understanding of how to prepare the cash flows from financing activities section of the statement of cash flows.

Check Your Learning

Write your answers to these questions on a sheet of notebook paper.

1. If a company borrows $75,000 cash by issuing a short-term note payable, do cash flows increase or decrease?
2. If a company redeems bonds for $60,000, do cash flows increase or decrease?
3. A corporation issues 1,000 shares of $125-par capital stock at $150. What amounts affect cash flows? Is each amount a cash inflow or a cash outflow?
4. If a corporation declares a cash dividend, does the transaction affect cash flows?

Compare your answers to those in the answers section. Reread the preceding part of the chapter to find the correct answers to any questions you may have missed.

You may want to have students complete Exercise 13-7 at this point.

The Schedule of Noncash Investing and Financing Transactions

Noncash investing and financing transactions involve long-lived assets, long-term liabilities, or capital stock. Noncash investing and financing transactions do not involve cash. Earlier you read about the noncash transaction recorded by the Johnson Corporation to issue bonds payable (long-term liabilities) for plant assets (long-lived assets). Since noncash transactions do not affect cash flows for the current accounting period, they are not included in the statement of cash flows. Noncash investing and financing transactions, however, will affect future cash flows. The Financial Accounting Standards Board decided, therefore, that a separate schedule of these noncash activities must be prepared.

Emphasize how this transaction will affect the cash flow during future accounting periods.

Look at the schedule of noncash investing and financing transactions that appears at the bottom of the statement of cash flows in Figure 13-1 on page 339. The schedule reports the Johnson Corporation's noncash transaction to issue $200,000 of bonds payable for plant assets.

Use demonstration problem 13-8 here.

Summary of Key Points

1. The statement of cash flows explains the increase or decrease in cash from one accounting period to the next by showing cash inflows and

cash outflows from operating activities, investing activities, and financing activities.

2. The statement of cash flows provides information about a business's cash receipts and cash payments during an accounting period.
3. The statement of cash flows is useful to business managers as well as to investors and creditors. These individuals use the statement to evaluate the company's ability to pay liabilities and dividends and to determine the company's need for additional investing and financing.
4. Income statement and balance sheet accounts must be analyzed to determine cash inflows and cash outflows.
5. When the accrual basis of accounting is used, amounts on the income statement must be converted to cash basis accounting. When the direct method is used for this conversion, each cash receipt and cash payment is listed separately in the cash flows from operating activities section. Then the amount of net cash flows from operating activities is calculated.
6. To determine the cash flows from investing activities that affect long-lived assets and short-term investments, the Marketable Securities and Plant Assets accounts are analyzed.
7. To determine the cash flows from financing activities, the Notes Payable, Bonds Payable, Capital Stock, Paid-in Capital in Excess of Par, Retained Earnings, and Dividends Payable accounts are analyzed.
8. Noncash investing and financing transactions involving long-lived assets, long-term liabilities, or capital stock are analyzed and reported separately on the statement of cash flows.

13 Review and Applications

Building Your Accounting Vocabulary

In your own words, write the definition of each of the following terms. Use complete sentences for your definitions.

cash equivalents
cash flows from financing activities
cash flows from investing activities
cash flows from operating activities
cash inflows
cash outflows
noncash investing and financing transactions
statement of cash flows

Reviewing Your Accounting Knowledge

1. What is the reason for preparing a statement of cash flows?
2. How is a statement of cash flows useful to business managers, investors, and creditors?
3. What are the three classifications of cash flows reported on a statement of cash flows?
4. What are the principal cash inflows and outflows for the operating activities section of the statement of cash flows?
5. Which financial statements provide information needed to prepare a statement of cash flows?
6. Why are cash receipts from sales to customers greater than the net sales reported on the income statement if the balance of Accounts Receivable decreases?
7. Which balance sheet account is used to determine cash receipts from interest income?
8. Which two balance sheet accounts are used to determine cash payments from purchases?
9. Why does depreciation expense reduce the cash flows for operating expenses?
10. Why is a gain on the sale of a plant asset not included on the statement of cash flows?
11. Which account is analyzed to determine cash flows from long-term borrowing?
12. Why did the Financial Accounting Standards Board decide that a separate schedule of noncash investing and financing transactions must be prepared?

Improving Your Decision-Making Skills

You are attending a training program with several people from your department to learn procedures for your company's new integrated computer system. You suddenly find that you do not understand what you are to do and why. Everyone else, however, seems to understand what the instructor is saying. In fact, practically no one is asking questions. What should you do? Give the reasons for your answer.

Applying Accounting Procedures

Exercise 13-1 Determining Cash Receipts from Sales to Customers

The Barnes Company's income statement reported net sales of $500,000 for the accounting period.

Instructions:

$525,000 **(1)** Determine the cash receipts from sales to customers if the balance of Accounts Receivable decreased $25,000 during the accounting period.

$484,000 **(2)** Determine the cash receipts from sales to customers if the balance of Accounts Receivable increased $16,000 during the accounting period.

Exercise 13-2 Determining Cash Receipts from Interest Income

The Fox Corporation's income statement reported interest income of $1,400 for the accounting period.

Instructions:

$1,200 **(1)** Determine the cash receipts from interest income if the balance of Interest Receivable increased $200 during the accounting period.

$1,650 **(2)** Determine the cash receipts from interest income if the balance of Interest Receivable decreased $250 during the accounting period.

Exercise 13-3 Determining Cash Payments for Purchases

Haywood Engineering's income statement reported cost of merchandise sold of $2,190,000 during the accounting period.

Instructions:

$2,110,000 **(1)** Determine the cash payments for purchases if the balance of Merchandise Inventory decreased $50,000 and the balance of Accounts Payable increased $30,000 during the accounting period.

$2,305,000 **(2)** Determine the amount of cash payments for purchases if the balance of Merchandise Inventory increased $70,000 and the balance of Accounts Payable decreased $45,000 during the accounting period.

Exercise 13-4 Determining Cash Payments for Operating Expenses

The income statement of Bonnette Information Services reported operating expenses of $170,900 for the accounting period.

$150,800 **Instructions:** Determine the cash payments for operating expenses if the balance of Prepaid Expenses increased $300, the balance of Accrued Liabilities increased $400, and there was $20,000 in depreciation during the accounting period.

Exercise 13-5 Determining Cash Payments for Interest Expense and Income Tax Expense

The income statement of Watts Accounting Services reported interest expense of $14,600 and federal income tax of $19,890 for the accounting period.

Instructions:

$14,900 **(1)** Determine the cash payments for interest expense if Interest Payable on the balance sheet decreased $300 during the accounting period.

$20,790 **(2)** Determine the cash payments for income tax expense if Federal Income Tax Payable on the balance sheet decreased $900 during the accounting period.

Exercise 13-6 Determining Cash Flows from Investing Activities

During the accounting period, the Monica Noland Clinic purchased marketable securities for $75,000. The clinic also purchased plant assets for $100,000 cash. Plant assets that originally cost $60,000 and had accumulated depreciation of $55,000 were sold for $7,000 cash.

Instructions: Determine the following amounts that should appear in the statement of cash flows. Place parentheses around dollar amounts that represent cash outflows.

($75,000) **1.** Purchases of marketable securities
($100,000) **2.** Purchases of plant assets
$7,000 **3.** Sales of plant assets
($168,000) **4.** Net cash flows from investing activities

Exercise 13-7 Determining Cash Flows from Financing Activities

At the end of the accounting period, some of the balance sheet accounts for Moore's House of Clothing, Inc., appear as shown in the T accounts that follow.

The company also declared and paid a cash dividend of $24,000 during the accounting period.

Notes Payable	
Dr.	Cr.
Pay. $25,000	Bal. $70,000
	Issue 10,000
	Bal. 55,000

Bonds Payable	
Dr.	Cr.
Pay. $75,000	Bal. $200,000
	Issue 50,000
	Bal. 175,000

Capital Stock	
Dr.	Cr.
	Bal. $800,000
	Issue 100,000
	Bal. 900,000

Paid-in Capital in Excess of Par	
Dr.	Cr.
	Bal. $30,000
	Issue 10,000
	Bal. 40,000

Instructions: Determine the following amounts that should appear in the statement of cash flows. Place parentheses around dollar amounts that represent cash outflows.

$10,000
($25,000)
$50,000
($75,000)
$110,000
($24,000)
$46,000

1. Cash receipts from issuing notes payable
2. Cash payments of notes payable
3. Cash receipts from issuing bonds payable
4. Cash payments of bonds payable
5. Cash receipts from issuing capital stock
6. Cash payments of dividends to stockholders
7. Net cash flows from financing activities

Problem 13-1 Preparing the Heading and Cash Flows from Operating Activities Section

The Hayes Corporation's income statement and comparative balance sheet for the current year are given in Figure 13-4 below and on page 360.

Hayes Corporation
Income Statement
For the Year Ended December 31, 199-

Net Sales			$820,000
Cost of Merchandise Sold			600,000
Gross Profit on Sales			$220,000
Operating Expenses (includes Depreciation of $15,000)			114,000
Operating Income			$106,000
Other Revenue:			
Gain on Sale of Plant Assets	$1,400		
Interest Income	1,200		
Total Other Revenue		$2,600	
Other Expenses:			
Interest Expense		4,800	
Net Deduction			2,200
Net Income Before Income Tax			$103,800
Federal Income Tax			37,600
Net Income			$ 66,200

Figure 13-4A Income Statement for Problem 13-1.

Hayes Corporation
Comparative Balance Sheet
December 31, 1993 and 1992

	1993	1992	Increase (Decrease)
Assets			
Current Assets:			
Cash in Bank	$172,600	$182,000	$ (9,400)
Marketable Securities	185,000	155,000	30,000
Interest Receivable	1,000	1,700	(700)
Accounts Receivable (net)	56,000	52,000	4,000
Merchandise Inventory	92,000	88,500	3,500
Prepaid Expenses	6,200	5,600	600
Total Current Assets	$512,800	$484,800	$ 28,000
Plant Assets:			
Plant Assets	$540,000	$464,000	$ 76,000
Less: Accumulated Depreciation	79,600	76,000	3,600
Total Plant Assets	$460,400	$388,000	$ 72,400
Total Assets	$973,200	$872,800	$ 100,400
Liabilities			
Current Liabilities:			
Notes Payable	$ 70,000	$100,000	$(30,000)
Accounts Payable	35,000	43,000	(8,000)
Accrued Liabilities	9,800	4,500	5,300
Interest Payable	2,400	3,500	(1,100)
Federal Income Tax Payable	21,000	18,000	3,000
Total Current Liabilities	$138,200	$169,000	$(30,800)
Long-Term Liabilities:			
Bonds Payable	200,000	150,000	50,000
Total Liabilities	$338,200	$319,000	$ 19,200
Stockholders' Equity			
Capital Stock, $100 Par	$500,000	$450,000	$ 50,000
Paid-in Capital in Excess of Par	60,000	50,000	10,000
Retained Earnings	75,000	53,800	21,200
Total Stockholders' Equity	$635,000	$553,800	$ 81,200
Total Liabilities and Stockholders' Equity	$973,200	$872,800	$ 100,400

Figure 13-4B Comparative Balance Sheet for Problem 13-1

Additional information found in the general ledger for the fiscal year ended December 31, 199-, follows.

1. Purchased marketable securities for $30,000 cash.
2. Sold plant assets for $20,000 cash that originally cost $30,000 and had accumulated depreciation of $11,400.

3. Purchased plant assets for $26,000 cash.
4. Paid $40,000 cash to repay notes payable.
5. Issued notes payable for $10,000 cash.
6. Issued bonds payable for $20,000 cash.
7. Redeemed bonds payable for $50,000 cash.
8. Issued bonds payable for $80,000 to acquire a plant asset. No cash was received for this transaction.
9. Issued 500 shares of $100-par capital stock at $120.
10. Declared and paid $45,000 in cash dividends to stockholders.

Instructions:

(1) Prepare the heading of a statement of cash flows for the Hayes Corporation.

NCF from OA, $71,600

(2) Prepare the cash flows from operating activities section of the statement of cash flows. Place parentheses around amounts that represent cash outflows.

Problem 13-2 Preparing the Cash Flows From Investing Activities Section

The income statement, balance sheet, and additional general ledger information for the Hayes Corporation are given in Problem 13-1. Use the information to complete this problem.

NCF from IA, ($36,000)

Instructions: Prepare the cash flows from investing activities section of a statement of cash flows. Place parentheses around amounts that represent cash outflows.

Problem 13-3 Preparing the Cash Flows from Financing Activities Section

The income statement, balance sheet, and additional general ledger information for the Hayes Corporation are given in Problem 13-1. Use the information to complete this problem.

NCF from FA, ($45,000)
Net Dec. in Cash, ($9,400)

Instructions: Prepare the cash flows from financing activities section of a statement of cash flows. Place parentheses around amounts that represent cash outflows.

Problem 13-4 Preparing the Schedule of Noncash Investing and Financing Transactions

The income statement, balance sheet, and additional general ledger information for the Hayes Corporation are given in Problem 13-1. Use the information to complete this problem.

Instructions: Prepare the schedule of noncash investing and financing transactions that would appear at the bottom of the statement of cash flows.

Problem 13-5 Preparing a Statement of Cash Flows

The Swain Corporation's income statement and comparative balance sheet for the year 199- are given in Figure 13-5A and B.

Swain Corporation
Income Statement
For the Year Ended December 31, 199-

Net Sales			$860,000
Cost of Merchandise Sold			518,000
Gross Profit on Sales			$342,000
Operating Expenses (includes Depreciation of $35,000)			275,000
Operating Income			$ 67,000
Other Revenue:			
Gain on Sale of Plant Assets	$5,000		
Interest Income	1,000		
Total Other Revenue		$6,000	
Other Expenses:			
Interest Expense		6,000	
Net Addition			0
Net Income before Income Tax			$ 67,000
Federal Income Tax			17,100
Net Income			$ 49,900

Figure 13-5A Income Statement for Problem 13-5.

Additional information found in the general ledger for the fiscal year ended December 31 follows.

1. Purchased marketable securities for $25,000.
2. Sold plant assets for $50,000 cash that originally cost $65,000 and had accumulated depreciation of $20,000.
3. Purchased plant assets for $20,000 cash.
4. Paid $40,000 cash to repay notes payable.
5. Issued notes payable for $55,000 cash.
6. Issued bonds payable for $20,000 cash.
7. Redeemed bonds payable for $80,000 cash.
8. Issued bonds payable for $65,000 to acquire a plant asset. No cash was received for the transaction.
9. Issued 1,000 shares of $50-par capital stock at $60.
10. Declared and paid a $37,000 cash dividend to stockholders.

NCF from OA, $74,000
NCF from IA, $5,000
NCF from FA, ($22,000)
Net Inc. in Cash, $57,000

Instructions: Prepare a statement of cash flows for the Swain Corporation for the year ended December 31, 199-. Refer to Figure 13-1 on page 339 if you need help in setting up the statement. Place parentheses around amounts that represent cash outflows.

Swain Corporation
Comparative Balance Sheet
December 31, 1993 and 1992

	1993	1992	Increase (Decrease)
Assets			
Current Assets:			
Cash in Bank	$ 204,800	$ 147,800	$57,000
Marketable Securities	375,000	350,000	25,000
Interest Receivable	3,500	4,000	(500)
Accounts Receivable (net)	45,000	41,000	4,000
Merchandise Inventory	135,000	137,000	(2,000)
Prepaid Expenses	9,000	10,200	(1,200)
Total Current Assets	$ 772,300	$ 690,000	$82,300
Plant Assets:			
Plant Assets	$ 730,000	$ 710,000	$20,000
Less: Accumulated Depreciation	175,000	160,000	15,000
Total Plant Assets	555,000	550,000	$ 5,000
Total Assets	$1,327,300	$1,240,000	$87,300
Liabilities			
Current Liabilities:			
Notes Payable	$ 75,000	$ 60,000	$15,000
Accounts Payable	66,000	72,000	(6,000)
Accrued Liabilities	21,000	24,000	(3,000)
Interest Payable	3,500	1,000	2,500
Federal Income Tax Payable	7,800	6,900	900
Total Current Liabilities	$ 173,300	$ 163,900	$ 9,400
Long-Term Liabilities:			
Bonds Payable	190,000	185,000	5,000
Total Liabilities	$ 363,300	$ 348,900	$14,400
Stockholders' Equity			
Capital Stock, $50 Par	750,000	700,000	50,000
Paid-in Capital in Excess of Par	150,000	140,000	10,000
Retained Earnings	64,000	51,100	12,900
Total Stockholders' Equity	$ 964,000	$ 891,100	$72,900
Total Liabilities and Stockholders' Equity	$1,327,300	$1,240,000	$87,300

Figure 13-5B Income Statement and Comparative Balance Sheet for Problem 13-5

Problem 13-6 Preparing a Statement of Cash Flows

As chief accountant for the Hargrave Construction Company, you are responsible for preparing the statement of cash flows. The income statement shown in Figure 13-6 on page 364 was prepared by a staff accountant. You reviewed the income statement, analyzed the balance sheet and some general ledger accounts, and compiled a list of additional information you would need to prepare the statement of cash flows.

Hargrave Construction Company
Income Statement
For the Year Ended September 30, 199-

Net Sales			$1,496,000
Cost of Merchandise Sold			673,200
Gross Profit on Sales			$ 822,800
Operating Expenses (includes Depreciation of $86,000)			598,400
Operating Income			$ 224,400
Other Revenue:			
Interest Income		$32,800	
Other Expenses:			
Interest Expense	$27,000		
Loss on Sale of Plant Assets	10,000		
Total Other Expenses		37,000	
Net Deduction			4,200
Net Income before Income Tax			$ 220,200
Federal Income Tax			82,700
Net Income			$ 137,500

Figure 13-6 Income Statement for Problem 13-6

Additional information is as follows:

1. The following balance sheet accounts changed as indicated during the accounting period.
   a. Cash in Bank decreased $101,500.
   b. Accounts Receivable increased $23,800.
   c. Interest Receivable increased $200.
   d. Merchandise Inventory increased $6,000.
   e. Prepaid Expenses decreased $2,000.
   f. Accounts Payable increased $5,000.
   g. Accrued Liabilities decreased $2,000.
   h. Federal Income Tax Payable increased $4,000.
   i. Interest Payable increased $1,000.

2. The following transactions were recorded during the accounting period.
   a. Purchased marketable securities for $150,000.
   b. Sold plant assets for $17,000 cash that originally cost $130,000 and had accumulated depreciation of $103,000. The income statement shows a loss of $10,000 on the sale.
   c. Purchased plant assets for $300,000 cash.
   d. Issued notes payable for $140,000 cash.
   e. Paid $90,000 cash to repay notes payable.
   f. Redeemed bonds payable for $75,000 cash.
   g. Issued bonds payable for $100,000 cash.
   h. Issued 1,500 shares of $100-par capital stock at $110.
   i. Declared and paid $122,000 cash dividends to stockholders.

NCF from OA, $213,500
NCF from IA, ($433,000)
NCF from FA, $118,000
Net Dec. in Cash, ($101,500)

Instructions: Prepare a statement of cash flows for the current year. Place parentheses around amounts that represent cash outflows.

Under the Table versus on the Level

Susanna wearily put away the tax paperwork her client had left a week ago—ten days before her client's taxes had to be filed. She double-checked the completed tax forms, signed them, then put them into an envelope and dropped them off at her client's home. Sorting through all of Mr. Chase's income statements, medical and charitable receipts, and interest records had been a nightmare. He certainly was keeping a lot of plates spinning, Susanna reflected. She hoped that in the future he would give her a little more time to organize the paperwork before expecting her to file his return. Apparently this was the first time he had used a CPA to prepare his taxes, although he used the services of many of the other members of Susanna's financial planning firm, and he was a valued client.

The next day, Susanna received a call from Mr. Chase, who had been looking over his copy of the tax return. He was furious; how could he owe so much money? Susanna should have realized that all of those income statements were not meant for the IRS. She would have to redo the return, leaving out some of the income she had "mistakenly" reported.

What is the ethical dilemma in this situation? What should Susanna do? By misrepresenting Mr. Chase's income, not only would Mr. Chase be held liable in an audit, but she would be, too. He was asking her to put her job and reputation on the line. On the other hand, Mr. Chase was a profitable client for Susanna's firm, and others in the company would lose business if he took his investments elsewhere. Should she consult with the others in her firm and get their advice, or would that violate Mr. Chase's rights as her client?

After listing and then evaluating all her options, Susanna was able to make a difficult decision.

To sort things out, Susanna decided to write down all the aspects of her problem. First, she documented the problem. Then she made a list of her options, noting for each one whether it was legal, whether it was morally defensible, whom it benefitted, and whom it injured. Then she made her decision, evaluating whether or not she could defend it to Mr. Chase, her boss, her co-workers, and herself. As Susanna called Mr. Chase to tell him her decision, she felt that it was one that would benefit the company in the long run, if not in the immediate future.

What would you have done in Susanna's place?

UNIT 4

ACCOUNTING FOR OTHER FORMS OF ORGANIZATION

So far in this textbook, you have studied the accounting procedures used by corporations. In this unit, you will look at two other types of organizations. In Chapter 14 and in Chapter 15, you'll learn how to record and report financial events that affect the ownership equity of partnerships. You will also look at the accounting procedures used by organizations that are not profit-oriented. Nonprofit organizations must also maintain accounting records and prepare reports on the results of their activities. In this unit, you will learn about the procedures nonprofit organizations use to plan for, control, and report on their operations.

Chapter 14

PARTNERSHIPS: FORMATION, DISSOLUTION, AND LIQUIDATION

As you know, the three forms of business organization are the sole proprietorship, the partnership, and the corporation. Many of the accounting procedures you have studied thus far in the textbook can be applied to any of these three types of organizations. For example, the sale of merchandise on account is recorded in the same manner by a sole proprietorship, a partnership, and a corporation. The major difference in accounting for the three types of business organization lies in accounting for ownership equity.

In this and the next chapter, you will examine the accounting procedures that apply to the partnership form of organization. You will learn about the characteristics of a partnership and how it is formed. You'll also learn how to record the journal entries required when a partnership forms, dissolves, or is liquidated.

Learning Objectives

When you have completed this chapter, you should be able to do the following:

1. List the major characteristics of a partnership.
2. List some of the advantages and disadvantages of the partnership form of business organization.
3. Journalize transactions involving partners' equity in a partnership.
4. Journalize the entries required when a partnership dissolves.
5. Journalize entries for the sale of assets when a partnership is liquidated.
6. Define the accounting terms presented in this chapter.

New Terms

partnership
mutual agency
partnership agreement
dissolution
liquidation
realization

Partnerships must maintain accounting records and report the results of their partnerships.

Accounting for a Partnership

The Uniform Partnership Act defines a **partnership** as an association of two or more persons to operate, as co-owners, a business for profit. It is a voluntary association; that is, no one can be forced into a partnership or required to remain in one. Although any type of business can be organized as a partnership, partnerships are often found in businesses that provide professional services, such as law or medicine. Each partner can maintain her or his own clients, yet share with the other partners the expenses of operating an office.

Point out that partnerships are not very common today.

Characteristics of a Partnership

Certain features of a partnership affect only the partners. Other features also affect persons outside the partnership. Let's examine some of these features.

Co-Ownership of Partnership Property

Tell students that this is the "what's mine is yours, and what's yours is mine" concept. Partners share ownership of all assets.

All partners are co-owners of the assets of the partnership. For example, Ben Bell and Ann Howe formed a partnership to operate Avco Delivery Service. The partnership owns two delivery vans. According to the co-ownership concept, Ben and Ann each own one-half of each van, as well as one-half of all the other assets of the business.

Limited Life

Make sure students realize that the death or withdrawal of a partner technically ends the partnership. Mention that the remaining partners can form a new partnership.

Unlike a corporation, a partnership has a limited life. It may be ended for a number of reasons. The death or withdrawal of any partner ends the partnership. Other factors that may bring about the end of a partnership include the bankruptcy or incapacity of a partner or the addition of a new partner. The partnership also ends when the time period specified in the partnership agreement expires or when the project for which the partnership was formed is completed.

Unlimited Liability

Give hypothetical examples to illustrate unlimited liability.

Just as a sole proprietor is personally liable for the debts of the proprietorship, each partner is personally liable for the debts of the partnership. In other words, if the partnership's creditors cannot be paid out of the partnership assets, a partner's personal assets may be used to pay the partnership's debts. A partner who withdraws from the business must issue a public notice of that withdrawal. If not, he or she may be held liable for debts the partnership incurs later.

Mutual Agency

Use the example of one partner entering into a contract to purchase a microcomputer system for the partnership.

Any partner can, in the name of the firm, enter into valid contracts that are binding on the partnership. This relationship is known as **mutual agency**. The partners may agree among themselves to limit the right of any partner to enter into certain contracts. Such an agreement, however, is not binding on outsiders dealing with the firm who are not aware of its existence.

Advantages of a Partnership

Discuss and give examples of each advantage.

The partnership form of business organization offers several advantages:

1. Partnerships provide an opportunity to pool the abilities, experiences, and resources of two or more persons.
2. A partnership is fairly easy to form. The only requirement is an agreement or mutual understanding by the partners.
3. Although the purpose of a partnership must be legal, there are few other legal restrictions on the types of business activities.
4. Federal income taxes are not levied against a partnership. A partnership, however, must file an informational tax return (Form 1065). This return contains an income statement, a balance sheet, and a report showing how the year's net income was allocated to each partner (Schedule K-1). Each partner must declare and pay personal income taxes on her or his share of the partnership's net income, whether or not this share was taken out of the business.

Disadvantages of a Partnership

Discuss and give examples of each disadvantage.

The partnership form of business organization also has some disadvantages:

1. General partners—those who actively and publicly participate in the firm's transactions—have unlimited liability for the partnership's debts.
2. A partnership has a limited life.

3. All of the partners may be held responsible for the actions of one partner (mutual agency).
4. It may be difficult for the partners to raise large amounts of capital.
5. The transfer of one partner's interest to another person must be agreed to by all the partners.

The Partnership Agreement

Emphasize the importance of a written agreement.

A partnership can be formed on the basis of a verbal agreement between two or more persons. However, it is much wiser to have a written partnership agreement. A **partnership agreement** is a written document that sets out the terms under which the partnership will operate.

Figure 14-1 shows a typical partnership agreement. Although there is no standard form of partnership agreement, the provisions listed on the next page are usually included.

PARTNERSHIP AGREEMENT

This agreement, made August 20, 199-, is between Tracy Gardner of 346 East Meadow Road, Plymouth, Colorado, and Lisa Roberts of 23 Lansing Street, Plymouth, Colorado.

1. The above named persons have this day formed a partnership to operate under the name of Creative Crafts, located at 834 Main Street, Plymouth, Colorado. The partnership business shall engage in the sale of crafts and related supplies.
2. This agreement shall run for a term of fifteen years, beginning on August 20, 199-, or for a shorter term if agreed upon in writing by both partners.
3. The initial investment by each partner shall be as follows: Tracy Gardner, assets and liabilities of Tracy's Crafts, valued at a capital investment of $40,000; Lisa Roberts, cash of $20,000. These investments are partnership property.
4. Each partner will give her time, skill, and attention to the operation of this partnership and will engage in no other business enterprise unless permission is granted in writing by the other partner.
5. The salary for each partner will be as follows: Tracy Gardner, $10,000 per year; Lisa Roberts, $8,000 per year. Neither partner may withdraw cash or other assets from the business without the express written permission of the other partner. All profits and losses of the business will be shared as follows: Tracy Gardner, three-fifths; Lisa Roberts, two-fifths.
6. Upon dissolution of the partnership due to the termination of this agreement, the written permission by each of the partners, or the death or incapacitation of one or both partners, a new contract may be entered into by the partners or the sole continuing partner has the option to purchase the other partner's interest in the business at a price that shall not exceed the balance in the terminating partner's capital account. The payment shall be made in cash in equal quarterly installments from the date of termination.
7. At the conclusion of this contract, unless it is agreed by both partners to continue the operation of the business under a new contract, the assets of the partnership, after the liabilities are paid, will be divided in proportion to the balance in each partner's capital account on that date.

Tracy Gardner (signed) — Tracy Gardner
Date: August 20, 199-

Lisa Roberts (signed) — Lisa Roberts
Date: August 20, 199-

Figure 14-1 Partnership Agreement

1. The date of the agreement
2. The names and addresses of the partners
3. The name, location, and nature of the business
4. The length of time the agreement is to run
5. The investment of each partner
6. The duties, rights, and responsibilities of each partner
7. The amount of withdrawals allowed each partner
8. The arrangement for sharing profits and losses
9. The procedure for dividing assets when the partnership is dissolved

Of course, each partner should sign the agreement.

Accounting for Partners' Equity

Accounting for a partnership is very similar to accounting for a sole proprietorship. The only difference lies in the owners' equity accounts. In a sole proprietorship, there is one capital account and one withdrawals account for the owner. Since a partnership has more than one owner, there is one capital account and one withdrawals account for *each* partner.

R — E — M — E — M — B — E — R

In a partnership, there are separate capital and withdrawals accounts for each partner.

ACCOUNTING Notes

If you think entrepreneurs don't need to work hard to make their businesses successful, consider the following. A recent survey of rapidly growing U.S. businesses found that fewer than one-third of the owners took more than two weeks' vacation per year.

Recording the Partners' Investments

When a partnership is formed, the cash and other items invested by each partner are listed in the partnership agreement. Then an entry is made to record the investment of each partner. Each partner's capital account is credited for the total amount of her or his investment.

Let's look at an example. Tracy Gardner and Lisa Roberts agreed to form a partnership to operate a crafts shop. Roberts is investing $20,000 in cash. Gardner presently owns and operates Tracy's Crafts. She is contributing the assets and liabilities of her sole proprietorship to the new partnership.

All partners must agree on the amounts at which noncash assets are recorded. For example, Tracy's Crafts has the following account balances:

Explain that items other than cash may be invested by partners.

Cash in Bank	$ 2,900
Accounts Receivable	18,300
Allowance for Uncollectible Accounts	300
Merchandise Inventory	21,700
Equipment	16,000
Accumulated Depreciation—Equipment	4,500
Notes Payable	1,600
Accounts Payable	9,300

The partners agree that $700 of the accounts receivable is definitely uncollectible and should not be recorded on the books of the new partnership. Of the remaining $17,600 of accounts receivable, $600 may not be collectible. The current market value of Gardner's merchandise is $20,500. The current market value of Gardner's equipment is $10,500. The entries to record each partner's investment appear in Figure 14-2.

GENERAL JOURNAL — PAGE ____

	DATE		DESCRIPTION	POST. REF.	DEBIT	CREDIT	
1	199– Aug.	20	Cash in Bank		20 000 00		1
2			Lisa Roberts, Capital			20 000 00	2
3			Memo 1				3
4		20	Cash in Bank		2 900 00		4
5			Accounts Receivable		17 600 00		5
6			Merchandise Inventory		20 500 00		6
7			Equipment		10 500 00		7
8			Allow. for Uncollectible Accounts			600 00	8
9			Notes Payable			1 600 00	9
10			Accounts Payable			9 300 00	10
11			Tracy Gardner, Capital			40 000 00	11
12			Memo 1				12

Figure 14-2 Journalizing the Partners' Initial Investments

Use demonstration problem 14-1 here.

Notice that Accounts Receivable is debited for only $17,600. Any customer accounts that are definitely uncollectible are not recorded in the accounting records of the new business. Allowance for Uncollectible Accounts is credited for the amount the partners estimate to be uncollectible. The partnership's Merchandise Inventory and Equipment accounts are debited for the amount of their *current market values*. As a result, the equipment's accumulated depreciation is not recorded. The current market value represents the new book value for the partnership.

You may want to have students complete Exercise 14-1 at this point.

R E M E M B E R

When a partner invests noncash assets in the business, the assets are recorded in the partnership records at their current market values.

Recording Additional Investments

Point out why additional investments are sometimes needed by a partnership.

Now let's say that seven months have gone by and the new partnership needs more cash. On March 1, each partner agrees to invest an additional $4,000. The entry appears in Figure 14-3.

GENERAL JOURNAL — PAGE 16

	DATE		DESCRIPTION	POST. REF.	DEBIT	CREDIT	
1	199– Mar.	1	Cash in Bank		8 000 00		1
2			Tracy Gardner, Capital			4 000 00	2
3			Lisa Roberts, Capital			4 000 00	3
4			Receipt 93				4

Figure 14-3 Journalizing an Additional Investment by the Partners

Explain that withdrawals by partners are recorded the same way as withdrawals made by a sole proprietor.

Recording Partners' Withdrawals

During the fiscal period, partners may withdraw cash or other assets for personal use, in accordance with the terms of the partnership agreement. Partners' withdrawals are recorded in the same manner as the withdrawals of a sole proprietor. The amount of the withdrawal is debited to the partner's withdrawals account and credited to the appropriate asset account. For example, on April 1, Tracy Gardner withdrew $200 cash for personal use and Lisa Roberts withdrew $148 in supplies for personal use. This transaction is illustrated in general journal form in Figure 14-4. Notice that the partners' withdrawals need not be equal.

GENERAL JOURNAL — PAGE 22

	DATE		DESCRIPTION	POST. REF.	DEBIT	CREDIT	
1	199– Apr.	1	Tracy Gardner, Withdrawals		200 00		1
2			Cash in Bank			200 00	2
3			Check 193				3
4		1	Lisa Roberts, Withdrawals		148 00		4
5			Supplies			148 00	5
6			Memo 27				6

Figure 14-4 Journalizing Withdrawals by the Partners

Before reading further, do the following activity to check your understanding of how to account for partners' equity.

Check Your Learning

Paul Stevko and Amy Simmons have agreed to form a partnership. Stevko plans to invest the assets of his old business. These assets include $7,500 cash, office equipment costing $53,800 with accumulated depreciation of $21,000, and accounts receivable of $18,400. The partners have agreed that the current market value of the equipment is $34,000. They have also agreed that 12% of the accounts receivable may be uncollectible.

Answer these questions on a sheet of notebook paper.

1. At what amount should the office equipment be recorded on the books of the new partnership?
2. What is the estimated uncollectible amount of accounts receivable?
3. What is Paul Stevko's total investment in the partnership?

Compare your answers to those in the answers section. Reread the preceding part of the chapter to find the correct answers to any questions you may have missed.

Dissolution of a Partnership

Remind students that this refers to the legal limited life. The business may continue its normal operations.

One disadvantage of a partnership mentioned earlier in the chapter is its limited life. A **dissolution** of a partnership occurs whenever there is a change in personnel of the partnership. When a partnership dissolves, the most visible result is a change in the membership. A new partnership agreement is drawn up, but the routine transactions of the business go on as usual. For example, suppose a partnership originally consisted of Adams, Brown, and Carver. Carver withdrew from the firm and a new partnership emerged: Adams and Brown. During the transition, business is carried on as usual. A dissolution may result from the admission of a new partner, the withdrawal of a partner, or the death of a partner.

R — E — M — E — M — B — E — R

When a partnership dissolves, the business continues in operation. The change occurs in the partnership's personnel.

Admission of a New Partner

Remind students that a disadvantage of a partnership is that it is not easy to admit a new partner.

The admission of a new partner dissolves an existing partnership because a new association has been formed. A new partner cannot be admitted, however, without the consent of all the old partners. When a new partner is admitted, a new partnership agreement must be drawn up describing the new arrangement.

An individual may be admitted to a partnership in two ways: (1) by purchasing an interest in the partnership from one or more of the original partners or (2) by investing assets in the partnership.

Purchase of a Partnership Interest with No Increase in Capital A partner may choose to sell her or his interest to a person outside the firm who is acceptable to the remaining partners. For example, Margaret Lange and Lee Merrill are partners in the firm of Lange & Merrill. At the end of the fiscal period, Margaret Lange has a capital balance of $33,240. She decides to sell her interest in the partnership to James Potter for $35,000. Figure 14-5 shows the entry to record the transfer of ownership.

Use demonstration problem 14-2 here.

GENERAL JOURNAL — PAGE 35

	DATE		DESCRIPTION	POST. REF.	DEBIT	CREDIT	
1	199- Dec.	31	Margaret Lange, Capital		33 240 00		1
2			James Potter, Capital			33 240 00	2
3			Memo. 69				3

Figure 14-5 Recording the Admission of a New Partner With No Increase in Capital

Be sure students understand that there is no change in total owners' equity.

Notice that the amount credited to James Potter's capital acount is the same amount as Lange's capital balance, not the amount Potter paid for Lange's interest. The difference between $35,000 and $33,240 represents a personal profit of $1,760 to Lange, not to the firm. There is no change in the partnership's assets or liabilities. As a result, there is no change in the total owners' equity. Remember, however, that for the business to continue, Lee Merrill (the other original partner) must be willing to accept James Potter as the new partner.

Use T accounts to illustrate this example. Total the capital in the T accounts to show the increase in owners' equity.

Use demonstration problem 14-3 here.

Investment of Assets by a New Partner When a new partner invests assets in the partnership, both the assets and the owners' equity of the firm increase. The assets the new partner invests increase the partnership's assets, which in turn increases total owners' equity.

For example, Melanie Bike and Joseph Petrone are partners whose capital accounts are $80,000 and $70,000, respectively. Christine Zima wishes to invest in the partnership. The two partners agree to admit Zima to the business for a $75,000 cash investment. The entry to record this investment appears in Figure 14-6. With the admission of Zima, the total equity of the business becomes $225,000.

GENERAL JOURNAL PAGE 19

	DATE		DESCRIPTION	POST. REF.	DEBIT	CREDIT	
1	199– July	1	Cash in Bank		75 000 00		1
2			Christine Zima, Capital			75 000 00	2
3			Receipt 114				3

Figure 14-6 Journalizing the Investment by a New Partner

R — E — M — E — M — B — E — R

If a new partner invests assets in a partnership, the total owners' equity of the business increases.

Withdrawal of a Partner

Ask students to give reasons why a partner may choose to withdraw from a partnership.

The partnership agreement should include the procedures to be followed when one of the partners withdraws. These procedures usually include an audit of the books and a revaluation of the partnership's assets to reflect current market values.

When a partner withdraws from the firm, he or she may withdraw (1) the book value of his or her equity, (2) more than the book value of his or her equity, or (3) less than the book value of his or her equity.

Partner Withdraws Book Value of Equity

Pat Eisen wants to retire from the partnership of Gray, Eisen, and Mott. The partnership agreement provides for an audit of the accounting records and a revaluation of assets if a partner retires. It also states that net income and net loss shall be divided equally.

After the audit and revaluation of assets, the total equity of the partnership is $86,500. The partners' capital accounts look like this:

Rachel Gray, Capital		Pat Eisen, Capital		Donald Mott, Capital	
Dr.	Cr.	Dr.	Cr.	Dr.	Cr.
	Bal. $35,700		Bal. $26,400		Bal. $24,400

Put these T accounts on the chalkboard. Then post the transaction shown in Figure 14-7 to the T accounts and have students verify the total owners' equity of the partnership.

Eisen can now withdraw cash equal to her equity in the partnership. Figure 14-7 shows the entry in general journal form. After Eisen's withdrawal, the total equity of the business is $60,100.

GENERAL JOURNAL — PAGE 26

	DATE		DESCRIPTION	POST. REF.	DEBIT	CREDIT	
1	199- Sept.	30	Pat Eisen, Capital		26 400 00		1
2			Cash in Bank			26 400 00	2
3			Check 1372				3

Figure 14-7 Recording the Withdrawal of Equity by a Partner

Partner Withdraws More Than Book Value of Equity

Sometimes a partner withdraws more than the book value amount of her or his capital account. There are two possible reasons for this: (1) The business is doing well and shows excellent potential for growth, or (2) the remaining partners are so eager for the partner to retire that they are willing to buy him or her out.

Keep the previous T accounts on the chalkboard as you illustrate this transaction.

Suppose that when Eisen announces that she wants to retire, Gray and Mott agree to pay her $27,000 for her interest in the partnership. The other partners' offer is $600 more than the balance of Eisen's capital account after the valuation. This $600 must be deducted from the capital accounts of the remaining partners. The same percentages used to divide profits and losses are used to divide the $600 decrease between the two partners. The entry to record Eisen's withdrawal appears in Figure 14-8.

Be sure to point out the difference in the total owners' equity between this situation and the previous example.

GENERAL JOURNAL — PAGE 26

	DATE		DESCRIPTION	POST. REF.	DEBIT	CREDIT	
1	199- Sept.	30	Pat Eisen, Capital		26 400 00		1
2			Rachel Gray, Capital		300 00		2
3			Donald Mott, Capital		300 00		3
4			Cash in Bank			27 000 00	4
5			Check 1372				5

Figure 14-8 Journalizing a Partner's Withdrawal at More Than Book Value of Equity

After Eisen's withdrawal, the total equity of the business is $59,500.

Rachel Gray, Capital	
Dr.	Cr.
$300	Bal. $35,700

Pat Eisen, Capital	
Dr.	Cr.
$26,400	Bal. $26,400

Donald Mott, Capital	
Dr.	Cr.
$300	Bal. $24,400

Again, keep the T accounts from the two previous situations on the board as you illustrate this transaction. Point out the difference in the total owners' equity.

Partner Withdraws Less Than Book Value of Equity

Sometimes a partner is so eager to retire that he or she is willing to take less than the book value of her or his equity in the business. Let's say that Eisen is willing to withdraw from the partnership for a payment of $25,000. Since the balance of Eisen's capital account after the revaluation is $26,400, the difference of $1,400 represents a profit to the remaining partners. That profit is recorded in the remaining partners' capital accounts. Figure 14-9 shows the entry to record this withdrawal situation.

Use demonstration problem 14-4 here.

GENERAL JOURNAL PAGE 26

	DATE		DESCRIPTION	POST. REF.	DEBIT	CREDIT	
1	19-- Sept.	30	Pat Eisen, Capital		26 400 00		1
2			Rachel Gray, Capital			700 00	2
3			Donald Mott, Capital			700 00	3
4			Cash in Bank			25 000 00	4
5			Check 1372				5

Figure 14-9 Journalizing a Partner's Withdrawal at Less Than Book Value of Equity

You may want to have students complete Exercise 14-2 at this point.

After Eisen's withdrawal, the total equity of the business is $61,500.

Rachel Gray, Capital	
Dr.	Cr.
	Bal. $35,700
	700

Pat Eisen, Capital	
Dr.	Cr.
$26,400	Bal. $26,400

Donald Mott, Capital	
Dr.	Cr.
	Bal. $24,400
	700

Emphasize that a deceased partner's heirs are entitled to receive the book value of his or her equity. They are not entitled to take the deceased partner's place in the partnership.

Death of a Partner

The death of a partner automatically ends the partnership, and the partner's heirs are entitled to receive the book value of her or his equity. Normally, the partnership's books are closed immediately, so that the business's net income for the current fiscal period can be determined. The partnership agreement also usually provides for an audit and revaluation of the assets. After the current book value of the deceased partner's capital account is determined, the remaining partners and the executor of the deceased partner's estate must agree on the method of payment. The journal entries are similar to those made for the withdrawal of a partner. To ensure that they have enough cash to meet such a demand, partnerships often carry life insurance policies on each partner.

Liquidation of a Partnership

A **liquidation** occurs when both the partnership and the business end. This final winding-up process involves selling assets, paying liabilities, and distributing the remaining cash to the partners. The closing entries are journalized and posted prior to the liquidation.

Make sure that the students understand the four accounting steps needed to liquidate a partnership.

It is difficult to predict how long the liquidation process will take. It could move quickly or it may take a long time to convert merchandise inventory and other assets into cash. The following four steps are necessary to liquidate a partnership:

1. The assets are sold for cash. This process is referred to as **realization**. Any losses or gains realized (earned) during the process are recorded in an account titled Loss or Gain on Realization. This account is a temporary account and is used only during the liquidation process. In this respect, it is similar to Income Summary. The account is debited for losses and credited for gains.
2. The total loss or gain is allocated among the partners. The balance of the Loss or Gain on Realization account is closed into the partners' capital accounts according to the terms on sharing profits and losses. This account is closed separately because it came into being *after* the regular closing entries had been journalized and posted.
3. Liabilities are paid. The business makes a final payment to each of its creditors.
4. The remaining cash is distributed to the partners based on the balances of their capital accounts.

Let's look at an example. Ronald Andrews, Miranda Blake, and Craig Conroy are partners in a gift shop called Carnivale. The partners share profits and losses as follows: Andrews, one-half; Blake, one-fourth; Conroy, one-fourth. Since business has been poor, the partners agree to liquidate the business. The account balances for the business are as follows:

Cash in Bank	$10,000
Merchandise Inventory	15,000
All other assets (net)	45,000
Accounts Payable	7,000
Ronald Andrews, Capital	27,000
Miranda Blake, Capital	24,000
Craig Conroy, Capital	12,000

Gain on Sale of Assets

Use T accounts to illustrate the four entries to liquidate the partnership.

Assume Carnivale sold its merchandise inventory for $20,000 and all other assets for $52,000, for a total of $72,000. First, the sale of these assets is recorded, including the $12,000 gain on realization ($72,000 – $60,000 recorded value). The Loss or Gain on Realization account is then closed into the partners' capital accounts, according to the terms of the partnership agreement. Next, the creditors are paid. Finally, the remaining cash is distributed to the partners. The journal entries for these transactions appear in Figure 14-10.

GENERAL JOURNAL PAGE 29

DATE		DESCRIPTION	POST. REF.	DEBIT	CREDIT
199- June	30	Cash in Bank		72 000 00	
		Merchandise Inventory			15 000 00
		Other Assets			45 000 00
		Loss or Gain on Realization			12 000 00
		Receipt 1917			
	30	Loss or Gain on Realization		12 000 00	
		Ronald Andrews, Capital			6 000 00
		Miranda Blake, Capital			3 000 00
		Craig Conroy, Capital			3 000 00
		Memo: 962			
	30	Accounts Payable		7 000 00	
		Cash in Bank			7 000 00
		Checks 2173–2179			
	30	Ronald Andrews, Capital		33 000 00	
		Miranda Blake, Capital		27 000 00	
		Craig Conroy, Capital		15 000 00	
		Cash in Bank			75 000 00
		Checks 2180–2182			

Figure 14-10 Liquidating a Partnership When There Is a Gain on Sale of Assets

Use demonstration problem 14-5 here.

After these entries are journalized and posted, the Cash in Bank and capital accounts appear as shown in the following T accounts:

Cash in Bank

Dr.	Cr.
Bal. $10,000	(3) $ 7,000
(1) 72,000	(4) 75,000

Ronald Andrews, Capital

Dr.	Cr.
(4) $33,000	Bal. $27,000
	(2) 6,000

Miranda Blake, Capital

Dr.	Cr.
(4) $27,000	Bal. $24,000
	(2) 3,000

Craig Conroy, Capital

Dr.	Cr.
(4) $15,000	Bal. $12,000
	(2) 3,000

R — E — M — E — M — B — E — R

When a partnership is liquidated, the cash is distributed to the partners based on the balances in their capital accounts.

Loss on Sale of Assets

Walk students through the liquidation procedure using T accounts.

Now suppose the partnership of Andrews, Blake, and Conroy sells its merchandise inventory for only $12,000 and its other assets for only $39,000. The business has realized a total of $51,000. When the sale of the assets is recorded, there is a $9,000 loss on realization ($60,000 – $51,000).

The Loss or Gain on Realization account is then closed into the three partners' capital accounts. All creditors are paid. Finally, the remaining cash is distributed to the partners. Figure 14-11 shows the journal entries for this situation.

GENERAL JOURNAL PAGE 29

DATE		DESCRIPTION	POST. REF.	DEBIT	CREDIT
199– June	30	Cash in Bank		51 000 00	
		Loss or Gain on Realization		9 000 00	
		Merchandise Inventory			15 000 00
		Other Assets			45 000 00
		Receipt 1917			
	30	Ronald Andrews, Capital		4 500 00	
		Miranda Blake, Capital		2 250 00	
		Craig Conroy, Capital		2 250 00	
		Loss or Gain on Realization			9 000 00
		Memo 962			
	30	Accounts Payable		7 000 00	
		Cash in Bank			7 000 00
		Checks 2173–2179			
	30	Ronald Andrews, Capital		22 500 00	
		Miranda Blake, Capital		21 750 00	
		Craig Conroy, Capital		9 750 00	
		Cash in Bank			54 000 00
		Checks 2180–2182			

Figure 14-11 Liquidating a Partnership When There Is a Loss on Sale of Assets

After these entries are journalized and posted, the Cash in Bank and capital accounts appear as shown in the following T accounts:

Use demonstration problem 14-6 here.

Cash in Bank

Dr.	Cr.
Bal. $10,000	(3) $ 7,000
(1) 51,000	(4) 54,000

Ronald Andrews, Capital

Dr.	Cr.
(2) $ 4,500	Bal. $27,000
(4) 22,500	

Miranda Blake, Capital

Dr.	Cr.
(2) $ 2,250	Bal. $24,000
(4) 21,750	

Craig Conroy, Capital

Dr.	Cr.
(2) $2,250	Bal. $12,000
(4) 9,750	

R—E—M—E—M—B—E—R

The Loss or Gain on Realization **account is used in the liquidation process only when a gain or a loss from the sale of partnership assets has been realized.**

Before reading further, do the following activity to check your understanding of how to record the liquidation of a partnership.

Check Your Learning

Write your answers to these questions on a sheet of notebook paper.

Stimson and Twan are partners who share profits and losses equally. The balances of the partnership's accounts are as follows:

Cash in Bank	$26,000
Noncash assets	97,000
Accounts Payable	7,000
Jo Stimson, Capital	60,000
Lee Twan, Capital	56,000

When they liquidate their partnership, Stimson and Twan sell the noncash assets for $71,000 and then pay all their liabilities.

1. What is the amount of the gain or loss on realization?
2. How much cash should be distributed to each partner?

You may want to have students complete Exercise 14-3 here.

Compare your answers to those in the answers section. Reread the preceding part of the chapter to find the correct answers to any questions you may have missed.

Summary of Key Points

1. A partnership is a voluntary association of two or more persons to carry on, as co-owners, a business for profit.
2. The actions of one partner acting on behalf of the partnership are binding on all the partners. This arrangement is known as mutual agency.
3. The main advantage of a partnership is that it allows the combining of people's abilities and investments to carry on a business. The primary disadvantage of a partnership is the unlimited liability each partner must assume.
4. In a partnership, separate capital and withdrawals accounts are set up for each partner.
5. A partnership is dissolved and reformed whenever there is any change in the composition of its membership. The effect on the business may simply be a change in the members listed in the partnership agreement and in the capital accounts. The normal transactions of the business go on as usual.
6. When a partnership liquidates, the business ends. Assets are sold, all liabilities are paid, and the remaining cash is distributed to the partners.

14 Review and Applications

Building Your Accounting Vocabulary

In your own words, write the definition of each of the following accounting terms. Use complete sentences for your definitions.

dissolution
liquidation
mutual agency
partnership
partnership agreement
realization

Reviewing Your Accounting Knowledge

1. Name four characteristics of the partnership form of organization.
2. List three advantages and three disadvantages of the partnership form of organization.
3. Jason Cott and Tanya Jones are partners in the firm of Cott & Jones. Cott signed a contract to purchase a word processing system for the business. Is the contract binding on the partnership? Why or why not?
4. Are partnerships required to pay federal income taxes? Why or why not?
5. Is it possible for one owner to lose more than the amount he or she has invested in the partnership? Why or why not?
6. What kind of information is usually included in a partnership agreement?
7. When assets other than cash are invested in a partnership by one of the partners, at what value are those assets recorded?
8. Name three situations that cause the dissolution of a partnership.
9. In what two ways may an individual be admitted to an already existing partnership?
10. How does the dissolution of a partnership differ from a liquidation?
11. What four steps are followed in the liquidation of a partnership?

Improving Your Analysis Skills

Line graphs are often used in business to illustrate sales figures over a period of time. The line graph on page 383 shows the sales figures for the True Ripe Fruit Company's canned peaches during the 1980s. Use the information on the graph to answer the following questions.

1. In what year were sales highest? In what year were they lowest?
2. Did the peaches sell better in 1983 or in 1987?
3. From looking at the graph, what general conclusion can you draw about the success of True Ripe peaches in the late 1980s?

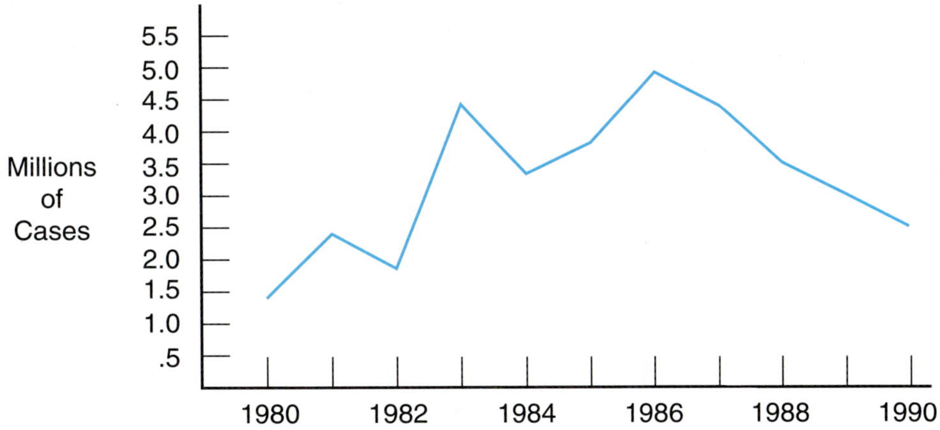

Figure 14-12 Line Graph Showing Sales Figures for True Ripe Fruit Company

Applying Accounting Procedures

Exercise 14-1 Calculating Initial Investments by Partners

Following are the initial investments planned by the members of several different partnerships.

Instructions: For each partnership, determine (1) the total amount of the investment by each partner and (2) the total partners' equity of the new partnership. Use plain paper or the form provided in the working papers.

Partnerships:

Total equity:
$80,350
$116,985
$83,805

1. *Abel:* cash, $25,000; supplies, $550; office equipment currently valued at $8,400
   Balzotti: store equipment currently valued at $7,900; building, current market value $35,000; land, current market value $3,500
2. *Alexander:* cash, $10,000; accounts receivable, $500; equipment, current market value $7,100
   Buresh: cash, $7,500; merchandise inventory, current market value $27,010; accounts payable, $1,575
   Carr: cash, $50,000; vehicle, current market value $16,450
3. *Archer:* cash, $12,750; merchandise inventory, current market value of 80% of $33,200 cost
   Bigelow: supplies, $1,980; equipment, current market value $8,600
   Cashman: cash, $30,000; accounts receivable, $1,900 of which 15% are estimated to be uncollectible; supplies, $2,300

SPREADSHEET PROBLEM

Exercise 14-2 Determining Total Equity after a Partner's Withdrawal

Rodgers, Stanhope, and Turner are partners in a carpet-cleaning business and share profits and losses equally. At the end of the fiscal period, the balances of the capital accounts are as follows: Rodgers, $36,400; Stanhope, $25,200; and Turner, $37,500. Turner wishes to withdraw from the partnership.

Instructions: Determine the balances in the remaining partners' capital accounts and the total equity of the business for each of the following situations.

Total equity:
$61,600
$67,100
$58,100

1. Turner retires, taking $37,500 in cash for her equity.
2. Turner retires, taking $32,000 in cash for her equity.
3. Turner retires, taking $41,000 in cash for her equity.

Exercise 14-3 Calculating a Gain or Loss on Realization

Nyugen, Otis, and Prince are partners in Child's Play, a children's furniture and furnishings store. Due to a mutual disagreement, they have decided to liquidate the business. The ending balances for the noncash assets are as follows.

Accounts Receivable	$ 1,600
Merchandise Inventory	24,300
Supplies	750
Equipment (net)	12,000

Instructions:

Acct. Rec., – $240
Mdse. Inv., – $1,550
Supplies, – $75
Equip. (net), $2,999
Total, $1,134

$378 each

(1) Determine whether the partnership has realized a gain or a loss on the sale of the assets. Merchandise inventory was sold for $22,750; supplies for $675; and equipment for $14,999. Of the business's accounts receivable, 85% of the amount due was collected.

(2) If the partners share profits and losses equally, what amount of the gain or loss should each partner receive?

COMPUTER PROBLEM

Problem 14-1 Recording Partners' Initial Investments

Maria Hosti and José Quinos agree to form a partnership to operate a business called Vision Software. Maria plans to invest cash and certain other assets. José plans to invest the assets and liabilities of his current business. All assets are listed at their current market values. The investments of the two partners follow.

	Maria Hosti	José Quinos
Cash	$17,000	$ 9,000
Accounts Receivable		1,800
Allowance for Uncollectible Accounts		150
Merchandise Inventory		19,300
Supplies	200	600
Office Equipment	6,400	
Accounts Payable		4,100

Instructions: Prepare the entries to record the initial investments of the partners on July 1. Use page 1 of a general journal and Memorandum 101 as the source document.

COMPUTER PROBLEM

Problem 14-2 Recording Partners' Equity Transactions

Margaret Johnson and Lou Miller are partners in MidPoint Travel. The following transactions took place during the month of March.

Instructions: Record the transactions on page 23 of a general journal.

Transactions:

Mar. 6 Johnson withdrew $400 in cash from the business, Check 295.

11 Miller invested an additional $1,000 in the business, Receipt 187.

21 Miller withdrew $300 in supplies from the business, Memorandum 119.

29 Johnson invested an additional $500 in cash plus office equipment valued at $1,200, Memorandum 121.

Problem 14-3 Admitting a New Partner

Pat Reilly and Barbara Saltus are partners in the firm of Reilly & Saltus. Their capital balances are $42,000 and $38,000, respectively. Reilly and Saltus agree to admit Kim Banks to the partnership for an investment of $40,000 cash (Receipt 385).

Instructions:

(1) On page 45 of a general journal, record the entry for the admission of Banks on July 1.

Total equity, $120,000

(2) Determine the total equity of the new partnership.

Problem 14-4 Recording the Withdrawal of a Partner

Brian Doonan, Karen Weller, and Peter Welsh are partners in ProBowl Lanes. The balances of their capital accounts are $32,000, $41,000, and $38,000, respectively. The three partners share profits and losses equally.

Weller wants to withdraw from the partnership. She agrees to accept $40,000 for her equity in the business—$25,000 in cash (Check 385) and a $15,000 note payable (Note 53).

Instructions:

(1) Journalize the entry to record the withdrawal of Weller on May 15. Use page 62 of a general journal.

Total equity, $71,000

(2) Determine the total equity of the new partnership between Doonan and Welsh.

Problem 14-5 Recording Entries Upon the Death of a Partner

Jennifer White, Courtney Silkwood, James Bruno, and Tom Penders are partners in Design Associates. The balances in their capital accounts are $85,000, $91,000, $70,000 and $80,000, respectively. The partners share profits and losses equally.

When Tom Penders died, the firm's assets were revalued. The revaluation indicated that the value of the following assets had changed.

	Book Value	Revaluation
Merchandise Inventory	$ 89,400	$ 85,600
Building (net)	164,000	172,000
Equipment (net)	27,200	29,800

Instructions:

(1) On general journal page 37, record the entry for the revaluation of the firm's assets. The date is November 15 and the source document is Memorandum 175.

(2) Record the payment of Penders' share of the partnership equity to his heirs, Check 824.

Total equity, $251,100

(3) Determine the total equity of the new partnership.

Problem 14-6 Journalizing and Posting the Entries for a Liquidation

Pam King, Ida Mazone, and John Rider are partners in a business called The Pan Handlers. Their capital balances are $52,800, $46,400, and $28,900, respectively. They share profits and losses equally.

The three partners have agreed to liquidate their business. The balances in the general ledger accounts are as follows.

Cash in Bank	$42,850
Accounts Receivable	7,580
Merchandise Inventory	76,350
Equipment (net)	19,410
Accounts Payable	18,090

Instructions: Journalize and post the following entries to liquidate the partnership. Use page 73 of a general journal. The opened general ledger accounts appear in the working papers.

1. The assets were sold and the accounts receivable collected (journalize separately).
   a. The merchandise was sold on February 10 for $74,900, Receipt 7381.
   b. The equipment was sold on February 12 for $18,200, Receipt 7382.
   c. Ninety percent of the accounts receivable were collected on February 14, Receipt 7383.
2. The gain or loss from realization was allocated to the partners' capital accounts on February 15 (Memorandum 295).
3. The creditors were paid on February 16, Checks 8327–8330.
4. The cash was distributed to the partners on February 18, Checks 8331–8333.

CHALLENGE PROBLEM

Problem 14-7 Liquidating a Partnership

Lee Abbott, Clarence Butler, and Lynn Craig are partners in the Blue Bird Boat Locker Company. Because business has been poor, the partners have decided to liquidate the business. The balances of the partnership accounts follow. The partners share profits and losses equally.

Cash in Bank	$ 6,900
Accounts Receivable	14,900
Equipment (net)	35,000
Boat Trailers (net)	24,800
All other assets	11,225
Accounts Payable	39,815
Lee Abbott, Capital	18,500
Clarence Butler, Capital	25,210
Lynn Craig, Capital	9,300

Instructions: Journalize the following entries to liquidate the partnership. Use page 86 of the general journal.

Transactions:

Apr.	3	Collected 65% of the accounts receivable, Receipt 3841.
	8	A competitor bought the equipment for $24,500, Receipt 3842.
	13	Sold the boat trailers for $15,200, Receipt 3843.
	15	The other assets were purchased by a neighboring business for $8,640, Receipt 3844.
	17	The gain or loss on realization was allocated to the partners' capital accounts, Memorandum 284.
	18	All creditors were paid the full amount owed, Checks 3821–3838.
	18	The remaining cash was distributed to the partners, Checks 3839–3840.

Computers in the Home/Office: Making Little Businesses Work Like Big Ones

Have you ever thought about working from your home instead of from an office? Millions of Americans are doing just that. The frustration of battling rush-hour traffic each day and the high cost of office space have caused many free-lance workers, as well as employees of larger companies, to consider working from home.

Although working from home may sound ideal, it can create problems. Typing and sending out letters, calculating financial reports, or keeping track of inventory are all time-consuming tasks that can greatly reduce a person's productivity. It could take all morning just to get a letter "right." With the aid of a computer, however, all these tasks can be handled speedily and efficiently.

People who work from home often must do their own writing, filing, bookkeeping, scheduling, and research. Computer programs for handling all of these tasks are available, however. Word processing programs enable a person to finish letters in just a few minutes. Database management software organizes files quickly, without taking up excessive space. Spreadsheet programs help complete bookkeeping and accounting tasks. There are even programs to help schedule a person's time.

Computers can also help a user create a more professional product while working at home. With the help of desktop publishing and graphics programs, a person can produce a proposal or brochure that looks as good as one done by a company ten times the size. Computer-aided design programs enable architects and designers to create designs of the same quality at home that they would otherwise have to do at the office. Estimating programs help small contractors prepare bids for jobs that only large companies could have tackled before computers. As our society and our work force become increasingly computerized, more and more workers will be using their homes as their offices. Modems will enable people to link home offices around the world. Then, perhaps, for the people who still must commute to work, maybe rush hour won't be so bad with all those people working at home!

Many people operate their businesses effectively in the home/office.

Chapter 15

PARTNERSHIPS: DIVISION OF PROFITS AND LOSSES

In Chapter 14, you were introduced to the partnership form of business organization. There you learned how to account for partners' equity. Each partner has her or his own capital account and withdrawals account. The capital account, as you know, is used to record the partners' investment in the business.

The capital account is also used to record the net income or net loss for a fiscal period. In a partnership, the amount of the net income or net loss must be divided among the partners. In this chapter, you will learn several methods for dividing a partnership's earnings among the partners. You'll learn how to record the closing entries for the division of net income or loss and how to prepare the partnership's financial statements.

Learning Objectives

When you have completed this chapter, you should be able to do the following:

1. List five methods of distributing a partnership's net income or loss.
2. Journalize the closing entry for a partnership to divide net income or loss.
3. Prepare the financial statements for a partnership.
4. Define the accounting terms presented in this chapter.

New Terms

salary allowance
interest allowance
statement of changes in partners' equity

Dividing Net Income or Net Loss

As you remember, the four closing entries for a sole proprietorship are as follows:

1. Close the revenue and contra cost accounts into Income Summary.
2. Close the contra revenue, cost, and expense accounts into Income Summary.
3. Close Income Summary into the capital account by the amount of the net income or loss.
4. Close the withdrawals account into the capital account.

The only differences between the closing entries for a sole proprietorship and those for a partnership are in steps 3 and 4. Instead of a single capital account and a single withdrawals account, each partner in a partnership has a capital account and a withdrawals account. Income Summary is closed into *all* of the capital accounts by the amount of the net income or loss. Each withdrawals account is closed into its respective capital account.

Remind students that the partnership agreement should spell out how profits and losses are to be divided among the partners.

Let's look more closely at step 3. The partners can divide the net income or loss by any method they wish. They may even choose to handle losses differently from profits. Any arrangements they make should be included in the written partnership agreement to avoid misunderstandings. If the partners do not set out a specific method, the law provides that partners share profits and losses equally.

Partners may use any one of a number of methods to divide the partnership earnings, or any combination of these methods. The method chosen should reflect the differences in the value of the services or investments contributed by individual partners. In this chapter, we will look at the following methods:

1. Dividing net income (or loss) equally.
2. Dividing net income on a fractional-share basis.
3. Dividing net income based on a capital investments ratio.
4. Dividing net income based on salary allowances.
5. Dividing net income based on interest allowances.

R — E — M — E — M — B — E — R

If the partnership agreement does not include a method for distributing net income or loss, net income or loss is shared equally among the partners.

To illustrate the various methods, we will use the partnership between Tracy Gardner and Lisa Roberts for the business called Creative Crafts. We will look at two examples of each method. In the first example of each method, we will assume the partnership has a net income of $24,000. In the second example, we will assume the partnership has a net *loss* of $3,600. We will use the same capital account balances throughout the examples. The balances of the capital accounts, of course, represent the partners' shares in the equity of the business. On December 31, the capital accounts for Gardner and Roberts have the following balances:

Tracy Gardner, Capital	
Dr.	Cr.
	Bal. $75,000

Lisa Roberts, Capital	
Dr.	Cr.
	Bal. $54,000

Emphasize the idea of equal investments "equal" division.

Dividing Net Income or Loss Equally

The easiest way to divide a partnership's net income or loss is equally. This method is frequently used when all partners spend the same amount of time in the business, contribute equal amounts of capital, and have similar managerial talents.

Net Income of $24,000 When the partnership has a net income of $24,000, the first step is to divide that amount equally between the two partners.

Gardner's share	$24,000 ÷ 2 = $12,000
Roberts's share	$24,000 ÷ 2 = $12,000

The effect of this division of the net income is shown in the following T accounts:

Tracy Gardner, Capital	
Dr.	Cr.
	Bal. $75,000
	Clo. 12,000

Lisa Roberts, Capital	
Dr.	Cr.
	Bal. $54,000
	Clo. 12,000

Use demonstration problem 15-1 here.

The closing entry to record this distribution of net income appears in Figure 15-1.

Students are used to seeing profit; therefore, be sure they understand the entry for a loss.

GENERAL JOURNAL PAGE 62

	DATE		DESCRIPTION	POST. REF.	DEBIT	CREDIT	
1			Closing Entries				1
2	199- Dec.	31	Income Summary		24 000 00		2
3			Tracy Gardner, Capital			12 000 00	3
4			Lisa Roberts, Capital			12 000 00	4

Figure 15-1 Closing Entry to Distribute Net Income Equally

ACCOUNTING *Notes*

Starting a new business may be a lot easier than making a new business successful. A recent study showed that over one-half of new businesses fail during the first five years—and often the failure is due to careless accounting practices.

Net Loss of $3,600 The division of a net loss is calculated in the same manner as the division of a net income. The parentheses indicate the negative amounts of a net loss.

Gardner's share	($3,600) ÷ 2 = ($1,800)
Roberts's share	($3,600) ÷ 2 = ($1,800)

The effect of this division of net loss on the partners' capital accounts is shown in the following T accounts:

Tracy Gardner, Capital	
Dr.	Cr.
Clo. $1,800	Bal. $75,000

Lisa Roberts, Captial	
Dr.	Cr.
Clo. $1,800	Bal. $54,000

Use demonstration problem 15-2 here.

Figure 15-2 shows the closing entry to record the equal division of the net loss.

GENERAL JOURNAL — PAGE 62

	DATE		DESCRIPTION	POST. REF.	DEBIT	CREDIT	
1			Closing Entries				1
2	199- Dec.	31	Tracy Gardner, Capital		1 800 00		2
3			Lisa Roberts, Capital		1 800 00		3
4			Income Summary			3 600 00	4

Figure 15-2 Closing Entry to Distribute Net Loss Equally

Dividing Net Income or Loss on a Fractional-Share Basis

Another way to divide net income or loss is to allot each partner a stated fraction of the total. The size of the fraction may take into consideration (1) the amount of each partner's investment and (2) the value of each partner's services.

Ask students to list reasons why the equal division of profits and losses might not be a fair method to use.

Net Income of $24,000 Let's assume the partnership agreement states that profits and losses are to be divided this way: three-fifths for Gardner and two-fifths for Roberts. To allocate the net income, the net income amount is multiplied by each partner's fractional share:

Gardner's share	$24,000 × 3/5 = $14,400
Roberts's share	$24,000 × 2/5 = $ 9,600

This fractional-share division of net income is shown in the following T accounts:

Tracy Gardner, Capital	
Dr.	Cr.
	Bal. $75,000
	Clo. 14,400

Lisa Roberts, Capital	
Dr.	Cr.
	Bal. $54,000
	Clo. 9,600

Use demonstration problem 15-3 here.

The division of net income is recorded as a closing entry as shown in Figure 15-3.

GENERAL JOURNAL — PAGE 62

	DATE		DESCRIPTION	POST. REF.	DEBIT	CREDIT	
1			Closing Entries				1
2	199- Dec.	31	Income Summary		24 000 00		2
3			Tracy Gardner, Capital			14 400 00	3
4			Lisa Roberts, Capital			9 600 00	4

Figure 15-3 Closing Entry for the Fractional-Share Division of Net Income

Net Loss of $3,600 The net loss is divided in the same manner the net income was divided:

Gardner's share	($3,600) × 3/5 = ($2,160)
Roberts's share	($3,600) × 2/5 = ($1,440)

This fractional-share division of the net loss is illustrated in the following T accounts:

Tracy Gardner, Capital	
Dr.	Cr.
Clo. $2,160	Bal. $75,000

Lisa Roberts, Captial	
Dr.	Cr.
Clo. $1,440	Bal. $54,000

The closing entry for the fractional-share division of the net loss is recorded as shown in Figure 15-4.

GENERAL JOURNAL PAGE 62

	DATE		DESCRIPTION	POST. REF.	DEBIT	CREDIT	
1			Closing Entries				1
2	199- Dec.	31	Tracy Gardner, Capital		2 160 00		2
3			Lisa Roberts, Capital		1 440 00		3
4			Income Summary			3 600 00	4

Figure 15-4 Closing Entry for the Fractional-Share Division of Net Loss

Be sure students understand how to convert fractions to percentages.

You may want to have students complete Exercise 15-1 at this point.

In these two examples, the fractional shares were stated as fractions: 3/5 and 2/5. The shares could also be expressed as percentages: 60% and 40%. They could also be expressed as a ratio: 3:2 (3 to 2).

Dividing Net Income or Loss Based on the Ratio of Capital Investments

Often partners divide net income or loss on the basis of their capital investment in the business. This method works well for businesses whose profits are closely related to the amount of money invested, such as businesses that buy and sell real estate.

Point out that the beginning, average, or ending capital investments could be used.

Suppose Gardner and Roberts have agreed to share profits or losses according to the ratio of their investments at the *beginning* of the period. Let's say Gardner's investment at the beginning of the year was $70,000 and Roberts's was $50,000, for a total investment of $120,000. Before any allocation can be made, the ratio of each partner's investment to the total partnership equity must be determined. The ratios of the two partners are calculated as follows:

Gardner's ratio	$70,000 ÷ $120,000 = 7/12
Roberts's ratio	$50,000 ÷ $120,000 = 5/12

Net Income of $24,000 Using the ratios just calculated, the distribution of net income is determined as follows:

Gardner's share	$24,000 × 7/12 = $14,000
Roberts's share	$24,000 × 5/12 = $10,000

Owners in a business share in the profits and losses of the business.

The division of net income based on the capital investment ratios is shown in the following T accounts:

Tracy Gardner, Capital	
Dr.	Cr.
	Bal. $75,000
	Clo. 14,000

Lisa Roberts, Capital	
Dr.	Cr.
	Bal. $54,000
	Clo. 10,000

The closing entry appears in Figure 15-5.

GENERAL JOURNAL PAGE 62

	DATE		DESCRIPTION	POST. REF.	DEBIT	CREDIT	
1			Closing Entries				1
2	199- Dec.	31	Income Summary		24 000 00		2
3			Tracy Gardner, Capital			14 000 00	3
4			Lisa Roberts, Capital			10 000 00	4

Use demonstration problem 15-4 here.

Figure 15-5 Closing Entry for the Division of Net Income Based on Capital Investments Ratio

Net Loss of $3,600 When the partnership has a net loss of $3,600, the distribution of the loss based on capital investments is calculated as follows:

Gardner's share	($3,600) × 7/12 = ($2,100)
Roberts's share	($3,600) × 5/12 = ($1,500)

The following T accounts show the effect of this division of the net loss on the capital accounts:

Tracy Gardner, Capital	
Dr.	Cr.
Clo. $2,100	Bal. $75,000

Lisa Roberts, Captial	
Dr.	Cr.
Clo. $1,500	Bal. $54,000

The closing entry for the net loss based on the capital investment ratio appears in Figure 15-6.

GENERAL JOURNAL PAGE 62

	DATE		DESCRIPTION	POST. REF.	DEBIT	CREDIT	
1			Closing Entries				1
2	199- Dec.	31	Tracy Gardner, Capital		2 100 00		2
3			Lisa Roberts, Capital		1 500 00		3
4			Income Summary			3 600 00	4

Figure 15-6 Closing Entry for the Division of Net Loss Based on Capital Investments Ratio

Before reading further, do the following activity to check your understanding of how to divide net income or loss based on the ratio of capital investments.

Check Your Learning

Write your answer to this question on a sheet of notebook paper.

Hilliard and Whitten are partners who share profits and losses according to the ratio of the balances of their capital accounts at the beginning of the year. Hilliard's beginning capital account balance was $40,000, and Whitten's was $30,000. If the net income for the current year is $27,900, what is each partner's share?

Compare your answer to that in the answers section. Reread the preceding part of the chapter to find the correct answer for any portion of the calculation you may have missed.

You may want to have students complete Exercise 15-2 at this point.

Dividing Net Income or Loss Based on Salary Allowances

Point out that this is a reward to certain partners for services provided to the partnership.

Stress that salary allowances are a means of allocating net income or loss. They are not expenses of the business nor are they withdrawals.

Partners do not always make equal contributions to the partnership. For example, one partner may work full time in the partnership while another participates only part time. Also, the services of one partner may be more valuable to the partnership than the services of the other partners. To account for these unequal contributions, some partnership agreements provide for salary allowances to the partners.

A **salary allowance** is an allocation of net income. It is used as a means of recognizing and rewarding differences in ability and time devoted to the business. A salary allowance is not a business expense nor is it the same as a withdrawal. Legally, partners do not work for salaries; they invest and work in the partnership to share in the business's earnings. As a result, when a partnership agreement provides for salary allowances, the partners must realize that the salary allowances are simply a means of sharing the profits and losses of the business.

Gardner and Roberts have a partnership agreement that provides for yearly salary allowances of $10,000 and $8,000, respectively (see page 370). Any remaining net income is divided three-fifths to Gardner and two-fifths to Roberts. Gardner and Roberts could have chosen to divide the remainder equally or on the basis of any other ratio.

R — E — M — E — M — B — E — R

Salary allowances to partners are not expenses of the business. They are allocations of net income or loss.

Net Income of $24,000 The first step in distributing the net income is to subtract the salary allowances from the net income of $24,000. Then the remaining amount is divided on the specified fractional-share basis. The calculations are as follows:

Net income		$24,000
Less salary allowances:		
Gardner	$10,000	
Roberts	8,000	–18,000
Amount remaining after salary allowances		$ 6,000

Gardner	$6,000 × 3/5 = $3,600
Roberts	$6,000 × 2/5 = $2,400

Each partner's share of the net income of $24,000 is determined by adding the partner's salary allowance and her or his share of the remaining net income.

Gardner's share	$10,000 + $3,600 = $13,600
Roberts's share	$ 8,000 + $2,400 = $10,400

This division of net income is shown in the following T accounts:

Tracy Gardner, Capital

Dr.	Cr.
	Bal. $75,000
	Clo. 13,600

Lisa Roberts, Capital

Dr.	Cr.
	Bal. $54,000
	Clo. 10,400

Use demonstration problem 15-5 here.

Figure 15-7 shows the closing entry.

GENERAL JOURNAL — PAGE 62

	DATE		DESCRIPTION	POST. REF.	DEBIT	CREDIT	
1			Closing Entries				1
2	199- Dec.	31	Income Summary		24 000 00		2
3			Tracy Gardner, Capital			13 600 00	3
4			Lisa Roberts, Capital			10 400 00	4

Figure 15-7 Closing Entry for the Division of Net Income with Salary Allowances

Net Loss of $3,600 When salary allowances are included in the partnership agreement, they must be allocated regardless of whether or not there is enough net income to take care of them. The division of the partnership's $3,600 net loss is calculated as follows. (Remember that the amounts enclosed in parentheses in the following calculations represent *negative* amounts:)

Net loss		($ 3,600)
Less salary allowances:		
Gardner	$10,000	
Roberts	8,000	−18,000
Amount remaining after salary allowances		($21,600)

Gardner	($21,600) × 3/5 = ($12,960)
Roberts	($21,600) × 2/5 = ($ 8,640)

Each partner's share of the net loss of $3,600 is determined by adding the partner's salary allowance and his or her share of the net loss after salary allowances.

Gardner's share	$10,000 + ($12,960) = ($2,960)
Roberts's share	$ 8,000 + ($ 8,640) = ($ 640)

The distribution of the net loss has the following effect on the partners' capital accounts:

Tracy Gardner, Capital	
Dr.	Cr.
Clo. $2,960	Bal. $75,000

Lisa Roberts, Captial	
Dr.	Cr.
Clo. $640	Bal. $54,000

As you can see, Gardner's capital account decreased by $2,960 and Roberts's capital account decreased by $640. This closing entry appears in Figure 15-8.

GENERAL JOURNAL — PAGE 62

	DATE		DESCRIPTION	POST. REF.	DEBIT	CREDIT	
1			Closing Entries				1
2	199- Dec.	31	Tracy Gardner, Capital		2 960 00		2
3			Lisa Roberts, Capital		640 00		3
4			Income Summary			3 600 00	4

Figure 15-8 Closing Entry for the Division of Net Loss with Salary Allowances

Before reading further, do the following activity to check your understanding of how to calculate the division of net income or loss based on salary allowances.

Check Your Learning

Write your answer to this question on a sheet of notebook paper.

The partnership agreement of Adams and Matthews provides for salary allowances of $14,000 a year for Adams and $10,000 a year for Matthews. They share the remaining net income or loss on the basis of three-fourths for Adams and one-fourth for Matthews. Calculate each partner's share of the net income of $49,000.

Compare your answer to that in the answers section. Reread the preceding part of the chapter to find the correct answer for any portion of the calculation you may have missed.

You may want to have students complete Exercise 15-3 at this point.

Dividing Net Income or Loss Based on Interest Allowances

Emphasize that this rewards partners for larger capital investments in the partnership.

Sometimes a partnership agreement includes an allowance for interest on the partners' capital investments. An **interest allowance** is a method of distributing net income that takes into account a partner's capital contribution. This provision acts as an incentive for partners to not only leave their investments in the business but even increase them.

For example, suppose Gardner and Roberts, in addition to their salary allowances of $10,000 and $8,000, are allowed 3% interest on their capital balances at the beginning of the fiscal year. Gardner is to receive three-fifths of the remaining net income and Roberts two-fifths.

R — E — M — E — M — B — E — R

An interest allowance is a distribution of net income. It is calculated on the balance of the partner's capital account.

Net Income of $24,000 With this method, the interest allowances must be calculated first. Gardner's and Roberts's capital balances at the beginning of the year were $70,000 and $50,000, respectively.

Gardner's interest allowance	$70,000 × .03 = $2,100
Roberts's interest allowance	$50,000 × .03 = $1,500

Next, both the salary allowances and the interest allowances are subtracted from the net income amount. Any remainder is divided equally between the partners according to the set fractional shares.

Net income		$24,000
Less:		
Salary allowances		
($10,000 + $8,000)	$18,000	
Interest allowances		
($2,100 + $1,500)	3,600	–21,600
Amount remaining after salary and interest allowances		$ 2,400

Gardner $2,400 × 3/5 = $1,440
Roberts $2,400 × 2/5 = $ 960

Each partner's share of the net income is determined by adding her or his salary allowance, interest allowance, and share of remaining net income.

Gardner's share $10,000 + $2,100 + $1,440 = $13,540
Roberts's share $ 8,000 + $1,500 + $ 960 = $10,460

This distribution of net income has the following effect on the partners' capital accounts:

Tracy Gardner, Capital	
Dr.	Cr.
	Bal. $75,000
	Clo. 13,540

Lisa Roberts, Capital	
Dr.	Cr.
	Bal. $54,000
	Clo. 10,460

Use demonstration problem 15-6 here.

The closing entry for this distribution of the net income would appear as in Figure 15-9.

GENERAL JOURNAL PAGE 62

	DATE		DESCRIPTION	POST. REF.	DEBIT	CREDIT	
1			Closing Entries				1
2	199– Dec.	31	Income Summary		24000 00		2
3			Tracy Gardner, Capital			13540 00	3
4			Lisa Roberts, Capital			10460 00	4

Figure 15-9 Closing Entry for the Division of Net Income with Interest Allowances

▲ Net Loss of $3,600

Interest allowances are handled the same way as salary allowances. Both must be allocated, even though there is a net loss.

Net loss		($ 3,600)
Less:		
Salary allowances		
($10,000 + $8,000)	$18,000	
Interest allowances		
($2,100 + $1,500)	3,600	–21,600
Amount remaining after salary and interest allowances		($25,200)

Gardner ($25,200) × 3/5 = ($15,120)
Roberts ($25,200) × 2/5 = ($10,080)

The total amount to be allocated to each partner's capital account is determined by adding the partner's salary allowance, interest allowance, and share of the total net loss.

Gardner's share	\$10,000 + \$2,100 + (\$15,120) = (\$3,020)
Roberts's share	\$ 8,000 + \$1,500 + (\$10,080) = (\$ 580)

The distribution of the net loss and the salary and interest allowances has the following effect on the partners' capital accounts:

Tracy Gardner, Capital	
Dr.	Cr.
Clo. \$3,020	Bal. \$75,000

Lisa Roberts, Captial	
Dr.	Cr.
Clo. \$580	Bal. \$54,000

As you can see, both Gardner's and Roberts's capital accounts decreased. Figure 15-10 shows the closing entry.

GENERAL JOURNAL PAGE 62

	DATE		DESCRIPTION	POST. REF.	DEBIT	CREDIT	
1			Closing Entries				1
2	199- Dec.	31	Tracy Gardner, Capital		3020 00		2
3			Lisa Roberts, Capital		580 00		3
4			Income Summary			3600 00	4

You may want to have students complete Exercise 15-4 at this point.

Figure 15-10 Closing Entry for the Division of Net Loss with Interest Allowances

R — E — M — E — M — B — E — R

Salary and interest allowances must be allocated to the partners regardless of whether enough net income is available.

Preparing Financial Statements for a Partnership

At the end of the fiscal period, financial statements for the partnership are prepared. For the partnership of Gardner and Roberts, these include an income statement, a statement of changes in partners' equity, and a balance sheet.

Income Statement

The income statement is prepared in the same way as for any merchandising business. The net income or net loss reported on the income statement may be divided between the partners and shown on the income statement. Accounting rules, however, do not require that the division of the net income or loss be shown on the income statement.

Illustrate the additional information that may by included on the income statement.

According to the partnership agreement between Gardner and Roberts, each partner receives a salary allowance. Then any remaining net income or loss is divided on a fractional-share basis. At the end of the fiscal period, Creative Crafts had a net income of $24,000. The division of that net income amount was calculated on page 396. If this division were included on the partnership's income statement, it would appear as shown in Figure 15-11.

Creative Crafts
Income Statement
For the Year Ended December 31, 199-

Net Income				24,000.00
Division of Net Income:				
Tracy Gardner			13,600.00	
Lisa Roberts			10,400.00	
Net Income				24,000.00

Figure 15-11 Reporting the Division of Net Income on the Income Statement

Statement of Changes in Partners' Equity

Point out that there is a column for each partner and a total column.

Changes in the balances of the partners' capital accounts are reported on the **statement of changes in partners' equity**. This report is very similar to the statement of changes in owner's equity for a sole proprietorship. The only difference is that on the statement of changes in partners' equity there is a separate column for each partner. In Figure 15-12, you can see that the net income has been divided between the partners as reported on the income statement.

Creative Crafts
Statement of Changes in Partners' Equity
For the Year Ended December 31, 199-

	Gardner	Roberts	Total
Beginning Capital, Jan. 1, 199-	70,000.00	50,000.00	120,000.00
Add: Investments	5,000.00	4,000.00	9,000.00
Net Income	13,600.00	10,400.00	24,000.00
Subtotal	88,600.00	64,400.00	153,000.00
Less: Withdrawals	11,000.00	7,000.00	18,000.00
Ending Capital, Dec. 31, 199-	77,600.00	57,400.00	135,000.00

Figure 15-12 Statement of Changes in Partners' Equity

Explain that the amount entered on a partner's personal income tax return is the share of net income the partner earned.

Unlike a corporation, a partnership does not pay income taxes as a separate entity. Each partner must pay federal income taxes on her or his share of the business's net income. For example, Tracy Gardner's taxable income from the partnership is $13,600, even though she withdrew only $11,000. She must report the $13,600 on her personal income tax return.

Balance Sheet

Point out that each partner's equity is listed separately on the balance sheet.

The only difference on the balance sheet of a partnership is that the owner's equity section is referred to as the Partners' Equity section. Each partner's capital account is listed separately, as shown in Figure 15-13. The account balances reported are taken from the statement of changes in partners' equity.

Creative Crafts Balance Sheet December 31, 199–		
Partners' Equity		
Tracy Gardner, Capital	77 600 00	
Lisa Roberts, Capital	57 400 00	
Total Partners' Equity		135 000 00
Total Liabilities and Partners' Equity		183 900 00

Figure 15-13 Partners' Equity Section of a Balance Sheet for a Partnership

Summary of Key Points

1. The partnership agreement should state how the net income or net loss is to be distributed to the partners. If it does not, net income or loss is shared equally.
2. The net income for a partnership can be divided by any of the following methods or by any combination of these methods: equally, on a fractional-share basis, based on the ratio of the partners' capital investments, based on salary allowances, and based on interest allowances. The method chosen should reflect the differences in the value of the services or investments contributed by the individual partners.
3. Salary allowances and interest allowances are distributions of net income or loss. They are not business expenses. Salary and interest allowances must be allocated to the partners regardless of whether net income is available.
4. The financial statements for a partnership include the income statement, the statement of changes in partners' equity, and the balance sheet.
5. The division of net income or loss among partners is reported on the statement of changes in partners' equity. It may also be reported on the income statement.

15 Review and Applications

Building Your Accounting Vocabulary

In your own words, write the definition of each of the following accounting terms. Use complete sentences for your definitions.

interest allowance	statement of changes in partners' equity
salary allowance	

Reviewing Your Accounting Knowledge

1. How do the closing entries for a partnership differ from those for a sole proprietorship?
2. How is net income or loss allocated to partners if no method is specified in the partnership agreement?
3. Name five methods by which partners can divide the partnership's net income or loss.
4. Under what circumstances might partners choose to divide net income or loss equally rather than by some other method?
5. When net income or loss is divided on a fractional-share basis, what factors are considered in establishing the size of the fractions?
6. What is the difference between a salary allowance and salary expense?
7. What is the advantage to the partnership of providing an interest allowance on the partners' capital investments?
8. Hunt and Wright are partners who share profits and losses in a 3:2 ratio. If the net income is $64,000, what is each partner's share?
9. What three financial statements are prepared for a partnership at the end of the fiscal period?
10. Must a partnership file a federal income tax return and pay federal income taxes? Why or why not?

Improving Your Human Relations Skills

Two of your fellow accounting clerks, Cathy Taylor and Latanya White, do not get along. They constantly complain to you about each other. Although you have urged them to work out their differences, their quarrels seem to be getting worse. Cathy and Latanya appear to be performing their work properly, but you're afraid their feud might affect a project that the three of you are scheduled to work on soon. Should you tell your supervisor your concerns or wait and see what happens? What other ways to deal with this potential problem can you think of?

Applying Accounting Procedures

Exercise 15-1 Allocating a Net Loss on a Fractional-Share Basis

The partnership agreement between Emily Ling and David Martin states that profits and losses are to be divided as follows: Ling, two-thirds, and Martin, one-third. During the current year, the company had a net loss of $12,375.

Ling, ($8,250)
Martin, ($4,125)

Instructions: Determine the amount of the net loss allocated to each partner. Use plain paper or the space provided in the working papers that accompany the textbook.

Exercise 15-2 Allocating Net Income Based on Capital Investments

The Clinton Company is a partnership established by Sam Armstrong, Jenny Brown, and Pat Chase. The partnership agreement states that the division of profits and losses is based on the original investment of each partner. These original investments were as follows: Armstrong, $60,000; Brown, $40,000; and Chase, $20,000.

Armstrong, $8,970
Brown, $5,980
Chase, $2,990

Instructions: Based on this information, determine each partner's share of the $17,940 net income.

Exercise 15-3 Allocating Net Income Based on Salary Allowances

José Hernandez, Maria Innes, and Lynn Jackson are partners in the Westerly Dental Center. Their partnership agreement provides for yearly salary allowances of $9,000, $13,000, and $11,000, respectively. Any remaining amount is to be divided equally.

Hernandez, $11,550
Innes, $15,550
Jackson, $13,550

Instructions: Determine the share for each partner if the profit for the fiscal period is $40,650.

SPREADSHEET PROBLEM

Exercise 15-4 Allocating Net Income Based on Interest Allowances

The Harvest Home Restaurant is a partnership owned by Stephen Rousch, Amanda Santos, and Jan Taylor. The partnership agreement calls for an interest allowance of 15% on the ending capital balances. Remaining income is to be allocated as follows: Rousch, 25%; Santos, 50%; Taylor, 25%. On December 31, the partners' capital balances were: Rousch, $55,500; Santos, $143,000; and Taylor, $51,000.

Rousch, $21,468.75
Santos, $47,737.50
Taylor, $20,793.75

Instructions: Calculate each partner's share of the net income of $90,000.

Problem 15-1 Journalizing the Closing Entry to Allocate a Net Loss

Harold Evans, Lucy Franklin, and Denise Grey are partners in the firm of Holly Crafts. Their partnership agreement states that profits will be shared equally, but it does not mention how losses are to be handled.

$3,145 each

The firm had a net loss of $9,435 for the fiscal period ended June 30.

Instructions: Journalize the closing entry to allocate the net loss among the partners.

Problem 15-2 Distributing Partnership Earnings on a Fractional-Share Basis

John Jenkins, Jim Kline, and Vivian Lee are partners in the firm of Potsfield Tool Supply. According to their partnership agreement, profits and losses are to be shared in a 2:2:1 ratio. Potsfield Tool Supply had a net income of $64,200 for the period.

Jenkins, $25,680
Kline, $25,680
Lee, $12,840

Instructions: On general journal page 46, record the closing entry to allocate the net income among the partners. Use December 31 as the date.

Problem 15-3 Allocating Net Income Based on a Capital Investments Ratio

Barbara Griffin and Dan McGuire are partners in a retail garden center called The Potting Shed. The partners started the business on January 2 by investing $40,000 and $70,000, respectively. The partnership agreement states that all profits and losses are to be allocated according to the balances of their capital accounts at the beginning of the year. The Potting Shed had a net income of $22,000 at the end of its first year of operations.

Instructions:

Griffin, $8,000
McGuire, $14,000

(1) Journalize the closing entry to allocate the net income between the partners. Use general journal page l4.

(2) Post the closing entry to the partners' capital accounts. The opened accounts are included in the working papers accompanying this textbook.

Problem 15-4 Distributing a Net Loss Based on Salary and Interest Allowances

Mary Kelly, Pat Lyons, and Tom Maxwell are partners in a business called Professional Placement Services. The balances of their capital accounts on December 31 (the end of the fiscal period) are $43,000, $35,000, and $38,000, respectively.

The partnership agreement states that Kelly is to receive a salary allowance of $9,000, Lyons a salary allowance of $8,000, and Maxwell a salary allowance of $12,000. The agreement also provides for an interest allowance of 5% on the balances of the capital accounts at the end of the fiscal period. Remaining profits or losses are to be divided equally.

Professional Placement Services had a net loss of $6,405 for the current fiscal period.

Instructions:

(1) Open the partners' capital accounts in the general ledger, using the December 31 balances.

$13,735 each

(2) Determine each partner's share of the net loss. On page 12, journalize the closing entry to allocate the net loss among the partners.

(3) Post the closing entry to the partners' capital accounts.

SPREADSHEET PROBLEM

Problem 15-5 Evaluating Methods for Distributing Partnership Earnings

Heather Dodds and Scott Morrow plan to form a partnership to operate a coffee shop. Dodds plans to work in the business full time, while Morrow will work part time. Dodds's initial investment will be $36,000, and Morrow will invest $24,000. They are considering the following plans for the division of profits and losses:

$21,600; $14,400
$21,600; $14,400
$22,420; $13,580

1. Division based on the ratio of their capital accounts.
2. Interest of 8% on the balances of their capital accounts at the beginning of the year and the remainder divided on a 3:2 basis.
3. Salary allowances of $12,000 to Dodds and $4,000 to Morrow, interest of 7% on the balances of their capital accounts at the beginning of the year, and the remainder divided equally.

Instructions: Determine the amount that would be allocated to Dodds and Morrow under each plan if their business had a net income of $36,000. Use the space provided in the working papers.

Problem 15-6 Preparing a Statement of Changes in Partners' Equity

Edward Ventura, Laura Wilson, and Kara Young are partners in a painting and wallpapering business called ELK Designs. The business had a net income of $74,660 for the current year.

The partnership agreement provides for the following salary allowances: Ventura, $13,000; Wilson, $11,000; and Young, $14,000. The agreement also provides for an interest allowance of 9% on the balances of the partners' capital accounts at the beginning of the year. The remaining profit or loss is to be divided equally.

At the beginning of the year, the balances in the capital accounts were $43,000, $32,000, and $38,500, respectively. During the year, Wilson invested an additional $5,000 in the business. The December 31 balances of the partners' withdrawals accounts were $13,000, $10,300, and $12,250, respectively.

Instructions:

Share of net income:
Ventura, $25,685
Wilson, $22,695
Young, $26,280

(1) Determine the share of the net income to be allocated to each partner.

(2) Prepare the statement of changes in partners' equity for ELK Designs.

Problem 15-7 Preparing End-of-Period Financial Statements for a Partnership

The following balances appear in the Adjusted Trial Balance section of the work sheet for the partnership of Holmes and Bond.

Account	Debit	Credit
Cash in Bank	$ 4,389	
Accounts Receivable	64,125	
Allowance for Uncollectible Accounts		$ 2,210
Merchandise Inventory	155,342	
Prepaid Insurance	864	
Equipment	88,605	
Accumulated Depreciation—Equipment		54,456
Accounts Payable		80,918
Notes Payable		24,000
William Holmes, Capital		72,000
William Holmes, Withdrawals	19,000	
Matthew Bond, Capital		57,000
Matthew Bond, Withdrawals	14,000	
Income Summary	14,130	
Sales		840,588
Sales Returns and Allowances	41,678	
Purchases	661,410	
Purchases Discounts		5,064
Purchases Returns and Allowances		30,542
Selling Expenses	81,543	
Administrative Expenses	17,575	
Interest Expense	4,117	

There were no changes in the partners' capital accounts during the year.

The partnership agreement provides for salary allowances of $22,000 for Holmes and $14,000 for Bond. It also provides for an interest allowance of 7% on the balances of the capital accounts at the beginning of the year. The remaining profit or loss is to be divided equally.

Net income, $55,741.00

Share of net income:
Holmes, $32,395.50
Bond, $23,345.50

BS totals, $256,659.00

Instructions:

(1) Prepare an income statement for the year ended December 31.
(2) Prepare a statement of changes in partners' equity.
(3) Prepare a balance sheet.

CHALLENGE PROBLEM

Problem 15-8 Allocating Partnership Earnings and Preparing a Statement of Changes in Partners' Equity

Draperies Plus is a partnership owned by Sally Chapin, Jan Foley, and James Lebowitz. The partnership agreement provides for salary allowances as follows: Chapin, $11,000; Foley, $10,000; and Lebowitz, $12,000. The agreement also includes an interest allowance of 4% on the balances of the partners' capital accounts at the end of the year. Any remainder is to be divided equally.

The balances in the partners' capital accounts at the beginning of the year were $81,500, $75,000, and $82,000, respectively. During the year, Jan Foley invested an additional $3,000 in the business. At the end of the year, the balances of the partners' withdrawals accounts were $12,000, $11,500, and $10,800, respectively.

Instructions:

(1) Prepare a statement of changes in partners' equity for Draperies Plus for the year ended December 31.
(2) On general journal page 35, record the December 31 closing entry to allocate the net loss of $2,700. Also prepare the entries to close the withdrawals accounts.

Share of net loss:
Chapin, ($860)
Foley, ($2,000)
Lebowitz, $160

FOCUS ON COMPUTERS

Teaching with Technology

As children today become increasingly computer-oriented, it becomes a challenge for teachers and schools to keep up with technology. When schools do not make use of the technology available today, however, students become bored with learning.

Although some people believe schools should not have to "teach" computers, teachers who have learned to use computers in the classroom say that it is not computers that they teach, but science—or math, history, language arts, music, and art. These teachers say that computers have become a way to interest students in learning a particular subject and, even more important, learning how that subject relates to other subjects and to world issues.

The many ways in which computers can be used, and are being used, to teach in the classroom only hint at the computer's vast potential for getting students involved in learning:

- Biology teachers are using computers to simulate dissections, illustrate cells, and trace genetic mutations.
- Earth science teachers are having students study the effects of acid rain by allowing them to share information with other research classrooms around the world.
- Computers make it possible for students to compose music that they can hear immediately. A computer hooked up to an electronic keyboard allows students to hear how their compositions sound.
- Students use interactive videos to combine moving images with the accompanying text, making term papers and book reports "come alive."
- Teachers are helping students compile information on databases, creating permanent records of topics such as the cultural backgrounds and folklore of people in the area or science issues affecting the community.

Teachers can use computers to involve students in learning science, music, language, and technology.

As teachers and students work together to discover how technology can expand their world, teachers become better guides and students become better learners.

Chapter 16

NOT-FOR-PROFIT ORGANIZATIONS: BUDGETING AND CONTROL

Up to this point in your study of accounting, you have learned to classify, record, and report accounting information for businesses that are organized to earn a profit. In this chapter and in Chapter 17, you'll look at a different type of organization—one with objectives other than earning a profit. Not-for-profit organizations include government agencies and organizations such as civic groups, professional associations, and social clubs. Unlike the business organizations you learned about earlier, the typical not-for-profit organization is organized to provide a service.

In this chapter, you will study the accounting system used by not-for-profit organizations. You will also learn about one tool not-for-profit organizations use to plan for and manage their funds.

Learning Objectives

When you have completed this chapter, you should be able to do the following:

1. Explain the difference between a not-for-profit organization and a profit-oriented business.
2. List the five principles of budgeting.
3. Name two methods that can be used to develop the revenue and expenditure projections for a budget.
4. Explain how a budget summary report can be used to control an organization's funds.
5. Prepare a budget summary report.
6. Define the accounting terms presented in this chapter.

New Terms

not-for-profit organization
fund
fund accounting
budget
budget period
revenue projection
expenditure projection
zero-base budgeting
surplus
budget summary report
free balance
budget adjustment

Characteristics of Not-for-Profit Organizations

Every business needs money (capital) to start its operations. To stay in operation, a business must earn a profit. The success of a typical business is usually measured by the amount of profit it earns.

Point out the main difference between profit-oriented and not-for-profit organizations.

Not all organizations are profit-oriented, however. The main goal of many organizations is to provide services to their members or to the general public. Examples of such service-oriented organizations include schools, libraries, museums, professional associations, civic groups, and public broadcasting stations. An organization with goals other than earning a profit for its organizers is called a **not-for-profit organization**.

It takes money to start and maintain the operations of a not-for-profit organization, just as it does for a for-profit business. The success of a not-for-profit organization is measured differently, however. Its success is measured not by the profits it makes but by the services it provides and by how well the public receives those services.

R E M E M B E R

Rather than trying to earn a profit for its organizers, the main purpose of a not-for-profit organization is to provide a service for its members or the general public.

Fund Accounting

Point out the meaning of the term "fund."

The word *fund* has several meanings in accounting. A change fund is an amount of money used for making change in cash transactions. A petty cash fund is an amount of money set aside for making small, incidental cash payments. A bond sinking fund consists of the cash and other securities set aside to pay off a bond issue when it comes due. *Fund* is used to refer to a corporation's working capital.

In not-for-profit organizations, *fund* has yet another meaning. A **fund** is a set of accounts (asset, liability, equity, revenue, and expense) used to record the transactions for a particular activity. A not-for-profit organization usually has a number of funds. For example, a university may have several scholarship funds, an investment fund, and a building fund. It also has a general fund. The general fund is used to account for all other, nonspecific activities. **Fund accounting**, then, is the accounting system used by not-for-profit organizations to account for the transactions of their various funds.

The Budgeting Process

To be successful and meet its goals, a not-for-profit organization must carefully plan for and manage its funds. Goals must be set, objectives established, and the purposes of the organization clearly defined. Part of the planning process includes preparing a budget.

Stress that preparing a budget requires planning, organization, and cooperation.

A **budget** is a formal, written statement of expected revenue and expenditures for a future period of time. This future time period is called the **budget period** and is usually 12 months. A budget is one of the most important financial tools a not-for-profit organization uses. First, it forces the managers or directors of the organization to look closely at the organization's goals. Second, it requires the cooperation of everyone in the organization to work toward and carry out those goals. Finally, by comparing the budget with the actual results, the organization can evaluate its performance and, if necessary, revise its goals.

Five basic principles are involved in the budgeting process:

1. Develop long-term goals.
2. Develop short-term goals.
3. Define budgeting responsibilities.
4. Establish budgeting guidelines.
5. Establish follow-up procedures.

To see how the budgeting process works, we will look at the operations of the Mountain View Recreation Center. The Mountain View Recreation Center is a community center that provides facilities and activities for the general public. These activities include swimming, golf, softball, baseball, basketball, tennis, exercise programs, and crafts.

Develop Long-Term Goals

Give several examples of long-term goals.

Long-term goals are the goals that an organization wants to accomplish over a long period of time, such as five or ten years. An organization's long-term goals are like highway markers. They point out the general directions that the organization can take. For example, a long-term goal for the Mountain View Recreation Center might be to build a new swimming pool in five years. To meet this goal, the organization must develop plans to estimate expenditures, to raise the money needed, and to hire personnel. An organization uses its long-term goals to develop its short-term goals.

Develop Short-Term Goals

Emphasize that short-term goals are used to meet an organization's long-term goals.

If an organization's long-term goals are like highway markers, its short-term goals are like street signs. They are the specific "routes" an organization can take to meet its long-term goals. Short-term goals are the goals that the organization wishes to accomplish within a short period of time, usually one year. For example, one of the Mountain View Recreation Center's short-term goals may be to raise $10,000 from a raffle. An organization uses its short-term goals to prepare its annual budget.

R — E — M — E — M — B — E — R

Long-terms goals are the goals that will be met over a long period of time, such as five or ten years. Short-term goals are expected to be accomplished within a year.

ACCOUNTING **Notes**
Training in accounting is important for many professions other than accounting. Tax collectors, appraisers, purchasing agents, and directors of not-for-profit organizations all use accounting in their jobs.

Define Budgeting Responsibilities

Developing the budget for an organization such as the Mountain View Recreation Center requires the cooperation of a number of people. Each person involved in the budgeting process must know what her or his responsibility is. For example, the director of the center's Little League baseball program must estimate the program's revenue and expenditure needs. The director, in turn, may ask the league manager to estimate the revenue that team entry fees or a particular fund-raising project is expected to bring in.

Stress that if one person fails on a given responsibility, the goals of a group may not be accomplished.

Give students several examples of guidelines (deadlines, planning, reporting, procedures).

Establish Budgeting Guidelines

No task can be accomplished without guidelines. In the budgeting process, it is important to set up methods for sharing information and to establish realistic deadlines for reporting budget data.

Preparing a budget requires detailed planning, organization, the cooperation of many people, and time. As a result, the Mountain View Recreation Center begins its budgeting process in January, six months before the beginning of its fiscal year on July 1.

Establish Follow-up Procedures

Emphasize the importance of follow-up.

Follow-up is very important in budgeting. Once a budget has been prepared and approved, it should be compared periodically with the actual revenue received and the expenditures made. For example, the Mountain View Recreation Center might want to compare the budget with the actual revenue and expenditures every month or every quarter. Then it can adjust its budget or its plans if revenue is lower or expenditures higher than expected.

While not-for-profit organizations are stuctured to provide a service, they must also plan for and manage their funds.

R — E — M — E — M — B — E — R

It is very important to compare a budget with actual revenue and expenditures to determine whether the budget must be revised.

Before reading further, do the following activity to check your understanding of the material you have just studied.

Check Your Learning

On a sheet of notebook paper, indicate whether the following statements are true or false.

1. A not-for-profit organization is an organization whose primary goal is to provide services to its members or the general public.
2. Goals that an organization hopes to accomplish within one year or less are called long-term goals.
3. Only the long-term goals of an organization are used to develop the budget.
4. A grocery store is an example of a not-for-profit organization.
5. Follow-up is one of the basic principles in the budgeting process.

Compare your answers to those in the answers section. Reread the preceding part of the chapter to find the correct answers to any questions you may have missed.

Preparing a Budget

Stress the importance of preparing a budget.

A budget is a one-year plan for the organization. It sets forth the specific short-term goals, the sources of revenue, and the uses of that revenue. A not-for-profit organization uses its budget to maintain control over its funds and their uses. Once it sets aside or budgets funds for a specific purpose, the organization cannot use those funds for any other purpose.

The budget for the Mountain View Recreation Center is actually composed of the budgets of all the individual programs the center offers. To see how a budget is developed, we will look at the budget prepared for the Little League baseball program. (The complete budget for the program appears in Figure 16-1 on page 419.)

During the budget preparation period, two important estimates are made: the estimate for revenue and the estimate for expenditures. Let's look first at how the director of the Little League baseball program estimated the revenue the program would receive.

R — E — M — E — M — B — E — R

Estimating the amount of revenue expected to be received and the amount of expenditures expected to be made is the heart of the budget process.

Revenue Projections

Point out the different sources of revenue for the Little League baseball program. Ask students to name sources of revenue for some other not-for-profit organization.

Every program needs cash to operate. Every program, therefore, must make **revenue projections** —estimates of the money to be received during a budget period. One common method of making revenue projections is to base those projections on the budget and the actual revenue amounts from the previous year.

Look at the following table, which shows the previous year's budget and actual revenue amounts for the Little League baseball program. The difference between the budget and the actual amount received for each revenue source appears in the last column. The actual revenue received last year from team entry fees was $4,500, the same as the budget amount. Because of bad weather, however, the program received only $868 from tournament entry fees, $632 less than had been estimated. Fund-raising projects brought in $9,825, $175 less than expected. The program, however, received $345 more than expected from gifts (donations). Finally, the program received $5,500 from the general fund, $500 less than budgeted. (A certain amount of money is contributed to each program from the Center's general fund. The amount contributed is the difference between the program's expenditures and its revenue from other sources.) As you can see, the Little League baseball program actually received $962 less than it had budgeted.

Revenue	Previous Year's Budget	Previous Year's Actual	Over (Under) Budget
Entry Fees—Teams	$ 4,500	$ 4,500	$ 0
Entry Fees—Tournaments	1,500	868	(632)
Fund-Raising Projects	10,000	9,825	(175)
Gifts	5,000	5,345	345
General Fund Contribution	6,000	5,500	(500)
Total Revenue	$27,000	$26,038	($962)

Since the difference between the two totals was so small, the program director can assume that last year's revenue projections were realistic. If there are no major changes planned for the coming year, the program director can reuse the previous year's revenue projections.

Review how the previous year's actual and budgeted amounts are used in estimating the current year's budget.

If, however, the program is going to change in some way, or if there is reason to believe enrollment will change, the revenue projections should be adjusted. When this happens, the revenue projections should be based on the previous year's *actual* amounts. Those amounts should be increased or decreased by the amount of the expected change.

The director of the Little League baseball program developed the revenue projections that follow. During the previous year, 50 teams had participated in the program. Since the entry fee was $90 per team, the Little League baseball program received $4,500 in entry fees. During the coming year, Mountain Valley plans to increase the entry fee to $100. As a result, the revenue projection for team entry fees is $5,000 ($100 × 50). This projection is $500 over the previous year's actual revenue amount.

The director is projecting tournament entry fees of $1,500. This projection is the same as the previous year's budget amount, $632 more than was actually received. The program director may be asked to justify this rather large increase.

During the coming year, the program director plans to hold the same fund-raising activities. As a result, the fund-raising revenue is estimated to be $10,000.

During the previous year, the Little League baseball program received $5,345 in gifts by "passing the hat" at each game. Spectators, however, were asked to give more last year, because tournament entry fees were down. Since entry fees are expected to increase this year, the revenue projection for gifts is again set at $5,000.

Use demonstration problem 16-1 here.

The Little League baseball program receives contributions from the center's general fund to make up the difference between the revenue actually received and the expenditures actually made. During the previous year, the program had expenditures of $26,038 and revenue of $20,538. Therefore, $5,500 was contributed to the Little League program from the general fund. This year, the director estimates that $6,000 will be needed from the general fund.

	Previous Year's Actual	Current Year's Budget	Over (Under) Actual
Revenue			
Entry Fees—Teams	$ 4,500	$ 5,000	$ 500
Entry Fees—Tournament	868	1,500	632
Fund-Raising Projects	9,825	10,000	175
Gifts	5,345	5,000	(345)
General Fund Contribution	5,500	6,000	500
Total Revenue	$26,038	$27,500	$1,462

You may want to have students complete Exercise 16-1 at this point.

As you can see, the program director estimates that the total revenue for the coming year will be $27,500. For the budget to be balanced, the Little League program's expenditures cannot exceed $27,500.

R — E — M — E — M — B — E — R

Revenue projections can be developed by using the previous year's budgeted and actual amounts.

Expenditure Projections

Once the revenue projections have been determined, the expenditures for the budget period are determined. Estimates of the amounts to be paid out during a budget period are called **expenditure projections**. *Expenditures* are the costs incurred for goods and services used to carry out the goals of a program or an organization.

Point out that expenditure projections should not exceed revenue projections.

The expenditure projections for the Little League baseball program are determined in the same way as the revenue projections—that is, the expenditure projections are based on the budget and actual expenditure amounts from the previous year. Expenditure projections, however, must be equal to or less than the revenue projections. Remember that for the Little League baseball program, expenditure projections can be no more than $27,500.

Point out that the Little League baseball program's expenditures are classified by type of expenditure.

The first step is to compare the previous year's budget and actual expenditures. These are shown in the following table. Let's look at the difference between the budgeted and actual expenditures.

Expenditures	Previous Year's Budget	Previous Year's Actual	Over (Under) Budget
Wages			
Umpires—League Games	$ 9,500	$ 9,240	$ (260)
Umpires—Tournaments	3,500	1,875	(1,625)
Scorekeepers—League Games	2,000	2,000	0
Scorekeepers—Tournaments	650	400	(250)
Field Maintenance	5,000	5,600	600
Total Wages	$20,650	$19,115	$(1,535)
Operating Services			
Postage	$ 100	$ 75	$ (25)
Utilities	1,200	2,020	820
Miscellaneous Repairs	450	525	75
Other	200	140	(60)
Total Operating Services	$ 1,950	$ 2,760	$ 810
Supplies			
Scorebooks	$ 100	$ 96	$ (4)
Paint	500	482	(18)
Baseballs	1,000	966	(34)
Trophies	1,400	1,428	28
Awards	600	582	(18)
Light bulbs	300	289	(11)
Other	200	88	(112)
Total Supplies	$ 4,100	$ 3,931	$ (169)
Equipment			
Umpires' Equipment	$ 100	$ 80	$ (20)
Home Plates	100	60	(40)
Bases (1st, 2nd, & 3rd)	100	92	(8)
Total Equipment	$ 300	$ 232	$ (68)
Total Expenditures	$27,000	$26,038	$ (962)

Last year, the total wages expenditure was $1,535 less than the budget amount. As you can see, the actual expenditure for umpires' wages during the tournaments was $1,625 less than the budget amount; for scorekeepers, it was $250 less. These wage costs were lower because two tournaments were rained out. Wages for field maintenance personnel, however, were $600 over the budget amount.

The total operating services expenditure was $810 over budget last year. The major reason for this was the increased utilities cost. If utilities costs continue to increase, the expenditure projection for utilities should be increased in the coming budget period.

The actual supplies expenditure was $169 less than the budget amount. As you can see, only the expenditure for trophies was over the budget amount. At first glance, it looks as though the previous year's expenditure projections for supplies were too high. The budget director may have canceled the purchases of some supplies, however, to offset the higher utilities costs.

The expenditure for equipment was fairly low. The total actual expenditure for equipment was $232, $68 less than the budget amount.

Show how the previous year's expenditures are used to develop the coming year's expenditure projections.

The program director can use the previous year's expenditures to develop the expenditure projections for the coming year. The expenditure projections for the Little League baseball program's budget appear in the following table:

Expenditures	Previous Year's Actual	Current Year's Budget	Over (Under) Budget
Wages			
Umpires—League Games	$ 9,240	$ 9,240	$ 0
Umpires—Tournaments	1,875	3,200	1,325
Scorekeepers—League Games	2,000	2,000	0
Scorekeepers—Tournaments	400	650	250
Field Maintenance	5,600	6,000	400
Total Wages	$19,115	$21,090	$ 1,975
Operating Services			
Postage	$ 75	$ 100	$ 25
Utilities	2,020	1,500	(520)
Miscellaneous Repairs	525	475	(50)
Other	140	200	60
Total Operating Services	$ 2,760	$ 2,275	$ (485)
Supplies			
Scorebooks	$ 96	$ 100	$ 4
Paint	482	500	18
Baseballs	966	1,000	34
Trophies	1,428	1,400	(28)
Awards	582	600	18
Light bulbs	289	300	11
Other	88	100	12
Total Supplies	$ 3,931	$ 4,000	$ 69
Equipment			
Umpires' Equipment	$ 80	$ 50	$ (30)
Home Plates	60	25	(35)
Bases (1st, 2nd, & 3rd)	92	60	(32)
Total Equipment	$ 232	$ 135	$ (97)
Total Expenditures	$26,038	$27,500	$ 1,462

The total expenditure projection for wages is $21,090, an increase of $1,975. This increase is a result of the plan to increase the number of tournaments over those held last year. Wages for field maintenance personnel must also be raised because of the increased cost of maintaining the playing fields.

The total expenditure projection for operating services is $2,275, a decrease of $485 from last year's actual expenditure. The major reasons for this decrease are that fewer miscellaneous repairs are expected during the coming budget period and the director has a plan to reduce utilities costs.

The total supplies expenditure projection is $4,000, an increase of $69. The supplies budget must be increased to offset the higher cost per item for the year.

The total expenditure projection for equipment is being decreased by $97. The program director plans to purchase less equipment during this budget year.

Use demonstration problem 16-2 here.

As you can see, when projections are based on the actual amounts from the previous year, the program director must carefully examine the previous year's budget before increasing or decreasing any amounts for the coming budget year. The budget committee may ask the program director to justify any increases or decreases in the budget amounts.

You may want to have students complete Exercise 16-2 at this point.

After the revenue and expenditure projections have been determined, the program director prepares the complete Little League baseball program budget request. This budget, shown in Figure 16-1, is then presented to the budget committee for review and approval.

R — E — M — E — M — B — E — R

Expenditure projections cannot be more than the revenue projections.

Before reading further, do the following activity to check your understanding of the material you have just studied.

Check Your Learning

Using Figure 16-1, the completed Little League baseball program budget request, answer these questions on a sheet of notebook paper.

1. Is the current year's total revenue projection over or under the previous year's? By what amount?
2. Is the amount budgeted for utilities expense increasing or decreasing? By what amount?
3. How much was actually spent for equipment during the previous year?
4. What amount is budgeted for field maintenance for the current budget year? Is this over or under the previous year?
5. What was the amount contributed by the general fund during the previous year?

Compare your answers to those in the answers section. Reread the preceding part of the chapter to find the correct answers to any questions you may have missed.

Zero-Base Budgeting

Emphasize that, with zero-base budgeting, projections are developed "from scratch."

Budget projections can also be developed without using the previous year's figures. When the coming year's projections are developed as though they were being done for the first time, **zero-base budgeting** is being used.

Mountain View Recreation Center
Little League Baseball Program
Budget Request
January 15, 199-

	Previous Year's Actual	Current Year's Budget	Over (Under) Actual
Revenue			
Entry Fees—Teams	$ 4,500	$ 5,000	$ 500
Entry Fees—Tournament	868	1,500	632
Fund-Raising Projects	9,825	10,000	175
Gifts	5,345	5,000	(345)
General Fund Contribution	5,500	6,000	500
Total Revenue	$26,038	$27,500	$1,462
Expenditures			
Wages			
Umpires—League Games	$ 9,240	$ 9,240	$ 0
Umpires—Tournaments	1,875	3,200	1,325
Scorekeepers—League Games	2,000	2,000	0
Scorekeepers — Tournaments	400	650	250
Field Maintenance	5,600	6,000	400
Total Wages	$19,115	$21,090	$1,975
Operating Services			
Postage	$ 75	$ 100	$ 5
Utilities	2,020	1,500	(520)
Miscellaneous Repairs	525	475	(50)
Other	140	200	60
Total Operating Services	$ 2,760	$ 2,275	$ (485)
Supplies			
Scorebooks	$ 96	$ 100	$ 4
Paint	482	500	18
Baseballs	966	1,000	34
Trophies	1,428	1,400	(28)
Awards	582	600	18
Light bulbs	289	300	11
Other	88	100	12
Total Supplies	$ 3,931	$ 4,000	$ 69
Equipment			
Umpires' Equipment	$ 80	$ 50	$ (30)
Home Plates	60	25	(35)
Bases (1st, 2nd, & 3rd)	92	60	(32)
Total Equipment	$ 232	$ 135	$ (97)
Total Expenditures	$26,038	$27,500	$1,462

Figure 16-1 Completed Little League Baseball Program Budget

Preparing Revenue Projections

Discuss each revenue projection.

Using zero-base budgeting, the program director of the Mountain View Recreation Center develops the revenue projections by preparing an itemized list of the expected revenue from each source. The itemized revenue projections that were developed for the Little League baseball program are as follows:

Entry Fees—Teams		
(50 teams @ $100 per team)		$ 5,000
Entry Fees—Tournaments		
(5 tournaments, 20 teams per tournament, $15 entry fee; 5 × 20 × $15)		1,500
Fund-Raising Projects		
Cake Sales		
(1,000 cakes @ $3 profit each)	$3,000	
Bar-B-Que Dinner		
(1,000 meals @ $3 profit each)	3,000	
Car Wash		
(10 car washes; total 4,000 cars washed @ $1 per car)	4,000	
Total Fund-Raising Projects		10,000
Gifts		
(A hat will be passed at each game until target goal is met.)		5,000
General Fund		
(A request will be made for $6,000 in funding from the General Fund of Mountain View Recreation Center.)		6,000
Total Revenue		$27,500

Use demonstration problem 16-3 here.

You may want to have students complete Exercise 16-3 at this point.

Notice that a goal has been established for each revenue source. For example, the goal for the number of Little League teams is 50. Five tournaments are planned, with 20 teams at each tournament. Goals were also set for each fund-raising project. Notice that the total revenue projection is the same as that developed earlier. What is different is how the program director reached that projection.

R — E — M — E — M — B — E — R

With zero-base budgeting, projections are developed "from scratch"; amounts from the previous year are not used.

Preparing Expenditure Projections

Point out that each expenditure line item must be justified.

Expenditure projections are developed in the same manner as revenue projections. Each expenditure projection is prepared as though for the first time. The program director usually must justify each expenditure item with a brief, concise explanation.

Let's look at three expenditure projections developed using the zero-base budgeting method:

Umpires for Little League Games

Request: $9,240

The Little League games will be held over a ten-week period. During this time, 385 games will be scheduled. Two umpires are required for each game, and each umpire receives $12 per game.

Number of Games	385
Cost of umpires per game ($12 × 2)	× $24.00
Total cost for league umpires	$9,240.00

Paint

Request: $500

Each of the four fields must be painted once a week for ten weeks. Field paint is $12.50 a gallon, and a gallon will paint one field.

Number of times fields will be painted (10 weeks × 4 fields)	40
Cost of paint to stripe one field	× $12.50
Total cost for paint	$500.00

Umpire Equipment

Request: $50

This year four umpire protection masks must be purchased at a cost of $12.50 per mask.

Cost per mask	$12.50
Number of masks needed	× 4
Total cost for masks	$50.00

Use demonstration problem 16-4 here.

These are just a few examples of how expenditure projections are determined using zero-base budgeting. As you can see, each expenditure item projection must be justified with facts and figures.

You may want to have students complete Exercise 16-4 at this point.

R — E — M — E — M — B — E — R

Revenue and expenditure projections can be based on the previous year's budget and actual amounts, or they can be developed using zero-base budgeting.

Summarizing the Program Budget Requests

Mention that the budget request summary combines all of the program budgets.

After each program's budget is approved, the budget director of the Mountain View Recreation Center prepares a cover sheet that summarizes all the program budgets. The budget request summary combines the revenue and expenditure projections of all the center's programs onto one sheet. The entire budget for the Mountain View Recreation Center appears on this one page. Specific details about each program can be found by examining the program budgets, which follow the summary page.

Figure 16-2 shows the budget request summary for the Mountain View Recreation Center.

Mountain View Recreation Center
Budget Request Summary
For the Fiscal Year Ended June 30, 199-

	Previous Year's Actual	Current Year's Budget	Over (Under) Actual
Revenue			
Membership Fees	$ 52,704	$ 55,000	$2,296
United Way	15,000	15,000	0
Entry Fees—Leagues	11,300	12,500	1,200
Entry Fees—Tournaments	3,845	5,000	1,155
Concession Stands	15,268	15,000	(268)
Tuition and Fees	10,120	11,000	880
Fund-Raising Projects	16,356	16,000	(356)
Gifts	6,276	6,000	(276)
Total Revenue Projections	$130,869	$135,500	$4,631
Expenditures			
Personal Services			
Director's Salary	$ 32,500	$ 35,750	$3,250
Wages	51,160	54,000	2,840
Total Personal Services	$ 83,660	$ 89,750	$6,090
Operating Services			
Postage	$ 975	$ 1,000	$ 25
Utilities	20,520	19,700	(820)
Miscellaneous Repairs	2,480	2,400	(80)
Other	842	1,000	158
Total Operating Services	$ 24,817	$ 24,100	$ (717)
Supplies			
Scorebooks	$ 740	$ 800	$ 60
Trophies	4,050	4,000	(50)
Awards	3,640	3,600	(40)
Instructional Supplies	8,325	8,500	175
Prepaid Supplies	1,660	2,000	340
Other	1,280	1,250	(30)
Total Supplies	$ 19,695	$ 20,150	$ 455
Capital Outlay Acquisitions	$ 1,400	$ 1,500	$ 100
Total Expenditure Projections	$129,572	$135,500	$5,928

Figure 16-2 Budget Request Summary

Notice that the actual revenue received last year was $130,869, while actual expenditures totaled $129,572. The difference of $1,287 represents a surplus to the center, which was carried over into the current budget period. A **surplus** occurs when the revenue received is more than the expenditures made.

Before reading further, do the following activity to check your understanding of the material you have just studied.

Check Your Learning

Write your answers to these questions on a sheet of notebook paper.

1. What are the two major projections that must be made when preparing a budget?
2. What are the costs incurred for goods and services used to carry out the goals of an organization called?
3. What are two methods that can be used to develop budget amounts?
4. If there are 300 baseball games scheduled and the two umpires required for each game are paid $10 each, what is the expenditure projection for umpire wages?

Compare your answers to those in the answers section. Reread the preceding part of the chapter to find the correct answers to any questions you may have missed.

Budget Control

Emphasize the importance of budget controls.

Once the budget has been approved, a not-for-profit organization must turn its attention to controlling the budget. The budget revenue projections represent amounts the not-for-profit organization expects to receive to be able to reach its goals. The budget expenditure projections are the maximum expenditures approved for each item. To control the budget amounts, the organization must set up procedures and periodically compare the budget amounts with the actual revenue and expenditures. By comparing the current year's budget and actual amounts with the previous year's actual amounts, the budget director can determine if the revenue and expenditure projections are realistic and within the limits set by the budget.

Like most not-for-profit organizations, the Mountain View Recreation Center prepares a budget summary report. A **budget summary report** summarizes and compares the current year's budget and actual revenue and expenditure amounts with the previous year's actual revenue and expenditure amounts.

Point out how the budget summary report is used to control the budget and to plan for any budget adjustments that may have to be made.

The budget summary report prepared by the center is shown in Figure 16-3. Notice that this report was prepared for the first three months of the center's fiscal period. Notice, too, that the report is cumulative; that is, it reports the *total* amounts that have been received or paid out as of September 30. The center prepares a budget summary report at the end of each month. The report prepared on October 31 would report the total revenue and expenditure amounts for the four months ended October 31. Budget summary reports can also be prepared to report and compare revenue and expenditure amounts for a single month. Budget summary reports—either monthly or cumulative—are also usually prepared for each of the center's programs.

Mountain View Recreation Center
Budget Summary Report
For the Three Months Ended September 30, 199-

	(1) Current Year Budget Amount	(2) Current Y-T-D Amount	(3) Free Balance Amount (1 – 2)	(4) Previous Y-T-D Amount	(5) Over (Under) Previous Y-T-D (2 – 4)
Revenue					
Membership Fees	$ 55,000	$51,680	$ 3,320	$50,800	$ 880
United Way	15,000	3,750	11,250	3,750	0
Entry Fees—Leagues	12,500	9,300	3,200	8,900	400
Entry Fees—Tournaments	5,000	2,600	2,400	2,500	100
Concession Stands	15,000	8,000	7,000	8,125	(125)
Tuition and Fees	11,000	3,400	7,600	3,250	150
Fund-Raising Projects	16,000	7,975	8,025	8,200	(225)
Gifts	6,000	3,600	2,400	3,510	90
Total Revenue	$135,500	$90,305	$45,195	$89,035	$1,270
Expenditures					
Personal Services					
Director's Salary	$ 35,750	$ 8,937	$26,813	$ 8,125	$ 812
Wages	54,000	18,600	35,400	18,750	(150)
Total Personal Services	$ 89,750	$27,537	$62,213	$26,875	$ 662
Operating Services					
Postage	$ 1,000	$ 280	$ 720	$ 275	$ 5
Utilities	19,700	5,728	13,972	5,504	224
Miscellaneous Repairs	2,400	796	1,604	828	(32)
Other	1,000	150	850	125	25
Total Operating Services	$ 24,100	$ 6,954	$17,146	$ 6,732	$ 222
Supplies					
Scorebooks	$ 800	$ 350	$ 450	$ 325	$ 25
Trophies	4,000	1,360	2,640	1,270	90
Awards	3,600	1,120	2,480	1,190	(70)
Instructional Supplies	8,500	1,850	6,650	1,750	100
Prepaid Supplies	2,000	350	1,650	325	25
Other	1,250	452	798	428	24
Total Supplies	$ 20,150	$ 5,482	$14,668	$ 5,288	$ 194
Capital Outlay Acquisitions	$ 1,500	0	$ 1,500	$ 500	$ (500)
Total Expenditures	$135,500	$39,973	$95,527	$39,395	$ 578

Figure 16-3 Budget Summary Report

Let's now look more closely at this report and the information it presents. The budget summary report has five columns:

1. The figures in the Current Year Budget Amount column are the approved budget amounts for each item for the current budget period.

These amounts are the same as those reported on the budget request summary (Figure 16-2).

2. The Current Year-to-Date (Y-T-D) Amount column reports the actual cumulative revenue and expenditure amounts—the actual amounts received or paid out up to the date the report was prepared. On this report, the column summarizes the revenue received and expenditures made for the months of July, August, and September.

Show students how to determine the free balance.

3. A **free balance** is the budgeted amount that remains to be collected or spent as of a specific date. The free balance for each budget item is determined by subtracting the current year-to-date amount from the current budget amount (Column 1-Column 2).

Current year budget amount
– Current year-to-date amount
= Free balance

As you can see, the Free Balance Amount column can be used to control the organization's—or a particular program's—expenditures. If a program has a $50 free balance for awards, that is the maximum amount that can be spent on awards for the rest of the budget period. The program director may have to eliminate some planned awards purchases to stay within the budget limit.

4. The Previous Year-to-Date (Y-T-D) Amount column reports the actual revenue and expenditure amounts for the same period during the *previous* budget year. By comparing the previous year-to-date amounts with the current year-to-date amounts, the budget director can spot major differences or trends.

Show students how to determine the over/under amounts.

5. The Over (Under) Previous Year-to-Date (Y-T-D) column reports the difference between the Current Year-to-Date Amount column and the Previous Year-to-Date Amount column. This column serves as a warning light to the budget director. If there is a large difference between the year-to-date amounts for the two periods, the budget director should investigate the cause of the difference. If the actual revenue received to date during the current year is less than the amount received to date during the previous year, there may be cause for concern. For example, so far this year the center has received $7,975 from fund-raising projects. This amount is $225 less than had been received during the same period last year. If that trend continues, the center will not reach its goal of $16,000. The budget director will want to determine exactly why less money has been received this year. If an expenditure is running ahead of, or over, the previous year's expenditure, the budget director will also want to investigate the causes for the difference. For example, utilities costs to date are $5,728, $224 more than for the same period last year. If utilities use cannot be adjusted, it may be necessary to decrease the budgeted amounts for other expenditure items.

Use demonstration problem 16-5 here.

R — E — M — E — M — B — E — R

The free balance represents the amount of revenue still to be received or the expenditure still to be spent during the remainder of the budget period.

You may want to have students complete Exercise 16-5 at this point.

Before reading further, do the following activity to check your understanding of the material you have just studied.

Check Your Learning

Using Figure 16-3, the budget summary report, answer the following questions on a sheet of notebook paper.

1. What is the total projected revenue for the current year?
2. How much cash has been received to date from membership fees?
3. What amount remains to be received from the United Way?
4. Is the current year-to-date postage expenditure over or under the previous year-to-date amount? By what amount?
5. Which current revenue items are less than the previous year-to-date amounts?
6. How many expenditure items are over the previous year-to-date expenditures?

Compare your answers to those in the answers section. Reread the preceding part of the chapter to find the correct answers to any questions you may have missed.

Budget Adjustments

Give students several situations that would require budget adjustments to be made.

After reviewing the budget summary report, the budget director may decide that the budget amounts for certain items are not adequate. When this occurs, budget adjustments should be made. A **budget adjustment** is a change made to a current budget amount because of decreased revenue or increased expenditures. Budget adjustments must usually be approved by the budget committee.

Let's look at an example of a budget adjustment. For the Mountain View Recreation Center, the actual expenditure for utilities as of September 30 is $5,728. Using this amount, the budget director estimates that the total utilities expenditure for the year will be about $20,100. The budgeted amount (the maximum amount the center is authorized to spend) is only $19,700. The budget director must make a budget adjustment to increase the utilities budget by $400. It may be possible to increase the center's revenue by $500 by asking for additional donations or by holding an additional fund-raising activity. If not, decreases must be made in the budgeted amounts of other expenditure items to provide for the increased utilities cost.

R—E—M—E—M—B—E—R

If revenue is less than expected or expenditures are greater than expected, the budget amounts may have to be adjusted.

Summary of Key Points

1. An organization with goals other than earning a profit for its organizers is called a not-for-profit organization.
2. Not-for-profit organizations use a fund accounting system. A fund is a set of accounts used to record the transactions for a particular activity.
3. One tool used by not-for-profit organizations is a budget. A budget is a formal, written statement of expected revenue and expenditures for a future budget period. The most common budget period is twelve months.
4. The five basic principles involved in the budgeting process are: (a) develop long-term goals, (b) develop short-term goals, (c) define budgeting responsibilities, (d) establish budgeting guidelines, and (e) establish follow-up procedures.
5. A budget consists of two estimates: revenue projections and expenditure projections. Expenditure projections must be equal to or less than revenue projections.
6. Revenue and expenditure projections can be based on the previous year's actual amounts or developed from scratch, using zero-base budgeting.
7. Once a budget has been approved, the not-for-profit organization must set up procedures to monitor the actual revenue and expenditure amounts. A budget summary report can be prepared to summarize and compare the current year's budgeted and actual revenue and expenditure amounts with the previous year's actual amounts.
8. The free balance is the budgeted amount that remains to be collected or spent as of a specific date. It is determined by subtracting the current year-to-date amount from the current year budget amount.
9. It is sometimes necessary to adjust budget amounts if revenue is lower or expenditures higher than expected. Budget adjustments must usually be approved by the budget committee.

16 Review and Applications

Building Your Accounting Vocabulary

In your own words, write the definition of each of the following accounting terms. Use complete sentences for your definitions.

budget
budget adjustment
budget period
budget summary report
expenditure projection
free balance
fund
fund accounting
not-for-profit organization
revenue projection
surplus
zero-base budgeting

Reviewing Your Accounting Knowledge

1. What is the difference between a not-for-profit organization and a profit-oriented business?
2. Why is it said that a budget is one of the most important tools a not-for-profit organization can use?
3. What are the five basic principles of budgeting?
4. What is the relationship between long-term and short-term goals?
5. Why is it important to develop follow-up procedures during the budgeting process?
6. What two estimates must be made during the budget preparation period?
7. Name two methods that can be used to develop the budget projections for revenue and expenditures.
8. What is the purpose of the budget summary report?
9. How is the free balance amount for an item on the budget summary report determined?
10. Why is it sometimes necessary to make budget adjustments?

Improving Your Communications Skills

Redundant expressions have more words than are necessary to get the meaning across. Rewrite the following phrases to eliminate the extra words.

1. original source
2. every now and then
3. few in number
4. depreciated in value
5. advance planning
6. may possibly
7. good benefit
8. first priority
9. quite unique
10. if and when

Applying Accounting Procedures

SPREADSHEET PROBLEM

Exercise 16-1 Calculating Revenue Projections

The Mason City Softball Program had the following budget and actual revenue amounts last year.

	Budgeted Revenue	Actual Revenue
Entry Fees—Leagues	$3,750	$3,600
Entry Fees—Tournaments	1,600	1,200

Fifty teams were budgeted for the league at $75 per team; only 48 teams participated. Four tournaments were scheduled, each with 16 teams at $25 per team. One tournament was canceled because of rain.

Instructions: Calculate the current year's revenue projections for league entry fees and tournament entry fees using the following information. Also show the amount by which the projections are over or under the previous year's actual revenue.

$5,700; $2,100
$1,920; $720

1. The league entry fees will increase by $20 per team. Sixty teams are expected to particpate.
2. Team entry fees for the tournaments will increase by 20%. Four tournaments of 16 teams each are planned.

COMPUTER PROBLEM

Exercise 16-2 Calculating Expenditure Projections

The Edgeview Senior Center is preparing next year's budget. Following are four of last year's budget and actual expenditure amounts.

	Budgeted Expenditures	Actual Expenditures
Travel	$ 2,000	$ 1,600
Supplies	20,000	19,100
Repair and Maintenance	12,000	14,800
Electricity	17,000	18,000

Instructions: Calculate the expenditure projections for the four expenditures, given the following changes.

$1,760; $160
$21,000; $1,000
$16,000; $4,000
$18,900; $900

1. Travel costs are expected to increase 10% over last year's actual expenditures.
2. Supplies should increase 5% over the previous year's budget amount.
3. Repair and maintenance costs are estimated to increase $4,000 over the previous year's budget amount.
4. The utility company is projecting a 5% increase in energy costs.

COMPUTER PROBLEM

Exercise 16-3 Using Zero-Base Budgeting for Revenue Projections

The Bell City Youth Center, which uses zero-base budgeting, developed the following itemized goals for two of its revenue sources.

Membership Fees:	200 individuals @ $150 per person
	400 families @ $225 per family
Concession Stands:	Basketball 20 days @ $150 per day
	Softball 40 days @ $175 per day
	Baseball 50 days @ $200 per day
	T-Ball 30 days @ $125 per day

Revenue proj.:
Fees, $120,000
Stands, $23,750
Total, $143,750

Instructions: Calculate the current year's revenue projections for membership fees and concessions stands.

Exercise 16-4 Using Zero-Base Budgeting for Expenditure Projections

The Lakeland Community Center uses zero-base budgeting and has developed the following guidelines for the wages and salaries expenditures for the current year's budget.

Expend. proj.:
$25,000
$24,800
$16,000
$6,580

1. The director, whose current salary is $22,000, will receive a $3,000 raise.
2. The maintenance person, who currently earns $16,000, will receive a 5% raise. A new, part-time employee will be added at $8,000 per year.
3. The center expects to pay wages for 4,000 hours at $4 per hour.
4. Employee benefits are estimated at 10% of total wages and salaries.

Instructions: Calculate the expenditure projections for the four budget items.

SPREADSHEET PROBLEM

Exercise 16-5 Calculating Free Balances

The following table lists the current year's budget amounts, the current year-to-date amounts, and the previous year-to-date amounts for revenue and expenditure items for the Leesville City Chamber of Commerce for the first six months of its fiscal year.

	Current Year's Budget Amount	Current Y-T-D Amount	Previous Y-T-D Amount
Total Revenue	$190,000	$175,000	$177,800
Total Personal Services	$100,000	$ 47,000	$ 42,000
Total Travel	10,000	7,000	6,200
Total Operating Services	55,000	31,000	28,100
Total Supplies	20,000	17,000	16,200
Total Capital Outlay Acquisitions	5,000	3,400	2,000
Total Expenditures	$190,000	$105,400	$ 94,500

Total revenue:
$15,000; ($2,800)

Total expenditures:
$84,600; $10,900

Instructions: Calculate the free balance amounts and the difference between the current year's and previous year's amounts.

SPREADSHEET PROBLEM

Problem 16-1 Preparing the Revenue Section of a Budget Request

Last year's revenue projections and actual receipts for the Jackson Park Commission are as follows.

	Previous Year's Budget	Previous Year's Actual
Revenue		
Entry Fees—Leagues	$ 4,500	$ 4,470
Entry Fees—Tournaments	2,875	2,700
Donations	750	900
Tuition and Fees	2,000	1,820
Concession Stand	2,500	2,400
General Fund Contribution	5,000	5,000
Totals	$17,625	$17,290

The park directors made the following changes in the revenue items. All other revenue items remain the same as last year's budget amounts.

1. All entry fees will be raised 25% (based on actual receipts).
2. A fund-raising campaign is expected to increase last year's actual donations amount by 10%.
3. Concession stand prices will be increased 15% (based on actual receipts).

Total revenue: $19,712.50; $2,422.50

Instructions: Prepare the Revenue section of the budget request for the Jackson Park Commission. Use June 1 as the date.

Problem 16-2 Preparing the Expenditure Section of a Budget Request

The budget committee of the River Walk Health Care Center has been working on next year's budget for the past three months. The previous year's expenditure projections and actual expenditures are listed in the following table.

	Previous Year's Budget	Previous Year's Actual
Expenditures		
Salaries and Wages	$150,600	$145,600
Employee Benefits	18,072	17,472
Travel	9,000	8,350
Repairs and Maintenance	10,000	12,685
Electricity	14,000	12,500
Water	500	450
Contracted Services	12,000	15,000
Lab Expenses	40,000	29,500
Dues and Subscriptions	1,200	1,200
Supplies	22,000	21,400
Miscellaneous	3,000	2,680
Lab Equipment	50,000	45,000
Totals	$330,372	$311,837

The budget committee has recommended the following changes. Items not mentioned will remain the same as last year's budget amount.

1. Salaries and wages and employee benefits should increase 5% over the previous year's budget amount. In addition, one new employee will be hired at a salary of $15,000, with estimated employee benefits of $1,800.
2. A 15% increase over the previous year's actual expenditures is expected for the following items: repairs and maintenance, contracted services, lab expenses, supplies, and miscellaneous.
3. Electricity costs are expected to increase 25% over the previous year's actual amount.
4. The lab equipment budget will be $30,000 and the travel budget $10,000.

Total expenditures: $344,686.00; $32,849.00

Instructions: Prepare the Expenditure section of the budget request for the River Walk Health Care Center. Use February 15 as the date, and round all amounts to the nearest whole dollar.

SPREADSHEET PROBLEM

Problem 16-3 Preparing the Revenue Section of a Budget Request Using Zero-Base Budgeting

The Bay City Youth Center uses zero-base budgeting. The director of the center has made the following revenue estimates for the coming budget period.

Membership Fees	125 individuals @ $125 per person
	175 families @ $225 per family
Donations	$8,000 for the budget period of one year
Entry Fees	
Basketball	20 teams @ $50 per team
Softball	30 teams @ $75 per team
Baseball	24 teams @ $75 per team
T-Ball	20 teams @ $50 per team
Crafts Tuition	52 classes of 30 persons each; tuition $15 per person per class
Racquet Ball Court Rental	$400 per month
Skate Rentals	$200 per month
Locker Rentals	25 lockers @ $5 per month
United Way Contribution	$5,000 requested

Total revenue, $106,150

Instructions: Prepare the Revenue section of the budget request for the Bay City Youth Center. Use June 15 as the date.

SPREADSHEET PROBLEM

Problem 16-4 Preparing the Expenditure Section of a Budget Request Using Zero-Base Budgeting

The Williams Community Center uses zero-base budgeting. The director of the center has asked you to develop the expenditure projections for the swimming pool. The pool is indoors and is used all year.The previous year's budget information is as follows.

	Previous Year's Budget	Previous Year's Actual
Salaries—Director	$ 18,000	$ 18,000
Salaries—Maintenance Personnel	15,000	15,000
Wages—Life Guards	16,000	15,500
Wages—Instructors	12,000	11,800
Employee Benefits	6,100	6,030
Repairs and Maintenance	4,000	3,825
Electricity	32,000	36,100
Water	2,000	1,800
Pool Supplies	6,000	6,200
Equipment	3,000	3,000
Miscellaneous	1,000	365
Totals	$115,100	$117,620

Additional information that you have collected for the coming year is as follows.

Salaries and wages:	
Director	To receive a $3,000 raise.
Maintenance personnel	To receive a 10% raise.
Life guards	4,000 hours @ $5 per hour.
Instructors	50 classes @ $300 per class.
Employee benefits	Estimated at 10% of total wages and salaries.
Repairs and maintenance:	
Filter system	$1,200
Pool	1,600
Heater for pool	1,500
Miscellaneous	500
Electricity	Expected to increase 15% over last year's actual expenditure.
Water	Averages $160 a month.
Pool supplies	Pool chemicals cost $150 a month. Miscellaneous cleaning supplies are expected to cost $40 a month. Towel service averages $350 a month.
Equipment	One of the diving boards will be replaced at a cost of $2,000. New lane markers will be purchased for $150.
Miscellaneous	$500 has been budgeted.

Total expend., $137,115

Instructions: Using the information given, prepare the Expenditures section of the budget request for the Williams Community Center. Date the request August 15.

Problem 16-5 Preparing a Budget Request

The previous year's budget and actual revenue and expenditure amounts for the Century Club of Hamilton are shown in the following table.

	Previous Year's Budget	Previous Year's Actual
Revenue		
Membership Fees	$20,000	$22,000
Fund-Raising Projects		
Car Wash	2,800	2,680
Fruit Cake Sale	1,000	960
Spring Dance	4,500	4,750
Surplus	750	750
Gifts	9,150	8,483
United Way Contribution	20,000	20,000
Totals	$58,200	$59,623
Expenditures		
Maintenance Personnel	$21,000	$21,000
Office Services	4,700	5,415
Travel	1,000	845
Insurance	1,200	1,200
Dues and Subscriptions	1,000	869
Craft Supplies	4,000	3,850
Office Supplies	1,000	1,036
Repair Supplies	3,000	2,800
Refreshments	1,500	1,625
Electricity	9,000	9,583
Water	300	285
Equipment	10,000	10,000
Miscellaneous	500	625
Totals	$58,200	$59,133

Total revenue: $59,889; $266

Total expenditures: $59,889; $756

Instructions: Use the previous year's amounts and the information that follows to prepare the complete budget request for the Century Club of Hamilton for the year ended June 30. Round all amounts to the nearest whole dollar.

The budget committee expects the following changes over the previous year's budget amounts.

1. The goal for this year's membership drive is $25,000.
2. The club plans to discontinue the fruit cake sale fund-raising project. Four car washes are planned; each is expected to raise $800. The spring dance should raise $5,000.
3. The club has a surplus of $490.
4. The club has requested $20,000 from the United Way.
5. The amount projected for gifts is the difference between the total expenditure projections and the projected revenue from other sources.
6. Salaries for maintenance personnel will increase 5%.
7. The estimate for part-time office help is 1,000 hours at $6 per hour.
8. Craft, office, and repair supplies are each expected to increase 15%.
9. Electricity costs are expected to be 20% above the previous year's actual expenditures.
10. The equipment list prepared by the director totals $6,000.

SPREADSHEET PROBLEM

Problem 16-6 Preparing a Budget Summary Report

The table that follows lists actual revenue and expenditure amounts for the Reeves Chamber of Commerce for the first three months of its fiscal year. The table also lists the current year's budget amounts and the year-to-date amounts for the previous budget year.

	Current Year Budget Amount	Current Y-T-D Amount	Previous Y-T-D Amount
Revenue			
Dues	$ 75,000	$52,000	$53,200
Interest	5,000	438	425
Sale of Services	12,000	1,250	1,000
Project Income	8,000	900	1,200
Contributions	23,000	8,250	9,400
Totals	$123,000	$62,838	$65,225
Expenditures			
Salaries	$ 42,000	$10,500	$ 9,850
Payroll Taxes	2,600	800	725
Employee Benefits	4,200	1,050	985
Travel	3,000	600	800
Rent	9,000	2,250	2,250
Electricity	6,000	1,268	1,055
Telephone	2,400	655	640
Office Cleaning	3,000	750	600
Insurance	6,000	2,000	2,000
Conferences	1,000	425	600
Membership Development	2,000	800	1,500
Dues	7,200	3,528	2,698
Printing	3,100	1,500	2,300
Office Supplies	7,000	900	1,250
Postage	5,000	2,100	2,010
Office Equipment	15,000	8,000	14,000
Audit	4,000	0	0
Miscellaneous	500	75	89
Totals	$123,000	$37,201	$43,352

Total revenue: $60,162; ($2,387)

Total expenditures: $85,799; ($6,151)

Instructions: Prepare a budget summary report for the Reeves Chamber of Commerce for the three months ended March 31. Determine the free balance amounts and the amount the current year's amounts are over or under the prior year's actual amounts. Use the form provided in the working papers.

CHALLENGE PROBLEM

Problem 16-7 Preparing a Revised Budget

The Beaumont Teen Center is a neighborhood center that provides services and recreational activities such as arts and crafts, dances, vocational instruction, counseling, and organized sports.

The center's budget director prepares an annual budget. Every three months, a budget summary report is prepared and analyzed. A portion of that report for the six months ended June 30 follows.

	Current Year Budget Amount	Current Y-T-D Amount	Free Balance Amount	Previous Y-T-D Amount
Revenue				
Membership Fees	$30,000	$14,800	$15,200	$14,200
United Way Contribution	10,000	5,000	5,000	5,000
Athletic Fees	15,500	8,600	6,900	8,300
Donations	9,000	5,600	3,400	4,200
Dances	8,300	3,000	5,300	5,000
Fund-Raising Projects	14,000	9,200	4,800	8,525
Total Revenue	$86,800	$46,200	$40,600	$45,225
Expenditures				
Personal Services				
Director's Salary	$30,000	$15,000	$15,000	$14,000
Wages	20,000	9,500	10,500	10,000
Total Personal Services	$50,000	$24,500	$25,500	$24,000
Operating Services				
Utilities	$ 7,000	$ 3,780	$ 3,220	$ 3,525
Office Supplies	2,500	1,200	1,300	1,600
Repairs	3,500	2,125	1,375	1,987
Postage	900	500	400	675
Insurance	1,200	600	600	600
Total Operating Services	$15,100	$ 8,205	$ 6,895	$ 8,387
Supplies				
Awards	$ 1,000	$ 800	$ 200	$ 400
Sports Equipment	2,500	1,700	800	1,200
Repair Supplies	4,000	2,580	1,420	1,156
Miscellaneous Supplies	1,200	600	600	725
Dance Supplies	2,000	895	1,105	1,568
Total Supplies	$10,700	$ 6,575	$ 4,125	$ 5,049
Capital Outlay Acquisitions				
Equipment	$ 8,000	$ 5,000	$ 3,000	$ 3,250
Furniture	3,000	0	3,000	2,000
Total	$11,000	$ 5,000	$ 6,000	$ 5,250
Total Expenditures	$86,800	$44,280	$42,520	$42,686

The budget director now expects that revenue from membership fees will be approximately 90% of the original budgeted amount and that revenue from dances will be only 75% of the original budgeted amount. Revenue from donations is expected to be 15% higher than originally projected.

The budget director has asked you to prepare a revised budget. Some of the expenditure projections will have to be adjusted to accommodate the revised revenue amounts.

Instructions: Prepare a revised annual budget that includes your recommendations for changes in the revenue and expenditure projections. Use the form provided in the working papers.

FOCUS ON CAREERS

Accounting in Government Circles

As everyone knows, businesses provide services with the goal of earning a profit for the owners. The federal government, on the other hand, offers services without operating on a profit basis. As a result of this difference, the accounting methods of government agencies vary somewhat from those in the business world. A federal agency's success is gauged in terms of how well it uses resources, such as people and equipment, rather than how much profit it earns. If the resources are being used effectively and the programs the agency implements are working, taxpayer dollars are being well spent.

Government agencies operate in many areas, providing both services and regulation. Agencies that produce products require many of the same accounting tasks performed by private accountants. For example, the Bureau of Engraving and Printing, an agency of the Department of the Treasury, prints money, postage stamps, and securities. Accountants for this agency prepare financial reports and make sure that the price charged for the agency's products is enough to cover expenses. If income exceeds expenses, the money is returned to operations. Accountants also look for ways to control costs and to use technological innovations to improve operations.

Many employment opportunities in accounting exist at all levels and branches of the federal government. If you are interested in government accounting, check to see what positions are available to you at city and state levels, too.

Accounting in government requires good use of resources—people and equipment.

Chapter 17

NOT-FOR-PROFIT ORGANIZATIONS: FINANCIAL REPORTING

In Chapter 16, you learned that some organizations are established to provide services for their members or the general public. These not-for-profit organizations use an accounting system called *fund accounting*.

Like profit-oriented businesses, not-for-profit organizations prepare financial statements that summarize their financial activities.

The financial statements of a not-for-profit organization communicate information to current and potential contributors and users to help them evaluate the services provided and the organization's ability to continue to provide these services. In this chapter, you'll learn about two financial statements commonly prepared by not-for-profit organizations.

Learning Objectives

When you have completed this chapter, you should be able to do the following:

1. Name and explain the purpose of two financial statements commonly prepared by a not-for-profit organization.
2. Prepare a statement of revenue, expenditures, and changes in fund balance for a not-for-profit organization.
3. Prepare a fund balance sheet for a not-for-profit organization.
4. Define the accounting terms presented in this chapter.

New Terms

fund balance
statement of revenue, expenditures, and changes in fund balance
self-generated revenue
support revenue
capital additions revenue
program expenditures
object expenditures
deficit

End-of-Period Reporting for Not-for-Profit Organizations

At the end of a fiscal period, a for-profit business prepares financial statements that summarize the financial condition of the business and the results of its operations. These statements are of interest to a number of people, including owners, employees, management, and creditors.

The financial statements a not-for-profit organization prepares are also of interest to many people. These individuals use the statements to measure the organization's service efforts and accomplishments and to determine whether existing services need to be expanded or discontinued. Management, contributors, and users of the organization study the financial statements when discussing and planning for future activities. Creditors, of course, are also interested in these statements; they want to know whether the organization can pay its debts.

Point out the major purpose of financial statements for not-for-profit organizations.

The major purpose of these financial statements is not to measure profit but to measure performance. The financial statements can answer questions such as: Did the organization stay within its budget? Were contributions used for the purposes for which they were intended? How well did management carry out its financial responsibilities? Are the services offered by the organization worth the cost?

Most not-for-profit organizations prepare two types of financial statements at the end of a fiscal period: (1) a statement of revenue, expenditures and changes in fund balance and (2) a balance sheet.

Statement of Revenue, Expenditures, and Changes in Fund Balance

In a profit-oriented business, the main measure of performance is the amount of profit the business has earned. The effectiveness of a not-for-profit organization is measured by the services it provides for the money it has available. Obviously, a not-for-profit organization tries to use the money it receives wisely to be able to meet its goals.

Review the purpose of fund accounting.

In Chapter 16, you learned that a not-for-profit organization usually has a number of funds (sets of accounts that summarize the transactions for particular activities). For example, a university might have a scholarship fund; a student loan fund; a property, plant, and equipment fund; and so on. The university will also have a *general fund,* a set of accounts that is not restricted to a specific purpose. The resources of the general fund can be used for any purpose designated by the director of the organization. The normal day-to-day transactions of the organization are usually recorded in the accounts of the general fund.

Discuss the term *fund balance* and compare it with owner's equity.

Readers of a not-for-profit organization's financial statements want to know the financial condition of the organization's various funds. They also want to know about the changes that have affected the fund balances. A **fund balance** is the difference between the assets and the liabilities of a particular fund. The fund balance is similar to the owner's equity of a profit-oriented business.

ACCOUNTING Notes
The chief executive officer of a corporation is the president or chairperson of the board of directors. The CEO of a not-for-profit organization is the director, mayor, or some other person designated for the position.

The financial statement that reports a not-for-profit organization's revenue and expenditures for a budget period as well as the change in the fund balance is called a **statement of revenue, expenditures, and changes in fund balance**. This statement is prepared for *each* fund that the not-for-profit organization has. A statement that combines the results for all of the organization's funds can also be prepared at the end of the fiscal period.

Let's look at the statement the Merryville Memorial Library prepared for its general fund. The library's statement of revenue, expenditures, and changes in fund balance is divided into three parts: sources of revenue, expenditures (by program and object), and changes in fund balance.

R — E — M — E — M — B — E — R

The fund balance is the difference between the assets and the liabilities of a particular fund.

Sources of Revenue Section

As you recall, a for-profit business earns revenue by providing services or selling goods to customers. A not-for-profit organization usually has several sources of revenue. For example, the Merryville Memorial Library has three sources of revenue: self-generated revenue, support revenue, and capital additions revenue.

Discuss the three sources of revenue.

Self-generated revenue is the revenue a not-for-profit organization earns from delivering or producing goods, providing services, or performing other activities. Examples of self-generated revenue include membership dues; rental, entry, or tuition fees; taxes; interest on investments; and the money received from fund-raising projects.

Support revenue for a not-for-profit organization refers to the contributions received from individuals, businesses, or other organizations. Support revenue includes gifts, donations, grants, money left to the organization in a will, and the contribution of services or facilities. The not-for-profit organization can use support revenue for any purpose. As a result, support revenue may also be called *unrestricted funds*.

Emphasize the difference between unrestricted and restricted revenue.

Capital additions revenue is the money a not-for-profit organization receives that is restricted to a particular use by the contributor. For example, a gift of $100,000 that must be used to build an art gallery is considered capital additions revenue. Money given to a college to be used for student loans is another example. Such revenue can be used only for the specific purpose outlined by the person or group donating the money.

Compare this Sources of Revenue section with the Revenue section on an income statement.

Now let's look at the Sources of Revenue section of the Merryville Memorial Library's statement of revenue, expenditures, and changes in fund balance, which appears in Figure 17-1. As you can see, the revenue is reported as either self-generated, support, or capital additions revenue.

The Merryville Memorial Library has three sources of self-generated revenue: fees for services (media center usage, copy machine usage,

Merryville Memorial Library
Statement of Revenue, Expenditures, and Changes in Fund Balance
General Fund
For the Budget Period Ended June 30, 199-

Sources of Revenue			
Self-Generated:			
Fees for services		$32,800	
Book rentals and fines		44,500	
Investment income		3,000	
Total Self-Generated Revenue			$80,300
Support:			
Grants			
Government	$75,000		
Other	15,000	$90,000	
Contributions		30,000	
Contributed services of volunteers		56,000	
Contributed use of facilities		24,000	
Total Support Revenue			200,000
Capital Additions:			
For books		$25,000	
For artwork		22,000	
Total Capital Additions Revenue			47,000
Total Revenue			$327,300

Figure 17-1 Sources of Revenue Section of a Statement of Revenue, Expenditures, and Changes in Fund Balance

rental of computer time, or library loan services), book rentals and fines, and investment income.

There are four sources of support revenue. During this fiscal year, the library received a government grant of $75,000 and other grants totaling $15,000. These funds are unrestricted; that is, they can be used for whatever purpose the director chooses. The director may want to use the funds to improve the library's services by increasing circulation or by buying new media equipment or computer terminals.

The contributions support revenue was received from a fund drive in which individuals were asked to pledge and give a certain amount. This revenue is also unrestricted although many organizations now specify how contributions from fund-raising projects will be used.

The contributed services of volunteers represents the time donated by various individuals to the library. Since these persons do not work for pay, their services represent a $56,000 donation to the library. The amount reported is the fair market value of the volunteers' services.

The contributed facilities support revenue of $24,000 is the amount of rent the library would have had to pay had it rented its facilities. Since the owner allows the library to use the building free of charge, the library is actually receiving a $24,000 donation. This revenue is also reported at the fair market value.

Use demonstration problem 17-1 here.

During the year, several individuals gave money to the library to buy books and artwork. Since the use of this revenue is restricted, it is reported as capital additions revenue. Notice that the specific purposes of the capital additions revenue are listed on the statement.

R — E — M — E — M — B — E — R

Self-generated revenue is the revenue earned from delivering or producing goods, rendering services, or performing other activities. Support revenue comes from the unrestricted contributions from individuals, businesses, or other organizations. Capital additions revenue consists of the restricted contributions received from individuals or groups.

Before reading further, do the following activity to check your understanding of sources of revenue for a not-for-profit organization.

Check Your Learning

Write your answers to these questions on a sheet of notebook paper.

1. A community health clinic is an example of a(n) __?__.
2. The __?__ reports on the revenue and the expenditures of a particular fund as well as the difference between the assets and liabilities of the fund.
3. The normal day-to-day transactions of a not-for-profit organization are recorded in the __?__ fund.
4. Money received from membership fees is considered to be __?__ revenue.
5. __?__ revenue can be used only for the purpose specified by the donor.

You may want to have students complete Exercise 17-1 at this point.

Compare your answers to those in the answers section. Reread the preceding part of the chapter to find the correct answers to any questions you may have missed.

Expenditures Section

Discuss object expenditures first.

Place the object expenditures on the board and point out that these expenditures are similar to those of profit-oriented businesses.

In Chapter 16, you learned that expenditures are the costs incurred for goods and services used to carry out the goals of an organization. Not-for-profit organizations often classify their expenditures by program or by object. **Program expenditures** are all of the expenditures made for a particular program of the organization. For example, the Merryville Memorial Library's programs include the circulating library, the research library, collections and exhibits, educational services, community services, fund raising, and general administration.

Object expenditures are the expenditures of an organization classified according to the type of cost. The object expenditures for the Merryville Memorial Library include the costs for personnel (wages, salaries, and fringe benefits), travel, purchased services (utilities, rent, insurance, and so on), supplies, equipment, and the books and artwork purchased for the library.

Use demonstration problem 17-2 here.

R — E — M — E — M — B — E — R

Program expenditures and object expenditures are two different methods of reporting the same expenditures.

On the statement of revenue, expenditures, and changes in fund balance, some organizations report their expenditures on a program basis, while others use the object basis. The Merryville Memorial Library reports its expenditures by both methods, as shown in Figure 17-2.

Expenditures		
Program Expenditures:		
Circulating library		$ 85,400
Research library		81,569
Collections and exhibits		46,686
Educational services		42,500
Community services		17,250
General administration		48,300
Fund raising		4,000
Total Program Expenditures		$325,705
Object Expenditures:		
Personnel:		
Salaries	$36,000	
Wages	56,000	
Fringe benefits	4,500	
Total Personnel		$ 96,500
Travel		4,100
Purchased Services:		
Rent	$24,000	
Utilities	19,300	
Maintenance contracts	15,750	
Subscriptions	33,200	
Insurance	4,500	
Other	4,200	
Total Purchased Services		100,950
Supplies		11,655
Equipment		5,500
Library Books		60,000
Capital Additions:		
Library books	$25,000	
Library artwork	22,000	
Total Capital Additions		47,000
Total Object Expenditures		$325,705

Figure 17-2 Expenditures Section of a Statement of Revenue, Expenditures, and Changes in Fund Balance

Introduce classifying expenditures according to a particular program of the organization.

Notice that the program expenditures include the costs of specific programs (circulating library, collections and exhibits, and so on) as well as the costs for management (general administration) and fund-raising. Users of the statement can easily review the costs for each program. For example, you can see that the total cost for the library's collections and exhibits program was $46,686. Reporting the library expenditures in this manner enables readers to compare a program's costs with the services it provides.

The object expenditures report all of the different types of costs incurred by the library. A user looking at this part of the statement can tell at a glance exactly how much was spent during the budget period for, say, purchased services or, more specifically, insurance or utilities.

Point out that object expenditures are prorated among the different programs of the organization.

Wages of $56,000 and rent of $24,000 are listed as object expenditures. These are the same amounts reported as support revenue in the first section of the statement (as contributed services of volunteers and contributed use of facilities). These amounts are also reported in the Expenditures section to give a truer picture of the operations of the library. They are the amounts the library would have had to pay out had the volunteers' services and the library facilities not been donated.

Stress that total object expenditures and total program expenditures will always be the same since they are two different methods of accounting for the same expenditures.

Use demonstration problem 17-3 to classify by program and object the expenditures given in demonstration problem 17-2.

You may want to have students complete Exercise 17-2 at this point.

Notice, also, that the amounts reported for total program expenditures and for total object expenditures are the same: $325,705. Remember that program expenditures and object expenditures are two different ways of classifying the *same* costs. The program expenditures include all of the costs classified as object expenditures. The object expenditures are allocated to the various programs. For example, personnel costs are allocated to the library's programs according to the time the staff spend on that program. If a staff member spends 20% of her or his time dealing with circulation services, 20% of that person's salary is allocated to the circulation program.

Before reading further, do the following activity to check your understanding of the material you have just studied.

Check Your Learning

On a sheet of notebook paper, indicate whether each of the following items represents a program expenditure or an object expenditure for the Glenview Community Center.

1. Fund raising
2. Craft classes
3. Utilities
4. Cleaning services
5. Community service
6. Note paper
7. Equipment
8. Insurance
9. Wages
10. Rent
11. Adult swimming
12. General administration
13. Basketball league
14. Maintenance contract
15. Exercise classes

Compare your answers to those in the answers section. Reread the preceding part of the chapter to find the correct answers for any items you may have missed.

Changes in Fund Balance Section

Point out that this portion of the statement is similar to a statement of retained earnings or a statement of changes in owner's equity.

The statement of revenue, expenditures, and changes in fund balance contains a section that reports the effect that the current year's operations have had on the fund balance. This section of the statement reports (1) the beginning fund balance, (2) the net increase or decrease in the fund balance for the budget period, and (3) the ending fund balance.

Review the meaning of fund balance.

Earlier in this chapter, we defined a fund balance as the difference between the assets and the liabilities of a particular fund. The operations of the not-for-profit organization during the budget period either increase or decrease the fund balance. The amount of the change in the fund balance for the budget period depends on the difference between revenue and expenditures. In a profit-oriented business, if revenue exceeds expenses, the ownership equity of the business increases. If expenses exceed revenue, the ownership equity of the business decreases. Likewise, in a not-for-profit organization, if revenue exceeds expenditures (a surplus), the fund balance increases. If expenditures exceed revenue, a **deficit** exists. A deficit decreases the fund balance.

Point out that the beginning fund balance for the current period was the ending fund balance of the previous year.

The revenue for the general fund of the Merryville Memorial Library for the budget period was \$327,300. As you've just seen, the fund's total expenditures were \$325,705. For this budget period, there is a surplus of \$1,595 (\$327,300 – \$325,705). There is, therefore, an increase in the fund balance of \$1,595. The final section of the statement of revenue, expenditures, and changes in fund balance reports this increase as shown in Figure 17-3. As you can see, the increase in the fund balance is added to the beginning fund balance amount. The resulting amount, \$97,395, is the ending fund balance amount for the budget period.

Beginning fund balance, July 1, 199-	\$ 95,800
Increase in fund balance	1,595
Ending fund balance, June 30, 199-	\$ 97,395

Figure 17-3 Reporting an Increase in the Fund Balance

Suppose, for example, that the total expenditures for the budget period had been \$330,600. In this case, expenditures exceed revenue by \$3,300 (\$330,600 – \$327,300). This deficit results in a decrease in the fund balance. The decrease would be reported in the final section of the statement as shown in Figure 17-4.

Beginning fund balance, July 1, 199-	\$ 95,800
Decrease in fund balance	3,300
Ending fund balance, June 30, 199-	\$ 92,500

Figure 17-4 Reporting a Decrease in the Fund Balance

Use demonstration problem 17-4 here.

As you have seen, the statement of revenue, expenditures, and changes in fund balance reports the results of the organization's current

Discuss the complete statement of revenue, expenditures, and changes in fund balance.

operations and the effects of those operations on the fund balance. The statement, then, combines the information that would be reported on a business's income statement and statement of changes in owner's equity (or statement of retained earnings). Figure 17-5 shows the complete statement for the Merryville Memorial Library.

Merryville Memorial Library
Statement of Revenue, Expenditures, and Changes in Fund Balance
General Fund
For the Budget Period Ended June 30, 199-

Sources of Revenue			
Self-Generated:			
Fees for services		$32,800	
Book rentals and fines		44,500	
Investment income		3,000	
Total Self-Generated Revenue			$ 80,300
Support:			
Grants			
Government	$75,000		
Other	15,000	$90,000	
Contributions		30,000	
Contributed services of volunteers		56,000	
Contributed use of facilities		24,000	
Total Support Revenue			200,000
Capital Additions:			
For books		$25,000	
For artwork		22,000	
Total Capital Additions Revenue			47,000
Total Revenue			$327,300
Expenditures			
Program Expenditures:			
Circulating library			$ 85,400
Research library			81,569
Collections and exhibits			46,686
Educational services			42,500
Community services			17,250
General administration			48,300
Fund-raising			4,000
Total Program Expenditures			$325,705
Object Expenditures:			
Personnel:			
Salaries		$36,000	
Wages		56,000	
Fringe benefits		4,500	
Total Personnel			$ 96,500

Figure 17-5 Completed Statement of Revenue, Expenditures, and Changes in Fund Balance

Travel		4,100
Purchased Services:		
Rent	$24,000	
Utilities	19,300	
Maintenance contracts	15,750	
Subscriptions	33,200	
Insurance	4,500	
Other	4,200	
Total Purchased Services		100,950
Supplies		11,655
Equipment		5,500
Library Books		60,000
Capital Additions:		
Library books	$25,000	
Library artwork	22,000	
Total Capital Additions		47,000
Total Object Expenditures		$325,705
Beginning fund balance, July 1, 199-		$ 95,800
Increase in fund balance		1,595
Ending fund balance, June 30, 199-		$ 97,395

You may want to have students complete Exercise 17-3 at this point.

Figure 17-5 Completed Statement of Revenue, Expenditures, and Changes in Fund Balance (cont.)

Balance Sheet

The second major financial statement prepared by not-for-profit organizations is a balance sheet. The balance sheet is prepared as of the end of the fiscal period and reports the balances of the asset, liability, and fund balance accounts of a particular fund. A separate balance sheet is prepared for each of the organization's funds. Most not-for-profit organizations prepare several balance sheets. A combined balance sheet, which reports the balances of all of the organization's funds, can also be prepared. In this chapter, you'll look at two balance sheets prepared by the Merryville Memorial Library: the general fund balance sheet and the property, plant, and equipment fund balance sheet.

Point out that not-for-profit organizations prepare a balance sheet for each fund and then prepare a combined balance sheet.

General Fund Balance Sheet

An organization's general fund represents the resources available to the organization that have no external limitations placed on their use. (*External limitations* are the restrictions on the use of the donated funds imposed by the contributors themselves.) The general fund can be used for any purpose designated by the organization's director or governing board. For example, the general fund can be used for current operations or to purchase certificates of deposit.

Point out how the Fund Balance section takes the place of owner's equity or stockholder's equity of a for-profit business.

Figure 17-6 shows the general fund balance sheet for the Merryville Memorial Library. As you can see, it is organized much like the balance sheet of a for-profit business.

Merryville Memorial Library
General Fund Balance Sheet
June 30, 199-

Assets			
Cash in Bank			$ 2,985
Certificates of Deposit (Note 2)			75,000
Grants Receivable (Note 1)			
Government		$30,000	
Other		5,000	35,000
Prepaid Expenses			3,000
Total Assets			$115,985
Liabilities			
Accounts Payable			$ 18,590
Fund Balance			
Designated by Governing Board			
Investments	$25,000		
Purchase of computer equipment	35,000		
Total Restricted Fund Balance		$60,000	
Undesignated Fund Balance		37,395	
Total Fund Balance			97,395
Total Liabilities and Fund Balance			$115,985

Figure 17-6 General Fund Balance Sheet

Discuss designated and undesignated funds.

In Chapter 10, you learned that the board of directors of a corporation may choose to appropriate (set aside) a part of Retained Earnings for some specific purpose. Likewise, the governing board of the library, which is similar to a corporation's board of directors, may decide to set aside a portion of the fund balance for specific purposes. For example, the governing board decided to invest $25,000 in a 12-month certificate of deposit and to purchase $35,000 in computer equipment. These internal designations of the fund balance should be reported on the general fund balance sheet.

Use demonstration problem 17-5 here.

Property, Plant, and Equipment Fund Balance Sheet

The Merryville Memorial Library also prepares a balance sheet for its property, plant, and equipment fund. Property, plant, and equipment, you'll remember, are long-lived assets that are used over several accounting periods. For the Merryville Memorial, this type of asset includes library books and artwork in addition to the more typical equipment.

Emphasize that capitalized expenditures are first reported as object expenditures—capital additions.

The purchase of several types of property, plant, and equipment assets were reported in the Expenditures section of the statement of revenue, expenditures, and changes in fund balance prepared for the general fund. These assets included the following:

Equipment	$ 5,500
Library books (unrestricted)	60,000
Library books (capital additions)	25,000
Artwork (capital additions)	22,000
Total	$112,500

Since these assets will be used for more than one year, they should also be recorded in the property, plant, and equipment fund accounts and reported on that fund's balance sheet. The process of transferring the general fund expenditures to the property, plant, and equipment fund is called *capitalizing an expenditure*.

Point out that capitalization takes place at the end of the accounting period.

For this budget period, general fund expenditures of $112,500 must be capitalized and reported as assets on the property, plant, and equipment fund balance sheet. The balance sheet that was prepared for the property, plant, and equipment fund of the Merryville Memorial Library appears in Figure 17-7.

Merryville Memorial Library
Property, Plant, and Equipment Fund Balance Sheet
June 30, 199-

	Previous Year's Balance	Current Year's Capitalization	Current Year's Balance
Assets			
Computer Equipment (Net)	$ 100,000	$ 0	$ 100,000
Library Books	1,250,000	85,000	1,335,000
Library Equipment (Net)	268,000	5,500	273,500
Artwork	98,300	22,000	120,300
Total Assets	$1,716,300	$112,500	$1,828,800
Liabilities and Fund Balance			
Liabilities	$ 0	$ 0	$ 0
Fund Balance	1,716,300	112,500	1,828,800
Total Liabilities and Fund Balance	$1,716,300	$112,500	$1,828,800

Figure 17-7 Property, Plant, and Equipment Fund Balance Sheet

Notice that the current year's expenditures for property, plant, and equipment assets are added to the beginning account balances. The new account balances are reported in the Current Year's Balance column.

Use demonstration problem 17-6 here.

The current year's capitalization amount is also added to the beginning fund balance amount. (The increase in the asset accounts results in an increase in the fund balance.) Since there are no liabilities, the total assets amount equals the ending fund balance amount.

Before reading further, do the following activity to check your understanding of the material you have just studied.

Check Your Learning

Write your answers to these questions on a sheet of notebook paper.

1. If revenue is less than expenditures, a fund has a(n) ___?___.
2. If the assets of a not-for-profit organization are $124,500 and the liabilities are $15,600, the fund balance is ___?___.
3. The governing board of a not-for-profit organization may designate a part or all of the ___?___ for a specific purpose.
4. The process of transferring general fund expenditures to the property, plant, and equipment fund is called ___?___.

Compare your answers to those in the answers section. Reread the preceding part of the chapter to find the correct answers to any questions you may have missed.

Services that volunteers contribute to not-for-profit organizations are reported as support revenue and as personnel expenditures at the fair market value.

Notes to Financial Statements

Point out the importance of the notes to the financial statement section.

In Chapter 11, you learned that businesses often present additional useful information on a separate sheet accompanying the financial statements. These notes to financial statements explain significant matters not disclosed in the financial statements and the accounting policies followed by the organization. Not-for-profit organizations also prepare these notes. The notes to the financial statements of the Merryville Memorial Library appear in Figure 17-8.

Merryville Memorial Library
Notes to Financial Statements
For the Budget Year Ended June 30, 199-

Note 1: Summary of Significant Accounting Policies

The financial statements of the Merryville Memorial Library have been prepared on the accrual basis.

The assets, liabilities, and fund balances are reported on two balance sheets.

General fund sources of revenue restricted by donor, grantor, or other outside party for particular purposes are reported as revenue in the year the money is spent.

Property, plant, and equipment acquisitions are accounted for as general fund expenditures and then added to the property, plant, and equipment fund and reported on that fund's balance sheet.

Plant and equipment assets are depreciated over their estimated useful lives by the straight-line method.

The library occupies, without charge, a building owned by the City of Merryville. The estimated fair rental value of the building is reported both as support revenue and as a purchased service expenditure for the budget period.

The library reports capital additions revenue from grants and donations in both the Revenue and Expenditures sections of the financial statement.

The values of donated books and artwork are based on the fair market value at the time the donations are received.

Contributed services of volunteers are reported as support revenue and as personnel expenditures at the fair market value.

Note 2: Investments

Investments are composed of certificates of deposit. A listing follows.

Lake City National Bank (10.5%)	$30,000
First National Bank (9.8%)	30,000
National Bank of Commerce (6.0%)	15,000
Total	$75,000

Note 3: Pension Plans

The library withholds FICA taxes and contributes the employer's share as required by law.

No other pension plan is in effect.

Note 4: Classification of Expenditures

The cost of providing library services is summarized by program and by object. Certain library program costs are allocated by actual expenditures and time devoted.

Library books, equipment, and art acquisitions are reported as general fund expenditures. These expenditures are added to the property, plant, and equipment fund during the same budget period.

Note 5: General

The library received a substantial amount of its support from federal, state, and local governments. A significant reduction in the level of their financial support would affect the library's programs and activities.

Figure 17-8 Notes to the Financial Statements of a Not-for-Profit Organization

Summary of Key Points

1. The two financial statements usually prepared by a not-for-profit organization are the statement of revenue, expenditures, and changes in fund balance and the balance sheet.
2. The fund balance is the difference between the assets and the liabilities for a particular fund. It is similar to the ownership equity of a for-profit business.
3. The statement of revenue, expenditures, and changes in fund balance reports the total revenue and expenditures of a particular fund for a budget period as well as the change in the fund balance.
4. A not-for-profit organization generally has three types of revenue: (a) self-generated, (b) support, and (c) capital additions.
5. The expenditures of a not-for-profit organization may be classified by program or by object.
6. If revenue for a budget period exceeds expenditures, there is a surplus, which increases the fund balance. If expenditures exceed revenue, there is a deficit, resulting in a decrease in the fund balance.
7. The balance sheet of a not-for-profit organization reports the balances of the asset, liability, and fund balance accounts of a particular fund.
8. Part or all of the fund balance can be designated for a certain purpose by the not-for-profit organization's governing board. The designation of the fund balance should be reported on the balance sheet.
9. Purchases of property, plant, and equipment assets are first reported as general fund expenditures on the statement of revenue, expenditures, and changes in fund balance. Each expenditure is capitalized and reported on the property, plant, and equipment fund balance sheet.

17 Review and Applications

Building Your Accounting Vocabulary

In your own words, write the definition of each of the following accounting terms. Use complete sentences for your definitions.

capital additions revenue
deficit
fund balance
object expenditures
program expenditures
self-generated revenue
statement of revenue, expenditures, and changes in fund balance
support revenue

Reviewing Your Accounting Knowledge

1. If a not-for-profit organization does not intend to earn a profit, why does it prepare financial statements?
2. Name two groups that may be interested in a not-for-profit organization's financial statements.
3. What two statements are normally prepared by a not-for-profit organization?
4. What is a general fund?
5. What are the three types of revenue for a not-for-profit organization? Give an example of each.
6. What is the difference between support revenue and capital additions revenue?
7. What are the two methods of classifying the expenditures of a not-for-profit organization?
8. How is the change in fund balance determined? When is the fund balance increased? When is the fund balance decreased?
9. What is meant by *capitalizing an expenditure*?
10. How does the property, plant, and equipment fund balance sheet differ from the general fund balance sheet?

Improving Your Problem-Solving Skills

You work in the accounting department of a wholesale auto parts supplier. You have become aware of several instances in which one branch manager submitted receipts from "nights out" with his spouse for reimbursement as selling expense by the central accounting office. What is the problem? What should you do?

Applying Accounting Procedures

Exercise 17-1 Identifying Sources of Revenue

The following list describes some of the revenue received by the DeRidder Community Center.

S-G SUP.

1. Interest from a savings account
2. The services of volunteer workers

CA **3.** Cash donated for a new baseball field (restricted)
S-G **4.** Entry fees for a tennis tournament
SUP. **5.** Use of contributed facilities
S-G **6.** Income from concession stands
S-G **7.** Money from a fund-raising car wash
S-G **8.** Tuition for craft classes
SUP. **9.** A grant from a local business (unrestricted)
S-G **10.** Dividends received from investments

Instructions: Classify each source of revenue as self-generated, support, or capital additions. Use plain paper or the form provided in the working papers.

Exercise 17-2 Classifying Expenditures by Object

The Greater Baldwin Chamber of Commerce made the following types of expenditures during the fiscal period.

1. Advertising
2. Computer equipment
3. Dues
4. Fringe benefits
5. Insurance
6. Office typewriter
7. Plane tickets
8. Postage
9. Printing
10. Rent
11. Salaries
12. Stationery
13. Telephone service
14. Utilities
15. Wages

Instructions: Classify the expenditures by object, such as Personnel, Travel, Purchased Services, Supplies, Equipment, or Capital Additions. Use plain paper or the space provided in the working papers.

Exercise 17-3 Calculating Changes in Fund Balances

The beginning fund balance, total revenue amount, and total expenditures amount for several not-for-profit organizations follow.

	A	B	C	D
Beginning fund balance	$ 90,000	$109,000	$ 84,500	$ 75,000
Total Revenue	568,000	775,020	365,800	134,000
Total Expenditures	549,987	792,390	400,900	86,700

A, $108,013
B, $91,630
C, $49,400
D, $122,300

Instructions: Calculate the ending fund balance for each organization. Use the form provided in the working papers.

Problem 17-1 Preparing the Revenue Section of the Statement of Revenue, Expenditures, and Changes in Fund Balance

Following is the general fund revenue received by the Colfax Community Center for the budget period ended September 30.

Tuition and fees	$ 7,967
Concession stand income	3,250
Contributed services of volunteers	31,500
Entry fees	800
Fund-raising projects	25,300
Grants for equipment purchases (restricted)	50,000

Interest on investments	4,568
Donation of land (restricted)	35,000
Federal government grant (unrestricted)	12,000
Use of contributed facilities	24,000
Donation for land improvements (restricted)	5,000
State grant (unrestricted)	20,000

Total S-G rev., $41,885
Total Sup. rev., $87,500
Total CA rev., $90,000
Total rev., $209,385

Instructions: Prepare the Sources of Revenue section of the statement of revenue, expenditures, and changes in fund balance for the center's general fund. Classify the revenue as self-generated, support, or capital additions.

Problem 17-2 Preparing the Expenditures Section of the Statement of Revenue, Expenditures, and Changes in Fund Balance

The following expenditures were made by the Greater Alexandria Chamber of Commerce during the budget period ended December 31.

Computer equipment (capital additions)	$15,000
Fringe benefits	8,850
Insurance	2,400
Maintenance services	3,600
Office equipment (capital additions)	8,900
Office machines	1,500
Postage	9,026
Printing	8,900
Rent	6,000
Salaries	72,600
Subscriptions	625
Supplies	4,265
Telephone	1,685
Travel	4,100
Utilities	5,986
Wages	15,900

These expenditures can be allocated to the various programs as follows.

Community development	$35,000
Education support	16,800
Fund-raising	5,800
General administration	63,913
Industrial development	31,589
Research	16,235

Expend. totals, $169,337

Instructions: Prepare the Expenditures section of the statement of revenue, expenditures, and changes in fund balance for the general fund of the Greater Alexandria Chamber of Commerce. Classify the expenditures by program and by object. Use the following headings for the object expenditures: Personnel, Travel, Purchased Services, Supplies, Office Equipment, Capital Additions.

SPREADSHEET PROBLEM

Problem 17-3 Preparing the Changes in Fund Balance Section of the Statement of Revenue, Expenditures, and Changes in Fund Balance

The beginning fund balance, the total revenue, and the total expenditures amounts for Haughton Community College's general fund and scholarship fund follow.

	General Fund	Scholarship Fund
Beginning fund balance	$ 98,590	$ 78,900
Total Revenue	21,450,000	750,000
Total Expenditures	21,497,876	748,325

GF End. bal., $50,714
SF End. bal., $80,575

Instructions: Prepare the Changes in Fund Balance section of the statement of revenue, expenditures, and changes in fund balance for the general fund and for the scholarship fund. The college's budget period ends on June 30.

Problem 17-4 Preparing a General Fund Balance Sheet

The following balances appeared in the general fund accounts of the Waco Civic Center on October 31.

Accounts Payable	$ 8,635
Accounts Receivable	1,685
Cash in Bank	15,800
Certificates of Deposit	100,000
Fund Balance	161,450
Grants Receivable—Government	35,000
Grants Receivable—Other	12,500
Prepaid Expenses	6,000
Wages Payable	900

During the October board meeting, the center's directors voted to designate a portion of the fund balance as follows:

1. $75,000 for a six-month certificate of deposit
2. $60,000 for a new computer system

BS totals, $170,985

Instructions: Prepare a balance sheet for the general fund of the Waco Civic Center.

Problem 17-5 Preparing a Property, Plant, and Equipment Fund Balance Sheet

The following amounts appeared on the balance sheet for the property, plant, and equipment fund of the Holt Pavilion for the previous year.

Movable Equipment	$ 236,500
Sound Equipment	26,000
Fixed Equipment	500,600
Building	1,500,000
Land Improvements	26,000
Land	90,000
Liabilities	0
Fund Balance	2,379,100

During the current budget period, the Pavilion purchased the following property, plant, and equipment items.

Tables (Movable Equipment)	$ 3,000
Chairs (Movable Equipment)	7,000
Additional auditorium seats (Fixed Equipment)	85,000
Land	75,000

Curr. yr. BS totals: $170,000; $2,549,100

Instructions: Prepare the balance sheet for the property, plant, and equipment fund of the Holt Pavilion. The organization's budget period ends on June 30.

Problem 17-6 Preparing Financial Statements for a Not-for-Profit Organization

The Vernon County Society for the Performing Arts had the following revenue and expenditures for its general fund for the budget period ended December 31.

Revenue:	
Contributed services of volunteers	$ 40,000
Contributed use of facilities	36,000
Contributions (unrestricted)	30,000
Donation for the purchase of land (restricted)	50,000
Donation for the purchase of production equipment (restricted)	25,000
Government grants (unrestricted)	20,000
Income from investments	12,400
Other grants	8,000
Refreshment stand income	18,555
Ticket sales	80,465
Tuition and fees	35,000

Expenditures:	
Fringe benefits	$ 7,200
Insurance premiums	3,600
Land (capital additions)	50,000
Lighting equipment (capital additions)	60,000
Maintenance contracts	7,542
Miscellaneous purchased services	1,236
Production equipment (capital additions)	25,000
Rent	36,000
Salaries	60,000
Subscriptions	4,200
Supplies	19,400
Travel	1,200
Utilities	9,845
Wages	40,000

The fund balance on January 1 was $130,034. The balances of the general fund accounts on December 31 are as follows.

Cash in Bank	$ 11,216
Certificates of Deposit	125,000
Accounts Receivable	16,483
Grants Receivable—Government	10,000
Grants Receivable—Other	3,000
Prepaid Expenses	1,800
Accounts Payable	7,268

Total revenue: $355,420

Total P/O expend.: $325,223

Ending fund balance: $160,231

BS totals, $167,499

Instructions:

(1) Prepare a statement of revenue, expenditures, and changes in fund balance for the organization's general fund. Report expenditures by program and by object. The expenditures can be allocated to the various programs as follows.

Ballet school	$73,358
General administration	76,631
Little Theater	27,800
Neighborhood productions	52,569
Production	94,865

The object classifications are Personnel, Travel, Purchased Services, Supplies, and Capital Additions.

(2) Prepare the general fund balance sheet. The governing board of the organization voted to make the following fund balance designations:

1. Invest $100,000 in a six-month certificate of deposit.
2. Purchase $35,000 of production equipment.

CHALLENGE PROBLEM SPREADSHEET PROBLEM

Problem 17-7 Analyzing the Financial Statement of a Not-for-Profit Organization

The statement of revenue, expenditures, and changes in fund balance for the Pine Tree Young Professionals Association follows. You have been asked to provide a breakdown of the various line items.

Total revenue: ($955); (1.2%)

Total expenditures: ($355); (0.5%)

Ending fund balance: ($600); (4.7%)

Instructions: Using the form provided in the working papers, calculate the difference between the actual revenue, expenditure, and fund balance amounts and the budgeted amounts. Then calculate the percentage the difference amount was over or under the budget amount. Round percentages to the nearest tenth of a percent.

Pine Tree Young Professionals Association
Statement of Revenue, Expenditures, and Changes in Fund Balance
General Fund
For the Budget Period Ended June 30, 199-

	Budget Amount	Actual Amount
Sources of Revenue		
Self-Generated:		
Membership fees	$36,500	$35,730
Seminar tuition	15,000	13,715
Total Self-Generated Revenue	$51,500	$49,445
Support:		
United Way	$ 8,000	$ 8,000
Contributed services of volunteers	18,000	19,100
Total Support Revenue	$26,000	$27,100
Total Revenue	$77,500	$76,545
Expenditures		
Personnel:		
Salaries	$27,000	$27,000
Wages	18,000	19,100
Total Personnel	$45,000	$46,100
Travel	$ 4,000	$ 3,800
Purchased Services:		
Insurance	900	900
Postage	1,000	950
Rent	4,000	3,600
Utilities	9,000	8,400
Total Purchased Services	$14,900	$13,850
Supplies	$ 5,900	$ 5,595
Equipment	$ 6,700	$ 6,800
Total Expenditures	$76,500	$76,145
Beginning fund balance	$11,850	$11,850
Increase in fund balance	1,000	400
Ending fund balance	$12,850	$12,250

Figure 17-9 Financial Statement for Problem 17-7

FOCUS ON

CAREERS

Balancing Costs and Benefits

As most taxpayers know, federal, state, and community projects usually involve very large amounts of money. Before deciding to go ahead with a project, government and industry planners use someone called a *cost-benefit analyst* to find out whether a project is worth the time and money that will go into it.

As their job title suggests, cost-benefit analysts calculate not only the cost of a project or a program but also its potential benefits. Although weighing costs against benefits may seem straightforward, it is actually a very difficult and complex process. This is primarily because costs and benefits must be stated in monetary terms, but many factors are difficult to measure in this way.

Let's look at an example. Suppose a multipurpose river development project combining electric power, flood control, irrigation, and river navigation is proposed by the U.S. Army Corps of Engineers. A cost-benefit analyst must evaluate factors such as the power that would be generated, the crops and property that would be saved, the increased crop production of the irrigated land, the impact on the environment, and the recreation and transportation benefits to the community. Although labor and materials have market values that can be stated in dollars, benefits such as beauty or enjoyment cannot be measured. These types of factors are assigned an estimate value called a *shadow price*. Once all the factors are assigned a dollar value, planners can estimate whether or not the project's benefits exceed its costs. If they do, the project is deemed cost-effective.

To do the type of work they do, cost-benefit analysts must be highly trained specialists. A background in cost accounting is necessary; however, cost-benefit analysts must have advanced knowledge in many other fields as well. If you like the idea of measuring the costs and benefits of proposed projects and programs and having a say in whether the money would be well spent, a career in cost-benefit analysis may be for you.

As a project progresses, analysts help planners determine if the project is worth the time and money involved.

UNIT 5

SPECIAL ACCOUNTING SYSTEMS

The accounting system a business uses must provide the information management needs to help plan, control, and evaluate the business's operations. In this unit, you will learn about the accounting systems used by businesses whose operations are divided into segments such as departments and branches. You will also examine a system businesses can use to control their purchases and cash payments. Finally, you'll learn about the accounting system used by a business that manufactures products. This accounting system is set up to accumulate data on all of the costs involved in manufacturing the business's products.

Chapter 18

DEPARTMENTAL ACCOUNTING SYSTEMS

Many businesses carry on more than one type of business activity. Some service stations, for example, do repair work in addition to selling gasoline and oil. Grocery stores have separate sections for produce, meat, frozen foods, and other items. Discount department stores sell everything from clothing to furniture to jewelry.

When a business carries on a number of different activities, it should separate those activities into departments. By organizing its operations into departments, a business can delegate authority to department managers, who are then responsible for their departments' activities. The business can also better measure each department's efficiency and profitability.

In this chapter, you will see how businesses organize their accounting data by department. You'll learn how to allocate revenue and costs among departments and how to prepare departmental income statements.

Learning Objectives

When you have completed this chapter, you should be able to do the folowing:

1. Explain why a business separates its operations into departments.
2. Determine gross profit on sales by department.
3. Allocate expenses among departments.
4. Prepare a departmental work sheet.
5. Prepare income statements that report departmental operating income and departmental contribution margins.
6. Define the accounting terms presented in this chapter.

New Terms

departmental accounting system
selling expenses
administrative expenses
contribution margin
direct expenses
indirect expenses

Accounting by Department

When a business has separated its operations into departments, management always wants to know how well each department is doing. They need to know how much of a contribution each department is making to the business's overall profit (or loss). The accounting system, therefore, must be set up to provide information on revenue and expenses by department. An accounting system that provides data for two or more departments is called a **departmental accounting system**.

Ask if any students work in a business having more than one department. If so, ask what kind of business and what departments.

While large companies are more likely to use a departmental accounting system, even small businesses can benefit from departmental accounting. For example, the MLM Company is a two-person business that sells office products and repairs office equipment. In the accounting system set up by the owners, Mark and Lara Mayberry, separate accounts are kept for sales and for repair income. At the end of the fiscal year, the Mayberrys can compare the income earned by each activity with the amount of time and attention they had to devote to it. This comparison can also help them decide whether to spend more or less time on each activity.

Point out that departmental income statements are generally for internal use only.

Financial statements for a departmentalized business as a whole are prepared from the information obtained for each department. Reports that are prepared for departmental operations are generally limited to income statements. The income statements may report departmental data through gross profit on sales. They may also be expanded to report each department's operating income.

Be sure students understand how gross profit on sales is determined. Take students through the determination of cost of merchandise sold.

For a merchandising business, gross profit on sales is one of the most important figures on the income statement. Gross profit on sales, remember, is the difference between net sales and the cost of merchandise sold. To be successful, a merchandising business must sell its goods for more than their cost to be able to pay expenses and have an adequate income left over.

Businesses that conduct more than one type of activity require organization of data to allocate funds.

Department managers are constantly making decisions that affect their departments' sales or cost of merchandise sold. For example, department managers determine which merchandise to purchase and what price to charge for that merchandise. Since sales and cost of merchandise sold are largely controlled by each department, an income statement reporting the gross profit on sales for each department is very useful.

To determine departmental gross profit on sales, departmental data must be available for each element entering into gross profit. There are two ways to do this:

1. Keep separate revenue and cost of merchandise accounts in the general ledger for each department. The balances of each department's accounts are then reported on the income statement.
2. Keep only one general ledger account for each revenue and cost of merchandise account, but maintain supplementary records for each department. The information from the supplemental records is used to prepare the income statement.

Emphasize that the most accurate way to determine how well each department is doing is to maintain separate revenue and cost of merchandise accounts for each department.

Maintaining Separate Departmental Accounts

Keeping separate revenue and cost of merchandise accounts for each department provides a company with the most accurate accounting data. Separate accounts for each department are set up for Sales, Sales Discounts, Sales Returns and Allowances, Purchases, Transportation In, Purchases Discounts, Purchases Returns and Allowances, and Merchandise Inventory.

For example, Custom Colors is a home decorating business with two departments: the Paint Department and the Wallpaper Department. It uses two Sales accounts: Sales—Paint and Sales—Wallpaper. It also has two Sales Returns and Allowances accounts, two Merchandise Inventory accounts, and so on. The company's special journals contain special amount columns for each departmental account.

Be sure students understand that the number of departmental accounts or the number of departmental columns in a special journal would depend upon the number of departments in the business.

Custom Color's sales journal appears in Figure 18-1. Notice that there are columns for the two departmental Sales accounts but only one for Sales Tax Payable. Sales Tax Payable is not part of the calculation of gross profit on sales. At the end of the month, the totals of the special columns are posted to the accounts named in the column headings.

SALES JOURNAL — PAGE 15

DATE		SALES SLIP NO.	CUSTOMER'S ACCOUNT DEBITED	POST. REF.	SALES PAINT CREDIT	SALES WALLPAPER CREDIT	SALES TAX PAYABLE CREDIT	ACCOUNTS RECEIVABLE DEBIT
199- Nov.	1	1850	Tim Evans	✓	140 00		8 40	148 40
	4	1851	Enrico Monzo	✓		350 00	21 00	371 00
	4	1852	Helen Parker	✓	90 00		5 40	95 40
	30		Totals		9,752 30	4,890 20	878 55	15,521 05
					(401)	(402)	(225)	(105)

Figure 18-1 Sales Journal for Custom Colors

Maintaining One General Ledger Account

When a business has only one general ledger account for each revenue and cost of merchandise account, the balance of each account must be

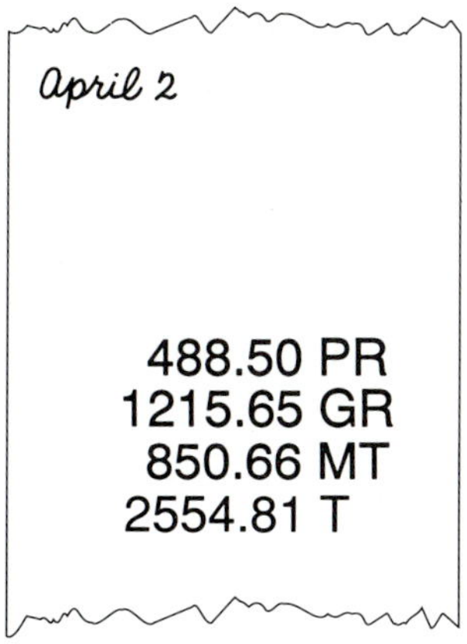

Ask students to bring in cash register tapes from a supermarket or store that identifies the merchandise by department.

distributed among the various departments at the end of the accounting period. To do this, supplementary records are kept to accumulate departmental information. For example, Anderson's Market has three departments: produce, grocery, and meat. As each item is sold, the checkout clerk strikes a department key on the electronic cash register. At the end of each day, the cash register provides the total sales amount, as well as a breakdown of those sales by department. The total sales amount is then recorded in a sales journal. The sales for each department are recorded on a departmental sales analysis sheet like the one shown in Figure 18-2.

ANDERSON'S MARKET
Departmental Sales Analysis Sheet

Date		Produce Department	Grocery Department	Meat Department	Total Sales
Apr.	1	$479.32	$ 993.70	$778.13	$2,251.15
	2	488.50	1,215.65	850.66	2,554.81

Figure 18-2 Departmental Sales Analysis Sheet

Remind students that separate departmental analysis sheets would be prepared for each account entering into the determination of gross profit.

Analysis sheets are also used to keep track of each department's sales returns, purchases discounts, purchases returns, and so on. At the end of the accounting period, these analysis sheets give departmental breakdowns for each item used to calculate gross profit on sales.

R — E — M — E — M — B — E — R

In a departmental accounting system, it is necessary to keep either separate accounts or supplementary records by department for each account involved in determining gross profit on sales.

Reporting Gross Profit by Department

As you can see, it is not difficult to organize the accounting system to report sales and cost of merchandise sold data by department. With this information, an income statement that reports gross profit on sales by department can be prepared. Figure 18-3 gives an example of such an income statement. This income statement for Custom Colors has separate sections for the Paint Department and the Wallpaper Department. Data from the two departments is combined and reported in the Total section.

Custom Colors
Income Statement
For the Year Ended December 31, 199-

	PAINT DEPARTMENT			WALLPAPER DEPARTMENT			TOTAL		
Revenue:									
Sales		470,000.00			310,000.00			780,000.00	
Less: Sales Returns & Allowances		13,100.00			6,200.00			19,300.00	
Net Sales			456,900.00			303,800.00			760,700.00
Cost of Merchandise Sold:									
Merch. Inventory, Jan. 1, 199-		97,500.00			91,650.00			189,150.00	
Purchases	298,000.00			175,900.00			473,900.00		
Less: Purchases Discounts	6,350.00			4,200.00			10,550.00		
Purchases Ret. & Allow.	10,200.00			5,800.00			16,000.00		
Net Purchases		281,450.00			165,900.00			447,350.00	
Merch. Available for Sale		378,950.00			259,550.00			636,500.00	
Less: Merch. Inv., Dec. 31, 199-		95,000.00			75,000.00			170,000.00	
Cost of Merchandise Sold			283,950.00			182,550.00			466,500.00
Gross Profit on Sales			172,950.00			121,250.00			294,200.00
Operating Expenses									
Selling Expenses:									
Advertising Expense							6,400.00		
Deprec. Expense–Store Equip.							5,600.00		
Miscellaneous Selling Exp.							1,375.00		
Sales Salaries Expense							138,900.00		
Total Selling Expenses								152,275.00	
Administrative Expenses:									
Bad Debts Expense							1,800.00		
Insurance Expense							4,000.00		
Misc. Administrative Exp.							775.00		
Office Salaries Expense							49,100.00		
Rent Expense							18,000.00		
Utilities Expense							5,300.00		
Total Administrative Exp.								78,975.00	
Total Operating Expenses									231,250.00
Operating Income									62,950.00
Other Revenue:									
Interest Income								5,900.00	
Other Expenses:									
Interest Expense								2,750.00	3,150.00
Net Income									66,100.00

Figure 18-3 Income Statement Showing Gross Profit by Department

As you can see, the accounting information is reported on a departmental basis only through gross profit on sales. Operating expenses are reported in the Total section only. It is not always easy to divide expenses among departments, particularly an expense such as Insurance Expense. For that reason, some businesses do not departmentalize their income statements beyond gross profit on sales.

Review the income statement in Figure 18-3 with students. Discuss why each expense is classified as either an administrative expense or a selling expense.

On this income statement, the operating expenses have been further classified as either selling expenses or administrative expenses. **Selling expenses** are the expenses incurred to sell or market the business's goods or services. Advertising expense and the salaries of salespeople are examples of selling expenses. **Administrative expenses** are costs related to the management of the business. For example, utilities expenses are considered to be administrative expenses, as are the salaries of office personnel. On an income statement, operating expenses are generally classified and reported as either selling or administrative expenses.

R — E — M — E — M — B — E — R

Gross profit on sales is determined by deducting the cost of merchandise sold from net sales.

Before reading further, do the following activity to check your understanding of how to calculate gross profit on sales by department.

Check Your Learning

Melody Products has three departments: Tapes & CDs, Videos, and Equipment. The business maintains separate revenue and cost of merchandise accounts for each department. At the end of the fiscal period, the accounting records showed the following information. Using this information, determine each department's gross profit on sales and the gross profit on sales for the business as a whole.

	Tapes & CDs	Videos	Equipment
Merchandise Inventory, Jan. 1	$250,000	$199,900	$302,450
Merchandise Inventory, Dec. 31	202,000	161,500	245,600
Sales	525,000	420,000	635,400
Sales Returns and Allowances	12,500	11,340	17,150
Purchases	350,000	280,000	425,800
Purchases Discounts	7,200	5,800	8,700
Purchases Returns and Allowances	10,500	8,500	12,700

Compare your answers to those in the answers section. Reread the preceding part of the chapter to find the correct answers for any calculations you may have missed.

Allocating Operating Expenses

If a business wishes to report departmental accounting data beyond gross profit on sales, it must allocate (divide) the various operating expenses among its departments. It is easy to allocate some operating expenses to a given department. For example, suppose Terry Mackin is a salesperson in the Paint Department of Custom Colors. Terry's salary, then, is an expense of the Paint Department only.

Other operating expenses, such as Rent Expense or Utilities Expense, are not restricted to one department. These expenses must be divided among the departments on some fair basis. Let's look at the operating expenses of Custom Colors and at the methods the company uses to allocate those expenses between its two departments. We'll look first at the company's selling expenses, then at its administrative expenses.

Advertising Expense

Point out that newspaper advertising is allocated according to the number of column inches each department uses in the ad.

Custom Colors advertises in newspapers and on the radio. The company's total advertising expense for the period was $6,400. The breakdown between the cost of the newspaper ads and the radio ads is as follows:

Newspaper advertising	$4,200
Radio advertising	2,200
Total advertising expense	$6,400

Custom Colors allocates the cost of newspaper advertising according to the number of column inches each department uses. (Newspaper advertising is billed according to the number of inches a particular ad covers; for example, a business purchases a 4-inch ad.) During the past year, Custom Colors bought 1,400 inches of newspaper advertising. The Paint Department had 840 column inches of advertising, or 60% of the 1,400 inches (840 ÷ 1,400). The Wallpaper Department had 560 column inches of advertising, or 40% (560 ÷ 1,400).

Be sure students understand how these percentages are determined.

The Paint Department's share of the cost of newspaper advertising is determined as follows:

$$\$4{,}200 \times .60 = \$2{,}520$$

The Wallpaper Department's share of the cost of newspaper advertising is calculated as follows:

$$\$4{,}200 \times .40 = \$1{,}680$$

Point out that radio advertising is allocated according to the amount of air time each department used.

Custom Colors allocates the cost of its radio advertising according to the amount of air time each department used. During the year, Custom Colors bought 400 minutes of radio time. The Paint Department ran 216 minutes of the ads, or 54% (216 ÷ 400). The Wallpaper Department ads ran for 184 minutes, or 46% (184 ÷ 400).

Go over these calculations with students.

The Paint Department's share of the cost of radio advertising is determined as follows:

$$\$2{,}200 \times .54 = \$1{,}188$$

The Wallpaper Department's share of the cost of radio advertising is calculated as follows:

$$\$2{,}200 \times .46 = \$1{,}012$$

The following table summarizes how Custom Colors allocated its advertising expense:

	Paint Department	Wallpaper Department	Total
Newspaper advertising	$2,520	$1,680	$4,200
Radio advertising	1,188	1,012	2,200
	$3,708	$2,692	$6,400

Depreciation Expense—Store Equipment

Explain that depreciation expense is charged directly to the department that maintains the plant asset.

Custom Colors maintains a plant asset subsidiary ledger that lists the department in which each piece of store equipment is located. The depreciation expense for each piece of equipment can then be easily identified by department. The total depreciation expense for the store equipment for the year is $5,600. The depreciation expense for the store equipment located in the Paint Department is $3,136. The depreciation expense for the store equipment located in the Wallpaper Department is $2,464.

Miscellaneous Selling Expense

Point out that the departmental sales method is used to allocate miscellaneous selling expenses and some other operating expenses.

The balance of the Miscellaneous Selling Expense account tends to vary according to the volume of sales. As a result, Custom Colors allocates the expense on the basis of the total sales of each department. Custom Colors also uses this departmental sales method to allocate some of its other operating expenses. The sales by department are as follows:

Paint Department sales	$470,000
Wallpaper Department sales	310,000
Total sales	$780,000

Be sure students understand these calculations.

The Paint Department's sales are 60% of the total sales ($470,000 ÷ $780,000). The Wallpaper Department's sales are 40% of total sales ($310,000 ÷ $780,000). The miscellaneous selling expense for the year is $1,375. It is allocated as follows:

Paint Department	$1,375 × .60 = $ 825
Wallpaper Department	$1,375 × .40 = 550
	$1,375

Sales Salaries Expense

Mention that because employees are identified by department in the payroll register their salaries can be allocated easily.

Custom Colors allocates the salaries of its salespeople to the department in which they work. The payroll register lists each employee by department. Of the $138,900 total sales salaries expense, the Paint Department's share is $90,000 and the Wallpaper Department's is $48,900.

Bad Debts Expense

Point out that the departmental sales method is used to allocate bad debts expense.

Bad Debts Expense also varies according to the volume of sales. Like Miscellaneous Selling Expense, it is allocated on the basis of departmental sales. The bad debts expense for the year is $1,800, which is allocated as follows:

Paint Department	$1,800 × .60 = $1,080
Wallpaper Department	$1,800 × .40 = $ 720

Insurance Expense

Mention that two different methods are used to allocate insurance expense.

Custom Colors carries two types of insurance policies to cover possible losses: (1) property insurance for damage to merchandise or equipment (annual premium $3,400) and (2) liability insurance for injuries to customers while on the premises (annual premium $600). The cost of the property insurance premium is allocated on the basis of the value of the inventory and equipment held by each department at the end of the year. The following table shows the breakdown by department:

Walk students through the calculations to allocate property insurance premiums.

	Paint Department	Wallpaper Department	Total
Merchandise inventory	$ 95,000	$75,000	$170,000
Equipment	18,000	16,000	34,000
	$113,000	$91,000	$204,000

The total value of the company's merchandise and equipment is $204,000. The Paint Department holds $113,000, or 55% of the total. The Wallpaper Department holds $91,000, or 45% of the total. Each department's share of the $3,400 property insurance expense is calculated as follows:

Paint Department	$3,400 × .55 = $1,870
Wallpaper Department	$3,400 × .45 = $1,530

Review the departmental sales method used to allocate liability insurance premiums.

The cost of the liability insurance premium is allocated according to departmental sales. Custom Colors allocates the $600 liability insurance expense as follows:

Paint Department	$600 × .60 = $360
Wallpaper Department	$600 × .40 = $240

The total insurance expense is allocated as follows:

	Paint Department	Wallpaper Department	Total
Property insurance	$1,870	$1,530	$3,400
Liability insurance	360	240	600
	$2,230	$1,770	$4,000

Miscellaneous Administrative Expenses

Like Miscellaneous Selling Expense, Miscellaneous Administrative Expense is allocated to the two departments according to sales. The expense for the year is $775. It is allocated as follows:

Paint Department	$775 × .60 = $465
Wallpaper Department	$775 × .40 = $310

Office Salaries Expense

Discuss the kinds of tasks these office workers might perform and why their time is allocated in this manner.

Office workers at Custom Colors were paid a total of $49,100 this past year. The company allocates office workers' salaries on the basis of the amount of time office personnel had to spend on each department. Custom Colors' management estimates that 60% of the office staff's time is devoted to the Paint Department and 40% to the Wallpaper Department. The office salaries expense is therefore allocated as follows:

Paint Department	$49,100 × .60 = $29,460
Wallpaper Department	$49,100 × .40 = $19,640

Rent Expense and Utilities Expense

Discuss why the company allocates rent and utilities expenses according to the floor space occupied by each department.

Custom Colors rents 40,000 square feet of floor space. It allocates the expenses for rent and utilities on the basis of the floor space occupied by each department. The Paint Department occupies 25,000 square feet, or 62.5% of the space (25,000 ÷ 40,000). The Wallpaper Department occupies 15,000 square feet, or 37.5% (15,000 ÷ 40,000).

The annual rent expense is $18,000. Each department's share of the total expense is calculated as follows:

Paint Department	$18,000 × .625 = $11,250
Wallpaper Department	$18,000 × .375 = $ 6,750

The total utilities expense for the year was $5,300. That amount is allocated as follows:

Use demonstration problem 18-1 here.

Paint Department	$5,300 × .625 = $3,312.50
Wallpaper Department	$5,300 × .375 = $1,987.50

Before reading further, do the following activity to check your understanding of how to allocate expenses.

Check Your Learning

Royer's Department Store occupies an area of 24,000 square feet. The store's departments and the floor space occupied by each are as follows. Royer's annual rent is $72,000. Allocate the rent expense among the four departments.

Men's Department:	8,000 square feet
Women's Department:	10,000 square feet
Children's Department:	4,000 square feet
Jewelry Department	2,000 square feet

You may want to have students complete Exercise 18-2 at this point.

Compare your answers to those in the answers section. Reread the preceding part of the chapter to find the correct answers for any calculations you may have missed.

Net Income From Operations by Department

A business may want to prepare an income statement that shows departmental information beyond gross profit on sales. Such an income statement may report departmental data through operating income or net income. Operating income, you'll remember, is gross profit on sales minus operating expenses.

Review how operating income is determined.

As you've seen, Custom Colors keeps separate revenue and cost of merchandise accounts for each department. It then allocates its operating expenses between the Paint Department and the Wallpaper Department using various methods. Once the operating expenses have been allocated, a departmental work sheet is prepared.

Preparing a Departmental Work Sheet

Point out the differences between this work sheet and those students have used up to this point.

The departmental work sheet for Custom Colors appears in Figure 18-4 on pages 472–473. Account balances are first entered in the Trial Balance columns of the work sheet. (Various asset, liability, and ownership equity accounts are not shown, but their balances are included in the totals.) The adjustments are calculated and entered in the Adjustments section. The amounts are then extended to either the Balance Sheet or the Income Statement section. Notice that this work sheet has three Income

Custom
Work
For the Year Ended

	ACCT. NO.	ACCOUNT NAME	TRIAL BALANCE DEBIT	TRIAL BALANCE CREDIT	ADJUSTMENTS DEBIT	ADJUSTMENTS CREDIT
1	101	Cash in Bank	30 654 00			
2	105	Accounts Receivable	72 500 00			
3	107	Allow. for Uncollectible Accts.		1 087 00		(a) 1 800 00
4	110	Merchandise Inv. - Paint	97 500 00			(b) 2 500 00
5	113	Merchandise Inv. - Wallpaper	91 650 00			(c) 16 650 00
6	115	Prepaid Insurance	6 200 00			(d) 4 000 00
10	155	Store Equipment	30 600 00			
11	157	Accum. Deprec. - Store Equip.		21 300 00		(e) 5 600 00
16	310	Income Summary			(b) 2 500 00	
17					(c) 16 650 00	
18	401	Sales - Paint		470 000 00		
19	403	Sales - Wallpaper		310 000 00		
20	405	Sales Ret. + Allow. - Paint	13 100 00			
21	407	Sales Ret. + Allow. - Wallpaper	6 200 00			
22	501	Purchases - Paint	298 000 00			
23	503	Purchases - Wallpaper	175 900 00			
24	505	Purch. Disc. - Paint		6 350 00		
25	507	Purch. Disc. - Wallpaper		4 200 00		
26	510	Purch. Ret. + Allow. - Paint		10 200 00		
27	513	Purch. Ret. + Allow. - Wallpaper		5 800 00		
28	601	Advertising Expense	6 400 00			
29	605	Bad Debts Expense	—		(a) 1 800 00	
30	610	Deprec. Exp. - Store Equipment	—		(e) 5 600 00	
31	615	Insurance Expense	—		(d) 4 000 00	
32	620	Misc. Admin. Expense	775 00			
33	625	Misc. Selling Expense	1 375 00			
34	630	Office Salaries Expense	49 100 00			
35	635	Rent Expense	18 000 00			
36	640	Sales Salaries Expense	138 900 00			
37	645	Utilities Expense	5 300 00			
38	710	Interest Income		5 900 00		
39	750	Interest Expense	2 750 00			
40			1,413 750 00	1,413 750 00	30 550 00	30 550 00
41		Operating Income				
42						
43		Net Income				
44						

Figure 18-4 Departmental Work Sheet (Left Side)

Statement sections. There is an Income Statement section for each of the two departments. The third Income Statement section is Nondepartmental. This section is used to record other revenue and other expense accounts.

Remind students that the work sheet is a tool of the accountant and should be prepared in pencil.

By the time the work sheet is prepared, Custom Colors has already allocated the operating expenses between its two departments. These allocations are the basis for the amounts extended to the departmental Income Statement sections. Notice that the operating income is calculated for each department. The Paint Department had an operating income of $27,483.50, while the Wallpaper Department's operating income was $35,466.50.

These two amounts are combined ($27,483.50 + $35,466.50 = $62,950.00) and extended to the Nondepartmental Credit column. Then the Nondepartmental Income Statement columns are totaled. The differ-

Colors
Sheet
December 31, 199–

Paint Department Income Statement		Wallpaper Department Income Statement		Nondepartmental Income Statement		Balance Sheet		
Debit	Credit	Debit	Credit	Debit	Credit	Debit	Credit	
						30 654 00		1
						72 500 00		2
							2 887 00	3
						95 000 00		4
						75 000 00		5
						2 200 00		6
						30 600 00		10
							26 900 00	11
2 500 00								16
		16 650 00						17
	470 000 00							18
			310 000 00					19
13 100 00								20
		6 200 00						21
298 000 00								22
		175 900 00						23
	6 350 00							24
			4 200 00					25
	10 200 00							26
			5 800 00					27
3 708 00		2 692 00						28
1 080 00		720 00						29
3 136 00		2 464 00						30
2 230 00		1 770 00						31
465 00		310 00						32
825 00		550 00						33
29 460 00		19 640 00						34
11 250 00		6 750 00						35
90 000 00		48 900 00						36
3 312 50		1 987 50						37
					5 900 00			38
				2 750 00				39
459 066 50	486 550 00	284 533 50	320 000 00					40
27 483 50		35 466 50			62 950 00			41
486 550 00	486 550 00	320 000 00	320 000 00	2 750 00	68 850 00	1,275 360 00	1,209 260 00	42
				66 100 00			66 100 00	43
				68 850 00	68 850 00	1,275 360 00	1,275 360 00	44

Figure 18-4 Departmental Work Sheet (Right Side)

ence between the two totals represents the company's net income for the period.

This departmental work sheet is used to prepare an income statement that reports the accounting data by department through operating income.

Reporting Operating Income by Department

Review this income statement with students. Point out the sections that are departmentalized and those that are not.

Custom Colors prepares the income statement shown in Figure 18-5 using the information on the departmental work sheet. This income statement reports financial information by department through operating income. Like the income statement in Figure 18-3, there is a set of

Custom
Income
For the Year Ended

	PAINT DEPARTMENT		
Revenue:			
Sales		470 000 00	
Less: Sales Returns + Allowances		13 100 00	
Net Sales			456 900 00
Cost of Merchandise Sold:			
Merch. Inventory, Jan. 1, 199-		97 500 00	
Purchases	298 000 00		
Less: Purchases Discounts	6 350 00		
Purchases Ret. + Allow.	10 200 00		
Net Purchases		281 450 00	
Merch. Available for Sale		378 950 00	
Less: Merch. Inv., Dec. 31, 199-		95 000 00	
Cost of Merchandise Sold			283 950 00
Gross Profit on Sales			172 950 00
Operating Expenses			
Selling Expenses:			
Advertising Expense	3 708 00		
Deprec. Expense-Store Equip.	3 136 00		
Miscellaneous Selling Exp.	825 00		
Sales Salaries Expense	90 000 00		
Total Selling Expenses		97 669 00	
Administrative Expenses:			
Bad Debts Expense	1 080 00		
Insurance Expense	2 230 00		
Misc. Administrative Exp.	465 00		
Office Salaries Expense	29 460 00		
Rent Expense	11 250 00		
Utilities Expense	3 312 50		
Total Administrative Exp.		47 797 50	
Total Operating Expenses			145 466 50
Operating Income			27 483 50
Other Revenue:			
Interest Income			
Other Expenses:			
Interest Expense			
Net Income			

Figure 18-5 Income Statement Showing Operating Income by Department (Left Side)

columns for each department. Data are then combined and reported in a set of columns labeled *Total*. Notice that the income statement follows this format.

Sales		
− Cost of Merchandise Sold		
= Gross Profit on Sales		Departmentalized
− Selling Expenses		
− Administrative Expenses		
= Operating Income		
+ Other Revenue		
− Other Expenses		Nondepartmentalized
= Net Income		

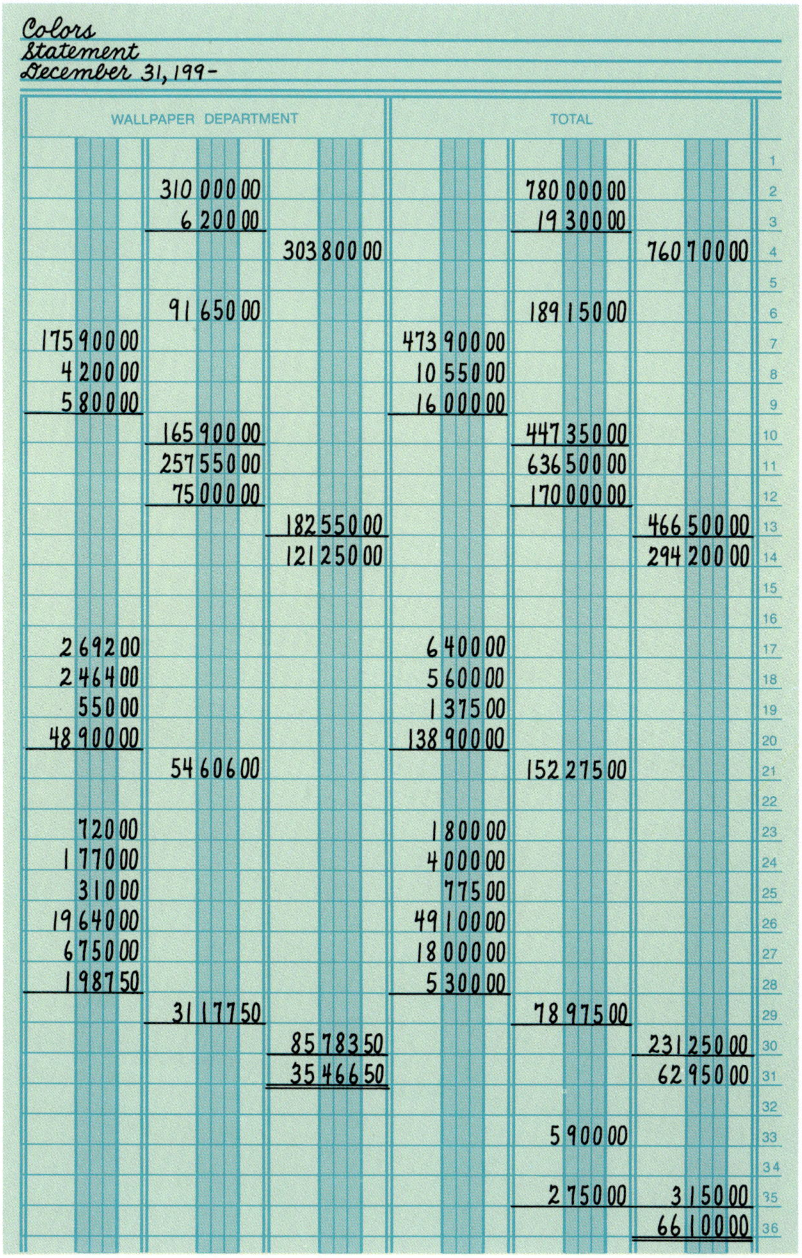

Colors
Statement
December 31, 199-

WALLPAPER DEPARTMENT			TOTAL			
						1
	310 000 00			780 000 00		2
	6 200 00			19 300 00		3
		303 800 00			760 700 00	4
						5
	91 650 00			189 150 00		6
175 900 00			473 900 00			7
4 200 00			10 550 00			8
5 800 00			16 000 00			9
	165 900 00			447 350 00		10
	257 550 00			636 500 00		11
	75 000 00			170 000 00		12
		182 550 00			466 500 00	13
		121 250 00			294 200 00	14
						15
						16
2 692 00			6 400 00			17
2 464 00			5 600 00			18
550 00			1 375 00			19
48 900 00			138 900 00			20
	54 606 00			152 275 00		21
						22
720 00			1 800 00			23
1 770 00			4 000 00			24
310 00			775 00			25
19 640 00			49 100 00			26
6 750 00			18 000 00			27
1 987 50			5 300 00			28
	31 177 50			78 975 00		29
		85 783 50			231 250 00	30
		35 466 50			62 950 00	31
						32
				5 900 00		33
						34
				2 750 00	3 150 00	35
					66 100 00	36

Figure 18-5 Income Statement Showing Operating Income by Department (Right Side)

R — E — M — E — M — B — E — R

Net income from operations is determined by subtracting the total operating expenses from gross profit on sales.

Contribution Margin

Some accountants believe that an income statement departmentalized through operating income does not realistically report each department's performance. They believe that the methods used to allocate operating

Custom
Income
For the Year Ended

	PAINT DEPARTMENT		
Revenue:			
Sales		470 000 00	
Less: Sales Returns + Allowances		13 100 00	
Net Sales			456 900 00
Cost of Merchandise Sold:			
Merch. Inventory, Jan. 1, 199-		97 500 00	
Purchases	298 000 00		
Less: Purchases Discounts	6 350 00		
Purchases Ret. + Allowances	10 200 00		
Net Purchases		281 450 00	
Merch. Available for Sale		378 950 00	
Less: Merch. Inv., Dec. 31, 199-		95 000 00	
Cost of Merchandise Sold			283 950 00
Gross Profit on Sales			172 950 00
Direct Expenses:			
Advertising Expense		3 708 00	
Bad Debts Expense		1 080 00	
Deprec. Expense-Store Equipment		3 136 00	
Insurance Expense (property)		1 870 00	
Sales Salaries Expense		90 000 00	
Total Direct Expenses			99 794 00
Contribution Margin by Department			73 156 00
Indirect Expenses:			
Insurance Expense (liability)			
Misc. Administrative Expense			
Misc. Selling Expense			
Office Salaries Expense			
Rent Expense			
Utilities Expense			
Total Indirect Expenses			
Operating Income			
Other Revenue:			
Interest Income			
Other Expenses:			
Interest Expense			
Net Income			

Figure 18-6 Income Statement Showing Contribution Margin by Department (Left Side)

Point out that contribution margin is the most accurate way to determine how much each department is contributing towards net income.

Gross profit on sales
− Direct expenses
= Contribution margin

Be sure students understand the difference between direct and indirect expenses.

expenses are arbitrary and that it is difficult to determine each department's "fair share" of the expenses. They also believe that a department should not be held responsible for expenses over which its manager has no control. For these reasons, income statements that report each department's contribution margin are often prepared. **Contribution margin** is the contribution that a given department makes to the net income of a business. It is determined by subtracting from gross profit on sales *only* those expenses that can be directly identified with each department.

To determine each department's contribution margin, you must first distinguish between direct expenses and indirect expenses. **Direct**

Colors
Statement
December 31, 199-

WALLPAPER DEPARTMENT			TOTAL			
						1
	310 000 00			780 000 00		2
	6 200 00			19 300 00		3
		303 800 00			760 700 00	4
						5
	91 650 00			189 150 00		6
175 900 00			473 900 00			7
4 200 00			10 550 00			8
5 800 00			16 000 00			9
	165 900 00			447 350 00		10
	257 550 00			636 500 00		11
	75 000 00			170 000 00		12
		182 550 00			466 500 00	13
		121 250 00			294 200 00	14
						15
	2 692 00			6 400 00		16
	720 00			1 800 00		17
	2 464 00			5 600 00		18
	1 530 00			3 400 00		19
	48 900 00			138 900 00		20
		56 306 00			156 100 00	21
		64 944 00			138 100 00	22
						23
				600 00		24
				775 00		25
				1 375 00		26
				49 100 00		27
				18 000 00		28
				5 300 00		29
					75 150 00	30
					62 950 00	31
						32
				5 900 00		33
						34
				2 750 00	3 150 00	35
					66 100 00	36

Figure 18-6 Income Statement Showing Contribution Margin by Department (Right Side)

expenses are expenses incurred for the sole benefit of a given department and, thus, under the control of the department head. **Indirect expenses** are expenses incurred for the business as a whole; indirect expenses are *not* under the control of one department head. Let's look at some examples.

Salespeople generally work in only one department. Sales Salaries Expense, therefore, is a direct expense; that is, the expense can be directly tied to a particular department. On the other hand, property taxes on real estate are incurred for the business as a whole. Property Tax Expense, then, is an indirect expense; it cannot be charged directly to one department.

Some operating expenses may be partly direct and partly indirect. For example, Insurance Expense usually includes both liability insurance (which benefits the company as a whole) and property insurance (which directly benefits each department). The premium for liability insurance is an indirect expense; the property insurance premium is a direct expense. If the advertising stresses the name and location of the company *and* focuses on one or both departments, Advertising Expense will be partly direct and partly indirect When classifying an expense as either direct or indirect, use this guideline: The expense must be *directly* related to the department. If the department did not exist, the expense would not exist.

You may want to have students complete Exercise 18-1 at this point.

Reporting Contribution Margins by Department

Discuss how this income statement is different from the one in Figure 18-5.

The income statement in Figure 18-6 shows each department's contribution margin. The format for such an income statement is as follows:

	Sales	By department
−	Cost of Merchandise Sold	
=	Gross Profit on Sales	
−	Direct Expenses	
=	Contribution Margin	
−	Indirect Expenses	Company totals
=	Operating Income	
+	Other Revenue	
−	Other Expenses	
=	Net Income	

The income statement in Figure 18-6 contains the same data as Figure 18-5; only the format has changed.

R — E — M — E — M — B — E — R

Direct expenses are the expenses incurred for the sole benefit of a department. If the department did not exist, the expenses would not have been incurred.

Use demonstration problem 18-2 here.

Contribution margin is the most realistic method of reporting the profitability of a department. If the business eliminates a department, its net income will decrease by the amount of that department's contribution margin. For example, the Wallpaper Department of Custom Colors had a contribution margin of $64,944.00. If Custom Colors eliminated the Wallpaper Department, its net income would decrease by $64,944.00.

On the work sheet in Figure 18-4 on pages 472–473, the Wallpaper Department had an operating income of $35,466.50. In calculating this income, a number of indirect expenses were assigned to the Wallpaper Department. If Custom Colors decided to eliminate the Wallpaper Department, these indirect expenses would still exist. They would then be assigned entirely to the Paint Department.

Before reading further, do the following activity to check your understanding of how to calculate contribution margin.

Check Your Learning

The following amounts for the Children's Books Department were taken from the work sheet of Porter's Reading Center. Determine the department's contribution margin.

Sales	$450,000
Sales Returns and Allowances	4,000
Merchandise Inventory (beginning)	150,000
Purchases	275,000
Purchases Returns and Allowances	3,000
Merchandise Inventory (ending)	102,000
Direct Expenses	76,000
Indirect Expenses	40,000
Interest Expense	2,000

You may want to have students complete Exercise 18-3 at this point.

Compare your answer to that in the answers section. Reread the preceding part of the chapter to find the correct answer for any portion of the calculation you may have missed.

The Usefulness of Contribution Margin

Discuss the various ways a company can use the contribution margin.

A business can use income statements showing contribution margin to help control its direct expenses. It can hold the manager of each department responsible for expenses directly chargeable to that department. If the manager can reduce direct expenses, the department's contribution margin will increase.

A manufacturing business can use the contribution margin concept to determine the profitability of a particular product. This is, in fact, one of the most important uses of the contribution margin.

Management can use an income statement reporting contribution margin as a tool for planning and analyzing future operations. Such an income statement may even indicate that a department should be eliminated. For example, the Merlino Company has five departments. Its net income last year was $243,000, which is about the same as it has been for the past four years. Merlino's income statement, in which all operating expenses are allocated to the various departments, shows that Department E had an operating loss of $17,000. The following results are shown in abbreviated contribution-margin format:

	Dept. E	Depts. A–D	Total, Depts. A–E	Total, Depts. A to D (with E Eliminated)
Sales	$210,000	$1,500,000	$1,710,000	$1,500,000
Cost of Mdse. Sold	–125,000	– 670,000	– 795,000	– 670,000
Gross Profit on Sales	$ 85,000	$ 830,000	$ 915,000	$ 830,000
Direct Expenses	– 70,000	– 420,000	– 490,000	– 420,000
Contribution Margin	$ 15,000	$ 410,000	$ 425,000	$ 410,000
Indirect Expenses	– 32,000	– 150,000	– 182,000	– 182,000
Net Income (Loss)	($17,000)	$ 260,000	$ 243,000	$ 228,000

ACCOUNTING *Notes*

"Once an accountant, always an accountant!" Research shows that most accountants and auditors are very satisfied with their profession. Fewer people leave this profession than is so for most other occupations.

Now suppose Merlino decides to eliminate Department E. Since Department E's contribution margin is $15,000, the net income of the company as a whole will decrease by $15,000 ($243,000 – $228,000). These results are shown in the fourth column in the preceding table.

Another factor Merlino should consider is the possible "spill-over sales" from Department E. In other words, customers of Department E may also shop in Departments A through D. If Department E is eliminated, those customers may choose to shop elsewhere.

Summary of Key Points

1. A departmental accounting system helps a business determine how well each department is doing by providing information on revenue, cost of merchandise sold, and expenses by department.
2. There are two ways to account for departmental gross profit: keeping separate revenue, cost, and expense accounts by department or keeping supplementary records on revenue, costs, and expenses for each department.
3. Operating expenses may be classified as either selling expenses or administrative expenses. Selling expenses are incurred to sell or market the business's goods or services. Administrative expenses are the costs of managing the business.
4. Operating expenses can be allocated among departments by various means. For example, Rent Expense is usually allocated according to floor space occupied, while Salaries Expense is allocated according to the number of employees in each department.
5. Income statements may be prepared showing each department's gross profit on sales or operating income.
6. Income statements prepared to show the contribution margin of each department may present a more realistic picture of each department's performance. Contribution margin is the contribution that each department makes to the net income of the business.
7. Operating expenses may be direct or indirect. Direct expenses are those expenses directly related to the operation of a particular department; indirect expenses are those incurred for the business as a whole.

18 Review and Applications

Building Your Accounting Vocabulary

In your own words, write the definition of each of the following accounting terms. Use complete sentences for your definitions.

administrative expenses	departmental accounting system	direct expenses
contribution margin		indirect expense
		selling expenses

Reviewing Your Accounting Knowledge

1. Why would a business such as a clothing store departmentalize its records?
2. Describe two methods a business can use to provide financial information by department.
3. What is a departmental analysis sheet? How is it used?
4. Describe two formats for preparing a departmental income statement.
5. On what basis would you allocate the following expenses to various departments: rent, depreciation of store equipment, salaries of office personnel, insurance?
6. In what ways does a departmental work sheet differ from an ordinary work sheet?
7. What information is entered in the Nondepartmental Income Statement columns of a departmental work sheet?
8. List two examples of direct operating expenses and two examples of indirect operating expense.
9. How is contribution margin calculated?
10. Describe two ways in which the concept of contribution margin may be useful to a business.
11. Why is contribution margin considered a more realistic portrayal of the profitability of a department than gross profit on sales or operating income?

Improving Your Math Skills

Banks charge a fee for handling a business's bank card sales. That fee is based on a percentage of the business's total bank card sales. The weekly bank card sales of Walsh Sporting Goods for the month of May were as follows: Week 1, \$1,727.40; Week 2, \$4,439.75; Week 3, \$10,655.40; Week 4, \$3,401.20; Week 5, \$2,554.75.

1. Calculate the weekly bank card expense if Walsh's bank charges a 4% fee.
2. What was the total bank card fee expense for the month?

Applying Accounting Procedures

Exercise 18-1 Classifying Expenses

Anchor Industries has the following operating expense accounts.

Advertising Expense
Bad Debts Expense
Cleaning Expense
Depreciation Expense—Office Equipment
Depreciation Expense—Store Equipment
Insurance Expense
Miscellaneous Administrative Expense
Miscellaneous Selling Expense
Office Salaries Expense
Rent Expense
Sales Salaries Expense
Supplies Expense
Utilities Expense

Instructions: Classify each operating expense as a selling expense, an administrative expense, a direct expense, or an indirect expense. Use a form similar to the one that follows, placing a check mark in each column that applies.

EXPENSE	Selling Expense	Admin. Expense	Direct Expense	Indirect Expense
Advertising Expense	√		√	√

SPREADSHEET PROBLEM

Exercise 18-2 Allocating Expenses

Moblay Industries has five departments: A, B, C, D, and E. The individual departments occupy the following space.

$24,000
$12,000
$4,800
$6,400
$12,800

Department A:	4,000 sq. ft. of first-floor space
Department B:	2,000 sq. ft. of first-floor space
Department C:	1,200 sq. ft. of second-floor space
Department D:	1,600 sq. ft. of second-floor space
Department E:	3,200 sq. ft. of second-floor space

Rent is $60,000 per year. Moblay allocates 60% of the total rent to the first floor and 40% to the second floor. Then the rent for each floor is allocated to the departments on that floor on the basis of the space occupied.

Instructions: Determine the rent expense to be allocated to each department. Use the space provided in the accounting stationery.

SPREADSHEET PROBLEM

Exercise 18-3 Calculating Contribution Margins

Gayle Marie's Boutique has three departments: Apparel, Shoes, and Jewelry. At the end of the fiscal period, the accounting records showed the following results.

	Apparel Department	Shoe Department	Jewelry Department
Net Sales	$340,000	$98,000	$75,000
Cost of Merchandise Sold	153,000	44,100	33,750

Direct expenses for the year totaled $150,000. Of that amount, 70% are chargeable to the Apparel Department, 20% to the Shoe Department, and 10% to the Jewelry Department. Indirect expenses for the year were $33,400.

Instructions: Using the form provided in the working papers,

Net income, $98,750

(1) Calculate each department's contribution margin.

(2) Determine the Boutique's net income for the fiscal period. (There were no other revenues or other expenses for the period.)

COMPUTER PROBLEM

Problem 18-1 Reporting Departmental Gross Profit on Sales

Renaldo's Home Center has two departments: the Video Department and the Appliance Department. Renaldo's maintains separate departmental accounts for its revenue and cost of merchandise accounts. The following amounts appear in those accounts on June 30, the end of the business's fiscal year.

Merchandise Inventory—Video, July 1	$138,600
Merchandise Inventory—Video, June 30	152,600
Merchandise Inventory—Appliance, July 1	182,400
Merchandise Inventory—Appliance, June 30	197,300
Sales—Video	295,400
Sales—Appliance	340,000
Sales Returns and Allowances—Video	16,800
Sales Returns and Allowances—Appliance	18,200
Purchases—Video	195,450
Purchases—Appliance	202,600
Purchases Discounts—Video	7,430
Purchases Discounts—Appliance	8,270
Purchases Returns and Allowances—Video	8,610
Purchases Returns and Allowances—Appliance	9,540

Total:
Net sales, $600,400
COMS, $335,300
Gross profit, $265,100

Instructions: Prepare a partial income statement through gross profit on sales.

Problem 18-2 Allocating Expenses and Completing a Departmental Work Sheet

R. J. Stevens is the owner/operator of Temp-Star Plumbing & Heating. Temp-Star has two departments: Plumbing and Air Conditioning/Heating. The business maintains separate accounts by department for its inventory, revenue, and cost of merchandise accounts.

The trial balance and adjustments have already been entered on the work sheet, which is included in the working papers.

Operating income:
Plumbing, $68,108.20
AC/Heat., $62,496.80

Net income, $127,885.00

Instructions: Complete Temp-Star's departmental work sheet. Allocate the operating expenses to the two departments as follows. Round percentages to the nearest whole percent.

1. Advertising Expense is allocated on the basis of the column inches bought: Plumbing Department, 4,000 column inches; Air Conditioning/Heating Department, 6,000 column inches.
2. Bad Debts Expense, Insurance Expense, Miscellaneous Expense, Salaries and Commission Expense, and Utilities Expense are allocated according to sales.
3. The depreciation expense is allocated according to the plant asset ledger: Plumbing Department, $1,800; Air Conditioning/Heating Department, $3,000.

4. Rent Expense is allocated according to the square footage occupied: Plumbing Department, 1,800 square feet; Air Conditioning/Heating Department, 3,200 square feet.

Problem 18-3 Reporting Departmental Data Through Operating Income

Use the work sheet you prepared in Problem 18-2 to complete this problem.

Instructions: Prepare an income statement for Temp-Star Plumbing & Heating showing departmental data through operating income. Classify the expenses as either selling expenses or administrative expenses.

Problem 18-4 Reporting Contribution Margins

The Trading Post has two departments: Wearing Apparel and Sporting Goods. The business maintains separate inventory, revenue, and cost of merchandise accounts for each department. The balances that follow appeared on The Trading Post's work sheet.

Merchandise Inventory—Wearing Apparel, Jan. 1	$152,935
Merchandise Inventory—Wearing Apparel, Dec. 31	158,670
Merchandise Inventory—Sporting Goods, Jan. 1	202,500
Merchandise Inventory—Sporting Goods, Dec. 31	190,750
Sales—Wearing Apparel	470,000
Sales—Sporting Goods	640,000
Sales Returns and Allowances—Wearing Apparel	21,350
Sales Returns and Allowances—Sporting Goods	25,900
Purchases—Wearing Apparel	298,400
Purchases—Sporting Goods	337,400
Purchases Discounts—Wearing Apparel	12,150
Purchases Discounts—Sporting Goods	9,830
Purchases Returns and Allowances—Wearing Apparel	7,320
Purchases Returns and Allowances—Sporting Goods	4,800
Advertising Expense	29,500
Bad Debts Expense	3,600
Depreciation Expense—Store Equipment	25,600
Insurance Expense	1,780
Miscellaneous Expense	2,860
Rent Expense	24,000
Sales Salaries Expense	250,530
Store Supplies Expense	1,440
Utilities Expense	6,800
Interest Expense	4,200

Contribution margin: $45,143; $99,762

Net income, $104,725

Instructions: Prepare an income statement that reports each department's contribution margin. Allocate direct expenses as follows. Round percentages to the nearest whole percent.

1. The Trading Post advertises in newspapers and on local radio. Newspaper advertising ($14,000) is allocated on the basis of the number of column inches used. Radio advertising ($15,500) is allocated on the basis of air time. The Wearing Apparel Department used 3,200 column inches and had 700 minutes of air time. The Sporting Goods Department used 2,800 column inches and had 800 minutes of air time.

2. Bad Debts Expense is allocated on the basis of net sales.
3. The $900 premium for property insurance and the depreciation expense are allocated on the basis of the value of the inventory and equipment located in each department. According to the plant asset ledger, the inventory and equipment located in the Wearing Apparel Department totals $310,750. The inventory and equipment in the Sporting Goods Department is $414,850.
4. Sales Salaries Expense is allocated as follows: Wearing Apparel, $102,700; Sporting Goods, $147,830.

CHALLENGE PROBLEM

Problem 18-5 Evaluating a Department's Contribution Margin

The Bowl and Board has four departments. Department A sells cards, stationery, candles, and potpourri; Department B sells rockers, chairs, and small wooden items; Department C sells small gift items; and Department D sells handmade crockery. The company is thinking about eliminating one of the departments.

The Bowl and Board allocates its indirect expenses to each department. The accounting records show the following.

	Dept. A	Dept. B	Dept. C	Dept. D
Net Sales	$87,418	$120,212	$68,600	$30,200
Cost of Merchandise Sold	45,457	62,510	35,296	18,704
Direct Expenses	20,035	28,648	18,850	10,175
Indirect Expenses Allocated	15,088	20,017	13,339	6,900

Instructions:

(1) Calculate the contribution margin and net income or loss for each department. Use plain paper or the form provided in the working papers.

(2) If the Bowl and Board eliminates Department D, what will be the store's total net income for the period?

(3) If the indirect expenses allocated to Department D are evenly distributed among the other three departments, what will be each department's net income or loss?

(4) If the indirect expenses allocated to Department D are distributed among Departments A, B, and C using a 2:2:1 ratio, what will be each department's net income or loss?

Computer Networking at Work

If you consider how you spend your time at work or in school, you will probably realize that most of your time is spent among limited groups of people. At school, these groups may include teachers, classmates, and friends. At work, they may include your immediate work group, customers, and a social group. In some workplaces, however, the number of groups with which an employee can interact is almost unlimited, because the organization has something called a *computer network*.

Computer networking allows users to share ideas and gather data from other users.

Computer networks are links among computers within an organization, whether the organization has only one location or is made up of offices worldwide. Networked organizations are very different from traditional workplaces. For one thing, computer-based communication is very fast—much faster than the mail and even the telephone. Today, it takes little time to communicate with someone across the globe. Group discussions can be held with people all over the world as easily as with people in adjoining offices. People can discuss company policies, health insurance, or a basketball game without ever meeting in person.

Organizations that have extensive computer networks experience both positive and negative effects. On the plus side, computer networks give workers unlimited access to data and to people. With a computer, it becomes a simple matter to communicate with people and to share ideas. Another positive outcome of computer networking is the freedom it gives people to express opinions and ask questions. Everyone in an organization, regardless of position, has a more equal say.

On the minus side, managers in networked organizations find it difficult to control employee access to the network. Employees may use the networks for non-work-related discussions. Managers have also found that increased democracy sometimes can interfere with decision making. If everyone has a say in a matter, it takes a long time to resolve something and more conflict can arise.

As more organizations become networked, many new possibilities will open up. The challenge will then be for employees to become more committed and responsible and for managers to find new ways to handle all the changes.

Chapter 19

BRANCH ACCOUNTING

Learning Objectives

When you have completed this chapter, you should be able to do the following:

1. Explain the difference between decentralized and centralized accounting systems.
2. Journalize transactions for a multistore business that uses a centralized accounting system.
3. Prepare financial statements for a multistore business that uses a centralized accounting system.
4. Define the accounting terms presented in this chapter.

In Chapter 18, you learned that when a business performs several activities, it often divides those activities into departments. By organizing its operations this way, the business can delegate authority to department managers and measure the profitability and efficiency of each department.

Businesses can also expand their operations by opening branches or stores in different locations. These multistore businesses are often referred to as *chain stores*. There may be several types of chain stores in your own community. Typical multistore businesses include grocery stores, drugstores, variety stores, fast-food restaurants, and service stations.

In this chapter, you'll learn about the accounting systems these multistore businesses use. You'll learn how to journalize transactions and how to prepare financial statements that report the individual and combined operations of the branches.

New Terms

multistore business
franchise
decentralized accounting system
centralized accounting system
interbranch transaction
combined income statement
combined balance sheet

Multistore Businesses

Give examples of franchise businesses in the local area. Identify several national franchises.

ACCOUNTING Notes
Franchises are important to the U.S. economy. For example, almost one-half of all eating establishments are franchises and about one-third of consumers' shopping dollars are spent at franchises.

Many businesses expand their operations to increase sales and income, to become more competitive, or to offer better services. One way to expand operations is to open a *branch*, another store in a different location. The branch may be in the same city, in another city, or even in another state. A business that has more than one store or branch is referred to as a **multistore business**. Many nationwide multistore businesses have started as one-store companies.

Some businesses expand by granting franchises. A **franchise** is a right, given by a company to an individual or another business, that allows that individual or business to use the company's name and to sell its goods or services in a specific area. The cost for a franchise varies, usually depending on how well known the original company is and how much support it provides. Often the *franchisee* (the individual or business buying the franchise) must purchase all products from the *franchiser* (the company granting the franchise). Many McDonald's restaurants, for example, are operated as franchises.

Other multistore businesses set up each branch as a separate corporation. The branch corporations share the same name and, usually, the same owner or group of owners. Branches that are set up as separate corporate entities are sometimes referred to as *brother-sister stores*.

For example, Riverside Gardens, Inc., is a multistore plant and garden business with two branches. One branch is located in the town of Jennings; the second branch is located in the neighboring town of Welch.

Businesses expand their operations by maintaining stores in several locations.

The owners of the Jennings branch and the Welch branch are the same. Each branch, however, was organized as a separate corporation. Each branch applied for and received a charter; therefore, each branch is a separate legal entity.

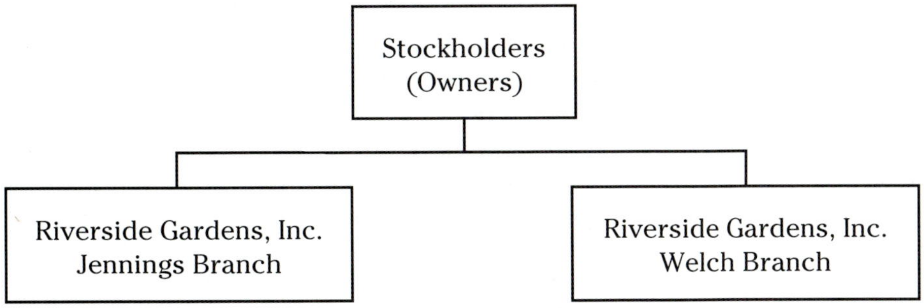

Discuss the advantages of organizing businesses as multistore operations.

This method of organizing a business offers several advantages. First, because each branch is a separate legal entity, the general liability of the multistore business is limited. Each branch is responsible for its own commitments and obligations. Second, creditors generally cannot look beyond the assets of a branch to satisfy their claims. Third, when one of the branches needs to borrow money, creditors can examine the combined financial statements of the multistore business. Creditors may then ask the other branch to guarantee the loan. Fourth, each branch has its own organizational structure (within limits). The principal owners of the multistore business maintain control over each branch by owning more than 50% of the stock of each branch. Each branch, however, can sell some shares of stock to employees and individuals in the community in which the business is located. Those persons then have a stake in the success of the branch.

In this chapter, you will learn about the accounting systems these multistore businesses use.

Accounting Systems for Multistore Businesses

Introduce the two basic types of accounting systems a multistore business may use.

The accounting procedures used vary from one multistore business to another. The system used depends to a great extent on the amount of responsibility and authority given to each branch by the management of the multistore business. The two basic types of accounting systems used by multistore businesses are referred to as *decentralized* and *centralized*. A business may also choose a variation of each type.

Decentralized Accounting System

An accounting system in which each branch of the multistore business maintains its own accounting records is called a **decentralized accounting system**. As a separate corporation, each branch is an independent business. Each, therefore, has its own journals and ledgers. The branches, however, use the same accounting procedures and chart of accounts. By doing so, their financial statements can easily be compared and combined at the end of the accounting period.

Point out the differences between a decentralized accounting system and a centralized accounting system.

Centralized Accounting System

The second, and probably more widely used, accounting system used by multistore businesses is the centralized accounting system. In a **centralized accounting system**, a central accounting office keeps the accounting records and performs the accounting functions for all branches. The central accounting office may be located in one of the branches or at an entirely separate location. Each branch sends its source documents (sales slips, purchase requisitions, receiving reports, deposit slips, and so on) to the central accounting office.

The central accounting office performs all accounting functions. It journalizes all transactions and maintains separate general ledger accounts for each branch. The central accounting office prepares separate financial statements for each branch. This accounting system is similar to a departmental accounting system. Each branch is treated like a separate department.

Give several advantages of using a centralized accounting system.

By using a centralized accounting system, a multistore business can usually decrease its expenses. The company may be able to lower its salary and training costs or it may need less equipment. Since an accounting office is not necessary at each branch, the duplication of activities is eliminated. Another advantage is that the accounting records and procedures used throughout all branches are consistent.

R—E—M—E—M—B—E—R

In a decentralized accounting system, each branch maintains its own accounting records. In a centralized accounting system, a central accounting office keeps all the accounting records and performs all accounting functions for all the branches.

Give several examples of accounting-related tasks performed by a branch.

Branch Accounting Tasks Although the central accounting office performs all of the accounting functions, each branch must handle some accounting-related tasks. An accounting clerk in the branch helps the branch manager in all matters that concern accounting. For example, the accounting clerk may prepare purchase requisitions, gather payroll information, batch sales slips, or prepare deposits. Each branch deposits the cash it receives in a special branch checking account. The branch can make deposits to this account, but it cannot write checks on it.

Chart of Accounts for a Centralized Accounting System In a departmental accounting system, separate revenue, cost of merchandise, and expense accounts are set up for each department. Since each branch in the multistore business is a separate entity, the central accounting office must separate each branch's operations. A complete set of asset, liability, stockholders' equity, revenue, cost, and expense accounts are maintained in the general ledger for each branch. For example, Riverside Gardens, Inc., uses a centralized accounting system. The business's chart of accounts includes a Cash in Bank—Jennings account and a Cash in Bank—Welch account. A portion of Riverside's chart of

Review the chart of accounts in Figure 19-1 with students.

accounts appears in Figure 19-1. You can see that within each classification, separate accounts are kept for each branch.

RIVERSIDE GARDENS, INC.
Chart of Accounts (Partial)

ASSETS	1011	Cash in Bank—Jennings
	1012	Cash in Bank—Welch
	1013	Cash in Bank—Payables
	1051	Accounts Receivable—Jennings
	1052	Accounts Receivable—Welch
	1071	Due from Welch
	1101	Merchandise Inventory—Jennings
	1102	Merchandise Inventory—Welch
	1151	Supplies—Jennings
	1152	Supplies—Welch
	1201	Prepaid Insurance—Jennings
	1202	Prepaid Insurance—Welch
	1501	Equipment—Jennings
	1502	Equipment—Welch
	1551	Accumulated Depreciation, Equipment—Jennings
	1552	Accumulated Depreciation, Equipment—Welch
LIABILITIES	2011	Accounts Payable—Jennings
	2012	Accounts Payable—Welch
	2031	Due to Jennings
STOCKHOLDERS' EQUITY	3011	Common Stock—Jennings
	3012	Common Stock—Welch
	3101	Retained Earnings—Jennings
	3102	Retained Earnings—Welch
	3201	Income Summary—Jennings
	3202	Income Summary—Welch
REVENUE	4011	Sales—Jennings
	4012	Sales—Welch
COST OF MERCHANDISE	5011	Purchases—Jennings
	5012	Purchases—Welch
	5202	Transfer Charges—Welch
EXPENSES	6011	Advertising Expense—Jennings
	6012	Advertising Expense—Welch
	6401	Salaries Expense—Jennings
	6402	Salaries Expense—Welch
OTHER REVENUE	7011	Transfer Fees Earned—Jennings

Figure 19-1 Partial Chart of Accounts for a Multistore Business

You may want to have students complete Exercise 10-2 at this point.

Notice that each branch's accounts can be identified. The first three digits of the account number identify the account. The last digit identifies the branch. For example, 401 is the account number for Sales. The "1" identifies the Jennings branch, and the "2" identifies the Welch branch. Therefore, 4011 is the Sales—Jennings account.

R — E — M — E — M — B — E — R

In a centralized accounting system, a complete set of accounts is maintained for each branch of the multistore business.

Before reading further, do the following activity to check your understanding of the material you have just studied.

Check Your Learning

Write your answers to these questions on a sheet of notebook paper.

1. A right granted by a company that allows another to use its name and to sell its goods or services is called a(n) __?__.
2. A business that has more than one store or branch is called a(n) __?__.
3. In a(n) __?__ accounting system, one accounting office keeps the accounting records and performs the accounting functions for all branches.
4. An accounting system in which each branch within the multistore business maintains its own accounting records is called a(n) __?__ accounting system.
5. When a four-digit coding system is used in a chart of accounts, the first three digits identify the __?__ and the last digit identifies the __?__.

Compare your answers to those in the answers section. Reread the preceding part of the chapter to find the correct answers to any questions you may have missed.

Journalizing Transactions in a Centralized Accounting System

Let's see how the central accounting office of Riverside Gardens, Inc., records the business transactions of its Jennings and Welch branches.

Recording Branch Cash Sales

Point out that each branch makes its own deposits.

Both the Jennings and Welch branches of Riverside Gardens use cash registers to record all cash sales. At the Jennings branch, for example, cash is removed from the cash registers during the day and at the end of the day and deposited in the branch's checking account. At the end of the business day, the accounting clerk prepares a special cash register report. The clerk sends this report, copies of the deposit slips, and the cash register tapes to the central accounting office.

The central accounting office verifies the cash register report, the tapes, and the deposit slips. A deposit verification report, shown in Figure 19-2, is prepared. As you can see, it lists the sales and sales tax recorded at each cash register. It also lists the two deposits made by the Jennings branch during the day. The total of the two deposits must equal the total amount reported on the top of the form.

Riverside Gardens, Inc.—Jennings Branch
Cash Register/Deposit Verification
November 10, 199–

Register No.	Time	Sales	Sales Tax Payable	Total
1	2:00 p.m.	$1,256.44	$ 94.23	$1,350.67
2	2:15 p.m.	590.40	44.28	634.68
1	8:00 p.m.	691.78	51.88	743.66
2	8:30 p.m.	840.20	63.02	903.22
Total		$3,378.82	$253.41	$3,632.23
		Cash Short or Over		0.00
		Total Cash Received		$3,632.23
		DEPOSITS		AMOUNT
		Deposit Slip 3589		$1,985.35
		Deposit Slip 3590		1,646.88
		Total Cash Deposited		$3,632.23

Figure 19-2 Deposit Verification Report

Mention that the deposit verification report is the source document for the journal entry.

The deposit verification report is the source document for the journal entry to record the branch's cash sales. The entry to record the cash sales of the Jennings branch is shown in general journal form in Figure 19-3. (This transaction could also be recorded in a cash receipts journal.)

GENERAL JOURNAL — PAGE 10

	DATE		DESCRIPTION	POST. REF.	DEBIT	CREDIT	
1	199– Nov.	11	Cash in Bank-Jennings		3 632 23		1
2			Sales-Jennings			3 378 82	2
3			Sales Tax Payable-Jennings			253 41	3
4			Deposit Verification Form 11/10				4

Figure 19-3 Journalizing Branch Cash Sales

You may want to have students complete Exercise 19-2 at this point.

The cash sales for the Welch branch are recorded in a similar manner; however, the Welch branch accounts are used.

Explain that when a computerized accounting system is used, sales on account data are captured and stored by a branch and transmitted to the central accounting office at scheduled intervals.

Recording Branch Accounts Receivable Transactions

When a branch sells merchandise on account to a charge customer, a sales slip is prepared, as in any other accounting system. At the end of each business day, the branch accounting clerk sends all the sales slips to the central accounting office.

Each branch's sales on account are journalized separately. For example, on November 12 the Welch branch sold $125.00 of merchandise on account to J. C. Watts, plus sales tax of $9.38. The entry to record this transaction appears in general journal form in Figure 19-4. (This transaction could also be recorded in the business's sales journal.)

GENERAL JOURNAL — PAGE 11

	DATE		DESCRIPTION	POST. REF.	DEBIT	CREDIT	
1	199- Nov.	12	Accts. Rec.—Welch/J. C. Watts	✓	134 38		1
2			Sales—Welch			125 00	2
3			Sales Tax Payable—Welch			9 38	3
4			Sales Slip 8421				4

Figure 19-4 Journalizing a Branch Sale on Account

Use demonstration problem 19-1 here.

The central accounting office sends monthly statements to charge customers of both branches. The customers, in turn, send their payments directly to the central accounting office. When it receives a payment from a charge customer, the central accounting office prepares a receipt and then records the transaction in the accounting records. For example, on November 14 Riverside's central accounting office received cash on account from J. B. Houston (a customer of the Jennings branch) and from Jane Brown (a customer of the Welch branch). The journal entries to record the cash receipts appear in general journal form in Figure 19-5.

GENERAL JOURNAL — PAGE 14

	DATE		DESCRIPTION	POST. REF.	DEBIT	CREDIT	
1	199- Nov.	14	Cash in Bank—Jennings		155 88		1
2			Accts. Rec.—Jennings/J. B. Houston	✓		155 88	2
3			Receipt 9488				3
4		14	Cash in Bank—Welch		59 87		4
5			Accts. Rec.—Welch/Jane Brown	✓		59 87	5
6			Receipt 9489				6

Figure 19-5 Journalizing Cash Receipts from Charge Customers by Branch

Recording Purchases on Account by Branch

Emphasize that all purchases must be authorized by the purchasing agent in the central accounting department.

In Riverside's centralized accounting system, all purchases must be authorized and placed by the central accounting office. Each branch prepares a purchase requisition for items it needs (merchandise, supplies, equipment, and so on) and sends it to the central accounting office. The purchasing agent in the central office decides what is to be bought, when it is to be purchased, and how many items are to be distributed to each branch. The central office then prepares purchase orders and sends them to appropriate suppliers. Often, to take advantage of special quantity discounts, the central office combines the requisitions from the two branches and places one large order.

When the branch receives the goods ordered, it returns the receiving report to the central accounting office, which compares it with the invoice. (The invoice is sent directly to the central accounting office.) After the invoice has been verified, it is journalized.

The central accounting office of Riverside Gardens received the following three invoices on November 15.

November 15: *Received Invoice 541 dated November 14 from Arton Nurseries, Inc., for merchandise purchased on account for the Jennings branch, $3,000.00; terms 2/10, n/30.*

November 15: *Received Invoice 1468 dated November 12 from American Paper, Inc., for supplies purchased on account for the Welch branch, $429.81; terms n/30.*

November 15: *Received Invoice 1202 dated November 13 from the LPB Equipment Company for computer equipment purchased on account for the Welch branch, $8,946.21; terms n/30.*

Figure 19-6 shows the three entries in general journal form. Notice that each purchase was charged to a particular branch's accounts.

GENERAL JOURNAL — PAGE 16

	DATE		DESCRIPTION	POST. REF.	DEBIT	CREDIT	
1	199– Nov.	15	Purchases–Jennings		3000 00		1
2			Accts. Pay.–Jennings/Arton Nur.	✓		3000 00	2
3			Invoice 541				3
4		15	Supplies–Welch		429 81		4
5			Accts. Pay.–Welch/Amer. Paper, Inc.	✓		429 81	5
6			Invoice 1468				6
7		15	Computer Equipment		8946 21		7
8			Accts. Pay.–Welch/LPB Equip. Co.	✓		8946 21	8
9			Invoice 1202				9

Figure 19-6 Journalizing Purchases on Account by Branch

Point out that costs from one big order must be allocated to the branches.

As mentioned earlier, the central office often combines the purchase requisitions from the two branches and places one large order. When it receives the supplier's invoice, the central accounting office allocates the cost of the items purchased between the two branches. Let's look at an example.

November 21: *Received Invoice 1480 from the National Wholesale Company for $12,468 for merchandise purchased on account; terms 3/10, n/30.*

By checking the original purchase order, the office determined that of the $12,468 total, $7,984 of the merchandise had been ordered for the Jennings branch and $4,484 for the Welch branch. When the central office receives only one invoice for items ordered for both branches, it writes an explanation of the allocation on the invoice. For example, the following note was placed on the invoice from National Wholesale:

Charge as follows:	
Jennings branch	$ 7,984
Welch branch	4,484
Total	$12,468

This transaction is recorded in the general journal form as shown in Figure 19-7.

GENERAL JOURNAL — PAGE 30

	DATE		DESCRIPTION	POST. REF.	DEBIT	CREDIT	
1	199- Nov.	21	Purchases–Jennings		7 984 00		1
2			Purchases–Welch		4 484 00		2
3			Accts. Pay.–Jennings/Nat. Whole.	✓		7 984 00	3
4			Accts. Pay.–Welch/Nat. Whole.	✓		4 484 00	4
5			Invoice 1480				5

Figure 19-7 Allocating a Purchase on Account between Two Branches

Use demonstration problem 19-2 here.

Before reading further, do the following activity to check your understanding of the material you have just studied.

Check Your Learning

Thompson's, Inc., is a multistore business with three branches that are organized as separate corporations. Thompson's uses a centralized accounting system and maintains separate accounts in the general ledger for each branch. Following are several transactions handled by the central accounting office on July 12. For each transaction, identify the accounts and determine the related amounts that would be debited and credited.

1. Branch 3 deposited $7,166.25 in its checking account for cash sales of $6,825.00 and sales taxes of $341.25.
2. Branch 1 sold $400.00 of mechandise on account, plus $20.00 sales tax, to John Dickerson.
3. The central accounting office received $735.00 on account from Kim Yu, a charge customer of Branch 2.
4. Received Invoice 2345 for $8,459.10 for merchandise purchased on account from the LaGrange Company for Branch 3.
5. Received Invoice 5690 for $1,245.10 from the National Supply Company for store supplies purchased for the three branches. The cost is allocated as follows: Branch 1, $360.00; Branch 2, $784.10; Branch 3, $101.00.

Compare your answers to those in the answers section. Reread the preceding part of the chapter to find the correct answers for any items you may have missed.

Recording Cash Payments for Branches

Discuss the advantages of making all cash payments to vendors from one checking account.

In a centralized accounting system, all cash payments are made by the central accounting office. Riverside's central accounting office maintains a special checking account that is used only for cash payments. This checking account is similar to the payroll checking account. As you recall, once the employees' total net pay is determined, a check is written on the business's checking account for the total net pay amount. That check is then deposited in the payroll checking account. Payroll checks are written to employees using the payroll checking account. After all payroll checks clear the bank, the payroll checking account has a zero balance.

Introduce the Cash in Bank—Payables account.

The cash payments checking account—called the Payables checking account—is used in the same way. Money is deposited in the Payables checking account from the two branch checking accounts. Checks written on the Payables account are used to make cash payments for *both* branches. A record of the transactions affecting the Payables checking account is maintained in a current asset account called Cash in Bank—Payables.

Cash in Bank—Payables	
Dr. Increase Side Balance Side (Transfers from Jennings and Welch Cash in Bank accounts)	Cr. Decrease Side (Payments on account and for expenses for both branches)

Now let's see how this Cash in Bank—Payables account is used in the centralized accounting system of Riverside Gardens, Inc.

R — E — M — E — M — B — E — R

In a centralized accounting system, all cash payments are made by the central accounting office. A special checking account is used to make all cash payments. A record of the transactions affecting this checking account is kept in the Cash in Bank—Payables account.

Transferring Funds to the Cash in Bank—Payables Account Once a week, an accounting clerk in the central office prepares a list of the cash payments that must be made for each of the branches. These cash payments may include payments to creditors or payments for expenses such as advertising, utilities, and rent. For example, on November 29 Riverside's central accounting office determined that cash payments totaling $16,840.28 had to be made for the Jennings branch. Cash payments for the Welch branch totaled $12,295.61.

Illustrate how cash is transferred to the Cash in Bank—Payables account for all checks that will be written to outside parties.

Next, an amount equal to the branch's cash payments is transferred from each branch's Cash in Bank account to the special Cash in Bank—Payables account. The amount can be transferred by a check written on the branch's checking account or, more likely, by using the electronic funds transfer system.

November 29: *Transferred into the* Cash in Bank—Payables *account $16,840.28 from the Jennings branch checking account and $12,295.61 from the Welch branch checking account, Electronic Funds Transfer (EFT) 1003.*

Cash in Bank—Payables is debited for $29,135.89 ($16,840.28 + $12,295.61), the total of the cash payments that must be made for the two branches. Cash in Bank—Jennings is credited for $16,840.28, the total cash payments to be made for the Jennings branch. Cash in Bank—Welch is credited for $12,295.61, the total cash payments to be made for the Welch branch.

Cash in Bank—Payables	
Dr.	Cr.
$29,135.89	

Cash in Bank—Jennings	
Dr.	Cr.
Bal. $20,460.00	$16,840.28

Cash in Bank—Welch	
Dr.	Cr.
Bal. $18,695.00	$12,295.61

Point out that after all of the checks in a check run clear the bank, the balance of the Cash in Bank—Payables account will be zero.

The entry to record the transfer of funds appears in general journal form in Figure 19-8. As you can see, this transaction simply moves cash from the two branch checking accounts into the special cash payments checking account. The Payables checking account now has enough cash to cover the checks that must be prepared that week.

GENERAL JOURNAL — PAGE 40

	DATE		DESCRIPTION	POST. REF.	DEBIT	CREDIT	
1	199– Nov.	29	Cash in Bank-Payables		29 135 89		1
2			Cash in Bank-Jennings			16 840 28	2
3			Cash in Bank-Welch			12 295 61	3
4			EFT 1003				4

Use demonstration problem 19-3 here.

Figure 19-8 Journalizing the Transfer of Funds

R — E — M — E — M — B — E — R

When cash payments must be made, the central accounting office transfers cash to the Cash in Bank—Payables account from the Cash in Bank accounts of the branches.

▲ Recording Cash Payments to Creditors on Account

When an invoice must be paid, a check is issued on the Cash in Bank—Payables checking account. Let's see how three of the cash payments made on November 29 are journalized.

__November 29:__ Issued Check 55666 for $349.54 to Ballard Bros. in payment of Invoice 4468 for supplies purchased on account for the Jennings branch.

Point out that all cash payments to outside parties are made from the Cash in Bank—Payable account.

In this transaction, Accounts Payable—Jennings and the Ballard Bros. account in the subsidiary ledger are debited for $349.54. Cash in Bank—Payables is credited for the same amount. Notice that the Cash in Bank—Payables account rather than the Cash in Bank—Jennings account is credited. This $349.54 cash payment is included in the $16,840.28 transferred from the Cash in Bank—Jennings account earlier (shown in Figure 19-8). The entry appears in general journal form on lines 5 through 7 in Figure 19-9.

GENERAL JOURNAL — PAGE 40

	DATE		DESCRIPTION	POST. REF.	DEBIT	CREDIT	
5	Nov.	29	Accts. Pay.- Jennings/Ballard Bros.	✓	349 54		5
6			Cash in Bank - Payables			349 54	6
7			Check 55666				7
8		29	Accts. Pay.- Welch/Venic, Inc.	✓	1 248 45		8
9			Cash in Bank - Payables			1 248 45	9
10			Check 55667				10
11		29	Accts. Pay.- Jennings/Baton Rouge Sales	✓	1 000 00		11
12			Accts. Pay.- Welch/Baton Rouge Sales	✓	500 00		12
13			Cash in Bank - Payables			1 500 00	13
14			Check 55668				14

Figure 19-9 Journalizing Cash Payments on Account

__November 29:__ Issued Check 55667 for $1,248.45 to Venic, Inc., in payment of Invoice 2468 for equipment purchased for the Welch branch.

Emphasize that when Accounts Payable is debited, the branch and the creditor must be identified.

In this transaction, Accounts Payable—Welch and the Venic, Inc., account in the subsidiary ledger are debited for $1,248.45. Cash in Bank—Payables is credited for $1,248.45. The entry is shown in general journal form on lines 8 through 10 in Figure 19-9. As you can see, this entry is very similar to the previous one. The Welch branch's Accounts Payable account and Venic, Inc.'s account, however, are debited in this transaction.

__November 29:__ Issued Check 55668 for $1,500.00 to Baton Rouge Sales in payment of Invoice 644 for merchandise purchased on account for the Jennings branch ($1,000.00) and for the Welch branch ($500.00).

Earlier you learned that a multistore business often combines the purchase requisitions from its branches and prepares one purchase order. When the invoice arrives, the central accounting offices makes a notation on the invoice indicating how the total amount is allocated between the two branches. When the invoice is ready to be paid, one check is drawn on the Cash in Bank—Payables account.

Review how the cash payment is allocated to the branches.

In the journal entry, the cash payment is allocated between the two branches according to the notation on the invoice. In this transaction, Accounts Payable—Jennings and the Baton Rouge Sales account are debited for $1,000.00; Accounts Payable—Welch and the Baton Rouge Sales account are debited for $500.00. The Cash in Bank—Payables account is credited for $1,500.00, the total amount of the cash payment. The entry is shown in general journal form on lines 11 through 14 in Figure 19-9.

R — E — M — E — M — B — E — R

In a centralized accounting system, the Cash in Bank—Payables account is credited for a cash payment rather than a branch's Cash in Bank account.

Remind students that certain expense payments are made without establishing a liability.

Recording Cash Payments for Expenses Expenses for branch operations are also paid out of the Cash in Bank—Payables account. These expenses include payments for utilities, advertising, and salaries. For example, one of the cash payments that must be made on November 29 is for an advertising bill of $864.29. The Alma Printing Company printed advertising circulars for both the Jennings branch and the Welch branch. The printing company sent one bill to the central accounting office for the services provided to both branches. Of the $864.29, $435.15 is allocated to the Jennings branch and $429.14 is allocated to the Welch branch. The entry to record the payment of the advertising bill appears in general journal form in Figure 19-10. Again, notice that Cash in Bank—Payables is credited for the total amount being paid.

GENERAL JOURNAL — PAGE 40

	DATE		DESCRIPTION	POST. REF.	DEBIT	CREDIT	
15	Nov.	29	Advertising Expense - Jennings		435 15		15
16			Advertising Expense - Welch		429 14		16
17			Cash in Bank - Payables			864 29	17
18			Check 55669				18

Figure 19-10 Journalizing the Cash Payment of an Expense

Interbranch Transactions

The branches of a multistore business occasionally conduct transactions with one another. Transactions among branches of the same multistore business are called **interbranch transactions**. One of the most frequent interbranch transactions is the transfer of merchandise.

The Jennings branch of Riverside Gardens, Inc., serves as a warehouse for both branches. When the central accounting offices places a large merchandise order, it is shipped to and stored at the Jennings branch.

Introduce and explain the interbranch accounts.

When the Welch branch needs merchandise, it completes a transfer request form. The Jennings branch sends the requested items to Welch and charges a 1% transfer fee to cover its handling, storage, and shipping expenses. The transfer fee is revenue for the Jennings branch. Whenever the Jennings branch ships merchandise to the Welch branch, the amount of the transfer fee is credited to an other revenue account called Transfer Fees Earned—Jennings.

Transfer Fees Earned—Jennings	
Dr. Decrease Side	Cr. Increase Side Balance Side

For the Welch branch, the amount of the transfer fee is considered to be an additional cost of merchandise purchased. In this respect, it is similar to the Transportation In account. Every time the Welch branch receives merchandise from the warehouse, the amount of the transfer fee is debited to a cost of merchandise account titled Transfer Charges—Welch.

Transfer Charges—Welch	
Dr. Increase Side Balance Side	Cr. Decrease Side

R — E — M — E — M — B — E — R

When merchandise is shipped from one branch to another, a transfer fee is charged. This fee is revenue for the branch shipping the goods and a cost of merchandise for the branch receiving the goods.

Point out that one branch serves as the warehouse.

Two other accounts are affected when merchandise is shipped from the Jennings warehouse to the Welch branch: Due from Welch and Due to Jennings. Due from Welch is a current asset account for the Jennings branch. The account is used to record the total amount the Jennings branch will receive from the Welch branch for the merchandise shipped. This total includes the cost of the merchandise and the amount of the transfer fee. Basically, a "Due from" account is a special Accounts Receivable account.

Due from Welch	
Dr. Increase Side Balance Side	Cr. Decrease Side

Due to Jennings is a current liability account for the Welch branch. The account is used to record the total amount the Welch branch owes the Jennings branch for the merchandise shipped. Like the "Due from" account, the amount recorded in the account includes the cost of the merchandise and the amount of the transfer fee. A "Due to" account is a special Accounts Payable account.

Due to Jennings	
Dr. Decrease Side	Cr. Increase Side Balance Side

Now let's look at an interbranch transaction involving the transfer of merchandise between the two branches.

November 30: *The Jennings warehouse shipped $20,000 of merchandise to Welch, transfer fee $200, Transfer Request 2826.*

Stress that two entries are required when merchandise is transferred.

When merchandise is shipped from the warehouse to the Welch branch, *two* journal entries must be made. The first entry records the transaction in the Jennings branch accounts. The second entry records the transaction in the Welch branch accounts.

Emphasize that this is the entry made for the branch that is shipping the merchandise.

Journalizing the Transfer of Merchandise Three Jennings branch accounts are affected by this transaction: Due from Welch, Purchases—Jennings, and Transfer Fees Earned—Jennings. Let's look at the entire transaction in T account form:

Due from Welch	
Dr.	Cr.
$20,200	

Purchases—Jennings	
Dr.	Cr.
Bal. $350,000	$20,000

Transfer Fees Earned—Jennings	
Dr.	Cr.
	$200

Due from Welch is being increased. It is, therefore, debited for $20,200, the total amount to be received from the Welch branch. Since merchandise is being transferred from the Jennings branch, Purchases—Jennings is being decreased. Purchases—Jennings is, therefore, credited for $20,000, the cost of the merchandise. Transfer Fees Earned—Jennings is credited for $200, the amount of the transfer fee. This transaction appears in Figure 19-11.

Discuss why Purchases is credited.

GENERAL JOURNAL					PAGE 42
DATE		DESCRIPTION	POST. REF.	DEBIT	CREDIT
199– Nov.	30	Due from Welch		20 200 00	
		Purchases-Jennings			20 000 00
		Transfer Fees Earned-Jennings			200 00
		Transfer Request 2826			

Figure 19-11 Journalizing the Transfer of Merchandise from the Shipping Branch

Journalizing the Receipt of Transferred Merchandise

Three Welch branch accounts are also affected by the interbranch transfer: Purchases—Welch, Transfer Charges—Welch, and Due to Jennings:

Purchases—Welch	
Dr.	Cr.
Bal. $169,000	
$20,000	

Transfer Charges—Welch	
Dr.	Cr.
$200	

Due to Jennings	
Dr.	Cr.
	$20,200

Emphasize that this is the entry made for the branch that is receiving the merchandise.

Since the Welch branch is receiving additional merchandise, its Purchases—Welch account is debited for the cost of the merchandise, $20,000. The amount of the transfer fee, $200, is debited to the Transfer Charges—Welch account. Due to Jennings, a liability account, is being increased. It is credited for $20,200, the total amount owed to the Jennings branch. The transaction is recorded as shown in Figure 19-12.

GENERAL JOURNAL					PAGE 42
DATE		DESCRIPTION	POST. REF.	DEBIT	CREDIT
Nov.	30	Purchases-Welch		20 000 00	
		Transfer Charges-Welch		200 00	
		Due to Jennings			20 200 00
		Transfer Request 2826			

Use demonstration problem 19-4 here.

Figure 19-12 Journalizing the Transfer of Merchandise to the Receiving Branch

R — E — M — E — M — B — E — R

"Due to" means an amount is owed. "Due from" means an amount will be received.

Settling Accounts Between Branches

Point out that "Due from" and "Due to" accounts are usually cleared once a month. Mention that they are offsetting.

At the beginning of each month, the central accounting office at Riverside Gardens, Inc., records an interbranch transaction to "pay" for the merchandise shipped to the Welch branch. Like the interbranch transaction for the transfer of merchandise, two journal entries are required for an interbranch cash payment. The first entry records the payment in the Welch accounts. The second entry records the receipt of cash in the Jennings branch accounts.

At the beginning of December, the Welch branch owes $20,200 to the Jennings branch for the merchandise transfer on November 30. Let's now look at the two journal entries required.

Remind students that all cash payments are made for the Cash in Bank—Payables account.

▲ Journalizing an Interbranch Cash Payment As you learned earlier, all cash payments must be made through the Cash in Bank—Payables account. Before an interbranch cash payment transaction can be made, cash must be transferred from the Cash in Bank—Welch account to the Cash in Bank—Payables account. At the beginning of the week, an accounting clerk in the central accounting office determined that the Welch branch had cash payments to be made totaling $24,038. This amount included the $20,200 owed to the Jennings branch. The account clerk transferred $24,038 to the Cash in Bank—Payables account from the Cash in Bank—Welch account. (Cash was also transferred from the Cash in Bank—Jennings account at the same time.) The interbranch cash payment can now be journalized.

December 4: *Paid $20,200 to the Jennings branch for merchandise transferred to the Welch branch, Electronic Funds Transfer (EFT) 1007.*

Point out that the payment is made by the branch receiving the merchandise.

The two accounts affected by this transaction are Due to Jennings and Cash in Bank—Payables. Since the amount owed is now being paid, Due to Jennings is debited for $20,200. Cash in Bank—Payables is credited for $20,200 because cash is decreasing.

Cash in Bank—Payables	
Dr.	Cr.
Bal. $31,723	$20,200

Due to Jennings	
Dr.	Cr.
$20,200	Bal. $20,200

The entry to record the interbranch cash payment appears in general journal form in Figure 19-13. Notice that the cash payment was made through the electronic funds transfer system. A check could have been written for the transaction, but the electronic transfer is much simpler.

GENERAL JOURNAL — PAGE 46

	DATE		DESCRIPTION	POST. REF.	DEBIT	CREDIT	
1	19-- Dec.	4	Due to Jennings		20200 00		1
2			Cash in Bank - Payables			20200 00	2
3			EFT 1007				3

Figure 19-13 Journalizing an Interbranch Cash Payment

Stress that a payment made by one branch becomes a receipt for the second branch.

▲ Journalizing an Interbranch Cash Receipt The cash received from the Welch branch must now be recorded in the Jennings branch accounts. The two accounts affected by the cash receipt are Due from Welch and Cash in Bank—Jennings. Cash in Bank—Jennings is debited for $20,200 because cash is being received. Due from Welch is credited for $20,200 because the asset is being decreased.

Remind students that two transactions are required for each interbranch transaction.

Cash in Bank—Jennings	
Dr.	Cr.
Bal. $15,619.72	
20,200.00	

Due from Welch	
Dr.	Cr.
Bal. $20,200.00	$20,200.00

Figure 19-14 shows the entry in general journal form.

GENERAL JOURNAL — PAGE 46

	DATE		DESCRIPTION	POST. REF.	DEBIT	CREDIT	
4	Dec.	4	Cash in Bank - Jennings		20200 00		4
5			Due from Welch			20200 00	5
6			Receipt 2841				6

Figure 19-14 Journalizing an Interbranch Cash Receipt

Use demonstration problem 19-5 here.

Before reading further, do the following activity to check your understanding of interbranch transactions.

Check Your Learning

On a sheet of notebook paper, record the following interbranch transactions in general journal form.

May 20 Store 1 transferred merchandise to Store 4, $40,000 plus transfer fee of $400, Transfer Request 111.

June 2 Store 1 received payment from Store 4 for the merchandise transferred on May 20, Receipt 113.

Compare your answers to those in the answers section. Reread the preceding part of the chapter to find the correct entries for any items you may have missed.

End-of-Fiscal-Period Procedures

While discussing the financial statements prepared for each of the branches, point out the interbranch accounts.

The end-of-fiscal-period procedures for a multistore business using a centralized accounting system are similar to the procedures followed by any other form of business organization. Separate work sheets and financial statements are prepared for each branch. Combined financial statements, which report the results of operations for both branches, are also prepared.

Riverside Gardens, Inc. - Jennings Branch
Income Statement
For the Year Ended December 31, 199-

Revenue:				
Net Sales				1,042 898 00
Cost of Merchandise Sold:				
Merch. Inv., Jan. 1, 199-			94 768 00	
Purchases	798 244 00			
Plus: Tran. In	2 725 00			
Cost of Delivered Merch.		800 969 00		
Less: Purch. Disc.	15 891 00			
Purch. Ret. + Allow.	6 135 00	22 026 00		
Net Purchases			778 943 00	
Cost of Merch. Avail.			873 711 00	
Less: Merch. Inv., Dec. 31, 199-			97 238 00	
Cost of Merch. Sold				776 473 00
Gross Profit on Sales				266 425 00
Operating Expenses				
Selling Expenses			125 201 00	
Admin. Expenses			80 452 00	
Total Operating Exp.				205 653 00
Operating Income				60 772 00
Other Revenue:				
Transfer Fees Earned				629 00
Net Inc. before Income Tax				61 401 00
Federal Income Tax				13 987 00
Net Income				47 414 00

Figure 19-15 Income Statement for Jennings Branch

Riverside Gardens, Inc. - Welch Branch
Income Statement
For the Year Ended December 31, 199-

Revenue:				
Net Sales				519 211 00
Cost of Merchandise Sold:				
Merch. Inv., Jan. 1, 199-			31 258 00	
Purchases		325 890 00		
Plus: Tran. In	840 00			
Transfer Charges	629 00	1 469 00		
Cost of Delivered Merch.		327 359 00		
Less: Purch. Discounts	3 259 00			
Purch. Ret. + Allow.	2 658 00	5 917 00		
Net Purchases			321 442 00	
Cost of Merch. Avail.			352 700 00	
Less: Merch. Inv., Dec. 31, 199-			29 450 00	
Cost of Merch. Sold				323 250 00
Gross Profit on Sales				195 961 00
Operating Expenses:				
Selling Expenses			85 652 00	
Admin. Expenses			71 250 00	
Total Operating Exp.				156 902 00
Operating Income				39 059 00
Federal Income Tax				6 259 00
Net Income				32 800 00

Figure 19-16 Income Statement for Welch Branch

Branch Income Statements

The income statements for the Jennings and Welch branches of Riverside Gardens, Inc., appear in Figures 19-15 and 19-16, respectively. Notice that on the income statement for the Jennings branch (Figure 19-15), Transfer Fees Earned appears in the Other Revenue section. On the Welch branch income statement (Figure 19-16), the Transfer Charges balance is reported in the Cost of Merchandise Sold section.

Combined Income Statement

After income statements are prepared for each of the branches, a combined income statement may be prepared. A **combined income statement** reports the revenue, costs, and expenses of all the branches of a multistore business. Data for the combined income statement are taken from the individual branch income statements.

The combined income statement for Riverside Gardens, Inc., appears in Figure 19-17. As you can see, the accounting data for the two branches are reported in the first two columns.

Riverside Gardens, Inc.
Combined Income Statement
For the Year Ended December 31, 199–

	Jennings	Welch	Eliminations Debit	Eliminations Credit	Combined
Revenue:					
Net Sales	1,042,898.00	519,211.00			1,562,109.00
Cost of Merchandise Sold:					
Merch. Inv., Jan. 1, 199–	94,768.00	31,258.00			126,026.00
Net Purchases	778,943.00	321,442.00		629.00	1,099,756.00
Cost of Merchandise Available	873,711.00	352,700.00		629.00	1,225,782.00
Less: Merch. Inv., Dec. 31, 199–	97,238.00	29,450.00			126,688.00
Cost of Merchandise Sold	776,473.00	323,250.00		629.00	1,099,094.00
Gross Profit on Sales	266,425.00	195,961.00		629.00	463,015.00
Operating Expenses:					
Selling Expenses	125,201.00	85,652.00			210,853.00
Administrative Expenses	80,452.00	71,250.00			151,702.00
Total Operating Expenses	205,653.00	156,902.00			362,555.00
Operating Income	60,772.00	39,059.00		629.00	100,460.00
Other Revenue:					
Transfer Fees Earned	629.00	—	629.00		—
Net Income before Income Tax	61,401.00	39,059.00	629.00	629.00	100,460.00
Federal Income Tax	13,987.00	6,259.00			20,246.00
Net Income	47,414.00	32,800.00	629.00	629.00	80,214.00

Figure 19-17 Combined Income Statement

Stress why the Eliminations section is needed.

The combined income statement also has debit and credit columns labeled *Eliminations.* These two columns are used to cancel the results of interbranch transactions. The combined income statement should not report the revenue earned or the added costs of merchandise that result from interbranch transactions. As a result, the Eliminations section on the combined income statement is used to cancel the Transfer Fees Earned and the Transfer Charges amounts.

Walk students through the preparation of the combined income statement in Figure 19-17.

Let's see how the Eliminations section is prepared. As you remember, the Transfer Charges balance of $629 was added to Purchases in the Cost of Merchandise Sold section of the Welch branch income statement. This amount must now be canceled (eliminated) from all affected totals on the combined income statement.

In the Cost of Merchandise Sold section, the transfer charges amount is included in the amounts used to calculate the Welch branch's net purchases, cost of merchandise available, and cost of merchandise sold. These amounts represent debit totals. To cancel the transfer charges from those amounts, $629 is entered in the Eliminations Credit column on those lines.

The transfer charges must also be eliminated from Welch's reported amounts for gross profit on sales, operating income, and net income before and after income taxes. Gross profit on sales, remember, is determined by subtracting the cost of merchandise sold from net sales. If cost of merchandise sold is decreased (by the $629 elimination), gross profit on sales and all subsequent income totals are *increased*. The amounts reported for gross profit on sales, operating income, and net income represent credit totals. To eliminate the transfer charges amount and increase the totals, $629 must be entered in the Eliminations Credit column on each of those four lines.

On the Jennings branch income statement, the Transfer Fees Earned amount of $629 was reported as other revenue. This amount must also be eliminated on the combined income statement. Since the Transfer Fees Earned amount represents a credit balance, $629 is entered in the Eliminations Debit column on the Transfer Fees Earned line.

If the transfer fees earned amount is eliminated from Jennings's other revenue, it must also be eliminated from Jennings's reported net income amounts. These amounts represent credit totals. To eliminate the transfer fees earned amount, $629 is entered in the Eliminations Debit column on the two net income lines.

The amounts reported in the Combined column are determined by totaling the amounts reported in the first four columns. Any amount canceled in the Eliminations columns is not carried across to the Combined column.

Use demonstration problem 19-6 here.

By combining the income statements of the branches, the owners can compare and analyze the operation of all branches. They can also evaluate the multistore business operation as a whole.

R — E — M — E — M — B — E — R

On a combined income statement, the Eliminations section is used to cancel the Transfer Fees Earned and Transfer Charges amounts.

Combined Balance Sheet

Separate balance sheets are prepared for each branch of Riverside Gardens, Inc. A combined balance sheet is also prepared. A **combined balance sheet** reports the total balances of the asset, liability, and stockholders' equity accounts of all branches of a multistore business. The combined balance sheet for Riverside Gardens, Inc., appears in Figure 19-18.

Riverside Gardens, Inc. Combined Balance Sheet December 31, 199–					
	Jennings	Welch	Eliminations Debit	Eliminations Credit	Combined
Assets					
Cash in Bank	29,257.00	12,813.00			42,070.00
Due from Welch	21,000.00	—		21,000.00	—
Accounts Receivable	78,256.00	31,600.00			109,856.00
Merchandise Inventory	81,598.00	28,457.00			110,055.00
Supplies	7,235.00	2,900.00			10,135.00
Prepaid Insurance	1,200.00	900.00			2,100.00
Equipment (Net)	152,000.00	185,000.00			337,000.00
Building (Net)	658,500.00	825,000.00			1,483,500.00
Land	75,000.00	100,000.00			175,000.00
Total Assets	1,104,046.00	1,186,670.00		21,000.00	2,269,716.00
Liabilities					
Accounts Payable	56,800.00	31,400.00			88,200.00
Notes Payable	90,000.00	425,000.00			515,000.00
Due to Jennings	—	21,000.00	21,000.00		—
Total Liabilities	146,800.00	477,400.00	21,000.00		603,200.00
Stockholders' Equity					
Common Stock	800,000.00	650,000.00			1,450,000.00
Retained Earnings	157,246.00	59,270.00			216,516.00
Total Stockholders' Equity	957,246.00	709,270.00			1,666,516.00
Total Liabilities + Stockholders' Equity	1,104,046.00	1,186,670.00	21,000.00		2,269,716.00

Figure 19-18 Combined Balance Sheet

Stress why the Eliminations section is needed.

The combined balance sheet also has an Eliminations section. The Eliminations section on the balance sheet is used to cancel the Due from Welch and Due to Jennings accounts. The combined balance sheet of a multistore business should not report an amount to be received from or paid to itself. The Eliminations columns of the combined balance sheet, therefore, are used to cancel the interbranch receivables and payables. As you can see, these amounts are the same, \$21,000. The "Due to" amount offsets the "Due from" amount.

Use demonstration problem 19-7 here.

The amounts recorded in the Combined column are determined by adding the totals of the first four columns. Notice that the \$21,000 balance of Due from Welch is canceled by the \$21,000 entered in the Eliminations Credit column.

R — E — M — E — M — B — E — R

A combined balance sheet should not include amounts to be received or paid that result from interbranch transactions. The Eliminations columns are used to cancel the Due to and Due from accounts.

Summary of Key Points

1. To increase sales and income, to be more competitive, or to offer better service, a business can expand its operations by opening branches in different locations. The branches are often incorporated as separate legal entities.
2. A multistore business can use either a decentralized accounting system or a centralized accounting system.
3. In a decentralized accounting system, each branch maintains its own accounting records. All branches, however, use the same procedures and chart of accounts.
4. In a centralized accounting system, all accounting functions for all branches are handled by a central accounting office. Separate general ledger accounts are maintained for each branch.
5. In a centralized accounting system, all cash payments are made from a special Payables checking account. Cash is transferred to the Payables checking account from the branch checking accounts.
6. Transactions among branches of the same multistore business are called interbranch transactions. When an interbranch transaction occurs, two journal entries are required.
7. Transfer fees represent revenue to the branch shipping the merchandise and an additional cost of merchandise for the branch receiving the merchandise.
8. A "Due from" account is a current asset account similar to Accounts Receivable. The "Due to" account is a current liability account similar to Accounts Payable.
9. At the end of the fiscal period, both separate and combined financial statements are prepared for the multistore business.
10. Transfer fees earned and transfer charges are eliminated on the combined income statement. "Due to" and "Due from" balances are eliminated on the combined balance sheet.

19 Review and Applications

Building Your Accounting Vocabulary

In your own words, write the definition of each of the following accounting terms. Use complete sentences for your definitions.

- centralized accounting system
- combined balance sheet
- combined income statement
- decentralized accounting system
- franchise
- interbranch transaction
- multistore business

Reviewing Your Accounting Knowledge

1. Name three advantages of incorporating the branches of a multistore business.
2. What is the difference between the two basic types of accounting systems that can be used by a multistore business?
3. How can a centralized accounting system decrease expenses for a multistore business?
4. How does the chart of accounts used in a decentralized accounting system of a multistore business differ from the chart of accounts used in a centralized accounting system?
5. What is a deposit verification report? How is it used?
6. How are purchases for the branches of a multistore business handled in a centralized accounting system?
7. What is the purpose of the Cash in Bank—Payables checking account used in a centralized accounting system?
8. When merchandise is shipped from one branch of a multistore business to another branch, why are two journal entries required?
9. Classify the following accounts: Cash in Bank—Payables, Transfer Fees Earned, Transfer Charges, Due to Store 1, and Due from Store 2.
10. What is the source of the data needed to prepare a combined income statement for a multistore business?
11. What is the purpose of the Eliminations columns on the financial statements of a multistore business?

Improving Your Decision-Making Skills

Matt Cobb operates a clothing store near a college campus. Many of his customers are students at the college. Until now, Matt has had a cash-only policy. Now he wonders whether he should allow his customers to use bank cards for their purchases. Many of his competitors accept all of the multipurpose bank cards, and some have even issued their own single-purpose credit cards. Make a list of the reasons *for* and *against* using the bank cards. Would you advise Matt to issue his own single-purpose card? What would you want to know about his store before you gave him any advice?

Applying Accounting Procedures

Exercise 19-1 Creating a Chart of Accounts for a Multistore Business

Stone Tire Center, Inc., is a multistore business with two branches in the towns of Stonewall and Taylor. The company plans to switch from a decentralized accounting system to a centralized system. Following are some of the accounts currently being used.

Cash in Bank	Sales Tax Payable
Accounts Receivable	Common Stock
Merchandise Inventory	Retained Earnings
Supplies	Income Summary
Prepaid Insurance	Sales
Equipment	Purchases
Accounts Payable	Utilities Expense

Instructions: Using these accounts, prepare a partial chart of accounts with four-digit account numbers for the centralized accounting system of Stone Tire Center. The Stonewall branch will be the warehouse for both branches. The company plans to use a special Payables checking account for all cash payments.

Exercise 19-2 Preparing a Deposit Verification Form

Deer Creek Antiques is a multistore business with two branches: Watkins and Martin. At the end of each business day, the accounting clerk at the Martin branch sends the cash register tapes and deposit slip copies to the central accounting office.

Total cash rec./dep., $4,322.45

Instructions: Using the following information, prepare a cash register/deposit verification report for the Martin branch for November 14. Use the form provided in the working papers.

Cash Register Tapes, Register 1
- Time 12:30 PM; Sales, $675.00; Sales Tax Payable, $40.50
- Time 8:45 PM; Sales, $989.45; Sales Tax Payable, $59.37

Cash Register Tapes, Register 2
- Time 1:00 PM; Sales, $1,357.12; Sales Tax Payable, $81.43
- Time 9:00 PM; Sales, $1,056.21; Sales Tax Payable, $63.37

Deposit Slip 34568: $2,154.05
Deposit Slip 34569: $2,168.40

Problem 19-1 Recording Transactions for a Multistore Business

The Changing Cycles Company is a multistore retail bicycle business with branches in the towns of Randolph, Slagle, and Walnut Hill. The company uses a centralized accounting system. The following transactions took place during March.

Instructions: Record these transactions on page 35 of the general journal.

Transactions:

Mar. 3 The Randolph branch had cash sales of $5,605.00 plus sales tax of $392.35, Deposit Verification R81.

9 The Slagle branch sold merchandise on account to Mary Johnson, $690.00 plus $48.30 sales tax, Sales Slip S789.

12 The central accounting office received Invoice 88994TC from Bossier's for $90,000.00 merchandise purchased on account for the Simpson branch; terms 2/15, n/45.

14 Janie Hightower, a charge customer of the Walnut Hill branch, sent a $900.00 payment on account to the central accounting office, Receipt W458.

19 The central accounting office received Invoice D2389 for $5,600.00 from L & M Company for a new computer (Computer Equipment) purchased on account for the Randolph branch; terms n/30.

22 Whitman Supplies sent Invoice X3487 for $856.00 for store supplies purchased on account for the Slagle branch; terms n/30.

30 The central accounting office received Invoice 9987 for $32,650.00 from Connors Accessories for merchandise purchased on account for the three branches. The merchandise cost is allocated as follows: Randolph, $15,010.00; Slagle, $12,250.00; Walnut Hill, $5,390.00.

Problem 19-2 Journalizing Interbranch Transactions

Mustang Feed Stores is a multistore business with branches in Martin and Waco. Following are some of the accounts used in the company's centralized accounting system.

Cash in Bank—Martin	Purchases—Martin
Cash in Bank—Waco	Purchases—Waco
Cash in Bank—Payables	Transfer Fees Earned—Martin
Due from Waco	Transfer Charges—Waco
Due to Martin	

Instructions: Journalize the following interbranch transactions on page 98 of the general journal.

Transactions:

Feb. 28 Transferred $12,400.00 of merchandise from the Martin warehouse to the Waco branch, Transfer Request 345. The warehouse charged a 2% transfer fee.

Mar. 3 Transferred $43,800.29 from the Waco branch's checking account to the special Payables checking account, EFT 33.

4 Issued Check 2876 to the Martin branch in payment for the merchandise transferred on February 28.

Problem 19-3 Making Cash Payments for a Multistore Business

Jamestown Products is a multistore business with two branches, one branch in Jonesboro and the other in Hodge. The company uses a centralized accounting system with a Cash in Bank—Payables account. On October 24, the following cash payments were made.

Instructions:

(1) Determine the amount that must be transferred from each branch's checking account to the Cash in Bank—Payables account. Record the entry on page 21 of the general journal (EFT 3456).

(2) Record the October 24 cash payments.

Transactions:

1. A $790.55 printing bill (Advertising Expense) from North Printers was allocated as follows: Jonesboro branch, $490.55; Hodge branch, $300.00; Check 4888.
2. Wrote Check 4889 for $3,600.00 to Ajax Insurance for the premiums on two six-month insurance policies (Jonesboro branch, $2,000.00; Hodge branch, $1,600.00).
3. Paid Esterwood Construction $7,250.00 on account for work performed at the Jonesboro branch, Check 4890. Charge to Jonesboro's Building account.
4. Prepared Check 4891 for $900.00 payable to The House of Equipment for a new copying machine (Equipment) purchased on account for the Hodge branch.
5. Paid $2,400.00 to Vaughn Realty for the November rent for the Hodge branch, Check 4892.
6. Issued Check 4893 for $12,300.00 to General Wholesale for the cash purchase of merchandise for the Jonesboro branch.
7. Purchased office supplies for the Hodge branch from Lake City Office Supply for $325.00 cash, Check 4894.

SPREADSHEET PROBLEM

Problem 19-4 Preparing Branch Income Statements

City Club Restaurants, a multistore business with two branches, uses a centralized accounting system. The following balances appeared on the company's work sheet for the year ended December 31.

	Income Statement	
	Debit	Credit
Income Summary—Westlake	$ 900	
Income Summary—Moss Bluff	900	
Sales—Westlake		$325,000
Sales—Moss Bluff		286,500
Purchases—Westlake	156,200	
Purchases—Moss Bluff	131,400	
Transfer Charges—Moss Bluff	7,000	
Selling Expenses—Westlake	71,000	
Selling Expenses—Moss Bluff	36,000	
Administrative Expenses—Westlake	15,000	
Administrative Expenses—Moss Bluff	7,100	
Transfer Fees Earned—Westlake		7,000
Income Tax Expense—Westlake	30,226	
Income Tax Expense—Moss Bluff	35,394	

Net income:
Westlake, $58,674.00
Moss Bluff, $68,706.00

In addition, the beginning inventory balances were as follows.

Merchandise Inventory—Westlake	$8,100
Merchandise Inventory—Moss Bluff	3,600

Instructions: Using the preceding information, prepare an income statement for the Westlake branch and an income statement for the Moss Bluff branch of City Club Restaurants.

SPREADSHEET PROBLEM

Problem 19-5 Preparing Combined Financial Statements

The balance sheets of the Westlake and Moss Bluff branches of City Club Restaurants appear in Figure 19-19.

City Club Restaurants—Westlake Branch
Balance Sheet
December 31, 199-

Assets		
Cash in Bank	$ 7,685.00	
Due from Moss Bluff	3,000.00	
Accounts Receivable	2,000.00	
Merchandise Inventory	7,200.00	
Kitchen Supplies	5,400.00	
Equipment (Net)	55,000.00	
Building (Net)	24,800.00	
Land	8,000.00	
Total Assets		$113,085.00
Liabilities		
Accounts Payable		$ 1,500.00
Stockholders' Equity		
Common Stock	$35,000.00	
Retained Earnings	76,585.00	
Total Stockholders' Equity		111,585.00
Total Liabilities and Stockholders' Equity		$113,085.00

City Club Restaurants—Moss Bluff Branch
Balance Sheet
December 31, 199-

Assets		
Cash in Bank	$13,356.00	
Accounts Receivable	900.00	
Merchandise Inventory	2,700.00	
Kitchen Supplies	3,700.00	
Equipment (Net)	45,000.00	
Building (Net)	38,300.00	
Land	18,000.00	
Total Assets		$121,956.00
Liabilities		
Accounts Payable	$ 9,000.00	
Due to Westlake	3,000.00	
Total Liabilities		$ 12,000.00
Stockholders' Equity		
Common Stock	$28,000.00	
Retained Earnings	81,956.00	
Total Stockholders' Equity		109,956.00
Total Liabilities and Stockholders' Equity		$121,956.00

Combined:
Gross profit, $322,100
Net income, $127,380

BS totals, $232,041

Figure 19-19 Balance Sheets for Problem 19-5

Instructions: Using the income statement you prepared in Problem 19-4 and the branch balance sheets, prepare a combined income statement and a combined balance sheet for City Club Restaurants.

CHALLENGE PROBLEM

Problem 19-6 Analyzing Transactions for a Multistore Business

The Jefferson Paint Company is a multistore business with branches in Fenton, Hathaway, and Lake Arthur. The Hathaway store is the warehouse for the other two branches.

On June 10, the Hathaway branch shipped $96,600 of merchandise to the Lake Arthur branch, charging a 5% transfer fee (Transfer Request 8895). It also shipped $32,700 of merchandise to the Fenton store, plus a 5% transfer fee (Transfer Request 8896). These entries were recorded as follows.

On June 24, the Lake Arthur store paid for the transferred merchandise. The transaction was recorded as follows.

GENERAL JOURNAL — PAGE 401

	DATE		DESCRIPTION	POST. REF.	DEBIT	CREDIT	
1	199- June	10	Due from Lake Arthur		101 430 00		1
2			Purchases—Hathaway			101 430 00	2
3			Transfer Request 8895				3
4		10	Due from Fenton		34 335 00		4
5			Purchases—Hathaway			34 335 00	5
6			Transfer Request 8896				6

GENERAL JOURNAL — PAGE 409

	DATE		DESCRIPTION	POST. REF.	DEBIT	CREDIT	
1	199- June	24	Cash in Bank—Hathaway		101 430 00		1
2			Due from Fenton			101 430 00	2
3			Receipt 7654				3

Figure 19-20 Transactions for Problem 19-6

Instructions: Prepare three entries, dated June 30, to correct the errors made on June 10 and June 24 (Memorandum 47890). Use page 411 of the general journal.

CHALLENGE PROBLEM

Problem 19-7 Allocating Expenses among Branches

The Boyce Home Furniture Center is a multistore business with branches in Flatwoods, Sharp, and Gorum. The company uses a centralized accounting system, with a Cash in Bank—Payables account.

On November 15, the central accounting office received a $6,470 bill from *The Daily News* for several recent advertisements. The ads feature sales items and list the locations of all three branches. The central accounting office allocates the advertising expense among the three branches according to the square footage occupied by the branches, which is as follows: Flatwoods, 9,959 square feet; Sharp, 5,196 square feet; and Gorum, 6,495 square feet.

Flat., $2,976.20
Sharp, $1,552.80
Gorum, $1,941.00

Instructions: Allocate the advertising expense among the three branches. Record the cash payment of the bill on November 21 on page 223 of the general journal (Check 1680).

FOCUS ON
ETHICS

Safety First

Imagine yourself a managerial accountant for a small manufacturing firm. Because of hard economic times, your firm is only just managing to make a profit; however, it is doing better than most other firms of its size because of its emphasis on safety. The firm's adherence to safety has kept it free of workman's compensation claims or employee litigation, problems the competitors are facing more and more as they try to cut expenditures.

Recently, your firm has received notification that new safety procedures must be implemented throughout your branch of manufacturing as a whole. The state regulatory agency has set up these procedures to combat the large number of injuries and resulting financial outlays that have been occurring. After sitting down with the books, however, you determine that the cost of implementing the new safety procedures would eat up any profit your compnay was making, and would even put it into debt.

During a management meeting, you present the numbers to the other members of your management team. The main problem seems to be the formal classes the regulatory agency demands be set up. Instructors would have to be paid, classrooms rented, and employees reimbursed for the time spent in class. Up until now, your firm has relied on a mentor program to promote adherence to safety procedures. In this program, a more experienced worker trains a less experienced one by example, demonstrating how to use equipment in a safe manner. Only when the new worker has shown his or her capability with a machine is he or she allowed to operate it alone. Not only has this method kept injuries in check, it has proven to be a very cost-effective way of training new people.

A careful review of all options is a key step in making tough decisions.

After discussing the general unfairness of the situation, someone on the team suggests sticking with the mentor system of training, and adjusting the books to make it look like the regulatroy agency's system was in place. The more this idea is discussed, the more logical it seems. What is the ethical dilemma here?

As in every situation, there are several options. One might be to outline the mentor program to the regulatory agency, citing the low injury rate as a measure of the program's success, and then petition the agency to allow the company to continue with this plan. Another option might be to research ways in which the new regulations could be implemented at a lower cost. For example, could an instructor be found among the more experienced employees? Could a space in the plant be used as a classroom? Might employees voluntarily give up their lunch hours to participate in the classes? As in every situation that involves tough decisions, it is wisest to evaluate all options before taking any action.

Chapter 20

THE VOUCHER SYSTEM OF ACCOUNTING

During your study of accounting, you have encountered the phrase *internal control* several times in discussions of cash receipts and cash payments. Internal control, refers to those procedures a business takes to protect its assets, especially cash. These procedures are intended to prevent errors, safeguard cash and other assets from theft or misuse, and manage the business's resources more efficiently.

In a small business, one individual—usually the owner or manager—is personally involved in most of the business's financial activities. As a business grows, it becomes difficult for only one person to handle all the financial responsibilities. As a result, those responsibilities are separated and delegated to different employees. For example, one person may be authorized to approve purchases and another person to approve cash payments. In these circumstances, internal control becomes even more important.

In this chapter, you will learn about one commonly used internal control system and how a business's transactions are recorded within that system.

Learning Objectives

When you have completed this chapter, you should be able to do the following:

1. Explain how the voucher system is used to control a business's cash payments.
2. Describe the components of a voucher system.
3. Record vouchers in a voucher register.
4. Record the payment of vouchers in a check register.
5. Define the accounting terms presented in this chapter.

New Terms

voucher system
voucher
voucher register
unpaid voucher file
voucher check
check register
paid voucher file
schedule of unpaid vouchers

The Voucher System

Emphasize that the voucher system's prime goal is to control purchases and cash payments.

The **voucher system** is a system for controlling purchases and cash payments. With a voucher system, the business's financial activities are delegated to various individuals or groups. One individual or group serves as a check on the activities of another. For example, the purchasing department is responsible for ordering merchandise. The receiving department verifies that the merchandise received is the merchandise that had been ordered. The accounting department is responsible for paying for that merchandise at the proper time. The activities of the various groups are controlled and monitored through the use of written documents.

The following four steps are basic to the voucher system:

1. All expenditures must be backed up by purchase orders or other authorizations.
2. Goods and services received must be inspected and approved.
3. Suppliers' invoices must be checked against their respective purchase orders and the accuracy of the amounts, shipping costs, and credit terms verified.
4. All payments must be made by check, except for payments made from petty cash.

The typical voucher system includes the following components:

- Vouchers
- Voucher register
- Unpaid voucher file
- Voucher checks
- Check register
- Paid voucher file
- General journal

Stress why the voucher system may not be suitable for all businesses.

When a voucher system is used, the Vouchers Payable account replaces the Accounts Payable account. For every cash payment that is to be made, a voucher is prepared requiring a credit to Vouchers Payable. As you might guess from the list of components, the voucher system generates quite a bit of paperwork. As a result, it is most appropriate for medium- to large-sized businesses. In other words, the business must have enough transactions to justify the extra paperwork. It also works best when the business pays its bills in full when they are due instead of making partial or installment payments.

Vouchers

The dictionary defines a voucher as a paper that serves as proof of a transaction. In the voucher system, a **voucher** is a document that serves as written authorization for each cash payment. It is also the source document for the entry.

Characteristics of Vouchers

Discuss the characteristics of a voucher.

Just as invoices vary from one business to another, vouchers vary among businesses. Some vouchers are single sheets, printed on both sides, that are attached to the invoices or bills. Other vouchers are in the form of envelopes or folders, which hold the supporting documents. Although vouchers differ, they usually have the following characteristics:

- Vouchers are prepared for every incoming invoice or bill and are numbered consecutively.
- The name and address of the payee or creditor appear on the voucher.
- The amount and credit terms of the invoice appear on the voucher.

Pro-Printers, Inc. Voucher No. 120

Payee Orange Computers — Date Prepared 11/2/--

Address 1410 Fifth Avenue

New York, NY 10126 — Date Due 11/11/--

Terms 2/10, n/20

Inv. Date	Invoice No.	Description	Amount
11/1/--	5710	Wide carriage printer	$950.00

Approved K. Harper, Controller — Approved A. J. Lester, Treasurer

(Front)

Account Debited	Acct. No.	Amount
Supplies	120	
Purchases	501	$950.00
Transportation In	505	
Salaries Expense	630	
Utilities Expense	640	

Account Credited	Acct. No.	Amount
Vouchers Payable	201	$950.00
Emp. Fed. Inc. Tax Payable	205	
Emp. St. Inc. Tax Payable	207	
Soc. Sec. Tax Payable	210	
Medicare Tax Payable	211	

Voucher No. 120

Payee Orange Computers

Address 1410 Fifth Ave.

New York, NY 10126

Inv. Total	$950.00
Less Disc.	19.00
Net	$931.00
Date Due	11/11/--
Date Paid	11/11/--
Check No.	487

(Back)

Figure 20-1 Front and Back of a Voucher

- The voucher lists the due date so that the business can take advantage of cash discounts.
- For internal control, vouchers require approval signatures before payments can be made.
- The payment information (date paid and check number) is recorded on the voucher.

A completed voucher, with the invoice or bill attached to it, thus describes an entire transaction, as well as the procedure for processing the voucher.

Pro-Printers, Inc., has just begun using the voucher system. The company's voucher appears in Figure 20-1.

Preparing and Processing Vouchers

Explain what information is recorded on a voucher.

Let's assume Pro-Printers, Inc., received from a supplier, Orange Computers, the invoice shown in Figure 20-2. Pro-Printers uses the invoice to prepare the voucher shown in Figure 20-1. The front of the voucher lists the details of the transaction: the name and address of the supplier, the credit terms, the date and number of the invoice, a description of the items purchased, and the invoice amount. The front of the voucher also has blanks for the signatures of those persons approving the purchase.

ORANGE COMPUTERS
1410 Fifth Avenue . New York, NY 10126

Invoice
5710

TO: Pro-Printers, Inc.
835 New Towne Plaza
New Haven, CT 06510

Date: Nov. 1, 199-
Order No.: PP389
Shipped By: Metro Lines
Terms: 2/10, n/30

QUANTITY	ITEM	UNIT PRICE	TOTAL
1	Wide carriage printer	$950.00	$950.00

Figure 20-2 Invoice Received by Pro-Printers, Inc.

The back of the voucher lists the accounts and amounts to be debited and credited; the name and address of the supplier; the invoice total, cash discount amount, and net amount; and the due date. There is also space for the payment information. The invoice is stapled to the voucher and circulated for the approval signatures.

Remind students that in the voucher system, the Vouchers Payable account replaces the Accounts Payable account.

In the voucher system, every voucher results in a credit to the Vouchers Payable account. The account to be debited depends, of course, on the type of goods or services purchased. For this invoice, because merchandise is being purchased on account, the transaction is recorded as a debit to Purchases and a credit to Vouchers Payable. Had Pro-Printers purchased a new display case, the transaction would have been recorded as a debit to Store Equipment and a credit to Vouchers Payable. A voucher is prepared every time a liability is incurred, including liabilities for expenses. For example, when the payroll must be paid, a voucher listing the Payroll Bank Account as the payee is prepared. On the voucher, Salaries Expense is debited for the gross payroll amount. Vouchers Payable is credited for the net payroll amount, and the amounts withheld from the employees' earnings are credited to the appropriate liability accounts.

You may want to have students complete Exercise 20-1 at this point.

R — E — M — E — M — B — E — R

A voucher is prepared for every invoice or bill received that requires a cash payment.

The Voucher Register

The **voucher register** is a book of original entry in which all vouchers are recorded, in numerical order. The voucher register is a special journal that, in the voucher system, expands on and replaces the purchases journal. The format of the voucher register varies depending on the size of the business and the number of accounts. Pro-Printers' voucher register, shown in Figure 20-3, has columns for the voucher number, creditor's name, and the payment information. Since every voucher requires a credit to Vouchers Payable, there is a Vouchers Payable Credit column. There are also a number of debit columns. As in any special

Emphasize that the voucher register replaces the purchases journal.

Point out that every transaction recorded in the voucher register results in a credit to Vouchers Payable for the amount of the voucher.

VOUCHER

	Date		Vou. No.	Creditor	Payment Date	Payment Ck. No.	Vouchers Payable Credit	Purchases Debit
1	199- Nov.	2	120	Orange Computers	Nov. 11	487	950 00	950 00
2		2	121	Empire Gas Co.	Nov. 2	482	120 00	
3		4	122	Laurel Office Supplies	Nov. 4	483	80 00	
4		5	123	Casey Insurance Co.	Nov. 5	484	300 00	
5		8	124	Challenge Software			1 400 00	1 400 00
6		9	125	Delta Carriers			725 00	
7		10	126	Challenge Software	Nov. 12	490	604 00	604 00
8		11	127	Ace Maintenance Co.	Nov. 11	488	30 00	
9		12	128	Store Equipment Outlet	Nov. 22	By note	1 185 00	
27		30	145	Payroll Bank Account	Nov. 30	506	2 229 50	
28								
29								
30								
31								
32		30		Totals			18 540 50	10 564 00
33							(201)	(501)

Figure 20-3 Voucher Register (Left Side)

journal, the special columns were selected because of their frequency of use. There is a Purchases Debit column because Pro-Printers makes a great many purchases of merchandise. In addition to the special debit columns, the voucher register has a General section for amounts that cannot be entered in special columns. Notice that the General section has both Debit and Credit columns.

Walk students through the steps followed to record Voucher 120.

Recording a Voucher

The first voucher recorded on page 2 of Pro-Printers' voucher register is the voucher in Figure 20-1, Voucher 120 for Orange Computers. The voucher date and number are recorded in the first two columns. The name of the supplier is entered in the Creditor column. The payment columns are not filled in at this time; they will be completed when the voucher is paid. The amount of the voucher is entered in the Vouchers Payable Credit column and in the Purchases Debit column.

If a voucher cannot be recorded in a special amount column, it is entered in the General section. The debit to Prepaid Insurance for Voucher 123 is recorded in the General Debit column.

ACCOUNTING Notes

In a voucher system, the written approval for each transaction leaves a chain of references that an accountant can use to trace a transaction through the accounting system back to the original source document. This trail of documentary evidence is called an *audit trail.*

R — E — M — E — M — B — E — R

Every voucher recorded in the voucher register requires a credit to Vouchers Payable.

Posting from the Voucher Register

Entries in the General Debit column are posted individually to the general ledger during the month, just as the General columns of the other

REGISTER PAGE 2

SUPPLIES DEBIT	UTILITIES EXPENSE DEBIT	GENERAL ACCOUNT	POST. REF.	GENERAL DEBIT	GENERAL CREDIT	
						1
	120 00					2
80 00						3
		Prepaid Insurance	125	300 00		4
						5
		Transportation In	505	725 00		6
						7
		Miscellaneous Expense		30 00		8
		Store Equipment	155	1 185 00		9
		Salaries Expense	630	3 000 00		27
		Emp. Fed. Inc. Tax Pay.	205		348 00	28
		Emp. State Inc. Tax Pay.	207		63 00	29
		Social Social Tax Pay.	210		186 00	30
		Medicare Tax Payable	211		43 50	31
		Ins. Premiums Payable	215		130 00	32
320 00	450 00			7 977 00	770 50	33
(120)	(640)			(✓)	(✓)	34

Figure 20-3 Voucher Register (Right Side)

Remind students that posting from the voucher register is similar to posting from special journals.

special journals are. At the end of the month, the voucher register is totaled, proved, and ruled like any special journal. The combined total of all the debit columns must equal the total of all the credit columns. The total of each special amount column is posted to the general ledger account named in the heading. When posting to the general ledger accounts, the letters *VR* are used to indicate the voucher register.

R — E — M — E — M — B — E — R

At the end of the month, the voucher register is totaled, proved, and ruled and the totals of the special amount columns are posted to the appropriate general ledger accounts.

Unpaid Voucher File

Emphasize that unpaid vouchers are filed according to due date and that the unpaid voucher file replaces the accounts payable subsidiary ledger.

After a voucher is recorded in the voucher register, it is placed in the unpaid voucher file. The **unpaid voucher file** contains all unpaid vouchers, filed according to their due dates. The unpaid voucher file helps the business forecast how much cash is needed to pay bills. It also helps ensure that the business pays its bills in time to take advantage of cash discounts.

In the voucher system, the unpaid voucher file takes the place of the accounts payable subsidiary ledger. As a result, the total of all the vouchers in the unpaid voucher file should equal the balance of the Vouchers Payable account after all posting has been completed.

Voucher Checks

Have samples of different types of voucher checks available for students to examine.

When the voucher system is used, every cash payment is made by check. Although regular checks can be used with a voucher system, many businesses use voucher checks. A **voucher check** is a special check with an attached stub or a special area on the face of the check that is used to list the details of the cash payment. Figure 20-4 shows the voucher check used by Pro-Printers. Voucher checks are prenumbered and are often prepared in duplicate. The original of the voucher check is sent to the payee. The business keeps the copy as a record of the payment.

Check Register

Point out that the check register replaces the cash payments journal.

In a voucher system, every check written in payment of a voucher is recorded in a check register. The **check register**, shown in Figure 20-5, is a special journal that, in the voucher system, replaces the cash payments journal. As you can see, the check register has columns in which to record the date of the check, the check number, the name of the

Pro-Printers, Inc.
835 New Towne Plaza
New Haven, CT 06510

New Haven National Bank
1012 Main Street
New Haven, CT 06510

32-13 / 455

No. 487

Pay to the Order of:

Orange Computers
1410 Fifth Avenue
New York, NY 10126

Date: November 11, 199-
DOLLARS: $931.00

K. Harper
CONTROLLER

DETACH THIS STUB BEFORE CASHING

INVOICE DATE	INVOICE NO.	DESCRIPTION	AMOUNT
11/1/9-	5710	Wide carriage printer	$950 00
		Less discount	– 19 00
		Total	$931 00

Figure 20-4 Voucher Check

payee, and the number of the voucher being paid. There are three amount columns: Vouchers Payable Debit, Purchases Discounts Credit, and Cash in Bank Credit. In a voucher system, checks are issued only in payment of approved, recorded vouchers. As a result, each check recorded in the check register requires a debit to Vouchers Payable and a credit to Cash in Bank. If Pro-Printers pays a voucher within the discount period, the amount of the discount is recorded in the Purchases Discounts Credit column.

Use demonstration problem 20-1 here.

CHECK REGISTER PAGE 2

	DATE		CK. NO.	PAYEE	VOU. NO.	VOUCHERS PAYABLE DEBIT	PURCHASES DISCOUNT CREDIT	CASH IN BANK CREDIT	
1	199- Nov.	2	482	Empire Gas Co.	121	120 00		120 00	1
2		4	483	Laurel Office Supplies	122	80 00		80 00	2
3		5	484	Casey Insurance Co.	123	300 00		300 00	3
4		8	485	Micro-Soft Systems	119	720 00		720 00	4
5		9	486	Mega-Byte Mftrs.	118	900 00	18 00	882 00	5
6		11	487	Orange Computers	120	950 00	19 00	931 00	6
7		11	488	Ace Maintenance Co.	127	30 00		30 00	7
8		12	489	Void					8
25		30	506	Payroll Bank Account	145	2 229 50		2 229 50	25
26		30		Totals		15 152 20	133 88	15 018 32	26
27						(201)	(510)	(101)	27

Figure 20-5 Check Register

Emphasize that the payment is also recorded in the voucher register and on the voucher.

As you can see, Check 487 was written to Orange Computers in payment of Voucher 120. After the check was recorded in the check register, the date and number of the voucher check were recorded in the Payment section of the voucher register and on the voucher itself. Look back at Figure 20-1 on page 520 and line 1 of Figure 20-3 on pages 522–523.

The check register also serves as a consecutive record of all of a business's checks. Notice that on line 8 in Figure 20-5, Check 489 was recorded in the check register even though it was voided. By entering all checks in the check register, a business can maintain control over these important documents.

At the end of the month, the check register is totaled, proved, and ruled. Then the column totals are posted to the three general ledger accounts. When posting, the letters *CK* are used to indicate the check register.

R — E — M — E — M — B — E — R

Every cash payment recorded in the check register requires a debit to Vouchers Payable **and a credit to** Cash in Bank**.**

Before reading further, do the following activity to check your understanding of the voucher system.

Check Your Learning

Write your answers to these questions on a sheet of notebook paper.

1. A(n) ___?___ is a written authorization for each cash payment.
2. In the voucher system, ___?___ replaces the Accounts Payable account.
3. In the voucher system, all cash payments are recorded in the ___?___.
4. In the voucher system, the unpaid voucher file replaces the ___?___.
5. A voucher register is used in place of the ___?___ journal.

Compare your answers to those in the answers section. Reread the preceding part of the chapter to find the correct answers to any questions you may have missed.

Paid Voucher File

Stress that vouchers in the paid voucher file are filed in numerical order.

Once a voucher check has been written and recorded, the payment information is recorded on the voucher. The voucher is then marked *paid* and filed. The **paid voucher file** contains all paid vouchers, filed in numerical order. Many businesses staple a copy of the voucher check to the paid voucher. The paid voucher file then contains a complete set of documents for every cash payment.

Schedule of Unpaid Vouchers

Compare the schedule of unpaid vouchers to a schedule of accounts payable. The two schedules are basically the same.

At the end of the month, Pro-Printers prepares a list of all unpaid vouchers, taking the information directly from the unpaid voucher file. The **schedule of unpaid vouchers,** shown in Figure 20-6, also lists the name of each creditor and the amount owed. As you can see, this document is similar to the schedule of accounts payable.

Pro-Printers, Inc.
Schedule of Unpaid Vouchers
November 30, 199-

Vou. No.	Name of Creditor		
124	Challenge Software	1400 00	
125	Delta Carriers	725 00	
130	Daily News	172 00	
142	New Haven National Bank	2541 00	
144	Empire Electronics	170 30	
	Total Vouchers Payable		5008 30

Figure 20-6 Schedule of Unpaid Vouchers

Situations Requiring Special Treatment

Point out that a general journal is still required in the voucher system.

When transactions do not fit into the fixed procedures of the voucher system, they are generally recorded in the general journal. Let's look at some of these transactions.

Handling Purchases Returns

If a busines has an efficient purchasing department, it identifies, and when necessary returns defective merchandise soon after it is received. A purchases return can be noted right on the supplier's invoice. Then the

Internal controls are used to manage the resources of a business more efficiently.

voucher is prepared for the original amount of the invoice *less* the purchases return. For example, on November 6 Pro-Printers bought $1,600 of merchandise on account from Challenge Software. Before the voucher was prepared, Pro-Printers returned $200 of the merchandise to Challenge. A debit memo was prepared and attached to the invoice, and $200 was deducted from the original amount of the invoice. Then Voucher 124 was prepared and recorded in the voucher register as a debit to Purchases for $1,400 and a credit to Vouchers Payable for $1,400.

Explain that if a voucher has been recorded, the issuance of the debit memo must be entered in the general journal and the voucher register.

Occasionally, however, merchandise is not returned until after the voucher has been prepared and recorded. For example, on October 27 Pro-Printers bought $1,200 of merchandise on account from Mega-Byte Manufacturers. Pro-Printers prepared Voucher 118 on October 28 and recorded the transaction in the voucher register as a debit to Purchases for $1,200 and a credit to Vouchers Payable for $1,200.

Use demonstration problem 20-2 here.

Two days later, Pro-Printers returned $300 of defective merchandise to Mega-Byte. Pro-Printers recorded this transaction in the general journal, as shown in Figure 20-7. The entry is basically the same as that for purchases returns you have recorded previously. Note, however, that in this entry Vouchers Payable is the account debited.

GENERAL JOURNAL — PAGE 22

	DATE		DESCRIPTION	POST. REF.	DEBIT	CREDIT	
1	199– Oct.	30	Vouchers Payable		300 00		1
2			Purchases Returns + Allowances			300 00	2
3			Debit Memo: 5 (Voucher 118)				3

Figure 20-7 Journalizing a Purchases Return in the Voucher System

Next, Pro-Printers deducted the amount of the purchases return from the total of Voucher 118 and stapled the debit memo to the voucher. The purchases return was then noted in the voucher register as shown in Figure 20-8. The date and number of the debit memo were entered in the Payment columns on the upper half of the line used to record the original voucher. On November 9, Pro-Printers paid the voucher by ising Check 486 for the original amount of the invoice less the purchases return and the discount. In the check register, Vouchers Payable was debited for $900, Purchases Discounts was credited for $18, and Cash in Bank was credited for $882. The date and number of the check were entered in the Payment columns of the voucher register as shown in Figure 20-8.

VOUCHER

	DATE		VOU. NO.	CREDITOR	PAYMENT DATE		PAYMENT CK. NO.	VOUCHERS PAYABLE CREDIT	PURCHASES DEBIT
30	Oct.	28	118	Mega-Byte Manufacturers	Oct. Nov.	30 9	DM5 486	1 200 00	1 200 00

Figure 20-8 Entering a Purchases Return and Payment in the Voucher Register

Issuing a Note Payable in Payment of a Voucher

Occasionally, a business issues a note payable in payment of a voucher. For example, on November 12 Pro-Printers issued Voucher 128 for

$1,185 of store equipment purchased on account from the Store Equipment Outlet. On November 22, to extend the payment period on Voucher 128, Pro-Printers issued a 60-day, 9% note payable for $1,185. The transaction was recorded in the general journal as a debit to Vouchers Payable and a credit to Notes Payable.

The issuance of the note was also entered in the voucher register. As you can see on line 9 of Figure 20-3 on pages 522–523, the date of the note was written in the Payment Date column and the words *By note* were entered in the Check Number column. Also, a notation was made on the voucher indicating that it had been canceled by the issuance of a note. The voucher was then placed in the paid voucher file.

Remind students to enter the payment of the voucher by a note payable in the voucher register.

On January 21 (the due date), Pro-Printers prepared a new voucher for the payment of the note plus the interest. This voucher was recorded in the voucher register as a debit to Notes Payable for $1,185.00, a debit to Interest Expense for $17.53, and a credit to Vouchers Payable for $1,202.53. Figure 20-9 illustrates this transaction.

VOUCHER

	DATE		VOU. NO.	CREDITOR	PAYMENT DATE		PAYMENT CK. NO.	VOUCHERS PAYABLE CREDIT	PURCHASES DEBIT
14	Jan.	21	195	Store Equipment Outlet	Jan.	21	549	1 202 53	
15									
16									

(Left Side)

REGISTER PAGE 4

SUPPLIES DEBIT	UTILITIES EXPENSE DEBIT	GENERAL ACCOUNT DEBITED	GENERAL POST. REF.	GENERAL DEBIT	GENERAL CREDIT	
		Notes Payable		1 185 00		14
		Interest Expense		17 53		15
						16

(Right Side)

Use demonstration problem 20-3 here.

Figure 20-9 Recording a Note Payable in the Voucher Register

Recording Installment Payments

Point out that a separate voucher must be prepared for each installment payment.

In a voucher system, vouchers are generally paid in full when they are due. Sometimes, however, management prefers to pay for an item in installments. When this happens, a separate voucher is prepared and recorded in the voucher register for each installment. For example, on December 5 Pro-Printers bought an executive office desk from the Modern Office Equipment Company for $1,500. Pro-Printers made a down payment of $500 and agreed to make two additional installments of $500 each, payable on December 15 and 30. Since a total of three checks will be needed, three vouchers (numbered 162, 163, and 164) are prepared and recorded in the voucher register, as shown in Figure 20-10.

VOUCHER

	DATE		VOU. NO.	CREDITOR	PAYMENT DATE		PAYMENT CK. NO.	VOUCHERS PAYABLE CREDIT	PURCHASES DEBIT
5	Dec.	5	162	Modern Office Equip. Co.	Dec.	5	520	500 00	
6		5	163	Modern Office Equip. Co.				500 00	
7		5	164	Modern Office Equip. Co.				500 00	

(Left Side)

REGISTER PAGE 3

SUPPLIES DEBIT	UTILITIES EXPENSE DEBIT	GENERAL ACCOUNT DEBITED	GENERAL POST. REF.	GENERAL DEBIT	GENERAL CREDIT	
		Office Furniture		1 500 00		5
						6
						7

(Right Side)

Figure 20-10 Recording Installment Payments in the Voucher Register

Use demonstration problem 20-4 here.

Each voucher has a due date that corresponds to the date the payment must be made. Voucher 162, which is for the December 5 down payment, is paid immediately. Vouchers 163 and 164 are filed in the unpaid voucher file according to their due dates, which are December 15 and December 30, respectively.

Correcting an Incorrect Voucher

Emphasize that the incorrect voucher is canceled and a new voucher is prepared.

The internal controls provided by the voucher system will not entirely eliminate errors. If an error is discovered after a voucher has been recorded in the voucher register, it must be corrected with a general journal entry. The general journal entry, in effect, cancels the original voucher by reversing the original voucher register entry. Then a new voucher for the correct amount is prepared.

For example, on October 26 Pro-Printers bought merchandise on account from Challenge Software totaling $640. Voucher 115 was prepared and recorded in the voucher register. In the entry, Purchases was debited for $640 and Vouchers Payable was credited for the same amount.

Use demonstration problem 20-5 here.

On November 10, an accounting clerk was double-checking the price extensions on the invoice and discovered an error. The correct amount of the invoice was $604. The general journal entry made to correct the error appears in Figure 20-11. As you can see, this entry reverses the original voucher register entry. Then a new voucher for the correct amount is issued. The entry for the new voucher (Voucher 126) is shown on line 7 of Figure 20-3.

GENERAL JOURNAL PAGE 22

	DATE		DESCRIPTION	POST. REF.	DEBIT	CREDIT	
	199-						
19	Nov.	10	Vouchers Payable		640 00		19
20			Purchases			640 00	20
21			Memo 30				21

Figure 20-11 Correcting an Error on a Voucher

The cancellation of the original voucher must also be noted in the voucher register. As you can see in Figure 20-12, the word *Canceled* is written in the Payment columns on the line for the original voucher (Voucher 115). The date and number of the new voucher are entered immediately below. The same notation is also written on Voucher 115. Voucher 115 is then placed in the paid voucher file.

VOUCHER

	DATE		VOU. NO.	CREDITOR	PAYMENT DATE	PAYMENT CK. NO.	VOUCHERS PAYABLE CREDIT	PURCHASES DEBIT
27	Oct.	26	115	Challenge Software	Canceled Nov. 10	V126	640 00	640 00

Figure 20-12 Recording the Cancellation of a Voucher

Before reading further, do the following activity to check your understanding of the material you have just studied.

Check Your Learning

Jetta Clothing Manufacturers uses the voucher system. During March, it had the following transactions.

Mar. 5 Purchased merchandise on account from Textiles Industries, \$12,500, terms 2/10, n/30, Voucher 4873.

10 Issued Debit Memo J101 to Textiles Industries for the return of defective merchandise purchased on March 5, \$500.

12 Issued Check 6743 in payment of Voucher 4873, minus the purchase return and the cash discount.

Write your answers to the following questions on a sheet of notebook paper.

1. In which journal or register would each of these transactions be recorded?
2. How is the issuance of the debit memo noted in the voucher register?
3. For what amount is Check 6743 written?

Compare your answers to those in the answers section. Reread the preceding part of the chapter to find the correct answers to any questions you may have missed.

The Voucher System as a Management Tool

The voucher system is one example of how an accounting procedure can be used as an internal control. It provides a systematic record of cash payments and aids in the efficient management of financial resources. In this respect, it has the following advantages:

Discuss the advantages of the voucher system for internal control.

1. Financial managers can use the information in the unpaid voucher file to plan for cash requirements.
2. Vouchers systematize the taking of cash discounts. Businesses can save money by making payments within the discount period. The unpaid voucher file contains the information the business needs to make timely payments.
3. Each cash payment corresponds to one specific voucher. This practice eliminates confusion that can lead to omitted payments or duplicate payments made for the same good or service.
4. Authority may be delegated and responsibility fixed. This advantage stems from the system of requiring approval signatures. Because the approval is given when the goods arrive or the service is received, something that is unsatisfactory receives immediate attention.

Summary of Key Points

1. The voucher system is a procedure for controlling a business's purchases and cash payments. The voucher system helps promote internal controls and enables management to handle its financial resources more efficiently.
2. In the voucher system, the Vouchers Payable account replaces the Accounts Payable account.
3. In a voucher system, a voucher is prepared for each invoice or bill received. The voucher, along with the invoice or bill, is circulated within the company for approval signatures.
4. All vouchers are recorded in the voucher register. The voucher register is a book of original entry that replaces the purchases journal.
5. In the voucher system, unpaid vouchers are filed chronologically by due dates in the unpaid voucher file, which replaces the accounts payable subsidiary ledger.
6. When the voucher system is used, all cash payments are made by check. A voucher check is a check with an attached stub or a special area on the front that is used to list the details of the cash payment.
7. In the voucher system, all checks are recorded in a check register, which replaces the cash payments journal.
8. Nonroutine transactions that do not fit into fixed procedures of the voucher system require special treatment, usually in the form of general journal entries.

20 Review and Applications

Building Your Accounting Vocabulary

In your own words, write the definition of each of the following accounting terms. Use complete sentences for your definitions.

check register
paid voucher file
schedule of unpaid vouchers
unpaid voucher file
voucher
voucher check
voucher register
voucher system

Reviewing Your Accounting Knowledge

1. How does the voucher system strengthen internal controls?
2. What are the seven components of a voucher system?
3. Why is the voucher system more appropriate for a medium- or large-sized business?
4. When a business uses the voucher system, for what types of transactions are vouchers prepared?
5. Which journal does the voucher register replace? How does it differ from that journal?
6. What is the purpose of the unpaid voucher file?
7. When a voucher system is being used, is the accounts payable subsidiary ledger necessary? Why or why not?
8. With a voucher system, why might a business prefer to use voucher checks rather than regular checks?
9. In the voucher system, which special journal does the check register replace?
10. How is a purchases return handled when the original voucher has already been recorded in the voucher register?
11. How are installment payments handled in the voucher system?
12. Briefly explain how the voucher system serves as a management tool.

Improving Your Analysis Skills

Bar graphs can be helpful in illustrating comparisons among businesses. The following bar graph compares the number of boats sold by five boat manufacturing companies in 1992. Use the graph to answer the following questions.

1. Which company had the highest sales in 1992?
2. Which two companies were closest in sales?
3. Which company had half as many sales as which other company?
4. What is the approximate total of all the boats sold by all five companies?

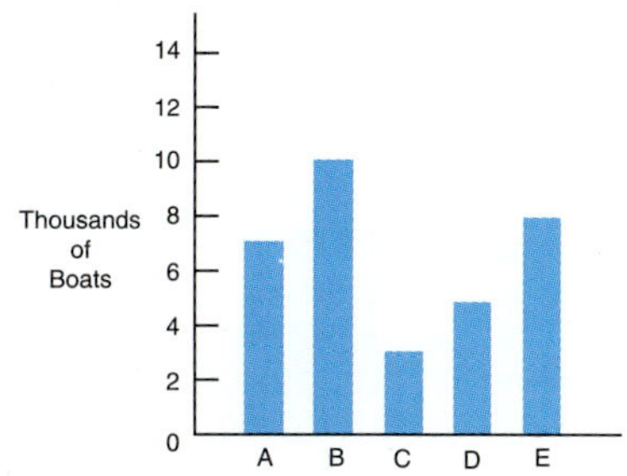

Applying Accounting Procedures

Exercise 20-1 Preparing a Voucher

Fox Enterprises, a supermarket wholesaler, uses the voucher system. On August 2, Fox received the following invoice from one of its suppliers.

HAWAII FRUIT GROWERS
132 Ala Moana Blvd./Honolulu, HI 96813

Invoice
558

Sold To: Fox Enterprises
6893 Skyway Blvd.
Seattle, WA 98101

Date: August 1, 199-
Order No.: 1057
Shipped By: Air express
Terms: 2/10, n/30

QUANTITY	DESCRIPTION	UNIT PRICE	TOTAL
200 cases	Pineapples	10.00	$2,000.00
400 cases	Sugar	15.00	6,000.00
100 cases	Figs	17.50	1,750.00
	TOTAL		$9,750.00

Figure 20-13 Invoice for Exercise 20-1

Instructions:

(1) Prepare Voucher 419, using the form provided in the working papers that accompany the textbook.

(2) Check 1358 was written in payment of Voucher 419 on August 9. Record the payment information on the voucher.

Problem 20-1 Recording Transactions in a Voucher Register

Uptime Technical Associates uses the voucher system. During April, the company had the transactions that follow.

Instructions:

(1) Record the April transactions on page 17 of a voucher register.

(2) Total, prove, and rule the voucher register at the end of the month.

VR totals:
Vouch. Pay., $18,718.50
Purchases, $8,570.00
Supplies, $185.50
Utilities Exp., $217.50
General Dr., $11,128.00
General Cr., $1,382.50

Transactions:

Apr. 1 Voucher 352 was issued in favor of Mark Realty Company for the April rent of $1,500.00.

3 Purchased merchandise on account from Murray Manufacturing Company, $3,600.00, terms 2/10, n/30, Voucher 353.

5 Received Invoice 877 from Basset, Inc., for supplies purchased on account, $185.50, terms n/30, Voucher 354.

9 Issued Voucher 355 to Piedmont Telephone Company for the monthly telephone service, $217.50.

12 Bought $4,970.00 of merchandise on account from Sea View Products, terms 2/10, n/EOM, Voucher 356.

17 Issued Voucher 357, payable to Alliance National Bank, for a note payable that matures today: principal, $4,400.00; interest, $65.10.

21 Received a bill for $137.90 from *Mountain View News* for recent advertisements; issued Voucher 358.

25 Issued Voucher 359 for $25.00 to Maids Unlimited for office cleaning services (Cleaning Expense).

30 Wrote Voucher 360 for $3,617.50 in favor of the Payroll Bank Account. The payroll data were total salaries expense, $5,000.00; employees' federal income tax, $900.00; employees' state income tax, $100.00; social security tax, $310.00; and medicare tax, $72.50.

Problem 20-2 Recording Transactions in the Voucher and Check Registers

The Gateway Manufacturing Company, which uses a voucher system, had the following unpaid vouchers on June 30. The vouchers appear in the voucher register in the working papers.

Voucher Number	Creditor	For	Date of Invoice	Amount
1230	Jennison Corp.	Merchandise	June 24	$12,490.00
1233	Allied Industries	Store equipment	June 28	5,645.00
1234	Mancini, Inc.	Merchandise	June 29	4,326.00

Instructions:

(1) Enter the July transactions on page 8 of a voucher register and page 7 of a check register.

(2) Total, prove, and rule the voucher register and check register at the end of the month.

VR totals:
Vouch. Pay., $22,236.35
Purchases, $15,780.00
Supplies, $125.00
Utilities Exp., $340.00
General Dr., $7,162.00
General Cr., $1,170.65

CR totals:
Vouch. Pay., $40,957.35
Purch. Disc., $583.92
Cash in Bank, $40,373.43

Transactions:

July 1 Issued Voucher 1235 in favor of All-World Insurance Company for a one-year premium on a fire insurance policy, $770.00; terms n/10.

2 Paid Voucher 1230 by issuing Check 989 for $12,240.20 ($12,490.00 less a 2% cash discount).

6 Issued Voucher 1236 to Rush Delivery Services for the transportation charges on merchandise purchased for the business, $92.00.

6 Paid Voucher 1236 by issuing Check 990 for $92.00.

7 Purchased $125.00 of supplies on account from The Office Supplier, terms n/15; issued Voucher 1237.

8 Received an invoice from Simmons Distributors for $1,580.00 of merchandise purchased on account, terms 2/10, n/30, issued Voucher 1238.

9 Issued Check 991 for $4,239.48 in payment of Voucher 1234 ($4,326.00 less a 2% discount).

9 Issued Check 992 for $770.00 in payment of Voucher 1235.

12 Prepared Voucher 1239 for $150.00 to Penn Communications Company for the monthly telephone service.

13 Received a bill from Hempfield Township for one year's property taxes of $2,200.00; issued Voucher 1240 (Property Tax Expense).

13 Issued Check 993 in payment of Voucher 1240 for $2,200.00.

15 Issued Voucher 1241 to the Payroll Bank Account for $2,929.35. The gross salaries expense was $4,100.00, less withholdings for federal income tax of $697.00, state income tax of $160.00, social security tax of $254.20, and medicare tax of $59.45.

15 Issued Check 994 for $2,929.35 in payment of Voucher 1241.

16 Paid Voucher 1238 by issuing Check 995 for $1,548.40 ($1,580.00 less a 2% discount).

16 Bought merchandise on account from Colonial, Inc., for $10,800.00, terms 2/10, n/30; issued Voucher 1242.

22 Issued Check 996 for $125.00 in payment of Voucher 1237.

23 Bought $3,400.00 of merchandise on account from Palmer Products, terms n/30; issued Voucher 1243.

25 Issued Check 997 for $10,584.00 in payment of Voucher 1242 for $10,800.00 less the 2% discount.

27 Issued Check 998 for $5,645.00 in payment of Voucher 1233.

28 Received the monthly utility bill from County Services, Inc.; issued Voucher 1244 for $190.00.

Problem 20-3 Handling Special Transactions within the Voucher System

The Colby Dynamics Corporation uses the voucher system. It had the following transactions during August.

Instructions: Record the transactions on page 23 of a general journal.

Transactions:

Aug. 1 Issued Debit Memo 17 for $250.00 for defective merchandise returned to Kerry Products. This merchandise was part of a purchase recorded on Voucher 101, which had totaled $1,500.00.

9 Issued Note 5 for $3,800.00 to Ellsworth Enterprises in payment of Voucher 110.

12 Voucher 115 (for the purchase of merchandise on account) was incorrectly issued for $827.00. The correct total was $872.00. Recorded the necessary entry to cancel Voucher 115 (Memorandum 45).

Problem 20-4 Preparing a Schedule of Unpaid Vouchers

A portion of the voucher register for Marvel Industries follows.

VOUCHER

	DATE		VOU. NO.	CREDITOR	PAYMENT DATE		PAYMENT CK. NO.	VOUCHERS PAYABLE CREDIT	PURCHASES DEBIT
1	199- Mar.	2	1076	GTAF Corporation	Mar.	9	2012	5,600 00	5,600 00
2		2	1077	Bell Real Estate	Mar.	2	2010	900 00	
3		5	1078	Max-Powers Industries				4,700 00	4,700 00
4		6	1079	Rocky Mt. Telephone Co.	Mar.	6	2011	187 60	
5		7	1080	Linden Hall Co.				8,400 00	8,400 00
6		9	1081	Sheraton Industries	Mar.	28	2016	3,900 00	3,900 00
7		12	1082	Archer Freight Corp.	Mar.	12	2013	142 00	
8		15	1083	Perez Insurance Agency	Mar.	15	2014	1,800 00	
9		16	1084	VOID					
10		20	1085	RJ Office Supplies				440 00	
11		22	1086	Ashley Industries				2,970 00	2,970 00
12		26	1087	Payroll Bank Account	Mar.	26	2015	3,752 40	
17		27	1088	Copper Products	Mar.	31	2017	1,866 00	
18		30	1089	Anchor Enterprises				3,650 00	3,650 00
19		31		Totals				38,308 00	29,220 00
20								(201)	(501)

Figure 20-14 Voucher for Problem 20-4

Vouchers Pay., $20,160.00

Instructions: Using the information in the voucher register, prepare a schedule of unpaid vouchers as of March 31.

Problem 20-5 Recording Transactions in a Voucher System

The Cannon Company uses a voucher system. During October of this year, it completed the following transactions.

Instructions:

(1) Record the transactions in the voucher register (page 10), the check register (page 8), and the general journal (page 5).

(2) Total, prove, and rule the voucher register and the check register at the end of the month.

(3) Post the amounts from the registers and the general journal to the Vouchers Payable account.

VR totals:
Vouch. Pay., $44,764.25
Purchases, $26,200.00
Supplies, $142.00
Utilities Exp., $172.00
General Dr., $20,535.75
General Cr., $2,285.50

CR totals:
Vouch. Pay., $24,717.25
Purch. Disc., $152.00
Cash in Bank, $24,565.25

Vouchers Pay., $13,247.00

Transactions:

Oct. 1 Prepared Voucher 1021 in favor of Keel Real Estate for the October rent of $1,700.00.

1 Wrote Check 2000 in payment of Voucher 1021.

2 Issued Voucher 1022, payable to the Somerset Company, for the purchase of merchandise totaling $6,600.00; terms n/30.

4 Purchased a microcomputer system (Equipment) for $7,500.00 from Compu-Serve, Inc., and arranged to make a down payment of $3,000.00 (Voucher 1023) and two additional payments of $2,500.00 (Voucher 1024) and $2,000.00 (Voucher 1025).

4 Issued Check 2001 in payment of Voucher 1023.

7 Received Invoice 333 from Hanover Enterprises for $142.00 of supplies purchased on account, terms n/20; issued Voucher 1026.

8 Prepared Voucher 1027 in favor of Cory Products for the purchase of merchandise on account, $3,200.00, Invoice 110 dated 10/7; terms 2/10, n/30.

10 Issued Voucher 1028 to Blue Motor Freight Company for transportation charges on purchased merchandise, $195.00.

10 Prepared Check 2002 in payment of Voucher 1028.

14 Purchased $4,600.00 in merchandise on account from Van Hughes Company, terms 2/10, n/30; prepared Voucher 1029.

15 Canceled Voucher 1022 (Memorandum 155) and arranged to pay the amount owed in two installments: $3,300.00 on November 1 (Voucher 1030) and $3,300.00 on November 15 (Voucher 1031).

16 Issued Debit Memo 83 to Cory Products for $200.00 of merchandise from Voucher 1027 returned for credit.

17 Issued Check 2003 for $2,940.00 in payment of Voucher 1027; $3,200.00 less the return and the cash discount.

21 Received the monthly telephone bill from Americana Telephone Company; issued Voucher 1032 for $172.00.

23 Issued Check 2004 for $4,508.00 in payment of Voucher 1029 for $4,600.00 less the 2% discount.

24 Issued Voucher 1033 for $75.00 to Brown Maintenance Service (Miscellaneous Expense).

24 Purchased merchandise on account from Berry Enterprises, $5,200.00, terms 3/10, n/30; issued Voucher 1034.

25 Paid Voucher 1026 by issuing Check 2005.

29 Issued Voucher 1035 to the Knox National Bank for a note previously recorded in the general journal: principal, $4,000.00 plus interest of $65.75.

29 Issued Check 2006 in payment of Voucher 1035.

31 Issued Voucher 1036 for $4,714.50 to the Payroll Bank Account. The total salaries expense was $7,000.00; deductions were for federal income tax of $1,540.00, social security tax of $434.00, medicare tax of $101.50, and state income tax of $210.00.

31 Paid Voucher 1036 by issuing Check 2007.

31 Wrote Check 2008 in payment of Voucher 1030.

Problem 20-6 Recording Voucher Transactions

The Riley Company, which uses a voucher system, had the following unpaid vouchers on November 30. These vouchers have already been recorded in the voucher register.

Voucher Number	Creditor	For	Date of Invoice	Amount
5803	Di-Matics, Inc.	Computer equipment	Nov. 27	$7,200.00
5805	Heidleberg Co.	Merchandise	Nov. 28	4,300.00

VR totals:
Vouch. Pay., $40,895.95
Purchases, $26,100.00
Supplies, $84.90
Utilities Exp., $202.00
General Dr., $16,168.05
General Cr., $1,659.00

CR totals:
Vouch. Pay., $26,826.05
Purch. Disc., $108.00
Cash in Bank, $26,718.05

Vouchers Pay.,
$10,769.90

Instructions:

(1) Record the following transactions in the voucher register (page 13), the check register (page 12), and the general journal (page 11).
(2) Total, prove, and rule the voucher register and the check register.
(3) Post the amounts from the two registers and the general journal to the Vouchers Payable account.
(4) Prepare a schedule of unpaid vouchers.

Transactions:

Dec. 1 Received the monthly electric bill of $202.00 from West Penn Power and issued Voucher 5806.
1 Paid Voucher 5806 by issuing Check 6100.
3 Issued Voucher 5807 to Boyer Enterprises in payment of a $6,000.00, 9.5%, 90-day note payable previously recorded in the general journal.
3 Prepared Check 6101 in payment of Voucher 5807.
4 Received Invoice 199A dated December 2 for $5,400.00 of merchandise bought on account from Taylor, Inc.; terms 2/10, n/30. Issued Voucher 5808.
9 Heidleberg Company agreed to accept a 60-day, 10% note in payment of the November 28 invoice; canceled Voucher 5805 and issued Note 167.
10 Issued Voucher 5809 for supplies purchased on account from King's Office Company, $84.90; terms n/30.
11 Wrote Check 6102 in payment of Voucher 5808 less the discount.
15 Issued Voucher 5810 for $435.00 in favor of Walters Express Company for freight charges on the merchandise purchased from Taylor, Inc.
15 Issued Voucher 5811 to the Payroll Bank Account. Salaries expense was $6,000.00; deductions were for federal income tax ($1,080.00), social security tax ($372.00), medicare tax ($87.00), and state income tax ($120.00).
15 Wrote Check 6103 in payment of Voucher 5811.
18 Purchased a three-year liability insurance policy from Executive Insurance Company, $2,400.00; prepared Voucher 5812.
18 Paid Voucher 5812 by writing Check 6104.
21 Bought merchandise on account from DiOrio Manufacturing Company totaling $10,500.00, terms n/45; issued Voucher 5813.
22 Discovered an error on the invoice from DiOrio Manufacturing that reduced the amount owed by $300.00. Canceled Voucher 5813 (Memorandum 112) and issued Voucher 5814 for $10,200.00.
24 Prepared Voucher 5815 for $1,142.50 to the First National Bank for the monthly mortgage payment (principal, $1,000.00; interest, $142.50).
24 Issued Check 6105 in payment of Voucher 5815.
24 Wrote Check 6106 in payment of Voucher 5803.
31 Issued Voucher 5816 for $50.00 in favor of The Window Cleaners for monthly services (Miscellaneous Expense).

CHALLENGE PROBLEM

Problem 20-7 Analyzing Voucher System Transactions

The Ealer Company uses the voucher system of accounting. In addition to the General columns, the company's voucher register has the following special columns: Vouchers Payable Credit, Purchases Debit, Supplies Debit, Transportation In Debit, and Miscellaneous Expense Debit. Several transactions that typically occur during an accounting period follow.

Instructions: Use plain paper or the form provided in the working papers. For each transaction, indicate the following.

1. The book of original entry in which the transaction would be recorded
2. The accounts that would be debited and credited
3. Whether the debit and credit amounts would be posted individually or as part of a column total

Transactions:

1. Received the monthly telephone bill.
2. Recorded the company's biweekly salary expense and the deductions for social security taxes, medicare taxes, state income taxes, and federal income taxes.
3. Paid the net amount of the payroll.
4. Received an invoice for merchandise purchased on account from the Truax Corporation.
5. Recorded the maturity value of an interest-bearing note payable.
6. Returned the complete shipment of merchandise purchased on account from the Truax Corporation.
7. Received a bill for freight charges on merchandise purchased.
8. Canceled a voucher because the totals on the original invoice (for merchandise) and on the voucher were incorrect.
9. Paid the amount owed to Holiday Products for merchandise purchased for cash.
10. Received a bill for supplies purchased on account.

FOCUS ON COMPUTERS

Speaking Out on Voice-Activated Computers

If you saw the movies *2001: A Space Odyssey* or *2010*, you saw Hollywood's version of what voice-activated computers may be like in the years 2001 and 2010. In these films, the voice-activated computers were somewhat eerie and unpredictable. They seemed more human than machine. The very real voice-activated computers of the 1990s, however, are different.

Voice-activated computers are systems that use speech as input. For example, instead of typing a letter on a computer keyboard, a person using a voice-activated computer talks into the system, and the computer converts the words into a series of bytes that become written text.

Since voice-activated computers are still new, they are somewhat limited. For example, most of these computers have a vocabulary of only about 1,000 words. The systems also require the speaker to pause after each spoken word, which makes using the system somewhat inconvenient.

Most voice-activated computers are programmed to recognize one particular voice. Since every person's voice has different speech patterns, tones, and inflections, it is difficult to program a computer to recognize a number of voices. Computers that can recognize more than one voice usually have a vocabulary that is limited to about 50 words.

The advantages of these high-tech computers are many, with more possibilities opening up as the systems improve. For instance, disabled people who have difficulty using a keyboard can use voice-activated computers to do the same variety of tasks that a word processor can perform. Cellular car phone users can use voice dialers to place calls on their car phones without taking their hands off the wheel or their eyes off the road. Medical professionals are testing voice-activated computers to see if medical documents can be transcribed more accurately and efficiently.

Although voice-activated computers are still limited and costly, it may not be long before they become common in businesses in which people do not have their hands free to operate a keyboard. As to what technology has in store for the years 2001 and 2010, only time will tell.

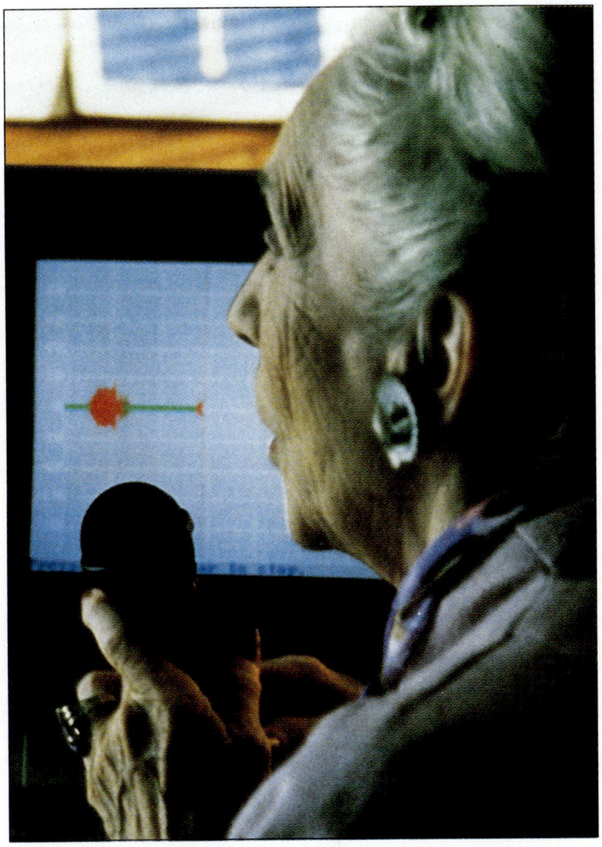

Voice-activated computers convert speech patterns into words.

Chapter 21

MANUFACTURING ACCOUNTING

So far in your study of accounting, you've learned about various accounting procedures as they apply to service and merchandising businesses. In this chapter and the next, you'll learn about the accounting procedures for a third type of business: a manufacturing business.

Manufacturing businesses carry on the same kinds of administrative activities that service and merchandising businesses do. They also make the products they sell to other businesses or individuals. The accounting system of a manufacturer, therefore, must include procedures to account for all of the costs that go into the production of a finished product.

In this chapter, you will learn how manufacturers determine the cost of the goods they manufacture and the cost of the goods they sell during an accounting period. You will also learn how to prepare the financial statements for a manufacturing business.

Learning Objectives

When you have completed this chapter, you should be able to do the following:

1. Identify the three major elements in the cost of a manufactured product.
2. Calculate the value of the ending inventories for a manufacturing business.
3. Complete a work sheet for a manufacturing business.
4. Prepare financial statements for a manufacturing business.
5. Journalize the adjusting and closing entries for a manufacturing business.
6. Define the accounting terms presented in this chapter.

New *Terms*

manufacturing business
direct materials
direct labor
factory overhead
indirect labor
factory supplies
work in process
finished goods
schedule of cost of goods manufactured

Manufacturing Operations

ACCOUNTING Notes
Merchandising businesses refer to their products as *merchandise;* manufacturing businesses refer to their products as *goods.*

Discuss the difference between a merchandising and manufacturing business.

Most of the procedures and examples discussed so far in this textbook have centered around merchandising businesses. As you know, a merchandising business buys goods—such as clothing, books, furniture, and so on—and then resells them to customers for a profit. A merchandising business doesn't process or change the goods before selling them. In contrast, a **manufacturing business** buys raw materials, such as wood or iron ore, and transforms those materials into finished products through the use of labor and machinery. A manufacturing business makes goods to sell; it does not buy finished goods to resell.

In other ways, merchandising and manufacturing businesses are similar. Both earn revenue by selling their products. Both types of businesses use many of the same asset, liability, and stockholders' equity accounts. Merchandising and manufacturing businesses also have similar selling and administrative expenses.

ACCOUNTING Notes
Manufacturing costs are sometimes classified by combining two of the three basic elements. If direct materials and direct labor are combined, they are referred to as *prime costs,* because they are the two major costs of producing a product.

A merchandising business, however, can determine the cost of the merchandise it has bought by simply looking at its Purchases account. A manufacturing business, in contrast, must keep track of a whole series of processing costs to determine the cost of the goods it produces.

In addition, determining the cost of goods sold for a manufacturing business is more complex. Instead of the one inventory account that a merchandising business uses, a manufacturing business has three inventory accounts.

Point out that a manufacturing business has three inventory accounts.

The major difference between accounting for a merchandising business and accounting for a manufacturing business is in accounting for inventories and the cost of merchandise or goods sold.

Elements of Manufacturing Costs

Mention that manufacturing costs are also referred to as product costs.

Regardless of the type of product a manufacturing business makes, its cost is made up of three basic elements: direct materials, direct labor, and factory overhead.

Direct Materials

Ask students to name the direct (raw) materials of some of the items in the classroom (desks, textbooks, clothes they are wearing).

All manufactured products require certain basic ingredients. These ingredients are called direct materials. **Direct materials** are the raw materials used to make a product that can be easily traced to the completed product. Suppose you manufacture pencils. The direct materials you need include wood, graphite (lead), paint, glue, erasers, and metal bands.

The direct materials of one manufacturer may be the finished goods of another manufacturer. For example, flour may be the finished product of a miller but part of the direct materials of a baker.

Direct Labor

The wage paid to an employee who actually works on a product—with either machinery or hand tools—is recorded as **direct labor**. Direct

To illustrate direct labor, ask students who may have been involved in the Junior Achievement program to share their experiences.

labor includes only the wages paid to workers who convert the direct materials into finished products. It does not include the wages and salaries paid to supervisors, office workers, maintenance personnel, or others who are not directly involved in the production process.

Factory Overhead

Point out that *factory overhead* is sometimes referred to as "factory burden" or "manufacturing overhead."

All other manufacturing costs that cannot be classified as direct materials or direct labor are referred to as **factory overhead**. Factory overhead includes a number of different types of production-related costs, such as

- Indirect labor.
- Factory supplies used.
- Supervisors' salaries.
- Payroll taxes on the wages and salaries of factory personnel.
- Heat, light, and power for the factory.
- Depreciation of factory equipment and factory buildings.
- Repairs and maintenance of factory equipment and factory buildings.
- Insurance on factory equipment and factory buildings.
- Property taxes on factory equipment and factory buildings.
- Cost of small tools.

Separate accounts are kept for each type of factory overhead cost. Some manufacturing businesses have so many factory overhead accounts that they use a Factory Overhead controlling account. The factory overhead subsidiary ledger would contain individual accounts for each production-related cost.

R — E — M — E — M — B — E — R

Factory overhead costs are those production-related costs that cannot be easily or directly traced to the products being manufactured.

Most of the costs just listed are self-explanatory. Two costs that need further discussion are indirect labor and factory supplies.

Indirect Labor As you just learned, direct labor is the wage paid to employees who actually convert the raw materials into finished products. A factory, however, cannot operate without the services of other types of employees. These other employees include maintenance personnel, timekeepers, security guards, forklift operators, and so on. The wage paid to the factory employees who do not physically work on the products is recorded as **indirect labor**.

Emphasize that indirect labor refers to the wages paid to employees who do not physically work on the products.

Indirect labor does not include the salaries paid to supervisors. *Salaries* are set amounts paid to employees each pay period. *Wages* are the amounts paid to employees at a specified per-hour rate. Wages can vary greatly depending on the number of hours employees work. Salaries do not vary; salaried employees receive the same amount each pay period regardless of the number of hours they work. Separate accounts are maintained for indirect labor and for supervisory salaries to further classify these costs.

▲ **Factory Supplies** Direct materials are not the only materials needed to complete the production process. Indirect materials such as the grease and oil for machinery, cleaning supplies, or the sandpaper used by a furniture maker are also needed. These indirect materials, which do not become part of the finished product, are referred to as **factory supplies.**

You may want to have students complete Exercise 21-1 at this point.

Before reading further, do the following activity to check your understanding of manufacturing costs.

Check Your Learning

Write the answers to these questions on a sheet of notebook paper.

1. The cardboard, paper, and ink of a book publisher are considered to be ___?___.
2. A wage paid to repair and janitorial workers is classified as ___?___; the wage paid to the employees who actually produce a product is classified as ___?___.
3. Depreciation of factory equipment, factory supplies used, and indirect labor cost are examples of ___?___.

Compare your answers to those in the answers section. Reread the preceding part of the chapter to find the correct answers to any questions you may have missed.

R — E — M — E — M — B — E — R

The cost of a manufactured product consists of the costs of direct materials, direct labor, and factory overhead.

Manufacturing Inventories

For a merchandising business, the ending balance of the Merchandise Inventory account represents the cost of all the merchandise on hand and available for sale at the end of the period. In a manufacturing business, however, the company's products are in various stages of completion at the end of the period. Some products are completed and available for sale, some are incomplete and still in the process of being manufactured, and some are still in the raw material stage.

Introduce and discuss the three inventory accounts.

As a result, a manufacturing business cannot allocate its costs (direct materials, direct labor, and factory overhead) to just one inventory account. Instead, a manufacturing business has three inventory accounts: Raw Materials Inventory, Work in Process Inventory, and Finished Goods Inventory.

The elements of manufacturing costs flow through these three inventories as shown in Figure 21-1.

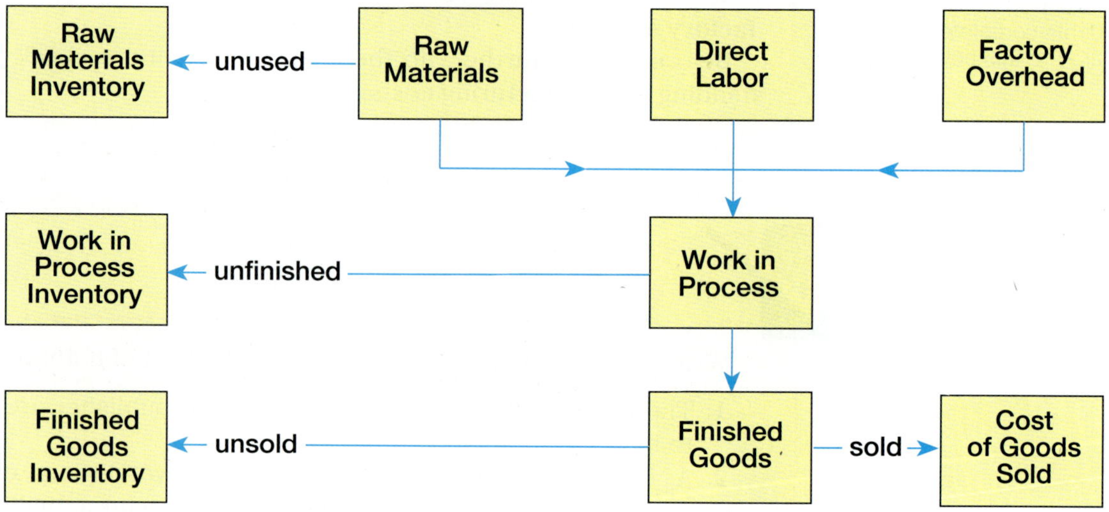

Figure 21-1 The Flow of Manufacturing Costs

Raw Materials Inventory

Mention that the raw materials inventory may also be called the direct materials inventory.

The raw materials inventory consists of the cost of the direct materials that have not yet been placed in the production process at the end of the fiscal period. The balance of the Raw Materials Inventory account is determined by taking a physical inventory and then assigning a cost to the materials on hand.

Work in Process Inventory

Point out that *work in process* is commonly called "WIP," pronounced "whip" or called the "whip" account.

At the end of a fiscal period, almost all manufacturing businesses have some products that are not yet finished. These partially completed products are called **work in process**. The balance of the Work in Process Inventory account consists of the costs of the products partially completed at the end of the period. These costs include the direct materials, direct labor, and factory overhead that have already been charged to the partially complete product. Work in Process Inventory has all of the cost elements of a finished product, but has not yet reached the end of the production process.

Finished Goods Inventory

Explain that finished goods inventory is most like merchandise inventory in a merchandising business.

The goods that a manufacturing business has completed and that are available for sale are its **finished goods**. The balance of the Finished Goods Inventory account, therefore, consists of the costs of all completed but unsold products. The Finished Goods Inventory account is very similar to the Merchandise Inventory account of a merchandising business.

R — E — M — E — M — B — E — R

A manufacturing business maintains three separate inventory accounts: Raw Materials Inventory, Work in Process Inventory, **and** Finished Goods Inventory.

Manufacturing Accounts

Let's look at the accounts commonly found in a manufacturing business before we examine the financial statements prepared by a manufacturing business. A partial chart of accounts for the High Point Corporation appears in Figure 21-2. The accounts listed are those that are typically found only in the general ledger of a manufacturing business. Other accounts unrelated to manufacturing that would normally appear on the chart of accounts have been omitted. For example, Figure 21-2 does not include asset accounts such as Cash in Bank and Accounts Receivable or the accounts for liabilities, stockholders' equity, and selling and administrative expenses.

HIGH POINT CORPORATION
Chart of Accounts (Partial)

	115	Raw Materials Inventory
	120	Work in Process Inventory
	125	Finished Goods Inventory
ASSETS	135	Factory Supplies
	160	Factory Equipment
	165	Accumulated Depreciation—Factory Equipment
	170	Factory Building
	175	Accumulated Depreciation—Factory Building
	501	Raw Materials Purchases (net)
	505	Depreciation Expense—Factory Equipment
	510	Depreciation Expense—Factory Building
	515	Direct Labor
	520	Factory Insurance Expired
COST OF GOODS	525	Factory Supplies Used
	530	Heat, Light, and Power
	535	Indirect Labor
	540	Miscellaneous Factory Costs
	545	Repairs and Maintenance
	550	Supervisory Salaries
	590	Manufacturing Summary

Figure 21-2 Accounts Common to a Manufacturing Business

Discuss the accounts that are common to a manufacturing business.

As you can see, Raw Materials Inventory, Work in Process Inventory, and Finished Goods Inventory appear in the Assets section of the chart of accounts. The Factory Supplies account also appears in this section. Factory Supplies is used to report the cost of items such as sandpaper or the oil or grease for lubricating machinery. At the end of the fiscal period, the account is adjusted in the same way Office Supplies is adjusted to reflect the cost of supplies still on hand.

Like a service or merchandising business, a manufacturing business has an Income Summary account. Income Summary is used at the end of the period during the adjusting and closing process in the same way as in any other business.

The Cost of Goods section of this chart of accounts contains many more accounts than does the Cost of Merchandise section of the chart of accounts for a merchandising business. The accounts shown in Figure 21-2 are all costs of producing High Point's finished products. The Raw Materials Purchases account is similar to the Purchases account of a merchandising business. Whenever High Point buys direct materials, the cost of those materials is debited to the Raw Materials Purchases account.

Emphasize that Manufacturing Summary is a cost of goods account, not a stockholders' equity account.

The Manufacturing Summary account is similar to the Income Summary account. It, too, is used only at the end of the fiscal period during the adjusting and closing process. This account, however, summarizes the costs associated with the goods manufactured during the period. The Raw Materials Inventory and Work in Process Inventory accounts are adjusted through this account. (Finished Goods Inventory is adjusted through the Income Summary account.) In addition, all cost of goods accounts are closed into Manufacturing Summary. Then the Manufacturing Summary account is closed into Income Summary.

R — E — M — E — M — B — E — R

At the end of the fiscal period, the Raw Materials Inventory and Work in Process Inventory accounts are adjusted through the Manufacturing Summary account.

Before reading further, do the following activity to check your understanding of the material you have just studied.

Check Your Learning

Write your answers to these questions on a sheet of notebook paper.

1. Products that have not yet been fully processed or completed are ____?____.
2. The products that a manufacturer has available for sale are called ____?____.
3. The cost of cleaning supplies, light bulbs, and machine oil are debited to the ____?____ account.
4. At the end of a fiscal period, Raw Materials Inventory and Work in Process Inventory are adjusted through the ____?____ account.

Compare your answers to those in the answers section. Reread the preceding part of the chapter to find the correct answers to any questions you may have missed.

Determining the Cost of Manufacturing Inventories

Remind students that physical inventory is an actual count.

At the end of a fiscal period, a manufacturing business must assign a cost to its ending inventories. It is fairly easy to do this for Raw Materials Inventory. A physical inventory of the direct materials is taken. Then the cost of the ending inventory is determined using one of the inventory costing methods (lifo, fifo, or weighted-average cost). The business may then apply the lower-of-cost-or-market rule.

Point out that *cost allocation* is also called cost application.

Assigning a cost to Work in Process Inventory and Finished Goods Inventory, however, is less routine. Remember, these inventories consist of the costs of direct materials, direct labor, and factory overhead. A manufacturing business can determine the total costs for direct materials, direct labor, and factory overhead. The accountant's task is to allocate these costs between work in process inventory and finished goods.

The High Point Corporation manufactures fine furniture. At the end of the fiscal period, the accounts show that the total costs for direct materials, direct labor, and factory overhead were as follows:

Direct materials	$240,000
Direct labor	595,000
Factory overhead	455,000

Tracing and charging direct materials and direct labor costs to work in process or finished goods is usually fairly easy. Since these items are easy to trace, they are called *direct* costs. The accountant determined that the direct materials and direct labor costs could be charged to work in process and finished goods as follows:

	Work in Process	Finished Goods
Direct materials	$28,008	$ 77,224
Direct labor	57,950	103,850

(The remaining direct materials and direct labor costs, $134,768 and $433,200, respectively, can be charged to goods that were completed and sold during the period.)

Ask students why factory overhead costs are not easily assignable to work in process and finished goods.

Factory overhead costs, however, cannot be easily traced to the product. A manufacturer must estimate the amount of factory overhead to allocate to work in process and finished goods. Factory overhead costs can be allocated in a number of ways. One method used when labor is a major cost of a product is to allocate the costs based on the percentage of direct labor costs assigned to each inventory. Direct labor costs are used because they generally vary in direct proportion to the level of production. If a product is labor-intensive, the direct labor costs increase as the number of products produced increases. Many factory overhead costs vary directly with the level of production. As production increases, the costs of indirect labor, utilities, factory supplies, and so on may also increase. Let's see how the factory overhead costs at High Point are allocated.

First, a factory overhead rate must be determined. A *factory overhead rate* is a percentage that will be used to allocate the factory overhead costs. The rate is calculated by dividing the total factory overhead costs by the total direct labor costs. The factory overhead rate for the High Point Corporation's manufacturing process is calculated as follows:

Use demonstration problem 21-1 here.

$$\text{Factory overhead rate} = \frac{\text{Factory overhead}}{\text{Direct labor}} = \frac{\$455{,}000}{\$595{,}000} = 76\%$$

The direct labor costs that have been charged to the two inventories become the base for allocating the factory overhead. The two direct labor amounts are then multiplied by the factory overhead rate. The resulting amounts are the factory overhead costs to be allocated to the Work in Process Inventory and Finished Goods Inventory accounts. The factory overhead costs to be allocated to High Point's two inventories are calculated as follows:

Use demonstration problem 21-2 here.

Work in Process Inventory = \$ 57,950 × .76 = \$44,042
Finished Goods Inventory = \$103,850 × .76 = \$78,926

R — E — M — E — M — B — E — R

Factory overhead costs cannot be easily or directly traced to the products being manufactured. The costs must be allocated to the work in process and finished goods inventories using the factory overhead rate.

You may want to have students complete Exercise 21-2 at this point.

End-of-Fiscal-Period Activities

At the end of a fiscal period, a manufacturing business completes the same end-of-period activities that a merchandising business does. These activities include

1. Preparing a trial balance (in the first two columns of a work sheet).
2. Completing the work sheet, including adjustments.
3. Preparing the financial statements.
4. Journalizing and posting the adjusting entries.
5. Journalizing and posting the closing entries.
6. Preparing a post-closing trial balance.

As you know, the work sheet is prepared before the financial statements. To enable you to better understand the flow of costs in a manufacturing business, we will look first at the financial statements and then at the work sheet.

Financial Statements for a Manufacturing Business

A manufacturing business usually prepares five financial statements at the end of a fiscal period. You are already familiar with four of them: the

Discuss the five financial statements prepared by a manufacturing business.

income statement, the statement of stockholders' equity, the balance sheet, and the statement of cash flows. The fifth statement is the schedule of cost of goods manufactured.

The statement of stockholders' equity and the balance sheet prepared by a manufacturing business differ very little from those prepared by a merchandising business. A manufacturing business, of course, will report three inventories rather than one. Since the statements are similar, they will not be discussed in this chapter. In the next two sections, we will look more closely at the schedule of cost of goods manufactured and the income statement.

Schedule of Cost of Goods Manufactured

Review the parts of the schedule of cost of goods manufactured.

Remind students that this is a supporting document for the income statement.

As the name indicates, the **schedule of cost of goods manufactured** reports all the costs of the goods completed during the fiscal period. The cost of goods manufactured will become an important part of determining income and will be reported on the income statement. The three elements of manufacturing costs are direct or raw materials, direct labor, and factory overhead. The schedule of cost of goods manufactured is organized to disclose these elements. The schedule of cost of goods manufactured for High Point Corporation appears in Figure 21-3. This schedule is prepared before and as a supporting statement for the income statement. The amounts reported on the schedule are taken from the Cost of Goods Manufactured section of the work sheet.

High Point Corporation
Schedule of Cost of Goods Manufactured
For the Year Ended December 31, 199-

Direct Materials:		
Raw Materials Inventory, Jan. 1, 199-	100 000 00	
Raw Materials Purchases (net)	245 000 00	
Cost of Raw Materials Available	345 000 00	
Less: Raw Materials Inventory, Dec. 31, 199-	105 000 00	
Cost of Direct Materials Used		240 000 00
Direct Labor		595 000 00
Factory Overhead:		
Depreciation Expense—Factory Equipment	31 000 00	
Depreciation Expense—Factory Building	26 000 00	
Factory Insurance Expired	23 000 00	
Factory Supplies Used	11 000 00	
Heat, Light, and Power	40 000 00	
Indirect Labor	125 000 00	
Miscellaneous Factory Costs	32 000 00	
Repairs and Maintenance	42 000 00	
Supervisory Salaries	125 000 00	
Total Factory Overhead Costs		455 000 00
Total Manufacturing Costs		1,290 000 00
Plus: Work in Process Inventory, Jan. 1, 199-		140 000 00
Total Cost of Work in Process in Period		1,430 000 00
Less: Work in Process Inventory, Dec. 31, 199-		130 000 00
Cost of Goods Manufactured		1,300 000 00

Figure 21-3 Schedule of Cost of Goods Manufactured

The total manufacturing costs are reported in the top portion of the schedule. First, the cost of direct materials used is reported. This is calculated in much the same way as the cost of merchandise sold.

  Beginning Raw Materials Inventory
+ Raw Materials Purchases (Net)
= Cost of Raw Materials Available
− Ending Raw Materials Inventory
= Cost of Direct Materials Used

Direct labor costs for the period are entered on the next line. Next, factory overhead costs are reported. As you can see, each factory overhead account is listed separately. If, however, there are many factory overhead costs, they may be listed on a separate statement. In that case, only the total factory overhead cost would be reported. The cost of direct materials used, direct labor, and total factory overhead costs are added to determine the total manufacturing costs.

Use demonstration problem 21-3 here.

In the final section of the schedule, the cost of goods manufactured is calculated. This amount is calculated as follows:

  Total Manufacturing Costs
+ Beginning Work in Process Inventory
= Total Cost of Work in Process in Period
− Ending Work in Process Inventory
= Cost of Goods Manufactured

You may want to have students complete Exercise 21-3 at this point.

It is the cost of goods manufactured amount that is carried over to and reported on the High Point Corporation's income statement.

Manufacturing businesses must account for all the costs that go into making the finished product.

R — E — M — E — M — B — E — R

The schedule of cost of goods manufactured is a supporting document for the income statement. The cost determined on this schedule is reported on the income statement as a part of the cost of goods sold section.

Income Statement

Emphasize the difference between the cost of goods manufactured and the cost of goods sold.

The income statement for a manufacturing business looks very much like that for a merchandising business. The Revenue, Operating Expenses, Other Revenue, and Other Expenses sections are very similar. The main difference appears in the Cost of Goods Sold section. The following tables illustrate the difference in how the cost of goods or merchandise sold is calculated:

Merchandising Business	Manufacturing Business
Beginning Merchandise Inventory	Beginning Finished Goods Inventory
+ Purchases (net)	+ Cost of Goods Manufactured
= Merchandise Available for Sale	= Goods Available for Sale
– Ending Merchandise Inventory	– Ending Finished Goods Inventory
= Cost of Merchandise Sold	= Cost of Goods Sold

Figure 21-4 shows the income statement for the High Point Corporation in condensed form.

High Point Corporation
Income Statement
For the Year Ended December 31, 19--

Revenue:		
Sales (net)		2,200 000 00
Costs of Goods Sold:		
Finished Goods Inventory, Jan. 1, 199-	500 000 00	
Cost of Goods Manufactured	1,300 000 00	
Goods Available for Sale	1,800 000 00	
Less: Finished Goods Inventory, Dec. 31, 199-	260 000 00	
Cost of Goods Sold		1,540 000 00
Gross Profit on Sales		660 000 00
Operating Expenses:		
Selling Expenses	300 000 00	
Administrative Expenses	142 000 00	
Total Operating Expenses		442 000 00
Operating Income		218 000 00
Other Expenses:		
Interest Expense		18 000 00
Net Income before Income Tax		200 000 00
Federal Income Tax		80 800 00
Net Income		119 200 00

Figure 21-4 Condensed Income Statement for a Manufacturing Business

As you can see from the discussion of these two financial statements, determining the cost of goods sold requires the use of all three manufacturing inventory accounts.

Before reading further, do the following activity to check your understanding of the material you have just studied.

Check Your Learning

Write your answers to these questions on a sheet of notebook paper.

1. What are the total manufacturing costs if the cost of direct materials used was $139,700, direct labor totaled $199,000, and total factory overhead costs were $156,350?
2. If the beginning raw materials inventory was $4,200, the net raw materials purchases were $26,430, and the ending raw materials inventory was $3,950, what was the amount of raw materials used during the period?
3. The beginning work in process inventory was $11,840, total manufacturing costs were $89,550, and the ending work in process inventory was $13,520. What was the cost of goods manufactured?

Compare your answers to those in the answers section. Reread the preceding part of the chapter to find the correct answers to any questions you may have missed.

Completing a Work Sheet for a Manufacturing Business

Remind students of the purpose of the work sheet.

As before, the work sheet is used to organize all the information needed to prepare the financial statements and to journalize the adjusting and closing entries. The work sheet used by the High Point Corporation, therefore, includes a Cost of Goods Manufactured section. Figure 21-5 shows this work sheet.

Stress that the Raw Materials and Work in Process inventory accounts are adjusted through the Manufacturing Summary Account; Finished Goods Inventory is adjusted through Income Summary.

Most of the adjustments entered on High Point's work sheet are similar to those for a merchandising business. For example, adjustments are made for estimated uncollectible amounts, supplies used, and insurance expired. The adjustments to the three manufacturing inventories, however, are handled slightly differently. Since the Raw Materials Inventory and Work in Process Inventory accounts are both used to determine the cost of goods *manufactured,* they are adjusted through the Manufacturing Summary account. Because Finished Goods Inventory is used to determine the cost of goods *sold,* it is adjusted through the Income Summary account.

The Raw Materials Inventory account is adjusted first. The beginning inventory amount, recorded on the Trial Balance section, was $100,000. At the end of the period, High Point determined that the cost of the ending inventory was $105,000. Since the ending inventory is $5,000 greater than the beginning inventory, Raw Materials Inventory is debited for the amount of the increase. Manufacturing Summary is credited for the same amount.

High Point Corporation
Work Sheet
For the Year Ended December 31, 199-

	ACCT. NO.	ACCOUNT NAME	TRIAL BALANCE DEBIT	TRIAL BALANCE CREDIT	ADJUSTMENTS DEBIT	ADJUSTMENTS CREDIT	COST OF GOODS MANUFACTURED DEBIT	COST OF GOODS MANUFACTURED CREDIT	INCOME STATEMENT DEBIT	INCOME STATEMENT CREDIT	BALANCE SHEET DEBIT	BALANCE SHEET CREDIT	
1	101	Cash in Bank	29 150 00								29 150 00		1
2	105	Accounts Receivable	180 000 00								180 000 00		2
3	110	Allow. for Uncoll. Accounts		2 500 00		(a) 3 500 00						6 000 00	3
4	115	Raw Materials Inventory	100 000 00		(b) 5 000 00						105 000 00		4
5	120	Work in Process Inventory	140 000 00			(c) 10 000 00					130 000 00		5
6	125	Finished Goods Inventory	500 000 00			(d) 240 000 00					260 000 00		6
7	130	Prepaid Insurance	25 000 00			(e) 23 000 00					2 000 00		7
8	135	Factory Supplies	16 000 00			(f) 11 000 00					5 000 00		8
9	150	Office Equipment	62 000 00								62 000 00		9
10	155	Accum. Depr.-Office Equip.		40 000 00		(g) 5 000 00						45 000 00	10
11	160	Factory Equipment	360 000 00								360 000 00		11
12	165	Accum. Depr.-Factory Equip.		218 000 00		(h) 31 000 00						249 000 00	12
13	170	Factory Building	500 000 00								500 000 00		13
14	175	Accum. Depr.-Factory Bldg.		250 000 00		(i) 26 000 00						276 000 00	14
15	180	Land	150 000 00								150 000 00		15
16	201	Notes Payable		40 000 00								40 000 00	16
17	205	Accounts Payable		82 000 00								82 000 00	17
18	210	Corporate Income Tax Payable		—		(j) 13 800 00						13 800 00	18
19	215	Dividends Payable		12 000 00								12 000 00	19
20	220	Bonds Payable		300 000 00								300 000 00	20
21	301	Common Stock		400 000 00								400 000 00	21
22	305	Paid-in Capital in Excess of Par		100 000 00								100 000 00	22
23	310	Retained Earnings		152 150 00								152 150 00	23
24	315	Dividends	12 000 00								12 000 00		24
25	320	Income Summary	—	—	(d) 240 000 00				240 000 00				25
26	401	Sales (net)		2,200 000 00						2,200 000 00			26
27	501	Raw Materials Purch. (net)	245 000 00				245 000 00						27
28	505	Depr. Exp.-Factory Equip.	—		(h) 31 000 00		31 000 00						28
29	510	Depr. Exp.-Factory Bldg.	—		(i) 26 000 00		26 000 00						29
30	515	Direct Labor	595 000 00				595 000 00						30
31	520	Factory Insurance Expired	—		(e) 23 000 00		23 000 00						31
32	525	Factory Supplies Used	—		(f) 11 000 00		11 000 00						32
33	530	Heat, Light, and Power	40 000 00				40 000 00						33
34	535	Indirect Labor	125 000 00				125 000 00						34
35		Carried Forward	3,079 150 00	3,796 650 00	336 000 00	363 300 00	1,096 000 00	—	240 000 00	2,200 000 00	1,795 150 00	1,675 950 00	35

Figure 21-5 Work Sheet for a Manufacturing Business

High Point Corporation
Work Sheet (Continued)
For the Year Ended December 31, 199-

	ACCT. NO.	ACCOUNT NAME	TRIAL BALANCE DEBIT	TRIAL BALANCE CREDIT	ADJUSTMENTS DEBIT	ADJUSTMENTS CREDIT	COST OF GOODS MANUFACTURED DEBIT	COST OF GOODS MANUFACTURED CREDIT	INCOME STATEMENT DEBIT	INCOME STATEMENT CREDIT	BALANCE SHEET DEBIT	BALANCE SHEET CREDIT	
1		Brought Forward	3,079 150 00	3,796 650 00	336 000 00	363 300 00	1,096 000 00	—	240 000 00	2,200 000 00	1,795 150 00	1,675 950 00	1
2	540	Miscellaneous Factory Costs	32 000 00				32 000 00						2
3	545	Repairs + Maintenance	42 000 00				42 000 00						3
4	550	Supervisory Salaries	125 000 00				125 000 00						4
5	590	Manufacturing Summary	—	—		(b) 5 000 00		5 000 00					5
6					(c) 10 000 00		10 000 00						6
7	601	Selling Expenses	300 000 00						300 000 00				7
8	610	Administrative Expenses	133 500 00		(a) 3 500 00				142 000 00				8
9					(g) 5 000 00								9
10	690	Income Tax Expense	67 000 00		(j) 13 800 00				80 800 00				10
11	750	Interest Expense	18 000 00						18 000 00				11
12			3,796 650 00	3,796 650 00	368 300 00	368 300 00	1,305 000 00	5 000 00					12
13		Cost of Goods Manufactured						1,300 000 00	1,300 000 00				13
14							1,305 000 00	1,305 000 00	2,080 800 00	2,200 000 00	1,795 150 00	1,675 950 00	14
15		Net Income							119 200 00			119 200 00	15
16									2,200 000 00	2,200 000 00	1,795 150 00	1,795 150 00	16

Figure 21-5 Work Sheet for a Manufacturing Business (Continued)

Raw Materials Inventory	
Dr.	Cr.
Bal. $100,000	
Adj. 5,000	

Manufacturing Summary	
Dr.	Cr.
	Adj. $5,000

Work in Process Inventory is adjusted in a similar manner. The ending balance was determined to be $130,000. The adjustment is shown in the following T accounts:

Work in Process Inventory	
Dr.	Cr.
Bal. $140,000	Adj. $10,000

Manufacturing Summary	
Dr.	Cr.
Adj. $10,000	Adj. $5,000

Finished Goods Inventory is adjusted through the Income Summary account. To reduce the balance to $260,000, Finished Goods Inventory is credited for $240,000.

Finished Goods Inventory	
Dr.	Cr.
Bal. $500,000	Adj. $240,000

Income Summary	
Dr.	Cr.
Adj. $240,000	

Make sure students understand which accounts are extended to the Cost of Goods Manufactured section.

After all the adjustments are entered on the work sheet, the adjustments section is totaled, proved, and ruled. Then the amounts are extended to the Cost of Goods Manufactured, Income Statement, or Balance Sheet section. As you can see in Figure 21-5, the cost of goods accounts—including Manufacturing Summary—are extended to the Cost of Goods Manufactured section. Income Summary and the revenue and expense accounts are extended to the Income Statement section.

After all amounts have been extended, the Cost of Goods Manufactured section is totaled. The difference between the Debit and Credit columns in this section ($1,300,000) is the cost of goods manufactured. That amount is entered in the Cost of Goods Manufactured Credit column *and* in the Income Statement Debit column. Then the Cost of Goods Manufactured section is totaled, proved, and ruled.

The last two sections of the work sheet are totaled and the amount of the net income is determined. This amount is the same as that shown on the income statement in Figure 21-4.

R — E — M — E — M — B — E — R

The cost of goods manufactured amount is extended to the Income Statement Debit column of the work sheet.

Journalizing the Adjusting and Closing Entries

At the end of the fiscal period, after the financial statements are prepared, the adjusting and closing entries are journalized and posted.

Adjusting Entries

As the work sheet in Figure 21-5 shows, the High Point Corporation had the following adjustments; these adjustments are journalized as shown in Figure 21-6.

Use demonstration problem 21-4 here.

- The estimated uncollectible amount using the aging method was $6,000 (a).
- Increased Raw Materials Inventory to reflect the ending balance of $105,000 (b).
- Decreased Work in Process Inventory to reflect the ending balance of $130,000 (c).
- Adjusted Finished Goods Inventory to reflect the ending balance of $260,000 (d).
- The expired factory insurance premium was $23,000 (e).
- The cost of the factory supplies used during the period was $11,000 (f).
- Depreciation of office equipment was $5,000 (g).
- Depreciation of factory equipment was $31,000 (h).
- Depreciation of the factory building was $26,000 (i).
- The additional income taxes owed are $13,800 (j).

GENERAL JOURNAL — PAGE 43

	DATE		DESCRIPTION	POST. REF.	DEBIT	CREDIT	
1			Adjusting Entries				1
2	199- Dec.	31	Administrative Expenses		3 500 00		2
3			Allow. for Uncollectible Accounts			3 500 00	3
4		31	Raw Materials Inventory		5 000 00		4
5			Manufacturing Summary			5 000 00	5
6		31	Manufacturing Summary		10 000 00		6
7			Work in Process Inventory			10 000 00	7
8		31	Income Summary		240 000 00		8
9			Finished Goods Inventory			240 000 00	9
10		31	Factory Insurance Expired		23 000 00		10
11			Prepaid Insurance			23 000 00	11
12		31	Factory Supplies Used		11 000 00		12
13			Factory Supplies			11 000 00	13
14		31	Administrative Expenses		5 000 00		14
15			Accum. Deprec.-Office Equip.			5 000 00	15
16		31	Deprec. Expense - Factory Equip.		31 000 00		16
17			Accum. Deprec.-Factory Equip.			31 000 00	17
18		31	Deprec. Expense - Factory Building		26 000 00		18
19			Accum. Deprec.-Factory Building			26 000 00	19
20		31	Income Tax Expense		13 800 00		20
21			Corporate Income Tax Payable			13 800 00	21

Figure 21-6 Adjusting Entries for a Manufacturing Business

Closing Entries

Point out the similarities and differences between these and the closing entries of a merchandising business.

Five closing entries are required for a manufacturing business:

1. Closed all cost of goods accounts into Manufacturing Summary. The cost of goods accounts appear in the Cost of Goods Manufactured Debit column of the work sheet.
2. Closed the Manufacturing Summary account balance into Income Summary. The amount for this closing entry is the cost of goods manufactured.
3. Closed the revenue account into Income Summary. For the High Point Corporation, the amount of the closing entry is shown as net sales.
4. Closed the expense accounts into Income Summary. In our example, the amount of the closing entry is the total of the selling expense, administrative expense, other expense, and Income Tax Expense accounts.
5. Closed Income Summary into Retained Earnings. The amount of the closing entry is the amount of the net income for the period.

If the manufacturing business is organized as a publicly held corporation, a sixth closing entry is required. In that closing entry, the balance of the Dividends account (or accounts) is closed into Retained Earnings. The High Point Corporation is a publicly held corporation and, therefore, makes this sixth closing entry.

Figure 21-7 illustrates the closing entries.

GENERAL JOURNAL — PAGE 44

DATE		DESCRIPTION	POST. REF.	DEBIT	CREDIT
		Closing Entries			
199- Dec.	31	Manufacturing Summary		1,295 000 00	
		Raw Materials Purchases (net)			245 000 00
		Deprec. Exp.-Factory Equip.			31 000 00
		Deprec. Exp.-Factory Bldg.			26 000 00
		Direct Labor			595 000 00
		Factory Insurance Expired			23 000 00
		Factory Supplies Used			11 000 00
		Heat, Light, and Power			40 000 00
		Indirect Labor			125 000 00
		Miscellaneous Factory Costs			32 000 00
		Repairs and Maintenance			42 000 00
		Supervisory Salaries			125 000 00
	31	Income Summary		1,300 000 00	
		Manufacturing Summary			1,300 000 00
	31	Sales (net)		2,200 000 00	
		Income Summary			2,200 000 00
	31	Income Summary		540 800 00	
		Selling Expenses			300 000 00
		Administrative Expenses			142 000 00
		Interest Expense			18 000 00
		Income Tax Expense			80 800 00
	31	Income Summary		119 200 00	
		Retained Earnings			119 200 00
	31	Retained Earnings		12 000 00	
		Dividends			12 000 00

Figure 21-7 Closing Entries for a Manufacturing Business

Discuss the Income Summary and Manufacturing Summary T accounts.

The effect of the adjusting and closing entries and the relationship between Manufacturing Summary and Income Summary are illustrated in the following T accounts:

Income Summary

Dr.		Cr.	
Adj.	$ 240,000	(3) Clo.	$2,200,000
(2) Clo.	1,300,000		
(4) Clo.	540,800		
(5) Clo.	119,200		

Manufacturing Summary

Dr.		Cr.	
Adj.	$ 10,000	Adj.	$ 5,000
(1) Clo.	1,295,000	(2) Clo.	1,300,000

Summary of Key Points

1. A manufacturing business converts raw materials into finished products through the use of labor and machinery.
2. The major difference between accounting for a merchandising business and accounting for a manufacturing business is in accounting for inventories and the cost of goods sold.
3. The three elements of manufacturing costs are direct materials, direct labor, and factory overhead. Direct materials are the raw materials used to make a product that can be directly traced to the completed product. Direct labor is the wages paid to employees who physically convert the raw materials into finished products. Factory overhead consists of all other manufacturing costs.
4. Two costs included in factory overhead are indirect labor and factory supplies. Indirect labor is the wages paid to factory employees who are not directly involved in converting raw materials into finished goods. Factory supplies, sometimes called indirect materials, are the costs of materials used in the manufacturing process that cannot be directly traced to the finished product.
5. A manufacturing business has three inventories: raw materials, work in process, and finished goods.
6. Factory overhead costs are often allocated to work in process and finished goods based on the percentage of direct labor costs assigned to the two inventories.
7. The Manufacturing Summary account is used only at the end of a fiscal period during the adjusting and closing process. The raw materials and work in process inventories are adjusted through Manufacturing Summary. The balances of all cost of goods accounts are closed into Manufacturing Summary.
8. At the end of the period, the finished goods inventory is adjusted through Income Summary.
9. The Manufacturing Summary account is closed, by the amount of the cost of goods manufactured, into Income Summary at the end of the fiscal period.
10. The schedule of cost of goods manufactured reports the costs of the goods completed during the period. It is a supporting statement for a manufacturing business's income statement.

21 Review and Applications

Building Your Accounting Vocabulary

In your own words, write the definition of each of the following accounting terms. Use complete sentences for your definitions.

direct labor
direct materials
factory overhead
factory supplies
finished goods
indirect labor
manufacturing business
schedule of cost of goods manufactured
work in process

Reviewing Your Accounting Knowledge

1. How does a manufacturing business differ from a merchandising business?
2. What are the three elements of manufacturing costs?
3. Give five examples of factory overhead costs.
4. What is the difference between direct labor and indirect labor?
5. Which three inventory accounts does a manufacturing business use?
6. Which inventory account for a manufacturing business is similar to the Merchandising Inventory account of a merchandising business?
7. Which accounts are summarized in a manufacturing business's Manufacturing Summary account? Which accounts are summarized in the Income Summary account of a manufacturing business?
8. Describe one method of allocating factory overhead costs to Work in Process Inventory and Finished Goods Inventory.
9. What five financial statements does a manufacturing business prepare at the end of a fiscal period?
10. Which inventory accounts appear on the schedule of cost of goods manufactured? on the income statement?
11. Why is the schedule of cost of goods manufactured prepared before the income statement?
12. How does the work sheet of a manufacturing business differ from the work sheet of a merchandising business?

Improving Your Human Relations Skills

Mary Gordon is the head of her company's human resources department. She has to give Paul Ford his performance appraisal. Mary has been very pleased with Paul's work. Because of the company's financial situation, however, she can afford to give Paul only a small raise.

How can Mary handle this situation? She wants to praise her employee and keep him highly motivated despite the small raise she is able to give him.

Applying Accounting Procedures

Exercise 21-1 Classifying Manufacturing Costs

The following items are typical costs incurred by Sleek Fashions, a company that manufactures women's clothing.

1. Depreciation of sewing machines
2. Zippers
3. Janitors' wages
4. Fabric
5. Shift supervisors' salaries
6. Patterns
7. Starch and fabric conditioners
8. Wages of seamstresses
9. Factory utility bills
10. Dyes for fabric

Instructions: Use a form similar to the one that follows. Classify each of the costs listed above as direct materials, direct labor, or factory overhead. If a factory overhead cost can be classified as indirect labor or factory supplies, place a check mark in the appropriate column.

Item	Direct Materials	Direct Labor	Factory Overhead	Indirect Labor	Factory Supplies
1			√		

Exercise 21-2 Allocating Factory Overhead Costs

At the end of the fiscal period, Wash Soap Products' total direct labor and factory overhead costs were as follows:

Direct labor costs	$544,900
Factory overhead costs	452,300

The company also determined that the following direct materials and direct labor costs could be assigned to its work in process and finished goods.

	Work in Process	Finished Goods
Direct materials cost	$37,000	$25,700
Direct labor cost	42,000	61,800

Instructions: Using the form provided in the working papers,

FO rate, 0.83

Ending inventory:
WIP, $113,860
FG, $138,794

(1) Determine the factory overhead rate based on direct labor costs.
(2) Allocate the factory overhead costs to work in process and finished goods using the factory overhead rate. Determine the cost of the ending work in process and finished goods inventories.

Exercise 21-3 Calculating Cost of Goods Manufactured Amounts

Instructions: For each group of figures that follows, determine the missing amounts.

$116,151.55
$1,735,616.44
$710,968.91
$212,790.90
$37,308.64

1. Cost of raw materials available	?
Ending raw materials inventory	$ 32,700.65
Cost of direct materials used	83,450.90
2. Beginning raw materials inventory	$ 304,500.36
Raw materials purchases (net)	?
Cost of raw materials available	2,040,116.80
3. Cost of direct materials used	$ 833,560.59
Direct labor	?
Factory overhead costs	300,000.80
Total manufacturing costs	1,844,530.30
4. Total manufacturing costs	?
Beginning work in process inventory	$ 7,585.60
Total cost of work in process in period	220,376.50
5. Total cost of work in process in period	$ 250,185.21
Ending work in process inventory	?
Cost of goods manufactured	212,876.57

SPREADSHEET PROBLEM

Problem 21-1 Preparing a Schedule of Cost of Goods Manufactured

The following amounts appeared on the work sheet of the Able Manufacturing Company for the month ended May 31.

Raw Materials Inventory, May 1	$ 18,000
Raw Materials Inventory, May 31	52,000
Work in Process Inventory, May 1	100,000
Work in Process Inventory, May 31	36,000
Raw Materials Purchases (Net)	250,000
Direct Labor	126,000
Factory Insurance Expired	3,000
Factory Supplies Used	6,401
Heat, Light, and Power	47,446
Indirect Labor	20,160
Miscellaneous Factory Costs	7,045
Repairs and Maintenance	4,944
Supervisory Salaries	19,450

COGM, $514,446

Instructions: Prepare a schedule of cost of goods manufactured for the Able Manufacturing Company.

SPREADSHEET PROBLEM

Problem 21-2 Preparing an Income Statement for a Manufacturing Business

The Norwood Manufacturing Company, Inc., makes glassware. The following amounts appeared on the company's work sheet for the year ended December 31.

	Income Statement	
Income Summary		$ 27,000
Sales		2,971,830
Sales Discounts	$ 22,600	
Sales Returns and Allowances	21,870	
Selling Expenses	293,390	
Administrative Expenses	230,520	
Interest Expense	27,350	
Loss on Disposal of Equipment	9,500	
Income Tax Expense	81,510	
Cost of Goods Manufactured	2,184,600	
	$2,871,340	$2,998,830
Net Income	127,490	
	$2,998,830	$2,998,830

Net sales, $2,927,360
COGS, $2,157,600
Gross profit, $769,760
Oper. Inc., $245,850
Net income, $127,490

Instructions: Prepare an income statement for the Norwood Manufacturing Company. The beginning balance of Finished Goods Inventory was $276,000.

Problem 21-3 Preparing a Work Sheet for a Manufacturing Business

Frisk Sales, Inc., is a manufacturing business that processes raw wool into yarn for both knitting and weaving. The Trial Balance section of the company's work sheet has already been completed and is included in the working papers that accompany the textbook.

Adjustments:
(a) $2,150.00
(b) $48.90
(c) $3,500.00
(d) $3,000.00
(e) $7,250.00
(f) $12,500.00
(g) $13,435.00
(h) $1,700.00
(i) $12,100.00
(j) $11,600.00
(k) $191.10

COGM, $1,141,475.00

Net income, $88,802.80

Instructions: Complete the work sheet for Frisk Sales, Inc. Data for the adjustments is as follows.

1. The estimated uncollectible amount, using the aging of accounts receivable method, is $2,400.
2. The 60-day, 8.5% note receivable was accepted on December 16.
3. The costs of the ending inventories are as follows.

Raw Materials Inventory	$35,000
Work in Process Inventory	60,000
Finished Goods Inventory	55,500

4. The expired premium on the factory insurance policy is $12,500.
5. The ending factory supplies inventory is $15,600.
6. Estimated annual depreciation on office equipment is $1,700.
7. Estimated annual depreciation on factory equipment is $12,100.
8. The total income tax liability for the year is $47,600.
9. The 90-day, 9% note payable was issued November 30.

Problem 21-4 Journalizing Adjusting and Closing Entries for a Manufacturing Business

Instructions: Using the work sheet you completed in Problem 21-3, record the adjusting and closing entries, beginning on general journal page 44.

Problem 21-5 Completing the End-of-Period Activities for a Manufacturing Business

The Oliver Products Corporation manufactures wicker laundry baskets. The Trial Balance section of the company's work sheet has already been completed; it is included in the working papers.

Instructions:

Adjustments:
(a) $1,750.00
(b) $2,100.00
(c) $6,650.00
(d) $1,560.00
(e) $1,300.00
(f) $1,410.00
(g) $400.00
(h) $9,500.00
(i) $190.00

COGM, $524,244.00

Net income, $24,744.00

Retained Earnings, $70,824.00

Total stock. equity, $272,224.00

BS totals, $303,765.00

(1) Complete the work sheet. Data for the adjustments are as follows.
  (a) Using the aging method, the total uncollectible amount is estimated to be $2,200.
  (b) The ending inventory amounts are as follows.

Raw Materials Inventory	$42,000
Work in Process Inventory	62,500
Finished Goods Inventory	68,100

  (c) The one-year factory insurance policy was purchased on November 1.
  (d) The inventory of factory supplies on December 31 was $1,500.
  (e) The estimated annual depreciation of office equipment is $400.
  (f) Estimated annual depreciation of factory machinery is $9,500.
  (g) The income tax liability for the year is $2,690.

(2) Prepare a schedule of cost of goods manufactured.
(3) Prepare an income statement.
(4) Prepare a statement of stockholders' equity. During the year, 500 shares of $10-par common stock were issued at $11.
(5) Prepare a balance sheet. Oliver's authorized capital stock consists of 25,000 shares of $10-par common stock.
(6) Journalize the adjusting and closing entries, beginning on page 61.
(7) Post the entries to the Manufacturing Summary and Income Summary accounts only.

CHALLENGE PROBLEM

Problem 21-6 Examining the Cost of Goods Manufactured

The Georgian Company manufactures several styles of bookcases. At the end of the fiscal period, the accounting records revealed the following information.

1. The direct materials cost, which is the same for all styles, is $33.40 per unit. (All materials are issued when the bookcase is started.)
2. The direct labor cost for the period totaled $144,316.
3. Factory overhead costs were $116,964.
4. During the fiscal period, 3,658 units were started. At the end of the fiscal period, 127 units had not yet been completed and 313 units were in the finished goods inventory.

5. The total direct labor cost assigned to the work in process was $7,903; the total direct labor cost assigned to the units in the finished goods inventory was $23,108.

Instructions: Based on this information, answer the following questions.

$122,177.20
$4,241.80
$10,454.20
81%
$6,401.43
$18,717.48
$107,481.20
$113,305.00

1. What is the total direct materials cost for the period?
2. What is the direct materials cost for work in process?
3. What is the direct materials cost for the finished goods inventory?
4. What is the factory overhead rate? (Round your answer to the nearest whole percent.)
5. What is the factory overhead cost for the work in process inventory?
6. What is the factory overhead cost for the finished goods inventory?
7. What is the direct materials cost for the units completed and sold during the period?
8. What is the direct labor cost for the units completed and sold during the period?

FOCUS ON CAREERS

Using Accounting Skills to Make Management Decisions

Managers use accounting skills to make financial decisions that affect the profitability of their companies.

Although many accountants work in the "public domain," many more work in private business. Private accountants can play many different roles within a company. One of the most important positions is that of the controller—the executive who oversees the business's accounting department.

The controller has a number of responsibilities. He or she supervises all the phases of general and cost accounting, prepares and evaluates budgets, and prepares taxes. The controller must also be experienced in data processing, credit and collection, and internal auditing.

Although controllers must have the same experience general accountants do, they are often more involved in making management decisions than they are in performing accounting duties. In the past, controllers usually were responsible only for reporting on the financial history of a business. Today, controllers are responsible for interpreting past financial operations and making future predictions to management. For example, a controller may prepare a corporation's budget or direct a feasibility study for establishing an overseas manufacturing plant. Similarly, a controller may evaluate the dollar return on the projects of other departments, such as research and development or marketing.

Controllers must be aware of all segments of an organization and be ready to offer suggestions for ways to maximize its profits. Since very little happens in an organization that does not relate to money and financial planning, a controller must be an integral part of a management team. As such, it is common for controllers to rise to high levels of management.

If using your accounting skills in a management capacity appeals to you, you will need keen analytical skills, sound judgment, creative problem-solving skills, leadership abilities, and supervisory qualities. Controllers usually have at least a bachelor's degree in accounting. Many also are CPAs, have advanced degrees, or have degrees in more than one field.

Chapter 22

PRODUCT COSTING: JOB AND PROCESS COST ACCOUNTING SYSTEMS

In Chapter 21, you learned about some of the differences between accounting for merchandising businesses and accounting for manufacturing businesses. You saw that the major difference lies in accounting for inventories and the cost of merchandise or goods sold.

Manufacturing costs consist of three elements: direct materials, direct labor, and factory overhead. In the general accounting system presented in Chapter 21, those costs were allocated at the end of the fiscal period to the three manufacturing inventories: raw materials, work in process, and finished goods. In that system, the periodic inventory system was used.

In this chapter, you will learn about two cost accounting systems that use a perpetual inventory system. You will learn how to accumulate costs in those two systems and how to determine the unit cost of the product.

Learning Objectives

When you have completed this chapter, you should be able to do the following:

1. Explain the purpose of cost accounting.
2. Explain the difference between a job order cost accounting system and a process cost accounting system.
3. Journalize entries within a job order cost system and a process cost system.
4. Apply factory overhead to work in process.
5. Account for overapplied and underapplied factory overhead.
6. Determine the unit cost of finished goods.
7. Prepare a cost of production report.
8. Define the accounting terms presented in this chapter.

New Terms

cost accounting system
job order cost accounting
process cost accounting
job cost sheet
materials requisition
job order time card
underapplied factory overhead
overapplied factory overhead
equivalent units
cost of production report

Cost Accounting Systems

ACCOUNTING **Notes** In contrast to financial accounting, which is designed to meet the needs of people outside a company, cost accounting is designed to meet the needs of people inside the company—namely management.

The purpose of a **cost accounting system** is to maintain accurate records of manufacturing costs. By using a cost accounting system, a business can maintain more control over the manufacturing process and can determine the unit cost of the product being manufactured. There are two basic types of cost accounting systems, which usually match the two basic kinds of production operations: job order and process.

Point out that a job may be a single order from a customer or a job to make additional products for stock.

Job order cost accounting systems are used by businesses that produce a certain quantity of identifiable items or whose products are easily identifiable as special orders. Job order systems would be used by businesses such as shipbuilders, building contractors, furniture makers, book printers, and shoe manufacturers that produce several distinct styles of shoes. In a job order system, costs are accumulated for each product or batch of products produced.

Process cost accounting systems are used by businesses that mass produce products that cannot be distinguished from one another during the production process; every unit produced is the same. Generally, the products are manufactured in a series of steps, or processes, with each process being handled by a separate department. The costs accumulated for each process or department are transferred on to the next process or department. Examples of businesses that use process cost accounting systems are automobile manufacturers, chemical producers, cement makers, food processors, and paint manufacturers.

Emphasize that the units produced are usually quite similar if not identical.

In some manufacturing businesses, a job order system may be used for some portions of production and a process system for other portions. In this chapter, we will look first at a job order cost accounting system and then at a process cost accounting system.

Ask students to name some manufacturing businesses in the community. Then, ask them what type of cost accounting system they think those businesses might use.

Have students complete Exercise 22-1 at this point.

R—E—M—E—M—B—E—R

In a job order cost accounting system, costs are accumulated for each product or batch of products. In a process cost accounting system, costs are accumulated for each manufacturing process or department.

Job Order Cost Accounting System

A job order cost accounting system is designed to accumulate manufacturing costs for a specific order or batch of products. As a result, each unique product or batch of products is assigned a job number. The costs of materials, labor, and factory overhead are then charged to and reported according to that job number.

Compare these subsidiary ledgers and controlling accounts with the accounts receivable ledger and the Accounts Receivable controlling account.

In a job order system, a perpetual inventory system is used. As a result, Raw Materials Inventory, Work in Process Inventory, and Finished Goods Inventory are controlling accounts. Subsidiary ledgers are maintained for each inventory account by type of material (Raw Materials Inventory), by job (Work in Process Inventory), and by work completed (Finished Goods Inventory). The inventory accounts are debited and credited during the year as materials, labor, and factory overhead are used.

Factory overhead costs are summarized in a controlling cost of goods account called Factory Overhead Control. Separate accounts are maintained in a factory overhead subsidiary ledger for the various types of overhead costs. As you know, factory overhead costs cannot be identified with a specific product or products. Factory overhead costs, therefore, are periodically allocated or applied to jobs using a *predetermined* factory overhead rate.

When a cost accounting system is used, the cost of manufacturing a product or batch of products is known as soon as the goods are finished. Therefore, it is possible to record the cost of the goods sold at the time the goods are sold. The cost is recorded in a cost of goods account called Cost of Goods Sold, which has a normal debit balance.

As you may have guessed by now, it is very important for a business using a job order cost accounting system to have set procedures for handling the flow of manufacturing costs. Let's now look at some of the internal source documents and journal entries of a job order cost accounting system.

Source Documents Used in a Job Order System

The Jamison Paper Company manufactures books according to specifications from various publishing companies. When Jamison receives an order from a customer, it assigns a job number to the order. For example, on January 28 Jamison received an order to print 9,000 copies of a book from the Westfall Publishing Company. Jamison assigned job order number 702 to this job.

Point out that job cost sheets are sometimes called job order sheets or job cost records.

▲ **Job Cost Sheets** A **job cost sheet** is used to record the various costs incurred for each job. The job cost sheet used by the Jamison Paper Company is shown in Figure 22-1. As you can see, the form has space at the top to record specific information about the job.

The middle section of the form is used to record the costs of the direct materials and direct labor used and the factory overhead applied in the completion of the job. As materials are needed, they are transferred from the materials warehouse and their cost is recorded in the Direct Materials column. Direct labor costs for the job are recorded in the Direct Labor column. When the job is completed, the amount of factory overhead applied to the job is recorded in the Factory Overhead column.

The bottom portion of the sheet summarizes all the costs incurred. It also has a line to record the selling price for the job. By deducting the total production costs from the sales price, Jamison can easily determine the amount of gross profit earned on the job.

Remind students that the job cost ledger is the subsidiary ledger for the Work in Process Inventory account.

A separate job cost sheet is prepared for each job. All the job cost sheets are maintained in a subsidiary ledger called the *work in process subsidiary ledger*.

Mention that material requisitions are sometimes called store requisitions.

▲ **Materials Requisition Forms** When direct materials are needed for a job, Jamison prepares a document called a materials requisition. A **materials requisition** authorizes the materials warehouse to

JOB COST SHEET

CUSTOMER Westfall Publishing Company JOB NO. 702

ITEM Vance: Accounting Theory QUANTITY 9,000

DATE ORDERED January 28, 199- DATE STARTED March 25, 199-

DATE EXPECTED April 1, 199- DATE COMPLETED March 29, 199-

DIRECT MATERIALS		DIRECT LABOR		FACTORY OVERHEAD	
3/25 #1842	$6,700.00	3/29	$1,600.00	3/29	$1,200.00
TOTAL	$6,700.00	TOTAL	$1,600.00	TOTAL	$1,200.00

COST SUMMARY

MATERIALS	$6,700.00	SELLING PRICE	$10,925.00
LABOR	$1,600.00		
FACTORY OVERHEAD	$1,200.00		
TOTAL COSTS	$9,500.00	PRODUCTION COSTS	$9,500.00
		GROSS PROFIT	$1,425.00

Figure 22-1 Job Cost Sheet

MATERIALS REQUISITION

NO. 1842

DATE March 25, 1990

JOB NO. 702 AUTHORIZED BY J. March

MATERIALS DESCRIPTION	QUANTITY	UNIT COST	AMOUNT
50# Ecolocote paper	10 rolls	350.00	$3,500.00
Black ink	95 gals.	1.00	95.00
Heavy cardboard backing	18,000	.09	1620.00
Tyvek coated cover stock	9,000	.165	1485.00
			$6,700.00

Figure 22-2 Materials Requisition Form

transfer materials to the factory. The materials requisition form used by the Jamison Paper Company appears in Figure 22-2.

Since each job is identified on the materials requisition form, it's easy to charge the cost of the materials issued to a particular job. For some jobs, materials may be requisitioned several times during the production process.

Job Order Time Cards Each factory worker has a job order time card. A **job order time card** is used to record the amount of time an employee spent on a particular job. It provides the hourly information needed to calculate the wages to be paid to the employee. Figure 22-3 shows the job order time card used by the Jamison Paper Company.

EMP. NO. 1122

JOB NO. 702

NAME ROLF MOORE

WEEK ENDING 3/29

DATE	IN	OUT	IN	OUT	TOTAL
3/25	8:00	11:00	12:00	5:00	8
3/26	7:30	11:30	12:00	5:00	9
3/27	8:00	11:00	12:00	5:00	8
3/28	8:30	11:00	12:00	5:00	$7\frac{1}{2}$
3/29	8:00	11:00	12:00	5:00	8
		TOTAL HOURS WORKED			$40\frac{1}{2}$

Figure 22-3 Job Order Time Card

Point out that time cards are used to "punch in" for a particular job worked on.

You can see that the time card lists the number of the job on which the employee is working. When an employee begins work on a new job, he or she receives a new time card with the new job number printed on it. The employee's wages can then be charged directly to a specific job.

Employees who do not work directly in the production process also have time cards. Their wages, however, are charged to Factory Overhead Control.

Before reading further, do the following activity to check your understanding of the material you have just studied.

Check Your Learning

Write your answers to these questions on a sheet of notebook paper.

1. An oil refinery would probably use a __?__ accounting system.
2. A __?__ cost accounting system would probably be used by an aircraft manufacturer.
3. In a job order system, a __?__ is used to accumulate the costs incurred in the production of a product or batch of products.
4. When direct materials are needed to produce an item, a __?__ is completed to authorize the transfer of materials to the factory.

Compare your answers to those in the answers section. Reread the preceding part of the chapter to find the correct answers to any questions you may have missed.

Remind students that when a perpetual inventory system is used, costs are debited directly to the Raw Materials Inventory and Work in Process Inventory accounts.

Journalizing Transactions in a Job Order System

When a perpetual inventory system is used with the job order cost accounting system, the Raw Materials Inventory, Work in Process Inventory, and Finished Goods Inventory accounts are debited and credited as jobs move through the production process.

Manufacturing businesses have to record the costs required to produce their products.

Journalizing Materials Transactions When raw materials are purchased, their cost is recorded directly in the Raw Materials Inventory account rather than in a Raw Materials Purchases account. For example, the Jamison Paper Company had the following transaction.

March 1: *Purchased 100 rolls of 50-pound Ecolocote paper on account from Bond Paper Mill, Invoice 741 for $35,000; terms n/30.*

In this transaction, Raw Materials Inventory is debited for $35,000, the cost of the materials purchased. Accounts Payable and Bond Paper Mill's account in the subsidiary ledger are credited for the same amount. The transaction is shown in general journal form in Figure 22-4. (This transaction could also be recorded in Jamison's purchases journal.)

GENERAL JOURNAL — PAGE 112

	DATE		DESCRIPTION	POST. REF.	DEBIT	CREDIT	
1	199- Mar.	1	Raw Materials Inventory		35 000 00		1
2			Accts. Pay./Bond Paper Mill	/		35 000 00	2
3			Invoice 741				3

Figure 22-4 Journalizing the Purchase of Raw Materials on Account

Relate the transactions to the physical flow of materials. When materials come into the warehouse, you debit Raw Materials Inventory. When materials leave the warehouse, you credit Raw Materials Inventory.

As you learned earlier, when the factory needs materials to complete a job, a materials requisition form is prepared. This form authorizes the warehouse to transfer the needed materials to the factory. The form is also the source document for the entry recording the transfer of materials. On March 25, the factory prepared the following materials requisitions:

Requisition No.	Job No.	Amount
1842	702	$6,700
1843	703	4,200
1844	704	5,400

When materials are issued to the factory, the cost of the materials is debited to Work in Process Inventory and credited to Raw Materials Inventory. Figure 22-5 illustrates the general journal entry made on March 25 to record the materials issued for all three jobs. The cost of materials issued for each job is also recorded on the individual job cost sheets.

GENERAL JOURNAL — PAGE 119

	DATE		DESCRIPTION	POST. REF.	DEBIT	CREDIT	
1	199– Mar.	25	Work in Process Inventory		16300 00		1
2			Raw Materials Inventory			16300 00	2
3			Materials Req. 1842-1844				3

Figure 22-5 Journalizing the Issuance of Raw Materials

Remind students of the difference between direct labor and indirect labor.

Journalizing Labor Transactions

At the end of each week, the employees' job order time cards are collected. Time cards for indirect-labor employees are also collected. The total hours worked by each employee are determined and each employee's gross pay is calculated. According to the time cards, Jamison's total gross wages for the week ending March 29 are as follows:

Indirect labor		$ 700
Direct labor		
Job 702	$1,600	
Job 703	1,100	
Job 704	1,200	3,900
Total		$4,600

March 29: *Recorded direct labor costs of $3,900 and indirect labor costs of $700 for the pay period, time cards.*

Point out that in most businesses some time elapses between the end of the pay period and the payment date.

As you learned earlier, the Work in Process Inventory account is increased for direct labor costs incurred. As a result, Work in Process Inventory is debited for $3,900, the total direct labor costs for the pay period. The Factory Overhead Control account is debited for $700, the total indirect labor costs for the pay period. At Jamison, employees are paid for their work on the Friday following the end of the pay period. On March 29, the employees' wages have been earned but not yet paid. The total amount of the payroll, therefore, is credited to the Factory Wages Payable account. The general journal entry for this transaction appears in Figure 22-6.

GENERAL JOURNAL — PAGE 120

	DATE		DESCRIPTION	POST. REF.	DEBIT	CREDIT	
1	199- Mar.	29	Work in Process Inventory		3 900 00		1
2			Factory Overhead Control		700 00		2
3			Factory Wages Payable			4 600 00	3
4			Time Cards				4

Figure 22-6 Journalizing Direct and Indirect Labor Costs

On April 5, Jamison had the following transaction.

April 5: *Wrote Check 4272 for $3,723.70 to the Payroll Checking Account for the net wages to be paid to employees for the pay period ended March 29. The following amounts were withheld: employees' federal income taxes, $450.80; employees' state income taxes, $73.60; social security taxes, $285.20, and medicare taxes, $66.70.*

Use demonstration problem 22-1 here.

The entry for this transaction appears in general journal form in Figure 22-7. Since the wages that had accrued are now being paid, Factory Wages Payable is debited for $4,600.00. Employees' Income Tax Payable is credited for $450.80, the total amount withheld. Employees' State Income Tax Payable is credited for $73.60, and FICA Tax Payable is credited for $351.90. Cash In Bank is credited for $3,723.70, the total net pay amount.

GENERAL JOURNAL — PAGE 125

	DATE		DESCRIPTION	POST. REF.	DEBIT	CREDIT	
1	199- Apr.	5	Factory Wages Payable		4 600 00		1
2			Emp. Fed. Income Tax Payable			450 80	2
3			Emp. State Income Tax Payable			73 60	3
4			Social Security Tax Payable			285 20	4
5			Medicare Tax Payable			66 70	5
6			Cash in Bank			3 723 70	6
7			Check 4272				7

Figure 22-7 Journalizing the Payment of Employees' Wages

R — E — M — E — M — B — E — R

In a cost accounting system, direct labor costs are debited to the Work in Process Inventory account and indirect labor costs are debited to the Factory Overhead Control account.

Point out that Factory Overhead Control is a controlling account and that the factory overhead subsidiary ledger contains a separate account for each type of factory overhead cost.

Journalizing Factory Overhead Transactions Since it has so many factory overhead accounts, Jamison uses a Factory Overhead Control account. Jamison's factory overhead subsidiary ledger has a separate account for each type of factory overhead cost. As factory overhead costs are incurred, the Factory Overhead Control account and the appropriate subsidiary ledger account are debited.

On March 29, Jamison Company had the following transactions.

March 29: *Purchased $700 of factory supplies on account from the Race Supply Center, Invoice 49; terms n/45.*

March 29: *Paid the monthly utilities bill of $840, Check 4192.*

March 29: *Received Invoice 401 from Airport Machinery for replacement parts for one of the printing presses purchased on account, $900; terms 2/10, n/45.*

March 29: *Allocated the monthly depreciation of $400 on the factory building, Memorandum 1822.*

Explain that when the electric bill is paid, Factory Overhead Control and the Heat, Light, and Power account in the factory overhead subsidiary ledger would be debited.

The entries to record these transactions are shown in general journal form in Figure 22-8. In each transaction, the Factory Overhead Control account was debited for the amount of the cost incurred. To simplify the explanation, only the Factory Overhead Control account was debited in the transactions. Normally, of course, the subsidiary ledger account would also be debited.

GENERAL JOURNAL PAGE 120

DATE		DESCRIPTION	POST. REF.	DEBIT	CREDIT
199-					
Mar.	29	Factory Overhead Control		700 00	
		Accts. Pay./Race Supply Center	✓		700 00
		Invoice 49			
	29	Factory Overhead Control		840 00	
		Cash in Bank			840 00
		Check 4192			
	29	Factory Overhead Control		900 00	
		Accts. Pay./Airport Machinery	✓		900 00
		Invoice 401B			
	29	Factory Overhead Control		400 00	
		Accum. Depr.-Factory Bldg.			400 00
		Memo. 1822			

Figure 22-8 Journalizing Factory Overhead Costs

The purpose of a job order cost accounting system is to accumulate job costs as the product or batch of products is being completed. It is very difficult, if not impossible, to determine the amount of factory overhead that has been incurred for each job. In addition, some factory overhead costs are not incurred or cannot be determined until the end of the fiscal period, after most of the jobs have been completed and sold to customers. It is necessary, therefore, to estimate the total factory overhead costs for the year and periodically apply a portion of that estimated amount to the Work in Process Inventory account and to the individual jobs. A predetermined factory overhead rate, often based on the relationship between direct labor costs and factory overhead costs, is used to allocate the factory overhead costs.

Emphasize that the amount of factory overhead applied to each job is an estimate, similar to the estimate made for bad debts expense.

To arrive at the predetermined factory overhead rate, the direct labor and factory overhead costs for the year first must be estimated. For example, the production manager at the Jamison Paper Company estimated that direct labor costs for the year would be $48,000 and that factory overhead costs would be $36,000. The production manager based the estimates on the previous year's actual costs and the estimated production for the coming year.

The predetermined factory overhead rate is found by dividing the estimated factory overhead costs by the estimated direct labor costs. Jamison's rate is calculated as follows:

$$\frac{\$36{,}000}{\$48{,}000} = .75 = 75\%$$

Have students complete Exercise 22-2 at this point.

In other words, for every $1.00 in direct labor costs charged to Work in Process Inventory, $.75 in factory overhead costs should also be charged.

At Jamison, factory overhead costs are applied to Work in Process Inventory at the end of each week.

March 29: *Applied factory overhead costs to Jobs 702–704 at 75% of direct labor costs, Memorandum 1823.*

The amount applied is calculated by multiplying the direct labor costs by the predetermined factory overhead rate, as follows:

Job	Direct Labor Costs	Predetermined Factory Overhead Rate	Factory Overhead Applied
702	$1,600	.75	$1,200
703	1,100	.75	825
704	1,200	.75	900
			$2,925

Discuss with students the use of the Factory Overhead Applied account.

Work in Process Inventory is debited for $2,925, the amount of factory overhead costs being applied. Although the $2,925 could be credited to Factory Overhead Control, accountants prefer to use a separate account titled Factory Overhead Applied. Factory Overhead Applied is a temporary contra cost of goods account. It is credited for $2,925. The entry to record the factory overhead costs applied appears in Figure 22-9.

GENERAL JOURNAL PAGE 120

	DATE		DESCRIPTION	POST. REF.	DEBIT	CREDIT	
	199–						
17	Mar.	29	Work in Process Inventory		2925 00		17
18			Factory Overhead Applied			2925 00	18
19			Memo. 1823				19

Figure 22-9 Applying Factory Overhead Costs

R — E — M — E — M — B — E — R

In a cost accounting system, a predetermined factory overhead rate is used to periodically allocate factory overhead costs to the Work in Process Inventory account.

Use demonstration problem 22-2 here.

Since the predetermined factory overhead rate is only an estimate, the factory overhead costs applied seldom agree with the factory overhead costs actually incurred. The factory overhead costs incurred may be more or less than was estimated, or direct labor costs may be more or less than was estimated at the beginning of the year. As a result, the balance of the Factory Overhead Applied account at the end of a fiscal period may be more or less than the balance of the Factory Overhead Control account.

Be sure students understand the difference between underapplied and overapplied factory overhead.

When the balance of Factory Overhead Applied is less than the balance of Factory Overhead Control, the difference is referred to as **underapplied factory overhead**. In other words, more factory overhead costs were incurred than were applied. When the balance of Factory Overhead Applied is greater than the balance of Factory Overhead Control, the difference is referred to as **overapplied factory overhead**. In other words, more factory overhead costs were applied than were actually incurred. The difference in either case is usually small. This difference, however, must be accounted for at the end of the fiscal period. The amount of the difference is eliminated through a closing entry. In the closing entry, the amount of the difference is transferred—as either a debit or a credit—to the Cost of Goods Sold account.

For example, suppose that at the end of the period, Jamison's Factory Overhead Control account has a debit balance of $38,500. This amount represents the actual factory overhead costs incurred during the period. The credit balance of the company's Factory Overhead Applied account is $38,225. This amount represents the amount of factory overhead costs that were applied to Work in Process Inventory during the period using the predetermined factory overhead rate.

Factory Overhead Control	
Dr.	Cr.
Bal. $38,500	

Factory Overhead Applied	
Dr.	Cr.
	Bal. $38,225

Emphasize that if factory overhead is underapplied, the cost of goods sold is too small and must be increased by a debit.

The difference between the two accounts is a debit amount of $275. In the closing entry, Factory Overhead Applied is debited for $38,225 and Factory Overhead Control is credited for $38,500. The Cost of Goods Sold account is debited for the difference of $275. This closing entry to eliminate the underapplied factory overhead is illustrated in Figure 22-10.

GENERAL JOURNAL PAGE 206

	DATE		DESCRIPTION	POST. REF.	DEBIT	CREDIT	
1			Closing Entries				1
2	199- Dec.	31	Cost of Goods Sold		275 00		2
3			Factory Overhead Applied		38 225 00		3
4			Factory Overhead Control			38 500 00	4

Figure 22-10 Closing Entry for Underapplied Factory Overhead

Emphasize that if factory overhead is overapplied, the cost of goods sold is too large and must be decreased by a credit.

$38,500
−38,225
$ 275

If the balance of Factory Overhead Applied had been $38,775, Jamison would have had overapplied factory overhead of $275. Cost of Goods Sold would have been *credited* for that amount in the closing entry.

R — E — M — E — M — B — E — R

The difference between the actual factory overhead costs and the factory overhead applied is transferred to the Cost of Goods Sold account at the end of the fiscal period.

Point out that Finished Goods Inventory is also a controlling account. Its subsidiary ledger consists of the job cost sheets for those jobs that have been completed but not yet sold.

Journalizing Finished Goods Transactions As a job is completed, its costs must be transferred from the Work in Process Inventory account to the Finished Goods Inventory account. For example, on March 29, the Jamison Paper Company completed work on Jobs 702 and 703. The costs of these two jobs, as indicated by the job cost sheets, are as follows:

	Job 702	Job 703	Totals
Direct materials	$6,700	$4,200	$10,900
Direct labor	1,600	1,100	2,700
Factory overhead applied	1,200	825	2,025
Total costs	$9,500	$6,125	$15,625

In the journal entry to transfer the costs, Work in Process Inventory is credited for $15,625 and Finished Goods Inventory is debited for the same amount. Figure 22-11 shows the general journal entry to record the transfer.

GENERAL JOURNAL — PAGE 120

	DATE	DESCRIPTION	POST. REF.	DEBIT	CREDIT	
	199–					
20	Mar. 29	Finished Goods Inventory		15 625 00		20
21		Work in Process Inventory			15 625 00	21
22		Job cost sheets 702-703				22

Figure 22-11 Journalizing the Transfer of Costs for Finished Goods

The job cost sheets for these two jobs are removed from the work in process subsidiary ledger and transferred to the finished goods subsidiary ledger.

Journalizing the Sale of Goods As you just saw, the costs incurred to manufacture or produce a product in a job order cost system are known as soon as the goods are finished. As a result, the total cost can be recorded in the Cost of Goods Sold account when the product is sold. For example, on March 29 the Jamison Paper Company shipped Job 702 to its customer.

March 29: *Shipped Job 702 to the Westfall Publishing Company, sales price $10,925, Sales Invoice 1291.*

Remind students that there are two entries every time a sale takes place—the perpetual inventory system.

This transaction is recorded in two entries. The first entry records the sale of the job to the customer. Since this transaction is on account, Accounts Receivable and Westfall's account in the accounts receivable subsidiary ledger are debited for $10,925. Sales is credited for the same amount. This transaction is shown in general journal form in Figure 22-12.

GENERAL JOURNAL PAGE 120

	DATE		DESCRIPTION	POST. REF.	DEBIT	CREDIT	
	199-						
23	Mar.	29	Accts. Rec./Westfall Publishing Co.	✓			23
24			Sales				24
25			Sales Invoice 1291				25
26		29	Cost of Goods Sold		9 500 00		26
27			Finished Goods Inventory			9 500 00	27
28			Sales Invoice 1291				28

Figure 22-12 Journalizing the Sale of Finished Goods

The second entry records the transfer of the finished goods into the Cost of Goods Sold account. Cost of Goods Sold is debited for $9,500, the total cost incurred by Jamison in printing the book. Finished Goods Inventory is credited for $9,500 to show the decrease in the account. This transaction is also shown in Figure 22-12. The job cost sheet is removed from the finished goods subsidiary ledger and filed with the sales invoice in the customer's file.

R — E — M — E — M — B — E — R

Cost of Goods Sold is used to record the total manufacturing costs for products completed *and* sold.

Use demonstration problem 22-3 here as a culminating activity.

Before reading further, do the following activity to check your understanding of the job order cost accounting system.

Check Your Learning

For each transaction that follows, indicate which accounts would be debited and which would be credited. Write your answers on a sheet of notebook paper.

1. Applied factory overhead costs to the Work in Process Inventory account.
2. Recorded the sale of goods for cash.
3. Recorded the direct labor costs for the pay period.
4. Completed the production of a specific job.
5. Paid the monthly utilities bill.

Compare your answers to those in the answers section. Reread the preceding part of the chapter to find the correct answers for any items you may have missed.

Process Cost Accounting System

Explain that the goal of the process cost system is to determine the cost of one unit of production.

For some manufacturing businesses, it is difficult to distinguish one unit produced from another. One pound of baking powder looks like the next one; all English muffins made are the same; one gallon of gasoline produced is just like the previous gallon produced. These products are usually manufactured in a series of steps, or processes, with each process being handled by a separate department. When more or less identical products are manufactured in a continuous series of steps, a business will usually use a process cost accounting system.

In a process cost system, costs are not accumulated for a specific job. Instead, materials, labor, and factory overhead costs are accumulated for a particular production step or department. As a result, a separate Work in Process Inventory account is maintained for each department. As a department incurs materials, labor, or factory overhead costs, those costs are charged directly to the department's Work in Process Inventory account. The flow of costs into the Work in Process Inventory account (or accounts) is very much the same in a job order cost system and in a process cost system.

Point out that job order costing collects costs separately for each job while process costing collects costs separately for each process.

The major difference between the two systems is in the way costs are assigned to products. In a job order cost system, most costs can be traced to and assigned to specific jobs and products. This cannot be done in a process cost system, because the products are almost identical. Instead, an average of the total manufacturing costs is determined and assigned to the goods completed by each department. In other words, the total costs accumulated by a department are divided by the number of units processed to determine the cost per unit. This unit cost is used to determine the manufacturing cost to be transferred from one department's Work in Process Inventory account to the next department's Work in Process Inventory account. Let's look at an example.

Emphasize that process costing units move from one department to another.

The Midwest Go Kart Company makes one cart model. Three processes are required and handled by three separate departments. Department A molds, welds, and paints the cart frames. Department B assembles the motors and attaches them to the frames. Department C completes the assembly by attaching the seats and wheels.

In January, Department A had the following costs:

Direct materials	$26,325
Direct labor	30,000
Factory overhead applied	15,000
Total costs	$71,325

During January, Department A processed 150 cart frames. The unit cost per frame is calculated by dividing the department's total costs by the number of frames processed. Department A's unit cost for January is calculated as follows:

$$\frac{\text{Total costs for Department A}}{\text{Total cart frames processed}} = \frac{\$71,325}{150} = \$475.50 \text{ per cart frame processed}$$

Stress that products flow from the work in process of one department to the work in process of another department.

When Department A completes its work, it transfers the cart frames to Department B for the next step in processing. The costs accumulated in

Department A ($475.50 per frame) are also transferred to Department B's Work in Process Inventory account.

REMEMBER

In a process cost system, a separate Work in Process Inventory account is maintained for each department.

Equivalent Units

Distinguish between fully completed and partially completed units.

You just learned how to calculate the unit cost of the cart frames completed in Department A of the Midwest Go Kart Company. The total costs incurred by Department A were divided by the number of cart frames processed. In that calculation, however, the number of frames processed was stated in equivalent units. **Equivalent units** are the number of units produced during a certain period, expressed in terms of fully completed units. Partially completed units are restated in terms of whole units.

Explain how units can be at different stages of completion.

At the end of January, Department A had fully completed and transferred to Department B 130 cart frames. Department A also had 30 cart frames that were not yet completed. These 30 cart frames must also be included in the calculations, because costs have been incurred during their processing. It is often difficult to determine exactly how "complete" the work in process is. Materials and labor may be added at various stages of a process. As a result, many companies use the *50% rule*. In other words, the work in process is considered to be 50% complete on the average. Some products are close to being completed; some are just being started; and some are halfway through the process. On the average, however, the work can be said to be 50% complete. By applying the 50% rule to Department A's work in process, the equivalent units are calculated as follows:

Completed and transferred	130 units
Partially completed: 30 × .50	15 units
Equivalent units	145 units

Some businesses do calculate equivalent units by determining how complete the work in process is. For example, Department A determined that the 30 cart frames were two-thirds completed. The number of equivalent units is determined as follows:

Have students complete Exercise 22-3 at this point.

Completed and transferred	130 units
Partially completed: $30 \times \frac{2}{3}$	20 units
Equivalent units	150 units

Journalizing Transactions in a Process Cost System

Remind students that costs are charged to departments not to jobs.

The process cost system is the same as a job order cost system in many ways. Costs, however, are accumulated by department (process) rather than by job. Each department accumulates and accounts for the costs of raw materials, direct labor, and factory overhead. As products move from one department to the next, all of the departmental costs accumulated up to that point are transferred to the costs accumulated in the next department.

As you read the following sections, you may wish to compare the journal entries for a process cost system with the journal entries for a job order cost system. Many of the entries are handled similarly.

▲ Journalizing Materials Transactions

As in a job order cost system, when raw materials are purchased, their cost is recorded in the Raw Materials Inventory account, not in a Raw Materials Purchases account.

January 4: *Purchased $62,300 of raw materials on account from the Jones Metal Products, Inc., Invoice 0281; terms n/30.*

In this transaction, Raw Materials Inventory is debited for $62,300, the cost of the raw materials purchased. Accounts Payable and Jones Metal Products' account in the subsidiary ledger are credited for the same amount. This transaction is shown in general journal form in Figure 22-13. (This transaction could also have been recorded in Midwest's purchases journal.)

GENERAL JOURNAL — PAGE ____

	DATE		DESCRIPTION	POST. REF.	DEBIT	CREDIT	
1	199- Jan.	4	Raw Materials Inventory		62 300 00		1
2			Accts. Pay./Jones Metal Products, Inc.	/		62 300 00	2
3			Invoice 0281				3

Figure 22-13 Journalizing the Purchase of Raw Materials on Account

In a process cost system, a materials requisition is also used to transfer direct materials from the warehouse to a production department. At the beginning of January, the three departments of Midwest Go Kart requisitioned direct materials as follows:

Requisition	Department	Amount
1130	A	$26,325
1131	B	20,550
1132	C	10,100
Total		$56,975

Begin using demonstration problem 22-4 here.

The cost of the direct materials requisitioned is charged to each department's Work in Process Inventory account. The combined entry to record the transfer of direct materials from the warehouse to the various departments appears in Figure 22-14.

GENERAL JOURNAL — PAGE 96

	DATE		DESCRIPTION	POST. REF.	DEBIT	CREDIT	
	199-						
4	Jan.	4	Work in Process Inventory -Dept. A		26 325 00		4
5			Work in Process Inventory -Dept. B		20 550 00		5
6			Work in Process Inventory -Dept. C		10 100 00		6
7			Raw Materials Inventory			56 975 00	7
8			Materials Req. 1130-1132				8

Figure 22-14 Journalizing the Issuance of Raw Materials

Remind students that labor costs are not charged to specific jobs.

Journalizing Labor Transactions A business that uses a process cost system may also have its direct- and indirect-labor employees complete time cards. There is no need, however, to allocate employees' wages to specific jobs. Most direct-labor employees work in only one department. Their wages are charged to the Work in Process Inventory account of the department in which they work. The wages of indirect-labor employees are charged to the Factory Overhead Control account. For example, during January Midwest Go Kart had the following labor costs:

Department A	$30,000
Department B	12,000
Department C	6,000
Indirect labor	3,500
Total	$51,500

January 31: *Recorded direct and indirect labor costs of $51,500 as follows: Department A, $30,000; Department B, $12,000; Department C, $6,000; indirect labor, $3,500; time cards.*

The entry to record the January labor costs is shown in Figure 22-15.

GENERAL JOURNAL — PAGE 116

	DATE		DESCRIPTION	POST. REF.	DEBIT	CREDIT	
1	199- Jan.	31	Work in Process Inventory-Dept. A		30 000 00		1
2			Work in Process Inventory-Dept. B		12 000 00		2
3			Work in Process Inventory-Dept. C		6 000 00		3
4			Factory Overhead Control		3 500 00		4
5			Factory Wages Payable			51 500 00	5
6			Time Cards				6

Figure 22-15 Journalizing Direct and Indirect Labor Costs

When employees are paid, a check is written to the payroll checking account.

February 7: *Wrote Check 6072 for $40,593.25 to the Payroll Checking Account for the net wages paid to employees for January. Withholdings were as follows: employees' federal income taxes, $5,150; employees' state income taxes, $1,817.00; social security taxes, $3,193.00, and medicare taxes, $746.75.*

Factory Wages Payable is debited for the amount of the monthly payroll. The various tax payable accounts are credited for the amounts withheld. Cash in Bank is credited for the total net pay amount. Figure 22-16 shows the entry to record the payment of the January payroll in general journal form.

GENERAL JOURNAL — PAGE 123

	DATE		DESCRIPTION	POST. REF.	DEBIT	CREDIT	
1	199- Feb.	7	Factory Wages Payable		51,500.00		1
2			Emp. Fed. Income Tax Payable			5,150.00	2
3			Emp. State Income Tax Payable			1,917.00	3
4			Social Security Tax Payable			3,193.00	4
5			Medicare Tax Payable			746.75	5
6			Cash in Bank			40,593.25	6
7			Check 6072				7

Figure 22-16 Journalizing the Payment of Employees' Wages

Journalizing Factory Overhead Transactions A factory overhead subsidiary ledger is also used with a process cost system. The subsidiary ledger contains separate accounts for each type of factory overhead cost. The balances of the individual accounts are summarized in the Factory Overhead Control account.

During January, Midwest Go Kart incurred factory overhead costs totaling $26,200. As each cost is incurred, it is journalized and charged to the Factory Overhead Control account. The transactions would be recorded in the same manner as in the job order system (see Figure 22-8 on page 576).

At the end of the month, factory overhead costs are applied to each department's Work in Process Inventory account. The factory overhead rates do not have to be the same for all departments. For example, Midwest Go Kart applies factory overhead costs at a 50% rate for Department A and at a 60% rate for Departments B and C. The company bases its factory overhead rates on the direct labor costs charged to each department. The calculations for each department are as follows:

Discuss the reason for the different factory overhead rates.

	Direct Labor Costs	Factory Overhead Rate	Factory Overhead Applied
Department A	$30,000	.50	$15,000
Department B	12,000	.60	7,200
Department C	6,000	.60	3,600
Total			$25,800

The general journal entry to record the factory overhead costs applied appears in Figure 22-17. The Work in Process Inventory account of each department is debited for the amount of that department's share of the factory overhead costs.

GENERAL JOURNAL — PAGE 116

	DATE		DESCRIPTION	POST. REF.	DEBIT	CREDIT	
	199-						
7	Jan.	31	Work in Process Inventory–Dept. A		15,000.00		7
8			Work in Process Inventory–Dept. B		7,200.00		8
9			Work in Process Inventory–Dept. C		3,600.00		9
10			Factory Overhead Applied			25,800.00	10
11			Memo 4841				11

Figure 22-17 Allocating Factory Overhead Costs

▲ Journalizing Transfer Transactions When a department completes its task, the processed products are transferred to the next department. At Midwest Go Kart, when Department A completes its work on the cart frames, it transfers the frames to Department B. When Department B had completed assembling and attaching the motors, it transfers the products to Department C. When Department C has completed the assembly process, it transfers the carts to the finished goods inventory.

Review how accumulated manufacturing costs are transferred from one Work in Process Inventory account to another.

When products are transferred from one department to another department or to the finished goods inventory, the accumulated manufacturing costs are also transferred. Let's look at some transfers that occurred at Midwest Go Kart.

During January, Department A completed its work on 130 cart frames and transferred them to Department B. Department A must also transfer the manufacturing costs for those frames to Department B. The entry is usually made at the end of the month. The unit cost of $475.50 calculated earlier is used to determine the amount of the entry.

$$130 \text{ units} \times \$475.50 = \$61,815.00$$

Figure 22-18 shows the general journal entry to record the transfer of the manufacturing costs from Department A to Department B. As you can see, the costs accumulated by one department become part of the costs (recorded in Work in Process Inventory) of the next department.

GENERAL JOURNAL PAGE 116

	DATE		DESCRIPTION	POST. REF.	DEBIT	CREDIT	
	199-						
12	Jan.	31	Work in Process Inventory-Dept. B		61,815.00		12
13			Work in Process Inventory-Dept. A			61,815.00	13
14			Memo. 4842				14

Figure 22-18 Journalizing the Transfer of Manufacturing Costs between Departments

Department B assembles the motors and attaches one to each frame transferred from Department A. During January, Department B assembled 142 equivalent units of motors. Its manufacturing costs for January were $44,020.00. The department's unit cost, therefore, is $310.00 ($44,020.00 ÷ 142 units).

During January, Department B was able to attach motors to 130 frames. The 130 units were then transferred to Department C for final assembly. An entry must be made to transfer the total manufacturing costs for the 130 units to Department C. To determine the amount of the journal entry, Department B's costs were added to the costs transferred from Department A as follows. The unit cost of the units transferred to Department C is $785.50.

Costs transferred from Department A:	130 units × $475.50 =	$ 61,815.00
Costs incurred by Department B:	130 units × $310.00 =	40,300.00
Total costs		$102,115.00

$$\text{Total unit cost} = \frac{\$102,115.00}{130 \text{ carts}} = \$785.50$$

The general journal entry to record the transfer of 130 carts from Department B to Department C appears in Figure 22-19.

GENERAL JOURNAL PAGE 116

	DATE		DESCRIPTION	POST. REF.	DEBIT	CREDIT	
	199-						
15	Jan.	31	Work in Process Inventory - Dept. C		102 1 1 5 00		15
16			Work in Process Inventory-Dept. B			102 1 1 5 00	16
17			Memo: 4844				17

Figure 22-19 Journalizing the Transfer of Manufacturing Costs

Department C completes the assembly of the go-carts by making and installing the seats and wheels. During January, Department C assembled 180 equivalent units of seats and wheels. The department had manufacturing costs of $19,980.00. The department's unit cost per cart, therefore, is $111.00 ($19,980.00 ÷ 180 units).

During January, Department C completed the assembly of 150 carts. This number includes 20 carts that had been transferred from Department B in December but not completed until January. It also contains the 130 frames transferred from Department B in January. The cost of the completed carts must now be transferred to the Finished Goods Inventory account. The amount of the journal entry is determined by adding the costs incurred by Department C to the costs transferred from Department B. The calculation is as follows. The unit cost of the carts transferred to the finished goods inventory is $891.85.

Costs transferred from Department B:	20 frames × $750.64 =	$ 15,012.80
	130 frames × $785.50 =	102,115.00
Costs incurred by Department C:	150 units × $111.00 =	16,650.00
Total costs		$133,770.80

$$\text{Total unit cost: } \frac{\$133{,}770.80}{150 \text{ carts}} = \$891.85$$

The entry to record the transfer of the 150 completed go-carts from Department C to Finished Goods Inventory appears in Figure 22-20.

GENERAL JOURNAL PAGE 116

	DATE		DESCRIPTION	POST. REF.	DEBIT	CREDIT	
	199-						
18	Jan.	31	Finished Goods Inventory		133 777 80		18
19			Work in Process Inventory-Dept. C			133 777 80	19
20			Memo: 4846				20

Figure 22-20 Journalizing the Transfer of Costs for Finished Goods

R — E — M — E — M — B — E — R

In a process cost system, when products are transferred from one department to another, the accumulated manufacturing costs are also transferred.

Illustrate the two entries used to record the sale of goods.

Use demonstration problem 22-5 here.

Go through the cost of production report with students. Explain where each cost came from and where each cost is going.

Journalizing the Sale of Goods

As in the job order system, the total manufacturing costs accumulated for finished goods in a process cost system are known as soon as the goods are transferred from the final processing department. Those costs can then be recorded in the Cost of Goods Sold account when the products are sold.

February 1: *Sold 145 go carts on account to the Ryan Cart Center at $1,000.00 per cart, Sales Invoice 2111.*

This transaction is journalized in two entries, as was done in the job order cost system. The first entry records the sale of the carts. Accounts Receivable and Ryan Cart Center's account in the accounts receivable subsidiary ledger are debited for $145,000.00, the total sales price (145 carts × $1,000.00 unit sales price). Sales is credited for $145,000.00. The entry is shown in general journal form on lines 1 through 3 of Figure 22-21.

GENERAL JOURNAL PAGE 117

	DATE		DESCRIPTION	POST. REF.	DEBIT	CREDIT	
1	199- Feb.	1	Accts. Rec./Ryan Cart Center	✓	145 000 00		1
2			Sales			145 000 00	2
3			Sales Invoice 2111				3
4		1	Cost of Goods Sold		129 318 25		4
5			Finished Goods Inventory			129 318 25	5
6			Sales Invoice 2111				6

Figure 22-21 Journalizing the Sale of Finished Goods

The second entry records the transfer of the finished goods to the Cost of Goods Sold account. The final unit cost of the carts assembled during January was $891.85. The cost of the 145 carts sold is $129,318.25 (145 × $891.85). The Cost of Goods Sold account is debited for this amount. Finished Goods Inventory is credited for the same amount. This entry appears on lines 4 through 6 of Figure 22-21.

Cost of Production Report

At the end of the month, each department at Midwest Go Kart prepares a cost of production report. The **cost of production report** summarizes (1) the units processed by the department and (2) the costs charged to the department. Figure 22-22 shows the cost of production report prepared by Department B.

The first section of the report summarizes the number of units processed during January. As you can see, the department had 24 uncompleted units (motors) in its Work in Process Inventory on January 1. It began work on 130 motors during the month. Of these 154 units, the department assembled and transferred 130 units to Department C. There

Midwest Go Kart Company
Cost of Production Report
Department B: Motors
For the Month Ended January 31, 199-

Quantity Schedule:		
Work in Process Inventory, January 1, 199-		24
New Units Started		130
Total Units to Be Accounted for		154
Transferred to Department C		130
Work in Process Inventory, January 31, 199-		24
Total Units Accounted for		154
Costs to Be Accounted for:		
Work in Process Inventory, January 1, 199- (24 @ 50% × $355.83)		$ 4,270.00
Costs transferred from Department A (130 @ $475.50)		61,815.00
Costs charged to the department:		
Direct materials	$20,550.00	
Direct labor	12,000.00	
Factory overhead applied (60% of direct labor)	7,200.00	39,750.00
Total costs to be accounted for		$105,835.00
Costs Accounted for as Follows:		
Costs transferred to Department C (130 @ $785.50)		$102,115.00
Work in Process Inventory, January 31, 199- (24 @ 50% × $310.00)		3,720.00
Total costs accounted for		$105,835.00
Department B Unit Processing Cost:		
($4,270.00 + $39,750.00) ÷ 142 units		$310.00
Total Unit Processing Cost:		
Department A	$ 475.50	
Department B	310.00	$785.50

Figure 22-22 Cost of Production Report

were also 24 uncompleted motors as of the end of the month. The equivalent units produced during January are calculated as follows:

Units completed and transferred to Department C:	130
Units in process (24 × .50)	12
Equivalent units	142

$ 4,270.00
61,815.00
39,750.00
$105,835.00

The second section of the report summarizes Department B's manufacturing costs for January. The cost assigned to the department's beginning Work in Process Inventory account is $4,270.00. That amount does not include any costs transferred from Department A; it includes only the costs incurred by Department B to assemble the go-cart motors. During January, Department A transferred manufacturing costs of $61,815.00 (130 units @ $475.50) to Department B's Work in Process Inventory account. During January, Department B incurred costs for materials, labor, and factory overhead totaling $39,750.00. The cost of the beginning work in process, the cost of the units transferred from Department A, and the department's January manufacturing costs are added to determine the total costs Department B must account for: $105,835.00.

The third section of the report summarizes how those costs were distributed. As you can see, Department B completed and transferred 130 units to Department C at a unit cost of $785.50. The value of the department's ending Work in Process Inventory is calculated by multiplying the 24 unfinished units by 50% and then by the January unit processing cost:

$$24 \times .50 \times \$310.00 = \$3{,}720.00$$

Explain the calculations for unit costs.

The final section of the report presents the calculations for the department's January unit cost and the total unit cost (up to this point in the production process). The unit cost for Department B is an average cost. The beginning work in process costs and the costs incurred during the month are added together and divided by the equivalent units completed.

$$\$4{,}270.00 + \$39{,}750.00 = \$44{,}020.00$$
$$\$44{,}020.00 \div 142 = \$310.00$$

Have students complete Exercise 22-4 at this point.

Before reading further, do the following activity to check your understanding of the process cost system.

Check Your Learning

For each transaction that follows, indicate which accounts would be debited and which would be credited. Write your answers on a sheet of notebook paper.

1. Applied factory overhead costs to Department A.
2. Paid the factory insurance bill for the month.
3. Transferred 1,250 units from Department A to Department B.
4. Transferred 1,000 units from Department B to finished goods.
5. Recorded the cost of finished goods sold to a charge customer.

Compare your answers to those in the answers section. Reread the preceding part of the chapter to find the correct answers for any items you may have missed.

Cost Accounting and Computers

The paperwork involved in a cost accounting system is often extensive and costly to control, even in the smallest of manufacturing businesses. Computers, however, have eliminated much of the time-consuming paper transfer problem. Input devices located throughout a factory can reduce the time used by workers to fill out time cards, materials requisitions, and job cost sheets. Each work station or department may have its own input terminal. For example, workers can simply insert a special card into the terminal when they start or finish a job or process. This method is fast, accurate, and efficient. Terminals can also be used to record the transfer of materials. The use of computers provides faster and more accurate information, which can be used when preparing production summaries.

Summary of Key Points

1. The purpose of a cost accounting system is to maintain more accurate records of manufacturing costs. The two basic types of cost accounting systems are job order cost accounting and process cost accounting.
2. The job order cost system accumulates costs for a particular product or batch of products. The process cost system accumulates manufacturing costs for a specific process or department. Both systems use the perpetual inventory method to determine the value of ending inventories.
3. Three source documents used in a job order cost system are the job cost sheet, the materials requisition form, and the job order time card.
4. In a cost accounting system, the Raw Materials Inventory, Work in Process Inventory, and Finished Goods Inventory accounts are debited and credited directly as costs are incurred and the products move through the production process.
5. As they are incurred, factory overhead costs are debited to the Factory Overhead Control account, which is the controlling account for the factory overhead subsidiary ledger.
6. In a cost accounting system, factory overhead costs are applied (allocated) to the Work in Process Inventory account(s) periodically. The costs are credited to the Factory Overhead Applied account.
7. Factory overhead costs may be overapplied or underapplied at the end of the period. The difference between the Factory Overhead Control account and the Factory Overhead Applied account is closed into the Cost of Goods Sold account.
8. When a cost accounting system is used, the cost of goods sold is known as soon as the production process is completed. As a result, when goods are sold, the cost of the goods can be recorded in the accounting records.
9. In a process cost accounting system, when units are transferred from one department to another, the costs incurred are also transferred from one department's Work in Process Inventory account to the next department's.
10. Equivalent units are a measure of the number of units processed during a certain period. Partially completed units are be restated in terms of whole units.

22 Review and Applications

Building Your Accounting Vocabulary

In your own words, write the definition of each of the following accounting terms. Use complete sentences for your definitions.

- cost accounting system
- cost of production report
- equivalent units
- job cost sheet
- job order cost accounting
- job order time card
- materials requisition
- overapplied factory overhead
- process cost accounting
- underapplied factory overhead

Reviewing Your Accounting Knowledge

1. What is the purpose of a cost accounting system?
2. What is the difference between the two types of cost accounting systems?
3. What type of account is Factory Overhead Control?
4. Explain the three source documents used in a job order cost system.
5. In a cost accounting system, which accounts are debited and which are credited when direct materials are purchased on account? Which accounts are involved when direct materials are requisitioned for the production process?
6. In a job order cost system, to which account are direct labor costs debited? Indirect labor costs?
7. How is the predetermined factory overhead rate calculated?
8. Why does a business using a job order cost system usually have either overapplied or underapplied factory overhead at the end of the fiscal period?
9. How is overapplied or underapplied factory overhead eliminated at the end of the period?
10. Which accounts are debited and which are credited when completed goods are sold?
11. How are equivalent units used in a process cost accounting system?
12. What is the purpose of the cost of production report?

Improving Your Communications Skills

The company you work for is participating in a program that gets businesses involved in local schools. The program sponsors field trips for students to learn about the career opportunities in your company. You are a senior accounting clerk and have been asked to describe your job to two separate school groups: (1) a fourth-grade class and (2) a tenth-grade business math class. The high school students will be able to understand the details of your job much better than the fourth-graders will. How will you plan your two presentations so that each one is appropriate for its listeners?

Applying Accounting Procedures

Exercise 22-1 Identifying Cost Accounting Systems

Instructions: Following is a list of several types of manufactured products. On a sheet of paper or on the form provided in the working papers that accompany the textbook, indicate whether each item would likely be produced in a job order cost system or in a process cost system.

PCS JOCS
JOCS PCS
PCS JOCS
JOCS JOCS
PCS JOCS
JOCS PCS

1. Sugar	7. Computers
2. Leather handbags	8. Metal furniture
3. Paint	9. Airplanes
4. Oriental rugs	10. Pianos
5. Paper boxes	11. Racing cars
6. Toys	12. Baseball bats

Item	Job Order Cost System	Process Cost System
1		√

Exercise 22-2 Calculating the Factory Overhead Rate

Instructions: The estimated direct labor costs and estimated factory overhead costs for six companies follow. Calculate the factory overhead rate for each company. Round your answers to the nearest whole percent.

32%
42%
14%
59%
60%
60%

	Estimated Direct Labor Costs	Estimated Factory Overhead Costs
1.	$ 837,584	$268,027
2.	1,200,000	500,000
3.	32,600	4,500
4.	160,000	95,000
5.	29,200	17,500
6.	377,500	228,300

Exercise 22-3 Calculating Equivalent Units

The Corcoran Umbrella Company uses a process cost accounting system. It also uses the 50% rule to determine the equivalent units produced in each department. The number of completed and partially completed units for the Framing Department for the first quarter of the year are shown in the following chart.

7,500
7,370
7,125

	Completed and Transferred	Partially Completed
January	6,900	1,200
February	6,460	1,820
March	6,385	1,480

Instructions: Determine the equivalent units produced by the Framing Department for each month. Use plain paper or the form provided in the working papers.

Exercise 22-4 Calculating Unit Manufacturing Costs

The Monroe Plastics Company uses a process cost accounting system. At the beginning of the month, Department A had a beginning inventory of $14,810. During the month, the department incurred the following costs:

$2.25

Direct materials	$488,900
Direct labor	155,600
Factory overhead applied	125,000

Instructions: Calculate Department A's unit manufacturing cost. There were 348,500 equivalent units produced during the month. Use plain paper or the space provided in the working papers.

SPREADSHEET PROBLEM

Problem 22-1 Completing a Job Cost Sheet

The Barry Company makes several styles of tables. The company uses a job order cost accounting system. On January 3, Woodcraft Home Products placed an order for 25 tables (style number 143) to be delivered by January 25. The job was assigned number J5. The job was started on January 8 and completed on January 19. The following costs were charged to the job:

1. Direct materials issued: January 8, $200.00; January 15, $50.00.
2. Direct labor costs: January 12, $116.00; January 15, $95.10.
3. Factory overhead was applied on January 12 and 19 at a rate of 75% of direct labor costs.

The selling price of the job was $800.00.

Instructions: Use the preceding information to complete the job cost sheet included in the working papers.

Problem 22-2 Applying Factory Overhead Costs

The Resort Company uses a job order cost accounting system. Resort applies factory overhead costs at the end of each month using a predetermined factory overhead rate of 80% of direct labor costs. The company also closes the Factory Overhead Control and Factory Overhead Applied accounts at the end of each month.

Instructions:

FOA, $74,011.20

(1) On page 29 of the general journal, record the May 31 entry to apply the month's factory overhead costs (Memorandum 403). Direct labor costs for May were $92,514.

(2) Record the entry to close Factory Overhead Control and Factory Overhead Applied on May 31. The balance of Factory Overhead Control is $78,100.

Problem 22-3 Recording Transactions in a Job Order Cost System

The Davis Metal Products Corporation uses the job order cost accounting system and the perpetual inventory method.

Instructions: Record the following transactions on page 23 of a general journal.

Transactions:

Mar. 5 Purchased raw materials for $12,030.00 cash, Check 1881.

7 Issued direct materials as follows: Job 109, $3,000.00 (Materials Requisition 109) and Job 110, $2,500.00 (Materials Requisition 110).

10 Purchased factory supplies on account from Lowtower, Inc., $705.00, Invoice D2117; terms n/30.

15 Recorded indirect labor costs of $1,200.00 and direct labor costs for Job 109 of $3,500.00 and for Job 110 of $2,000.00; time cards.

17 Issued Check 1902 for $5,430.35 for the net pay due employees. The following amounts were withheld: employees' federal income taxes, $569.50; employees' state income taxes, $187.60; social security taxes, $415.40; and medicare taxes, $97.15.

18 Applied factory overhead costs to Jobs 109 and 110 at 45% of direct labor costs, Memorandum 207.

22 Completed Job 109 and transferred the costs to finished goods.

25 Sold Job 109 for $8,700.00 cash (Receipt 2121) and transferred the costs to Cost of Goods Sold.

Problem 22-4 Examining Costs in a Process Cost System

The Work in Process Inventory account for Department A of the World Manufacturing Company follows in T account form.

Work in Process Inventory—Department A

Dr.		Cr.
Bal.	$ 35,000	Transferred out $410,000
Dir. Materials	120,000	
Dir. Labor	210,000	
Fact. Overhead	105,000	

Instructions:

(1) Using the information in the T account, record the following entries on page 36 of a general journal.

(a) The issuance of the direct materials on November 6 (Materials Requisition 3065)

(b) The direct labor costs on November 11 (time cards)

(c) The application of factory overhead on November 30 (Memorandum 6233)

(d) The transfer of the products to Department B on November 30 (Memorandum 6234)

FO rate, 50%

(2) Calculate the predetermined factory overhead rate used.

Problem 22-5 Recording Transactions in a Process Cost System

The Mag Electronics Company uses a process cost accounting system with the perpetual inventory method.

Instructions: Record the following transactions beginning on page 54 of a general journal.

Transactions:

Jan. 2 Purchased $3,750.00 of raw materials on account from Samson's, Inc., Invoice AB115; terms 2/10, n/30.

4 Issued direct materials as follows, Materials Requisitions 971–973.

Department A	$1,500.00
Department B	750.00
Department C	1,000.00

10 Recorded labor costs as follows (time cards).

Direct labor	
Department A	$2,600.00
Department B	2,100.00
Department C	1,200.00
Indirect labor	200.00

15 Issued Check 2101 for the net pay due employees. Amounts withheld were as follows: employees' federal income taxes, $518.50; employees' state income taxes, $207.40; social security taxes, $378.20; medicare taxes, $88.45.

17 Paid the utilities bill of $910.00, Check 2109.

20 Issued Check 2115 for $2,075.50 for repairs to factory equipment.

31 Applied factory overhead to the three departments at a rate of 55% of direct labor costs, Memorandum 4300.

31 Transferred 1,080 units, at a unit cost of $5.02, from Department A to Department B, Memorandum 4301.

31 Transferred 1,320 units, at a unit cost of $8.03, from Department B to Department C, Memorandum 4302.

31 Transferred 1,400 units, at a unit cost of $10.07, from Department C to finished goods, Memorandum 4303.

31 Sold 1,300 units at $15.00 per unit (cost, $10.07 per unit) on account to the Marks Company, Sales Invoice 3110.

SPREADSHEET PROBLEM

Problem 22-6 Preparing a Cost of Production Report

The manager of Department A of the Fine Metal Company gathered the following information about the department's January operations.

Beginning inventory (100 units @ 50% @ $15.00)	$ 750
Costs incurred:	
Direct materials	16,375
Direct labor	22,510
Factory overhead applied	10,135
Work in process units, January 1	100
New units started	3,200
	3,300
Transferred to Department B	3,000
Work in Process, January 31	300
Units completed and transferred out	3,000
Units in process (300 @ 50%)	150
Equivalent units	3,150

Units accounted for, 3,300

Costs accounted for, $49,770.00

Dept. A UPC, $15.80

Instructions: Using this information, prepare a cost of production report for Department A of the Fine Metal Company.

CHALLENGE PROBLEM

Problem 22-7 Recreating a Cost of Production Report

United Products, Inc., manufactures small sailboats. The company has four departments: Department A makes the hull, Department B paints the hull and attaches the hardware, Department C makes the sails, and Department D inspects the final product and packages it for shipping.

Recently the sprinkler system accidently went off in Department B's office. Several of the monthly statements and other production reports were ruined. You have been asked to help reconstruct one of these statements.

The following information was obtained from other departments and from documents not ruined by water.

Units accounted for, 406

Costs accounted for, $142,041.73

Dept. B UPC, $75.77
Total UPC, $378.37
Equivalent units, 389

1. On July 1, the work in process inventory was valued at $1,276.93 and consisted of 34 units that were 50% complete.
2. During July, 372 units were completed and transferred to Department C.
3. The July 31 work in process was 50% complete.
4. Manufacturing costs charged to the department during July were:
   a. Direct materials of $5,335.10
   b. Direct labor of $14,750.00
   c. The factory overhead applied was estimated at 55% of the direct labor cost for the month.
5. The costs transferred from Department A during July totaled $112,567.20 for 372 units.
6. The costs transferred to Department C during July were $140,753.64.

Instructions: Based on this information, recreate a cost of production report for the month ended July 31.

Using Computers to Run High-Tech Dairy Farms

People outside the farming community may not think of farming as a business. Producing enough high-quality food products to meet consumer demand and still pay the bills, however, involves a lot of management. As computers become more affordable and specialized software becomes more accessible, farmers are increasingly able to reap the benefits of computerizing their businesses.

One of the fastest growing areas of farm computerization is the dairy industry. Dairy farmers have found that computers can help them keep track of many details and assist in nearly every task. One Washington farmer uses computers to keep track of 1,200 cows, each of which is milked three times a day. The computers record how much milk each cow produces and what each cow's health status is, as well as which cows are due to breed, which are pregnant, and which need vaccinations.

A dairy farmer in Idaho found that his computer helps him avoid management slip-ups. Each of his 500 cows is electronically identified. Workers in the milking parlor can record milking statistics at each milking, as well as check whether any of the cows should not be milked at a particular time.

Keeping track of a herd's health is an important function of the software used in dairy farming. Computers can keep track of vaccinations, when veterinary checkups are due, whether milk production is dropping, and which cows have a higher than average body temperature. Keeping track of such information is critical in ensuring that milk sold to the public is high in quality and disease-free.

Dairy farmers can also use computers to keep track of how much feed each cow consumes, how much feed to buy each month, and how much of a particular crop to grow during the next growing season. Farm business and payroll data are also easily accessed by computer.

By computerizing their records, farmers can realize increased productivity.

As we move further into the 1990s, the picture of farming will change more and more. Instead of seeing a farmer hand-milking a cow in a drafty old barn, we're much more likely to see a farmer sitting at a computer, tracking his cows that are being milked electronically in a high-tech milking parlor.

Mini Practice Set

APPLICATION ACTIVITY 5

Preparing Financial Statements for a Manufacturing Business

In Chapters 21 and 22, you learned about the accounting procedures and financial statements of a manufacturing business. Now you will have the opportunity to apply what you have learned as you complete the work sheet and prepare the end-of-period financial statements for the Express Manufacturing Company, Inc.

When you have completed this activity, you will have done the following:

COMPUTER PROBLEM

1. Calculated and entered adjustments for a manufacturing business on a ten-column work sheet.
2. Completed the work sheet.
3. Prepared a schedule of cost of goods manufactured.
4. Prepared an income statement.
5. Prepared a statement of stockholders' equity.
6. Prepared a balance sheet.
7. Journalized and posted the adjusting and closing entries.

Express Manufacturing Company, Inc.

The Express Manufacturing Company, Inc., manufactures paper products for the office. The company sells its products to local retail office supply stores. Express Manufacturing is a publicly held corporation with authorized capital of 200,000 shares of $5-par common stock.

Completing End-of-Period Work

Before going on vacation, another accounting clerk at Express Manufacturing prepared the year-end trial balance. It is included in the working papers that accompany this textbook. You have been asked to complete the work sheet and prepare the financial statements. Express's fiscal year ends on December 31.

Adjustments:
(a) $4,864.23
(b) $6,000.00
(c) $1,500.00
(d) $3,500.00
(e) $2,000.00
(f) $1,600.00
(g) $6,000.00
(h) $30,000.00
(i) $2,900.00
(j) $6,500.00
(k) $1,700.00
(l) $15,780.00
(m) $2,625.00
(n) $3,700.00

Instructions:

(1) Complete the work sheet. Data for the adjustments is as follows.

(a) Express Manufacturing estimates that its uncollectible accounts will be .35% of net sales.

(b) Express Manufacturing uses the periodic inventory system to determine the cost of its ending inventories. The ending inventory amounts are as follows.

Raw Materials Inventory	$20,000
Work in Process Inventory	57,000
Finished Goods Inventory	78,000

(c) The ending factory supplies inventory on December 31 is $3,400.

COGM, $750,100.00

Net income, $298,110.77

Retained Earnings, $395,130.77

Total stock. equity, $995,130.77

BS totals, $1,188,935.77

(d) The amount of the expired insurance premium is as follows: factory insurance, $700; office insurance, $900.

(e) Express Manufacturing uses the straight-line method to determine the annual depreciation amounts. Depreciation for the year is as follows.

Office equipment	$ 6,000
Factory machinery	30,000
Office building	2,900
Factory building	6,500

(f) The December factory power bill of $1,700 has not yet been recorded or paid. (Credit this to Accounts Payable.)

(g) The federal income tax liability for the year is $151,780.

(h) On October 1, the company borrowed $100,000 from the Pacific States Trust Company by issuing a 10.5%, 6-month note payable.

(i) Accrued wages are as follows: direct labor, $2,500; indirect labor, $1,200.

(2) Prepare a schedule of cost of goods manufactured.

(3) Prepare an income statement.

(4) Prepare a statement of stockholders' equity. During the year, the company issued 10,000 shares of common stock at $7.50.

(5) Prepare a balance sheet. (Place the Assets section on the first page of the report form and the Liabilities and Stockholders' Equity sections on the second page.)

(6) Journalize the adjusting and closing entries, beginning on page 73 of the general journal.

(7) Post the entries to the Retained Earnings, Income Summary, and Manufacturing Summary accounts only.

UNIT 6

ACCOUNTING FOR BUSINESS DECISIONS

Owners and managers of businesses must make decisions about which product the business should produce and sell and what price to charge. To make sound decisions and have a successful business, owners and managers must understand costs and how they behave. In this unit, you will learn how costs change in relation to changes in business activities. You will also learn how to analyze the relationships among costs, volume, and profits. Finally, you will learn how to establish the selling price for a product or service.

Chapter 23

MANAGERIAL COST CONTROL

The manager or owner of a business—whether the business is large or small—needs cost and expense information to make informed decisions. Information about costs or expenses may be collected for different purposes and classified in many different ways. In Chapter 21, you learned how to classify costs by *function*; that is, costs and expenses were summarized by the business functions of selling, administration, and manufacturing and used to prepare financial statements. In Chapter 22, you learned about product costs and the systems used to record and report them. You learned how to collect job order costs and report the cost of a production process. Costs may be classified in other ways as well, depending on the objective or activity involved. For example, costs may be classified as either direct costs or indirect costs and reported as total costs or unit costs. In this chapter, you will learn how to separate and classify costs and expenses from the viewpoint of cost behavior.

Learning Objectives

When you have completed this chapter, you should be able to do the following:

1. Explain the meaning of cost behavior and its importance to decision making.
2. Describe the difference among variable, fixed, and mixed costs.
3. Separate the fixed and variable parts of a mixed cost.
4. Apply the equations for variable, fixed, and mixed costs.
5. Identify costs as variable, fixed, or mixed.
6. Define the accounting terms presented in this chapter.

New Terms

cost behavior
variable costs
fixed costs
relevant range
committed fixed costs
discretionary fixed costs
mixed costs
high-low method

Cost Planning and Control

Managers and owners are required to make decisions involving costs. They need to know, therefore, how costs behave in relation to changes in the business's activities, such as volume of production and labor hours. As they are planning and preparing budgets, managers might ask accountants the following questions: If we decide to increase the production and sales level, which costs will increase? Which costs will decrease? Will any costs remain the same? The managerial accountant provides the answers by analyzing the behavior of all costs.

Accurate and complete information about costs and expenses helps managers make informed decisions.

Cost Behavior

Discuss the meaning of cost behavior.

The term **cost behavior** refers to the way a cost changes in relation to a change in a business activity level. As a business activity level, such as volume of production, changes, costs may increase, remain the same, or follow some other pattern of change. Let's look at three basic classifications of costs: variable costs, fixed costs, and mixed costs.

A primary interest of an owner or manager is in how costs change or do not change with a business decision. The managerial accountant, therefore, needs to classify all costs as either variable or fixed. Not all costs fall easily into these two classifications. Some costs are mixed and must be separated into their variable and fixed components. By forcing all costs into either a variable or a fixed classification, the accountant can

Emphasize that the distinction between variable and fixed costs is necessary if the accountant is to provide information on how costs change as output increases or decreases.

analyze total cost behavior. The following total cost equation is used for this anaylsis:

$$\text{Total Cost} = \text{Fixed Costs} + \text{Variable Costs}$$

$$TC = FC + VC$$

As you study this and the next chapter, you will learn how this cost equation is used to analyze cost behavior. You will also learn how important it is to classify all costs as either variable or fixed.

Variable Costs

Stress that variable costs vary in total but variable cost per unit is constant.

Variable costs are costs that vary in direct proportion to an activity level such as volume of production. The total variable cost increases as the activity level increases. The variable cost assigned to each unit, however, remains unchanged. Direct materials, direct labor, factory supplies expenses, and some utility expenses are examples of variable costs. To illustrate variable costs, let's assume Albert Hayes operates the Hayes Hairbrush Company, a business that manufactures hairbrushes. If the wood used to produce one hairbrush costs \$3.50, the total direct material cost (variable cost) increases by \$3.50 for each hairbrush (unit) produced. If 10 hairbrushes are produced, the total variable cost, therefore, will be \$35.00 (10 × \$3.50 = \$35.00). The \$3.50 variable cost assigned to each unit is the same regardless of the number of units produced. The graph in Figure 23-1 illustrates this variable cost behavior.

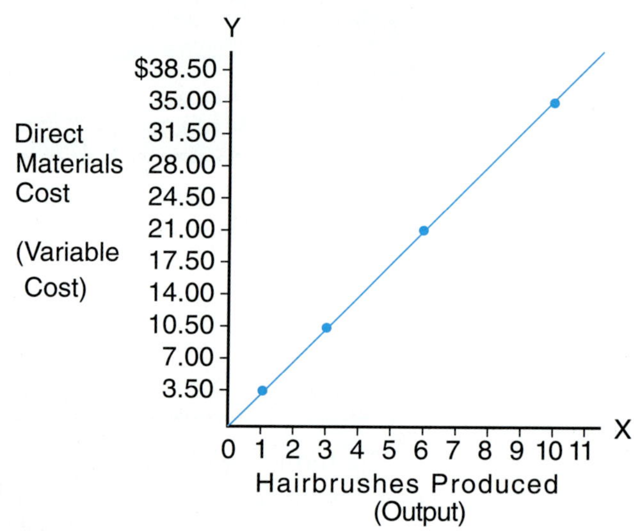

Figure 23-1 Variable Cost Behavior Graph

Review the examples in the graph and table to be sure students understand variable cost behavior.

In Figure 23-1, the variable cost is shown on the left (the Y axis) and the output is reported along the bottom (the X axis). As the output increases, total variable cost also increases. If output is 1 hairbrush, the variable cost per unit is \$3.50 and the total variable cost is also \$3.50. If output increases to 3 hairbrushes, the total variable cost increases to \$10.50. The unit cost, however, is still \$3.50 (\$10.50 ÷ 3 = \$3.50). If the output increases to 6 hairbrushes, the total variable cost increases to $21.00, but the unit cost is still $3.50 ($21.00 ÷ 6 = $3.50). If the output increases to 10 hairbrushes, the total variable cost increases to $35.00, but the unit cost is still $3.50 ($35.00 ÷ 10 = $3.50).

The variable cost behavior may also be reported in table form as shown in Figure 23-2. Some accountants prefer the table format because it illustrates more clearly the relationship between variable costs and output. The table in Figure 23-2 reports the same cost information shown on the graph in Figure 23-1, but in a different format. As output increases from 1 to 11 hairbrushes, the unit variable cost of $3.50 remains unchanged. The total variable cost, however, increases from $3.50 to $38.50. The amount of increase is in direct proportion to the number of units produced. The accountant will be sure to point out that if no units are produced, no variable costs are incurred.

Units Produced (Output)	Unit Direct Materials Cost	Total Direct Materials Cost
0	0	0
1	$3.50	$ 3.50
2	3.50	7.00
3	3.50	10.50
4	3.50	14.00
5	3.50	17.50
6	3.50	21.00
7	3.50	24.50
8	3.50	28.00
9	3.50	31.50
10	3.50	35.00
11	3.50	38.50

Figure 23-2 Variable Cost Behavior Table

Be sure students understand the variable cost equation.

The behavior of variable costs may be expressed in equation form as follows:

$$\text{Total Variable Cost} = \text{Unit Variable Cost} \times \text{Activity Level}$$

$$\text{TVC} = \text{UVC} \times \text{AL}$$

Using the preceding hairbrush example, the unit variable cost is $3.50. The activity level represents units of output. If 35 hairbrushes are produced, the equation, therefore, appears as follows:

$$\text{TVC} = \text{UVC} \times \text{AL}$$

$$\$122.50 = \$3.50 \times 35$$

R — E — M — E — M — B — E — R

As the units of output increase, the variable cost assigned to each unit remains unchanged but the total variable cost increases.

Before reading further, do the following activity to check your understanding of variable costs.

Check Your Learning

Write your answers to these questions on a sheet of notebook paper.

1. What are two examples of variable costs?
2. If $34.00 is the total variable cost for 20 units produced, what is the unit variable cost?
3. Explain the following equation in your own words: TVC = UVC × AL

Compare your answers to those in the answers section. Reread the preceding part of the chapter to find the correct answers to any questions you may have missed.

Fixed Costs

Stress that fixed costs are fixed in total but fixed cost per unit changes as output changes.

Fixed costs are costs that remain constant even if an activity level such as volume of production changes. The total fixed cost remains the same regardless of the number of units produced. The fixed cost per unit, however, varies as the volume of production changes. Costs such as depreciation, advertising, insurance, and administrative salaries are examples of fixed costs. To illustrate fixed costs, let's assume the plant in which hairbrushes are made is leased for $300 per month. Regardless of the number of hairbrushes produced in a month, the total fixed cost rent expense will remain $300. This fixed cost behavior is illustrated in Figure 23-3.

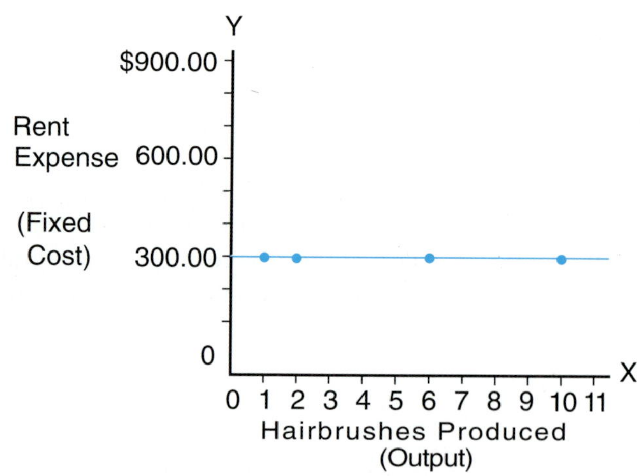

Figure 23-3 Fixed Cost Behavior Graph

In the graph, the fixed cost is shown on the left (the Y axis) and the output is reported along the bottom (the X axis). Note that the total fixed

Review the examples in the graph and table to be sure students understand fixed cost behavior.

cost, $300, remains the same regardless of the output. The fixed cost per unit, however, decreases as the output increases. If output is 1 hairbrush, total fixed cost is $300 and the fixed cost per unit is also $300. If the output increases to 2 hairbrushes, the total fixed cost is still $300. The fixed cost per unit, however, decreases to $150 ($300 ÷ 2 = $150). If the output increases to 6 hairbrushes, the total fixed cost is still $300, but the fixed cost per unit decreases to $50 ($300 ÷ 6 = $50). If the output increases to 10 hairbrushes, the total fixed cost is still $300 and the fixed cost per unit decreases to $30.00 ($300 ÷ 10 = $30).

The fixed cost behavior may also be reported in table form as shown in Figure 23-4. Some accountants prefer this method of reporting because it illustrates more clearly the relationship between fixed costs and output. As output increases from 1 to 11 units, total fixed cost remains constant at $300. The fixed cost assigned to each unit, however, decreases from $300.00 to $27.27. This reduction is an important characteristic of fixed costs. The managerial accountant points out that as more units are produced from the same fixed cost, the cost per unit decreases. If the unit cost decreases, a greater percentage of each sales dollar generated by these units will go to net income. The accountant will also point out that if no hairbrushes are produced, the fixed cost of $300 remains.

Units Produced (Output)	Unit Rent Cost	Total Rent Cost
0	0	$300.00
1	$300.00	300.00
2	150.00	300.00
3	100.00	300.00
4	75.00	300.00
5	60.00	300.00
6	50.00	300.00
7	42.86	300.00
8	37.50	300.00
9	33.33	300.00
10	30.00	300.00
11	27.27	300.00

Figure 23-4 Fixed Cost Behavior Table

Be sure students understand the fixed cost equation.

The following equation is useful for solving problems involving fixed costs:

$$\textit{Total Fixed Cost} = \textit{Fixed Costs}$$

$$\text{TFC} = \text{FC}$$

Using the hairbrush example, the total fixed cost would be $300 regardless of the number of hairbrushes produced. If 1 or 35 hairbrushes are produced, the fixed cost equation will appear as follows:

$$\text{TFC} = \text{FC}$$
$$\$300 = \$300$$

Use demonstration problems 23-1 and 23-2 here to help students classify costs and calculate variable and fixed unit costs.

R — E — M — E — M — B — E — R

As the units of output increase, the total fixed cost remains unchanged, but the fixed cost assigned to each unit of output decreases.

Before reading further, do the following activity to check your understanding of fixed costs.

Check Your Learning

Write your answers to these questions on a sheet of notebook paper.

1. What are two examples of fixed costs?
2. If $34.00 is the total fixed cost for producing 20 units, what is the total fixed cost for producing 25 units?
3. Explain the following equation in your own words: TFC = FC.

Compare your answers to those in the answers section. Reread the preceding part of the chapter to find the correct answers to any questions you may have missed.

You may want to have students complete Exercise 23-2 at this point.

The Relevant Range

Explain that relevant range is a band of activity in which the specific relationship between a cost and a unit of output is valid.

Cost behavior is valid only within a level of activity called the **relevant range**. A fixed cost is fixed only over a given range of activity and a given period of time. For example, the $2,100 fixed cost for packaging and shipping 0 to 150 cartons of hairbrushes is the warehouse supervisor's salary. It is possible that if the activity level exceeds 150 cartons a month, an additional supervisor will be needed to supervise the additional work. The fixed cost for packaging and shipping more than 150 cartons a month will jump to $4,200, the salary of two warehouse supervisors. Figure 23-5 shows that the relevant range for the fixed cost of $2,100 is 0 to 150 cartons. If output exceeds 150 cartons, the fixed cost jumps to $4,200, creating a new relevant range. Fixed costs that jump or step up at different levels of activity are often called *step-fixed costs.*

Be sure students understand what causes a relevant range to change.

Considering the relevant range of a fixed cost is important for planning. If the planning period is one year, the fixed cost is usually considered fixed for the year. Before deciding to increase the shipping capacity of the warehouse, the manager, therefore, must look at the relevant range of the fixed cost. The manager's decision can be influenced by the amount of increase in the fixed cost.

Discuss how the relevant range is used in planning.

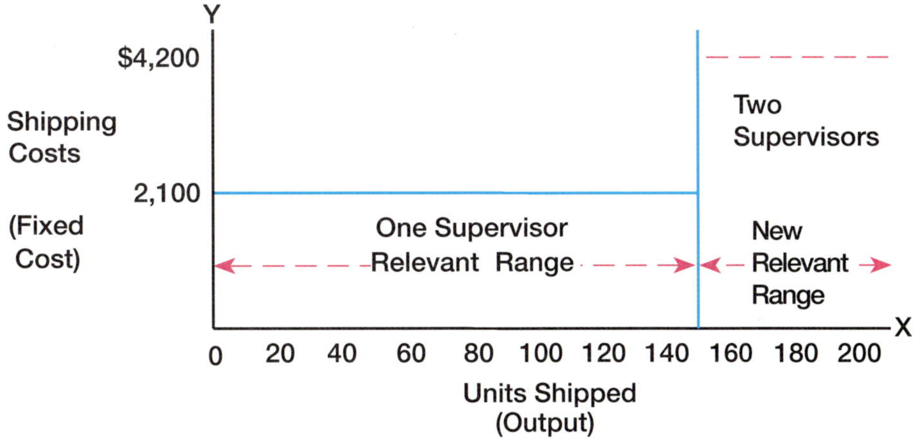

Figure 23-5 Relevant Range

ACCOUNTING *Notes*
Accountants need self-confidence and tact to ask clients sensitive questions and recommend changes. They don't want to offend their clients.

Point out the difference between committed and discretionary fixed costs.

Committed and Discretionary Fixed Costs

Fixed costs are sometimes classified as either committed or discretionary costs. **Committed fixed costs** cannot be eliminated easily and are associated with long-range investments in plant, equipment, and the business itself. Decisions to construct buildings, buy equipment, and hire staff to run the business cannot be quickly reversed, and they represent long-range commitments. The day-to-day operations of the business should generate enough revenue to justify these long-range investments. The business must show evidence of being a going concern.

Discretionary fixed costs are usually based on decisions for a fiscal period and can be increased or decreased during the annual budgeting process. Examples of discretionary fixed costs are costs associated with advertising, training, health care, and services.

Owners and managers are very concerned about controlling fixed costs. Because of the amount of revenues and the length of time required to recover the investments, they review any decisions to make fixed cost commitments very carefully.

Mixed Costs

Emphasize that mixed costs have both variable and fixed elements.

When costs cannot be explained by a single cost behavior pattern, the costs are called **mixed costs**. Mixed costs are part variable and part fixed. Examples of mixed costs are truck rental charges, telephone charges, copy machine leases, and repairs and maintenance costs. For decision-making purposes, managers and owners prefer that mixed costs be separated into variable costs and fixed costs. For some mixed costs, the fixed portion is the amount paid to have a service provided. The variable portion is the cost for the use of that service. For example, Albert Hayes leases a truck at a fixed cost of $300 per month. He also pays a variable cost charge of $.04 for every mile driven over 5,000 miles. Figure 23-6 illustrates this mixed cost behavior for the truck rental contract.

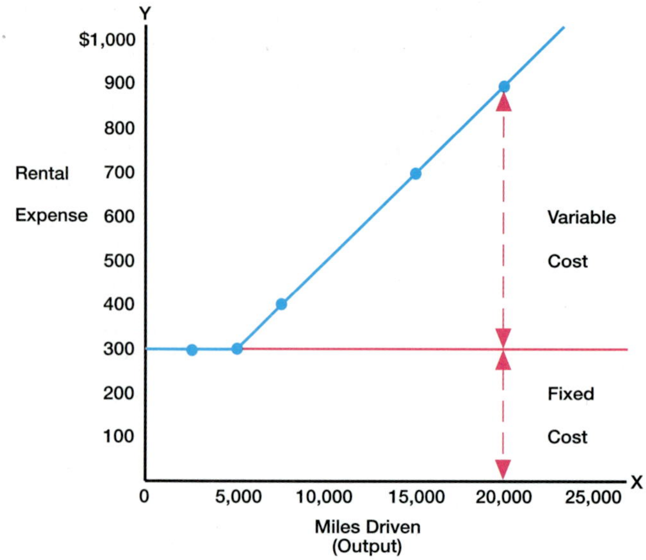

Figure 23-6 Mixed Cost Behavior Graph

Explain that the fixed portion of a mixed cost represents the minimum cost of obtaining a service, while the variable element is the result of a change in the activity level.

In this graph, the fixed and variable costs are easily identified. If the truck is driven from 0 to 5,000 miles, the total truck rental cost is the $300 monthly fixed cost. If the truck is driven 7,500 miles, the $400 total truck rental cost becomes a mixed cost. The mixed cost is separated as $300 fixed cost and $100 variable cost. The variable cost is calculated by multiplying the number of miles in excess of 5,000 by the $.04 variable cost charge (2,500 × $.04 = $100). If the truck is driven 15,000 miles, the $700 total truck rental cost is separated as $300 fixed cost and $400 variable cost (10,000 miles × $.04 = $400). If the truck is driven 20,000 miles, the $900 total truck rental cost is separated as $300 fixed cost and $600 variable cost (15,000 miles × $.04 = $600). After the initial 5,000 miles, the variable cost increases as the number of miles driven increases.

Have students complete Exercise 23-1 at this point.

Sometimes the variable and fixed components of certain mixed costs are difficult to identify. A widely used method for finding the variable and fixed parts of a mixed cost is the **high-low method**. Repair cost data provided by Albert Hayes to his accountant follow:

Month	Repair Costs	Labor Hours
June	$310	44
July	275	30
August	380	72
September	350	60
October	415	86
November	345	58
December	375	70

Discuss how the accountant determines that these are mixed costs.

The accountant will first identify the total cost behavior revealed by the data. The cost data shows that there is some change in the activity level (labor hours) and a corresponding change in total cost (repair costs). As the labor hours for making repairs change, the total repair costs also change. A fixed cost behavior pattern would not show changes such as these. In addition, the total cost changes are not in direct proportion to the changes in activity level as they would be in a variable cost behavior pattern. Since the costs cannot be explained as either fixed costs or variable costs alone, they must be mixed costs. Now the accountant must identify the variable and fixed cost parts of the mixed cost.

Walk students through calculations used to apply the high-low method.

To apply the high-low method of finding the variable and fixed costs, select the highest and the lowest costs and calculate the difference for those two months. The high cost was in October and the low cost was in July. The differences in the total cost and the activity level for those two months are calculated as follows:

Month	Total Cost (Repair Costs)		Activity Level (Labor Hours)	
October	High	= $415	High	= 86 hours
July	Low	= 275	Low	= 30 hours
	Difference	= $140	Difference	= 56 hours

Now the unit variable cost can be determined. The difference in total cost, $140, is divided by the difference in activity level, 56 hours:

$$\$140 \div 56 = \$2.50 \text{ variable cost per labor hour}$$

For every labor hour worked on repairs, the cost increased by $2.50. The unit variable cost is $2.50. Using this unit amount and the variable cost equation (TVC = UVC × AL), the total variable cost for each month can be determined.

Be sure students understand how to use this equation.

The next step is to determine the fixed costs. A variation of the total cost equation (TC = FC + VC) is used:

$$\textit{Total Cost} = \textit{Fixed Cost} + (\textit{Unit Variable Cost} \times \textit{Activity Level})$$

$$TC = FC + (UVC \times AL)$$

or

$$FC = TC - (UVC \times AL)$$

Emphasize that fixed costs are the same for any month.

Total cost, $415, unit variable cost, $2.50, and activity level, 86 hours, are inserted in the equation to determine total variable cost and fixed cost for the high-cost month of October. The total variable cost for October is $215, and the fixed cost is $200.

$$\begin{aligned} TC &= FC + (UVC \times AL) \\ FC &= TC - (UVC \times AL) \\ FC &= \$415 - (\$2.50 \times 86) \\ FC &= \$415 - \$215 \\ FC &= \$200 \end{aligned}$$

As the following calculations show, the fixed cost is the same for any month in which the total cost, unit variable cost and activity level are used in the equation. The total variable cost for September is $150.

$$\begin{aligned} TC &= FC + (UVC \times AL) \\ FC &= TC - (UVC \times AL) \\ FC &= \$350 - (\$2.50 \times 60) \\ FC &= \$350 - \$150 \\ FC &= \$200 \end{aligned}$$

R — E — M — E — M — B — E — R

Use demonstration problem 23-3 here.

Mixed costs are costs that cannot be described by a single cost behavior pattern and have both variable and fixed costs.

Before reading further, do the following activity to check your understanding of mixed costs.

Check Your Learning

Write your answers to these questions on a sheet of notebook paper.

1. What are two examples of mixed costs?
2. John's water bill reads $10 per month plus $.01 per gallon. Why is John's cost a mixed cost?
3. Explain the following equation in your own words: TC = FC + (UVC × AL)

Compare your answers to those in the answers section. Reread the preceding part of the chapter to find the correct answers to any questions you may have missed.

Have students complete Exercise 23-3 at this point.

Summary of Key Points

1. Information about costs may be collected for different purposes and classified in different ways.
2. Cost behavior is used to classify costs.
3. Variable costs are costs that vary in direct proportion to an activity level.
4. As units of output increase, the variable cost assigned to each unit remains unchanged.
5. As units of output increase, the total variable cost also increases.
6. Fixed costs are costs that do not vary in direct proportion to an activity level.
7. As units of output increase, the fixed cost assigned to each unit decreases.
8. As units of output increase, the total fixed cost remains unchanged.
9. A fixed cost is fixed only within the relevant range.
10. Committed and discretionary fixed costs represent commitments that require large amounts of revenue and time to recover. Decisions regarding fixed cost commitments, therefore, must be made care fully.
11. Mixed costs are costs that cannot be explained by a single cost behavior pattern.
12. Mixed costs are part variable costs and part fixed costs.

23 Review and Applications

Building Your Accounting Vocabulary

In your own words, write the definition of each of the following accounting terms. Use complete sentences for your definitions.

committed fixed costs
cost behavior
discretionary fixed costs
fixed costs
high-low method
mixed costs
relevant range
variable costs

Reviewing Your Accounting Knowledge

1. Why is an owner or manager of a business concerned about cost behavior patterns?
2. What effect may a change in a business activity level have on costs?
3. Explain the equation TC = FC + VC.
4. What effect does an increase in output have on the total variable cost?
5. What effect does an increase in output have on the variable cost assigned to each unit produced?
6. What effect does an increase in output have on the total fixed cost?
7. What effect does an increase in output have on the fixed cost assigned to each unit produced?
8. Why should the owner or manager of a business be concerned about the relevant range of a fixed cost?
9. Why should the owner or manager of a business be concerned that some fixed costs can be either discretionary or committed?
10. How does an accountant know that cost data are mixed rather than fixed or variable?
11. Give an example of a variable cost, a fixed cost, and a mixed cost.

Improving Your Problem-Solving Skills

You are an accountant in the purchasing department of a construction company. When you got home from work on December 22, you found a large ham in a box marked "Happy Holidays! It's a pleasure to work with you." The gift is from a supplier who has bid on a contract your employer is going to award next week. What is the problem? How should you handle this situation?

Applying Accounting Procedures

Exercise 23-1 Identifying Cost Behavior

The following graphs show different cost behavior patterns in relation to units of output.

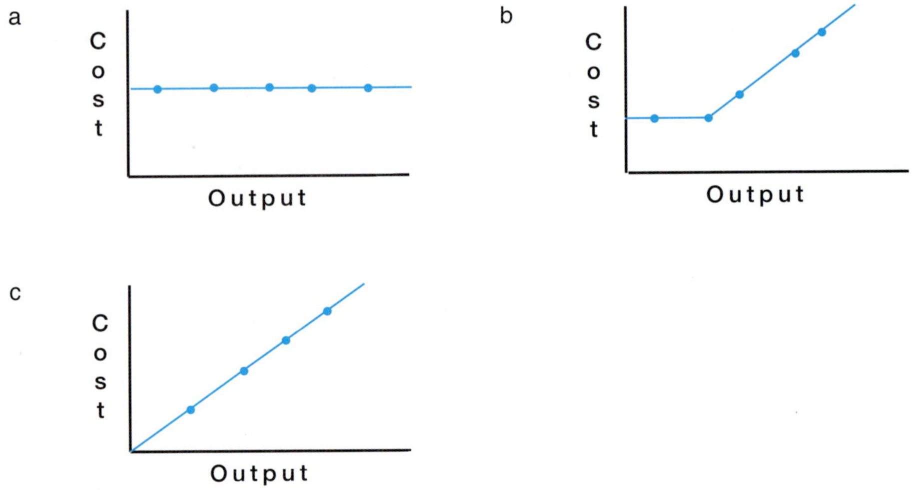

Figure 23-7 Graphs of Cost Behavior Patterns for Exercise 23-1

C
A
B

Instructions: Select the graph that best illustrates the behavior of the following costs: (1) variable costs, (2) fixed costs, (3) mixed costs.

Exercise 23-2 Calculating Variable and Fixed Costs

Instructions: Complete the following summary of cost information by filling in the missing amounts for each situation.

$260
$2.60
125
$25.00
80

	Variable Cost		
Situation	Units Produced	Unit Cost	Total Cost
1	100	$2.60	?
2	75	?	$195
3	?	$2.60	$325
4	25	?	$625
5	?	$5.25	$420

$300
$4.00
120

	Fixed Cost		
Situation	Units Produced	Unit Cost	Total Cost
1	100	$3.00	?
2	75	?	$300
3	?	$2.50	$300

Exercise 23-3 Using the High-Low Method

The owner of a small business wants to know the variable and fixed components of the labor costs for the year ended December 31.

VC, $4
FC, $100,000

Instructions: Using the high-low method, find the variable and fixed costs from the following data.

January—Low	$244,000 labor cost for 36,000 hours
June—High	$300,000 labor cost for 50,000 hours

Problem 23-1 Analyzing Cost Behavior

The Fayetteville Construction Company is concerned about its advertising costs. The advertising cost data for the last eight months shows a fixed advertising cost of $2,000 per month and a variable cost of $.02 per $1.00 of sales.

Instructions:

TC = FC + (UVC x AL)
$3,600
$42,000

(1) Write the cost equation used to determine the company's total monthly cost for advertising.
(2) Using the cost equation, estimate the total monthly cost for advertising if sales for May are projected to be $80,000.
(3) Using the cost equation, estimate the total annual cost for advertising if sales for the year are projected to be $900,000.

SPREADSHEET PROBLEM

Problem 23-2 Using the High-Low Method

The cost information for repairs on a small printing machine in the office of April Harris follows.

Repair No.	Machine Hours	Repair Cost
1	22	$25.50
2	23	26.00
3	19	24.00
4	12	20.50
5	7	18.00
6	9	19.00
7	11	20.00
8	14	21.50

Instructions:

$.50
$14.50

(1) Using the high-low method, calculate the unit variable cost.
(2) Using the total cost equation, calculate the fixed cost for each repair.

SPREADSHEET PROBLEM

Problem 23-3 Calculating Costs

During the past year, the Small-But-Quality Manufacturing Company collected the following cost data for manufacturing garden tools.

Month	Labor Hours	Manufacturing Costs
January	4,300	$26,000
February	4,500	27,000
March	3,000	19,500
April	3,700	23,000
May	4,000	24,500
June	5,500	32,000

Instructions:

$5
$4,500; $21,500
$29,500

(1) Using the high-low method, calculate the unit variable cost.
(2) Using the total cost equation, calculate the fixed costs and total variable costs for January.
(3) Estimate the total manufacturing costs for July if the company works 5,000 hours that month.

CHALLENGE PROBLEM

Problem 23-4 Analyzing Cost Data

Mary Evans wants to make and sell pottery. She asked her local CPA to estimate the cost of making one piece of pottery. Mary estimates she can produce 1,000 pieces of pottery each month. Assume a four-week month.

$12.45 **Instructions:** Using the following cost data, calculate the cost of one piece of pottery.

Variable costs per unit produced:	
Clay	$ 2.25
Paint	.50
Fixed cost per month:	
Depreciation on equipment	$200.00
Rent	600.00
Electric and gas	100.00
Mixed cost for wages:	
High week: 48 hours	$392.00
Low week: 40 hours	360.00

Each piece of pottery requires 2 hours of labor.

FOCUS ON
COMPUTERS

Decision Support Systems: The Edge of Profitability

Managers often use special computer support systems to increase profitability.

Decision support system (DSS) is a general name for special computer systems designed to help executives make better decisions. At their most basic level, these systems allow people to use interactive computer terminals to track and manipulate information. For example, an accountant can sit down at a terminal and find out which toy in a manufacturer's product line is the most profitable. If one toy line is a clear leader, production lines for other toys may be switched over to increase production.

Computer decision support systems also allow accountants and managers to play games of "what if." The computer can make projections of what would happen if various component combinations in an operation were changed. For example, would profits increase if sales prices were raised 10%? If manufacturing were automated? If shipments were made by truck instead of by rail? Some DSS programs allow users to input and manipulate dozens of variables and get an answer in seconds that would take a team of accountants a month to calculate.

Computer modeling is also part of a DSS. Some car manufacturers use computerized models to try out a product before creating it. For example, they create a model to anticipate how a car might perform. Similarly, airline engineers use DSSs to calculate maintenance schedules that will minimize ground time.

Critics of DSSs claim that these systems don't consider all the human factors involved in making decisions, and the resulting decisions will be only as complete as the data put into the program. For example, DSS data may indicate that it's a great idea to move a manufacturing plant to another state. If most of the employees are unwilling or unable to move, however, it's not such a good idea.

As in all computer applications, having lots of data doesn't necessarily mean that a good decision will result automatically. Good decisions depend on human reasoning and interpretative skills. A DSS merely provides more information in an organized manner, allowing executives to make decisions based on facts rather than on guesswork.

Chapter 24

COST-VOLUME-PROFIT RELATIONSHIPS

In Chapter 23, you learned that owners and managers are very interested in the way costs behave. They can perform many useful analyses with cost behavior information. To respond to their interest in cost behavior, accountants are expected to classify costs as either variable or fixed. Even when the behavior pattern is mixed, the owner or manager wants the accountant to separate each cost into variable or fixed components. In this chapter, you will learn that by classifying *all costs* as either fixed or variable, the owner or manager can analyze the relationships among costs, volume, and profits. Understanding these relationships is important when making business decisions about what to sell, what to produce, and what production facilities to use.

Learning Objectives

When you have completed this chapter, you should be able to do the following:

1. Explain the meaning of contribution margin and prepare a contribution income statement.
2. Calculate the contribution margin ratio.
3. Calculate the break-even point in units and dollars.
4. Calculate the target profit and margin of safety.
5. Apply C-V-P analysis to business decisions.
6. Define the accounting terms presented in this chapter.

New Terms

cost-volume-profit (C-V-P) analysis
contribution margin
contribution income statement
unit contribution margin
contribution margin ratio
break-even point
target profit
margin of safety
margin of safety ratio

Cost-Volume-Profit Relationships

Point out that C-V-P analysis is valid only for a single product and a single set of costs.

To understand the relationships among costs, volume, and profit, managers and owners use cost-volume-profit analysis. **Cost-volume-profit (C-V-P) analysis** uses costs to determine the effect of changes in volume on the profit that results. This analysis is useful for planning. For C-V-P analysis, all costs must be classified as either variable costs or fixed costs. To understand cost-volume-profit relationships, look at some new concepts: contribution margin, break-even point, and profit planning.

By analyzing costs, owners can make better decisions about what to sell, what to produce, and what facilities to use.

The Contribution Margin

Emphasize that the contribution margin is sales revenue minus all variable costs.

After all costs have been separated into their variable and fixed parts, the accountant can determine the contribution margin. In Chapter 18, you learned that contribution margin is the contribution that a given department makes to the net income of a business. In this chapter, we will expand the definition of **contribution margin** to include the contribution that a given product or department makes to paying for fixed costs and adding to the business's profit. The contribution margin is calculated by subtracting total variable costs from total revenues. The contribution margin is useful when trying to determine the impact of changes in sales, costs, and volume on profits.

Explain that the contribution income statement is a report based on cost behavior.

The Contribution Income Statement For internal reporting, the managerial accountant may decide to prepare an income statement that presents contribution margin information. On a **contribution income statement,** all selling, administrative, and manufacturing costs are classified as either fixed or variable costs. This format differs from that of a standard income statement that classifies costs by *function*—

selling, administrative, or manufacturing. The standard format is used for external reporting. Figure 24-1 presents a comparison between the standard income statement and the contribution income statement for a small manufacturing business.

Scott Motors, Inc.
Standard and Contribution Income Statements
For the Month Ended December 31, 199-

Standard Income Statement (for external reporting)			Contribution Income Statement (for internal reporting)		
Sales (200 motors)		$15,000	Sales (200 motors)		$15,000
Less: Cost of Goods Sold		9,000	Less Variable Costs:		
Gross Profit on Sales		$ 6,000	Manufacturing	$6,000	
Less Operating Expenses:			Administrative	1,800	
Administrative	$2,600		Selling	2,200	
Selling	2,900		Total Variable Costs		10,000
Total Operating Expenses		5,500	Contribution Margin		$ 5,000
			Less Fixed Costs:		
Net Income		$ 500	Manufacturing	$3,000	
			Administrative	800	
			Selling	700	
			Total Fixed Costs		4,500
			Net Income		$ 500

Figure 24-1 Comparison of Standard and Contribution Income Statements

As you study Figure 24-1, note that the total costs are the same on both statements. The amount of net income is also the same. The major difference between the two statements is in the format used for classifying and reporting costs and expenses. The standard format reports manufacturing costs as cost of goods sold ($9,000). The contribution format separates and reports manufacturing costs as variable and fixed ($6,000 + $3,000 = $9,000). If the variable and fixed administrative costs on the contribution statement are totaled, the total is the same as the amount of administrative expenses shown on the standard statement ($2,600). Also, the total of variable and fixed selling costs on the contribution statement equals the amount of selling expenses on the standard statement ($2,900). Note that the gross profit on sales and the contribution margin are different. Gross profit on sales is the difference between total revenues and cost of goods sold (manufacturing costs); the contribution margin is the difference between total revenues and total variable costs.

Have students complete Exercise 24-1 at this point.

R — E — M — E — M — B — E — R

The contribution margin is the difference between total revenues and total variable costs. A contribution income statement separates and lists all costs as either variable or fixed.

Before reading further, do the following activity to check your understanding of the material you have just studied.

Check Your Learning

Write your answers to these questions on a sheet of notebook paper.

1. Why are variable selling and administrative costs added to variable manufacturing costs when preparing a contribution income statement?
2. Why do a standard income statement and a contribution income statement report the same net income figure?
3. If a company has $27,000 sales, $12,500 total variable costs, and $2,000 total fixed costs, what is its contribution margin?

Compare your answers to those in the answers section. Reread the preceding part of the chapter to find the correct answers to any questions you may have missed.

Illustrate how the unit contribution margin is determined.

The Unit Contribution Margin To make cost-volume-profit analysis easier, the contribution margin is commonly expressed as a per-unit amount. The **unit contribution margin** is the difference between the unit selling price and the unit variable costs. The unit selling price, unit variable costs, and unit contribution margin are reported in a separate column on the contribution income statement, as illustrated in Figure 24-2. Two important facts can be learned from this contribution income statement. First, for a business to make a profit, the total contribution margin must exceed total fixed costs. Second, the total contribution margin is equal to the unit contribution margin multiplied by the sales volume.

Scott Motors, Inc.
Contribution Income Statement
For the Month Ended December 31, 199-

		Total	Unit
Sales (200 motors)		$15,000	$75
Less Variable Costs:			
Manufacturing	$6,000		
Administrative	1,800		
Selling	2,200		
Total Variable Costs		10,000	50
Contribution Margin		$ 5,000	$25
Less Fixed Costs:			
Manufacturing	$3,000		
Administrative	800		
Selling	700		
Total Fixed Costs		4,500	
Net Income		$ 500	

Figure 24-2 Contribution Income Statement with Unit Contribution Margin

Explain the use of "what if" questions.

By reviewing the contribution income statement shown in Figure 24-2, the accountant can reach some important conclusions as well as ask some important questions about the performance of the business. The total contribution margin of $5,000 is adequate to cover the total fixed costs of $4,500 and leave Scott Motors, Inc., a profit of $500. *What if* the total contribution margin is only $4,000? The $4,000 will not cover total fixed costs of $4,500; therefore, Scott Motors, Inc., will report a loss of $500.

The accountant may also use the unit contribution margin to analyze the performance of the business. The sale of 200 units with a unit contribution margin of $25 results in a total contribution margin of $5,000 (200 units × $25 = $5,000) and a profit of $500. *What if* only 185 units are sold? The total contribution margin will be $4,625 (185 units × $25 = $4,625). The $4,625 will be enough to cover the total fixed costs of $4,500 and give Scott Motors, Inc., a profit of $125. The proof follows:

Sales (185 × $75 unit selling price)	$13,875
Less: Variable costs (185 × $50 unit variable costs)	9,250
Contribution margin (185 × $25 unit contribution margin)	$ 4,625
Less: Fixed costs	4,500
Net income (loss)	$ 125

Discuss how the unit contribution margin is used to examine C-V-P relationships.

What if the sales volume falls to 150 units? The total contribution margin will be $3,750 (150 units×$25 = $3,750). The $3,750 will not be enough to cover the fixed costs of $4,500. Scott Motors, Inc., therefore, will report a loss of $750. The proof follows:

Sales (150 × $75 unit selling price)	$11,250
Less: Variable costs (150 × $50 unit variable costs)	7,500
Contribution margin (150 × $25 unit contribution margin)	$ 3,750
Less: Fixed costs	4,500
Net income (loss)	($ 750)

By using a contribution margin income statement and asking "what if" questions, the accountant is able to provide a clearer picture about the cost- volume-profit relationships for Scott Motors, Inc.

R — E — M — E — M — B — E — R

The unit contribution margin is the difference between the unit selling price and the unit variable costs. The total contribution margin is equal to the total units sold multiplied by the unit contribution margin.

The Contribution Margin Ratio In addition to stating selling prices, variable costs, and contribution margin in unit dollar amounts, the accountant can state the same information as percentages. The percentage of contribution margin to sales is called the **contribution margin ratio.** Using information from the income statement in Figure 24-2, the contribution margin ratio of 33.3% would be reported in the percentage column shown on the next page.

	Total	Unit	Percentage
Sales (200 motors)	$15,000	$75	100.0%
Less: Total variable costs	10,000	50	66.7%
Contribution margin	$ 5,000	$25	33.3%
Less: Total fixed costs	4,500		
Net income	$ 500		

Be sure students know how to calculate the contribution margin ratio.

The contribution margin ratio is calculated by dividing the amount of contribution margin, $5,000, by the amount of sales, $15,000. The 33.3% contribution margin ratio means that $.333 of every $1.00 of sales is available to pay fixed costs and earn a profit. Later in this chapter, you will learn how to use the contribution margin ratio to calculate cost-volume-profit relationships.

Before reading further, do the following activity to check your understanding of the material you have just studied.

Check Your Learning

Write your answers to these questions on a sheet of notebook paper.

1. Why are "what if" questions so important to accountants?
2. If the unit contribution margin is $34 and 400 units are sold, what is the total contribution margin?
3. If the total contribution margin is $7,500 and the unit contribution margin is $150, how many units must be sold to equal the total contribution margin?

Compare your answers to those in the answers section. Reread the preceding part of the chapter to find the correct answers to any questions you may have missed.

The Break-Even Point

Explain that the idea behind the break-even point is to determine the number of units that must be sold to generate a total contribution margin large enough to cover total fixed costs.

To predict the effect of changes in costs and sales volume on the business's profit, the accountant determines the break-even point. The **break-even point** is the point at which total revenues equal total costs. At the break-even point, there is neither a loss nor a profit. A break-even point may be computed for a single product, a group of products, or the entire business entity.

The Break-Even Equation Sales, fixed costs, and variable costs are used to determine the break-even point. The following equation illustrates what you learned about the contribution income statement:

*S*ales – *V*ariable *C*osts – *F*ixed *C*osts = *N*et *I*ncome

or

S – VC – FC = NI

The break-even equation is based on this equation. As you just learned, the break-even point is the point at which total revenues (sales) equal total costs (variable and fixed). There is neither net income nor a net loss. The break-even equation, therefore, is written as follows:

$$\textit{B}\text{reak-}\textit{E}\text{ven S} = \text{VC} + \text{FC}$$

or

$$\text{BES} = \text{VC} + \text{FC}$$

To illustrate the break-even equation, let's assume Scott Motors, Inc., plans to introduce a new small electric motor. The expected selling price is $125 per motor. The variable cost per motor is expected to be $85. Two new pieces of equipment with a total fixed cost of $12,000 will be required to build the motor. One of the first questions to ask is: How many motors will Scott Motors need to sell to break even?

Illustrate how the break-even equation is used to calculate the break-even point in units.

From the preceding information, we know the unit selling price (USP), the unit variable cost (UVC), and the total fixed costs. If we let X equal the number of units needed to break even, we can use the break-even equation to calculate the break-even point in units, as follows:

$$\begin{aligned}
\text{BES} &= \text{VC} + \text{FC} \\
&\text{or} \\
\text{USP(X)} &= \text{UVC(X)} + \text{FC} \\
\$125\text{X} &= \$85\text{X} + \$12{,}000 \\
\$125\text{X} - \$85\text{X} &= \$12{,}000 \\
\$40\text{X} &= \$12{,}000 \\
\text{X} &= \frac{\$12{,}000}{\$40} \\
\text{X} &= 300 \text{ units needed to break even} \\
300 \text{ units @ } \$125 &= \$37{,}500 \text{ sales needed to break even}
\end{aligned}$$

Scott Motors, Inc., must sell at least 300 of the new motors to break even. The proof of these calculations in the contribution income statement format follows:

	Total	Unit
Sales (300 × $125)	$37,500	$125
Less: Variable costs (300 × $85)	25,500	85
Contribution margin	12,000	$ 40
Less: Fixed costs	12,000	
Net income (loss)	0	

Review how the unit contribution margin is calculated.

Notice that the break-even equation calculates the unit contribution margin (unit selling price, $125, less unit variable cost, $85, equals unit contribution margin, $40). Total fixed costs, $12,000, are then divided by the unit contribution margin, $40, to determine the number of units needed to cover the fixed cost amount. You can see from these calculations that a quick way to determine the break-even point in units is to use the equation shown on the next page.

$$\textit{Break-Even Point} = \textit{Fixed Costs} \div \textit{Unit Contribution Margin}$$

or

$$\begin{aligned} BEP &= FC \div UCM \\ BEP &= \$12{,}000 \div \$40 \\ BEP &= 300 \text{ units} \end{aligned}$$

Point out that once the break-even point has been reached, profit will increase by the unit contribution for each additional unit sold.

Now let's examine some "what if" questions related to sales volume and profit. For example, if Scott Motors, Inc., will break even with sales of 300 units, how much profit or loss will it experience if its sell 302 units? At 300 units with a UCM of $40, Scott Motors will break even. Two more units sold, therefore, will contribute $80 (2 × $40 UCM) beyond the BEP, resulting in a profit of $80. The proof follows:

	Total	Unit
Sales (302 × $125)	$37,750	$125
Less: Variable costs (302 × $85)	25,670	85
Contribution margin	$12,080	$ 40
Less: Fixed costs	12,000	
Net income (loss)	$ 80	

What if Scott Motors, Inc., can sell only 280 new motors? It will break even at 300 units with a UCM of $40. Therefore, 20 fewer units sold will contribute $800 (20 × $40 UCM) less than needed to break even, resulting in a loss of $800. The proof follows:

	Total	Unit
Sales (280 × $125)	$35,000	$125
Less: Variable costs (280 × $85)	23,800	85
Contribution margin	$11,200	$ 40
Less: Fixed costs	12,000	
Net income (loss)	($ 800)	

R — E — M — E — M — B — E — R

The break-even point is the point at which total revenues equal total costs, resulting in neither a profit nor a loss.

Have students complete Exercise 24-2 at this point.

Review with students the equation used to calculate the contribution margin ratio.

Using the Contribution Margin Ratio to Calculate the Break-Even Point As you know, the contribution margin ratio is the percentage of contribution margin to sales. The contribution margin ratio for 300 motors sold by Scott Motors, Inc., is calculated by dividing the contribution margin, $12,000, by the amount of sales, $37,500. The 32% contribution ratio is reported as follows:

	Total	Unit	Percentage
Sales (300 × $125)	$37,500	$125	100%
Less: Variable costs (300 × $85)	25,500	85	68%
Contribution margin	$12,000	$ 40	32%
Less: Fixed costs	12,000		
Net income (loss)	0		

Illustrate how the contribution margin ratio is used to calculate the break-even point in dollars.

In the preceding illustration, the fixed cost amount is $12,000 and the contribution margin ratio is 32%. This information and the following equation are used to calculate the break-even point in sales dollars:

$$\text{Break-Even Sales} = \text{Fixed Cost} \div \text{Contribution Margin Ratio}$$

or

$$\begin{aligned} BES &= FC \div CMR \\ BES &= \$12{,}000 \div .32 \\ BES &= \$37{,}500 \end{aligned}$$

Use demonstration problem 24-1 here.

The 32% contribution margin ratio means that $.32 of every $1.00 of sales is available to pay fixed costs and earn a profit. For every $1.00 of sales beyond the break-even point, therefore, the company will increase its profit by $.32. For example, if the break-even point is $37,500 and sales are $38,000, the profit will be $160 ($500 × $.32 = $160).

R — E — M — E — M — B — E — R

The contribution margin ratio is the percentage of the contribution margin to sales.

Before reading further, do the following activity to check your understanding of the material you have just studied.

Check Your Learning

Write your answers to these questions on a sheet of notebook paper.

1. Write out the break-even equation.
2. If fixed costs are $12,000 and the unit contribution margin is $60, what is the break-even point in units?
3. If fixed costs are $18,000 and the contribution margin ratio is 40%, what is the break-even point in dollars?

Compare your answers to those in the answers section. Reread the preceding part of the chapter to find the correct answers to any questions you may have missed.

Profit Planning

Discuss the importance of the target profit to a business.

Part of the planning process for business managers is setting goals. One goal may be to increase the amount of net income or profit. The net income goal is called the **target profit** (also called *target net income*). *What if* the manager of Scott Motors, Inc., wants to earn a profit of $1,800 on the new motor? How many motors must the company sell to achieve this target profit? To answer this question, the accountant uses the general equation presented earlier in the chapter:

$$S - VC - FC = NI$$

or

$$S = VC + FC + NI$$

Show students how to calculate target sales in units and dollars.

As in the earlier example, the unit selling price (USP) is $125, the unit variable cost (UVC) is $85, and the total fixed cost is $12,000. The target profit of $1,800 will represent net income (NI) in the equation. If we let X equal the number of units needed to achieve the target profit, the amount of sales needed to achieve the target profit is calculated as follows:

$$\begin{aligned} USP(X) &= UVC(X) + FC + NI \\ \$125X &= \$85X + \$12{,}000 + \$1{,}800 \\ \$125X - \$85X &= \$12{,}000 + \$1{,}800 \\ \$40X &= \$13{,}800 \\ X &= \$13{,}800 \div \$40 \\ X &= 345 \text{ units} \\ 345 \text{ units @ } \$125 &= \$43{,}125 \text{ sales to earn } \$1{,}800 \text{ profit} \end{aligned}$$

The proof of this calculation is shown by inserting the amounts in the original equation. Total variable cost is $29,325 (345 × $85 = $29,325).

$$\begin{aligned} S &= VC + FC + NI \\ \$43{,}125 &= \$29{,}325 + \$12{,}000 + \$1{,}800 \end{aligned}$$

Have students complete Exercise 24-3 at this point.

Notice that when the general equation is used to calculate the target sales in units, the unit contribution margin is calculated (USP − UVC = UCM). You can quickly calculate the sales in units needed to achieve the target profit by adding the fixed costs to the target profit and dividing the total by the unit contribution margin. You can quickly calculate the sales in dollars needed to achieve the target profit by adding the fixed costs to the target profit and dividing the total by the contribution margin ratio.

R — E — M — E — M — B — E — R

When calculating target sales in units, the target profit is added to the fixed costs and the total is divided by the unit contribution margin. When calculating target sales in dollars, the target profit is added to the fixed costs and the total is divided by the contribution margin ratio.

When analyzing target sales and profits, the manager must consider what will happen if the amount targeted, or budgeted, is not reached. How far can sales drop before the business experiences a loss? For this analysis, the manager looks for the margin of safety. The **margin of safety** is the excess of target sales over break-even sales. The higher the margin of safety, the lower the risk of falling below the break-even point and experiencing a loss. Managers, therefore, look for a high margin of safety in their sales projections and budgets.

Explain that margin of safety is used as a judgment of risk: high margin—low risk or low margin—high risk.

Point out that margin of safety may be expressed in units or dollars or as a percentage.

Once again, let's use the example of the new motor Scott Motors, Inc., wants to manufacture. The accountant determined that sales of $37,500 are needed to break even and sales of $43,125 are needed to achieve the target profit of $1,800. The margin of safety, therefore, is $5,625 (target sales, $43,125, less break-even sales, $37,500, equals margin of safety, $5,625). This means that sales of the new motor can be $5,625 less than targeted before the company experiences a net loss. The margin of safety may also be expressed in units. For example, target sales, 345 units, less break-even sales, 300 units, equals margin of safety, 45 units. This means that sales can be 45 units less than targeted before the company experiences a loss.

Use demonstration problem 24-2 here.

Have students complete Exercise 24-4 at this point.

The margin of safety may also be stated as a percentage of target sales. The **margin of safety ratio** is calculated by dividing the margin of safety by the target sales. For the new motor, the margin of safety ratio is 13% ($5,625 ÷ $43,125 = 13%). This means that if sales fall more than 13%, the company will experience a loss. Since the margin of safety is small, the manager and owner of Scott Motors, Inc., will need to be very careful when making decisions to change any cost-volume-profit relationships.

Applying C-V-P Analysis

Now that you understand cost-volumne-profit relationships and have the basic tools needed to perform C-V-P analysis, let's look at some additional situations. In the following section, C-V-P analysis will be used to answer "what if" questions about plans that would change fixed costs, variable costs, the selling price, and sales.

ACCOUNTING *Notes*

Electronic spreadsheets are very helpful tools in "what if" analysis. Spreadsheets can quickly and automatically recalculate all amounts when any one number changes. Managers can use spreadsheets to see the effects of changes on the business.

The following data for electric motor number 437 manufactured by Scott Motors, Inc., will be used for the analysis:

	Total	Unit	Percentage
Sales (6,000 units)	$1,050,000	$175	100%
Less: Variable costs	630,000	105	60%
Contribution margin	$ 420,000	$ 70	40%
Less: Fixed costs	350,000		
Net income	$ 70,000		

BEP in units = 5,000 ($350,000 ÷ $70)
BEP in sales dollars = $875,000 ($350,000 ÷ 40%)

Using the preceding information, let's look at some changes Scott Motors might consider when planning the future production and sales of motor number 437.

Changing Fixed Costs

Question: What will happen to the break-even point if a supervisor with an annual salary of $22,750 is added to the production line for motor number 437?

Analysis:

1. Determine the new amount of fixed costs.

$350,000 + $22,750 = $372,750 fixed costs

2. Determine the new break-even point in units and in dollars.

Explain that an increase in total fixed costs will result in an increase in the break-even point.

$372,750 ÷ $70 = 5,325 units needed to break even = an increase of 325 units (5,325 units – 5,000 units = 325 units)
$372,750 ÷ 40% = $931,875 in sales needed to break even = an increase of $56,875 in sales ($931,875 – $875,000 = $56,875)

Answer: To break even if a new supervisor is added, the company must sell 325 more units, thus increasing break-even sales by $56,875.

R — E — M — E — M — B — E — R

To break even if fixed costs increase, more sales are needed to cover the additional fixed costs. To break even if fixed costs decrease, fewer sales are needed to cover the lower fixed costs.

Changing Variable Costs

Question: What will happen to the break-even point if a better quality of material that costs $10 per unit more is used for motor number 437?

Analysis:

1. Determine the new amount of unit variable costs.

$105 + $10 = $115 unit variable costs

2. Determine the new unit contribution margin and contribution margin ratio.

$175 – $115 = $60 unit contribution margin

$60 ÷ $175 = 34% contribution margin ratio

3. Determine the new break-even point in units and in dollars.

$350,000 ÷ $60 = 5,834 units needed to break even = an increase of 834 units (5,834 units – 5,000 units = 834 units)
$350,000 ÷ 34% = $1,029,412 in sales needed to break even = an increase of $154,412 in sales ($1,029,412 – $875,000 = $154,412)

Explain that an increase in the unit variable cost leads to a decline in the unit contribution margin and an increase in the break-even point.

Note that some amounts were rounded to simplify calculations.

Answer: To break even if a higher-quality material is used, the company must sell 834 more units, thus increasing break-even sales by $154,412.

R — E — M — E — M — B — E — R

To break even if variable costs increase, more sales are needed because each unit contributes less. To break even if variable costs decrease, fewer sales are needed because each unit contributes more.

Changing the Selling Price

Question: What will happen to the break-even point if the selling price of motor number 437 is increased to $180?

Analysis:

1. Determine the new unit contribution margin and contribution margin ratio.

$180 – $105 = $75 unit contribution margin
$75 ÷ $180 = 42% contribution margin ratio

2. Determine the new break-even point in units and in dollars.

$350,000 ÷ $75 = 4,667 units needed to break even = a decrease of 333 units (5,000 units – 4,667 units = 333 units)
$350,000 ÷ 42% = $833,333 in sales needed to break even = a decrease of $41,667 in sales ($875,000 – $833,333 = $41,667)

Note that some amounts were rounded to simplify calculations.

Explain that an increase in the selling price will raise the contribution margin and decrease the break-even point.

Answer: To break even if the selling price is increased, the company can sell 333 fewer units, thus decreasing break-even sales by $41,667. The manager and owner must be very careful when deciding to increase the selling price. Customers may be unwilling to pay the additional amount, thus reducing the sales volume more than 333 units and creating a loss.

R—E—M—E—M—B—E—R

To break even if the selling price increases, fewer sales are needed because each unit contributes more. To break even if the selling price decreases, more sales are needed because each unit contributes less.

Before reading further, do the following activity to check your understanding of the material you have just studied.

Check Your Learning

Write your answers to these questions on a sheet of notebook paper.

1. What is the equation for calculating target profit?
2. What is meant by a margin of safety ratio of 25%?
3. What happens to the break-even point when fixed costs are increased?
4. What happens to the break-even point when variable costs are increased?
5. What happens to the break-even point when the selling price is increased?

Compare your answers to those in the answers section. Reread the preceding part of the chapter to find the correct answers to any questions you may have missed.

Use demonstration problem 24-3 here.

Changing Fixed Costs, Resulting in an Increase in Sales

Question: What will happen to profits if the advertising budget for motor number 437 is increased by $20,000, resulting in an increase in sales of 350 units?

Analysis:

1. Determine the new total sales amount.

$$6{,}000 + 350 = 6{,}350 \text{ units} \times \$175 = \$1{,}111{,}250$$

2. Determine the new total variable costs.

$$6{,}350 \text{ units} \times \$105 = \$666{,}750$$

3. Determine the new contribution margin.

$$\$1{,}111{,}250 - \$666{,}750 = \$444{,}500$$

4. Determine the new fixed costs.

$$\$350{,}000 + \$20{,}000 = \$370{,}000$$

5. Determine the new net income.

$$\$444{,}500 \text{ CM} - \$370{,}000 \text{ FC} = \$74{,}500 \text{ NI} = \text{an increase of } \$4{,}500$$
$$(\$74{,}500 - \$70{,}000 = \$4{,}500)$$

Emphasize that the increase in the contribution margin must be large enough to cover the increase in fixed costs before profits will increase.

Answer: The $20,000 increase in the fixed cost advertising budget will result in a $61,250 increase in sales and a $24,500 increase in the contribution margin. The increase in the contribution margin will offset the increase in fixed costs, resulting in a $4,500 increase in profits. Based on the C-V-P analysis, the change in the advertising budget should be approved.

Changing Variable Costs, Resulting in an Increase in Sales

Question: What will happen to profits if a better quality of material is used for motor number 437 that costs $5 more per motor, resulting in an increase in sales of 500 units?

Analysis:

1. Determine the new total sales amount.

$$6{,}000 + 500 = 6{,}500 \text{ units} \times \$175 = \$1{,}137{,}500$$

2. Determine the new unit and total variable costs.

$$\$105 + \$5 = \$110 \text{ UVC} \times 6{,}500 \text{ units} = \$715{,}000 \text{ TVC}$$

3. Determine the new unit and total contribution margins.

$$\$175 - \$110 = \$65 \text{ UCM} \times 6{,}500 \text{ units} = \$422{,}500 \text{ TCM}$$

4. Determine the new net income.

$422,500 CM – $350,000 FC = $72,500 NI = an increase of $2,500
($72,500 – $70,000 = $2,500)

Answer: The C-V-P analysis demonstrates that an increase in material costs of $5 per unit will result in a reduced unit contribution margin. The projected increase in sales based on a better-quality product, however, should actually increase profits by $2,500. The increase in profits, along with the increase in the quality of the product, supports a decision to go forward with this plan.

Emphasize that the increase in sales must be large enough to cover the decrease in unit contribution margin before profits will increase.

Changing Selling Price, Resulting in a Decrease in Sales

Question: What will happen to profits if the selling price of motor number 437 is increased by $5 per unit, resulting in a decrease in sales of 10%?

Analysis:

1. Determine the new selling price.

$175 + $5 = $180

2. Determine the new sales amount.

6,000 units × 10% = 600 units
6,000 – 600 = 5,400 units × $180 = $972,000

3. Determine the new unit and total contribution margins.

$180 – $105 = $75 UCM × 5,400 units = $405,000 TCM

4. Determine the new net income.

$405,000 CM – $350,000 FC = $55,000 NI = a decrease of $15,000
($70,000 – $55,000 = $15,000)

Answer: If increasing the selling price by $5 results in a decrease in sales of 600 units, profits will decrease by $15,000. The C-V-P analysis, therefore, shows that the selling price should not be increased.

Point out that an increase in the selling price may reduce the sales volume, resulting in a decrease in total contribution margin and profit.

R — E — M — E — M — B — E — R

A change in one component in the C-V-P relationship usually results in a change in another C-V-P component.

Summary of Key Points

1. Business owners and managers use cost-volume-profit analysis to relate activity levels to changing costs and profits.

2. The contribution margin is determined by subtracting total variable costs from total revenues.
3. The contribution income statement reports all costs as either fixed or variable and is used for internal reporting.
4. The unit contribution margin is the difference between the unit selling price and the unit variable costs.
5. The percentage of the contribution margin to sales is called the contribution margin ratio.
6. The break-even point is the point at which total revenues equal total costs, resulting in neither a profit nor a loss.
7. The target profit is the net income goal established by the manager.
8. The margin of safety measures the difference between the budgeted sales and the break-even sales.
9. The break-even point will change if fixed costs, variable costs, and the selling price change.

24 Review and Applications

Building Your Accounting Vocabulary

In your own words, write the definition of each of the following terms. Use complete sentences for your definitions.

- break-even point
- contribution income statement
- contribution margin
- contribution margin ratio
- cost-volume-profit (C-V-P) analysis
- margin of safety
- margin of safety ratio
- target profit
- unit contribution margin

Reviewing Your Accounting Knowledge

1. How must costs be classified for C-V-P analysis?
2. How does a contribution income statement differ from a standard income statement?
3. How does the contribution margin differ from the gross profit on sales?
4. How does the contribution margin ratio differ from the unit contribution margin?
5. The break-even point can be calculated using the unit contribution margin or the contribution margin ratio. How do the results differ?
6. Why is a target profit important in C-V-P analysis?
7. What does it mean when the the margin of safety for a product is $6,500?
8. What does it mean when the margin of safety ratio for a product is 25%?
9. The managerial accountant uses C-V-P analysis to look into the future. Explain.
10. What will happen to the break-even point in each of the following situations?
    a. Fixed costs increase.
    b. The selling price decreases.
    c. Variable costs decrease.

Improving Your Math Skills

When you reduce the selling price of an item, the reduction is called a *markdown*. The *markdown rate* is expressed as a percentage of the regular selling price of the item. Calculate the amount of the markdown and the sale price for each of the following items.

1. Luggage, regular price $110.00, markdown 55%
2. Table lamp, regular price $69.99, markdown 36%
3. Bookcase, regular price $239.95, markdown 17%
4. Answering machine, regular price $79.99, markdown 20%
5. Hair dryer, regular price $18.99, markdown 25%

Applying Accounting Procedures

Exercise 24-1 Preparing a Contribution Income Statement

The following revenue and cost data are from the records of the Martin Bird House Company.

Sales	$11,000
Variable manufacturing costs	4,000
Variable administrative costs	750
Variable selling costs	1,200
Fixed manufacturing costs	2,000
Fixed administrative costs	1,000
Fixed selling costs	300

CM, $5,050
FC, $3,300
Net income, $1,750

Instructions: Prepare a contribution income statement for the month ended May 31, 199-.

SPREADSHEET PROBLEM

Exercise 24-2 Calculating Break-Even Point

Product number 2398 sells for $2.00 per unit, has unit variable costs of $1.50, and has fixed costs of $6,000.00.

12,000;
$24,000

Instructions: Calculate the break-even point in units and in dollars.

SPREADSHEET PROBLEM

Exercise 24-3 Calculating Contribution Margin Ratio, Break-Even Point, and Target Sales

The Davis Company manufactures and sells an adjustable computer table that sells for $150 per unit and has unit variable costs of $30. Fixed costs for this computer table are $120,000 per year.

Instructions: Answer the following questions.

80%
$150,000
1,000
1,375

1. What is the contribution margin ratio?
2. What is the break-even point in dollars?
3. What is the break-even point in units?
4. How many units must the company sell to make a target profit of $45,000?

Exercise 24-4 Calculating Break-Even Point and Margin of Safety

The following contribution income statement shows the projected revenue and cost data for Lou's Pizza House for the coming year.

Lou's Pizza House
Contribution Income Statement
Projected for 199-

Sales (25,000 units)	$200,000
Less: Variable Costs	120,000
Contribution Margin	$ 80,000
Less: Fixed Costs	57,600
Net Income	$ 22,400

Instructions:

18,000; $144,000 (1) Calculate the break-even point in units and in dollars.
28% (2) Calculate the margin of safety ratio.

Problem 24-1 Calculating Break-Even Point, Target Sales, and Margin of Safety

The SurfBoard Company, owned and operated by Mary Willis, produces a surfboard that sells for $150. The board requires a variable cost of $105 per unit to produce and fixed costs of $459,000. Willis wants to earn $25,000 profit from the sales of the surfboard.

Instructions:

10,200; $1,530,000 (1) Calculate the break-even point in units and in dollars.
10,756; $1,613,400 (2) Calculate the amount of unit and dollar sales required to reach the target profit.
$83,400 (3) Calculate the margin of safety in dollars.

SPREADSHEET PROBLEM

Problem 24-2 Analyzing Changes in Variable Costs and Sales

Robert Macks sells 400 dictionaries per month at a price of $25.00 each. Currently he pays $15.00 per dictionary but believes he can buy a new dictionary at $12.50. The selling price of the new dictionary will remain $25.00. However, he expects sales to fall by about 50 dictionaries per month because of the reduced quality of the new dictionary. His monthly fixed costs will not change.

Instructions: Should Macks buy and sell the $12.50 dictionary? Why or why not?

SPREADSHEET PROBLEM

Problem 24-3 Analyzing Changes in Fixed Costs, Selling Price, and Sales

Assume the same information as in Problem 24-2. Now Robert Macks is considering reducing the price of the dictionary by $2 and increasing his advertising budget by $1,000. He expects that doing so will increase sales by 100 units.

Instructions: If Macks makes these changes, will he be making a good decision or a bad decision? Why?

SPREADSHEET PROBLEM

Problem 24-4 Analyzing Changes in Variable Costs, Fixed Costs, and Sales

Assume the same information as in Problem 24-2. Now Robert Macks believes that if he hires a part-time salesperson at $7,500 a year, he can double his sales of dictionaries from 400 to 800 units per month. The increase in volume would allow him to buy dictionaries at $12 rather than $15. The selling price would remain at $25 per unit.

Instructions: Do you agree or disagree with Robert Macks's reasoning? Why?

Problem 24-5 Identifying C-V-P Relationships

Instructions: Fill in the missing amounts in the following cost and price information.

$54
$40,000
$60,000

	Situation (1)	Situation (2)	Situation (3)
Unit selling price	$ 20	$ 70	$ 50
Unit variable costs	13	?	34
Fixed costs	80,000	30,000	?
Target profit	?	10,000	12,000
Target unit sales	20,000	2,500	3,250

CHALLENGE PROBLEM

Problem 24-6 Applying C-V-P Analysis

Roberta Smith owns a sandwich shop that sells about ten different sandwiches at the same price. Smith is an absentee owner, so she pays the sandwich clerk a commission per sandwich sold plus an annual salary. The following cost and revenue data are available from the owner.

Selling price per sandwich		$ 3.95
Variable costs:		
Ingredients		$ 2.00
Commission per sandwich		.25
Fixed costs:		
Advertising	$ 1,250	
Shop rent	7,700	
Salary	$14,000	

Instructions: Answer the following questions.

13,500; $53,325
$2,550
Yes, profits increase.
Yes, profits increase.

1. Calculate the break-even point in units and in dollars.
2. If the shop is open 6 days a week for 50 weeks each year and sells an average of 50 sandwiches a day, how much profit or loss will Roberta Smith report for the year?
3. Smith is considering paying the sandwich clerk an additional $.10 per sandwich for each sandwich sold beyond the current break-even point. She believes this new incentive will increase sales by 10 sandwiches per week. Should Smith pay the $.10? Why or why not?
4. Ms. Smith is considering increasing the annual salary level to $16,000 and doing away with all commissions. Do you think she should? Why or why not?

FOCUS ON
COMPUTERS

Electronic Spreadsheets Open a Window to Business Opportunities

By using electronic spreadsheets, business owners can track data and make informed decisions.

Spreadsheets, reference tables that systematically arrange data in rows and columns, are widely used by businesses and individuals. Spreadsheets allow people to keep track of data such as bank statements, budgets, tax records, profit-loss statements, expense diaries, payroll records, strategic plans, scientific tabulations, and inventory control records. Spreadsheets that can be produced on a computer have become very valuable.

Consider the hard tasks a restaurant owner faces at least once a year. The owner must figure out the price structure for the coming year. First, she prepares a cost analysis by listing on a spreadsheet her various expense categories: projected wholesale prices; percentage of fixed overhead, including equipment and property depreciation, insurance, utilities, and maintenance; finance charges; operating costs; projected sales volume; taxes; profit margin; and any other cost-affecting variables. Next, she looks through her books for the figures and pencils them in. Then come long hours of manually calculating the data. If she finds, after doing the calculations, that the figures come out too high, the owner must experiment with alternatives. When changing just one variable, she must recalculate all of the figures on the spreadsheet.

Enter electronic spreadsheeting—the use of an almost unlimited work sheet that allows the user to enter data, calculate it, and change it with just a few keystrokes. Once the data are entered, the computer performs all the calculations. "What if" scenarios become painless. When one cell in the spreadsheet is changed, the program automatically adjusts the other figures. Instead of spending time recalculating all the figures, the restaurant owner can consider which of the possible scenarios to implement.

Electronic spreadsheeting gives businesspeople more than answers; it gives them a range of options that allow informed decision making.

Chapter 25

USING COST DATA FOR PRICING DECISIONS

In the last two chapters, you learned about the ways in which costs behave. Owners or managers classify costs on the basis of behavior. They can then compare costs that vary with a particular activity level with costs that do not vary. You also learned about managerial decisions based on the relationships among cost, volume, and profit.

In this chapter, you will learn about one of the most important decisions a manager or owner must make—the pricing decision. The manager or owner must decide what the selling price should be for a product or service the business sells. When making pricing decisions, owners and managers must always consider costs, economic conditions, and competition.

Learning Objectives

When you have completed this chapter, you should be able to do the following:

1. Explain some of the influences on pricing decisions.
2. Calculate product price based on four cost-plus pricing methods.
3. Calculate service price based on labor and materials pricing.
4. Define the accounting terms presented in this chapter.

New Terms

pricing
cost-plus pricing
product cost-plus
full cost-plus
standard cost-plus
cost variance
variable cost-plus
billing rate for labor
materials loading charge

Major Influences on Pricing

Remind students that cost is a key factor in pricing decisions but not the only factor.

Almost all the situations you have studied in this textbook thus far have dealt with understanding and recording costs, expenses, and revenues. In this chapter, you will be concerned with the pricing decisions for the products and services provided by a business. **Pricing** means assigning a selling price to a product or service. Decisions regarding the prices to be charged for a product or service are complex. They involve factors such as costs, target profit, type of product or service, government regulations, and competitors' actions.

Point out that some products have price elasticity; that is, the sales price greatly affects sales volume.

Remind students that when fixed costs are high, the firm may be "locked in" for a long period of time and not enjoy much pricing flexibility.

A manager must always examine pricing problems through the eyes of the customer. A manager must have an understanding of what the customer is willing to pay. If the selling price is too high, the customer will not buy the product or service. Reactions by competitors also will influence the selling price. If a competitor lowers the selling price, the customer will probably buy the product or service from the competitor. Of course, product or service costs and the target profit have the greatest influence on the price charged. If the selling price is not high enough to cover costs, the business will not make a profit and may suffer a loss. In general, the selling price must be high enough to (1) cover the costs of buying or manufacturing the product, (2) cover the operating expenses of the business, and (3) provide a net profit. The price must be high enough for the business to continue in operations but low enough to meet the competition and attract customers.

Some managers or owners may not face a pricing challenge. For example, a farmer may not have to make a pricing decision at all. The selling price of farm products is usually dictated by the market or by the government. All corn and beans may sell at the same national or international price per bushel. The farmer, therefore, will not make a pricing decision

Prices paid by consumers are based on production costs, economics, and analyses of the competition.

but will make a decision about what and how much to plant each year.

Other examples of businesses that may not have to make pricing decisions are hospitals and utility companies. The selling prices of their products and services may be set by a federal or state agency. Prices set by governmental agencies make up a very long list. Although farmers and managers of these other businesses may not have to make pricing decisions, many other types of businesses must. The methods of pricing presented in this chapter are commonly used by owners and managers to make their pricing decisions regardless of business size.

Common Pricing Methods

Pricing decisions are approached in a number of ways. Owners or managers typically select from among the commonly used pricing methods the one they believe will work best for their situation. In this chapter, you will learn about the following pricing methods:

1. Cost-plus pricing
   a. Product cost-plus
   b. Full cost-plus
   c. Standard cost-plus
   d. Variable cost-plus
2. Labor and materials pricing

Cost-Plus Pricing

Explain that prices calculated using cost-plus methods are target prices. Actual prices may be lower or higher depending on the market.

Cost-plus pricing is widely used because it is easy to explain and to understand. In **cost-plus pricing**, a dollar amount or a percentage of the cost is added to the base cost to arrive at the selling price. As you learned in Chapter 5, this added amount is referred to as the *markup*. Let's see how a selling price is established by adding a markup to product cost, full cost, standard cost, and variable cost.

Product Cost-Plus One of the most commonly used methods of calculating a selling price is to add a markup to the product cost. This pricing method is called **product cost-plus**. Product cost-plus pricing may be used for either purchased products or manufactured products.

When a retail business buys merchandise for resale, the invoice purchase price (cost) is the product cost. For example, the Speedy Bicycle Shop prices all bicycles based on invoice purchase cost plus a 40% to 50% markup. The markup percentage must be large enough to cover the administrative and selling expenses and provide a reasonable profit. The following price list illustrates cost-plus pricing of purchased products:

Speedy Bicycle Shop
Price List

Model No.	Purchase Cost	Markup %	Markup $	Selling Price
7375-A	$477.80	40% =	$191.12	$668.92
7374-B	637.70	40% =	255.08	892.78
7575-C	321.95	45% =	144.88	466.83
7655-D	235.50	50% =	117.75	353.25

Review the calculations to determine the markup and selling price.

The selling price for each model was calculated as shown below for Model 7375-A using the product cost-plus method of pricing:

Purchase cost	$477.80
+ Markup (.40 × $477.80)	+191.12
Selling price	$668.92

Discuss the differences between the product cost-plus pricing used by a retail business and a manufacturing business.

Product cost-plus pricing may also be used for a product that has been manufactured rather than purchased. Since there is no invoice purchase price for the product, the unit manufacturing cost is used as the product cost for pricing. The following illustration shows how Alex Chairs, Inc., a manufacturer of plastic chairs, determines the unit manufacturing cost for Model 7454-C:

	Total Manufacturing Costs	Units Produced	Unit Manufacturing Costs
Direct materials	$29,725	1,250	$23.78
Direct labor	13,850	1,250	11.08
Overhead applied	13,350	1,250	10.68
Total	$56,925	1,250	$45.54

Note that selling and administrative costs are not included in the cost base.

The pricing of Model 7454-C is based on the unit manufacturing cost plus a 40% markup. Administrative and selling costs are not included in the manufacturing costs. The markup, therefore, must be large enough to cover these operating costs and provide a reasonable profit. Using the product cost-plus method of pricing, the selling price for Model 7454-C is calculated as follows:

Manufacturing cost	$45.54
+ Markup (.40 × $45.54)	+18.22
Selling price	$63.76

Assuming Alex Chairs, Inc., expects to incur $14,452.59 in administrative and selling costs to sell 1,250 units of Model 7454-C, the *projected* or target profit would be $8,322.41, as follows:

Alex Chairs, Inc.
Projected Net Income for
Model No. 7454-C

Sales (1,250 @ $63.76)	$79,700.00
Less: Cost of goods sold (1,250 @ $45.54)	56,925.00
Gross profit on sales	22,775.00
Less: Selling and administrative expenses	14,452.59
Net income (estimated)	$ 8,322.41

Use demonstration problems 25-1 and 25-2 here.

Markup percentages should be reviewed as economic and business conditions change. The owner, manager, and accountant must all stay alert to changing cost-volume-profit relationships.

R — E — M — E — M — B — E — R

When a business uses the product cost-plus pricing method, the markup must be large enough to cover all administrative and selling costs and provide a profit.

Before reading further, do the following activity to check your understanding of the material you have just studied.

Check Your Learning

Write your answers to these questions on a sheet of notebook paper.

1. If a retailer pays $345.78 to purchase a product for resale and adds a 45% markup based on the purchase cost, what is the selling price?
2. If a manufacturer incurs costs of $12,000 for direct materials, $10,000 for direct labor, and $8,500 for applied overhead to make 125 water pumps, what is the unit manufacturing cost? If a 60% markup is added based on the manufacturing cost, what is the selling price of the product?

Compare your answers to those in the answers section. Reread the preceding part of the chapter to find the correct answers to any questions you may have missed.

Have students complete Exercises 25-1 and 25-2 at this point.

Full Cost-Plus

Full cost-plus combines the product cost with the operating costs associated with the product to establish a full or total cost base. Then a markup is added to the full cost to provide a reasonable profit. The full cost-plus approach is a popular pricing method used for government contracts. This is because the government frequently purchases new products, such as tanks and jet fighters, for which there is no other market. The purpose of the full cost-plus method is to provide a fair price for the government and a fair profit for the manufacturer. The full cost-plus method allows the contractor to bill for full cost plus a reasonable profit.

Discuss why the full cost-plus pricing method is used for govenment contracts.

One of the greatest difficulties the manufacturer and government face is the determination of the full cost of the special product. Which costs incurred by the business were incurred for the special government contract, and how were the costs allocated? The government provides special and complex rules and procedures that the manufacturer must follow in pricing a full cost-plus product.

Let's assume the government has issued a contract for 200 small patrol boats. The contract (selling) price includes a markup that is 11% of the full cost. This 11% is the allowance for a reasonable profit. The contract also states that full cost means product manufacturing costs plus 25% of operating costs (nonmanufacturing costs). Using the full cost-plus method, the contract price would be determined as follows:

Be sure students understand how to allocate operating costs and determine the profit allowance.

Estimated Costs for Contract No. 23456-B-67

Product manufacturing costs:	
Direct materials	$ 45,989.00
Direct labor	45,678.25
Factory overhead applied	65,789.90
Total product manufacturing costs	$157,457.15
Operating costs (nonmanufacturing)	$987,989.00

Calculating the Contract Price

Product manufacturing costs	$157,457.15
+ Allocated operating costs (.25 × $987,989)	246,997.25
Full cost	$404,454.40
+ Profit allowance (.11 × $404,454.40)	44,489.98
Total contract price	$448,944.38

Use demonstration problem 25-3 here.

Since the contract is for 200 small patrol boats, the contract price per boat is $2,244.72 ($448,944.38 ÷ 200).

R — E — M — E — M — B — E — R

When a business uses the full cost-plus pricing method, the price is set at product cost plus allocated operating costs plus a markup for profit.

Before reading further, do the following activity to check your understanding of the material you have just studied.

Check Your Learning

Write your answers to these questions on a sheet of notebook paper.

A manufacturer estimated the following costs to produce 75 motors on a government contract.

Direct materials	$34,890.00
Direct labor	25,678.90
Factory overhead applied	8,756.00
Operating costs (nonmanufacturing)	13,432.78

The contract states that the profit allowance is 8% of the full cost. It also states that full cost means product manufacturing costs plus 30% of nonmanufacturing operating costs.

1. What is the amount of profit the company will earn from this contract?
2. What is the contract price for one motor?

Compare your answers to those in the answers section. Reread the preceding part of the chapter to find the correct answers to any questions you may have missed.

Standard Cost-Plus You just learned that when the full cost-plus method is used, the profit allowance is based on a percentage of product manufacturing costs plus allocated operating costs. When manufacturing costs increase, profits increase. Because of this situation, the manufacturing company may not be concerned about operating efficiently and trying to cut manufacturing costs. The company can pass along the excess manufacturing costs and be rewarded with a higher profit. To help guard against rewarding inefficient manufacturing operations, the standard cost-plus method of pricing is used.

Discuss the concept of standard costs and the standard cost-plus method of pricing.

Standard cost-plus uses predetermined costs for direct labor, direct materials, and factory overhead as the basis for pricing. The standard cost-plus method allows the manufacturer to bill for the total standard costs plus a reasonable profit. The standard costs are established in cooperation with management and manufacturing and represent appropriate costs for the industry. Standard costs are difficult to establish for new products for which there is no historical cost data.

Point out the difference between standard costs and actual costs and the reason for determining cost variances.

When the standard cost-plus method is used, the actual manufacturing costs are compared with the standard costs to determine how efficient the manufacturing process has been. The difference between a standard cost and an actual cost is called a **cost variance.** The cost variance is *favorable* if the actual cost is lower than the standard cost. If the actual cost is higher than the standard cost, the variance is *unfavorable*. Frequent unfavorable cost variances would point out areas of inefficient operation that need to be corrected. The variances, however, might also indicate a standard cost that is inappropriate and should be changed. Variances are not added to or deducted from the cost base unless the standards need to be changed.

The following illustration shows how the price of one unit of Model 3456 is calculated using the standard cost-plus method and a 40% profit allowance. The favorable and unfavorable cost variances are also shown.

	Standard Cost	Actual Cost	Variance from Standard
Direct materials	$25.00	$24.50	–$ .50 F
Direct labor	12.50	13.75	+ 1.25 U
Overhead applied	9.00	9.25	+ .25 U
Total	$46.50	$47.50	+$1.00 U

Standard cost	$46.50
+ Profit allowance (.40 × $46.50)	+18.60
Unit price	$65.10

If the unit price is figured using the actual cost plus an allowance for a profit, the calculations appears as follows:

Actual cost	$47.50
+ Profit allowance (.40 × $47.50)	+19.00
Unit price	$66.50

Use demonstration problem 25-4 here.

If the actual costs were used, the manufacturer would pass along the $1.40-per-unit higher cost. This higher price could make a substantial difference as the number of units contracted increases.

R — E — M — E — M — B — E — R

When the standard cost-plus pricing method is used, the cost variances do not affect the base used for pricing unless the standard is determined to be inappropriate and is changed.

Be sure students understand that the variable cost-plus pricing method uses just the variable costs assigned to the product as the base for pricing.

Emphasize the differences between this method and the product cost-plus method.

Variable Cost-Plus

Variable cost-plus uses only the variable costs assigned to the product as the base for pricing. The cost base is made up of the variable manufacturing, administrative, and selling costs. The variable costs plus the markup establish the selling price. The markup must be large enough to cover fixed costs and provide a reasonable profit.

Suppose Alex Chairs, Inc., calculates the base cost of Model 7454-C using the variable cost-plus method rather than the product cost-plus method. Let's begin by using the manufacturing cost data presented in the product cost-plus illustration shown below. The same amounts are used because direct materials and direct labor are variable costs. The variable parts of factory overhead and administrative and selling costs must be separated from their fixed components. When this is done, the total and unit variable costs for Model 7454-C will appear as follows:

	Total Variable Costs	Units Produced	Unit Variable Costs
Direct materials	$29,725.00	1,250	$23.78
Direct labor	13,850.00	1,250	11.08
Overhead applied	3,350.00	1,250	2.68
Administrative and selling costs	2,887.50	1,250	2.31
Total	$49,812.50	1,250	$39.85

Let's assume the pricing of Model 7454-C is based on the unit variable cost plus a 60% markup. The fixed costs of $21,565.09 are not included in the unit variable cost. The markup, therefore, must be large enough to cover the fixed costs and provide a reasonable profit. Using the variable cost-plus pricing method, the selling price for Model 7454-C is calculated as follows:

Variable costs	$39.85
+ Markup (.60 × $39.85)	+23.91
Selling price	$63.76

The projected net income generated from the sale of 1,250 Model 7454-C chairs at the $63.76 unit selling price follows:

Alex Chairs, Inc.
Projected Net Income for
Model No. 7454-C

Sales (1,250 @ $63.76)	$79,700.00
Less: Variable costs (1,250 @ $39.85)	49,812.50
Contribution margin	$29,887.50
Less: Fixed costs	21,565.09
Net income (estimated)	$ 8,322.41

Use demonstration problem 25-5 here.

Notice that the projected net income is the same as that using the product cost-plus method of pricing. As you can see, determining the percentage of markup is very important. The markup must be large enough to cover the base costs, cover additional costs not included in the base costs, and provide a reasonable profit. By using the variable cost-plus method, the company can apply the concepts of cost-volume-profit analysis and adjust the selling price based on the expected volume of sales.

R — E — M — E — M — B — E — R

When a business uses the variable cost-plus pricing method, the price is set at unit variable cost plus a markup to cover fixed costs and provide a profit.

Before reading further, do the following activity to check your understanding of the material you have just studied.

Check Your Learning

Write your answers to these questions on a sheet of notebook paper.

1. If the standard cost to make a tool is \$4.56 and the actual cost is \$5.01, what is the selling price if a markup of 45% is based on the standard cost? What is the amount of the cost variance? Is the variance favorable or unfavorable?
2. The following unit variable costs were incurred to make a telephone: direct materials, \$35.78; direct labor, \$18.75; and overhead, \$7.89. In addition, the unit variable administrative and selling costs were \$3.25. If the owner prices products based on variable costs plus a 45% markup, what is the selling price of the telephone?

Compare your answers to those in the answers section. Reread the preceding part of the chapter to find the correct answers to any questions you may have missed.

Have students complete Exercise 25-3 at this point.

ACCOUNTING Notes

Accounting firms are made up of partners, who must be CPAs, and staff accountants, who hope to become partners someday. Accounting firms vary in size from large firms with hundreds of partners to small, two-person firms.

Labor and Materials Pricing

When you receive an invoice or bill from a repair business, such as lawn mower, shoe, or auto repair, you are charged for the time required to do the work and for the parts or materials used. For professional services provided by accountants, doctors, and lawyers, you are charged a fee for the amount of time they visited with you or for the work they did on your behalf. The amounts charged by repair and service businesses are more than just an hourly pay rate and the purchase costs of materials and parts. The amounts charged must be large enough to cover administrative and selling expenses and provide a reasonable profit.

The **billing rate for labor** is a per-hour amount charged customers

Explain what costs are used to calculate a billing rate for labor.

that covers direct labor costs, benefits, and selling and administrative costs and provides a profit. Let's look at how the owner of Jack's Shoe Repair determines the billing rate for labor for his shop. The annual administrative and selling costs for the shop follow:

Annual administrative and selling costs:	
Owner's salary plus benefits	$22,000
Store supplies used	3,000
Depreciation on equipment	2,000
Miscellaneous costs	1,000
Total administrative and selling costs	$28,000

The shop has one employee, who earns $5.10 per hour. This employee works 44 hours a week for 50 weeks for a total of 2,200 hours a year. The cost of the employee's benefits is 25% of the hourly rate. The benefits are $1.28 ($5.10 × .25). The owner wants to make a $3.00 profit for every hour the employee works. Using all of the preceding information, the owner computes the billing rate for labor as follows:

Employee's hourly rate plus benefits ($5.10 + $1.28)	$ 6.38
Administrative and selling costs ($28,000 ÷ 2,200 hours)	12.73
Target profit	3.00
Billing rate for labor	$22.11

Based on these calculations, the shop will charge customers $22.11 per hour for labor on a repair job. As you can see, this amount is a lot higher than the $5.10 hourly wage the employee receives.

Discuss the purpose of the materials loading charge.

The **materials loading charge** is the amount added to the purchase cost of parts and materials used on a job to determine the amount the customer will be billed. The materials loading charge is stated as a percentage of the purchase cost and generally covers overhead costs (such as the costs of ordering, handling, and carrying an inventory) and provides for a profit. A materials loading charge may add as much as 50% to the purchase cost of parts and materials. The owner of Jack's Shoe Repair determines the materials loading charge for his shop. The annual overhead costs for the materials inventory for the shop follow:

Annual overhead costs for materials inventory:	
Utilities	$1,100
Insurance	850
Rent	6,000
Total overhead costs for materials inventory	$7,950

Be sure students understand how to determine the percentage of markup to cover overhead.

The owner now knows that the annual overhead costs for the materials inventory is $7,950. He also knows that the materials inventory runs about $32,000 a year. Therefore, 25% of the purchase cost of materials must be added to the customer's bill to cover overhead costs ($7,950 ÷ $32,000 = 25%). In addition, the owner expects a 10% profit on all materials purchased. The materials loading charge for Jack's Shoe Repair, therefore, will be 35% (25% to cover overhead plus 10% for desired profit).

The owner has set the billing rate for labor at $22.11 per hour and the materials loading charge at 35% of the purchase cost of materials used on a repair job. With this information, he would determine the amount to charge a customer as follows:

Labor charges:		
(.75 hours × $22.11 billing rate for labor)		$16.58
Materials charges:		
Purchase cost of materials	$4.76	
+ Materials loading charge (.35 × $4.76)	1.67	6.43
Total bill for shoe repair		$23.01

Of course, the actual bill handed to the customer will not show the billing rate for labor and the materials loading charge; these items are for internal use only. The bill the customer receives will appear as follows:

Jack's Shoe Repair
43 Apple Street

Date: 7/2/93	Tag: #5678
Labor	$16.58
Materials	6.43
Total	$23.01

Use demonstration problem 25-6 here.

R — E — M — E — M — B — E — R

To calculate the amount to charge a customer for labor, use a billing rate for labor that covers direct labor costs, benefits, and selling and administrative costs and provides a profit. To calculate the amount to charge a customer for materials and parts, add a materials loading charge to the purchase cost of the materials and parts to cover overhead and provide a profit.

Before reading further, do the following activity to check your understanding of the material you have just studied.

Check Your Learning

Write your answers to these questions on a sheet of notebook paper.

1. Assume a mechanic's wage per hour, including benefits, is $12.00; the selling and administrative costs per hour are $2.50; and the desired profit per hour for service is $2.50. What is the billing rate for labor?
2. Assume the purchase cost of a part is $34.67 and the company uses a materials loading charge of 50% (30% to cover overhead and 20% for desired profit). For what amount will the customer be billed for the part?

Compare your answers to those in the answers section. Reread the preceding part of the chapter to find the correct answers to any questions you may have missed.

Summary of Key Points

1. Pricing decisions are influenced by costs, competition, and economic conditions.
2. Pricing is the assigning of a selling price to a product or service sold by a business.
3. In general, the selling price must be high enough to cover costs and provide a reasonable profit.
4. Cost-plus pricing is widely used by merchandising and manufacturing businesses.
5. Four common cost-plus pricing methods are product cost-plus, full cost-plus, standard cost-plus, and variable cost-plus.
6. A markup is added to the base cost to arrive at the selling cost.
7. Service and repair businesses use a pricing method that covers costs of labor and materials or parts and provides a profit.

25 Review and Applications

Building Your Accounting Vocabulary

In your own words, write the definition of each of the following accounting terms. Use complete sentences for your definitions.

- billing rate for labor
- cost-plus pricing
- cost variance
- full cost-plus
- materials loading charge
- pricing
- product cost-plus
- standard cost-plus
- variable cost-plus

Reviewing Your Accounting Knowledge

1. What are the major influences on price?
2. Why might a farmer not have to make pricing decisions?
3. What is the difference between purchase price and selling price?
4. How do you think a business would select a markup percentage?
5. Why would a government contract allow a manufacturer to use full-cost pricing?
6. Who establishes a standard cost in manufacturing?
7. Would you expect standard cost and actual cost to differ? Why or why not?
8. What is the major difference between the product cost-plus and variable cost-plus pricing methods?
9. What is the advantage of the variable cost-plus pricing method?
10. Why would an auto repair shop add a materials loading charge to the billing charge for parts?
11. How might an accounting firm set its billing rate?

Improving Your Decision-Making Skills

You have been offered two very similar accounting jobs. One job pays $3,000 a year less than the other, but it offers better health insurance benefits, including eye and dental care. Assuming you would like either job equally well, your decision will rest on whether you find the higher salary or the better benefits more appealing.

Which of the following factors should influence your decision, and why are they significant?

1. The balance in your savings account
2. Whether or not you have children
3. The state of your health
4. How much money your neighbor makes
5. The condition of your car
6. Whether you are married and whether your spouse has good insurance
7. Whether you own or rent your home
8. Your age

Applying Accounting Procedures

Exercise 25-1 Using Product Cost-Plus Pricing

A dealer bought shirts for $25.76 each and sold them at a markup on purchase cost of 20%. The dealer also bought a dozen neckties for $96.00. The markup on purchase cost for the neckties is 25%.

$30.91; $10.00

Instructions: Determine the selling price for one shirt and for one tie based on the product cost-plus pricing method.

Exercise 25-2 Using Product Cost-Plus Pricing

Treetop, Inc., a bird feed company, prices its products at manufacturing cost plus a 60% markup. The cost data for 60,000 pounds of bird seed is as follows:

Direct materials	$9,000
Direct labor	3,000
Overhead applied	6,000
Selling costs	1,000

$.48

Instructions: Use the data given to calculate the selling price per pound based on the product cost-plus pricing method.

Exercise 25-3 Using Cost-Plus Pricing

The Cool-Off Company manufactures office fans. The cost data to make one Model A-46 office fan based on 500 units of production is as follows:

Manufacturing Costs	Standard Cost	Actual Cost
Direct materials	$23.00	$26.00
Direct labor	18.00	15.00
Overhead (variable)	2.00	3.00
Overhead (fixed)	4.50	5.00

Administrative and selling costs (variable)	$ 750
Administrative and selling costs (fixed)	1,500

Instructions: Compute the selling price for one Model A-46 office fan
$71.05 based on each of the following pricing methods: (1) product cost-plus
$68.88 with 45% markup; (2) standard cost-plus with 45% markup; (3) variable
$70.53 cost-plus with 55% markup.

Problem 25-1 Using Cost-Plus Pricing

The Ajazz Music Company needs to determine a price for one of the products it manufactures. Cost data for the product follows:

Direct materials	$12.00
Direct labor	16.00
Overhead applied (variable)	5.00
Overhead applied (fixed)	9.00
Administrative and selling costs (variable)	2.00
Administrative and selling costs (fixed)	5.00

Instructions: Calculate the selling price for one item using the following
$63 pricing methods: (1) product cost-plus with 50% markup; (2) variable
$63 cost-plus with 80% markup;.

Problem 25-2 Using Full Cost-Plus Pricing

A manufacturer has a contract with the government to produce 250 engines. The contract states that the profit allowance is 8% of the full cost. It also states that full cost means product manufacturing cost plus 25% of nonmanufacturing operating costs. The manufacturer incurred the following costs to produce the 250 engines.

Direct materials	$143,980
Direct labor	152,860
Factory overhead (applied)	18,650
Operating costs (nonmanufacturing)	131,340

Instructions:

$27,866 **(1)** Calculate the amount of profit the manufacturing company will make.
$1,504.76 **(2)** Calculate the contract price for one engine.

Problem 25-3 Using Labor and Materials Pricing

The Runever Lawn Mower Repair Shop employs three people who work 40 hours a week for 50 weeks a year. The shop incurs the following costs to operate.

Employees' hourly rate	$ 10.00
Employees' benefits per hour	2.00
Target profit per hour	5.00
Administrative, selling, and other costs	10,000.00

The owner of the shop has determined that 20% must be added to cover handling and storage of materials (overhead costs). In addition, the owner expects a 12% profit on materials.

Instructions:

$18.67 **(1)** Calculate the billing rate for labor.
32% **(2)** Calculate the materials loading charge.
$179.15 **(3)** The shop took 5 hours to repair a large riding mower. New parts costing $65 were installed. Calculate the amount to be billed the customer for labor and parts for the job.

CHALLENGE PROBLEM

Problem 25-4 Using Cost-Plus Pricing

A retired schoolteacher decides to make bird feeders to keep busy and make a few extra dollars. She charges enough to cover the cost of lumber plus a little extra for her efforts. A friend tells her that she is not charging enough to cover costs. The teacher collected the following information.

Manufacturing costs (per feeder):	
Lumber	$ 20.00
Paint	1.50
Nails, glue, supplies, etc.	3.00
Total materials per feeder	$ 24.50
Fixed costs:	
Annual depreciation on equipment	$310.00

The teacher makes 50 bird feeders a year and sells them for $30 each. It takes her 10 hours to make one bird feeder.

Instructions:

$30.70
$40.70
$42.05

(1) If the teacher wants to cover total costs, what should be the selling price per feeder?

(2) If the teacher wants to cover total costs plus make $1 per hour for labor per feeder, what should be the selling price per feeder?

(3) If her business grows to 200 feeders a year, the teacher will need to rent a garage for storage at $1,200 per year. She still wants to make $1 per hour for labor per feeder. What should be the selling price per feeder to cover total costs plus labor?

Computers and the Physically Challenged

For most of us, computers are a luxury. They can help make our work easier by doing many of the tedious tasks we would otherwise do by hand. For people who are physically challenged, however, computers may become a necessity. Computers have helped the handicapped take the CPA exam, testify in court, do their jobs better, and communicate with those around them.

As computer technology advances, more and more hardware and software are being adapted to aid the physically challenged. Voice-activated computers enable users to give commands without having to use their hands. In the workplace, robotic arms can be controlled through a computer to complete tasks.

Communicating with others can be difficult for those who are deaf or have suffered from a disease such as cerebral palsy or Down's syndrome. Deaf students, who often have difficulty learning to read because they have never heard the words aloud, have been using a computer program that displays sign language alongside written words. The students can understand the meaning of the text by matching the signs with the words.

Many children with Down's syndrome or cerebral palsy are language-disabled. Their ability to communicate with the people around them is limited. Today, however, computer programs are available to enable them to share their feelings with others. With the use of a voice synthesizer, the computer becomes a voice for the child, simultaneously saying and displaying each letter, word, and sentence the child types on the keyboard.

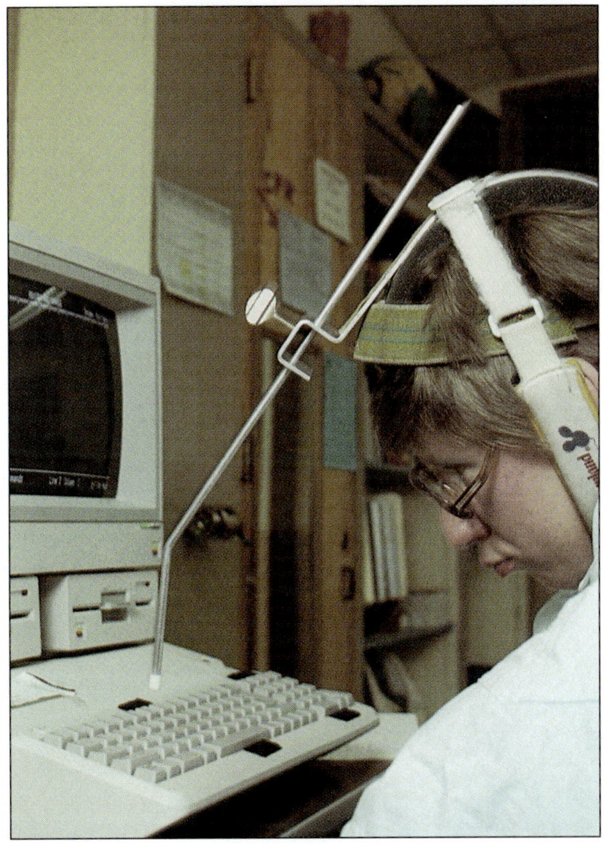

Advances in computer technology improve quality of life for the physically challenged.

With the aid of computers, physically challenged people can become more independent and better able to do the things they wish to do.

Additional Reinforcement Problems

Chapter 1, Problem 1A Analyzing the Effects of Posting

The bookkeeper for the Mercer Corporation was in charge of posting all amounts from the four special journals and the general journal for the month ended June 30. Amounts were to be posted to the general ledger and to the accounts receivable and accounts payable subsidiary ledgers. In her haste, the bookkeeper forgot to post the *entire* sales journal to all ledgers.

Instructions: Use a form similar to the one that follows. For each numbered item, use a check mark to indicate whether the amount would be overstated, understated, or not affected by the posting error.

Items:

1. Net sales for the period
2. Total liabilities as of June 30
3. Ending balance in the Cash in Bank account
4. Total amount owed to the state in sales tax
5. Total of the Trial Balance section of the work sheet
6. Total of the schedule of accounts payable
7. Ending balance in the Sales account
8. Ending balance in the Sales Discounts account

Number of Item	Overstated	Understated	Not Affected
1.		✓	

Chapter 2, Problem 2A Identifying Accounts on Financial Statements Affected by Adjusting and Closing Entries

Instructions: Use a form similar to the one that follows. Write *yes* or *no* in each column to indicate on which financial statement(s) each of the following accounts would appear. Also, indicate whether each would be included in the adjusting entries or in the closing entries.

Cash in Bank
Insurance Expense
Sales Discounts
Social Security Tax Payable
Medicare Tax Payble
Transportation In
Beginning Merchandise Inventory
Cost of Merchandise Sold
Net Income
Ending Merchandise Inventory
Sales Tax Payable
Income Summary
Bank Card Fees Expense
Purchases Discounts
Prepaid Insurance
Cost of Delivered Merchandise
Sales
Rent Expense
Accounts Payable
Office Equipment
Payroll Tax Expense

Account or Amount	Income Statement	Statement of Retained Earnings	Balance Sheet	Included in Adjusting Entries	Included in Closing Entries
Cash in Bank	No	No	Yes	No	No

Chapter 3, Problem 3A Aging Accounts Receivable

Jo's Parts House uses the accounts receivable aging method to estimate its uncollectible accounts. At the end of the fiscal period (June 30), a co-worker began to prepare the aging schedule. When that person went on vacation, you were asked to complete the schedule. The following customer accounts remain to be aged.

Account	Amount	Due Date
R. Roberts	$ 845	June 4
M. Smith	3,949	May 2, $2,000; June 23, $1,949
C. Tate	200	March 12
S. Watkins	1,941	February 28
T. Young	600	July 12

Instructions:

(1) Complete the accounts receivable aging schedule included in the working papers.

(2) Calculate the total estimated uncollectible amount using the following percentages.

Not yet due	1%
1–30 days past due	3%
31–60 days past due	30%
61–90 days past due	40%
Over 90 days past due	60%

(3) Determine the amount of the adjustment if Allowance for Uncollectible Accounts has a debit balance of $291.

Chapter 3, Problem 3B Determining the Adjustment for Uncollectible Accounts

The Sports Equipment Center opened for business five years ago. For the first four years, the company used the direct write-off method of accounting for uncollectible accounts. With net sales this year of $698,420, the center decided to switch to the allowance method.

The company plans to use the percentage of net sales method to estimate the adjustment for bad debts expense. Accounting information for the first four years follows.

	Net Sales	Total Actual Bad Debts Losses
Year 1	$127,800	$ 1,728
Year 2	314,900	8,100
Year 3	429,604	7,241
Year 4	586,214	11,139

Instructions: Answer the following questions.

1. Based on the figures for the first four years, what percentage of net sales would you suggest be used for the adjustment?
2. What new account must be placed in the chart of accounts when Sports Equipment Center switches to the allowance method?
3. Using the percentage suggested in Question 1, what should be the amount of the adjustment?
4. If Accounts Receivable has a year-end balance of $95,280, what is the book value of accounts receivable?
5. Record the December 31 adjusting entry for bad debts expense on page 40 of a general journal.

Chapter 4, Problem 4A Accounting for a Dishonored Discounted Note Receivable

During the current year, the Frosty Refrigeration Company completed the transactions that follow.

Instructions: Record the transactions in the cash receipts journal, page 26; the cash payments journal, page 45; and the general journal, page 21.

Transactions:

Oct. 18 Accepted a 30-day, 10.50%, $3,850 note receivable, dated October 18, from Dari-Delite in place of its accounts receivable amount, Note 9.

Oct. 29 Discounted Note 9 at the Federal National Bank at a 9.75% discount rate, Receipt 440.

Nov. 17 Received notice from Federal National Bank that Dari-Delite had dishonored its note on the maturity date. Federal National charged Frosty Refrigeration Company a $10 protest fee. Removed the dishonored note receivable from the accounting records (Memorandum 97) and recorded the payment of the note plus the interest and the protest fee (Check 837).

Chapter 5, Problem 5A Determining Gross Profit

The Terrace Corporation uses the periodic inventory system. On December 31, the end of the fiscal period, the accounting records provided the following amounts.

Merchandise inventory, January 1	$ 73,000
Net purchases	148,000
Net sales	195,000
Total expenses	39,000

A physical inventory revealed that the ending inventory was $89,000. However, the ending inventory was incorrectly reported as $82,000 in the accounting records.

Instructions:

(1) Use a form similar to the one that follows. For each numbered item, use a check mark to indicate whether the amount would be overstated, understated, or not affected by the error.

Items:

1. Cost of merchandise available for sale
2. Cost of merchandise sold
3. Gross profit on sales
4. Beginning inventory for the next fiscal period
5. Net income

Number of Item	Overstated	Understated	Not Affected
1.			√

(2) Using the correct amount of ending merchandise inventory, determine the cost of merchandise sold, the gross profit, and the net income for the year ended December 31. Show your results in income statement form.

Chapter 6, Problem 6A Disposing of a Plant Asset

The Bruno Corporation traded in an old delivery truck for a new truck. The following accounts were affected by the transaction.

Delivery Equipment	$19,300	
Accumulated Depreciation—Delivery Equipment	7,600	
Loss on Disposal of Plant Assets	600	
Cash in Bank		$ 9,500
Delivery Equipment		18,000

Instructions: Answer the following questions. Use plain paper or the space provided in the working papers.

1. What was the original purchase price of the old truck?
2. How much has the old truck depreciated?
3. What is the value of the new truck?
4. How much cash was paid for the new truck?
5. What is the amount of the trade-in allowance for the old truck?
6. Explain why there was a loss on this transaction.

Chapter 7, Problem 7A Issuing and Paying an Interest-Bearing Note Payable

Keystone Communications carried out the transactions that follow.

Instructions: Record these transactions in a purchases journal (page 31), cash payments journal (page 42), and general journal (page 25).

Transactions:

Mar. 3 Purchased merchandise on account from King's Store Suppliers, $8,000, terms n/30; Invoice 5873.

Apr. 2 Issued an $8,000, 30-day, 7.75% note payable to King's Store Suppliers as an extension on an amount recorded as an account payable, Note 14.

May 2 Issued Check 667 to King's Store Suppliers for the principal and interest due on Note 14.

Chapter 7, Problem 7B Issuing and Paying a Non-Interest-Bearing Note Payable

Interior Designs, Inc., borrowed $7,500 from the Fresno Bank, issuing a 30-day, non-interest-bearing note payable that the bank discounted at 9.75%.

Instructions: Use a cash receipts journal (page 8) and a cash payments journal (page 12) to prepare the entries for the following.

1. The issuance of the note payable (Note 3) on July 17.
2. The payment of Note 3 on the maturity date (Check 320).

Chapter 8, Problem 8A Evaluating and Redeeming a Bond Issue

Five years ago on April 1, the Champion Manufacturing Company issued $4,000,000 of 20-year, 10% callable bonds, call price 103. Interest payments have been made each year for the past five years. The company wants to redeem these 10% bonds and issue $4,000,000 of 8.5%, 15-year bonds.

Instructions:

(1) Answer the following questions.

- (a) Over the next 15 years, how much interest would be paid on the 10% bond issue?
- (b) Over the next 15 years, how much interest would be paid on the 8.5% bond issue?
- (c) How much interest expense would Champion save over the next 15 years if it redeemed the old bonds and issued the new bonds at face value?
- (d) How much would it cost Champion to redeem the original bond issue?
- (e) Considering the premium the company would have to pay for redeeming the existing bonds, how much would Champion save over the next 15 years?

(2) Record the following transactions on page 64 of a cash receipts journal and page 51 of a cash payments journal.

Transactions:

Apr. 1 Redeemed the complete bond issue at the call price, Check 2445.

15 Issued $4,000,000 of 8.5%, 15-year bonds at 101, Receipt 379.

Chapter 8, Problem 8B Issuing Bonds and Recording Bond Sinking Fund and Mortgage Note Transactions

On July 1, the Georgetown Mall Corporation issued $5,000,000 of 8.5%, 20-year bonds with interest payable on June 30 and December 31. The company has a bond sinking fund to which it makes annual deposits.

Instructions:

(1) Record the following transactions in the cash receipts journal (page 36), cash payments journal (page 47), and general journal (page 32).

Transactions:

1991		
July	1	Issued $5,000,000 of 20-year, 8.5% bonds at 101 (face value, $1,000), Receipt 755.
Dec.	31	Deposited $200,000 in the bond sinking fund, Check 1214.
	31	Paid the semiannual bond interest, Check 1215.
	31	Recorded the adjusting entry for the amortization of the bond premium.
	31	Closed the Bond Interest Expense account.
1992		
Jan.	5	Used $180,000 from the bond sinking fund to purchase various securities, Check 1220.
June	30	Paid the semiannual bond interest, Check 1302.
July	5	Received $9,000 income from sinking fund investments, Receipt 487.
	27	Used $15,000 from the bond sinking fund to purchase various securities, Check 1320.
Sept.	17	Signed a 5-year mortgage note with the Farmington Bank to borrow $50,000 at 9% interest, Receipt 510.
Oct.	31	Received $9,750 income from sinking fund investments, Receipt 522.
Nov.	15	Made the first mortgage payment of $1,269.86 to the Farmington Bank; interest, $369.86; principal, $900.00; Check 1400.
	30	Deposited $200,000 in the bond sinking fund, Check 1430.
Dec.	1	Received $205,000 from the sale of various sinking fund investments that originally cost $195,000, Receipt 535.
	15	Made the second mortgage payment of $1,263.21 to the Farmington Bank; interest, $363.21; principal, $900.00; Check 1445.
	31	Paid the semiannual bond interest, Check 1456.
	31	Recorded the adjusting entry for the amortization of the bond premium.
	31	Closed the Sinking Fund Income and Bond Interest Expense accounts.

(2) Post the transactions to the general ledger accounts that are given in the working papers.

Chapter 9, Problem 9A Recording Stock Transactions

The Skate Shop has authorized capital of 3,000 shares of $50-par preferred 7% stock and 18,000 shares of $20-par common stock. The following transactions were completed during the first year of operation.

Instructions: Record the transactions on page 1 of a cash receipts journal and page 2 of a general journal.

Transactions:

Mar.	8	Issued 1,200 shares of preferred 7% stock at par and 9,000 shares of common stock at par, Receipt 10.
	20	Issued 750 shares of common stock in exchange for office equipment valued at $6,000 and delivery equipment valued at $9,000, Memorandum 8.

22 Issued 350 shares of common stock to the organizers of the corporation, Memorandum 12.

Apr. 4 Issued 4,000 shares of $20-par common stock at $22, Receipt 25.

21 Received subscriptions to 2,000 shares of $20-par common stock at $23 per share, with a down payment of 50% of the subscription price, Memorandum 22 and Receipt 30.

Chapter 10, Problem 10A Recording Stockholders' Equity Transactions

The following balances appeared in the general ledger accounts of the Burton Corporation on January 1.

Preferred 7% Stock, $25 par, 10,000 shares authorized, 4,400 shares issued	$110,000
Paid-in Capital in Excess of Par—Preferred	2,500
Common Stock, $20 par, 100,000 shares authorized, 45,000 shares issued	900,000
Paid-in Capital in Excess of Par—Common	50,000
Retained Earnings	170,000

Instructions: Record the following transactions on page 37 of the cash receipts journal, page 42 of the cash payments journal, and page 63 of the general journal.

Transactions:

Feb. 23 The board of directors declared the regular quarterly cash dividend for preferred stockholders of record on March 15, payable on March 31, Minute Book page 268.

Mar. 31 Paid the cash dividend declared on February 23, Check 2481.

Apr. 24 Declared a 5% stock dividend to common stockholders of record on April 15, distributable on May 31, Minute Book page 304. The market price of the stock on April 15 is $24 per share.

May 31 Distributed the stock dividend declared on April 24, Minute Book page 304.

Nov. 28 Purchased 1,000 shares of own common stock at $25 per share, Check 4981.

Dec. 15 Sold 300 shares of treasury stock for $27 per share, Receipt 3998.

Dec. 31 The board of directors voted to appropriate $100,000 of retained earnings each year for six years to provide for purchase of new equipment. Recorded the closing entry for the appropriation.

Chapter 11, Problem 11A Correcting Errors on the Work Sheet

You are an accounting clerk for the Reynolds Corporation. A co-worker started preparing the work sheet for the fiscal period ended December 31. The Trial Balance section has been totaled, proved, and ruled. However, there are some mistakes in the Adjustments section.

Instructions: Using the information that follows, find and correct the errors in the Adjustments section of the work sheet that appears in the working papers. Draw a line through any incorrect amounts, and write the correct amounts above the incorrect data.

1. The ending merchandise inventory is $33,000.
2. The ending supplies inventory is $100.
3. On March 1, the company paid $300 for a one-year insurance policy.
4. Uncollectible accounts are estimated by using 2% of the balance of Accounts Receivable.
5. On November 1, the company borrowed $8,000 from the County Bank, issuing a 120-day, non-interest-bearing note discounted at 12%.
6. Estimated depreciation on delivery equipment for the year is $1,600.
7. Of the $10,000 in rental income that was collected this year, $3,000 has not been earned.
8. Salaries totaling $600 have accrued since the last payroll was paid.
9. Total federal income tax expense for the year is $3,800.

Chapter 11, Problem 11B Analyzing Errors on the Work Sheet

Errors made while calculating or recording adjustments on the work sheet may affect the amounts reported on the financial statements. The following list includes several different types of errors.

Instructions: Indicate what effect each error will have on the amounts reported on the financial statements for the year ended December 31. Using the chart provided in the working papers, enter an *O* for "overstated," a *U* for "understated," and an *N* for "no effect."

Errors:

1. The ending merchandise inventory was understated by $5,000.
2. Uncollectible accounts are estimated by using a percentage of net sales. When calculating the adjustment, a net sales amount of $54,600 was used rather than the correct amount of $45,600.
3. The amount of supplies used during the period was calculated at $1,760; the correct amount was $1,670.
4. The adjustment for the additional $750 owed in corporate federal income taxes was omitted.
5. On December 1 the company accepted a $4,000, 60-day, 8.5% note receivable. When calculating the accrued interest income for the period, an 8.75% interest rate was used.
6. The adjustment for the portion of the prepaid insurance premium that expired was omitted.
7. When making the adjustment for other income, Unearned Rent was credited and Rental Income was debited.
8. The adjustment for accrued salaries was omitted.
9. When recording the adjustment for depreciation, the Equipment account was credited rather than the Accumulated Depreciation—Equipment account.

[continued]

10. Uncollectible accounts are estimated by using 2% of the balance of Accounts Receivable. The $800 estimated uncollectible amount was added to the $200 credit balance of Allowance for Uncollectible Accounts.

Chapter 12, Problem 12A Interpreting Financial Data

Jason's Foot Wear sells athletic shoes for women and men. You are interested in purchasing a large number of shares of the company's stock for investment purposes. In order for you to make a thorough financial analysis of the business, the following information covering the past three years has been supplied.

	1991	1992	1993
Current assets	$784,000	$821,000	$900,000
Total liabilities	$370,000	$380,000	$410,000
Current ratio	3:1	3.4:1	4:1
Quick ratio	1:1	1.5:1	2.3:1
Ratio of stockholders' equity to liabilities	3.5:1	4:1	4.2:1

Instructions: Based on this information, answer the following questions. Use plain paper or the form provided in the working papers. Round your answers to the nearest whole dollar.

1. What are the current liabilities for each of the three years?
2. What are the long-term liabilities for each of the three years?
3. What are the quick assets for each of the three years?
4. What is the total stockholders' equity for each of the three years?
5. What is the working capital for each of the three years?
6. By what amount did the quick assets increase from 1991 to 1993?
7. By what amount did working capital increase from 1991 to 1993?

Chapter 13, Problem 13A Completing a Statement of Cash Flows

The accountant for Superior Electronics, Inc., completed the cash flows from operating activities section of the statement of cash flows. The accountant then analyzed the general ledger accounts to determine which transactions would affect the cash flows from investing and financing activities sections. You have been asked to complete the statement of cash flows.

Instructions:

(1) Prepare the heading of the statement of cash flows and record the amount of net cash flows from operating activities, $164,200.
(2) Using the information from the following transactions, prepare the cash flows from investing activities and the cash flows from financing activities sections. Place parentheses around amounts that represent cash outflows.
(3) Determine the amount of net increase (or decrease) in cash.

Transactions:

		Debit	Credit
(a)	Plant Assets	$ 40,000	
	Cash in Bank		$ 40,000
	Purchased new delivery truck		
(b)	Notes Payable	$ 10,000	
	Interest Expense	200	
	Cash in Bank		$ 10,200
	Repaid a note payable		
(c)	Marketable Securities	$100,000	
	Cash in Bank		$100,000
	Purchased Treasury bills		
(d)	Cash in Bank	$ 22,000	
	Accumulated Depreciation	60,000	
	Loss on Sale of Plant Asset	3,000	
	Plant Assets		$ 85,000
	Sold two old delivery trucks		
(e)	Cash in Bank	$ 12,500	
	Capital Stock		$ 10,000
	Paid-in Capital in Excess of Par		2,500
	Issued 500 shares of $20-par capital stock		
(f)	Plant Assets	$ 55,000	
	Cash in Bank		$ 55,000
	Purchased new delivery truck		
(g)	Cash in Bank	$ 5,000	
	Notes Payable		$ 5,000
	Issued a note payable		
(h)	Dividends Payable	$ 15,000	
	Cash in Bank		$ 15,000
	Paid cash dividend to stockholders		
(i)	Cash in Bank	$ 30,000	
	Bonds Payable		$ 30,000
	Issued bonds payable		

Chapter 14, Problem 14A Recording Partnership Transactions

On February 1, 1991, Sara Long and James Duncan became partners in Fairfax Gifts. The following transactions took place during a period of three years.

Instructions: Record the transactions on page 1 of a general journal.

Transactions:

1991

Feb. 1 Long and Duncan initially invested $15,000 each to form the partnership, Memorandum 1.

May 5 Duncan withdrew $200 in supplies from the business, Memorandum 15.

1992

Jan. 1 Long and Duncan agreed to admit Jessica Gilman to the partnership for an investment of $18,000 cash, Receipt 60.

Sept. 20 Long withdrew from the partnership and was paid $1,000 more than the balance of her capital account after revaluation, $18,000, Check 317. The $1,000 was divided equally between the remaining partners.

Dec.	15	Duncan invested an additional $2,000 in the business, Receipt 85.
1993		
Aug.	1	Duncan and Gilman liquidated their business. Partners share profits and losses equally. (No journal entry was recorded on this date.)
	15	Sold merchandise valued at $25,000 for $23,000 cash and other assets valued at $17,000 for $20,800 cash, Receipt 205.
	15	Allocated the gain or loss from realization to the partners capital accounts, Memorandum 83.
	17	Paid creditors $12,500, Checks 440–442.
	20	Distributed the cash to the partners as follows: Duncan, $22,500; Gilman, $20,000; Checks 443–444.

Chapter 15, Problem 15A Allocating Net Income Based on Salary and Interest Allowances

José Quinto and Alma Brown are partners in Letters & Things. The balances of their capital accounts on December 31 (the end of the fiscal period) are $36,000 and $42,000, respectively. Letters & Things has a net income of $34,700 for the current fiscal period.

The partnership agreement provides for salary allowances of $10,000 for Quinto and $14,000 for Brown. The agreement also states that each partner is to receive a 5% interest allowance on the balances of their capital accounts at the end of the fiscal period. Any remaining net income or loss is to be divided equally.

Instructions: Determine each partner's share of net income. On general journal page 91, record the closing entry to allocate the net income to the partners.

Chapter 16, Problem 16A Preparing a Revised Budget

The Bay City Youth Center is a neighborhood center that provides services and recreational activities such as arts and crafts, dances, vocational instruction, counseling, and organized sports. The center's budget director prepares an annual budget. Every three months, a budget summary report is prepared and analyzed. A portion of that report for the six months ended June 30 follows.

The budget director now expects that revenue from membership fees will be approximately 85% of the original budgeted amount and that revenue from dances will be 90% of the original budgeted amount. Revenue from donations is expected to be 10% higher than originally projected.

The budget director has asked you to prepare a revised budget. Some of the expenditure projections will have to be adjusted to accommodate the revised revenue amounts.

	Current Year Budget Amount	Current Y-T-D Amount	Free Balance Amount	Previous Y-T-D Amount
Revenue				
Membership Fees	$ 70,000	$32,000	$38,000	$33,000
United Way Contributions	50,000	25,000	25,000	25,000
Athletic Fees	17,900	8,000	9,900	7,000
Donations	20,000	11,300	8,700	9,000
Dances	10,000	4,000	6,000	5,000
Fund-Raising Projects	20,000	12,000	8,000	11,500
Total Revenue	$187,900	$92,300	$95,600	$90,500
Expenditures				
Personal Services				
Director's Salary	$ 60,000	$30,000	$30,000	$28,000
Wages	50,000	22,000	28,000	25,000
Related Benefits	25,000	11,100	13,900	10,500
Total Pers. Serv.	$135,000	$63,100	$71,900	$63,500
Operating Services				
Utilities	$ 9,000	$ 4,100	$ 4,900	$ 5,000
Office Supplies	2,000	1,400	600	1,500
Repairs	8,000	4,500	3,500	2,800
Postage	1,000	600	400	700
Insurance	2,400	1,200	1,200	1,200
Total Oper. Serv.	$ 22,400	$11,800	$10,600	$11,200
Supplies				
Awards	$ 2,500	$ 1,500	$ 1,000	$ 1,700
Sports Equipment	4,000	2,300	1,700	2,100
Repair Supplies	6,000	4,300	1,700	2,600
Misc. Supplies	2,000	1,200	800	1,500
Dance Supplies	3,000	2,200	800	1,200
Total Supplies	$ 17,500	$11,500	$ 6,000	$ 9,100
Cap. Outlay Acquisitions				
Equipment	$ 10,000	$ 6,000	$ 4,000	$ 3,500
Furniture	3,000	1,000	2,000	500
Total	$ 13,000	$ 7,000	$ 6,000	$ 4,000
Total Expenditures	$187,900	$93,400	$94,500	$87,800

Instructions: Prepare a revised annual budget that includes your recommendations for changes in the revenue and expenditure projections. Use the form provided in the working papers.

Chapter 17, Problem 17A Analyzing the Financial Statement of a Not-for-Profit Organization

The statement of revenue, expenditures, and changes in fund balance for the Smithville Chamber of Commerce follows. You have been asked to provide a breakdown of the various line items.

Smithville Chamber of Commerce
Statement of Revenue, Expenditures, and Changes in Fund Balance
General Fund
For the Budget Period Ended September 30, 199-

	Budget Amount	Actual Amount
Sources of Revenue		
Self-Generated:		
Membership fees	$ 66,000	$ 66,100
Seminar tuition	20,000	19,600
Total Self-Generated Revenue	$ 86,000	$ 85,700
Support:		
United Way	$ 15,000	$ 15,000
Contributed services of volunteers	27,100	26,800
Total Support Revenue	42,100	41,800
Total Revenue	$128,100	$127,500
Expenditures		
Personnel:		
Salaries	$ 50,000	$ 50,000
Wages	35,000	34,200
Total Personnel	$ 85,000	$ 84,200
Travel	$ 5,000	$ 5,250
Purchased Services:		
Insurance	1,200	1,200
Postage	1,800	1,700
Rent	6,000	6,000
Utilities	9,600	10,200
Total Purchased Services	$ 18,600	$ 19,100
Supplies	$ 7,500	$ 8,000
Equipment	$ 10,000	$ 9,200
Total Expenditures	$126,100	$125,750
Beginning Fund Balance	$ 29,225	$ 29,225
Increase in Fund Balance	2,000	1,750
Ending Fund Balance	$ 31,225	$ 30,975

Instructions: Using the form provided in the working papers, calculate the difference between the actual revenue, expenditure, and fund balance amounts and the budgeted amounts. Then calculate the percentage the difference amount was over or under the budget amount. Round percentages to the nearest tenth of a percent.

Chapter 18, Problem 18A Reporting Departmental Gross Profit on Sales

Fischer Decorating has two departments: the Rugs Department and the Lamps Department. Fischer Decorating maintains separate departmental accounts for its revenue and cost of merchandise accounts. The following amounts appear in those accounts on June 30, the end of the business's fiscal year.

Merchandise Inventory—Rugs, July 1	$402,000
Merchandise Inventory—Rugs, June 30	395,000
Merchandise Inventory—Lamps, July 1	386,000
Merchandise Inventory—Lamps, June 30	382,000
Sales—Rugs	650,000
Sales—Lamps	595,000
Sales Returns and Allowances—Rugs	8,290
Sales Returns and Allowances—Lamps	5,860
Purchases—Rugs	275,000
Purchases—Lamps	259,000
Purchases Discounts—Rugs	1,870
Purchases Discounts—Lamps	1,465
Purchases Returns and Allowances—Rugs	4,900
Purchases Returns and Allowances—Lamps	3,750

Instructions: Prepare a partial income statement through gross profit on sales.

Chapter 18, Problem 18B Evaluating a Department's Contribution Margin

Holiday Fair has four departments. Department A sells greeting cards, wrapping paper, and ribbon; Department B sells toys, puzzles, and small gift items; Department C sells paperback books and magazines; and Department D sells house plants, decorative pots, and potting soil. The company is thinking about eliminating one of the departments.

The company allocates its indirect expenses to each department. The accounting records show the following.

	Dept. A	Dept. B	Dept. C	Dept. D
Net Sales	$90,400	$112,600	$73,800	$28,800
Cost of Merchandise Sold	52,500	58,900	33,600	15,600
Direct Expenses	19,300	27,400	18,400	8,200
Indirect Expenses Allocated	14,200	19,100	13,350	7,500

Instructions:

(1) Calculate the contribution margin and net income or loss for each department. Use plain paper or the form provided in the working papers.

(2) If Holiday Fair eliminates Department D, what will the store's total net income for the period be?

(3) If the indirect expenses allocated to Department D are evenly distributed among the other three departments, what will each department's net income or loss be?

(4) If the indirect expenses allocated to Department D are distributed to Departments A, B, and C using a 2:2:1 ratio, what will each department's net income or loss be?

Chapter 19, Problem 19A Allocating Expenses Among Branches

The Golden Triangle Home Decorating Center is a multistore business with branches in Orange, Port Arthur, and Beaumont. The company uses a centralized accounting system with a Cash in Bank—Payables account.

On June 4, the central accounting office received the following invoices from suppliers of services or goods.

1. Received Invoice 4287 from Comet Broadcasting Company for $7,945 for several advertisements. The ads featured sales items and listed the location of all three branches. The central accounting office allocates advertising expenses among the three branches according to the square footage occupied by the branches. Orange occupies 12,000 sq. ft.; Port Arthur, 18,000 sq. ft.; Beaumont, 30,000 sq. ft.
2. Received a premium notice, Invoice 3131, from WeCare Insurance Company for $7,500 for a six-month insurance policy. The accounting office was instructed to set up the liabilities for the premium and allocate the cost on the basis of square footage occupied by each branch.
3. Received Invoice 2488 from the Southstreet Construction Company for $16,900 for work performed at each branch (Major Repair—Buildings). Cost on the invoice was allocated to each branch as follows: Orange, $2,700; Port Arthur, $3,800; Beaumont, $10,400.

Instructions:

(1) Allocate the costs among the three branches. Record the necessary transactions on June 4 on page 48 of the general journal.

(2) Determine the amount that must be transferred from each branch's checking account to the Cash in Bank—Payables account. Record the entry on June 5 on page 49 of the general journal (Electronic Funds Transfer 4448).

(3) Record the cash payment of the three invoices on June 5 on page 49 of the general journal (Checks 4876, 4877, and 4878).

Chapter 20, Problem 20A Recording Voucher Transactions

Greentree Industries, which uses a voucher system, had the following unpaid vouchers on June 30. These vouchers have already been recorded in the voucher register provided in the working papers.

Voucher No.	Creditor	For	Date of Invoice	Amount
1520	Bel-Air Corporation	Merchandise	June 26	$3,200.00
1521	Zippi Industries	Merchandise	June 27	6,800.00

Instructions:

(1) Record the following transactions in the voucher register (page 27), the check register (page 25), and the general journal (page 17).

(2) Total, prove, and rule the voucher register and the check register.

Transactions:

July	1	Issued Voucher 1522 in favor of Ford Office Equipment Company for office equipment purchased, $2,100.00.
	2	Purchased $10,400.00 in merchandise on account from Reed Products, terms 2/10, n/30; issued Voucher 1523.
	3	Purchased a microcomputer (Equipment) for $3,300.00 from Phoenix Computers and arranged to make three equal payments of $1,100.00 each; prepared Vouchers 1524, 1525, and 1526.
	3	Issued Check 1630 in payment of Voucher 1524.

5 Issued Debit Memo 65 to Reed Products for $200.00 of merchandise from Voucher 1523 returned for credit.
7 Purchased $14,600.00 in merchandise on account from Alpha Corporation, terms 2/10, n/30; issued Voucher 1527.
7 Issued Check 1631 for $3,136.00 in payment of Voucher 1520 for $3,200.00 less the cash discount.
8 Received monthly telephone bill from County Telephone Company; issued Voucher 1528 for $250.00.
8 Zippi Industries agreed to accept a 60-day, 10% note in payment of the June 27 invoice; canceled Voucher 1521 and issued Note 12.
8 Issued Check 1632 for $9,996.00 in payment of Voucher 1523; $10,400.00 less the return and the cash discount.
12 Purchased $125.00 in supplies from Brentwood Supply Company; issued Voucher 1529.
15 Issued Voucher 1530 for $60.00 to Mr. Fix-It for emergency plumbing repairs (Miscellaneous Expense).
20 Wrote Check 1633 in payment of Voucher 1525.
20 Issued Voucher 1531 to the First National Bank for a note recorded in the general journal in June: principal, $5,600.00, plus interest of $92.05.
20 Wrote Check 1634 in payment of Voucher 1531.
22 Purchased $1,275.00 in merchandise on account from Omega Systems; issued Voucher 1532.
23 Issued Voucher 1533 for $112.00 to Dash Delivery for delivering merchandise.
25 Discovered an error on the invoice from Omega Systems that reduced the amount owed. Canceled Voucher 1532 (Memorandum 66) and issued Voucher 1534 for $1,257.00.
31 Issued Voucher 1535 for $7,015.00 to the Payroll Bank Account. The total salaries expense was $10,000.00; deductions were for federal income tax of $2,000.00, state income tax of $220.00, social security tax of $620.00, and medicare tax of $145.00.
31 Wrote Check 1635 in payment Voucher 1535.

Chapter 21, Problem 21A Preparing a Schedule of Cost of Goods Manufactured

The following amounts appear on the work sheet of Wright Manufacturing, Inc., for the month ended June 30.

Raw Materials Inventory, June 1	$ 21,000
Raw Materials Inventory, June 30	49,000
Work in Process Inventory, June 1	97,000
Work in Process Inventory, June 30	40,000
Raw Materials Purchases (Net)	247,000
Direct Labor	130,000
Factory Insurance Expired	4,000
Factory Supplies Used	5,300
Heat, Light, and Power	51,600
Indirect Labor	19,240
Miscellaneous Factory Costs	8,000
Repairs and Maintenance	3,125
Supervisory Salaries	21,000

Instructions: Prepare a schedule of cost of goods manufactured for Wright Manufacturing.

Chapter 21, Problem 21B Preparing an Income Statement for a Manufacturing Business

The following amounts appear on the work sheet of the Central Manufacturing Company for the year ended December 31.

	Income Statement	
Income Summary		$ 30,000
Sales		2,891,380
Sales Discounts	$ 23,300	
Sales Returns and Allowances	20,500	
Selling Expenses	282,710	
Administrative Expenses	235,420	
Interest Expense	30,500	
Income Tax Expense	84,620	
Cost of Goods Manufactured	2,113,830	
	$2,790,880	$2,921,380
Net Income	130,500	
	$2,921,380	$2,921,380

Instructions: Prepare an income statement. The beginning balance of Finished Goods Inventory was $264,000.

Chapter 22, Problem 22A Preparing a Cost of Production Report

The manager of the assembly department of the Alpine Manufacturing Company gathered the following information about the department's April operations. There was no beginning work in process inventory.

Costs incurred:	
Direct materials	$ 55,100
Direct labor	49,875
Factory overhead applied	45,125
Assembly costs to account for	$150,100
New units started	10,000
Transferred to Finished Goods	9,000
Work in Process, April 30	1,000
Units completed and transferred out	9,000
Units in process (1,000 @ 50%)	500
Equivalent units	9,500

Instructions: Using this information, prepare a cost of production report for the assembly department for Alpine Manufacturing Company.

Chapter 23, Problem 23A Analyzing Cost Behavior

The Able Retail Company had the following selling expenses and sales during the first six months of the year.

Month	Selling Expenses	Sales
January	$15,600	$300,000
February	13,400	205,000
March	16,900	280,000
April	19,800	365,000
May	17,300	262,000
June	18,200	259,000

Instructions:

(1) Using the high-low method, calculate unit variable costs and fixed costs.

(2) Estimate the total selling expenses for December if the estimated sales for the month are $250,000.

Chapter 24, Problem 24A Calculating Break-Even Point, Profit, and Margin of Safety

The Tennon Company plans to market a new product. Based on its market information, the company estimates it can sell 6,000 units of the new product during the next fiscal period. The selling price is set at $4 per unit. Variable costs are estimated at 70% of the selling price. Fixed costs are estimated at $6,000 for a year.

Instructions: Answer the following questions.

1. What is the break-even point in units and in dollars?
2. What is the expected profit if sales reach 6,000 units?
3. What is Tennon's margin of safety in units and in dollars?

Chapter 24, Problem 24B Applying C-V-P Analysis

Mary Chavez makes sweaters at a cost of $49.95 each. She cannot sell the sweaters herself. Therefore, she pays an employee a $5,000 salary plus a $3.00 commission for each sweater sold. Mary provided the accountant with the following data:

Selling price per sweater	$85.00
Variable costs:	
Materials	$48.00
Commission per sweater	3.00
Fixed costs:	
Rent	$6,000
Advertising	1,750
Salary	5,000

Instructions: Answer the following questions.

1. What is the break-even point in units and in dollars?
2. If Chavez sells 1,250 sweaters a year, how much profit or loss will she report for the year?
3. Chavez believes that if she raises her employee's salary to $7,500, the incentive will increase sales to 1,500 sweaters a year. Should she increase the salary? Why or why not?

Chapter 25, Problem 25A Using Cost-Plus Pricing

The Smith Lamp Company manufactures desk lamps. Cost data to make one lamp follows.

Manufacturing costs:	
Materials	$12.00
Direct labor	4.50
Overhead (variable)	3.00
Overhead (fixed)	10.50
Administrative and selling costs (variable)	$ 4.00
Administrative and selling costs (fixed)	5.00

Instructions: Calculate the selling price for one item using the following pricing methods: (1) product cost-plus with 40% markup; (2) variable cost-plus with 80% markup

Chapter 25, Problem 25B Using Labor and Materials Pricing

The Auto Repair Garage employs four auto mechanics who work 40 hours per week for 50 weeks a year. The garage reports the following operating costs.

Auto mechanics' hourly wage	$ 15.95
Auto mechanics' benefits per hour	3.30
Target profit per hour	4.00
Overhead costs	8,500.00

The shop follows industry practice and adds 25% to cover handling and storage costs for parts. In addition, the owner expects 10% profit on parts used.

Instructions:

(1) Calculate the billing rate for labor.
(2) Calculate the materials loading charge.
(3) The garage took 4.75 hours to repair a car and used parts costing $78.85. Calculate the amount to be billed the customer for labor and parts for the repair job.

Answers to "Check Your Learning" Activities

Chapter 1, Page 7

1. liabilities, stockholders' (or owner's) equity
2. basic accounting equation
3. chart of accounts
4. asset
5. credit

Chapter 1, Page 16

1. sales slip
2. First, add the totals of all debit columns. Then add the totals of all credit columns. Compare the two totals; if they agree, the equality has been proved.
3. Purchases is debited; Accounts Payable and the supplier's account are credited.
4. The special journals are ruled at the end of the month. A single rule is drawn under all amount columns. When the equality of the journal has been proved, a double rule is drawn below the totals.
5. purchases returns, purchases allowances, sales returns, sales allowances, correcting entries, employer's payroll taxes

Chapter 1, Page 18

1. daily
2. Accounts Receivable
3. accounts payable subsidiary ledger

Chapter 1, Page 24

1. Special journals save time in posting because the totals of the special amount columns are posted to the general ledger accounts named in the headings. Amounts entered in the special columns are not posted individually.
2. After posting, the account number of the general ledger account is entered in parentheses, below the column total. A check mark, in parentheses, indicates that a column total is *not* posted.
3. The accuracy of the subsidiary ledgers is proved by preparing a schedule of accounts receivable and a schedule of accounts payable. The ledgers are proved if the totals of these schedules match the balances of their controlling accounts.
4. $10,500; cash has *not* been proved—a $500 error has occurred somewhere.

Chapter 2, Page 41

1. $2,411.93; Merchandise Inventory is debited and Income Summary is credited.
2. $1,920.27; Supplies Expense is debited and Supplies is credited.
3. $1,950.00; Insurance Expense is debited and Prepaid Insurance is credited.

Chapter 2, Page 46

1. $9,978.91
2. $54,118.89
3. $19,455.68

Chapter 2, Page 51

1. statement of retained earnings
2. Adjustments section of the work sheet
3. three
4. Income Summary

Chapter 3, Page 72

1. Cash is short by $10.
2. Debits: Supplies, $21; Advertising Expense, $9; Delivery Expense, $16; Miscellaneous Expense, $8; Cash Short and Over, $4. Credit: Cash in Bank, $58.

Chapter 3, Page 76

June 10	Bad Debts Expense		200.00	
	Accts. Rec./Jason LeBleu	/		200.00
	Memo. 44			
14	Acct. Rec./Sue Hicks	/	98.00	
	Bad Debts Expense			98.00
	Memo. 45			
14	Cash in Bank		98.00	
	Accts. Rec./Sue Hicks	/		98.00
	Receipt 1947			

Chapter 3, Page 84

1. $644.70
2. $1,370.00

Chapter 4, Page 99

1. December 15
2. June 23
3. May 17
4. October 8
5. August 30

Chapter 4, Page 101

1. $47.32
2. $66.16
3. $144.86
4. $315.62
5. $416.10

Chapter 4, Page 103

1. a. Notes Receivable is debited for $3,600.00; Accounts Receivable and Rick Rossi's account are credited for $3,600.00.
   b. March 16
2. a. $3,647.34
   b. Cash in Bank is debited for $3,647.34; Notes Receivable is credited for $3,600.00 and Interest Income is credited for $47.34.

Chapter 4, Page 107

1. 30 days
2. 60 days
3. $2,049.32
4. $32.00
5. $2,017.32
6. $17.32 interest income

Chapter 5, Page 123

1. Cost of Merchandise Sold; Current Assets
2. physical inventory
3. perpetual
4. online

Chapter 5, Page 127

1. 19
2. $77.22
3. fifo, $78.85 (19 × $4.15); lifo, $76.00 (19 × $4.00)

Chapter 5, Page 131

1. markup
2. retail method
3. gross profit method

Chapter 6, Page 145

1. $69,172
2. Land, $81,000; Building, $189,000

Chapter 6, Page 151

1. Straight-line method, $3,140
2. Units-of-production method, $3,330
3. Double-declining-balance method, $6,700
4. Sum-of-the-years'-digits method, $5,024

Chapter 6, Page 156

1. $625.00
2. $416.67
3. Depreciation Expense—Office Equipment is debited; Accumulated Depreciation—Office Equipment is credited.

Chapter 6, Page 160

1. true
2. false
3. false
4. true

Chapter 7, Page 179

1. a. Accounts Payable and Frontier, Inc. are debited for $3,000.00.
   b. Notes Payable is credited for $3,000.00.
2. a. The accounts debited are Notes Payable for $3,000.00 and Interest Expense for $49.32.
   b. Cash in Bank is credited for $3,049.32.

Chapter 7, Page 183

1. a. Cash in Bank, $5,866.85; Discount on Notes Payable, $133.15
   b. Notes Payable, $6,000.00
2. a. Notes Payable, $6,000.00; Interest Expense, $133.15
   b. Discount on Notes Payable, $133.15; Cash in Bank, $6,000.00

Chapter 8, Page 203

1. false
2. false
3. true
4. false
5. false

Chapter 8, Page 210

1. at a premium
2. Cash in Bank was debited for $618,000; 8% Bonds Payable was credited for $600,000, and Premium on Bonds Payable was credited for $18,000.
3. $24,000
4. a. yes, for the bond premium
   b. Premium on Bonds Payable is debited for $3,600, and Bond Interest Expense is credited for $3,600.

Chapter 8, Page 212

1. $960,000
2. $3,000
3. $15,000

Chapter 8, Page 217

1.	Year 5				
	July	27	Bond Sinking Fund	460,000.00	
			Sinking Fund Investments		450,000.00
			Gain on Sale of Sink. Fund Inv.		10,000.00
			Receipt 660		
2.		31	Bond Sinking Fund	40,000.00	
			Cash in Bank		40,000.00
			Check 997		
3.	Aug.	1	Bonds Payable	500,000.00	
			Bond Sinking Fund		500,000.00
			Check 498		

Chapter 9, Page 236

1. Corporations are taxed on the amount of their net income. Stockholders are taxed on the dividends they receive. Dividends are paid out of the corporation's retained earnings.
2. Capital Stock; Retained Earnings
3. 250 (500 shares ÷ 10,000 = 5%; 5,000 shares × 5%)

Chapter 9, Page 242

199-				
Apr.	2	Cash in Bank	200,000.00	
		Common Stock		200,000.00
		Receipt 101		
	6	Organization Costs	50,000.00	
		Common Stock		50,000.00
		Memo. 3		
June	5	Cash in Bank	103,000.00	
		Common Stock		100,000.00
		Paid-in Capital in Excess of Par		3,000.00
		Receipt 226		

Chapter 9, Page 245

1. $48,000
2. Cash in Bank is debited for $48,000; Common Stock is credited for $48,000.
3. Cash in Bank is debited for $48,000; Common Stock is credited for $40,000, and Paid-in Capital in Excess of Stated Value is credited for $8,000.

Chapter 9, Page 249

1. The company issued shares of common stock at a price above the stated value.
2. The company had subscriptions for shares of its common stock at a subscription price above the stock's stated value.
3. The company received $9,500 of the subscription price from subscribers.
4. The company received the remaining $12,500 of the subscription price from subscribers.
5. The company issued the common stock subscribed to earlier.

Chapter 10, Page 262

1. $4,500
2. $375
3. January 12 and February 20

4. 199-

Jan. 12	Dividends	4,500.00	
	Dividends Payable		4,500.00
	Minute Book, p. 505		
Feb. 20	Dividends Payable	4,500.00	
	Cash in Bank	4,500.00	
	Check 1834		

Chapter 10, Page 269

1. 117,000 shares
2. 5,500 shares
3. a credit balance of $2,250

Chapter 11, Page 290

1. $200; Income Tax Expense; Federal Income Tax Payable
2. Depreciation Expense—Office Equipment; Accumulated Depreciation—Office Equipment
3. Interest Receivable; Interest Income
4. Interest Expense; Discount on Notes Payable
5. $5,400; Unearned Rent; Rental Income

Chapter 11, Page 297

1. work sheet
2. Other Revenue
3. net addition
4. statement of stockholders' equity
5. balance sheet
6. statement of stockholders' equity
7. Current Assets

Chapter 12, Page 320

Cash in Bank	55.67%
Notes Receivable	(16.13%)
Equipment (Net)	(5.52%)
Retained Earnings	14.75%

Chapter 12, Page 324

1993: 5.87 times/year; 62 days
1992: 5.30 times/year; 69 days

Chapter 13, Page 343

1. $175,000
2. $249,000
3. $4,800
4. $5,500

Chapter 13, Page 345

1. $670,000
2. $560,000
3. $255,000
4. $370,000
5. $802,000

Chapter 13, Page 349

1. $165,500
2. $3,600
3. $9,770

Chapter 13, Page 351

1. decrease
2. amount of sale, $21,000
3. decrease
4. to show cash outflows

Chapter 13, Page 354

1. increase
2. decrease
3. $125,000 credit to Capital Stock; $25,000 credit to Paid-in Capital in Excess of Par; cash inflow
4. no

Chapter 14, Page 373

1. $34,000
2. $2,208
3. $57,692

Chapter 14, Page 381

1. $26,000 loss
2. $45,000

Chapter 15, Page 395

Hilliard: $15,942.86
Whitten: $11,957.14

Chapter 15, Page 398

Adams: $14,000 + $18,750 = $32,750
Matthews: $10,000 + $ 6,250 = $16,250

Chapter 16, Page 413

1. true
2. false
3. false
4. false
5. true

Chapter 16, Page 418

1. over by $1,462
2. decreasing by $520
3. $232
4. $6,000; over by $400
5. $5,500

Chapter 16, Page 423

1. revenue projections and expenditure projections
2. expenditures
3. basing estimates on the previous year's budgeted and actual amounts; zero-base budgeting
4. $6,000

Chapter 16, Page 426

1. $135,500
2. $51,680
3. $11,250
4. over by $5
5. concession stands, fund-raising projects
6. 9 (director's salary, postage, utilities, other operating services, scorebooks, trophies, instructional supplies, prepaid supplies, and other supplies)

Chapter 17, Page 442

1. not-for-profit organization
2. statement of revenue, expenditures, and changes in fund balance
3. general
4. self-generated
5. capital additions

Chapter 17, Page 444

1.	program	**9.**	object
2.	program	**10.**	object
3.	object	**11.**	program
4.	object	**12.**	program
5.	program	**13.**	program
6.	object	**14.**	object
7.	object	**15.**	program
8.	object		

Chapter 17, Page 450

1. decrease in fund balance
2. $108,900
3. fund balance
4. capitalizing an expenditure

Chapter 18, Page 467

Tapes & CDs	$132,200
Videos	104,560
Equipment	157,000
Total	$393,760

Chapter 18, Page 471

Men's Department	$24,000
Women's Department	30,000
Children's Department	12,000
Jewelry Department	6,000
	$72,000

Chapter 18, Page 479

$50,000

Chapter 19, Page 492

1. franchise
2. multistore business
3. centralized
4. decentralized
5. account; branch

Chapter 19, Page 496

1. Debit Cash in Bank—Branch 3 for $7,166.25; credit Sales—Branch 3 for $6,825.00 and Sales Tax Payable—Branch 3 for $341.25.
2. Debit Accounts Receivable—Branch 1 and John Dickerson's account in the accounts receivable subsidiary ledger for $420.00; credit Sales—Branch 1 for $400.00 and Sales Tax Payable—Branch 1 for $20.00.
3. Debit Cash in Bank—Branch 2 for $735.00; credit Accounts Receivable—Branch 2 and Kim Yu's account in the accounts receivable subsidiary ledger for $735.00.
4. Debit Purchases—Branch 3 for $8,459.10; credit Accounts Payable—Branch 3 and LaGrange Company's account in the accounts payable subsidiary ledger for $8,459.10.
5. Debit Purchases—Branch 1 for $360.00, Purchases—Branch 2 for $784.10, and Purchases—Branch 3 for $101.00; credit Accounts Payable—Branch 1 and National Supply Company's account for $360.00, Accounts Payable—Branch 2 and National Supply Company's account for $784.10, and Accounts Payable Branch 3 and National Supply Company's account for $101.00.

Chapter 19, Page 505

199-				
May	20	Due from Store #4	40,400	
		Purchases—Store 1		40,000
		Transfer Fees Earned—Store 1		400
		Transfer Request 111		
	20	Purchases—Store 4	40,000	
		Transfer Charges—Store 4	400	
		Due to Store 1		40,400
		Transfer Request 111		
June	2	Due to Store 1	40,400	
		Cash in Bank—Payables		40,400
		EFT 624		
	2	Cash in Bank—Store 1	40,400	
		Due from Store 4		40,400
		Receipt 113		

Chapter 20, Page 526

1. voucher
2. Vouchers Payable
3. check register
4. accounts payable subsidiary ledger
5. purchases

Chapter 20, Page 531

1. The Mar. 5 transaction would be recorded in the voucher register; the Mar. 10 transaction would be recorded in the general journal; the Mar. 12 transaction would be recorded in the check register and voucher register.
2. The notation *DMJ101* would be entered in the Payment column on the line for voucher 4873.
3. $11,760

Chapter 21, Page 545

1. raw materials
2. indirect labor; direct labor
3. factory overhead

Chapter 21, Page 548

1. work in process
2. finished goods
3. Factory Supplies
4. Manufacturing Summary

Chapter 21, Page 554

1. $495,050
2. $26,680
3. $87,870

Chapter 22, Page 572

1. process cost
2. job order
3. job cost sheet
4. materials requisition

Chapter 22, Page 580

1. Debit Work in Process Inventory; credit Factory Overhead Applied.
2. Debit Cash in Bank; credit Sales.
3. Debit Work in Process Inventory; credit Factory Wages Payable.
4. Debit Finished Goods Inventory; credit Work in Process Inventory.
5. Debit Factory Overhead Control; credit Cash in Bank.

Chapter 22, Page 590

1. Debit Work in Process Inventory—Department A; credit Factory Overhead Applied.
2. Debit Factory Overhead Control; credit Cash in Bank.
3. Debit Work in Process Inventory—Department B; credit Work in Process Inventory—Department A.
4. Debit Finished Goods Inventory; credit Work in Process Inventory—Department B.
5. Debit Cost of Goods Sold; credit Finished Goods Inventory.

Chapter 23, Page 606

1. Direct labor; direct materials
2. $1.70
3. Total variable cost is equal to the unit variable cost multiplied by the number of units produced (activity level).

Chapter 23, Page 608

1. Insurance; monthly rent
2. $34.00
3. Total fixed costs equal the fixed cost.

Chapter 23, Page 612

1. copy machine costs; telephone charges
2. It contains both a fixed cost, $10 per month, and a variable cost, $.01 per gallon.
3. Total cost equals fixed costs plus variable costs. Unit variable cost is multiplied by the number of units produced (activity level) to determine variable costs.

Chapter 24, Page 621

1. Variable selling and administrative costs are added to variable manufacturing costs to determine total variable costs, which is subtracted from total revenues to determine the contribution margin.
2. Although the costs are classified differently, the total costs are the same on both statements. Therefore, the net income is the same.
3. $14,500

Chapter 24, Page 623

1. The answers to "what if" questions show cost-volume-profit relationships that help managers and owners make better business decisions.
2. $13,600
3. 50 units

Chapter 24, Page 626

1. Break-Even Sales = Variable Costs + Fixed Costs
2. 200 units
3. $45,000

Chapter 24, Page 630

1. Sales-Variable Costs-Fixed Costs = Net Income (Target Profit), or Sales = Variable Costs + Fixed Costs + Net Income (Target Profit)
2. If sales fall more than 25% below target sales, the business will experience a loss.
3. The break-even point increases.
4. The break-even point increases.
5. The break-even point decreases.

Chapter 25, Page 643

1. $501.38
2. $244.00; $390.40

Chapter 25, Page 644

$5,868.38 ($73,354.73 × .08);
$1,056.31 ($79,223.11 ÷ 75)

Chapter 25, Page 647

1. $6.61; $0.45; unfavorable
2. $95.22

Chapter 25, Page 649

1. $17.00
2. $52.01

Glossary

a

accelerated cost recovery system (ACRS) a depreciation method established by Congress in which a plant asset's cost is written off over a specified number of years (Ch. 6)

account a record of the increases and decreases in and the balance for a specific item such as supplies (Ch. 1)

accounts payable subsidiary ledger a subsidiary ledger that contains accounts for all of a business's creditors (Ch. 1)

accounts receivable subsidiary ledger a subsidiary ledger that contains accounts for all of a business's charge customers (Ch. 1)

accounts receivable turnover a ratio that indicates how quickly a company collects its average accounts receivable; calculated by dividing net credit sales by average net accounts receivable (Ch. 12)

accounting cycle the activities a business completes within a fiscal period to keep its accounting records in order (Ch. 1)

accrual the recognition of revenue or expenses that have gradually increased over time but that have not yet been recorded (Ch. 11)

accrual basis of accounting an accounting method in which revenue is recognized when earned and expenses when incurred (Ch. 4)

accrued expense an expense incurred in one fiscal period but not paid until a later fiscal period (Ch. 7)

accrued revenue revenue earned but not yet received and recorded (Ch. 4)

accumulated depreciation total depreciation recorded up to a specific point in time (Ch. 6)

adjusting entries journal entries made at the end of the fiscal period to update the balances of all general ledger accounts affected by adjustments (Ch. 2)

adjustment an amount that is added to or subtracted from an account balance to bring that balance up to date (Ch. 2)

administrative expenses expenses related to the management of the business, such as utilities expenses (Ch. 18)

aging of accounts receivable method a method of estimating the uncollectible amount in which each customer's account is examined and aged and each age group total is multiplied by a percentage deemed uncollectible (Ch. 3)

allowance method a method of accounting for uncollectible accounts in which the business makes an adjustment at the end of the period for the estimated uncollectible amount (Ch. 3)

amortize to write off a portion of a bond discount or premium over the life of the bond issue (Ch. 8)

appraisal value estimated worth (Ch. 6)

appropriated retained earnings the restriction of a certain amount of retained earnings for a specific purpose (Ch. 10)

articles of incorporation an application to organize a business as a corporation made to appropriate state officials (Ch. 9)

assets items of value owned or controlled by a business (Ch. 1)

authorized capital stock the maximum number of shares of stock a corporation may issue according to its charter (Ch. 9)

b

balance sheet the financial statement that reports the final, updated balances of all asset, liability, and stockholders' equity accounts as of a specific date (Ch. 1)

bank discount the amount of interest deducted in advance when a promissory note is discounted (Ch. 4)

base year the year used for comparison in financial statement analysis (Ch. 12)

basic accounting equation Assets = Liabilities + Owner's/Stockholders' Equity (Ch. 1)

beginning inventory the merchandise on hand at the beginning of the fiscal period (Ch. 2)

billing rate for labor a per-hour amount charged customers that covers direct labor costs, benefits, and selling and administrative costs and still provides a profit (Ch. 25)

board of directors a group of individuals, elected by stockholders, who govern and are responsible for the affairs of the corporation (Ch. 9)

bond a long-term liability in which the corporation promises to repay a certain amount at a specified date and to pay interest at set times (Ch. 8)

bond certificate a document that serves as evidence of the corporation's debt (Ch. 8)

bond indenture the binding agreement between the corporation and bondholders that defines the rights, privileges, and limitations of bondholders (Ch. 8)

bond issue the total amount of bonds issued at the same time (Ch. 8)

book value the value of a plant asset according to the records of the business; original cost minus accumulated depreciation (Ch. 6)

book value of accounts receivable the amount a business can reasonably expect to collect from its charge customers (Ch. 3)

book value of notes payable the difference between the balance of the Notes Payable account and the Discount on Notes Payable account (Ch. 7)

break-even point the point at which total revenues equal total costs (Ch. 24)

budget a formal, written statement of expected revenue and expenditures for a future period of time (Ch. 16)

budget adjustment a change made to a current budget amount to take into account decreased revenue or increased expenditures (Ch. 16)

budget period the period of time covered by a budget (Ch. 16)

budget summary report a report that summarizes and compares the current year's budgeted and actual revenue and expenditure amounts with the previous year's actual revenue and expenditure amounts (Ch. 16)

C

call price the amount at which the corporation agrees to redeem bonds (Ch. 8)

callable bond a bond that a corporation has the option to redeem at a certain price (Ch. 8)

capital additions revenue the revenue a not-for-profit organization receives that is restricted to a particular use by the contributor (Ch. 17)

carrying value the amount at which the corporation is carrying the bond issue in the accounting records; the present value of a bond issue (Ch. 8)

cash discount a reduction in the amount owed, given because of prompt payment (Ch. 1)

cash dividend cash distribution of earnings paid by a corporation to stockholders as a reward for their investment (Ch. 10)

cash equivalents short-term, highly liquid investments such as money market accounts and certificates of deposit (Ch. 13)

cash flows from financing activities a section of the statement of cash flows that shows transactions affecting certain liability and stockholders' equity accounts (Ch. 13)

cash flows from investing activities a section of the statement of cash flows that shows transactions affecting the marketable securities and plant asset accounts (Ch. 13)

cash flows from operating activities a section of the statement of cash flows that shows cash transactions that are used to determine net income; includes both cash inflows and cash outflows (Ch. 13)

cash inflows cash receipts (Ch. 13)

cash outflows cash payments (Ch. 13)

cash payments journal a special journal used to record all transactions in which cash is paid out or decreased (Ch. 1)

cash receipts journal a special journal used to record all transactions in which cash is received (Ch. 1)

centralized accounting system an accounting system in which a central accounting office keeps the accounting records and performs the accounting functions for all branches of a multistore business (Ch. 19)

change fund an amount of money, consisting of varying denominations of bills and coins, used to make change in cash transactions (Ch. 3)

chart of accounts a complete list of a business's accounts (Ch. 1)

charter the approved articles of incorporation (Ch. 9)

check register a special journal in which every check written is recorded and that replaces the cash payments journal in the voucher system (Ch. 20)

closely held corporation a corporation owned by a small group of stockholders (Ch. 9)

closing entries journal entries made at the end of the fiscal period to transfer the balances of the temporary capital accounts to a permanent general ledger account (Ch. 2)

combined balance sheet a financial statement that reports the total balances of the asset, liability, and stockholders' equity accounts of all branches of a multistore business (Ch. 19)

combined income statement a financial statement that reports the revenue, costs, and expenses of all branches of a multistore business (Ch. 19)

committed fixed costs fixed costs that cannot be eliminated very easily and that are associated with long-range investments in plant, equipment, and the organization itself (Ch. 23)

common stock a title given to stock when only one class is issued by the corporation (Ch. 9)

common-size statements financial statements on which all items are reported as percentages of a key item on the statement (Ch. 12)

comparability an accounting characteristic that refers to financial information that can be compared from one fiscal period to another or from one business to another (Ch. 12)

conservatism an accounting guideline that states that when reporting the financial position of a business, it is best to present amounts that are least likely to overstate income or assets (Ch. 4)

contingent liability the liability an endorser has for the payment of a note (Ch. 4)

contra account an account whose balance decreases another account's balance (Ch. 1)

contract rate the rate of interest stated in the bond indenture (Ch. 8)

contribution income statement an income statement in which all selling, administrative, and manufacturing costs are classified as either fixed costs or variable costs (Ch. 24)

contribution margin the contribution that a given department makes to the net income of a business (Ch. 18); the contribution that a given product or department makes to paying for fixed costs and adding to the profit of a business; calculated by subtracting total variable costs from total revenues (Ch. 24)

contribution margin ratio the relationship between contribution margin and sales; calculated by dividing the amount of contribution margin by net sales (Ch. 24)

controlling account an account whose balance must equal the total of all of the account balances in a subsidiary ledger (Ch. 1)

copyright an exclusive right granted by the federal government for literary, musical, or artistic materials (Ch. 6)

corporation an artificial legal entity that has rights and responsibilities of its own (Ch. 9)

correcting entry an entry made to correct an error discovered after it has been posted to the ledger (Ch. 1)

cost of merchandise the actual cost to the business of the merchandise to be resold to customers (Ch. 1)

cost accounting system a system used to maintain accurate records of manufacturing costs (Ch. 22)

cost behavior refers to the way a cost changes as the level of a particular business activity changes (Ch. 23)

cost of merchandise sold the actual cost to the business of the merchandise sold to customers; beginning inventory plus net purchases minus ending inventory (Ch. 2)

cost of production report a report that summarizes the number of units processed by a manufacturing department and the costs charged to that department (Ch. 22)

cost variance the difference between standard and actual cost (Ch. 25)

cost-plus pricing a pricing method in which a dollar amount or a percentage of the cost is added to the base cost to arrive at the selling price (Ch. 25)

cost-volume-profit (C-V-P) analysis a method of using costs to determine the effect of changes in volume on the profit that results (Ch. 24)

coupon bonds a bond issue that has interest coupons attached to each bond certificate (Ch. 8)

credit an amount entered on the right side of an account (Ch. 1)

credit limit the maximum amount of credit extended (Ch. 3)

cumulative preferred stock preferred stock that accumulates any dividends passed in earlier years (Ch. 9)

current assets assets that are used up or converted to cash during the normal operating cycle of a business (Ch. 6)

current liabilities liabilities that a business expects to pay off in one year or within the normal operating cycle, whichever is longer (Ch. 7)

current ratio the relationship between a company's current assets and its current liabilities; calculated by dividing the dollar amount of current assets by the dollar amount of current liabilities (Ch. 12)

d

debenture an unsecured bond (Ch. 8)

debit an amount entered on the left side of an account (Ch. 1)

decentralized accounting system an accounting system in which each branch of a multistore business maintains its own accounting records (Ch. 19)

deferral a delay in recognizing revenue for cash already received or an expense for a bill already paid (Ch. 11)

deficit the result of having a greater amount of expenditures than revenue received (Ch. 17)

departmental accounting system an accounting system that provides data for two or more departments (Ch. 18)

depreciable cost the total amount of the cost of a plant asset to be depreciated; original cost less disposal value (Ch. 6)

depreciation a systematic procedure for allocating the cost of a plant asset to the accounting periods in which the firm receives service from that asset (Ch. 6)

direct labor wages paid to employees who actually work on a manufactured product (Ch. 21)

direct expenses expenses incurred for the sole benefit of a given department and thus under the control of the department head (Ch. 18)

direct materials the raw materials that are used to make and can be easily traced to the finished product (Ch. 21)

direct write-off method a method of accounting for uncollectible accounts in which the uncollectible amount is removed from the accounts receivable subsidiary ledger and from the controlling account when the business's management decides that the account is not going to be paid (Ch. 3)

discount the amount by which the face value of a bond exceeds the issue price of the bond (Ch. 8)

discount period the period of time between the discount date and the maturity date of a note (Ch. 4)

discounting notes payable deducting the interest on a note payable at the time the note is issued (Ch. 7)

discounting notes receivable selling a note receivable to a bank rather than holding it until maturity (Ch. 4)

discretionary fixed costs fixed costs that are usually based on decisions made for a fiscal period and that can be increased or decreased during the annual budgeting process (Ch. 23)

dishonored note a promissory note that the maker fails to pay or renew on the maturity date (Ch. 4)

dissolution a change in the membership of a partnership (Ch. 14)

dividends a distribution of earnings that a corporation makes to its stockholders (Ch. 10)

double-declining-balance method a method of calculating depreciation in which the asset's book value is multiplied by a rate twice the straight-line rate (Ch. 6)

double-entry accounting an accounting system in which every business transaction affects the balance in at least two accounts (Ch. 1)

double taxation the situation in which both the earnings of a corporation and the distribution of those earnings made to stockholders are taxed (Ch. 9)

e

earnings per share a measure of the amount of profit that could be assigned to each share of common stock; calculated by dividing net income by the number of outstanding shares of common stock (Ch. 12)

ending inventory the merchandise on hand at the end of the fiscal period (Ch. 2)

equity financial claims to assets (Ch. 1)

equity per share the amount that would be paid on each share of stock if the corporation liquidated and the assets were sold for their book value; calculated by dividing the total stockholders' equity by the number of shares of common stock outstanding (Ch. 12)

equivalent units the number of units produced during a certain period, expressed in terms of fully completed units (Ch. 22)

expenditure projection an estimate of the amount to be paid out for goods and services during a budget period (Ch. 16)

expenses amounts paid for goods and services used to operate a business (Ch. 1)

f

face value the amount written on the "face" of a promissory note (Ch. 4); the amount received when the contract rate and the market rate of bonds are the same (Ch. 8)

factory overhead all other manufacturing costs that cannot be classified as direct materials or direct labor (Ch. 21)

factory supplies indirect materials that do not become part of the finished product (Ch. 21)

finance charge interest on the unpaid balance of a charge account or installment sale (Ch. 3)

finished goods goods that a manufacturing business has completed and that are available for sale (Ch. 21)

first in, first out method (fifo) a method of assigning a cost to the ending inventory in which it is assumed that the first items purchased were the first items sold; the ending inventory then consists of the last items purchased (Ch. 5)

fiscal period the time covered by an accounting report (Ch. 1)

fixed costs costs that remain the same even though the level of a particular business activity changes; that is, the costs remain constant regardless of the number of units produced (Ch. 23)

franchise a right to conduct business under a contracted name (Ch. 6, 19)

free balance the budgeted amount that remains to be collected or spent as of a specific date (Ch. 16)

full cost-plus a pricing method by which a markup amount is added to the full cost, which is the product cost plus the operating costs associated with the product (Ch. 25)

fund in a not-for-profit organization, a set of accounts used to record the transactions for a particular activity (Ch. 16)

fund accounting the accounting system used by not-for-profit organizations to account for the transactions of their various funds (Ch. 16)

fund balance the difference between the assets and the liabilities of a particular fund (Ch. 17)

g

general journal a two-column journal in which all types of transactions can be recorded (Ch. 1)

general ledger all of a business's accounts (Ch. 1)

goodwill the good reputation of a company (Ch. 6)

gross profit method a method of estimating the cost of the ending inventory in which the net sales amount is multiplied by the percentage of gross profit made over a period of time (Ch. 5)

gross profit on sales the amount of profit made during the fiscal period before expenses are deducted; net sales minus the cost of merchandise sold (Ch. 2)

h

high-low method a method used to determine the variable and fixed parts of a mixed cost (Ch. 23)

horizontal analysis the comparison of dollar amount changes and percentage changes for the same items on a company's financial statements for two or more periods (Ch. 12)

i

income statement the financial statement that reports the net income or net loss earned by a business during the fiscal period (Ch. 2)

indirect expenses expenses incurred for the business as a whole and not under the control of a department head (Ch. 18)

indirect labor wages paid to factory employees who do not physically work on the products (Ch. 21)

installment sale a sale in which the customer makes a cash down payment and a series of equal monthly payments (Ch. 3)

intangible assets long-lived assets that have no physical substance (Ch. 6)

interbranch transaction a transaction that occurs between two or more branches of the same multistore business (Ch. 19)

interest the fee charged for the use of money (Ch. 4)

interest allowance a method of distributing net income that takes into account a partner's capital contribution (Ch. 15)

interest-bearing note a promissory note requiring the payment of the principal plus interest on the maturity date (Ch. 4)

interest rate the amount of interest expressed as a percentage of the principal (Ch. 4)

internal controls the procedures a business sets up to protect its cash and other assets (Ch. 3)

investments long-term assets that are not intended to be converted to cash or to be used in the normal business operations within the next accounting period (Ch. 5)

issue date the date a promissory note is written (Ch. 4)

issued shares those shares of stock that the corporation has sold to stockholders (Ch. 9)

j

job cost sheet a document used to record the various manufacturing costs incurred for each job (Ch. 22)

job order cost accounting a cost accounting system in which costs are accumulated for each product or batch of products produced (Ch. 22)

job order time card a document used to record the amount of time an employee spent on a particular job (Ch. 22)

journal a chronological record of a business's transactions (Ch. 1)

l

land improvements amounts paid out for improvements that are not as permanent as the land or not directly associated with a building (Ch. 6)

last in, first out method (lifo) a method of assigning a cost to the ending inventory in which it is assumed that the last items purchased were the first items sold; the ending inventory then consists of the first items purchased (Ch. 5)

legal capital the minimum amount of contributed capital that a corporation must keep in the business (Ch. 9)

leverage the ability to earn a greater return on the money borrowed than must be paid out in interest (Ch. 8)

liabilities creditors' claims to the assets of a business (Ch. 1)

liquidation the process of ending a partnership and the business (Ch. 14)

liquidity the ease with which an asset can be converted to cash (Ch. 3)

long-term investments investments made for a period of one year or more (Ch. 5)

long-term liabilities liabilities that are not due during the next fiscal period or operating cycle (Ch. 7)

lower-of-cost-or-market rule an accounting guideline that states that a business can report the cost of its ending inventory at the calculated cost or at market value, whichever is lower (Ch. 5)

m

maker one who issues a promissory note (Ch. 4)

manufacturing business a business that buys raw materials and transforms them into finished products through the use of labor and machinery (Ch. 21)

margin of safety the amount by which target sales exceed break-even sales (Ch. 24)

margin of safety ratio the relationship between target sales and break-even sales stated as a percentage; calculated by dividing the margin of safety by the target sales (Ch. 24)

market interest rate the interest rate a corporation is willing to pay and investors are willing to accept for the use of money (Ch. 8)

market value the current price that is being charged for an item in the marketplace (Ch. 5)

marketable securities short-term investments that usually include government securities such as Treasury bills and the securities of large corporations (Ch. 3)

markup an amount added to the cost of an item to arrive at its selling price (Ch. 5)

matching principle an accounting principle that states that revenue for a fiscal period must be matched against the expenses incurred in earning that revenue during the period (Ch. 3)

materials loading charge the amount added to the cost of parts and materials used on a job to determine the amount the customer will be billed (Ch. 25)

materials requisition a document authorizing the materials warehouse to transfer raw materials to the factory (Ch. 22)

maturity date the due date of a promissory note (Ch. 4)

maturity value principal plus interest; the amount that must be repaid on the maturity date (Ch. 4)

medicare a federal program that provides certain health insurance benefits to retired people. (Ch. 1)

merchandise inventory turnover the number of times a company's inventory is sold during a given year; calculated by dividing the cost of merchandise sold by the average merchandise inventory (Ch. 12)

mixed costs costs that are part variable costs and part fixed costs; costs that cannot be explained by a single cost behavior pattern (Ch. 23)

modified accelerated cost recovery system (MACRS) a revision of the accelerated cost recovery system in which the number of years over which depreciation could be calculated was increased (Ch. 6)

mortgage a formal, legal agreement in which the borrower agrees to repay the amount owed plus interest over a 5–30 year period; the creditor usually has the right to repossess the mortgaged asset if the mortgage is not repaid (Ch. 8)

multistore business a business that has more than one store or branch (Ch. 19)

mutual agency the ability of any partner in a partnership to enter into valid contracts that are binding on the partnership (Ch. 14)

n

net amount method recording invoices in the accounting records at their net amount (total amount less cash discount); based on the assumption that the business always takes advantage of cash discounts offered (Ch. 7)

net income the amount left after expenses for the period are subtracted from revenue (Ch. 2)

net loss the amount resulting when expenses are greater than the gross profit on sales for the period (Ch. 2)

net pay the amount actually paid to employees; gross pay minus deductions (Ch. 1)

net purchases the amount of all costs related to merchandise purchased during the period; Purchases plus Transportation In minus Purchases Discounts minus Purchases Returns and Allowances (Ch. 2)

net sales the amount resulting when the contra revenue accounts are subtracted from total sales; Sales minus Sales Discounts minus Sales Returns and Allowances (Ch. 2)

noncash investing and financing activities transactions affecting long-lived assets, long-term liabilities, or capital stock that do not involve cash; must be reported on the statement of cash flows (Ch. 13)

noncumulative preferred stock preferred stock that does not accumulate any passed dividends (Ch. 9)

non-interest-bearing note payable a note payable from which the interest has been deducted in advance (Ch. 7)

nonparticipating preferred stock preferred stock that is limited to the established dividend amount (Ch. 9)

no-par stock stock that does not have a value printed on the stock certificate (Ch. 9)

not-for-profit organization an organization with goals other than earning a profit for its organizers (Ch. 16)

note payable a promissory note issued by a person or business (Ch. 7)

note receivable a promissory note accepted by a person or business (Ch. 4)

notes to financial statements information added to financial statements that explains significant matters not disclosed in the financial statements and the accounting policies followed by the organization (Ch. 11)

o

object expenditures the expenditures of a not-for-profit organization classified according to the type of cost (Ch. 17)

operating expenses the cash spent or the assets consumed to earn revenue for the business (Ch. 2)

operating income the taxable income of a corporation; the amount of income before federal income taxes; gross profit on sales minus total operating expenses (Ch. 2)

organization costs costs directly related to establishing a corporation (Ch. 6)

other revenue nonoperating revenue; revenue a business receives or earns from activities outside its normal operations (Ch. 3)

outstanding stock stock that is actually in the hands of stockholders (Ch. 9)

overapplied factory overhead occurs when more factory overhead costs were applied during the period than were actually incurred (Ch. 22)

owner's equity the owner's claims to the assets of a business; usually used with a sole proprietorship (Ch. 1)

p

paid voucher file a file that contains all paid vouchers, filed in numerical order (Ch. 20)

participating preferred stock preferred stock eligible for dividends beyond the stated amount (Ch. 9)

partnership an association of two or more persons to operate, as co-owners, a business for profit (Ch. 14)

partnership agreement a written document that sets out the terms under which the partnership will operate (Ch. 14)

par-value stock stock that has a specific value printed on the stock certificate (Ch. 9)

patents exclusive rights granted by the federal government for particular products or processes (Ch. 6)

payee one to whom a promissory note is issued (Ch. 4)

percentage of net sales method a method of estimating the uncollectible amount in which the net sales amount for the period is multiplied by a certain set percentage (Ch. 3)

periodic inventory system an inventory system in which the amount of goods on hand is determined by periodically counting them (Ch. 5)

permanent account an account whose balance is carried forward from one accounting period to the next (Ch. 1)

perpetual inventory system an inventory system in which the business keeps a constant, up-to-date record of the amount of merchandise on hand (Ch. 5)

petty cash fund an amount of cash on hand used to make small cash payments (Ch. 3)

petty cash voucher a receipt that serves as proof of a payment from the petty cash fund (Ch. 3)

physical inventory an actual count of the merchandise on hand (Ch. 2)

plant asset records a detailed record of the purchase information and depreciation schedule for a plant asset (Ch. 6)

post-closing trial balance a report prepared to prove the equality of debits and credits in the general ledger after the adjusting and closing entries have been posted (Ch. 2)

posting the process of transferring amounts from a journal to ledger accounts (Ch. 1)

pre-emptive right each stockholder's right to purchase additional shares of new stock issues in proportion to her or his present holding (Ch. 9)

preferred stock stock that has preferences over common stock, usually in relation to dividends (Ch. 9)

premium the amount received when bonds are issued for more than their face value (Ch. 8)

prepaid expense an expense paid in advance, such as the bank discount on a non-interest-bearing note (Ch. 7)

price-earnings ratio a measure used to determine whether the market price of a corporation's stock is reasonable; calculated by dividing the market price per share by the earnings per share (Ch. 12)

pricing assigning a selling price to a product or service (Ch. 25)

principal the amount of money borrowed (Ch. 4)

proceeds the amount of cash actually received when a promissory note is discounted; maturity value minus bank discount (Ch. 4)

process cost accounting a cost accounting system in which costs are accumulated for each process or department and then transferred on to the next process or department (Ch. 22)

product cost-plus a pricing method by which the markup is added to the product cost (Ch. 25)

profitability a company's ability to earn a reasonable profit on the owners' investment (Ch. 12)

program expenditures all of the expenditures made for a particular program of a not-for-profit organization (Ch. 17)

promissory note a written promise to pay a certain sum of money on demand or on a specified date; a formal legal document serving as proof of a debt (Ch. 4)

property, plant, and equipment long-lived assets that are used in the production or sale of other assets or services over several accounting periods; plant assets (Ch. 6)

protest fee a fee charged when a discounted note is dishonored (Ch. 4)

proving cash the process of determining whether the cash reported in a business's accounting records and in its checkbook agree (Ch. 1)

publicly held corporation a corporation whose stock is widely held, has a large market, and is usually traded on a stock exchange (Ch. 3)

purchases journal a special journal used to record the purchase of all items bought on account (Ch. 1)

q

quick ratio the relationship between a company's short-term liquid assets and its current liabilities; calculated by dividing the company's quick assets by its current liabilities (Ch. 12)

r

ratio analysis the comparison of two amounts on a financial statement resulting in a percentage that shows the relationship between the two amounts (Ch. 12)

realization the process of selling assets for cash (Ch. 14)

registered bonds a bond issue in which the bondholders' names are on file with the issuing corporation (Ch. 8)

relevant range the given range of activity and/or period of time for which cost behavior is fixed (Ch. 23)

retail method a method of estimating the cost of the ending inventory in which the retail value of the ending merchandise inventory is multiplied by a figure representing the relationship between the cost of the merchandise available for sale and its retail value (Ch. 5)

revenue the income earned from the sale of goods and services (Ch. 1)

revenue projection an estimate of the money to be received during a budget period (Ch. 16)

s

salary allowance an allocation of net income that recognizes differences in ability and time devoted to the business by partners (Ch. 15)

sales journal a special journal used to record only the sale of merchandise on account (Ch. 1)

salvage value the estimated value of a plant asset at the time of its disposal (Ch. 6)

schedule of accounts payable a report prepared to prove the accuracy of the accounts payable subsidiary ledger; the total of this schedule must match the balance of the Accounts Payable account (Ch. 1)

schedule of accounts receivable a report prepared to prove the accuracy of the accounts receivable subsidiary ledger; the total of this schedule must match the balance of the Accounts Receivable account (Ch. 1)

schedule of cost of goods manufactured a financial statement that summarizes all the costs of the goods completed during the financial period; this statement is prepared before and as a supporting document for the income statement (Ch. 21)

schedule of unpaid vouchers a report that lists all unpaid vouchers by number and name of creditor; the total of this schedule must match the balance of the Vouchers Payable account (Ch. 20)

secured bonds a bond issue that is covered or backed up by corporate assets such as buildings or equipment (Ch. 8)

self-generated revenue the revenue that a not-for-profit organization earns from delivering or producing goods, providing services, or other activities (Ch. 17)

selling expenses expenses incurred to sell or market a business's goods or services (Ch. 18)

serial bonds a bond issue that has a series of maturity dates (Ch. 8)

short-term investments investments made for a few weeks or months (Ch. 5)

sinking fund a special fund used to pay off a bond issue when it comes due (Ch. 8)

source document a paper prepared as evidence that a business transaction took place (Ch. 1)

special journal a multicolumn journal that has columns reserved for the recording of a specific type of transaction (Ch. 1)

specific identification method a method of assigning costs to the ending inventory in which the actual cost of each item in the ending inventory is determined and assigned to the item (Ch. 5)

standard cost-plus a pricing method in which the markup is added to predetermined costs for direct labor, direct materials, and factory overhead to determine the selling price (Ch. 25)

stated value the value assigned to a share of no-par stock by the board of directors (Ch. 9)

statement of cash flows the financial statement that reports how cash was affected by the operating, investing, and financing activities of a business during the fiscal period (Ch. 13)

statement of changes in partners' equity the financial statement that reports the changes in the balances of the partners' capital accounts during the fiscal period (Ch. 15)

statement of retained earnings the financial statement that reports the changes that have taken place in the Retained Earnings account during the fiscal period (Ch. 2)

statement of revenue, expenditures, and changes in fund balance the financial statement that reports a not-for-profit organization's revenue and expenditures for a budget period as well as the change in the fund balance (Ch. 17)

statement of stockholders' equity the financial statement that reports the changes that have taken place in all of the stockholders' equity accounts during the fiscal period (Ch. 11)

stock shares of ownership in a corporation (Ch. 9)

stock certificate a document showing how many shares of corporation stock are owned (Ch. 9)

stock dividend a distribution of shares of its own stock that a corporation makes to its stockholders (Ch. 10)

stock split a deliberate split in the par or stated value of a corporation's stock and the issue of a proportionate number of additional shares (Ch. 10)

stock subscription the process of selling stock to investors on an installment basis (Ch. 9)

stockholder an owner of a corporation (Ch. 9)

stockholders' equity owners' (stockholders') claims to the assets of a corporation (Ch. 1, 9)

stockholders' ledger a subsidiary ledger or supplementary record showing the name and address of each stockholder and the number of shares owned by each (Ch. 9)

straight-line method a method of calculating depreciation in which an equal amount of depreciation is charged off for each year of the asset's useful life (Ch. 6)

subsidiary ledger a ledger or book that is summarized in a controlling account in the general ledger (Ch. 1)

sum-of-the-years'-digits method a method of calculating depreciation in which a plant asset's depreciable cost is multiplied by fractions related to the length of the asset's useful life (Ch. 6)

support revenue the unrestricted contributions a not-for-profit organization receives from individuals, businesses, or other organizations (Ch. 17)

surplus the result of receiving more revenue than the expenditures paid out (Ch. 16)

t

target profit the net income goal of a company (Ch. 24)

taxable income the income on which taxes are assessed (Ch. 7)

temporary capital account an account used for only one accounting period; an account whose balance is closed into a permanent account at the end of the fiscal period (Ch. 1)

term the amount of time between the issue date and the maturity date of a promissory note (Ch. 4)

term bonds a bond issue in which all the bonds have the same term or maturity date (Ch. 8)

trade-in allowance the amount given for an old asset when traded in on a new asset (Ch. 6)

trademark a registered symbol or name identifying a certain product or service (Ch. 6)

treasury stock stock that has been issued by a corporation and then reacquired and held (Ch. 10)

trial balance a report prepared to prove the equality of debits and credits in the general ledger (Ch. 1)

u

uncollectible account an account receivable that cannot be collected (Ch. 3)

underapplied factory overhead occurs when more factory overhead costs are incurred than were applied during the period (Ch. 22)

underwriter an investment firm that handles the sale of a bond issue to the general public (Ch. 8)

unearned revenue revenue received in advance but not yet earned (Ch. 7)

unit contribution margin the difference between the unit selling price and the unit variable cost (Ch. 24)

units-of-production method a method of calculating depreciation in which the estimated depreciation per unit of use is determined and then multiplied by the actual units of use for the period (Ch. 6)

unpaid voucher file a file of all unpaid vouchers filed according to their due dates (Ch. 20)

unsecured bonds bonds that are issued on the corporation's credit standing and not backed up by the assets of the corporation (Ch. 8)

useful life the length of time a plant asset is used (Ch. 6)

v

variable cost-plus a pricing method in which the markup is added to the variable costs to determine the selling price (Ch. 25)

variable costs costs that vary in direct proportion to the changes in a particular business activity; that is, as the business activity increases, the total variable cost increases (Ch. 23)

vertical analysis the comparison of financial statements in which every dollar amount reported on a financial statement is also stated as a percentage of a base amount on the same statement (Ch. 12)

voucher a document that serves as written authorization for each cash payment (Ch. 20)

voucher check a special check with an attached stub or a special area on the face of the check that is used to list the details of the cash payment (Ch. 20)

voucher register a book of original entry in which all vouchers are recorded in numerical order (Ch. 20)

voucher system a system to control purchases and cash payments in which a voucher is prepared for each expenditure and approved by appropriate personnel (Ch. 20)

W

weighted average cost method a method of assigning a cost to the ending inventory in which an average unit cost is assigned to all like items in the inventory (Ch. 5)

work in process products that are not yet finished being manufactured (Ch. 21)

work in process subsidiary ledger a subsidiary ledger composed of the job cost sheets (Ch. 22)

work sheet a working paper used to collect information from the general ledger needed to prepare the financial statements (Ch. 2)

working capital the amount by which current assets exceed current liabilities (Ch. 12)

Z

zero-base budgeting a method of developing budget projections that is not based on the previous year's amounts; amounts are developed as though being done for the first time (Ch. 16)

Credits

Cover Photographs: Marble background, Otto Rogge/The Stock Market
Building, Kunio Owake/The Stock Market

1 © Aaron Haupt/David R. Frazier, Photolibrary
3 © Will & Deni McIntyre/Photo Researchers
14 © Gary L. Benson/Allstock
35 © KS Studios
36 © Telegraph colour library/FPG International
38 © Courtesy IBM Corporation
38 © Courtesy IBM Corporation
59 © KS Studios
60 © Robert Frerck/Woodfin Camp and Associates
65 © John Terence Turner/FPG International
68 © Robert Mullenix
74 © Doug Martin
94 © Barbra Filet/Tonystone Images
95 © Comstock
97 © Barbra Filet/Tonystone Images
118 © KS Studios
119 © Donald Johnston/Tony Stone Images
122 © Billy E. Barnes
141 © Ed Wheeler/The Stock Market
142 © Benelux Press/Westlight
156 © Photo Researchers, Inc.
170 © Uniphoto
171 © Comstock
173 © Jay Freis/The Image Bank
178 © Henley & Savage/Tony Stone Images
197 © Matt Meadows Photography
198 © Wendell Metzen/Bruce Coleman
200 © Richard Braine/Tony Stone Images
225 © NASA
226 © Frederick Mckinney/FPG International
230 © Bill Strode/Woodfin Camp and Associates
231 © Culver Pictures
257 © Courtesy of H&R Block, Inc.
258 © Joan Laconetti/Bruce Coleman
263 © Uniphoto
279 © 1989 Comstock, Inc.
280 © Charles Gupton/Uniphoto
287 © SuperStock
307 © Michael Ventura/Bruce Coleman
308 © K.S. Studios
313 © Steve Chenn/Westlight
314 © Bill Bachmann/Allstock
315 © Doug Martin
335 © Jane Shaw/Bruce Coleman
336 © Drew Jimsan/Tony Stone Images
338 © Gabe Palmer/The Stock Market
365 © (Computer) Courtesy Apple Computers, Inc./Will Mosgrove, (Screen) Courtesy Broderbund Software, Inc.
365 © Matt Meadows Photography
366 © Gabe Palmer/The Stock Market
367 © Michael Krasowitz/FPG International
368 © Jon Gray/Tony Stone Images
388 © Larry Williams/Masterfile
389 © Tim Brown/Tony Stone Images
394 © Superstock
408 © Don & Pat Valenti/Tony Stone Images
409 © Robert E. Daemmrich/Tony Stone Images
412 © Cathlyn Melloan/Tony Stone Images
437 © Runk/Schoenberger/Grant Heilman
438 © Jeff Greenberg/Photo Researchers, Inc.
450 © Michal Heron/Woodfin Camp and Associates
460 © Comstock
461 © Andy Sacks/Tony Stone
462 © Michael Shopenn/Allstock
463 © Doug Martin
486 © John Henley/The Stock Market
487 © Ron Blakeley/Photo Resources
488 © (All) Doug Martin
517 © Matt Meadows Photography
518 © Chris Johns/Allstock
527 © Doug Martin
541 © Courtesy IBM Corporation
542 © Phil Degginger/Picture Perfect
552 © Doug Martin
567 © Jose L. Pelaez/The Stock Market
568 © Charles Gupton/Allstock
573 © David R. Frazier/Photolibrary
598 © Larry Lefever/Grant Heilman
599 © Superstock
601 © Dallas and John Heaton/Westlight
602 © Stock Imagery
603 © KS Studios
617 © Michael Keller/The Stock Market
618 © Tom Stewart/The Stock Market
619 © Henley and Savage/The Stock Market
638 © Matt Meadows Photography
639 © Jacques Chenet/Woodfin Camp & Associates
640 © Doug Martin
655 © Robert E. Daemmrich/Tony Stone Images

Index

d

n

t